BERTRAND RUSSELL

The Ghost of Madness

1921–1970

RAY MONK

THE FREE PRESS

NEW YORK · LONDON · TORONTO · SYDNEY · SINGAPORE

fP
THE FREE PRESS
A Division of Simon & Schuster, Inc.
1230 Avenue of the Americas
New York, NY 10020

First Free Press Edition 2001
Published by arrangement with Jonathan Cape Ltd.
Originally published in Great Britain in 2000
by Jonathan Cape Ltd.

Manufactured in the United States of America

10 9 8 7 6 5 4 3 2 1

Library of Congress Cataloging-in-Publication Data

Monk, Ray.
    Bertrand Russell, 1921–1970 : the ghost of madness / Ray Monk.
        —1st Free Press ed.
            p. cm.
    Originally published: London : J. Cape, 2000.
    Includes bibliographical references (p.) and index.
    1. Russell, Bertrand, 1872–1970. 2. Philosophers—England—
        Biography. I. Title: Ghost of madness. II. Title.
B1649.R94 M66 2001
192—dc21   00-053556
[B]

ISBN 0-7432-1215-0

To my children: Zala, Danika, Zeno, and Myron

The greatness of a man can be measured by his intelligence minus his vanity.

Attributed to Prince Otto von Bismarck

Madness alone is truly terrifying.

Joseph Conrad, The Secret Agent

CONTENTS

PREFACE AND ACKNOWLEDGEMENTS

The publication of this book brings to completion a task that has occupied me for more than ten years, during which I have read thousands of documents and met dozens of people in order to construct a coherent account of Bertrand Russell's life. When I began I had no idea what a taxing task this would prove to be. One reason for this, of course, is the sheer quantity of available documentation, which, as I remarked in the Introduction to *The Spirit of Solitude*, is almost unbelievably daunting. Another reason – perhaps the main one – that this has been a difficult book to write has been my growing realisation of the tragedy of Russell's life. It may seem odd to describe as tragic a life so full of achievements. After all, Russell's early work on logic and the philosophy of mathematics has established for him a permanent place in the history of philosophy as one of the very few indisputably *great* philosophers of the twentieth century, and in the second half of his life he was the recipient of a number of distinguished honours, including the Nobel Prize for Literature and the Order of Merit.

And yet 'tragedy' still seems to me the right word. I do not just mean that there was sadness in Russell's life, though, to be sure, the degree of suffering he endured – and caused – has been one of the hardest revelations of my work on this book. To research Russell's private life, I discovered, is to pick one's way through a long trail of emotional wreckage, and to put oneself in the position of someone close to Russell has often been a heartbreaking experience. But what I mean when I speak of tragedy is principally that Russell's life seems to have been inexorably drawn towards disaster, determined on its course by two fundamental traits of character: a deep-seated fear of madness and a quite colossal vanity. To so many questions that one wants to ask about Russell's behaviour – how could he have been so *cold* towards those who loved him? how could he have treated his son, John, as he did? how could he have written so much second-rate journalism? – the answers seem to lie in one or other (or both) of these character traits.

In writing this book I have had to confront, in a way that is new to me, my own reactions to my subject. For ten years I have, as it were, lived with Russell, and, for the most part, it has been an uncomfortable experience. I find him inexhaustibly fascinating and there are things about him that I

admire tremendously, but, as I have worked on this volume, two thoughts
have dominated my reactions to him, which, I am aware, may have distorted
my account of his life. The first is just how *bad* most of his writing on
political, social and moral questions is. Few who know Russell from his
great writings on logic have taken the trouble to read the vast quantity of
journalism that he produced in the second half of his life; those who do
would, I think, be shocked at how sloppy and ill-considered much of it is.

The second thought that has come to dominate my reaction to Russell,
particularly in the latter half of his life, is how emotionally maimed he was.
He was, it sometimes seems, simply not capable of loving another human
being. Russell had what he considered to be an exalted conception of love –
which he expressed in *Marriage and Morals* and in numerous other places –
according to which love takes the form of 'merging' one ego with another. In
many of his political writings this notion reappears as the duty to love
humanity in the sense of regarding all mankind as, in some sense,
coextensive with one's own ego. One might regard this as a harmlessly
fanciful way of urging people to empathise with each other, but Russell's
relations with those close to him suggest another interpretation: that he was
unable to conceive of loving a person unless he could regard that person as
part of himself. In other words, loving *another* was, for him, inconceivable.
He was, as it were (as, indeed, his epistemology maintains we all are),
trapped inside the boundaries of his own ego. He could imagine – and
frequently did imagine – extending those boundaries, but what he could not
imagine was reaching out *beyond* them. Would that this were only a
theoretical problem, but the experience of Russell's wives, children and
friends suggests that, on this point, theory and practice combined in the
most devastating manner.

What I present here is a picture of the second half of Russell's life shaped
largely by these two dominating thoughts. The extent to which it is
distorted by them I am no longer able to judge, though I am conscious that
other pictures could be drawn in which Russell is presented in a very
different light.

In writing this book, I have been helped by a large number of people. My
greatest debt is to Russell's daughter, Kate, whom I have met on numerous
occasions and with whom I have discussed at great length Russell's character
and his family life. Kate very generously gave me access to the large
amounts of family correspondence she inherited from her mother, Dora, as
well as allowing me to read an extensive commentary she herself has written
on her own correspondence with her father. It should not be imagined,
however, that I have taken my view of Russell from Kate, who (one is
tempted to say 'despite everything') has an undying admiration of and love
for him. In understanding the tangled affairs of the Russell family, I have
also benefited enormously from the kindness and hospitality of Russell's
adoptive granddaughter, Felicity (formerly Anne), who has discussed with
me her painful memories of her parents, her upbringing and the unbearably
sad story of her sister, Lucy. Further light on the family was shed by
Harriet Ward, Dora's daughter, whom I met several times and who was kind
enough to show me her unfinished memoir of her father, Griffin Barry. I

would also like to thank Russell's son, Conrad, his granddaughter, Sarah, and his grandsons, Ben and Andrew Tait, for agreeing to talk to me about their family. Friends of various family members, too, have shared their memories with me, including Susan, Euan and Siân Cooper-Willis, Christopher Wordsworth, Chris Eve and Jack Pole, to all of whom I would like to extend my thanks. I am particularly grateful to the Cooper-Willises for extending to me their hospitality and for allowing me access to the heart-rending collection of papers left behind at Portmeirion by Lucy Russell. I am also grateful to Susan Russell's brother, Nicholas Lindsay, for giving me some insight into her character and their own family background.

Kevin Holland, Daphne Phelps, Frances Partridge and Sir Peter Strawson were all kind enough to tell me of their own contacts with Russell, and Kevin Holland was especially generous in providing me with copies of his interesting correspondence with Russell.

For information on Russell's later political activities I am very grateful to Pat Pottle and the late Nicholas Walter, both of whom were leading members of the Committee of 100, and to Tariq Ali, Robin Blackburn, Ken Coates, Christopher Farley and Quentin Hoare, all of whom were associated with the Bertrand Russell Peace Foundation. Christopher Farley was especially generous with his time and I am grateful to him for answering with unfailing good grace and patience my many bewildered questions about the last phase of Russell's political life. For helping to make some sense of this extraordinary period I am also grateful to Andrew Collier, Richard Gott, Christopher Roper and Adam Roberts. Ralph Schoenman, alas, felt unable to co-operate, but I am sure I am not alone in eagerly looking forward to his own account of his work with Russell, which, he has told me, he is currently preparing.

For enlightening discussions of all aspects of Russell's life and work I am very grateful to Kenneth Blackwell, whose knowledge of Russell's manuscripts is unparalleled, and to Charles Pigden, with whom I have had, over the years, many stimulating conversations about Russell's personality and the value of his later work. Most of these conversations have been conducted by e-mail, but Charles was kind enough to arrange for me to spend three weeks at his own university, Otago, in Dunedin, New Zealand, where I had the opportunity to pester him in person about his inexplicable fondness for Russell's journalism and to discuss with him, among many other things, his pioneering work on Russell's theoretical ethics. In the later stages of writing this book I have also had the opportunity to discuss my work with James Conant, whose own work I admire deeply, and who has been the most sympathetic and perceptive critic that a friend could hope for. I have also benefited from discussions of Russell's work with Peter Hacker of St John's College, Oxford, and Louis Greenspan, Nicholas Griffin, Richard Rempel, Carl Spadoni and Sheila Turcan of McMaster University, Hamilton, Ontario.

My publishers, Dan Franklin of Jonathan Cape and Stephen Morrow of the Free Press, have been inexhaustibly patient during the prolonged writing of this book, and I am very grateful to both of them for the encouragement and support they have given me. The support of my agent, Gill Coleridge, has, as ever, been indispensable.

For comments on an earlier version of this book, I would like to thank

Louis Greenspan, Charles Pigden, James Conant, Kate Tait, Aaron Ridley, and my copy-editor, Mandy Greenfield, all of whom have saved me from a number of infelicities of style and content.

This book is dedicated to my children, who, together with my partner, Jenny, have had to endure my distractions, absences and obsessions throughout the writing of it, and have done so with far better grace than I have any right to expect.

Southampton
April 2000   RAY MONK

LIST OF ILLUSTRATIONS

Bertrand and Dora Russell in 1922
Dora with baby John (*Katharine Tait*)
Russell, John and Dora, 1924 (*Katharine Tait*)
The Russells in Cornwall, 1925 (*Katharine Tait*)
Alice Stücki, Russell, John and Kate (*Katharine Tait*)
Telegraph House (*McMaster University*)
Dora with the children at Beacon Hill School (*Katharine Tait*)
Griffin Barry and Dora with Harriet, 1930 (*Katharine Tait*)
Dora, John, Kate, Harriet and Roddy, 1932 (*Katharine Tait*)
Griffin Barry, Harriet, Peter and Russell, 1932 (*Katharine Tait*)
Kate, Peter and John at Hendaye, 1932 (*Katharine Tait*)
Griffin Barry and John at Hendaye (*Katharine Tait*)
Paul Gillard (*Katharine Tait*)
Patricia (Peter) Russell (*McMaster University*)

Russell lecturing at UCLA, 1939 (*McMaster University*)
Peter and Conrad, 1938 (*Katharine Tait*)
Pat Grace, Dora, Harriet and Roddy, 1939 (*Katharine Tait*)
John and Kate in Los Angeles, c. 1940 (*Katharine Tait*)
Russell, Peter, Conrad, and Kate, 1939 (*Katharine Tait*)
Russell and Dr Albert C. Barnes, 1941 (*Temple University*)
Russell, Conrad and Peter, 1944 (*McMaster University*)
John in Washington, 1945 (*Katharine Tait*)
Kate at Radcliffe, 1947 (*Katharine Tait*)
John and Susan, 1946 (*Katharine Tait/Nicholas Lindsay*)
Susan Russell, c. 1951 (*Nicholas Lindsay*)
Plas Penrhyn
Russell in his study, 1957 (*Hulton Getty*)
Ralph Schoenman, Russell and Edith, 1961 (*Hulton Getty*)
Ralph Schoenman and Russell, 1962 (*Hulton Getty*)
Sarah, Russell, Anne, Edith and Lucy, 1956 (*Katharine Tait*)
Lucy Russell, 1968

The author and publishers are grateful to the above sources for permission to reproduce illustrations.

Part III
1921–38

FALLEN ANGEL: RUSSELL AT FORTY-NINE

'My brain is not what it was. I'm past my best – & therefore, of course, I am now celebrated.'

As Russell approached his fiftieth birthday, this was the kind of wittily self-deprecating remark he was prone to make. On this occasion he was speaking to Virginia Woolf, next to whom he found himself sitting on 3 December 1921 at a dinner party in Chelsea given by his old Cambridge friend (now a successful and wealthy barrister) Charles Sanger. Sitting among such friends, Russell could not help but be deeply conscious of the fact that he had changed a great deal since the days when he and Sanger had been mathematics students together thirty years earlier, and, under Virginia Woolf's gentle but persistent prompting ('Bertie is a fervid egoist,' Woolf wrote that night in her diary, 'which helps matters'), he began to reflect on these changes. He still regarded mathematics as 'the most exalted form of art', he told her, but it was not an art that he himself expected ever to practise again: 'The brain becomes rigid at 50 – & I shall be 50 in a month or two' (actually, he would be fifty the following May). He might write more philosophy, he said, but 'I have to make money', and so most of his writing would henceforth be paid journalism. The days when he could devote himself solely to serious intellectual work were over. Between the ages of twenty-eight and thirty-eight, he told Woolf, he had 'lived in a cellar & worked', but then 'my passions got hold of me'. Now, he had come to terms with himself, and 'I don't expect any more emotional experiences. I don't think any longer that something is going to happen when I meet a new person.'

Virginia Woolf recorded all this in her diary without judgment or comment, but other friends noted the changes in Russell with dismay. At a dinner party two months later at the Webbs' home in Grosvenor Road, Russell was described by Beatrice Webb as 'cynical and witty', 'brilliantly intellectual' and yet 'not at peace either with himself or the world'. From a political point of view, she was inclined to regard him as a lightweight: 'He never seems serious, and his economic and political views follow on his temperamental likes and dislikes . . . He is too indolent or impatient to work out the problems of maximising freedom by deliberate social action.' All in all, she considered, he had gone downhill:

> His present role of a fallen angel with Mephistophelian wit, and his brilliantly analytic and scoffing intellect, makes him stimulating company. All the same, I look back on this vision of an old friend with sadness. He may be successful as a *littérateur*; I doubt whether he will be of value as a thinker, and I am pretty well certain he will not attain happiness of love given and taken and the peacefulness of constructive work. When one remembers the Bertrand Russell of twenty years ago, with his intense concentration on abstract thought, his virile body and chivalrous ways, his comradeship and pleasant kindly humour, the perfect personal dignity with a touch of puritanism, it is melancholy to look at this rather frowsy, unhealthy and cynical personage, prematurely old, linked to a . . . girl of light character and materialist philosophy whom he does not and cannot reverence.

Beatrice Webb had always been a perceptive chronicler of Russell's changing personality, and this is an especially acute portrait, distorted to some extent, perhaps, by her loyalty to Alys, Russell's first wife, and her consequent dismissal of his second wife, Dora ('a singularly unattractive little person'), who, though half Alys's age, was, at twenty-seven, a little old to be called a 'girl'.

What is striking about these glimpses of Russell from the diaries of Virginia Woolf and Beatrice Webb is the sense they give of Russell's old friends needing in 1921 to catch up with the changes in his life and personality. Much had happened to him since the outbreak of war in 1914 that they had not been part of, and, since the end of the war, he had been out of the country for much of the time, first in Soviet Russia and then in China. Now he was back in their midst with a new wife, a new career as a journalist and public speaker and, in some fundamental respects, a new attitude to life. It is therefore no wonder that he seems to have spent much of his time with his friends reflecting on these changes, trying to explain what had happened to the Bertrand Russell they had known in the 1890s, the earnest, priggish young man, whose chief passion was the contemplation of the abstract truths of logic and mathematics.

Russell liked to say that his life before 1910 and his life after 1914 were as sharply separated as Faust's life before and after he met Mephistopheles. The First World War, he said, 'changed everything' for him, leaving him with a completely different, and much darker, view of human nature: 'I became convinced that most human beings are possessed by a profound unhappiness venting itself in destructive rages . . . I learned an understanding of instinctive processes which I had not possessed before.' But, as Russell himself often emphasised, in teaching him about the power of 'instinctive processes', the war had merely continued a transformation in his outlook and personality that had begun several years earlier with the release of his own instincts, triggered by his passionate love for Ottoline Morrell.

Many of the changes in Russell noticed and lamented by Beatrice Webb were already apparent before the war started. The Russell who, in the spring of 1914, inspired T. S. Eliot's 'Mr Apollinax' (reminding Eliot of 'Priapus in the shrubbery/Gaping at the lady in the swing'), would have been as unfamiliar a figure to Russell's friends of the 1890s as the 'fallen angel' described by Beatrice Webb in 1921.

By the early 1920s, the Russell described by Webb – the cynical and witty *littérateur*, who had opinions on everything without ever thinking seriously about *anything* – had become almost a stock figure in fiction. One recognises him as Mr Scogan in Aldous Huxley's *Crome Yellow*, Melian Stokes in Gilbert Cannan's *Pugs and Peacocks*, Joshua Malleson in D. H. Lawrence's *Women in Love*, and again as Bertie Reid in Lawrence's short story, 'The Blind Man'. What these caricatures (all written by people who knew Russell personally) have in common is their portrayal of a man who, though extraordinarily intelligent, had somehow lost his way; a fallen character who, having lost his faith in everything – God, ideas, people – had lost, too, any serious sense of purpose. Russell considered himself to have found, first in his love for Ottoline and then in his work for peace during the war, a higher, nobler purpose than that which had inspired his great work in mathematics, but this is not how it was perceived by others, who could not take him quite seriously, either as a lover or as a political reformer. In both roles he appeared incongruous and therefore a trivial, diminished figure compared to the intense, august and incontestably great author of *The Principles of Mathematics* and *Principia Mathematica*. Gilbert Cannan, for example, describes Melian Stokes as having, in his youth, 'achieved that obscure but illustrious fame which is given to mathematicians and men of science', and having then turned to politics, where the very qualities that made him a great mathematician and philosopher prove to be his undoing. It falls to his wise old aunt to tell him:

You are the same Melian with the difference only that you are working at a subject which the rest of us can reach, and the philosophic method in politics is, to say the least, alarming. You see, in politics, there is nothing to be proved. It is purely a matter of falling dexterously out of one muddle into another, and, my dear, you have no practice in falling. At a time like this, how can you be either witty or logical? And if you are neither – where is Melian?

Echoes of these sentiments can be heard again and again in the words of Russell's friends, most brutally, perhaps, in the oft-repeated saying of G. M. Trevelyan, who knew Russell well when they were undergraduates together in the 1890s: 'He [Russell] may be a genius in mathematics – as to that I am no judge; but about politics he is a perfect goose.'

As a philosopher of mathematics, Russell had achieved rare greatness; as a journalist and political commentator, he was to produce a staggering amount of second-rate writing. The problem, as many of his friends identified, was partly that he approached politics with the logician's desire for absolute clarity, and thus, impatient with the messy realities of political life, was inclined to oversimplify every issue. But partly, also, it was, as Beatrice Webb saw, that he did *not* bring to politics the qualities that made him a great philosopher and logician. His best philosophical writing is subtle, nuanced and unafraid of complexity. He supports his views with rigorous and sophisticated arguments, and deals with objections carefully and respectfully. In most of the journalism and political writing that he produced in the second half of his life, however, these qualities are absent, replaced with empty rhetoric, blind dogmatism and a cavalier refusal to take the views of his opponents seriously. The gulf in quality between Russell's writings on logic and his writings on politics is cavernous. The question that must be raised, therefore, is why he abandoned a subject of which he was one of the greatest practitioners since Aristotle in favour of one to which he had very little of any value to contribute.

There is a story that on one of his lecture tours of America, Russell found himself at dinner sitting next to the principal of a respectable girls' college, who asked him: 'Why did you give up philosophy?' To which he is supposed to have replied: 'Because I discovered I preferred fucking.' The story is probably apocryphal, though it chimes with many things that Russell did say, including his remark to Virginia Woolf that his devotion to serious intellectual work came to an end when 'my passions got hold of me'. There is no doubt that Russell's love for Ottoline, and his subsequent romantic adventures, helped to weaken the hold on him of his absorption in the philosophy of mathematics. What finally killed his interest in mathematics, however, as he himself acknowledged, was the impact of Ludwig Wittgenstein, which, as Russell was to write in *My Philosophical Development*, 'came in two waves'.

The first wave came in the summer of 1913, when Wittgenstein temporarily destroyed Russell's philosophical self-confidence through his devastating attack on Russell's theory of judgment. The second wave came in 1919, after Russell had to some extent rebuilt his self-confidence, when he read Wittgenstein's *Tractatus Logico-Philosophicus* and became convinced by it that the view of logic that had motivated his own work on the philosophy of mathematics was fundamentally wrong. Up until his reading of Wittgenstein's *Tractatus*, Russell took a more or less Platonist view of logic, regarding it as the study of objective and eternal truths. After reading Wittgenstein, Russell became convinced that, on the contrary, logic was purely linguistic, so-called 'logical truths' being nothing more than tautologies. Though this might sound a fairly recondite matter, it is almost impossible to exaggerate its effect on Russell's life. Russell's great work on the philosophy of mathematics was inspired by the dream of arriving at truths that were demonstrable, incorrigible and known with absolute certainty. Logic, he thought, was such a body of truth, and his ambition of proving that mathematics was but a branch of logic was driven by his desire to show that a substantial body of knowledge, namely mathematics, was impervious to sceptical doubt. If logic was not a body of truth, but merely – as Russell put it immediately after his conversion to a Wittgensteinian view

– a matter of giving 'different ways of saying the same thing', then this dream vanished and with it the hope of arriving at *any* absolutely certain knowledge. Neither logic nor mathematics had the philosophical interest that Russell had attributed to them, and that, fundamentally, was why he abandoned the philosophy of mathematics.

But why should he turn his attention instead to hack journalism and political writing? Partly for the reason he gave to Virginia Woolf: that, with a wife and child to support, he needed to earn money. As the child of an aristocratic family, he had inherited enough to live on without an earnt income, but he had given this inheritance away, some of it to the London School of Economics and some of it to T. S. Eliot. He had also rejected the offer of a lectureship from Trinity College, Cambridge, apparently believing that, having been divorced by his first wife for adultery, he was no longer respectable enough to survive in academic life (though it seems likely that his diminished interest in academic philosophy also had something to do with it). In any case, he believed, rightly, that he could earn more money from freelance writing than he could as a university lecturer. He had also come to believe that he could do more good as a political commentator writing for a wide audience than as an academic writing for the very few who understood mathematical logic. It was perhaps in this respect that the war had its most profound and far-reaching effect upon him.

After the war, Russell was famous, not for his philosophy but for his politics. His passionate and brave stand against the war, and particularly against conscription, had made him a hero among the younger generation, and the series of public lectures that he gave in 1915, published as *Principles of Social Reconstruction*, had established him as someone who might provide intellectual leadership to the Socialist and pacifist movements. His second wife, Dora, was one of many who came to admire him as a political leader rather than as a philosopher, and she encouraged him in his belief that he had something important and relevant to contribute to political life, a belief that was reinforced during their year in China when he lectured on political subjects more often than on logic and was hailed, somewhat ludicrously, as 'the greatest social philosopher of [the] world'.

Russell knew, of course, that this was nonsense, but if the world (outside the circle of his more discerning friends) was prepared to regard his hastily written lectures and articles as great social and political thought, and if, by supplying the seemingly inexhaustible demand for this material, he was able to provide well for his wife and son, then he was prepared to keep producing it at an ever more prolific rate. In his more self-critical moments, he might reflect that he was being celebrated for work that was manifestly and incomparably inferior to his writing on logic, but, for the most part, he was happy to make light of this irony. As his fiftieth birthday loomed, he knew that he was past his best as a serious thinker, but, for the moment, this mattered less to him than the fact that he had, at last, achieved his most heartfelt ambition: he had become a father.

2

MORAL TRAINING IN THE WASTE LAND

The day Russell became a father, 16 November 1921, was quite possibly the happiest day of his life. Having a child, and preferably a son, was the strongest desire he had had for about twenty years, and now that the desire was fulfilled the child became the very centre of his life. Everything else that mattered to Russell – philosophy, mathematics, romantic love, politics – took second place in his affections to his beloved son, John Conrad. John gave him, as Russell himself put it, 'a new emotional centre' to his life and, for the first ten years at least, was the source of Russell's greatest hopes and happiness. Russell might have loved his previous lovers, Ottoline Morrell and Constance Malleson ('Colette'), more deeply than he loved Dora, but Dora had given him a son, and because of that he was prepared to overlook every other consideration. Because Dora had been willing to bear his children, he had married her in preference to Colette, and because he needed to provide for Dora and the child he was prepared to abandon his academic career in favour of the more lucrative business of freelance writing. *Everything* in his life was arranged around his desire to bring up a son and to see that son grow up to be the pride of his father. Even Beatrice Webb, who thought little of Dora, or of Russell for marrying her, conceded that 'the boy may keep them together'. 'For', she added, 'Bertie seems inclined to dote on his son and heir.'

Indeed he did. Shortly after the birth, Russell, in a parody of the aristocratic custom, but with a pride that was entirely genuine, hired a horse and carriage to take himself and Dora around London, showing their son off to the populace. Russell, his new wife and their baby son lived in a small terraced house in Sydney Street, Chelsea, which they furnished with rugs brought back from China and the meticulously designed wooden furniture that Russell had bought from Wittgenstein in 1919 (Russell's son was born in Wittgenstein's bed). A bust of Voltaire stood on the mantelpiece of Russell's ground-floor study, and portraits of the Earls and Dukes of Bedford (Russell's ancestors), and of Leibniz and Spinoza (his 'spiritual ancestors', as he liked to say), adorned the walls. In Chelsea, the Russells were surrounded by old friends, including Alfred North Whitehead, Charles Sanger and Desmond MacCarthy. They received dinner invitations, too,

from the Webbs in Grosvenor Road (a short walk away) and from the
Woolfs, John Maynard Keynes and Ottoline Morrell in Bloomsbury.
'Bloomsbury dinners were alarming to a novice,' Dora has recalled, 'the talk
was allusive, often learned, exchanges swift. Modesty required listening
rather than talk; in any case it would have been difficult to get a word in
edgeways.' Russell's own talk, like his letters at this time, dwelt on just two
subjects: the changes in him that events had wrought since the war and his
son.

Working as a freelance writer had, for Russell, the advantage that he was
hardly ever more than a few yards away from John. 'I lead a queer life,' he
wrote to Ottoline Morrell on 31 January 1922. 'Most days I hardly go
outside the house, reading and writing about the Far East, and at intervals
studying the child.' The baby, Russell noted ruefully, looked just like
Immanuel Kant, though others noticed an almost comically exact likeness to
Russell himself. 'I am amazed to find', he told Ottoline, 'how much
passionate affection one can give to a little creature who as yet is only
stimulated to activity by greed and stomach-ache.' When he said that he
spent the intervals between writing in studying his son, he was not speaking
lightly. John, he reported to Ottoline, had, at the age of two months, 'all the
characteristics that as a psychologist I should have expected. He has learnt to
follow things with his eyes, but hasn't found out yet that he can do it by
turning his head and he has not found out that the things he sees are the
same as the things he touches.'

Russell was determined to be a model parent. Unfortunately for poor
John, however, his birth happened to coincide with Russell's adoption of a
fervent interest and faith in 'scientific' psychology, his utopian hopes for
which recall his earlier hopes for mathematics. Just as he had earlier dreamt
of reducing all knowledge to mathematics, so he now looked to psychology
to provide solutions to the ethical, social and political problems raised by the
First World War. The war having aroused his interest in the study of
instinct, Russell believed that, if we were to prevent such wars in the future,
we would have to understand, and thus overcome, the instinctual drives that
led men to fight. If we had a scientific understanding of human psychology,
he thought, we could use it to create a new type of person. If people believe,
he wrote, 'that there is no way of producing an adult population whose
behaviour will be radically different from that of existing populations', then
'they are flying in the face of all modern psychology'.

He talked of creating young people 'freed from fear and inhibitions and
rebellious or thwarted instincts' and implied that this could be achieved
within a generation. 'A generation educated in fearless freedom', he claimed,
'will have wider and bolder hopes than are possible to us, who still have to
struggle with the superstitious fears that lie in wait for us below the level of
consciousness.' War, famine and even fear itself, he implied, could be
abolished if we brought up our children correctly. 'Scientific' psychology
would enable us to do this, he believed, by showing us how we could 'train
the instincts' to produce 'a harmonious character, constructive rather than

destructive, affectionate rather than sullen, courageous, frank and intelligent'. All this, he claimed, 'can be done with a great majority of children; it is actually being done where children are rightly treated':

> If existing knowledge were used and tested methods applied, we could, in a generation, produce a population almost wholly free from disease, malevolence and stupidity. We do not do so, because we prefer oppression and war.

For Russell, 'scientific' psychology meant behaviourism, particularly the work of John B. Watson, whose writings Russell began to study in 1918. The influence of Watson on Russell's general thinking about mental phenomena is revealed in *The Analysis of Mind*, published in 1921. But, by a further misfortune for John, just as he was born, Watson began to turn his attention specifically to the subject of infant development. In December 1921, the month after John's birth, Watson published, in collaboration with his wife, an article called 'Studies in Infant Psychology', which was to have a decisive influence on Russell's conception of the correct method of parenthood. The article contained a report of the Watsons' experiments on young children, and sought to show how emotional reactions could be 'conditioned'. Most famously, the Watsons reported on their successful attempts to induce in 'little Albert', an eleven-month-old baby, a fear of rats. Introduced to a white rat, Albert showed to begin with only curiosity in it, reaching out to touch it and being pleased when the rat pressed its nose against him. By frightening the child with a loud noise whenever the rat appeared, however (they banged a steel bar with a heavy hammer above his head), the Watsons reversed this reaction, causing the boy to whimper whenever the rat appeared. Upon such experimental data was Russell's faith in the 'training of the instincts' based, and upon John's infant shoulders came to rest the burden of that faith.

Inspired by Watson's work, Russell began to think that parenting itself could be provided with a scientific foundation. 'The child is to be trained from the first in the habits we wish him to acquire,' he announced, and, if we wish to know *how* to train the child, we should look, not to the accumulated wisdom of mothers and nurses, but to the 'science of child psychology'. 'Mothers and nurses', Russell wrote, 'were supposed to know by instinct what was good for the child. As a matter of fact, they did not know.' Reviewing Watson's book, *The Psychological Care of Infant and Child*, he suggested that it might be retitled 'How to Make Mothers Harmless' and expressed himself to be 'in a considerable measure of agreement' with Watson's chapter on the 'Dangers of Too Much Mother Love'.

What Russell thought should replace the traditional methods of motherly love was outlined by him in the chapter on 'The First Year' in his 1926 book, *On Education*. From this, a rather grim picture emerges of how John spent his infancy. To Watson's already rather austere notions of how infants should be treated,[1] Russell added his own emphasis on undermining the child's sense of his or her own importance. 'To the devoted parent,' he writes, 'the child is immensely important':

Unless care is taken, the child feels this, and judges himself as important as his parents feel him . . . Do not let the child see how much you do for it, or how much trouble you take . . . Above all, we should not give the child a sense of self-importance which later experience will mortify, and which, in any case, is not in accordance with the facts.

The origin of this attitude (if we resist the temptation to attribute it to a more general misanthropy, a jealousy of his son or a fear of the enormous importance that his son had for him) seems to lie in Russell's conviction that the essence of morality is the overcoming of egoism, together with his belief that: 'The right moment to begin . . . moral training is the moment of birth.' Egoism, the root cause of almost all immorality, could, he appears to have thought, be nipped in the bud during infancy.

Thus, while John was, in fact, the emotional centre of his life and the object of Russell's unceasing devotion and attention, Russell took great pains to disguise this fact from him, in order, 'scientifically', to make his son a better person. Much of the advice that Russell gives for looking after babies (stated with an astonishing dogmatic finality) is based upon the premise that the all-important thing is to prevent the infant from acquiring an inflated view of itself. In order to accomplish this, we have to unlearn the methods traditionally used by mothers and trust in the use of conditioning to instil habits of behaviour:

Take such a matter as sleep. All mothers wish their children to sleep, because it is both healthy and convenient when they do so. They had developed a certain technique: rocking the cradle and singing lullabies. It was left for males, who investigated the matter scientifically, to discover that this technique is ideally wrong, for though it is likely to succeed on any given day, it creates bad habits. Every child loves to be made a fuss of, because its sense of self-importance is gratified. If it finds that by not sleeping it secures attention it will soon learn to adopt this method. The result is equally damaging to health and character. The great thing here is the formation of habit: the association of the cot with sleep.

The 'scientific' way is thus to place the baby in the cot and ignore its cries for attention. Babies, in Russell's view, are cunning little creatures: they cry when they are not in pain, simply because they want affection; they seek praise for doing things, like eating and sleeping, that are not in the least praiseworthy; and they demand to be amused when they ought to be sleeping. Accordingly:

---

[1] As Russell (approvingly) summarises them, Watson's views are that: 'Mothers are not to kiss their children except once in a way on the forehead; fathers are not to take them on their knee; two children must never sleep in the same room, nor should a child sleep in the same room with an adult after the first stages of infancy.'

... if it [the baby] cries when there is no adequate physical cause, it must be left to cry; if not, it will quickly develop into a tyrant. When it is attended to, there should not be too much fuss: what is necessary must be done, but without excessive expressions of sympathy.

It is easy and agreeable to amuse an infant by dandling it or singing to it. But it learns with amazing rapidity to demand more and more of such amusements, which soon interfere with necessary sleep – and sleep ought to occupy almost all the day except meal-times.

... do not minister to the child's self-importance by letting it see that you mind if it does not sleep or eat or evacuate as it should ... Never let the child think that a necessary normal action, such as eating, which ought to be a pleasure, is something that you desire, and that you want it to do to please you. If you do, the child soon perceives that it has acquired a new source of power, and expects to be coaxed into actions which it ought to perform spontaneously.

'Some of these precepts may seem harsh,' Russell concedes, 'but experience shows that they make for the child's health and happiness.' Many years later, his daughter, Kate, born two years after John, retorted: 'Whose experience? Not mine, either as an infant or as a mother.'

In view of what later happened to John, Russell's confidence in his parental methods appears tragically misplaced. Of course, the links between cause and effect here are very difficult to determine, and one should be wary of attributing John's later misfortunes directly to his upbringing; but, at the very least, one can say, as Russell himself conceded, that he was 'unduly optimistic' about the power of behaviouristic conditioning to produce the habits of character he sought to instil in his son. 'I think now that the methods I proposed with very young children were unduly harsh,' he admitted in his old age. John did not grow up to be fearless, independent and free, as Russell's theory demanded that he should, but rather inhibited, withdrawn and anxious. It is only in retrospect, however, that we can say: 'No wonder'.

Some initial signs that John was not exactly thriving on the 'moral training' imposed upon him from the moment of his birth appear in Dora's autobiography, *The Tamarisk Tree*. 'John had not been doing too well after the first month or two,' she recalls. They decided that this was due to living in London, and they therefore began to look for a house in Cornwall in which they could spend at least part of the year. Dora chose a house called 'Sunny Bank' in Porthcurno, near Penzance. The name would obviously not do (one of their first visitors, Vera Meynell, remarked incredulously that the Russells lived in 'simple domestic bliss' in a house 'actually called Sunny Bank'), and it was changed to 'Carn Voel' after a nearby headland. It was (and is), as Dora put it, 'a funny house', full of small rooms that betray its origins as a boarding house. But it was only a short walk away from the lovely little beach at Porthcurno, and it had a distant view of the sea. In any case, Dora was delighted with it, and Russell agreed to buy it.

'It is lovely here,' Russell wrote to Ottoline from Cornwall in May 1922:

The birds sing all day. There are larks and thrushes and blackbirds and cuckoos and curlews and seagulls all round the house, and ships sail by, and at night one hears the sea in the distance booming on the rocks, and there is blackthorn and whitethorn, and bluebells and buttercups, and green fields and gorse moors, all without stirring from the house.

'The boy thrives amazingly,' he told her. 'He is quite a different creature from what he was when we came. He is full of fun and very roguish and I love him beyond measure.' The following week, he wrote again. 'The house is hideous,' he conceded, 'and the garden entirely bare. But we are going to buy it, as it suits both us and the boy.' John, now six months old, was flourishing, 'and we keep wondering whether he really is intelligent and beautiful or whether we only think so. I don't know.' In Cornwall that summer, Russell was perhaps happier than he had ever been. 'In my memory,' he wrote, 'which, of course, is fallacious, it was always sunny.' Forgetting, for the moment, to study and train his son, he gave himself up to the simple enjoyments of being with a young child at the seaside: playing on the sands, boating on the sea and climbing on the rocks. 'I want him to be an outdoor boy,' he wrote to Ottoline. Dora remembers them both being 'infatuated with our firstborn', who 'throve on Cornish milk and air from the start, and was soon cheerful and sunburnt'. Russell, too, was 'robust again, sunburnt and happy', even 'rather beefy', and the two of them 'unrepentantly lay in the sun, swam as early as May, tramped all round the marvellous West Penwith coast, and thought nothing of pushing John in his pram four miles across country to Sennen Cove'.

At the end of the summer, the Russells travelled to the Continent to stay with Russell's sister-in-law, the novelist Elizabeth von Arnim, at her chalet in Switzerland, stopping *en route* in Austria to visit Wittgenstein, whom Russell had not seen since the end of 1919, when they met to go through Wittgenstein's then unpublished book, *Tractatus Logico-Philosophicus*. Since then the book had been published, and Wittgenstein, like Russell, had abandoned philosophy – in his case for a life as an elementary schoolteacher in rural Austria. They met in Innsbruck, where, according to Dora's recollection: 'We all tramped the streets trying to find rooms in which to stay':

Wittgenstein was in an agony of wounded pride at the state of his country and his inability to show some sort of hospitality. In the end we found one room, in which Bertie and I occupied the bed and Wittgenstein a couch. But the hotel had a terrace, where it was pleasant enough to sit while Bertie discussed how to get Wittgenstein to England.

'It has been suggested that they quarrelled on this occasion,' Dora wrote. 'Wittgenstein was never easy, but I think any differences must have been over their philosophical ideas . . . The circumstances of the time made this a troubled meeting.'

In fact, this was the last time the two met as friends. In his autobiography, Russell alludes to the meeting in a rather condescending manner, describing Wittgenstein as being then 'at the height of his mystic ardour'. Though Wittgenstein 'assured me with great earnestness that it is better to be good than clever', Russell scoffs, 'I found him terrified of wasps, and, because of bugs, unable to stay another night in lodgings we had found in Innsbruck. After my travels in Russia and China, I was inured to small matters of that sort, but not all his conviction that the things of this world are of no account could enable him to endure insects with patience.' The tone of mocking superiority is misplaced (having fought on the Eastern and Italian Fronts, and been held captive by the Italians, Wittgenstein had surely endured conditions at least as harsh as anything Russell had experienced in Russia and China), and perhaps Russell's emphasis on Wittgenstein's alleged fear of insects serves to distract from what really made this meeting uncomfortable: the fact that he was severely criticised by Wittgenstein for preferring cleverness to moral integrity, a criticism that echoes those made earlier in the year by Beatrice Webb when she complained of Russell's lack of seriousness.

Wittgenstein's friend, Paul Engelmann, has recalled how, at Innsbruck, Wittgenstein rebuked Russell fiercely for his concern with 'peace and freedom'. 'Well, I suppose *you* would rather establish a World Organisation for War and Slavery,' Russell is said to have retorted. 'Yes, rather that, rather that!' came the uncompromising reply. The exchange carries echoes of D. H. Lawrence's fierce denunciation of Russell in 1915 ('to come as the angel of peace – no, I prefer Tirpitz a thousand times in that role'), and my guess is that, after their meeting at Innsbruck, Russell chose to dismiss Wittgenstein as he had earlier dismissed Lawrence, as an irrationalist, a 'mystic', whose criticisms of his character ought not to be given any credence. Russell's descriptions of Lawrence and Wittgenstein run strangely parallel: Lawrence was 'a man of a certain imaginative genius', Wittgenstein 'perhaps the most perfect example I have ever known of genius as traditionally conceived'; Lawrence was 'an essentially timid man, who tried to conceal his timidity', Wittgenstein was afraid of wasps. Both were mystics, and both, to some extent, figures of fun; neither could *quite* be taken seriously.

Like Lawrence, too, Wittgenstein does not seem to have realised that his friendship with Russell could not survive his denunciation of him. Among some papers of Wittgenstein's were found two letters to Russell, perhaps unsent, written after their meeting in Innsbruck. Both are couched in a friendly tone, asking Russell to write with news of himself, his wife and his baby, and both begin: 'It is a long time since I have heard from you.' It is in keeping with Wittgenstein's personality that he made a strenuous effort at Innsbruck to improve Russell's character; it is in keeping with Russell's that he took this as a sign that Wittgenstein no longer wished to be his friend.

Between Wittgenstein and Russell there was a fundamental clash of ethical sensibilities. When Wittgenstein was once asked what one can do to improve the world, he replied: 'Improve yourself; that is the only thing you can do to improve the world.' In his letters to Ottoline Morrell during the war, and elsewhere in his writings, Russell had raised the same dilemma and had come down on the other side: the important thing, for him, was not to improve his own character, but to do what he could to improve the world. In asking him to abandon his concern for 'peace and freedom', Wittgenstein was asking Russell to abandon his entire *Weltanschauung*. In the massive amounts of journalism that Russell produced after deciding to become a freelance writer, he wrote not only for money (though certainly for that as well), but also to influence the world to take what he considered to be a more sane course. What he was expressing in this writing was a 'philosophy of life' of a kind that typically does not, and cannot, find expression in articles written for academic philosophy journals.

Nowhere is this more apparent than in the flood of articles he wrote between 1921 and 1922 on the subject of China, many of which were used as chapters in his book *The Problem of China*. Since his visit there the previous year, China had held a special place in Russell's heart. It had for him a symbolic significance, representing the frail hope that civilisation might triumph over the barbarism that had been unleashed by the First World War. Russell's attitude to the war was, and still is, often misrepresented as 'pacifist'. In fact Russell, as he tried to make clear in several of his writings during the war, was never a pacifist. He did not think war itself was wrong; what he thought was wrong was that two of the most civilised nations in the world, Germany and Britain, were at war with each other. This, he thought, threatened civilisation itself, and pointed to the need to think afresh the structure of our society, establishing new forms of government, new methods in education and a more sceptical attitude to the authority of religious and political leaders. And, especially, he believed, it obliged us to think carefully about the power conferred upon us by the advancement of science. Science was the surest guide to truth, but, precisely because of that, it could be used to catastrophically destructive ends, as was witnessed on the Western Front.

What Russell found in China was a poignant symbol of this dilemma. The Chinese, he believed, were the most civilised nation on earth: 'The Chinese are gentle, urbane, seeking only justice and freedom. They have a civilisation superior to ours in all that makes for human happiness . . . I think they are the only people in the world who quite genuinely believe that wisdom is more precious than rubies.' The Chinese, as Russell saw them, had a great love of literature, art and music, a healthily sceptical attitude to religion, an exquisite code of manners and a delightfully mischievous sense of fun. What they lacked was science, technology and industry, and, for this reason, they fell prey to the military dominance of Japan and the Western powers. As the post-war future of China was being discussed at the Washington Conference in 1922, therefore, something more was at stake for Russell than the immediate political question of whether the Western powers could agree to respect China's national sovereignty. The fundamental question, *the* problem of China, was: 'Can Chinese virtues be preserved? Or must China, in order to survive, acquire, instead, the vices which make for success, and cause misery to others only?'

To some extent, Russell recognised, China had to become Westernised; that is, it had to become industrialised: 'The . . . danger is that they may become completely Westernised, retaining nothing of what has hitherto distinguished them, adding merely one more to the restless, intelligent, industrial and militaristic nations which now afflict this unfortunate planet.' The war 'showed that something is wrong with our civilisation'; China could help to show us *what* was wrong: 'The Chinese have discovered, and have practised for many centuries, a way of life which, if it could be adopted by all the world, would make all the world happy. We Europeans have not.' China had problems that 'demand Western science. But they do not demand the adoption of the Western philosophy of life.' The problem of China, therefore, was the problem facing us all: of whether civilisation itself could survive. Could the benefits of science, technology and industry be given to a society without it also importing the aggressive militarism that characterises the Western nations?

> . . . if, when they have become safe at home, they can turn aside from the materialistic activities imposed by the Powers, and devote their freedom to science and art and the inauguration of a better economic system – then China will have played the part in the world for which she is fitted, and will have given to mankind as a whole new hope in the moment of greatest need. It is this hope that I wish to see inspiring Young China. This hope is realisable; and because it is realisable, China deserves a foremost place in the esteem of every lover of mankind.

Much of Russell's other writing during this time could be regarded as variations on the same theme: what must be done if civilisation is to survive? For example, in 'Obstacles to Free Thought', which he delivered as a public lecture in March 1922 and then published as two articles in *The Freeman*, Russell argued that the greatest threat to civilisation comprised the credulity and irrationalism that characterise the mass of people in advanced countries, who are unable, or unwilling, to think freely and clearly. This could be overcome, he insists, only by encouraging people to question and doubt the things they are told by politicians and priests, by persuading them to adopt a sceptical, scientific outlook:

> My plea throughout this essay has been for the spread of the scientific temper, which is an altogether different thing from the knowledge of scientific results. The scientific temper is capable of regenerating mankind and providing an issue for all our troubles. The results of science, in the form of mechanism, poison gas and the Yellow Press, bid fair to lead to the total downfall of our civilisation. It is a curious antithesis, which a Martian might contemplate with amused detachment. But for us it is a matter of life and death. Upon its issue depends the question whether our grandchildren are to live in a happier world, or are to exterminate each other by scientific methods, leaving perhaps to negroes and Papuans the future destinies of mankind.

The visceral racism evident in Russell's mention of 'negroes' in this context reappears in many other places in his writing and, more overtly, in his conversation. Its main function here, though, is of course symbolic: the vision of the world led by negroes standing as an image of the catastrophic consequences of civilisation killing itself.

In 'Hopes and Fears as Regards America', published in two parts in *The New Republic* at about the same time, Russell developed another variation on the same theme, dwelling this time on the role that America must now take as the leading defender of the civilised world, and on the importance of Socialism as the only political doctrine that could prevent civilised countries from once again going to war with each other. 'Apart from the Russian Revolution,' he argued, 'the most striking result of the war has been the world-supremacy of the United States.' This was a hopeful development, in that America's foreign policy was more enlightened than that of the European powers, but fearful, in that America was the most stridently *capitalist* country in the world, and capitalism was 'by its very nature contrary to justice, freedom and democracy'. 'Practically all advanced opinion in Europe', Russell claimed, 'believes that the world's ills can only be cured by socialism.' America, in this respect, was somewhat less advanced: 'American radicals . . . are somewhat less radical than those of some other countries.'

As is clear from almost everything he wrote during this period, Russell's conversion to Socialism was itself driven by his fundamental concern with the preservation of civilisation. Capitalism, he believed, bred the kind of aggressive rivalry that made war inevitable. As he had put it in *The Problem of China*: 'it is impossible to make a silk purse out of a sow's ear, or peace and freedom out of capitalism'. As peace between civilised countries is a necessary precondition of the survival of civilisation, it follows that capitalism and civilisation are incompatible. Given the world dominance of America, it further follows that a 'complete collapse of civilisation' could be averted only if 'the American belief in capitalism can be shaken'.

In two articles published in the summer of 1922, 'Socialism in Undeveloped Countries' and 'Socialism in Advanced Countries', Russell provided a lofty, but in many ways perceptive, analysis of the prospects for international Socialism. 'The ultimate victory of Socialism', he argued, 'will have to come from the advanced countries.' Because their industries were undeveloped, Russia and China would not be able to stand up to the might of the United States, and thus would have, eventually, to 'relapse under the economic dominion of the Western Powers'. Similarly, Britain would not be able to take the lead, because 'We cannot . . . as things stand at present, adopt any economic policy, even in home affairs, which is displeasing to our American masters.' Therefore 'The future of mankind depends upon the action of America during the next half-century.' If America continues 'upon the path of capitalist imperialism which is indicated by present tendencies and opportunities', there will be an international class-war between it and the oppressed nations of the world, and, whether the European countries are on the side of the oppressor or the oppressed, the result will be a world war 'so long and destructive that nothing would be left of European civilisation at the end'. Civilisation itself will be destroyed, in America as well as in Europe, so that 'After reverting for centuries to the life of Red Indians, the Americans might be re-discovered by a second Columbus hunting wild beasts with bows and arrows on Manhattan Island.'

The only hope for mankind, therefore, is to see in America 'a belief in socialism, or at least a disbelief in capitalism, spread from individual to individual'. Such a belief is so in accord with reason and common sense that it is not unreasonable to expect it to so spread, once it is realised that Socialism need not necessarily lead to a diminution of individual liberty and that it is 'capable of increasing the happiness of all but an infinitesimal section in an advanced industrial community'. For this to happen, Socialists must put their faith in reasoned arguments rather than propaganda and 'abandon the class outlook hitherto prevailing among socialists'. The adoption of a class point of view 'breeds strife, oppression and bitterness, and cannot be expected to appeal to members of other classes'. Socialism must be seen to be 'a gain to the community, not only to the wage-earners in the lower ranks of labour'. The case for such a 'scientific socialism' will have such persuasive force that all but a tiny handful of capitalists will accept it: 'It is in this way, and in this way only, that socialism can be made to prevail in a country like the United States.'

As to what, exactly, he meant by 'Socialism', Russell was rather sketchy. His definition contained three basic tenets: 1. 'All land and capital must be the property of the State'; 2. 'what is paid for each kind of work must be fixed by a public authority, with a minimum of what is required for bare necessaries, and a maximum of what will give the greatest incentive to efficient work'; and 3. 'all sane adults should have an equal share of ultimate political power'. The implications of the first of these are, of course, huge, but Russell does not dwell on them beyond spelling out that, of course, they would include the nationalisation of all major industries and the confiscation without compensation of all private capital. His conviction that all but a tiny number of millionaires would accept these measures once the arguments for them had been presented, seems a little fanciful. However, given tenet number three, such widespread acceptance would have to be a necessary condition for the other two tenets to be enforced. What Russell seemed to envisage was the overwhelming majority of paid employees, in whatever industry, on whatever level of pay and at whatever level of managerial seniority, voting to become civil servants. They would do this, he seemed to think, because they would see that the alternative was class-war and the destruction of civilisation.

It was perhaps this tendency of Russell's to approach political questions from a position of lofty generality that prompted Beatrice Webb's criticism of his being 'too indolent or impatient to work out the problems of maximising freedom by deliberate social action', and her dismissal of him as a mere *littérateur*. And perhaps this explains too why, despite expressing his fervent allegiance to the Labour Party in many of his public utterances, he was kept somewhat at arm's length by the leaders of the party. As the election of 1922 approached, Russell was suggested as a candidate for the perfectly winnable seat of London University, by the chairman of the University Labour Party, R. H. Tawney. Tawney had objected to the candidature being offered instead to H. G. Wells on the grounds that, as Beatrice Webb put it, 'Bertrand Russell is a gentleman and H. G. a cad', but, she sniffed, such a consideration was 'hardly relevant if it is sexual morality which is to be the test'.

Russell was offered instead the candidature in his home constituency of Chelsea, one of the safest Tory seats in the country. He had no chance of winning against the sitting MP, Sir Samuel Hoare, and, indeed, did not want to; he only agreed to stand, he said, to make propaganda for the causes in which he believed. In his electoral address he pledged his 'complete agreement' with the programme of the Labour Party, and emphasised, in particular, his support for nationalisation of the mines and railways, his conviction that the best solution to unemployment lay in restoring 'normal life' to Europe, and his strong opposition to 'all suggestions of violent revolution'. In the course of the campaign, however, he made propaganda for the less orthodox and more controversial cause of birth control, a cause to which Dora was becoming passionately committed. Dora seemed to enjoy the campaign more than he did. The count, on 15 November, was, she recalls, a thrilling experience: 'As I watched those piles of voting papers in that, my first election, I felt tense excitement.' The election was won by the Tories, led by Bonar Law, but the Labour Party doubled its number of MPs and became, for the first time, the second-largest party in the House. At its first meeting in Parliament it elected as its leader the anti-war campaigner, Ramsay MacDonald. 'I am delighted with the general results,' Russell wrote to Ottoline. 'Our UDC friends got in everywhere.'

As the Labour Party was now more powerful than it had ever been before, and as many of the people Russell had campaigned alongside during the war now occupied influential positions within the party, one might have expected Russell, at this point in his life, to have become more actively involved in it: helping to shape its policy, sitting on its committees, even writing its propaganda. In fact, he remained a rather marginal figure in the party, supporting it through his journalism, but excluded from its policy-making decisions and somewhat distant from its leadership. It is difficult to know to what to attribute this distance. There is little sign that the party tried to woo Russell into becoming more closely involved, but equally little sign that he wanted to become so. His unhappy experience of acting as 'substitute chairman' of the No-Conscription Fellowship during the war was no doubt still fresh in his mind. 'Writing and speaking are easy to me,' he had written then, 'but administration is impossible.' For all his desire to see the Labour Party pursue the policies in which he believed, perhaps he recognised that he was not a committee man.

In any case, he had more than enough 'writing and speaking' to keep him occupied. As well as his heavy load of journalism and the occasional public lecture, Russell endeavoured to keep in touch with the world of academic philosophy by reviewing books and replying to criticisms. One of the most interesting of these replies was the one he published in *The Journal of Philosophy* in November 1922 in response to the review of *The Analysis of Mind* by the Oxford pragmatist philosopher F. C. S. Schiller. Schiller had attacked Russell's theory of the mind for being too abstract and analytical, and his general approach to philosophy for being 'atavistic', seeing in it, at bottom, a return to Hume and accusing Russell of ignoring the revolution in philosophy inaugurated by Kant's criticisms of Hume. In reply, Russell took up the challenge to fight on a broad front and dismissed 'the whole romantic movement, beginning with Rousseau and Kant, and culminating in pragmatism and futurism', as 'a regrettable aberration'. He would, he proclaimed, take 'Back to the eighteenth century' as his battle cry. The romantic emphasis on the feelings of the heart, rather than the thinking of the mind, was a disaster:

> I dislike the heart as an inspirer of beliefs; I much prefer the spleen. I take comfort in Freud's work, because it shows what we are to think of the heart, which, he says, makes us desire the death of our parents, and therefore dream that they are dead, with a hypocritical sorrow in our very dreams. The heart is the cause of the anti-rational philosophy that begins with Kant and leads to the 'will to believe'. The heart is the inspirer of atrocities against negroes, the late war, and the starvation of Russia.

Defending the behaviourist reliance upon what Schiller had called 'the standpoint of an extraneous observer', Russell insisted that it was the only *scientific* way of investigating the mind; self-knowledge, he was convinced, was 'precarious and deceptive': 'What little I know about myself I owe to the observations of candid friends.' (One wonders here whether he would have included Lawrence and Wittgenstein among those 'candid friends'.) In his defence of the method of analysis against 'mystics' ('as one may call the opponents of analysis'), Russell again emphasised the importance of scientific inquiry, to the point at which he came close to abolishing any role for philosophy at all. The more science advances, he wrote, 'the more abstract and analytical it becomes; and the more abstract and analytical it becomes, the more it is able to increase our knowledge of the world':

> I do not believe that there is any way of obtaining knowledge except the scientific way. Some of the problems with which philosophy has concerned itself can be solved by scientific methods; others cannot. Those which cannot are insoluble.

The same note was struck in the paper entitled 'Vagueness', which Russell presented at a meeting of the Jowett Society in Oxford on 22 November 1922. 'Physics, in its modern forms,' he claimed, 'supplies materials for answers to all philosophical questions that are capable of being answered.' The traditional problems of knowledge 'are really problems of physics and physiology; moreover, I believe that physiology is only a complicated branch of physics':

People do not say that a barometer 'knows' that it is going to rain; but I doubt if there is any essential difference in this respect between the barometer and the meteorologist who observes it.

With an unacknowledged allusion to his pre-Wittgenstein belief in the objective of 'logical forms', Russell declared: 'almost all thinking that purports to be philosophical or logical consists in attributing to the world the properties of language'. The study of language would not produce any *positive* philosophical results, but: 'By studying the principles of symbolism we can learn not to be unconsciously influenced by language, and in this way can escape a host of erroneous notions.'

The topic of vagueness is a case in point. 'All language is vague', but those who talk of 'the flux and the continuum and the unanalysability of the Universe' and who insist that, as our language becomes more precise, it becomes less adapted to represent this flux, are simply committing the fallacy of 'mistaking the properties of words for the properties of things'. Vagueness, in Russell's definition, is a 'one-many' relation between a word and its possible meanings. All words of ordinary language, even proper names, are vague in this sense, since it is not possible to determine precisely their application to just one thing or person (even if a person's name is unique, Russell argues, there are still grey areas about *when* it is applicable to that person, since birth and death are both gradual processes). The only form of language that would not be vague is the kind of 'intolerably prolix' language that he had described in his earlier *Lectures on Logical Atomism*, a language in which each thing in the world had its own unique name. Such a language is an unreachable ideal, but the language of science, in becoming more analytical, approaches it: 'Science is perpetually trying to substitute more precise beliefs for vague ones.'

Schiller was among Russell's audience on this occasion and had been asked to open the discussion. Thinking it to be a manifest flaw in Russell's argument, Schiller drew attention to the fact that, in Russell's view, a language free from vagueness would be 'almost wholly unintelligible'. Russell, however, was unmoved. 'When', recalled Schiller, 'I pointed out this consequence, Russell cheerfully accepted it, and I retired from the fray':

Russell had rightly diagnosed what was the condition of exactness. But he had ignored the fact that his cure was impracticable and far worse than the alleged disease. Nor had he considered the alternative, the inference that therefore the capacity of words to convey a multitude of meanings must not be regarded as a flaw, but that a distinction must be made between plurality of meanings and actual ambiguity.

'Vagueness' is arguably the weakest piece of philosophical writing that Russell had yet produced. What it adds to what he had already said on the subject in *Lectures on Logical Atomism* is only a crude caricature of the views of his opponents. There is evident in it a tendency that characterises much of his work during this period to dismiss all those who disagree with him as 'mystics'. Regarding his belief in Socialism, his opposition to the war, his faith in science and his commitment to the analytic method in philosophy as being in some way all of a piece, Russell became inclined to talk as if there were broadly only two groups of thinkers: those who believed in science, Socialism, peace and analysis, and those who believed in religion, capitalism, war and synthesis. If anybody did not agree with his opinions – whether it be on the situation in China, the correct way to bring up babies, the nature of philosophy, or whatever – then he tended to assume that this was because they looked to tradition, authority or intuition to support their views, rather than to reason. But so hurriedly were many of his writings produced, and so quickly did he move from one subject to the next, that, in his impatience, his conviction that reason was on his side was too often presupposed rather than demonstrated.

The truth is that, with all his other commitments, Russell no longer had the time to produce serious, original philosophy. When he wrote his great philosophical work before the war, he could devote himself entirely to his work. Now he had to find time in between looking after his son, writing journalism, giving lectures and satisfying the increasing demand to write popular books. In 1923, Cambridge University Press expressed an interest in reprinting *Principia Mathematica*, and Russell wanted to take the opportunity to add to it an Introduction, discussing the work that had been published on mathematical logic since 1910. In particular, he wanted to work out the consequences for the theory of *Principia* of accepting Wittgenstein's views on logic. He thought that he could get this done in Cornwall during the summer, but in September he had to admit defeat and ask for more time.

In the short term, there was little incentive for Russell to subject himself to the rigours of original philosophical thinking. Writing popular books was not only easier, but also more lucrative. True, *The Problem of China* had not sold very well, and *The Prospects of Industrial Civilization*, put together from the articles he had written on Socialism during and immediately after his visit to China,[2] had done only slightly better. But *The ABC of Atoms*, written in 1923, was a much bigger financial success, going through several reprints within a few years. It was published, not by Unwin, but by Kegan Paul, for whom C. K. Ogden, Dora's old friend, worked as an editor. Ogden had offered Russell generous terms to write a philosophical book on the principles of physics, which would provide an analysis of matter to complement *The Analysis of Mind*. Such a book was a large undertaking and Russell did not complete it until 1927. In the meantime, he felt obliged to

---

[2] The book was published as being by 'Bertrand Russell with Dora Russell', and a jointly written preface declared it to be 'so much a product of mutual discussion, that the ideas contained in it can scarcely be separately assigned'. It remains true, however, that many of the chapters were originally published as articles under Russell's name alone. My feeling is that the extent of Dora's influence on the work varies from chapter to chapter. It is discernible in the book's discussions of industrialism and its concern to oppose 'a mechanistic conception of society', but much less so in the chapters on Socialism, which are more concerned with the very Russellian theme of the survival of civilisation than with the book's purported central theme of the social effects of mechanised industry.

offer Ogden *The ABC of Atoms*, a little book, popularising recent developments in subatomic physics, based on a series of articles that he published in the spring of 1923.

The ABC of Atoms has become famous for Russell's apparent anticipation in it of the development of nuclear weapons. 'It is probable', he writes, 'that it [the recent work on the structure of the atom] will ultimately be used for making more deadly explosives and projectiles than any yet invented.' It is a remarkably prescient remark, but it is possible to make too much of its prophetic insight. Russell did not foresee the development of nuclear fusion; his remark was based on more general considerations of the military uses to which scientific discoveries are apt to be put, together with his knowledge of Ernest Rutherford's attempts to split nitrogen atoms and the potential applications of such work in generating electrical power ('The outcome may in time revolutionise industry'). In general, however, the book avoids such speculation and concentrates on explaining, in as non-technical a way as possible, the work of Rutherford, Planck and Bohr that led to the creation of quantum physics. Even the philosophical consequences of quantum theory are not discussed at any great length; instead, Russell guides the reader through specific scientific topics such as the wave-theory of light, the theory of energy 'quanta', the discoveries of X-rays and radioactivity, and the problems of reconciling quantum theory with relativity theory. For a popular book, it is fairly heavy-going, written in a sober prose that eschews the exaggerations and witty, polemical asides that characterise his political journalism, and even his philosophical writing, at this time.

It ends with a question close to Russell's heart: does the counter-intuitive, scarcely intelligible behaviour of subatomic particles described by quantum theory (one of its founders, Niels Bohr, once famously remarked that anyone who claims to understand quantum theory has not understood it) suggest that the world itself is, fundamentally, mysterious?

> Is the world 'rational', i.e., such as to conform to our intellectual habits? Or is it 'irrational', i.e., not such as we should have made it if we had been in the position of the Creator? I do not propose to suggest an answer to this question.

The implications of this question would echo through many of Russell's numerous later discussions of modern physics and its popularisers.

The success of *The ABC of Atoms* was part of a more general phenomenon that erupted in the 1920s and has persisted ever since: the boom in demand for popular books on science, particularly theoretical physics. The desire to understand the abstract and difficult theories of modern physics, once those theories have been stripped of what makes them abstract and difficult (namely, mathematics), is, of course, destined to remain unsatisfied. When physical theories are stripped of the mathematics upon which they are based, they lose their essential character and become rather puzzling statements in ordinary language about space, time, matter, energy, and so on. Translating a physical theory from the language of mathematics to the language of everyday life is not like translating a novel from, say, French into English: the concepts of higher mathematics are simply not expressible in everyday language, and neither, therefore, are the ideas of mathematical physics.

Russell was fully aware of this problem and did not try to disguise it from his readers. In *The ABC of Atoms* he alludes to it often, and tries to overcome it, first by trying to explain some of the mathematics used in quantum theory (the book contains far more mathematical symbols than has since become the norm in works of popular science), and second by reminding the reader that what he is trying to convey cannot quite be conveyed in ordinary language. The book abounds with such remarks as: '. . . although this statement would not be accurate, it gives, as nearly as is possible in non-mathematical language, a general idea of the sort of thing that is affirmed by the modern form of the quantum theory'. The concepts of theoretical physics are highly abstract, Russell emphasises, but:

> Our imagination is so incurably concrete and pictorial that we have to express scientific laws, as soon as we depart from the language of mathematics, in language which asserts much more than we *mean* to assert.

Shortly after *The ABC of Atoms* was published, a note of exasperation crept in when Russell was asked by Unwin for a reader's report on yet another popular exposition of relativity theory. 'I am prepared to write future reports of popular books on relativity at a reduced fee without seeing the books,' he wrote to Unwin:

> They will be as follows: 'This book gives an admirable popular exposition of Einstein's views, which non-mathematicians will think they understand unless they are fairly intelligent. Four years ago, the book would have been worth publishing; now, multitudes of other books contain all that is to be found in it.'

This attitude did not, however, prevent Russell from adding to the crowded market of popular books on relativity the very next year, when his own *The ABC of Relativity* was published. Popular science earnt money and, for the moment, earning money was high on Russell's list of priorities. His letters to Unwin repeatedly ask how his books are selling, and he was loath to turn down any requests for newspaper or magazine articles.

In the spring of 1923, Dora discovered that she was pregnant again, and Russell felt under greater pressure than ever to make money. He began to make plans for a lecture tour of the United States the following year – not, this time, giving papers at universities on logic and epistemology, but public lectures on topical, controversial subjects for which an entrance fee would be charged. Further money would be made by selling tickets for dinners at which paying guests would have the opportunity to meet the famous philosopher for themselves. There was an element of prostitution in this method of selling himself, and a part of Russell felt contempt for the whole business. Another part of him, however, welcomed with open arms what proved to be a lucrative source of extra income.

Russell had waited a long time to have children, and now that he had one and was expecting another he was prepared to do almost anything to ensure that they would grow up to become the model citizens he felt certain he was capable of producing. That spring he left London for Cornwall ahead of Dora, who stayed behind to put the Chelsea house in order for tenants. He took John, now a healthy and apparently happy sixteen-month-old toddler, with him. When he arrived, he immediately wrote Dora an affectionate letter, dwelling on John's reaction to being back in Cornwall:

> When he got here, he ran in & out of all the rooms, & at last began climbing the stairs to the attic, thinking he would find his old nursery there . . . He is wild with delight at the daffodils here; he cries to be held up to the window where he can see them. They *are* nice.
> . . . It is heavenly here. The blackthorn is out. The daffodils & gorse are glorious, & the elm undergrowth is getting green. Gulls in flocks are in all the fields round the house. There is no wind, & it is very warm.
> . . . I miss you dreadfully, my Darling. It is so lovely here. How heavenly it will be when you come.

To Ottoline a few months later, he described his day-to-day routine in Cornwall: 'I work all morning and after tea . . . In the afternoon we go to some part or other of the coast, which is extraordinarily beautiful; if it is not very cold we bathe. The air makes one feel sleepy after dinner, and so the day is gone.' 'When I have any time to spare,' he added, 'I spend it playing with John, whom I love beyond all reason and measure. He is very full of life. He has not been even slightly unwell for over a year (unberufen!). He is full of gallant energy, and marches against the wind till it blows him over. He has an amazing passion for flowers; the sight of a garden full of them sends him into an ecstasy. I keep thinking they will kill him in the next war, and have thoughts of becoming a Norwegian to prevent it.'

Russell had just finished *The ABC of Atoms* ('they are fascinating') and was half-inclined to assert the superiority of matter over mind:

> I don't like human beings in the mass; I think of becoming an inverted Manichaean, and maintaining that matter is the good principle and spirit the evil one.

He was, I think, only partly joking.

With *The ABC of Atoms* out of the way, Russell tried to concentrate on the new Introduction to *Principia Mathematica*. In this he was encouraged by Ottoline, who (according to her biographer, Miranda Seymour), was by this time 'bored and depressed by the degree of Dora's influence over Bertie'. Ottoline visited the Russells in Carn Voel that summer and had spent a thoroughly miserable five days, 'sitting among heaps of nappies and struggling to wean the conversation away from the all-absorbing topic of baby John'. Later, on a visit to Freiburg to be treated by a psychoanalyst called Dr Marten, Ottoline was impressed by how highly Russell's work on logic and mathematics was regarded by the mathematicians and philosophers whom she met, and could not help thinking what a waste it was that this internationally eminent friend of hers was now preoccupied with looking after his baby son. 'I have seen several people here,' she wrote to Russell. 'Mathematicians who are *very* interested in your work and in you.' Despite such encouragement, Russell made little headway and decided, after two more or less fruitless months' work, to leave the Introduction till the following year. It 'involves reading all that has been done in recent years on the subject', he wrote to his publisher at Cambridge University Press, 'most of which, unfortunately, is by Polish mathematicians, whose language is unknown to me'. He turned instead to journalism and the preparation of his American lecture tour.

Ironically, at a time when he was working harder than ever, Russell now began to use his journalism to preach the value of indolence. In an article published in August 1922 on 'Leisure and Mechanism', he had proclaimed: 'I have hopes of laziness as a gospel.' If we were all lazy, he argued, we would all be much happier. And, the disinterested pursuit of knowledge that motivates the best work in science cannot thrive in a culture that constantly demands short-term rewards in the form of increased wealth and production; it requires leisure. Thus: 'If excellence is to survive, we must become more leisurely.' A comparison of the work he did between 1900 and 1909 and the work he was doing now might well have been at the back of his mind.

During the summer, while Russell wrote, Dora struggled against the Cornish wind to establish a garden at Carn Voel. It was an uphill task made more difficult by her pregnancy, which gave her more trouble than she had experienced the first time: 'Somehow it set up pressure on the sciatic nerve; I was in pain most of the summer and spent nearly two months lying down most of the day.' She was, in any case, somewhat disgruntled about becoming pregnant again, as it put paid to hopes that had been aroused during the winter in London of reviving her ambitions for a career on the stage. After experiencing, during the election campaign of 1922, what she described as 'the intoxication of the acclaim of a great crowd of people and the knowledge that I did have the power to move and even inspire them', she became convinced that, 'given a real chance', she could be a success as an actress. She spent some months as an understudy during the rehearsals of Lewis Casson's production of Shaw's *Saint Joan*, but the end of the season coincided with her discovery that she was pregnant. 'Farewell to the theatre for many months,' she wrote to Ogden, 'baby expected at Christmas.' In fact, she wrote later, 'I knew I was facing the end of my theatrical ambitions.'

The Russells returned to Chelsea at the end of August, anxious at the prospect of Russell having to leave for the United States in the New Year, as soon as – or, just possibly, before – the new baby was born. Despite this anxiety, and despite too his preparatory work on his US lectures, the steady stream of articles from Russell's pen continued to flow, most of them recycling themes and ideas he had already published: a discussion of subatomic theory for the *Guardian*, an essay on behaviourism for *Vanity Fair*, an attack on moral puritans for *The Freeman*, and so on. In October, he managed to find time, a rare 'breathing space', for a weekend visit to Garsington Manor, Ottoline's home (without Dora, who was now seven months pregnant and suffering – so Russell told Ottoline – from a bad leg). It was, he wrote to Ottoline afterwards, 'delightful' to back in Garsington: 'I get so busy that I have little time for anything civilised.' He found it particularly exciting 'to get hold of Eliot's *Wasteland*', which had just been published as a book by the Woolfs' Hogarth Press, having been published the previous year in Eliot's journal, *Criterion*. On his return to London, Russell wrote to Eliot to express his appreciation, and received in response a warm reply:

> It gives me very great pleasure to know that you like *The Waste Land*, and especially Part V which in my opinion is not only the best part, but the only part that justifies the whole, at all. It means a great deal to me that you like it.
>
> I must tell you that 18 months ago, before it was published anywhere, Vivien wanted me to send you the MS to read, because she was sure that you were one of the very few persons who might possibly see anything in it. But we felt that *you* might prefer to have nothing to do with *us*: It is absurd that we wished to drop you.
>
> Vivien has had a frightful illness, and nearly died, in the spring – as Ottoline has probably told you. And that she has been in the country ever since. She has not come back.
>
> Dinner is rather difficult for me at present. But might I come to tea with you on Saturday? I should like to see you very much – there have been *many times* when I have thought that.

Russell had not seen the Eliots since the New Year of 1919, when Vivien had written to him to say that, disliking 'fading intimacies', she wished to 'break completely' with him (in the summer of the same year he called round at the Eliots' flat to recover some of his possessions, but, on that occasion, had failed to see Vivien, since she stayed in the bathroom, shouting to him through the door). He had heard nothing from them since Vivien wrote to congratulate him on John's birth. Since then, Vivien's health and the Eliots' marriage had deteriorated sharply, while Eliot's reputation as a poet had increased enormously. For what Eliot considered to be the wrong reasons, *The Waste Land* had established him as the leading poet of his generation. Russell later claimed that the image of London as an 'Unreal City', which recurs throughout Eliot's poem, had been taken from a nightmarish vision that he used to have during the war and had discussed with Eliot:

After seeing troop trains departing from Waterloo, I used to have strange visions of London as a place of unreality. I used in imagination to see the bridges collapse and sink, and the whole great city vanish like a morning mist. Its inhabitants began to seem like hallucinations, and I would wonder whether the world in which I thought I had lived was a mere product of my own febrile nightmares.

For both Eliot and Russell, the unreality of London was an image of the collapse of civilisation, which, in an intriguing way, forms the starting point for the post-war thinking of both. This, however, then diverged, sending them in diametrically opposed directions. For Russell, the central question was: what are we to do if civilisation is to survive? For Eliot, it was: what are we to do now that civilisation has died? The 'waste land' – the land in which people were more dead than alive, in which hopes, fears, beliefs and values had collapsed 'in a handful of dust' – was, for Russell, a danger; for Eliot, it was a reality. Among the things that represent 'that part of the present which is already dead', Eliot was later to write, was the creed that Russell outlined in his essay *What I Believe*. The belief in civilisation, in the ability of mankind to create for itself a system of values and an ordered, rational world, was, in Eliot's bleak view, part of the malaise of modern life, which could be overcome only by a recognition of sin and the need for divine redemption.

In the autumn of 1923, Eliot had not yet joined the Anglican Church, nor had he begun the direct attacks on Russell's thinking that would repeatedly appear in his essays in the coming decades. But already there was enough in his public utterances – and, indeed, in *The Waste Land* – to suggest an unbridgeable gulf between his outlook and Russell's. Eliot had, for example, already announced himself, in a letter to the *Daily Mail*, as a sympathiser of Mussolini's Blackshirts and, in a circular sent out to attract new subscribers to *Criterion*, he explained that the journal stood for a 'pure Toryism' that rejected the 'suburban democracy' of a previous age in favour of 'reaction' and 'revolution'. This was not a flag around which Russell was likely to rally, and, although Eliot evidently went to tea with the Russells at Sydney Street (he is mentioned in Dora's autobiography as one of the people who came, but otherwise the meeting goes unrecorded), it is perhaps hardly surprising that this did not lead to a renewal of their friendship.

The death of civilisation, real or imagined, was a topic that dominated British intellectual life in the aftermath of the First World War. In October 1923, the Fabian Society ran a series of public lectures under the title 'Is Civilization Decaying?' Among those who contributed were Sidney Webb, George Bernard Shaw, Harold Laski, R. H. Tawney and Russell, whose lecture, 'The Effect of Science on Social Institutions', was published in four parts in George Lansbury's *Daily Herald* under the title 'Science and Civilization'. It later formed the basis for his little book *Icarus or the Future of Science*, which Kegan Paul published the following February. The *Herald* trumpeted it as: 'The conclusions of one of the most eminent philosophers and men of science of the day on such subjects as civilisation, war, industrialism, and the possibility of finding a way out of our troubles by common sense and kindliness', though what strikes one now about it is the *inconclusive*, deeply ambivalent nature of its argument.

Russell's purpose was to emphasise the 'dangers inherent in the progress of science while we retain our present political and economic institutions', and his lecture consisted for the most part of a series of dire warnings on the uses to which scientific discoveries might be put. For instance, he foresaw the universal adoption of birth control 'among the white races . . . at a time when uncivilised races are still prolific', leading to the employment of these 'more prolific' races as mercenaries, and thus to the opposition of governments to the teaching of birth control among Africans: 'The result will be an immense numerical inferiority of the white races, leading probably to their extermination in a mutiny of mercenaries.'

He also imagined governments acquiring the right to sterilise those who are not considered desirable as parents: 'This power will be used, at first, to diminish imbecility, a most desirable object. But probably, in time, opposition to the government will be taken to prove imbecility, so that rebels of all kinds will be sterilized.' The effects of 'scientific' psychology, he prophesied, would include 'the possibility of controlling the emotional life through the secretions of the ductless glands', and then 'we shall have the emotions desired by our rulers'.

The moral of all this is that scientific progress is not *in itself* a good thing; it depends upon the use that is made of scientific knowledge. In the Greek myth, the inventor Daedalus showed Icarus how to fly, but he could not prevent Icarus from using that knowledge to fly too close to the sun. Similarly, modern-day scientists will have no control over the use to which governments put their discoveries:

> Science enables the holders of power to realise their purposes more fully than they could otherwise do. If their purposes are good, this is a gain: if they are evil, it is a loss.

Thus: 'Science is no substitute for virtue: the heart is as necessary for a good life as the head.' If men were rational, 'intelligence would be enough to make the world almost a paradise'. But men are not rational, they are 'bundles of passions and instincts'. That being so, the future of civilisation rests upon the triumph of 'kindly impulses' over aggressive and rivalrous ones. Thus 'it is of the greatest importance to inquire whether any method of strengthening kindly impulses exists', and here science may, after all, help, since 'I have no doubt that their strength or weakness depends upon discoverable physiological causes.' But, even then, science itself is not sufficient, because 'even if we knew how to produce kindliness we should not do so unless we were already kindly'. And we are not: 'Men's collective passions are mainly evil; far the strongest of them are hatred and rivalry.' So one should not pin one's hopes on kindliness, after all, but on the victory of one aggressive nation, say the United States, over all others, 'leading to the gradual formation of an orderly economic and political world-government'.

Is this outcome, then, to be desired? Possibly not: 'perhaps, in view of the sterility of the Roman Empire, the collapse of our civilisation would in the end be preferable to this alternative'.

That such a great logician could produce such a simplistic and confused argument is extraordinary. What 'conclusions' are we to draw from it? Its apparent conclusion is that science offers us a paradise, but we will choose, instead, to use it to create a hell. We will do this because we, and especially our 'rulers', are wicked and stupid. It is no good becoming less stupid if we remain so wicked, and we are not likely to do that, so the only practical alternative to the collapse of our civilisation is the 'sterility' of world dominance by whoever happens to be the most powerful industrial nation. Surely, though, the moral that Russell *wished* us to draw was that the only real hope of preserving a civilisation worth living in lies in sufficient numbers of people being prepared to be 'kindly' enough to use scientific psychology to 'train the instincts' of the next generation, in the way that he was doing with John.

Russell's tendency to attribute the ills of the world to the wickedness and stupidity of governments continued throughout his life and imposed great limits on his ability to offer convincing analyses of political events, often giving the impression that everything would be all right if only our rulers were as clever and kind as Bertrand Russell. But, apart from the superficiality (not to say vanity) entailed in this way of looking at things, there was also a deep tension running throughout his writing concerning the relative importance of the head and the heart, intelligence and 'kindliness', stupidity and wickedness. How, for example, can one reconcile his view in *Icarus* that 'the heart is as necessary for a good life as the head' with his vitriolic attack on 'the heart' in his earlier reply to Schiller? And how does his emphatic assertion here that men are not, and cannot be, rational square with his view in 'Can Men Be Rational?' – published in the same month as his lecture on 'Science and Civilization' – that 'all solid progress in the world consists of an increase in rationality'?

In 'Can Men Be Rational?' Russell had argued that: 'To preach an altruistic morality appears to me somewhat useless, because it will appeal only to those who already have altruistic desires. But to preach rationality is somewhat different, since rationality helps us to realise our own desires on the whole, whatever they may be.' Yet in 'Science and Civilization', he seems to argue the opposite: that science, by helping us to realise our desires, 'threatens to cause the destruction of our civilisation', a threat that can only be avoided by the promotion, or 'training', of altruistic desires (either that or the 'sterility' of world domination by the United States, which may, in any case, be *worse* that the destruction of civilisation!).

In the face of this morass of contradictions, one can understand Beatrice Webb's exasperation when she complained: 'That's the worst of Bertie; he refuses to verify any of his conclusions':

He has not the patience for observation, inference and verification. Each successive book contains a series of original and witty impressions or suggestions, flashed out as his mind comes into contact with some outstanding fact – usually these flashes are denunciations of what exists. Frequently these judgments or descriptions contradict each other; he seems to have no care for consistency; he does not care even if they do contradict each other. It amuses him to watch the bewilderment of disciples who have no sense of humour! And why should he trouble himself to produce a thought-tight philosophy of life? As a lecturer he commands a big price ... He is disintegrating prejudice and 'rattling' people out of old conventions. Upsetting people's thoughts is good fun; and it is very agreeable being brilliant in thought and expression. Of all forms of mental superiority it is quite the most agreeable for the possessor, the most soothing to his self-esteem.

It is a devastating and penetrating piece of criticism. And, though it sounds odd to accuse a great logician of being impatient with inference and indifferent to contradiction, it is impossible to read Russell's lectures and articles of this period without feeling the justice of Webb's complaints.

Much to the Russells' dismay, in November 1923, the Prime Minister, Stanley Baldwin, suddenly announced a general election for 6 December. Baldwin had become Prime Minister the previous May, when Andrew Bonar Law resigned due to ill health. By the autumn, he had come to the conclusion that protective tariffs were necessary for the sake of curbing the growing problem of unemployment, and, as this was contrary to the programme on which the Tories were elected in 1922, he felt that an election was necessary over the issue. Russell was again asked to be the Labour candidate for Chelsea, and, says Dora, though neither of them was in the mood to fight another election, they 'felt it would be faint-hearted not to do so'. Dora was by this time eight months pregnant, but, even so, seemed once again to enjoy the campaign more than Russell, who was the target for much personal abuse from the Tories, which revived in him the misanthropy to which he always prone. 'Their whole campaign consisted of whispered slanders designed to save their pockets at the cost of the lives of the poor,' he complained to Ottoline. 'Human nature is so vile that I am ashamed of not being one of the brutes.'

Russell, of course, lost again to Sir Samuel Hoare, but the Labour Party as a whole did even better than in the previous year, increasing its number of seats from 142 to 191. The Tories had 258 seats, but, as this was not enough to secure an overall majority, they were vulnerable to being outvoted by the Liberal and Labour Parties acting together, which duly happened on 21 January 1924. The following day, King George V sent for Ramsay MacDonald to become Prime Minister. For the first time in its history, Britain had a Labour Government, albeit one perpetually vulnerable to the kind of co-operation between the other two parties that had defeated the Tories.

Coming at a time when he was already overburdened, the election took a heavy toll on Russell's health. Weakened by overwork, he went down with pneumonia and, having been advised that his proposed winter trip to

America could possibly prove fatal, he postponed his lecture tour until April. He was thus spared the ordeal of leaving the country just as his second child was born. On 29 December, Dora gave birth to a baby girl, whom they named Katharine, after Russell's mother. 'The child is fat and large,' Russell wrote to Ottoline, 'weighed 8 lbs 6 oz, and seems very healthy.'

The three months' breathing space that Russell had bought by rescheduling his American trip no doubt seemed all too short, and much of it, as ever, was taken up with keeping up his incessant flow of journalism. Despite the grave warnings he had issued in 'Science and Civilization', much of his writing continued to evangelise on behalf of science. One such article roused T. S. Eliot to fire the first shot in a sniping campaign against Russell that he would keep up throughout the next two decades. It was entitled 'A Motley Pantheon', and was a review by Russell of a book called *Creative Spirits of the Nineteenth Century*, a collection of twelve essays by the German writer Georg Brandes. The 'creative spirits' chosen by Brandes included Garibaldi, Swinburne, Napoleon, Ibsen, Renan and Flaubert, but, to Russell's displeasure, not a single scientist. This provoked him into a characteristic piece of overstatement:

When one views the Nineteenth Century in perspective, it is clear that science is its only claim to distinction. Its literary men were mostly second-rate, its philosophers sentimental, its artists inferior to those of earlier times. Science ruthlessly forced novelties upon it, while men of 'culture' tried to preserve the old picturesque follies by wrapping them in a mist of muddled romanticism. Until 'culture' has made its peace with science, it will remain outside the main current of events, feeble and querulous, sighing for the past. The world that science has been making may be disgusting, but it is the world in which we have to live; and it condemns to futility all who are too fastidious to notice it.

In his next editorial for *Criterion*, the 'fastidious' Eliot quoted these lines and responded to them with chilly disdain:

One is immediately struck by the arrogance of the scientist. No literary man would pretend to sweep aside the whole of science of any century with the magnificence with which Mr Russell dismisses the nineteenth-century literature and art. And the truth seems to us to be exactly the reverse of Mr Russell's implication. The man of letters or the man of 'culture' of the present time is far too easily impressed and overawed by scientific knowledge and ability; the aristocracy of culture has abdicated before the demagogy of science. In consequence, a mathematician like Mr Russell, or even some pretender to scientific authority without Mr Russell's achievement, can more easily persuade the populace in literary opinion than will the man with a genuine competence in literature . . .

One draws furthermore from Mr Russell's paragraph an edifying commentary on the ability of the scientist to think clearly outside of his own sphere. It is curious that in a paragraph which begins with a reference to Flaubert, Mr Russell should have accused men of culture of trying 'to preserve the old picturesque follies by wrapping them in a mist of muddled romanticism'. This is the most remarkable criticism of Flaubert that we have ever heard. Of course, culture is increasingly rare, and the detection of culture from its numerous imitations is a task requiring technical skill. Yet Mr Russell, who is a great philosopher, has himself made at least two contributions of inestimable value to culture, *The Philosophy of Leibniz* and *Principles of Mathematics*. It is all the more to be regretted that he should have formed such a vulgar conception of culture, and it is deplorable that any article bearing Mr Russell's name should end with a phrase of sentimental brutality.

A few weeks before he set sail for New York, Russell attended a dinner given by his old student (and Virginia Woolf's sister-in-law), Karin Stephen. Once again, he is captured to good effect in Virginia Woolf's diaries, where, yet again, he is described talking about himself, telling her about his parents' early deaths, the loneliness of his life at Pembroke Lodge, and so on. He also tried to persuade her that, contrary to the accepted Bloomsbury view, G. E. Moore's *Principia Ethica* was not a great work and, indeed, was markedly inferior to Moore's earlier essay, 'On the Nature of Judgment'. Woolf listened to this with interest and recorded as much of it as she could remember, but concluded:

One does not like him. Yet he is brilliant of course; perfectly outspoken; familiar; talks of his bowels; likes people; & yet & yet – He disapproves of me perhaps? He has not much body of character. This luminous vigorous mind seems attached to a flimsy little car, like that on a large glinting balloon. His adventures with his wives diminish his importance. And he has no chin & he is dapper. Nevertheless, I should like the run of his headpiece. We parted at the corner of the Square; no attempt to meet again.

There is distance here, even a disdain, that chimes with Ottoline's horror at Russell's domestic enslavement, Eliot's denunciation of his opinions on culture and Beatrice Webb's accusations of glibness and intellectual laziness. Slowly, but inexorably, his old friends were withdrawing from him, united in their view that the Russell of the 1920s was a diminished figure from the important philosopher they had known before the war. In place of their friendship and respect, however, he had the admiration of his growing readership and, above all, his family. His closest friend and comrade was now Dora; with her he had built up a shared conviction that, in their defiance of the conventions of society, in their commitment to Socialism and in their jointly held hopes for their children, they were marching on the side of progress. His departure for the United States on 22 March was a day of sadness for them both. He would not be back until June, and he hated being away for so long from Dora, John – now a talkative and charming two-year-old – and his new-born baby, Kate. 'I can never think of that leave-taking without a pang,' Dora has written:

I see his desperately unhappy face at parting from the three of us as he gets into the taxi and drives away, and I stand feeling equally forlorn at our front door. Living and working together day by day, very much in harmony about our beliefs and purposes, we had become almost part of each other.

3

HOW TO BE FREE AND HAPPY

Russell's lecture tour of the United States in 1924 was an exhausting and, for the most part, unhappy experience. In the space of just under two months (he arrived in New York on 1 April and left at the end of May), he gave more than fifty lectures, travelling from town to town throughout the eastern, southern and midwestern states, sometimes lecturing in one state in the morning and another in the evening. Most of his time, he later said, was spent either in trains or lecture halls. His routine, as he described it to Ottoline, typically went like this: 'On arrival in a town, I was first surrounded by journalists all morning (after being turned out of the train at 6 a.m.), then had an enormous lunch with businessmen who unrolled slow platitudes that reminded one of the mills of the gods, then had tea (if I was lucky) with a crowd of sentimental ladies, then a heavy dinner with another crowd of businessmen, then a lecture, and then a train for the night.'

His audiences were large and appreciative, but he had little respect either for them or for himself in pandering to them. 'I am really a species of mental male prostitute,' he wrote to Dora. 'It is infinitely disgusting ... I cannot flatter myself that my lectures are any use at all.' He was contemptuous of the people who wanted to hear him lecture but did not bother to read his books, and still more so of the people who paid to dine with him ('The people I meet would all be better dead'; 'there is something about Americans that makes one feel them unimportant'). American ladies, in particular, he told Dora, 'are *quite* dreadful':

> They all rush up to me after a lecture ... Poor things, they get no male companionship, & they want it. They have to put up with nothing but sleepy copulation. So they try to rape the mind of every lecturer who comes along. That is why they are willing to pay for lectures.

'I don't feel there is the *slightest* point in the work,' he wrote, 'it is merely a source of money.' When he got depressed, he thought of 'the money growing more & the days to come growing less – otherwise I have no consolations'. Despite his contempt, however, he found that he was good at giving his audiences what they wanted: 'I have no difficulty in feeling what a meeting wants, & supplying it. It is grossly dishonest, but it will equip John & Kate with a good education.'

Russell was probably exaggerating, for Dora's benefit, what a miserable time he was having, and no doubt he gave an entirely different impression to his hosts. There were, after all, compensations in being received with admiration and flattery wherever he went, not the least of which were the sexual opportunities it provided (he later confessed to Dora of at least one 'small and insignificant *affaire*'). And he did meet at least some people whom he liked. In New York, for example, he stayed with the philosopher H. M. Kallen, 'a nice host . . . with quiet rooms full of books, a man wholly without prejudices', a description evidently not quite applicable to Russell himself, judging from the description he gave to Ottoline of Kallen as 'a Jew, whose friends are all Jews. All were kind, but I began to long for the uncircumcised.' In Chicago he stayed with T. S. Eliot's brother, 'a pathetic lonely soul, like all nice people in this country', at whose flat he met again the wretched Helen Dudley, who had once considered herself to be Russell's fiancée:

To my great relief, I found she had no wish for anything amatory. She is in a dreadful situation, with a disease like Barbellion's which is slowly bringing on paralysis, with recurrent insanity, yet she keeps us bravely, hates no one, is full of artistic interests. She is really a very nice person. I treated her very badly in the first days of the war & one might expect her to hate me, but she doesn't, & she also doesn't love me, which is a mercy.

'I see it would be a bearable country if one could choose one's friends,' Russell told Dora. 'What makes it trying for me is having to meet 100 new bores every day, all enthusiastic & stupid.' In another letter he said that 'the lack of sincerity & truth is what is most trying. Everybody wants to be flattered, & is willing to flatter.' But, clearly, what was *most* trying was that he was missing his family. With John just learning to talk, and baby Kate beginning to smile, he resented having to be thousands of miles away, surrounded by strangers. After his very first night away, he recorded a dream in which 'I was away from home & they came & told me John was dead – then I dreamt that I woke up & found he wasn't, & he & I started rolling together down the steep hill at Pembroke Lodge that I always rolled down as a child, & I vowed not to go to sleep again for fear of having the dream again. And then I really woke up.' Later, he told Dora: 'I dream about you & John & Kate every night as regularly as clockwork.' The first thing he did when he arrived somewhere, he said, was to spread out the pictures he had of the three of them. Dora kept him informed about the children, and he worried at the news that John was 'nervy', but delighted at her descriptions of Kate 'smiling deliciously'. 'I long to see how she has developed,' he wrote. 'I wonder how much John will remember of me?'

'Little Kate is well & happy,' Dora reassured him, '& so is darling John – I peeped at him asleep at Grandma's today – a cherub, with long & lovely legs – & his face a sheer delight – it is growing so handsome – More babies for us, I think, my Treasure. They are such perfect creations.'

When Russell complained at the lack of sincerity and truth, he was perhaps thinking of himself as much as the people with whom he mixed. After all, what room was there for sincerity and truth in an enterprise that involved being charming to people whom he considered 'better off dead', and lecturing to others whom he despised for being 'enthusiastic and stupid' enough to pay to hear him? Actually, the degree of contempt that he felt towards his audiences varied. He had, he told Dora, basically three types of audience: academic, open forums and women's clubs:

I like the academic audiences best. I always get on with the students. The open forums are rather admirable; they always have very lively questions & discussions afterwards, & they are gradually teaching Yanks to keep their tempers when they hear opinions they don't agree with. But the women's clubs are utterly horrible. I doubt if the human race produces anything more repulsive than the American rich woman of middle age, very fat, very ugly, very expensively dressed, telling you that the pearls she is wearing are imitation, the real ones being at the Bank on account of recent robberies, boasting that her most intimate friend married a Serbian prince, & at intervals maintaining that pure American womanhood does wonders for morals. If I ever come again, I shall tell Feakins to charge the women's clubs extra.

William B. Feakins, a self-styled 'transcontinental tour agent for lectures by Men of Fame', had arranged Russell's programme. Taking a commission of 50 per cent for himself, he charged $200 a lecture. The women's clubs were used to this kind of arrangement and entirely happy with it, but some Socialist organisations that wished to hear Russell speak were puzzled to discover that he seemed to be less interested in spreading his ideas than in earning money. The result was that Russell often found himself addressing people who knew little about him and were unsympathetic to his ideas. On these occasions, he tailored his material to suit his audience; otherwise, he told Dora, 'John & Kate would suffer in their education'.

Russell arrived in America with a stock of manuscript lectures that drew on his journalism of the last few years, dealing with now familiar themes: 'Mechanism and Life', 'What is Wrong with Western Civilization?', 'How to Secure World Peace', 'Causes of Modern War', and so on. Sometimes he simply read these lectures out; at other times, he relied on notes; and sometimes he improvised completely. Wherever he went – New York, Boston, Washington, St Paul, Milwaukee, Chicago – the local newspapers reported his lectures, usually finding in them at least one or two sentences guaranteed to outrage conservative opinion. The *New York Times* gave a full report of Russell's address to the League for Industrial Democracy, in which, 'in the presence of several hundred liberals, radicals, social workers, university professors and students of sociology', Russell explained that he had 'very reluctantly' come to the conclusion that world government would be formed, if at all, not by voluntary federation, but by American economic imperialism. Then, like Huxley's Mr Scogan dressed up as Sesostris the Sorceress, he gave his paying customers a thrillingly horrifying glimpse of the future that awaited them:

I foresee at no distant date an extension of the American financial empire over the whole American continent, the whole of Western Europe and also the Near East . . . The empire of American finance will be in the highest degree illiberal and cruel. It will crush trade unionism, control education, encourage competition among the workers while avoiding it among the capitalists. It will make life everywhere ugly, uniform, laborious and monotonous. Men of ability in all countries will be purchased by high salaries. The world will enjoy peace, broken only by the dropping of bombs from airplanes on strikers, but it will look back to the old days of war as a happy memory almost too bright to be true.

It may have afforded some amusement to Russell that the very accusation for which he had been imprisoned in 1918 – that US military might would be used against strikers – was here being made in an absurdly exaggerated form, and, not only was it being taken entirely seriously, but he was being paid handsomely to make it!

In Harvard, Russell ran into trouble when he came to the defence of the American radical, Scott Nearing, whom, he was told, had been prevented from speaking at the Harvard Student Union by the university's Board of Trustees. Interviewed by the student newspaper, *Crimson*, Russell launched an attack on boards of trustees in general. 'When an institution of learning is governed by a group of financiers and businessmen,' he was quoted as saying, 'any interests are served but those of liberalism.' It was, he said, part of the larger problem that he had been emphasising in his lectures, namely that America was governed to its detriment by industry and the banks: 'America is not ruled by the Washington government. It is oil and Morgan that rule you.' On this occasion, however, Russell had got his facts wrong, as Lawrence A. Lowell, the President of Harvard, explained in a letter to the *New York Times* the following day: 'The Harvard Union is an association of students and graduates over which the Governing Boards exercise no more control than the authorities of Oxford and Cambridge do over the question of who shall speak, or what shall be said, in the Oxford and Cambridge Unions.'

In many of the places that Russell visited he was asked his opinion on the new Labour Government in Britain. In the month before his visit, he had given an address on the 'Philosophy of Socialism' at the Oxford Union, and was quoted by the American newspapers as saying on that occasion that Britain could never achieve Socialism unless the United States also adopted it, for: 'If we had socialism and through it lost our empire, we could get no oil and would eventually all be proletarians working for America.' In America, judging by newspaper reports (the texts of these talks have not survived, if they ever existed), he was more cautious, confining himself to reassuring Americans that the Labour Party was *not* revolutionary, insisting that Ramsey MacDonald's plans for social reform were moderate and practical, and defending MacDonald's recent decision to recognise the Soviet Union.

On 5 May, he took part in a public debate in Carnegie Hall, New York, with the American Socialist, Morris Hillquit, on the question: 'Is the British Labour Party Revolutionary?' ('he says "yes," Russell told Dora, 'fancy how different things look at a distance'). According to his account to Dora, there were 3,000 people at the meeting: 'I got the best of it til the last five minutes, when I felt it intolerable to criticise our Labour Party & deliberately gave him points.' Two weeks later, he took part in an even more widely publicised debate with Scott Nearing on: 'Is the Soviet Form of Government applicable to Western civilisation?', with Nearing answering 'yes' and Russell 'no'. Later in the year, a verbatim report of the debate was published in *Life and Letters* under the heading 'The International Debate of the Day!'

His last engagement was an address (which he gave free of charge) to the Young People's Socialist League in New York on the subject of 'How to be Free and Happy'. On this occasion, Russell promised Dora beforehand, 'I will have my fling – free love, atheism, etc.'; 'to them I am going to be indiscreet, as I shall be gone when the storm breaks, & it will have blown over if I should ever have to come again'. Actually, there was no storm: the lecture went entirely unreported. Verbatim notes were, however, kept and these were later published as a pamphlet by the Rand School of Social Science. When this came to the attention of his publisher Stanley Unwin, Russell explained that it was part of the terms of the lecture that the organisers should have the copyright, adding: 'I did not say what I thought on the subject, viz. "Embark for Europe". I don't really know what I did say, as the lecture was extempore.' What he did in fact say was that, under Socialism, no one ought to work more than four hours a day, the rest of the time being devoted to the pursuit of freedom and happiness. 'In America I have spent most of my time by preaching idleness,' he told his audience. 'I made up my mind when I was young that I would not be restrained from preaching a doctrine merely because I have not practised it. I have not been able to practise the doctrine of idleness, because the preaching of it takes up so much time.' He set sail for home on 31 May. 'My time was very successful,' he wrote to Ottoline from on board the SS *Celtic*, 'everybody was enthusiastic, and I cleared £1,450 to invest. But oh! it was beastly.'

After he had gone, an odd piece appeared in a Chicago journal called *Unity*, heaping upon Russell the kind of uncritical acclaim reminiscent of that accorded to the leaders of dictatorial regimes by newspapers loyal to them. Russell's visit was, *Unity* claimed, 'one of the most impressive tours ever made in this country by a distinguished foreigner ... Everywhere Professor Russell spoke, he was greeted by great audiences with rapturous enthusiasm, and listened to with a touching interest and reverence ... Throngs of eager men and women crowded the auditoriums where he appeared, and vied with another in paying homage to the distinguished man

whom they so honoured.' Even more oddly, considering the extensive
coverage that Russell received in the American newspapers, the piece
claimed that 'the great public at large' had been allowed to know nothing
'about this famous Englishman and the message which he brought across the
seas to us Americans . . . The silence of our newspapers was well-nigh
complete.' It went on to chastise American universities for not offering him
honorary degrees, adding: 'how many colleges in America officially invited
him to their halls?' (the answer to which was: as many as he could cope
with). 'Here is Mr Russell,' *Unity* concluded, getting into its stride, 'the
ablest and most famous mathematical philosopher of modern times – for
long an honored Fellow of Cambridge, England – author of learned essays
and treatises which are the standard authorities in their field – at least, a
great scholar, at the most, one of the greatest of scholars!' And yet:
'Practically speaking, Professor Russell was ignored' by American universities. 'A better measure of the ignorance, cowardice and Pharisaism of
American academic life we have never seen!'

The report gives some indication of what Russell may have had in mind
when, on his return to England, he wrote to Ottoline that: 'Americans have
such a passionate love of humbug.' 'It is *so* delicious to be at home and not
be a public character and not have to pretend,' he told Ottoline; 'little John
is much more shrewd in seeing through humbug than any American'. The
writer in *Unity* may have thought that what Russell had delivered to
America was an important 'message' informed by great scholarship, but
Russell himself knew better. 'Anyone who takes these debates and lectures
of ours seriously', he said on a later tour to one of his debating partners,
'must be an idiot.' If he had been lecturing on mathematical logic, the
philosophy of mathematics or epistemology, then the respect shown to him
would have been entirely deserved, but his thoughts on Socialism,
capitalism, the Labour Government and the future of American politics
were worth little more than those of any other political journalist; nor did he
have any special expertise on the subject of 'how to be free and happy'. He
knew this, and it aroused in him a certain nausea for the whole business –
the 'humbug' in which he had become involved.

'I should like to chuck politics altogether,' Russell had written to Dora
from America, '& make a living out of popular science. Everybody here
knows *The ABC of Atoms*.' The fragility of the minority Labour
Government threatened yet another general election, but, Russell said, 'I
dread getting nominated.' He hoped Chelsea would choose another
candidate and leave him, as he put it in a letter to Kallen, 'to retire from the
world & cultivate my garden'. But, he added, 'that is not lucrative enough to
pay for one's children's education'. As he had repeatedly said to Dora, the
only thing that had enabled him to get through the 'pretence' of his lecture
tour was the thought that it was in the best interests of John and Kate. Now
that it was over, he simply wanted to be with his family and concentrate on
writing something that would restore some self-respect.

On his arrival back in Liverpool, Russell was met by Dora, and, after a
night in London, the two of them went straight to Cornwall. John, Russell

wrote to Ottoline, 'was delicious when I arrived. He was waiting by the gate
and received me with the greatest delight. Then he took me indoors &
showed me a photograph of myself & said "that is Dada" & set to work to
compare it with the original. I thought he would have half forgotten me but
he remembered everything we used to do together & insisted on doing it all
again.' Kate had just recovered from measles, and 'is just as nice as John
was, though not so nice as he is, because she is too young'.

To Russell's great consternation, John, now two and a half, was not the
fearless child he had set out to produce; he was frightened of, among other
things, shadows, mechanical toys, dogs, cats, the dark and even, to begin
with, his baby sister. Since Russell accepted Watson's view that all fears are
acquired (apart from the fear of loud noises and that of being dropped), he
decided that John must have acquired these fears from the nurse who looked
after him, 'who was generally timid and especially afraid of the dark'. The
nurse was thus dismissed and Russell set out to repair the damage, working
on the principle that, if John understood the things that frightened him, he
would no longer be afraid of them. Thus:

> I cured him [of his fear of shadows] by making shadows on the wall and
> the floor with my fingers, and getting him to imitate me; before long, he
> felt that he understood shadows and began to enjoy them. The same
> principle applied to mechanical toys; when he had seen the mechanism he
> was no longer frightened.

Similarly, John's fear of the dark was cured (so Russell claims – one
cannot help feeling sceptical about this) by talking to him 'very carefully
about the absence of danger in the dark' and letting him know that, if he
cried out in the dark, no one would come to comfort him. ('If we had been
more indulgent, we should probably have made him sleep badly for a long
time, perhaps for life.') 'I think an irrational fear should never be simply let
alone,' Russell declared, 'but should be gradually overcome by familiarity
with its fainter forms.'

The strongest test of this precept was provided by John's fear of the sea.
Puzzled that his son should have acquired a fear of something that he
himself loved, Russell decided that *this* fear was instinctive: 'I am fairly
certain there had been no suggestion to cause it.' He nevertheless set out to
overcome it by placing John in shallow pools away from the sea to get him
used to the cold water, and by getting him to notice that waves went out as
well as in. It did not work: John still cried when he was placed in deep pools
where the water came up to his waist, and nothing would induce him to go
into the sea. The following year, Russell adopted a different method:

> When he showed cowardice, we made him feel that we were ashamed of
> him; when he showed courage, we praised him warmly. Every day for
> about a fortnight, we plunged him up to the neck in the sea, in spite of
> his struggles and cries. Every day they grew less; before they ceased, he

began to ask to be put in. At the end of a fortnight, the desired result had been achieved; he no longer feared the sea.

Thus, perhaps, was John's 'irrational' fear of the sea replaced by an entirely rational fear of his parents.

True to the desire he had expressed to Dora of 'chucking politics', Russell wrote almost no political journalism during the summer of 1924. He turned his experience of America into two articles, 'Impressions of America' and 'The American Intelligentsia', but in neither did he indulge in speculations about the future; he simply recorded what he had seen – the high standard of living, the bigotry of the Ku-Klux-Klan, the prominence of Jews, the power of finance, the burden of administration placed upon American academics, and so on – and concluded, blandly but sensibly, that 'there is reason for fear as well as for hope, and no man can say whether fear or hope will be justified by the event'. He also reviewed Kallen's book, *Culture and Democracy in the United States*, but, when Kallen took exception to his criticisms, Russell admitted: 'I know so little of America that I can't really argue against you.' For the moment he was finished with pretending that he had answers to every problem, whether American or European, political, social, economic or ethical. Sesostris the Sorceress, the foreteller of futures, had, for the time being, closed her tent.

What little political journalism Russell did publish in the summer of 1924 was mostly on the subject of China, a subject upon which his expertise was now recognised by the British Government. Waiting for him when he returned from his lecture tour was a letter from the Prime Minister, Ramsay MacDonald, asking him to join a Government advisory committee that was being set up to discuss the question of how best to spend the Boxer Indemnity. This was an annual payment that the Chinese were obliged to make to the European powers under the terms of the treaty that had been imposed upon them after the Boxer Uprisings had been put down in 1900. The punitive nature of this arrangement was something of an embarrass-ment to the Labour Government of 1924, and MacDonald thus sought ways of using the money for 'purposes mutually beneficial to British and Chinese interests' (as the proposed Boxer Indemnity Bill put it).

The prevailing progressive opinion, and one that Russell held passion-ately, was that the money should be used to improve education in China. Despite his wish to 'chuck politics', Russell was eager to use this rare opportunity to have an influence on Government policy and drafted a 'Memorandum on the Boxer Indemnity', urging the Government to add the words 'connected with education' to the bill after the word 'purposes'. Before this suggestion was adopted, however, the Labour Government was defeated at the general election of October 1924, and, by the end of the year, Russell had been sacked from the committee by the incoming Tory Government, while the Boxer Indemnity continued to be used to further the aims of British industry. Even before he was sacked, Russell's position on the committee was made difficult by its Chairman, Lord Phillimore, who urged MacDonald to get rid of him on the grounds that he was 'a highly immoral character' who held 'views on education subversive of accepted theories of conduct'. MacDonald refused to yield to Phillimore, but the experience of serving on a committee headed by such a man can hardly have done much to rekindle Russell's taste for practical politics.

Partly, one suspects, as a reaction to his distaste for public life, Russell – now aged fifty-three – made efforts during the summer to return to serious philosophical work. The money he had earnt from his American lecture tour eased the pressure to produce journalism at the rate he had been doing, but another problem remained: living outside academic life, he had no one to discuss philosophy with. Moore, Whitehead and Wittgenstein, the three people with whom he had enjoyed his most fruitful philosophical contacts, were all now estranged from him. Moore had never quite *liked* Russell, and, though he was now in a position of great influence in British philosophy – the editor of *Mind* and soon to become Professor of Philosophy at Cambridge – he was not likely to be of much use to Russell. Whitehead's philosophical interests were moving sharply away from Russell's; the work that he had published since the First World War, particularly *The Concept of Nature* (published in 1922), showed indeed a sympathy for the very kind of metaphysics – the kind associated with the French philosopher, Henri Bergson – that Russell had repeatedly attacked as 'mystical' and as being of a piece with the 'irrationalism' that had led to the war. In any case, in the New Year of 1924, Whitehead left England to take up a post teaching philosophy at the University of Harvard. Russell maintained his respect for Wittgenstein's work, but their meeting in Innsbruck in 1922 had shown that there was little intellectual sympathy left between them.

Ironically, just as Russell became isolated from other philosophers, philosophy itself was becoming more Russellian. The 'analytic' style of philosophy that he and Moore had developed was now becoming dominant, and interest in the logical and philosophical foundations of mathematics was growing ever greater. The 1920s saw a fierce debate developing between rival philosophies of mathematics – formalist, constructivist and logicist – and Russell's work was the starting point for much of the discussion. A number of articles, conference papers and books were now being written, by mathematicians and philosophers, that assumed familiarity with Russell's views. *The Principles of Mathematics*, 'On Denoting' and *Principia Mathematica* (its first volume, anyway) were becoming essential reading to those who wished to follow contemporary developments in philosophy. In the debates that raged between the constructivists, led by the Dutch mathematician, L. E. J. Brouwer, the fomalists, led by the German, David Hilbert, and the 'logical positivists', led by Moritz Schlick in Vienna, Russell might have become a prominent participant. But, although his name was often invoked, it was the Russell of 1900–10 who played a part in these debates, and not the Russell of the 1920s. Beset with many other demands on his time, Russell failed to keep up with the literature that his own work had inspired, and became an increasingly peripheral figure in the developments of philosophy that he himself had inaugurated.

Some hope of overcoming this isolation was offered in the summer of

1924 by the proposal to establish a 'School of Philosophy' in London, with
the purpose of encouraging philosophical studies by giving public lectures
and publishing a philosophical journal that was less austerely professional
than those that catered only for academics. Though it would be a non-
academic institution, it would, of necessity, have links with the leading
figures in British academic philosophy. This body, which became the British
Institute of Philosophy and, later, the Royal Institute of Philosophy,
seemed, in many ways, tailor-made for Russell's participation, giving him
the opportunity to repeat the success of his earlier public lectures in
philosophy, 'The Philosophy of Logical Atomism' and 'The Analysis of
Mind'. From the very first, Russell was an ardent advocate of it, writing
letters in the summer to his friends enlisting their support, and agreeing, at
its inaugural meeting on 10 November, to join its General Committee.
During the next two years, Russell gave two courses of lectures at the
institute, each consisting of twenty lectures, spread over two academic
terms. They did not make the same impact as his earlier public lecture
courses, and the money he earnt from them was trifling compared to what
he made from his American lecture tours, but at least they gave him an
opportunity to lecture, without pretence, on subjects in which he had quite
genuine expertise.

The problems Russell faced in returning to the abstruse, technical work
on which his reputation as a philosopher was primarily based are illustrated
by his work on the second edition of *Principia*, which he completed at the
end of the summer of 1924. Russell's ambitions for this second edition were
large – much larger than, in his present state, he was capable of realising. He
wanted to write an Introduction that would discuss the growing body of
recent literature on the subject and work out the technical consequences of
the fundamental changes to the basic theory of logic in the book that would
be required by an acceptance of Wittgenstein's work. This was a flawed
ambition in many respects. First, Russell had not read most of the recent
technical literature on the subject, and had neither the time nor the
inclination required to master it. Second, a complete acceptance of
Wittgenstein's work would require, not just changes to the system of
Principia, but its complete abandonment. Third, as *Principia Mathematica*
was co-written with Whitehead, this new edition would also have to be
published under both their names, and Whitehead was deeply unsympathetic to Wittgenstein's work and thus to the general lines on which Russell
sought to 'improve' their joint undertaking.

In the face of these difficulties, what Russell produced was a piece of
work that was unsatisfactory in almost every respect, one that failed to
realise any of its aims, made no significant technical advances to the subject
and was disliked by both Wittgenstein and Whitehead. After the second
edition of *Principia* had been published, Whitehead wrote to *Mind*
dissociating himself from the new material that Russell had added to it. He
had been under the impression, he insisted, that a general statement would
appear in the new edition, making it clear that Russell alone was responsible
for the new additions. In fact, Russell sent Whitehead a manuscript of the

new Introduction and the three new Appendices before they were published. When Whitehead (as was his wont) did not reply, Russell sent the new material to the publishers, apparently assuming that Whitehead would have no objections to it being published under his name. When the suggestion to produce a new edition had first been made, Russell had written to Whitehead asking for his opinions, and had then (May 1923) received a rare reply from Whitehead, agreeing with Russell's basic plan to leave the text unaltered but to add a new Introduction, and agreeing, too, that the Theory of Types in the original book was not 'quite right'. Before he left for his American lecture tour, Russell also wrote to Cambridge University Press asking them to send Whitehead proofs of the new edition (for, although the basic text remained unaltered, it all had to be reset and thus proofread again).

Russell could, then, be cleared of any impropriety in his dealings with Whitehead over the new edition; he kept his co-author informed and allowed him a chance to object to the new material. But, still, as he must have realised, the new material represented his, not Whitehead's, further thoughts on the system of *Principia*. In so far as Russell had a collaborator on this new work, it was not Whitehead, but Frank Ramsey, a brilliant young mathematician and philosopher at King's College, Cambridge. Ramsey *ought* to have been the perfect collaborator for the work that Russell wanted to do: he had a thorough knowledge of the recent work in mathematical logic and a deep understanding of Wittgenstein's work (as an undergraduate, he had helped C. K. Ogden with the translation of *Tractatus Logico-Philosophicus*, and had then written a long review of the book, which remains one of the most penetrating discussions of it ever published). Moreover, he was committed to defending the 'logicist' philosophy of mathematics of *Principia Mathematica* against its constructivist and formalist rivals.

Despite all this, Ramsey was to prove a half-hearted partner in Russell's project. Though a great admirer of Russell's previous work, Ramsey had little respect for the plans for a new edition of *Principia*. In this, he was no doubt influenced by Wittgenstein. In the summer of 1923, Ramsey visited Wittgenstein in Trattenbach, the Austrian village in which Wittgenstein was then working as a schoolteacher, in order to discuss with him the ideas of the *Tractatus*. In a letter to his mother written on 20 September 1923, Ramsey reported that Wittgenstein was 'a little annoyed that Russell is doing a new edit[ion] of Principia because he thought he had shown R that it was so wrong that a new edition would be futile. It must be done altogether fresh.'

Ramsey did not at this stage know that he would become involved in Russell's plans for a new edition, but in February 1924, he was taken by Ogden to meet Russell at his home in Sydney Street. Ramsey was then in the process of applying for a research scholarship at King's, and went to meet Russell hoping, as he put it in his diary, that 'if I get on well with Russell, he might be a reference'. At the meeting, Ramsey's diary records, he and Russell 'talked about identity, propositional functions, etc.':

Russell amusing and very intelligent, but doesn't seem to assimilate what you say, only understand it and out it goes again. Og talked his rot and Russell thought it silly.[3]

From Russell's point of view, the meeting with Ramsey was a success, and he evidently decided there and then to make Ramsey his collaborator. He lent Ramsey a typescript by the logician, H. M. Sheffer, that he intended to use for his new Introduction, and arranged to meet the following day for a more exhaustive discussion. The next day, Ramsey's diary records:

> . . . to lunch with Russell, and afterwards for a walk with him, he is nice and amusing, discussed partly types, partly identity. He is rather good against W's identity, poor on types; doubts Dedekindian section as he can't prove it, though he can Math Induction without Axiom of Reducibility. Og and Mrs R came back to tea, saw their son John; seemed intelligent and very articulate for 2, but they seemed to me to talk about him sillily in front of him. He comes a great deal into R's conversation by himself too.

On this occasion, Russell gave Ramsey his preliminary draft of the new Introduction and asked him to look through it for mistakes. As indicated by Ramsey's remarks, Russell's new Introduction suggested major revisions to the original theory of *Principia*: it dropped the Axiom of Reducibility and adopted Wittgenstein's system of logic in *Tractatus*, according to which *all* propositions are analysable into truth-functional compounds of an initial stock of 'elementary propositions'. The consequences of these changes were drastic: large parts of mathematics, in particular the theory of real numbers ('Dedekindian section'), were no longer provable from within the system. This meant, in effect, abandoning Volumes II and III of the original work.

Despite this major surgery, Ramsey did not think Russell's changes went far enough in Wittgenstein's direction. 'I went to see Russell a few weeks ago,' he wrote to Wittgenstein on 20 February, 'and am reading the manuscript of the new stuff he is putting into the Principia':

> You are quite right that it is of no importance; all it really amounts to is a clever proof of mathematical induction without using the axiom of reducibility. There are no fundamental changes, identity just as it used to be. I felt he was too old; he seemed to understand and say 'yes' to each separate thing, but it made no impression so that 3 minutes afterwards he

---

[3] Ogden's 'rot' was almost certainly the causal theory of meaning that he had outlined in the book he had recently co-authored with the poet and critic, I. A. Richards, *The Meaning of Meaning*. Though privately Russell thought little of the book, he had, in a review for *The Nation and the Athenaeum*, described it as 'undoubtedly important and valuable'. This phrase was then used by the publishers for promotional purposes, shocking Wittgenstein, who had earlier pronounced it 'a miserable book', one that showed merely 'how easy it is to write a thick book'. Wittgenstein was no doubt still more shocked to be told later by Ramsey that Russell 'does not really think *The Meaning of Meaning* important, but he wants to help Ogden by encouraging the sale of it'.

talked on his old lines. Of all your work he seems now to accept only this: that it is nonsense to put an adjective where a substantive ought to be which helps in his theory of types.

To Russell himself, Ramsey was more polite, sending him a list of corrections to the manuscript, together with a reading list of recent work in mathematical logic.

Ramsey was possibly less forthcoming than he might have been in helping Russell, because he was himself engaged on a piece of work that he regarded as a rival to Russell's. This emerges in a letter he wrote to G. E. Moore on 6 February 1924, in which he tried to convince Moore of the importance of his research by contrasting it with the relative futility of Russell's:

I am working on the basis of Wittgenstein's work, which seems to me to show that Principia is wrong not merely in detail but fundamentally. I have got Russell's manuscript of the stuff that he is inserting into the new edition, and it seems to take no account of Wittgenstein's work at all. There is a new theory of types without the axiom of reducibility, on which however Russell hasn't succeeded in proving a lot of ordinary mathematics, whose truth, he concludes, remains doubtful. But I have got on W's principles a new theory of types without any special doubtful axiom which gives all the results of Russell's old one, and solves all the contradictions.

When Russell left for his American lecture tour in March, Ramsey left Cambridge for Vienna, partly to be psychoanalysed, partly to spend more time with Wittgenstein. He was still in Vienna in September, when Russell sent him the final draft of his Introduction, incorporating the corrections that Ramsey had made. Russell also sent him the three new Appendices he had written during the summer for the new edition. Ramsey agreed to proofread Russell's new work, but otherwise made little comment on it. When the new edition was published the following year, however, Ramsey wrote a terse and unenthusiastic review of it for *Mind*, pointing out its failure to provide logical foundations for large parts of ordinary mathematics.

In fact, from the point of view of Russell's original hopes for mathematical logic, the second edition of *Principia Mathematica* represents a major step backwards. For the parts of mathematics that cannot be proved using the new system are *precisely* those that had first inspired his Herculean endeavours to reduce mathematics to logic.[4] The work, that is, of the German mathematicians, which in 1900 Russell had described as 'the greatest achievement of which our age has to boast' – Dedekind's definition

---

[4] The logician and Russell scholar, Nino Cocchiarella, goes further: the system of logic in the new edition of *Principia Mathematica*, he claims, is incapable of defining numbers at all, or, anyway, incapable of preserving any analogue of Russell's original definition of numbers as 'classes of classes' (see Nino B. Cocchiarella, 'Russell's Theory of Logical Types and the Atomistic Hierarchy of Sentences', in Savage and Anderson (eds), *Rereading Russell: Essays in Bertrand Russell's Metaphysics and Epistemology*).

of real numbers, Weierstrass's definition of continuity and Cantor's transfinite set theory – cannot be established using the new theory. Had Russell (as Ramsey implies in his letter to G. E. Moore) decided that this work was not, after all, part of mathematics? No, for in his new Introduction he says: 'the theory of real numbers is an integral part of ordinary mathematics, and can hardly be the object of a reasonable doubt'. Nor had he given up the claim that all mathematics can be reduced to logic. His hope, he says in the new Introduction, is that some new logical axiom will be discovered that will enable the theory of real numbers to be deduced without the Axiom of Reducibility, 'but we have not succeeded in finding such an axiom'. In other words, there must be a theory of logic upon which the whole of mathematics can be built – only not that which Russell was now offering to the public. Not surprisingly, this new edition of *Principia* did little to further Russell's reputation as a technical philosopher, which remained more firmly than ever based on the work he had published before the First World War.

One senses that Russell's heart was not fully in this attempted return to technical work. He later told Beatrice Webb that he 'had exhausted his interest in mathematical reasoning and found getting out a new edition of his great book intellectually boresome'. As soon as it was finished, he turned to the relatively undemanding task of writing a 10,000-word essay on 'Philosophy in the Twentieth Century' for *The Dial*. This went over well-trodden ground and gave Russell another opportunity to hit out at his philosophical opponents. Twentieth-century academic philosophy, Russell claimed, divided into three groups: 1. Hegelian and Kantian Idealists; 2. pragmatists and Bergsonians; and 3. 'those who attach themselves to the sciences, believing that philosophy has no special brand of truth and no peculiar method of arriving at it'. These last, among whom, of course, he included himself, he called 'realists'. As he admitted, there was some intermingling between these groups; after all, 'Dr Whitehead's recent books employ the methods of realists in defence of a more or less Bergsonian metaphysic', and many philosophers considered modern science to provide confirmation of Kantian Idealism. Nevertheless, these distinctions 'are useful as affording a framework for the classification of opinions'.

Passing over Hegelianism very quickly, and saying almost nothing about Kantianism, Russell rehearsed his objections to the pragmatist theory of truth, before launching a spirited attack on Bergsonians, whom he caricatured as people who believed that the brain got in the way of intuitive wisdom: 'Bergson, like the pragmatists, prefers action to reason, Othello to Hamlet; he thinks it better to kill Desdemona by intuition than to let the King live because of intellect.' A great part of Bergson's philosophy, he declared, 'is merely traditional mysticism expressed in slightly novel language'. A Bergsonian is 'a temperamentally inactive man with a romantic admiration for action. Before 1914, the world was full of such people.' In contrast are the realists (Russell does not devote any space to explaining Whitehead's Bergsonianism – presumably he considered it entirely inexplicable), who believe in logical analysis rather than intuition and who hold

that 'all knowledge is scientific knowledge'. Although influenced in its
beginnings by pure mathematics, the most important influence on this new
philosophy now, Russell claimed, is physics, which had upset our old
notions of space, time and matter. The aim of the 'new realism' is not to
prove or disprove the 'great truths of religion', but only to clarify 'the
fundamental ideas of the sciences'. In this way, perhaps, Russell's
popularisations of modern physics might be regarded as the very epitome of
the new philosophy.

Although, ostensibly, it purports to champion the 'new philosophy', the
striking thing about this article is how little Russell says about recent
developments in philosophy itself. The only post-war philosophical works
he mentions are those of Whitehead. He never mentions Wittgenstein, or
Moore, or the recent philosophical controversies about the nature of
mathematics. In its preoccupations with William James and Henri Bergson,
the essay seems curiously anachronistic, harking back to the controversies in
which Russell had been engaged before the war. His emphasis on the
influence of physics on modern philosophy seems similarly out of touch. In
the 1920s, it is true, many philosophers did write analyses of the ideas and
methods of contemporary physics (one thinks, for example, of C. D. Broad's
Scientific Thought, which Russell had reviewed in 1923), but the work of
Moore or Wittgenstein could hardly be characterised in this light, and, in
his concentration on physics, Russell neglects to mention the concern of
philosophers with logic and language, which was already beginning to loom
large and was to become ever more dominant over the following decades.

Whatever its faults, 'Philosophy in the Twentieth Century' might be seen
as indicative of Russell's desire during the summer of 1924 to return to
philosophy. It is significant, I think, that, after working on *Principia*, Russell
wrote to the editor of *The Dial*, offering to write a survey of philosophy
since 1900, rather than, say, a piece on some more topical or political
subject. Russell's mood during this summer was one of disenchantment with
public affairs and a desire to absorb himself in private, contemplative
matters. In this, however, he was – for the first time in their married life –
out of step with Dora. For, just when Russell had become tired of practical
politics and with being a public figure, Dora was becoming intoxicated with
the pleasures of both.

While he was away in America, Dora had established herself as a left-
wing political activist in her own right. The previous year, both Dora and
Russell had become involved in the case of Rose Witcop and Guy Aldred,
whose pamphlet on sex education and birth control – sold cheaply and
specifically aimed at working-class women – had been seized by the police as
'obscene'. The Russells wrote letters to the Press about the case and tried to
get the banning order overturned, which, with the change of government in
1924, duly happened. During Russell's absence, Dora became involved in
the subsequent campaign to establish birth-control clinics for working-class
people. In 1924, any doctor or health visitor who offered advice on birth
control faced the threat of dismissal. Together with H. G. Wells and others,
Dora organised a deputation to the Ministry of Health to discuss the issue.

The deputation met on 9 May, and the pleas of Dora, Wells, and others were rejected on the grounds that the authority of Parliament was needed to change the government's policy. Taking up the challenge, the birth-control reformers, with Dora prominent among them, raised the issue at the next meeting of the Labour Women's Conference on 14 May, where they succeeded in passing a resolution backing the provision of birth-control advice.

By this time, the campaign was attracting much publicity and Dora's speech to the conference was reported in all the newspapers. Even as far away as Boston, Massachusetts, Russell was able to read of Dora's success. 'I have been watching your career in the American papers,' he wrote to her; 'they reported the interview of "Mrs Bertrand Russell's Birth-control Committee" & the remarks of H. G. It seems to me that you have done very well.' The conference led to the creation of the Workers' Birth Control Group within the Labour Party and a great deal of public debate on the issue, in which, naturally, Dora played a leading part. 'All through 1924 we buzzed and stung,' Dora wrote. 'We found the pages of the *Daily Herald*, the *New Leader*, the *Manchester Guardian*, *The Nation and the Athenaeum* open to us.' One important effect on Dora of the campaign was to draw her much closer to the left wing of the Labour Party, particularly the *Daily Herald* circle of writers, MPs and activists led by George Lansbury, the MP for Bow and Bromley. Lansbury was one of many left-wingers who had attacked Russell for his anti-Soviet stance, but on this issue, as on many others, he and Dora were at one.

Russell thus returned from America to find his wife happily engaged in the very kind of public life from which he now wished to retire, and treating as friends and comrades the very people from whom he had become alienated because of his opposition to the Soviet Union. Dora, in her own words, had now received her 'true political education', and, soon after the family were reunited in Cornwall, she left to attend the Independent Labour Party's Summer School in Scarborough, where she took an active part in the debates, contributed an article on birth control to the Summer School's discussion booklet, and sympathised with the Communists in their efforts to gain affiliation to the Labour Party.

All this was a long way indeed from Russell's concerns, but to compound matters, Dora's political activities brought with them opportunities for sexual dalliances that she was scarcely likely to resist for very long. While Russell was away, she had already attracted the attention of a writer and member of the Lansbury circle called Roy Randall. Their affair did not begin until a few years later, but, Randall later told Dora, he had fallen in love with her in 1924. Russell must have sensed something of the sort from Dora's letters, for in one of his letters from the United States he had reassured her: 'I don't feel I should be jealous about anything you did in my absence because I shouldn't feel it showed a preference of others to me. And altogether when people are as secure as you & I are, jealousy is impossible.'

In the event, however, Russell became impotent with Dora at around this time, thus ensuring that both her sexual appetites and the desire for more children that she had expressed in her letter to him of 19 May would have to be satisfied, if at all, by other men. In retrospect, therefore, it is possible to see the origins of the break-up of their marriage in the aftermath of Russell's lecture tour in 1924. Sexual jealousy no doubt played a part in Russell's changed attitude to his wife, but a greater part was perhaps played by Russell's sense that the Dora to whom he had waved goodbye in March was not the Dora to whom he returned in June. This latter was a more independent figure, dissatisfied with a merely domestic life and only too eager to enter the world of newspaper interviews, political journalism and public lectures and debates, from which he now recoiled in disgust.

As Russell had feared, a general election – the third in three years – was called in October 1924. For many months, the Government had suffered strong criticism from opposition parties over its foreign policy, particularly over its desire to establish diplomatic and trading links with the Soviet Union (which, following Lenin's death in January, was now led by Stalin, Kamenev and Zinoviev). Following his recognition of the Soviet regime in March, Ramsay MacDonald had announced plans to grant the Soviets a loan to help their economic reforms, a move that led to much 'No money for Bolshevik murderers' rhetoric among opposition MPs and the conservative Press. The issue on which the Government finally fell, however, was a relatively minor, domestic question concerning the prosecution of J. R. Campbell, the editor of the Communist paper *Workers' Weekly*, for alleged sedition in publishing an open letter to the armed forces, urging them not to allow themselves to be used against strikers. The Attorney-General first charged Campbell and then dropped the charge, under pressure from the Government to do so, whereupon the Liberals and Conservatives combined to pass a motion of censure against the Government, forcing an election.

On 9 October, the day the election was called, Russell, still in Cornwall, wrote to Dora in London that he wished 'the Election had been on the Russian Treaty. It is beastly having it on a small issue, & in defence of an asinine scoundrel. However, the issue of free speech is involved, & is important.' Important or not, he could not be persuaded to go through the ordeal of yet another campaign, but, wrote Dora: 'fortunately, the local supporters were unanimous in wanting me to stand in his place'. 'Naturally,' she said, 'I was excited and proud to be in a position to fight for a seat in Parliament, young as I was. I knew there was no chance of winning, but I could carry on my crusade for social justice and the rights of women.' Dora, in fact, was only just old enough to vote, having the previous spring become thirty years old – the age limit imposed on women by the 1918 Act that first gave women the vote.

The campaign was the most bitter in which the Russells had yet fought, and was dominated by the fear of Communism, which both the Liberals and the Conservatives used to discredit the Labour Government. On 21 October, just a week before polling day, the Foreign Office released to the Press a letter purportedly written by Zinoviev, the President of the Third International, to the British Communist Party, urging them to press ahead with revolutionary and subversive measures. This 'Red Letter' (later shown

to be a forgery) provoked much indignation in the Press and added much to
the atmosphere of hysterical anti-Communism in which the election was
fought. Far from being daunted by this, Dora found the whole thing
invigorating. She gloried in being smeared a 'Red', and spiritedly defended
MacDonald's Soviet policy, while roundly denouncing the Zinoviev letter as
a forgery planted on, or by, the Foreign Office.

The result of the election was a huge victory for the Conservatives, who
now, with 412 seats, had a comfortable majority in the House of Commons.
Labour were down to 151 seats, but the real losers of the campaign were the
Liberals, who, with only forty seats, were reduced to the small minority
party they have remained ever since. Dora, of course, lost to Sir Samuel
Hoare, but, she later claimed: 'I was told by an elector who had supported
me in that election that I had gained the highest vote ever obtained for
Labour in Chelsea.' For her, the campaign had been a triumph, increasing
still further her taste for the hurly-burly of political controversy and
confirming her in her belief that she had an important part to play in public
life, a part that would compensate for her earlier disappointment in having
to abandon her theatrical ambitions. 'For me personally,' she wrote in her
autobiography, '1924 had been a great year':

> There had been enough drama and platform appearances to satisfy my
> theatrical instincts. I had begun to earn a reputation as a convincing and
> moving speaker, whilst the press controversy had given me malicious
> delight in detecting my enemies' weak points and replying in brief,
> sarcastic sentences. I suppose it would be said by psychiatrists that I had
> found a constructive outlet for my aggression. However that may be, all
> my life I have enjoyed this kind of controversial pamphleteering, begun in
> that exciting year.

For Russell, the year had been dispiriting rather than exciting. He took no
pleasure in the furore created by the Zinoviev letter, and could not happily,
as Dora could, regard himself as a friend and comrade of the beleaguered
Communists in the Labour movement. Nor, equally, could he align himself
with the right wing of the Labour Party. The MacDonald ministry had
disappointed him in not bringing in more Socialist measures, and still more
in what he regarded as its craven subservience to the Foreign Office. In a
short piece for *The New Republic* called 'British Labour's Lesson', published
at the end of 1924, he attacked MacDonald for failing to stand up to the
Foreign Office, a failure that he attributed to MacDonald's snobbish respect
for 'gentlemen'. While Labour leaders continued to feel 'an inferiority
complex' in dealing with their permanent officials, Russell maintained, the
prospects of diminishing social inequality, even if Labour got into power
again, would remain bleak.

The election served only to confirm Russell in his distaste for politics and
his desire to withdraw from public life ('Since the General Election I have
been too disgusted with politics to take any interest,' as he put it in a letter
to Ottoline). At Christmas, he and Dora escaped from London – and their

children – for a week alone together in a hotel room in Lynton, North Devon. 'In London,' Russell wrote to Ottoline, 'what with babies and household and callers and local Labour Party and birth control, Dora never gets a moment to herself.' In Lynton, it rained all week, and the two of them spent most of their time sitting either side of the fire, writing. Both had been commissioned by Ogden to write short books for the Kegan Paul series, 'To-day and To-morrow'. Russell's was called *What I Believe*, and was completed comfortably within the week. Eschewing all discussion of politics or current affairs (except, here and there, a reference to the importance of birth control), *What I Believe* is written from a rather Olympian viewpoint. Beginning with the 'philosophy of nature', Russell urges mankind as a whole to learn the lesson he had tried to instil in his own son of recognising its own unimportance:

> the earth is merely one of the smaller planets of one of the smaller stars of the Milky Way. It would be ridiculous to warp the philosophy of nature in order to bring out results that are pleasing to the tiny parasites of this insignificant planet.

Passing next to the 'philosophy of value', Russell summarises his ethical view in a single, subsequently oft-quoted, sentence: 'The good life is one inspired by love and guided by knowledge.' The knowledge in question is, of course, *scientific* knowledge, and Russell ends with his now-familiar vision of how psychological science might contribute to bringing about 'the good life':

> There is probably no limit to what science can do in the way of increasing positive excellence . . . When we have discovered how character depends upon physiological conditions, we shall also be able, if we choose, to produce far more of the type of human being that we admire. Intelligence, artistic capacity, benevolence – all these things no doubt could be increased by science.
> . . . Nature, even human nature, will cease more and more to be an absolute datum: more and more, it will become what scientific manipulation has made it. Science can, if it chooses, enable our grandchildren to live the good life, by giving them knowledge, self-control and characters productive of harmony rather than strife.

Dora's little book, *Hypatia or Woman and Knowledge*, written in the same week for the same series, struck a very different note. While Russell addressed mankind from a great height, Dora did so with her feet planted firmly on the earth; while Russell avoided topical issues, Dora rushed headlong into the controversies of the day; while Russell dealt in large generalities like love, knowledge and nature, Dora dealt in specifics, spelling out exactly what she thought modern feminists should demand: a happy, uninhibited and guilt-free sex life, free birth control, maternity leave from work and the vote at twenty-one. Linking the sex-war with the class-war,

Dora declared that 'it is the progressive working woman rather than the woman of the middle class who will in the future make the most important contribution to the thought of feminism and to a solution of our practical difficulties'. Her book is a spirited defence of Socialist feminism, its language not that of a dry political tract, but rather that of a Lawrentian sexual liberator, eager to break with convention in destroying the polite silence that customarily surrounds the subject of sexual enjoyment, particularly that of women:

> Let us freely admit that we have but been playing mock modesty, and that to us the body is no mere box to hold the mind, but a temple of delight and ecstasy . . . To me the important task of modern feminism is to accept and proclaim sex . . . during the years of war, young women took the last step towards feminine emancipation by admitting to themselves and their lovers the mutual nature of sex-love between man and woman. It sounds a platitude, but is, in fact, a revolution.

Dora's enthusiasm for the cause of birth control was strongly linked to her desire to destroy the conventional view that the purpose of sex was to have children. 'We want better reasons for having children,' she writes in *Hypatia*, 'than not knowing how to prevent them.' Sex was not a means to an end, but an end in itself:

> Men and women are not creatures of clay, nor disembodied spirits; but things of fire intertwining in understanding, torrents leaping to join in a cascade of mutual ecstasy. There is nothing in life to compare with this united purpose of minds and bodies in men and women who have laid aside hostility and fear and seek in love the fullest understanding of themselves and the universe.

This conjures up a rather different picture of 'the good life' than that promised by Russell's somewhat clinical vision of the happiness produced by advances in physiological science. Where one wishes to train the instincts, the other wishes to unleash them. Knowing that Russell was at this time impotent with Dora, one cannot help wondering whether, in her characterisation of the sexlessness of the intellectual man, there was an implied rebuke to her husband:

> The intellectual . . . does all that he can to forget the needs of the body. Woman counts as one of them. She is a burden, a responsibility, a distraction, an incursion of the material into a world of contemplation . . . An instinctive life – so he thinks – is possible only in spasms, if at all, for a man with serious mental work to accomplish. If woman persists in keeping him company, then she must shoulder the burdens, tend him and care for him, and leave him alone when he doesn't want her.

The differences in tone and content between *What I Believe* and *Hypatia* illustrate the gulf that was beginning to open up between Dora and Russell. While Dora railed against the chains of domesticity and the aridness of the merely contemplative life, all Russell wanted to do was be with his children and recover his belief that he did indeed have 'serious mental work to accomplish'. When they returned to London, Dora threw herself once more into political activism, standing as a candidate for the London County Council in order to help change its policies on birth control. The basement in Sydney Street became a meeting place for local Labour Party activists and the Workers' Birth Control Group. Dora revelled in being at the centre of this frenetic activity, but Russell remained aloof, writing to Ottoline of the 'smelly young men' who now invaded his home and, when the results of the local election were announced, reporting triumphantly that 'Dora was badly beaten for LCC thank heaven'.

'I am getting back to philosophical work,' Russell told Ottoline on 20 February 1925. 'I have undertaken a popular book on relativity, a book on education, one on the stars (popular), and one on matter – so I have plenty to do. Also they are starting a philosophical institute in London where I shall lecture, beginning in the autumn.' A few weeks previously, he had been to Holland to deliver a paper to the Amsterdam Philosophical Society on 'The Philosophical Analysis of Matter'. This contained his most careful and considered statement yet on the relationship between philosophy and physics, and on the task that remained for philosophy to accomplish after it had recognised that all genuine knowledge was scientific. He identified three sorts of problems that fell to the philosopher, rather than to the physicist, to solve regarding the analysis of matter: logical, epistemological and ontological:

> The logical problems are concerned with the organisation of physics as a deductive system and the consideration of possible pre-physical premises from which the postulates of physics, as a logical whole, can be deduced. The epistemological problems are concerned with the evidence for the truth of physics – not for this or that particular physical law, but for the main postulates upon which the science depends. The ontological problems are concerned with the status of matter in relation to what actually exists: here we have to discuss four principal theories: dualism, materialism, idealism, and neutral monism.

Russell's lecture then went through these problems, each in turn, concluding that 'what we call a piece of matter is merely a certain crinkle in space-time, i.e., a certain complicated mathematical relation among events throughout space-time'. Filling out what, exactly, that meant would be the central task of *The Analysis of Matter* that he had promised to write for Ogden, a task that would provide the central focus of his philosophical thinking for the next few years.

Russell showed far more relish for this task than he had shown for that of producing a new edition of *Principia Mathematica*, largely, I believe, because he could think of it as a contribution to *knowledge*. Since his conversion by

Wittgenstein to a linguistic view of logic, Russell had regarded mathematics, not as a body of knowledge, but as a set of tautologies. This robbed it of its interest, and made it appear trivial. Several times from the 1920s onwards, Russell expressed the wish that he had been a physicist rather than a mathematician; given that it was now too late to make a contribution to physics, he could do the next best thing and make a contribution to the *understanding* of physics, a piece of 'serious mental work' for which his mathematical training would equip him well. As he himself realised, his expertise in mathematics and mathematical philosophy gave him no authority whatever for pronouncing on political matters. Indeed, it may even have been a disadvantage, producing in him a desire for cut-and-dried conclusions where none was to be found and leading him to the impatience with detail and nuance of which Beatrice Webb complained. His mathematical training did, however, give him an advantage in understanding the arcane theories of modern physics, and that, combined with his remarkable gift for rendering difficult technical ideas intelligible to the non-specialist, made him the ideal person to negotiate, as it were, between physicists and philosophers, explaining relativity theory and quantum physics to the philosopher, and pointing out to physicists the philosophical problems raised by their work.

If no other factors had been involved, Russell would have devoted his time entirely to this task, writing work of interest only to professional philosophers and physicists. But other factors *were* involved, not the least of which was the need to earn money. One way of solving this problem, without 'prostituting' himself as he had on his 1924 lecture tour, seemed to be to write books of popular science that would, at the same time, provide material for the philosophical task he had set himself of analysing the presuppositions, logical structure and ontological consequences of modern physics. This involved him in treading a difficult line between market forces and intellectual integrity, but the public demand for popular science seemed to offer some hope that this line could be trodden. After all, *The ABC of Atoms* was not the only best-selling book he had written since his return from China, but also by a long way the most intellectually honest and serious. His offer to Ogden to write a companion volume on Einstein's work, therefore, though it rather flew in the face of his remarks to Unwin about the superfluity and pointlessness of producing yet more popularistions of relativity theory, seemed to offer the best hope of something that would sell, while further pursuing his philosophical work. Thus, when he returned to Cornwall in March, he began work on *The ABC of Relativity*.

Because he had agreed to deliver a book on education to Unwin during the summer, *The ABC of Relativity* had to be written very quickly. Russell was also concerned that it should not be too intellectually difficult. In this, he was possibly influenced by the reaction he had received to his Amsterdam lecture. It was, he told Dora, 'above the heads of most of the audience' (about the Dutch generally, Russell remarked: 'One gets the impression that ever since the 17th century they have lived below their income & invested their savings prudently'). The result, delivered to Kegan Paul in May, was a book that sold very well but contained little that Russell could use in his projected philosophical book, *The Analysis of Matter*. As Russell wrote to Ottoline: 'There never seems to be time for the things one really wants to do.'

As soon as *The ABC of Relativity* was out of the way, Russell began work on *On Education*. The problem he faced in writing this particular book was that he did not actually know very much about education, or rather, as he put it to Unwin: 'I know a lot about education up to the age of 3, but not much yet about the later years.' His solution was to add to the book's title the words 'especially in early childhood', and to concentrate on what he had learnt from his experience of bringing up John and Kate. In fact, the book is not about education at all in the usual sense, but about parenting, giving the lessons about 'moral training' that he had learnt from Watson and other psychologists. 'I have begun to understand how to manage moral education without superstition,' he claimed to Ottoline, 'at any rate we seem to succeed so far with John and Kate. I think moral education should be nearly finished by the age of six.'

The greater part of the book, then, is taken up with the 'education of character', and displays Russell's astonishing confidence in the 'science' of psychology, the application of which, he appeared to believe, would enable us to produce within a generation children free from fear, stupidity, anxiety, dishonesty and all other weaknesses of character. Dominating the book is the question of how to conquer fear. Fear, Russell seems to suggest, is at the root of almost all the evils of the world; if we could only eliminate fear, there would be no barriers in the way of living the 'good life', inspired by love and guided by knowledge. 'A thousand ancient fears obstruct the road to happiness and freedom,' he writes. 'Shall we let them [our children] be twisted and stunted and terrified in youth, to be killed afterwards in futile wars which their intelligence was too cowed to prevent?' Unless we are prepared to say 'yes' to this question, he claims, 'the way is clear', and that way is to begin moral training from the moment of birth on the lines suggested by Watson's experimental work on the causes of fear.

From a commercial point of view, *On Education* proved to be one of Russell's most successful books. It has been reprinted dozens of times and translated into twenty foreign languages. The reasons for its success, however, remain somewhat mysterious. After all, it has almost nothing to say about school and university education, its chapters on these subjects being short, bland and unoriginal (so much so that, on its first appearance, it was rejected for publication in periodicals on the grounds of its 'lack of novelty'). And its claims for the 'science of child psychology' are transparently overstated, if not entirely spurious. Did Russell's readers *really* believe that 'If existing knowledge were used and tested methods applied, we could, in a generation, produce a population almost wholly free from disease, malevolence and stupidity', and that 'We do not do so, because we prefer oppression and war'? Could Russell himself really have believed it? Perhaps parents bought *On Education* for advice on how to bring up their children. But why should they have accepted Russell as an authority on the subject? Because he had written path-breaking work on the philosophy of mathematics? One is reminded of the many people who wrote to Einstein asking him how they should vote in US elections, presumably on the grounds that, if he was clever enough to think up the theory of relativity, he was surely clever enough to work out which economic, domestic and foreign policies the United States should adopt!

From Russell's point of view, it was probably fortunate that he wrote *On Education* at a time when he had no doubts about the correctness of his methods of parenting. During the summer that he wrote *The ABC of Relativity* and *On Education*, Russell enjoyed the kind of family life he had always dreamt of. 'I feel so happy', he wrote to Ottoline in August, 'that I feel frightened, like Polycrates. I feel fate must have something bad in store.'[5] Both children appeared to be flourishing, especially Kate, who from an early age was showing signs of exceptional intelligence, in which Russell took great pride. Still less than two years old, she could already recite many nursery rhymes and spoke, much earlier than John had done, in whole sentences. One night, Russell was delighted to hear her saying as she went to sleep: 'Last year I used to dive off the diving board – I *did*.' He took equal delight in his son's early grasp of syllogistic logic, demonstrated when Dora once alarmed him by angrily shouting at a cow on their lawn. 'Mummy is angry, she is angry with the cow. John is not a cow,' said John with Aristotelian precision.

Despite writing more than 2,000 words a day, Russell spent much time with his children. A vivid evocation of family life at Carn Voel that summer has been left by Dora:

> Day after day we would lie on the white sand, steep ourselves in the green and purple water. The garden began to prosper. I started to grow tomatoes in my greenhouse: John was toddling about and playing with his father, fishing with my whole ball of string in my watering can.

The only blot on this otherwise perfect serenity was that Dora would often have to leave Carn Voel to attend political meetings. Whenever she left, Russell would write her short affectionate letters, telling her what John and Kate had been up to and how much he was missing her. 'Life is short,' he wrote, '& I grudge every day of possible happiness lost.' Though he encouraged her in her fight to get the Labour Party to commit itself to the provision of birth control, he evidently felt rather distant from her work and would really have preferred her to stay at home, cultivating the garden (in both a literal and metaphorical sense).

When, in October, the time came to return to London, Russell did so reluctantly. *On Education* was still not quite finished, he had to prepare the

---

[5] Polycrates was the Samoan tyrant who enjoyed such good fortune that he was advised to throw away something he valued highly, so as to avoid nemesis. Accordingly, he threw away a precious gold ring, but a few days later the ring was discovered in the belly of a fish that had been presented to him. Nemesis duly arrived when he was crucified by the Persians.

course of philosophical lectures he was to give that autumn at the British
Institute of Philosophy and, all the time, he was longing to get down to the
serious philosophical task of writing *The Analysis of Matter*. Dora,
meanwhile, was working harder than ever with the Workers' Birth Control
Group, which now began a campaign of lobbying Members of Parliament
and local authority health officers. 'We are both overworked,' Russell wrote
to Ottoline, 'and it is hateful being back in London.' 'Politics are
depressing,' he added. 'I can't believe in any of the politicians.'

John, now nearly four, was sent to a Montessori nursery school in
London. 'John loves his school,' Russell told Ottoline, 'but only does
kindergarten things. He has not quite grasped that it is not his province to
teach – on arriving one morning he gave the headmistress a lecture on
Saturn's rings. Another day he suddenly piped up: "Have you been round
the world?" and when she said no he said "my daddy has".' Because John
used the Montessori apparatus for making trains rather than for its intended
purpose, Russell was told that his son had a 'disordered imagination', a
suggestion that Russell laughed off: on the contrary, he retorted, what John
had was a love of trains acquired from his father. Russell also arranged for
John and Kate to spend an afternoon at the famous nursery school for
working-class children in Deptford, South London, run by the Socialist and
educational reformer, Margaret McMillan. In *On Education* Russell had
lavished praise upon Miss McMillan's school, claiming, among other things,
that, 'in spite of the fact that, at night, and on Sundays, they [McMillan's
pupils] have to be in poverty-stricken homes, perhaps in cellars with
drunken parents, their physique and intelligence become equal to the best
that middle-class children achieve'. Seeing her school for themselves, Dora
and Russell became even more fervent converts of her style of teaching,
which emphasised free play and a healthy regime of good diet and outdoor
exercise.

Throughout the autumn and winter months of 1925–6, Russell delivered
his lectures on 'Problems of Philosophy' for the British Institute. They were
held at the London School of Economics every Wednesday to a fee-paying,
non-academic audience. As such, they were deliberately non-technical;
indeed, the syllabus seemed to follow the basic structure of *What I Believe*,
distinguishing the 'world of values' from the 'world of facts', asking 'What
can we know about the universe as a whole?' and ending with 'The Good
Life' and 'The Value of Philosophy'. Some of the material was later
incorporated into Russell's 1927 book, *Outline of Philosophy*, an uninspired
popular guide to the subject that never quite achieved the success of his
earlier (1911) popular book, *The Problems of Philosophy*.

Despite his nauseous reaction to his lecture tour of 1924, and his
subsequent determination to return to philosophy, Russell agreed to give
several public lectures on political themes in the autumn of 1925, in which
one can see the intellectually serious tone of his Amsterdam lecture at the
beginning of the year giving way to the glib superficiality and outrageous
simplifications that had alternately delighted his American audiences and
offended the American Press. On 16 October, for example, he gave a lecture

called 'Psychology and Politics' to the 1917 Club, in which he delivered
himself of such pronouncements as the following:

> In the present age, some people think society is a machine and some think
> it is a tree. The former are Fascisti, imperialists, industrialists,
> Bolsheviks; the latter constitutionalists, agrarians or pacifists. The
> argument is just as absurd as that of the Guelfs and Ghibellines, since
> society is in fact neither a machine nor a tree.

The theme of the lecture was that, as 'political opinions are not based
upon reason', they are not to be changed by rational argument, but rather by
the application of psychology. Indulging in his now familiar overstatements
about the power of 'scientific' psychology to mould the characters of the
young, Russell added to it a simplistic, crudely reductive psychological
analysis of the wickedness of political leaders. The reason why the world is
not better governed, he claimed, is because the people who run it are
sexually and emotionally frustrated, and the reason for *this* is that they have
not studied scientific psychology and thus do not understand what
happiness is. Thus:

> In such important acts as choosing a career, a man is greatly influenced by
> theory. If a wrong theory [of what constitutes happiness] prevails,
> successful men will be unhappy, but will not know why. This fills them
> with rage, which leads them to desire the slaughter of younger men,
> whom they envy unconsciously. Most modern politics, while nominally
> based on economics, is really due to rage, caused by lack of instinctive
> satisfaction; and this lack, in turn, is largely due to false popular
> psychology.

The cause of the war, then, was the frustrated emotional life of people like
Sir Edward Grey, and, now that we know what leads to such frustration,
putting an end to war is easy: we just have to bring people up without fear,
rage and hatred. And we know just how to do *that*, for psychology has made
education a science, a simple matter of effecting changes in 'organisms':

> The essence of education is that it is a change (other than death) effected
> in an organism to satisfy the desires of the operator . . . Now there are
> many ways of altering an organism. You may change its anatomy, as in
> the fish that has lost an eye, or the man that has lost an appendix. You
> may alter its metabolism, for instance by drugs. You may alter its habits
> by creating associations. Ordinary instruction is a particular case of this
> last.

Armed with the information concerning how to create the habits we wish
to create, it 'would be easy, with our present knowledge, to make instinctive
happiness almost universal, if we were not thwarted by the malevolent
passions of those who have missed happiness and do not want anyone else to

get it'. Easy? Our *present* knowledge? It is extraordinary that the man who wrote this credulous nonsense was, at the same time, lecturing his audiences at the British Institute on the value of sceptical doubt.

The wild exaggerations and crass oversimplifications of 'Psychology and Politics' would be easier to accept if one could regard them as casual, off-the-cuff remarks. But the evidence is that Russell was prepared to let the essay stand as representing his considered opinion. He repeated the lecture at the London School of Economics in November, and yet again at a meeting of the Independent Labour Party in February 1926. He then had it published as an article in *The Dial*, and as a chapter in his collection *Sceptical Essays*, a collection that, with glorious cheek and unconscious irony, he prefaced with an Introduction stating as his central doctrine that 'it is undesirable to believe a proposition when there is no ground whatever for supposing it true'.

Still worse was to come. On 22 October 1925, just five days after he had delivered 'Psychology and Politics', Russell gave a Fabian lecture called 'Freedom in Society' that was, if anything, still more intellectually careless; packed with the kind of half-serious, half-humorous epigrams that flowed so easily from his pen and were to become characteristic of his journalism of the 1920s and 30s:

> Americans need rest, but do not know it. I believe this to be a large part of the explanation of the crime wave in the United States.

> The British police hold that no one must know the truth about anything.

> Miss McMillan at Deptford is training children who become capable of creating a free community. If her methods were applied to all children, rich and poor, one generation would suffice to solve our social problems.

> The people in Dostoevsky are no doubt not quite like real Russians, but at any rate they are people whom only a Russian could have invented. They have all sorts of strange, violent desires, from which the average Englishman is free, at least so far as his conscious life is concerned.

If one shows Russell's sense of humour, it is possible to enjoy the glibness and wilful shallowness of these remarks (and thousands like them that he was to publish in the following decades), but it is surely not possible to see in them a serious attempt to cast light on the subject in hand.

One reason, one suspects, for the superficiality of Russell's writing on politics at this time was that, politically, he had nowhere to go. As he had told Ottoline, he could 'not believe in any of the politicians'. As he surveyed the political landscape of the 1920s, there were no organised groups, and few causes even, to which he could give his allegiance. The reason he found the politics of this time 'disgusting' was not just because of the acrimony, the deceit and the viciousness with which they were conducted, but also because, as the battle lines were being drawn, he could not place himself wholeheartedly on *either* side. British politics at this time was dominated by class, the great issues being unemployment, the rise of trade unionism, the conditions and pay of manual labourers, and the perceived threat of Communist revolution.

Russell's sympathies in these struggles were with the Socialists, but *not* with the working class and especially not with the Communists. He had not become a Socialist because of any sense of identification with working-class people, and he had no sympathy with any talk of the working class *winning* their battles against the bourgeoisie. He was no class warrior. On the contrary, he had become a Socialist partly because he thought Socialism was the only way of *avoiding* class-war and thus preserving civilisation. He disliked the hysterical fear of Communism that had brought the Conservatives to power in 1924, not because he liked the Communists any more than the Conservatives did, but because he despised the politics of fear and because a political issue that he did care passionately about – namely, freedom – was involved. Thus, as Baldwin's Conservatives continued to play upon fears of 'Bolshevism' while in office, Russell found himself defending the rights of people whose politics he despised. For example, when twelve Communist Party leaders, including Wal Hannington and Arthur McManus, were tried and imprisoned at the end of 1925, Russell took part in the demonstration against their imprisonment, but he took care to make clear that what he was defending was not the men themselves, or their views, but the principle of free speech.

As Britain continued its slide into the class-warfare that produced the General Strike of 1926, Russell could, with some justification, present himself as being, in his own words, 'a moderately reasonable being in a totally unreasonable scheme'. It was perhaps this that prompted him to fantasise about the ability of scientific methods of education to produce other 'reasonable beings' – it was the only hope he could see. If this led him, on the one hand, to a startling credulity about what might be achieved by decent nursery education, it also gave his political pronouncements an air of cynical detachment that could easily be misrepresented as complete scepticism. There was, too, the problem that, in his thinking about Socialism, he had argued himself into political paralysis. His argument, stated many times in many different forms, went like this: Socialism was the only way of averting a class conflict that would destroy civilisation, but Socialism could not be achieved in Britain unless America also adopted it, for otherwise America would blockade Britain and we would all starve. So, the only hope was to see Socialism triumph in America. But, if this argument is sound (and, of course, this is a big 'if'), what, in the meantime, should British Socialists do while they waited for America to turn Socialist? Russell had no answer to this question, which is why, perhaps, he stopped writing about Socialism and started writing instead about how to produce 'reasonable' human beings.

The fact that Russell's analysis of the prospects for Socialism provided little guidance as to what Socialists in Britain ought to be doing emerges clearly from his controversy with Leon Trotsky in 1926. In a review of

Trotsky's *Where is Britain Going?*, Russell praised Trotsky for pointing out that the British Labour Party lacked a 'coherent theoretical outlook', but took him to task for his vision of Britain's future. When a Labour Government with a clear majority is finally elected in Britain, Trotsky prophesied, the Labour leaders will be swept aside by a Communist revolution, leading to civil war and, eventually, to the 'revolutionary dictatorship' of the proletariat. This, Russell writes, 'is a programme that could only be advocated by an enemy or a fool; and Trotsky is not a fool'. 'It is obvious', he claims, 'that French (if not British) aeroplanes and American (if not British) warships would soon put an end to the Communist regime; or, at the very lowest, an economic blockade would destroy our export trade and therefore deprive us of our food supply.' Until 'Soviet Russia can place a fleet in the Atlantic stronger than that of America', British Socialists would be unwise to take a course of action that was intolerable to the United States. If Trotsky 'really desired the spread of Communism, and not merely the collapse of England, it is time for him to turn his attention to the American Federation of Labour'.

In his reply, Trotsky fired off some splendidly vituperative abuse at Russell, whom he described as 'a philosopher of mathematicians, a mathematician of philosophers, an aristocrat of democracy and a dilettante of socialism':

> And this man, worm-eaten through and through with scepticism, egoistic, reclusive and aristocratic, considers himself called upon to give advice to the British proletariat and to warn it against our communist intrigues!

He also scored a polemical bull's-eye by reminding Russell that 'In his pamphlet *Icarus* he openly expresses his conviction that the best outcome would be the destruction of all our civilisation.' Otherwise Trotsky was ineffectual, choosing to centre his reply on a defence of violent revolution against Russell's 'pacifism'. This was misguided in two respects: first, Russell was not a pacifist (as Trotsky might have gathered by Russell's appeal to militarily strategic arguments) and, second, Russell's argument – whether he himself realised it or not – had nothing to do with revolution. Russell envisaged an American blockade of a Socialist Britain, not because the Americans dislike revolutions, but because they dislike Socialism. His argument, if sound at all, would apply – as he himself had applied it previously – to parliamentary methods of establishing Socialism as much as to revolutionary methods. (Equally, of course, the argument in itself gives no reason for objecting to a revolution *in America*.) Thus, if Trotsky's programme could only be advocated by 'an enemy or a fool', it would seem to follow that *anybody* who advocated Socialism in Britain, without first turning their attention to the American Federation of Labor, was acting against Britain's best interests.

Trotsky was therefore wide of the mark when he described Russell as 'a sceptic through and through', one of 'those bourgeois sceptics who imagine themselves to be socialist only because they from time to time vomit in the atmosphere of rotting bourgeois society'. The problem was not Russell's scepticism; on the contrary, in his visions of a future in which fear was eliminated and happiness universal, he might more justly be accused of a starry-eyed utopianism. The problem was, rather, that Russell had argued himself into a belief that the best form of government for Britain was also one that, if implemented before the United States turned Socialist, would lead to its starvation. This was clearly not a point of view likely to inspire fervent agitation for the politics in which he believed.

Dora was much better placed to play an active part in British politics; not only because her love of the Soviet Union enabled her to feel solidarity with the British Communists, nor simply because in birth control she had found a cause to which she could ardently devote herself, but also because, unlike Russell, she did have an instinctive sympathy for the working class. At home, this showed itself in their different attitudes to servants. Though the Russells were not especially wealthy, they employed – as was common in Britain until after the Second World War – a number of servants: a cook, a housemaid, a gardener, a chauffeur and a nanny. For Russell, despite his Socialism, this raised no problems. He had, Dora has remarked, 'an aristocratic attitude to servants, which I had always minded'. When the servants were there, life ran smoothly; when they were not, he complained of the inconvenience. But, either way, though he was a perfectly decent employer, Russell took little interest in them, taking the class divide that separated him from them as part of the natural order of things. Dora's attitude was entirely different – she complained that 'the class basis of "service" as it used to be too often poisoned the relations between master and man, mistress and maid'. She was uncomfortable at being separated from other people by class, and sought to overcome the gulf through sympathy and friendship. In many cases, she succeeded: 'when the class question was out of the way, people who first came as staff, or in a domestic capacity, later became my life-long friends'.

In public life, this difference manifested itself in Dora's growing tendency to see British politics in class terms and in her increasing identification with the struggles of the working class. Both processes were accelerated in 1926, when Dora, possibly for the first time, learnt something at first hand of how working-class families in Britain lived. In February, a bill, sponsored by the Workers' Birth Control Group, was presented to Parliament that would have enabled local authorities to spend money on birth-control advice. That it was defeated was no surprise, given the large Conservative majority, but what upset the group was that a large number of Labour MPs voted against it. It therefore began a campaign to shame those MPs into supporting the movement, first by producing a leaflet naming the Labour members who had voted against the bill, and then by visiting their constituencies to agitate on behalf of birth control.

Dora took a leading part in this campaign, which entailed her visiting the mining areas of Durham and South Wales, and the steel town of Motherwell in Scotland. At these places she was put up by working-class Labour activists, and saw for herself what it meant to be poor. In Consett, County Durham, for example, she discovered that her host, a miner's wife, 'pregnant at the time, had to carry coals up several flights of stairs and cook on an open grate'. In Motherwell, her host was a steelworker called John Wilson, who 'lived in a flat with the typical "butt and ben" beds in the kitchen-living room'. She was taken to see the steelworks, and 'was, as always, filled with admiration for the men who work day after day in such places'. When she returned home, she found that she had caught scabies – 'For this I insinuate no blame whatever to kind and courageous hosts' – which she passed on to Russell and they both 'had to suffer the unpleasant cure together'. More importantly, she returned with an even stronger feeling of solidarity with the working class, which, if it contained a certain degree of sentimentality, was none the less real and was to remain an important part of her make-up for the rest of her life.

As the Russells prepared to leave for Cornwall in the spring of 1926, Britain was already moving inexorably towards its biggest class conflict yet. A General Strike had been threatened the previous summer, when the Government withdrew its subsidy of the mining industry, and the mine-owners thus informed their workers that they would have to take a cut in pay. At that time Baldwin had capitulated, restoring the subsidy for a year, and commissioning a Government report on the issue from Sir Herbert Samuel, the ex-Home Secretary. The Samuel Report was published in March, and recommended an end to subsidy and the immediate reduction of wages. The mine-owners added to this the demand that miners work longer hours, prompting the miners' leader, A. J. Cook, to his famously defiant slogan: 'Not a penny off the pay, not a minute on the day'. The existing subsidy ran out at the end of April and, as deadlock had been reached in the negotiations between the miners and the owners, the miners stopped working. On 3 May, the TUC declared a General Strike.

By this time, the atmosphere throughout the country was charged with talk of revolution. 'A general strike is not an industrial dispute,' thundered the *Daily Mail*. 'It is a revolutionary movement intended to inflict suffering upon the mass of innocent persons in the community and thereby to put possible constraint on the government . . . It cannot be tolerated by any civilised government.' Baldwin's Government took the same view and was determined to break the strike. In this it was supported by the mass of middle-class people in Britain, many of whom volunteered for the 'Organisation for the Maintenance of Supplies' in order to keep going a skeleton transport service of amateur train, tram and bus drivers. Troops were stationed in Whitehall and used to help transport food and other supplies.

The battle lines drawn, Dora was in no doubt which side she was on and was eager to enter the fray. 'My first impulse', she wrote, 'was to help the cause of the workers in any way that I could.' At the first news of the strike, she got on her bike and cycled to Penzance – a hilly and arduous nine-mile trek – looking for strikers to whom to declare her support. At the harbour, she met a man sitting on an upturned boat.

> Rather nervously I asked: 'Are the men out down here?' 'They are.' 'Do you think they are likely to go back?' 'Be fools if they do.' 'Could you perhaps direct me to the Strike Committee?'

The Strike Committee received her warmly, and the following day she and Russell visited the strikers together, declared their support and contributed towards the strike fund.

After that, Dora was made a member of the Strike Committee (the only woman on it) and, every day, cycled to St John's Hall in Penzance, where the strikers assembled to hear news (there were no newspapers during the strike, of course, because the printers, too, were out on strike), listen to speeches, sing songs and generally keep their spirits up. It is apparent from her account that Dora revelled in the excitement of those heady days, when it began to seem possible that in this fight between organised labour and the Tory Government, the Tories would lose. Satisfying both her theatrical streak and her sense of working-class solidarity, she was taken to local meetings outside Penzance, where she delivered stirring and encouraging speeches, on one occasion quoting Milton's lines:

> Oh, how comely it is and how reviving
> To the spirits of just men long opprest
> When God into the hands of their deliverer
> Puts invincible might.

'She is a born proletarian leader, and will probably die on a barricade,' Russell wrote to Ottoline of his wife, with obvious pride, but also, perhaps, a touch of condescension. While Dora travelled around Cornwall, exhorting the strikers to stay firm, Russell stayed at home, writing. Though 'heart and soul with the strikers', as he put it to Ottoline, he felt that there was nothing useful he could do to help them. Writing on 10 May, when the strike had been on for a week, Russell's analysis of the future that awaited the strikers was bleak:

> I think the Govt deliberately provoked the strike in order to smash trade unionism; I think if it wins it will put all the leaders in prison, make trade unionism illegal, and perhaps disenfranchise all who struck, on the ground that they are criminals.

These predictions look far-fetched, but, at a time when there were no newspapers, people had to rely on hearsay, and rumours were rife that the Government had decided to arrest the TUC leaders and to repeal the Trades Disputes Act, making the illegality of the strike beyond question. This followed the statement in the House of Commons on 8 May by the former Attorney-General, Sir John Simon ('that foul beast', as Russell called him in his letter to Ottoline: 'I have loathed him ever since I once dined with him in Soho in 1916'), that he considered the General Strike to be against the law. Simon's judgment was challenged by legal experts, but it was sufficient to worry the TUC leaders, who were also becoming alarmed at the prospect of having started a revolution. On 12 May, therefore, the TUC announced an unconditional end to the strike.

The miners, feeling bitterly betrayed by the TUC, stayed on strike until they were forced by poverty and near-starvation to return to work in the winter. During this period, the Russells had two miner's daughters to stay with them at Carn Voel. They were, Russell wrote to Ottoline, 'nice, but dull'. When A. J. Cook, the miners' leader, came to Penzance to speak, he stayed at Carn Voel and turned out to be, Russell wrote, 'a most lovable man, simple, modest, humane, and full of fun, quite the opposite of what he is said to be. I am heart and soul with him.' Cook was put up in the best attic bedroom, the beams of which had recently been painted red. 'To this day', Dora writes in her autobiography, 'I have seen to it that those beams have remained red in honour of the man and the time.'

Dora, of course, was furious at what she called 'the sell-out by Bevin and his colleagues'. To the ex-strikers in the Penzance district, she became, according to Russell, 'a sort of Jeanne D'Arc', doing what she could to protect them against any threat of victimisation from their employers. Politically, in the aftermath of the strike, she moved even further to the left, disgusted with the Labour Party's 'lack of courage', and more sympathetic than ever towards the Communists. Russell, too, was disgusted with the Labour Party; 'half scoundrels and the other half cowards', as he put it to Ottoline, but, he added: 'I can't join the Communists, so I can only be an onlooker.'

In fact, Russell's attitude to the General Strike was extremely ambivalent. His 'heart and soul' may have been with the strikers, but his mind was not. This emerges from an article he wrote for *The New Leader* on 28 May, called 'On the Use of a General Strike'. The Government, he maintained, saw the real issue raised by the strike more clearly than did the TUC. The latter claimed that it was aimed only at preventing a reduction in miners' wages, but, in truth:

A General Strike is a trial of strength, and the victors can use the threat of another battle to enforce future concessions in addition to those involved in the settlement. If the strikers had proved that they were stronger than the Government, the Government would have been forced in future to yield to any demands made by the TUC with the support of the rank and file. The taste of power would have altered the mentality of the Trade Union movement, and made it bolder. It might have come to demand nationalisation of mines and railways without compensation; in time it might even have insisted upon complete Socialism. The Government would have found subsequent resistance almost impossible if they had been defeated in a fight to the finish. This was the real issue, as the Government saw from the first. The TUC took nine days to perceive it, and when they perceived it, they surrendered at discretion.

Were the TUC leaders *wrong* to surrender, then? Dora's answer would have been an emphatic 'yes!' Russell's answer, reading between the lines of his article, seems to be that they were right to have called off the strike and (therefore) wrong to have called the strike in the first place. 'I hold', he writes, 'that a General Strike is justifiable if it succeeds and unjustifiable if it fails.' The rub comes when he spells out the conditions, as he sees them, for success:

> . . . a General Strike cannot hope to succeed in this country unless the strikers are more willing than the Government to face widespread starvation and ruin . . .
> It is hardly possible for a General Strike to succeed unless its leaders are prepared to face the possibility of civil war.

The TUC were not prepared to face these things, and, implies Russell, nor should they have been. A fight with Baldwin's Government over the pay of miners was hardly worth risking starvation, ruin and civil war for. That being so, Russell's argument goes, the General Strike was unjustifiable. A General Strike, he writes, 'is too tremendous a weapon to be used lightly'. It has its place, he insists, though that place is 'to be resistance to Fascism after a Socialist Government has been democratically elected. In such a situation, it would probably succeed. In any other, in this country, it is very likely to fail. And, if it fails, it is wholly regrettable.'

Despite his show of support for the strikers, therefore, and his contribution to the strike fund, Russell's analysis of the situation was that the General Strike was futile, which is presumably why, at a time when Dora was throwing herself wholeheartedly into the fight, he stayed at home. There is here an analogy with his general analysis of the prospects for Socialism in Britain, which he believed to be at once desirable and yet unobtainable (and even positively dangerous, destructive and 'regrettable' – like a failed General Strike) without the support of America. In a lecture to the Fabian Society in autumn 1926, called 'The Danger of Creed Wars', he repeated this analysis in its strongest form yet:

> I do not think that the socialistic outlook is likely to become common in America at any time in the next hundred years, and unless America is socialistic in opinion, no nation within its economic orbit will be allowed to practise even a modicum of Socialism.

The theme of the lecture was that the world was in danger of being engulfed in a 'creed war' between the capitalism of the United States and the Communism of the Soviet Union, a war analogous to that between Protestantism and Catholicism at the time of the Counter-Reformation. In a

statement that echoed his description of himself to Ottoline as an 'onlooker',
Russell declared:

> I look upon the coming strife as Erasmus did, without the ability to join
> wholeheartedly with either party. No doubt I agree with the Bolsheviks
> on many more points than with the American magnates, but I cannot
> believe that their philosophy is ultimately true or capable of producing a
> happy world.

'As to the methods of diminishing the ferocity of the struggle,' Russell
told his audience, 'I do not know of anything better than the old Liberal
watchwords, yet I feel that they are likely to be very ineffective. What is
needed is freedom of opinion, and opportunity for the spread of opinion.'

There is an air of detachment in this lecture, as in most things that
Russell wrote at this time. It is as if he is gazing down at mankind and
shaking his head at its capacity for stupidity ('Perhaps in time men may
come to feel that intelligence is an asset to a community, but I cannot say
that I see much sign of any movement in this direction'). He looks at Britain
and he sees it dividing between the working class and the middle class, he
looks at the world and sees it dividing between American capitalism and
Soviet Communism, and in neither case can he identify himself with either
side of the divide. On the day the First World War ended, Russell had
walked among the jubilant crowds and felt, he said, 'strangely solitary amid
the rejoicings, like a ghost dropped by accident from some other planet'.
Now, it is as if, casting his eyes over the world's masses, intoxicated this
time, not by victory, but by class loyalty and ideology, he feels much the
same ghostly solitariness.

Where the Russell of the 1920s differed from the Russell of 1918 was
that, in his love for his children, he now had some escape from this feeling
of detachment. In 'The Danger of Creed Wars' he stressed that his refusal
to accept *either* American capitalism or Soviet Communism sprang in part
from their emphasis on economic rather than biological relations between
people. Indeed, he said, the 'fundamental delusion of our time' is 'the
excessive emphasis upon the economic aspects of life', and:

> I do not expect the strife between Capitalism and Communism as
> philosophies to cease until it is recognised that both are inadequate
> through their failure to recognise biological needs.

The 'groupings that are consonant with human instinct are biological',
and chief among these is the family.

There is in this argument, I think, a strongly autobiographical element.
The strongest loyalty Russell felt was that towards his family, and, as he
watched Britain and the world divide into warring factions from which he
felt remote, the one thing that prevented him feeling *completely* isolated
from the mass of mankind was his love for John and Kate. In his letter to
Ottoline, written during the General Strike, Russell had dwelt on his

children as much as on public matters, and had painted a picture of himself turning away from the horror of the conflict and towards his family. 'One feels disaster impending,' he wrote. 'Perhaps it is the downfall of England. But we cultivate our garden':

> We all flourish. John can read words of 3 syllables, do simple sums, and dance the hornpipe. Kate composes 'vers libres' to herself. One day when there was a cold wind Dora and I both overheard her saying to herself:
>
>> The North Wind blows over the North Pole,
>> The daisies hit the grass,
>> The wind blows the bluebells down,
>> The North Wind blows to the wind in the south.
>
> Her age was $2\frac{1}{4}$. We wrote it down then and there, so I know we got it right. We have a Swiss governess to teach John French.

The following month, writing to the American philosopher and educationalist John Dewey to thank him for his favourable review of *On Education*, Russell told him: 'What you say about the effect of my children on me is quite just. I am as pessimistic as ever about politics, but I have now something else to think about. I seriously think of emigrating, as I expect disaster in England before my children are grown up.' In a letter to Ottoline of 8 September, this gloomy view of England had extended to encompass the whole world:

> We all flourish. I think John will be a scientist and Kate a pet – they do lessons every morning for $1\frac{1}{2}$ hours and learn a lot. I find myself increasingly anxious to escape from the world, which I despair of.

While Russell was despairing of the modern world, Dora was celebrating it. In the summer of 1926, she wrote her second book, *The Right to be Happy*, the theme of which was that, behind the various struggles 'against national, class and sexual oppression' that characterised the world of the 1920s, there was 'a consistent new philosophy'. 'People of our time', Dora declares, 'are expressing a new ethics and metaphysics against which the old ones may be weighed and found wanting.' At the centre of this 'new philosophy' is a rejection of the 'religion of asceticism, suffering, poverty, and submission' that has hitherto dominated Europe. This religion is represented most obviously by Christianity (the book's epigraph is a quotation from the Rev. E. Lyttleton, ex-headmaster of Eton, in which he says that the belief in the right to be happy is 'the perversion of true religion, self-denial and obedience'), but Dora sees traces of it also in any view that celebrates the mind over the body, including that of the intellectual men she had earlier disparaged in *Hypatia*. The view that 'contemplation is the supreme good' and the prejudice against manual labour in favour of intellectual work, Dora argues, have their roots in the notion that the body is horrible and bodily processes are to be despised. We will never shake off this asceticism, she concludes, 'till we no longer believe this world a vale of tears'.

Theoretically, Russell was in agreement with much of what Dora was saying, but, feeling no instinctive admiration for people who earnt their living in steel factories and mines rather than by writing books, and feeling strongly himself the desire to turn away from the world and lead a contemplative life, he was unable to share Dora's enthusiasm for the social and political movements inspired by the 'new philosophy' that she triumphantly extolled. Indeed, he spent the turbulent summer of 1926 concentrating on writing *The Analysis of Matter*, the largest and most ambitious piece of philosophical writing he had produced since he abandoned *The Theory of Knowledge* in 1913.

The Analysis of Matter occupies a curious place in Russell's canon. Despite being the culmination of over ten years' thought, and one of the two or three most substantial works of philosophy that he published during the second half of his life, it has been almost completely neglected, not least by Russell himself (in *My Philosophical Development* and in his *Autobiography* it gets only the briefest of mentions). The reason for this, I believe, is that, soon after it was published, its central thesis was subjected to a devastating criticism by the Cambridge mathematician, M. H. Newman, who, in an article for *Mind* entitled 'Mr Russell's "Causal Theory of Perception"', demonstrated a fundamental flaw in Russell's theory.

The Analysis of Matter is an attempt to fulfil the promise of Russell's Amsterdam lecture in 1925 by presenting a philosophical analysis of the methods and results of physics. Its central thesis is that the objects that form the subject matter of physics – electrons, protons, points in space-time, and so on – are 'logically complex structures' of 'events', and these events should be thought of as neither material nor mental, but something 'neutral' between the two. Thus 'matter is less material, and mind is less mental, than is commonly supposed', and 'the traditional separation between physics and psychology, mind and matter, is not metaphysically defensible'.

'Physics', Russell says, 'is exceedingly abstract, and reveals only certain mathematical characteristics of the material with which it deals.' That 'material' is provided by observation, by perceptions, and is, in this way, psychological; but, if we are not to be trapped in some form of Idealism, we have to assume that these perceptions have 'extra-psychical causes', and, in this way, we have brought physics within psychology and psychology within physics, so that both together 'can be included in one science'. What we know about these 'extra-psychical causes' is *only* their structure – that is, 'what can be expressed by mathematical logic' – and thus 'The only legitimate attitude about the physical world seems to be one of complete agnosticism as regard all but its mathematical properties.' Russell's idea was that, starting with perceptions, we construct an elegant mathematical model of their relations to one another. This mathematical model is physics, and what it tells us about the physical world is only that between the things in the world (whatever they may be – for we can know nothing about their intrinsic properties) there are relations structurally similar to those in our model.

What Newman pointed out is that if we can know *only* the structure of the things in the physical world, then we can know next to *nothing* about it. For from a formal, mathematical point of view, similarity of structure is a fairly trivial matter. If two groups of objects have the same number of members, it immediately follows that both can be arranged in a structurally similar way. So, to know only that there is a relation between one group of objects (say, the things in the world) that is structurally similar to a relation between another group (the 'events' of physics) is to know only that they have the same number of objects. Surely physics tells us more than this. However, in order to do that, it must tell us not only that *there is a relation* between physical objects structurally similar to our theory of them, but also *what kind* of relation. And, if we know what kinds of relations exist between the objects of the world, then we know something more than its bare, mathematical structure. This is implicitly assumed in Russell's causal theory of perception, which postulates *causal* relations between the things in the world and our perceptions of them. But, Newman points out, this postulation is inconsistent with Russell's 'structuralist' theory of physics, for – if true – it would suggest that we do, after all, know more about the things in the world than their bare structure.

When Russell read Newman's article, he wrote to him, graciously admitting the validity of his argument:

> Many thanks for sending me the off-print of your article about me in *Mind*. I read it with great interest and some dismay. You make it entirely obvious that my statements to the effect that nothing is known about the physical world except its structure are either false or trivial, and I am somewhat ashamed at not having noticed the point for myself.

Whether anything could be rescued from his theory, Russell was not quite sure. He was 'at the moment too busy to give the matter proper thought', and so he remained for many years.

Possibly still more dismaying for Russell was that his 'structuralist' theory of physics was accepted and applauded by the astronomer, A. S. Eddington, who saw in it confirmation of his own tendency to think that physics was, ultimately, subjective. In his review of *The Analysis of Matter* for the *Journal of Philosophical Studies*, Eddington hailed it as an 'important book' that showed that 'the physicist cannot get behind structure'. As Russell points out, Eddington wrote: 'By physical inquiry we cannot learn anything as to the nature of the ultimate elements constituting the world; we can only learn how they are woven together', and thus 'it may be left vague, whether we are discussing an objective world of inscrutable nature or a subjective counterpart derived from data in someone's consciousness'. But, although the physicist cannot get behind structure, the philosopher, Eddington implies, can, and, on the basis of Russell's analysis of matter, the 'ultimate elements constituting the world' have to be regarded as essentially mental.

This reading of his theory must have horrified Russell, since it destroys altogether the notion of science as an objective study of impersonal facts, which was the very core of his *Weltanschauung*.

In his subsequent reviews of Eddington's popular books on science, Russell took every opportunity to distance himself from Eddington's Idealism, which he objected to, not only on intellectual grounds but also emotionally. The idea that 'physics was not really concerned with an external world' he described as a 'haunting nightmare', which removed the consolation of thinking that 'the cruelty, the meanness, the dusty fretful passion of human life' was but 'a little thing, set, like some resolved discord in music, amid the splendour of the stars and the stately procession of geological ages'. The emotional importance to Russell of picturing human life as an unimportant speck in a vast, impersonal universe is little understood in the published work written on him, though he himself made innumerable efforts to convey it. In *My Philosophical Development*, for example, he quoted Frank Ramsey as saying:

Where I seem to differ from some of my friends is in attaching little importance to physical size. I don't feel the least humble before the vastness of the heavens. The stars may be large, but they cannot think or love; and these are qualities which impress me far more than size does. I take no credit for weighing nearly seventeen stone.

My picture of the world is drawn in perspective, and not like a model to scale . . . Humanity, which fills the foreground of my picture, I find interesting and on the whole admirable.

In this passage, Russell wrote, Ramsey had expressed precisely 'what I do *not* feel . . . I find little satisfaction in contemplating the human race and its follies. I am happier thinking about the nebula in Andromeda than thinking about Genghis Khan. I cannot, like Kant, put the moral law on the same plane as the starry heavens.' Such an attitude seems so alien that many have supposed that Russell could not have been quite serious when he said such things. The evidence suggests, however, that he was entirely earnest in his misanthropy, which was both deeply felt and enduring. Very late in life, Russell was asked what he thought of space travel, and replied that he considered it to be a kind of 'cosmic impiety'. He hated to think of humanity extending its perniciousness beyond the 'insignificant planet' that was its humble and rightful place.

Not that Russell was entirely consistent in holding this attitude, and indeed sometimes he expressed exactly the opposite point of view regarding the relative importance of the starry heavens and the moral law. In an article he published in April 1927 entitled 'Bertrand Russell's Confession of Faith', for example, he included a paragraph that echoes Ramsey's so closely that it might be regarded as a piece of (perhaps unconscious) plagiarism:

To return to the emotion of awe. Kant and others have told us that we

ought to feel this when we gaze upon the starry heavens. I confess that I
am quite at a loss to see why we should. No doubt the starry heavens are
large, but so is a hippopotamus. I fail to see why mere size should be
considered so impressive. To my mind the proper objects of respect are
those which have value, and the inanimate world has in itself no value
either good or bad. In the world we know good and bad are confined to
human beings, and if either exists in the stellar spaces we have at any rate
no evidence that this is so.

That Russell was 'quite at a loss' to see why people should feel awe when
gazing at the stars is, of course, entirely untrue, and one is tempted to
dismiss this whole passage as not only derivative but insincere. More
charitably, one could say that whether Russell found the moral law or the
starry heavens more exalted depended upon his mood, but that his
misanthropic mood was the one that more frequently took control of him.
Side by side with his distaste for Idealist interpretations of physics went
Russell's dislike of any attempt to bring religion and science together. As far
as he was concerned, the scientific outlook was the very repudiation of
religion, and he therefore looked on in dismay as many of the popularisers of
science in the 1920s strove to show that the new physics – the relativity and
quantum theories – were more consonant with religion than traditional
physics. Among the writers involved in this were the very ones whose
explanations of the recent developments in physics Russell had relied upon
in writing his own popular books. These included not only Eddington, but
also Russell's erstwhile collaborator, Alfred Whitehead, whose 1922 book,
The Principle of Relativity, was one of the main sources Russell used in both
The ABC of Relativity and *The Analysis of Mind*. Russell had looked askance
at Whitehead's Bergsonian metaphysics in his subsequent book, *The Concept
of Nature*, but when in 1925 Whitehead published *Science and the Modern
World*, which argued that God is 'the ground of rationality', Russell was
moved to direct polemics. In a review of the book for *The Nation and the
Athenaeum*, Russell ridiculed Whitehead's God as 'metaphysically old-
fashioned' and declared his dissent from Whitehead's attempt to use modern
science to 'restore the consolations of religion to a world desolated by
mechanism'.
During the autumn of 1926, Russell was practically a full-time lecturer.
On Mondays, he lectured on 'The Problems of Philosophy' at the British
Institute, on Wednesdays on 'Mind and Matter' to the same body, and on
Fridays he travelled up to Cambridge to deliver parts of *The Analysis of
Mind* as the Tarner Lectures, a series of eight public talks which he had
been invited to give at Trinity College. No doubt, of these, the Tarner
Lectures gave him the greatest pleasure, but his other writing of the time –
his journalism, correspondence and other public lectures – suggests that,
during the period when he was delivering these three series of philosophical
lectures, his thoughts moved away from technical philosophy to moral and
cultural themes. To some extent, his public utterances during this time
show him taking up the cudgels of the struggle against conventional views

heralded in Dora's *The Right to be Happy*. Gone were the earnest proselytising on behalf of Socialism and the dark, foreboding prophecies of the downfall of civilisation that had marked his journalism in the early 1920s, and in its place was a series of mischievous attacks on conventional morality and religion.

'He is disintegrating prejudice and "rattling" people out of old conventions,' as Beatrice Webb put it. What she did not appear to notice was that one of people whom Russell was trying to 'rattle' out of old conventions was himself. This is most apparent in an essay called 'Behaviourism and Values', which he published in *The Century Magazine*. There he seems to respond directly to Dora's attack on the contemplative life as a residue of European medievalism, with its implied criticism of himself. Despite its title, the essay is scarcely about behaviourism at all. As Russell had made very clear on innumerable other occasions, he accepted behaviourism scientifically, and here he repeats his view that 'If you want a child to learn to behave in a certain way, you will often be wise if you follow Dr Watson's advice rather than (say) Freud's.' But, he adds, 'this is a scientific matter, not an ethical matter'. From an ethical point of view, behaviourism, in this essay, is taken to be representative of an outlook that sees little value in the life of the mind – the outlook, Russell says, that is characteristic of 'modern-minded men'. It is also, of course, the outlook of Dora's 'new philosophy', but, writes Russell, it is not one to which he can fully subscribe, for 'ever since the year in which I saw Russia and China, I have realised that I am not up to date':

Objective self-criticism, however, compels me to admit that it would be better if I were. In this essay I want to set forth certain difficulties which are felt by persons like myself, who, while accepting what is modern in science, have difficulty in divesting themselves of mediaevalism as regards what is worth living.

In this 'older outlook', Russell writes, 'feeling and knowing are considered as important as doing; art and contemplation are thought to be as admirable as altering the positions in space of large quantities of matter'. It is not entirely clear what Russell has in mind with this last phrase, but manual work and, particularly mining and steelworking, would be a reasonable guess. What is clear is that, despite his claim to accept that it would be better if he were more 'modern', Russell was extremely reluctant to give up this older outlook, and one sees in this essay the Russell of an earlier period, of what in 1902 he had called the 'religion of contemplation', struggling to come to terms with the world extolled by Dora, a world that dismisses all vestiges of the religious outlook and celebrates the body above the mind, and action above thought. While admiring the irreverent spirit of this modern world, Russell cannot quite bring himself to share its values: 'I cannot cease to admire "useless" knowledge, and art which has no purpose except to give delight.'

One imagines Russell being stirred into writing this defence of contemplation and the life of the mind by such things as the telegram Dora received from H. G. Wells in October 1926, saying: 'Bertie thinks, I write, but you DO.' The occasion for this was Dora's triumph at the Labour Party Conference in Margate, where she and her colleagues in the Workers' Birth Control Group finally succeeded in getting the party to commit itself to a policy of providing birth-control advice at health centres. Ironically, this triumph coincided with Dora's disillusionment with Labour Party politics. 'The surrender of the General Strike', she writes in her autobiography, 'had badly shaken the nerve of the Party. Indeed, I think that it was in that year that the revolutionary hopes and mood of the Party were lost forever, and reformism took its place.' From this time on, her zeal was channelled, not into party politics, but into attempts to change the attitudes of society at large towards, among other things, sex, religion, the role of women and education.

Despite his reservations about some aspects of the modern outlook that he had described in 'Behaviourism and Values', Russell was emphatically on its – and Dora's – side in the struggle against conventional morality and the established order. This he made clear in an article he published in *Harper's* in October, called 'The Harm that Good Men Do'. A 'good' man is one who:

does not drink or smoke, avoids bad language, converses in the presence of men only exactly as he would if there were ladies present, attends church regularly, and holds the correct opinions on all subjects. He has a wholesome horror of wrongdoing, and realises that it is our painful duty to castigate Sin. He has a still greater horror of wrong thinking, and considers it the business of the authorities to safeguard the young against those who question the wisdom of the views generally accepted by middle-aged successful citizens.

A 'bad' man, on the other hand, is one who:

. . . is known to smoke, and to drink occasionally . . . His conversation is not always such as could be printed, and he sometimes spends fine Sundays out-of-doors instead of at church . . . In the matter of wrongdoing, he takes a scientific attitude, such as he would take towards his motorcar if it misbehaved . . . In the matter of wrong thinking he is even more perverse. He maintains that what is called 'wrong thinking' is simply thinking, and what is called 'right thinking' is repeating words like a parrot; this gives him a sympathy with all sorts of undesirable cranks . . . it is even possible that in the matter of 'morals' he may not conceal his lapses as carefully as a truly virtuous man would do, defending himself by the perverse contention that it is better to be honest than to pretend to set a good example.

This is recognisably a self-portrait. Russell's argument, predictably, is that 'good' men do harm and 'bad' men good, which is to say that 'the standards of "goodness" which are generally recognised by public opinion are not those which are calculated to make the world a happier place'. Thus, public opinion needs to change, so that the virtues of 'bad' men like Russell are properly appreciated. 'Official morality', which 'has always been oppressive and negative', needs to give way to 'a morality based upon love of life, upon pleasure in growth and positive achievement, not upon repression and prohibition'. A man should be regarded as 'good', not because he conforms to conventional codes of, for instance, sexual morality, but because 'he is happy, expansive, generous and glad when others are happy'.

With Dora having become disillusioned with party politics, and Russell prepared to bury his residual 'religion of contemplation' in favour of the outlook of Dora's *The Right to be Happy*, the stage was set for the two of them to work together – instead of, as had been the case since Russell's return from his American lecture tour, pulling in opposite directions. Dora would give up her committee work, and Russell would give up philosophy, and together they would show the world how to be 'free and happy'.

4
THE NEW MORALITY

By the end of 1926, the gulf that seemed to be opening up between Russell and Dora had, to some extent, been bridged. The harmony between their 'beliefs and purposes', which Dora had mentioned as existing up until Russell's departure for America in March 1924 – and which meant a great deal to both of them – had, apparently, been restored. From Dora's point of view, the cost of achieving this was the loss of what had promised to be an exciting and fulfilling career as a left-wing Labour Party activist. From Russell's side, the cost was the temporary abandonment of his aspirations to write more technical philosophy, and a reconciliation with a philosophy of life – that of Dora's *The Right to be Happy* – which disparaged the very thing he had previously regarded as having the greatest value: abstract, intellectual contemplation.

The focus for this new-found sense of harmony and joint purpose was provided by the plans they developed during the Christmas period of 1926 to establish a school together. On the face of it, this was a madly ambitious project: neither of them had any experience of schoolteaching, and neither had shown much taste or aptitude for administrative chores, of which, inevitably, there would be great many if they were to run a school. Why should they have been even tempted to embark on such an arduous and potentially perilous venture?

The first reason was to provide for John and Kate the kind of education in which Russell and Dora, as parents, believed. Traditional public schools, of course, would not do for a couple who regarded themselves as pioneers in defiance of conventional attitudes, and nor would ordinary State schools. As Dora has put it: 'Bertie rather feared the imposition of orthodoxy and the stifling of unusual talent. He was inclined to think that children of exceptional ability – or views – should have an upbringing suited to themselves.' In other words, Russell did not want *his* children being educated alongside the common herd. There were, of course, fee-paying progressive schools, most notably A. S. Neill's Summerhill, but the academic standards at these were considered by Russell and Dora to be too low. Then there was the option of employing private tutors, or of educating John and Kate themselves at home, but this was rejected because Russell did not want to inflict on his children the kind of isolation he himself had suffered as a child. The solution seemed to be to educate John and Kate themselves, but *with other children*.

The other reason for starting the school – taken more seriously, no doubt, by Dora than by Russell – was a genuine desire to become educational pioneers, showing to society at large what could be achieved by educating children in the light of the 'new philosophy', rather than under the yoke of the old superstitions of religion, patriotism and conventional morality. When Russell wrote *On Education*, he had no thought of becoming an educationalist himself, but running a school would seem to provide the best possible means of testing his claim that, by applying modern psychology to education, one could produce fearless, courageous and creative individuals. Moreover, since he had been applying this theory to John and Kate since their birth, he would have what was practically the best-controlled experiment he could wish for, safe in the knowledge that they had not been contaminated by any pre-scientific methods of moral training. This led him open to the possibility of being faced with a decisive refutation of his theories, if John and Kate did not, after all, develop the characters predicted by him, but this was a risk he was willing to take.

More surprisingly, perhaps, it was a risk other people were prepared to take, too. The idea to start the school grew out of conversations during the Christmas holiday in Lynton, which the Russells shared with many of their friends, including Miles and Joan Malleson, Vera and Francis Meynell, Clifford and Joan Allen, John Strachey and Cyril Joad. In the evening, when the children had gone to bed, there was much talk of all aspects of the 'new philosophy'. They discussed the results of the General Strike, where 'progressives' were to go from here, sex and marriage reform, the rights of women and, above all, education. One evening, Russell encouraged Dora to read aloud from *The Right to be Happy*. 'He thought well of the book and wanted to see how others reacted,' Dora remembers. For the most part, it seems, they were impressed.

Of their fellow-guests at Lynton, both the Mallesons and the Allens decided to send their children to the Russells' school. In this, they demonstrated more confidence in the Russells than did the Bloomsbury Group, from whom, despite Strachey's presence in Lynton on this occasion, Russell was now largely isolated. 'We were disappointed by the attitude of many of the Bloomsbury set,' writes Dora, 'who treated the school as matter for merriment, making up tales about it for dinner table conversation.' Still, the school was intended to be small, and, now that they could count on Polly Allen and Nicky Malleson to join John and Kate, they had roughly one-third of what would be the total school-pupil population when it opened in September 1927. The other eight or nine pupils would come mostly from America, where belief in Russell's prescriptions for a happy life was, on the whole, stronger than in Bloomsbury.

Recognising this, and recognising also that setting up the school would require a great deal of money, Russell began to target his popular writing specifically at American audiences. In the summer of 1927, he produced his *Outline of Philosophy*, 'chiefly for the Americans', as he put it to Ottoline, and an anthology called *Selected Papers of Bertrand Russell*, which was sold only in America. For this last, Russell wrote a special Introduction called 'Things that Have Moulded Me', in which he appeared to argue that his interest in education was the result of political despair. For years, Russell had argued that Socialism was so obviously to the advantage of everybody but a handful of millionaires that it was only a matter of time before public opinion demanded its imposition upon that tiny minority. Why had this not happened? Why, as he puts it in this new Introduction, 'do the ninety-nine per cent not combine to overcome the resistance of the privileged one per cent?' The answer, he suggests, is that they have been educated incorrectly, and thus 'can be swayed by appeals to hatred, fear and envy' to ignore measures that would be in their best interests. 'A radical reform of education is, therefore, an essential preliminary to the creation of a better world . . . All that is needed is to give men a just conception of what constitutes their own happiness':

> Morality, therefore, should not be based upon self-sacrifice, but upon correct psychology. There is less pleasure to be derived from keeping a beggar hungry than from filling your own stomach. This may not sound a very exalted maxim, but if it were acted upon war and oppression would cease throughout the world.

For the most part, the pieces chosen for this new collection were fairly 'safe' ('A Free Man's Worship', 'Mysticism and Logic', extracts from *The Practice and Theory of Bolshevism* and *The Analysis of Mind*, and so on), but at around this time Russell also entered into negotiations with his American publisher, Horace Liveright, for a book provisionally called *Sex Freedom* (later changed to *Marriage and Morals*) which, he knew, would cause controversy and thus sell well. Exploiting the golden goose still further, Russell overcame his reactions to his lecture tour of 1924 and arranged another one, beginning in September 1927. This would have the huge disadvantage of taking him out of the country at the very time his school was due to open, but, as Feakins wrote to him after swiftly arranging a packed itinerary, 'you will take home with you a lot more money than you did last time'.

In what looks suspiciously like a further attempt to ingratiate himself with the American people, in May 1927 Russell published in the *New York Times Magazine* an article called 'The New Philosophy of America', in which the very aspects of American thought and life that had previously inspired his disgust – its mechanised efficiency, its concern with action over thought – are extolled as intrinsic parts of 'a philosophy of life which, whether we like it or not, is obviously more suited to the modern world than that of most Europeans'. The 'best work that has been done anywhere in philosophy and psychology during the present century', Russell announces, 'has been done in America'. Russell's explanation of why this should be so resolves the tension of his previous article, 'Behaviourism and Values', and reveals, perhaps, his final submission to the outlook of Dora's 'new philosophy'. The merit of America's philosophers and psychologists, he says:

> is due not so much to the individual ability of the men concerned as to their freedom from certain hampering traditions which the European man of learning inherits from the Middle Ages.
>
> Perhaps these traditions can be summed up in the one word – contemplation. European universities were originally places for the training of monks, and monks, though they tilled the soil, existed primarily for the sake of the contemplative life. A modern European professor does not till the soil, but he continues to believe in contemplation. In him, this belief takes the form of admiration for pure learning, regardless of its practical applications. I am myself sufficiently European to feel this admiration in a far higher degree than it is felt by the typical American. Nevertheless, I perceive that it is psychologically connected with an attitude of reverence towards the universe which is hardly compatible with the belief in man's omnipotence through the machine.

This last belief, Russell argues, is at the centre of the hope of eradicating traditional fears and superstitions and replacing them with a confident mastery over nature (including human nature), which would be 'so great a boon that it is worth-while to pay even a high price in order to achieve it'. The admiration for pure learning, the awed delight in contemplating the vastness of the universe and all forms of reverence are, then, to be cheerfully abandoned in the pursuit of mastering ourselves and the world. The one regret Russell admits to in this process is the loss of respect for individual liberty that would inevitably accompany the growth of a collective and industrialised world, but even this he is prepared to accept as an affordable price of the triumph of the 'new philosophy of America'.

It is as if, after the despair of the previous summer, when he wanted to escape from a world he found increasingly alien and unsympathetic, Russell had decided that, faced with the tides that were threatening to obliterate altogether the things he most cherished, he had better swim with the current than risk drowning. Rather than rail against the modern world, he would become modern himself, even if this meant embracing with enthusiasm a view of life he had previously found repugnant. If some of his fundamental attitudes were threatened by this view of life, well, he would simply change his attitudes, learning, for example, to dismiss the spirit that had informed his earlier great work in philosophy as merely the residue of an outmoded medievalism. This meant, of course, accepting that philosophy itself as he had always understood it – the disinterested contemplation of the truth – belonged to an earlier age, but at least it would overcome, or anyway postpone, the feeling that *he* belonged to an earlier age.

Previously, Russell had believed that the future lay with Socialism; now he believed that the future lay with America. The Americanisation of the world, he believed, was inevitable and, being inevitable, it had better come quickly and painlessly, rather than after a cataclysmic war with its only real rival, Soviet Communism. This he argued in a series of four articles for the *Jewish Daily Forward* in the summer of 1927, collectively called 'The Future', which showed an uninhibited and full-blooded return to the crystal ball-gazing of Sesostris the Sorceress. Among the things he predicted were the abolition of the family ('Biologically, this seems inevitable'), the subsequent loss of interest in sex and romance, and the establishment by the State of 'Official Feelers', who 'will decide what emotions are to be propagated in school, theatres, churches. etc.' The central theme of the four articles, however, is the necessity of establishing a 'central authority to control the whole world', a process that he now believes more likely to be achieved through the power of American finance than through the ideals of Socialism: 'I am an international socialist, but I expect to see international-ism realised sooner than socialism.' Once world unity has been achieved, *then* socialism will become inevitable, since the alternative, as he had argued many times, was the destruction of civilisation: 'if our civilisation continues for much longer to pursue the interests of the rich, it is doomed. It is because I do not desire the collapse of civilisation that I am a socialist.' It follows that what he had said in *Icarus* and elsewhere was wrong: world domination by American capitalism would *not* be worse than the destruction of civilisation; on the contrary, it was a necessary step to international Socialism and, therefore, to the preservation of civilisation.

So, on the principle of first things first, it was necessary to applaud and encourage the Americanisation of the world, rather than to keep banging one's head against the brick wall in the way of a non-American Socialist utopia. This argument kept Russell strategically at arm's length from Dora, whose sympathies in a fight between American capitalism and Soviet Communism would always be unequivocally with the latter, and whose chosen path to international Socialism was the liberalisation of Soviet-style Communism, rather the Socialisation of American world hegemony. But, practically, it brought the two of them together, since what Russell regarded as the 'new philosophy *of America*' was a recognisable variant of the 'new philosophy' of *The Right to be Happy*, and in both Dora's and Russell's conceptions of how Socialism was to be achieved one of the most important and immediate necessary steps was the overcoming of all vestiges of European monasticism, including traditional attitudes to religion and sexual morality.

Thus a bemused world was treated to the spectacle of a man in his mid-fifties, whose Edwardian dress, courtly manners and Victorian patterns of speech had become almost comically outmoded, proclaiming at every turn his allegiance to the 'modern view of life'. When, in March 1927, Russell and Dora placed an advertisement for their school in the (US) *Nation*, it was headed: 'To *Modern* Parents', and in the same month Russell delivered the lecture that would establish for the rest of his life his reputation as the scourge of traditional values and conventional religion: 'Why I Am Not a Christian'. The lecture was delivered at Battersea Town Hall on 6 March under the auspices of the Secular Society, and then published as a booklet by the Rationalist Press. It was subsequently reprinted in many anthologies, and has probably never been out of print. It is, perhaps, the most widely read piece of writing that Russell ever produced, attracting roughly equal measures of opprobrium and admiration.

The theme of the lecture is closely allied to that of 'The New Philosophy of America': advances in science have enabled us to understand and control nature (including our own), so that we have no need any longer to fear it. As religion is based 'primarily and mainly upon fear', we ought to learn to live without it. The power of science ought to make us proud and self-assertive, dismissing the humility preached by Christianity. The 'whole conception of God' is 'quite unworthy of free men':

> When you hear people in church debasing themselves and saying they are miserable sinners, and all the rest of it, it seems contemptible and not worthy of self-respecting human beings.

A loss of faith does not make people wicked; on the contrary, 'the Christian religion, as organised in its Churches, has been and still is the principal enemy of moral progress in the world'.

Russell presents the traditional arguments for the existence of God one by one, and meets each of them with an almost equally traditional refutation. Then he acknowledges that 'the sort of intellectual arguments that I have been talking to you about are not what really moves people'. The *real* reasons people have for believing in Christianity, he argues, are that they were brought up to believe in it, that they are afraid of life, or death, or nature, or that they have 'a sort of feeling that there is a big brother who will look after you'. In a scientific age, there is no need for any of this; in a scientific age 'We want to stand upon our own feet and look fair and square at the world . . . see the world as it is, and be not afraid of it.'

The lecture was intended as a rallying-call and it succeeded in establishing Russell both as the hero of secularists throughout the world and as one of the principal targets for defenders of religion. Among the latter was now T. S. Eliot, recently confirmed as a member of the Anglican Church and a devout believer both that 'the recognition of the reality of Sin is a New Life', and that 'humility is the beginning of anything spiritually or even culturally worthwhile'. In a withering review in the *Criterion*, Eliot poured scorn on what he insisted on regarding as Russell's 'religion'. A few months earlier, in an article for *The Dial*, Eliot had responded to Russell's *What I Believe* by commenting upon the dogmatic certitude with which Russell declared his creed. 'Mr Russell believes that when he is dead he will rot,' he remarked. 'I cannot subscribe with that conviction to *any* belief.' Now, Eliot dismissed Russell as 'essentially a low Churchman', aware no doubt that, in the face of Russell's determined modernity, this was about as wounding a description as he could give. Russell 'should know, as well as anyone', Eliot wrote, 'that what matters is not what he *thinks*, but how he *behaves*, in the psychologist's sense of Behaviour'. Eliot does not spell out what he means by this, what 'behaviour' of Russell's he is thinking of, but a reasonable guess is that he was alluding to Russell's incessant preaching of the 'paradise' to be attained on earth through moral improvement. This, anyway, is what would seem to be suggested by his concluding remarks:

> Just as Mr Russell's Radicalism in politics is merely a variety of Whiggery, so his Non-Christianity is merely a variety of Low Church sentiment. That is why his pamphlet is a curious, and a pathetic, document.

The unedifying background to Eliot's conversion to Anglicanism, and to this public spat with Russell, was the wretched deterioration in the mental and physical health of his wife, Vivien. 'Everything has turned out as you predicted 10 years ago,' Eliot had written to Russell in April 1925. 'You are a great psychologist.' A few weeks later, he spelt out something of what had turned out. Vivien's health, he told Russell, 'is a thousand times worse . . . I need the help of someone who understands her – I find her perpetually baffling and deceptive. She seems to me like a child of 6 with an immensely clever and precocious mind.' Vivien was suffering from severe rheumatism and neuralgia, was constantly in pain and often unable to move at all. She needed continual attention and, because Eliot was often away working, she felt desperately lonely and abandoned, clutching at him whenever he threatened to leave her sight.

In his desperation, Eliot asked Russell's advice. Unfortunately, only Eliot's side of the correspondence has become available, so we do not know what advice Russell actually gave, but whatever it was, it seems to have met with Eliot's approval. 'What you suggest seems to me of course what should have been done years ago,' he wrote to Russell on 7 May 1925. 'Her only alternative would be to live quite alone – if she could. And the fact that living with me has done her so much damage does not help me to come to any decision.' What had Russell suggested? Given his faith in the science of psychology, his fear of insanity and the way he later dealt with the mental illness of relations, the most likely answer would seem to be: to have Vivien certified and confined to a psychiatric hospital. This, in any case, is what Eliot eventually did, but it took him a few more years to reach that decision. In the meantime, he withdrew from her, mentally, physically and spiritually, and, as he found refuge in the Church, she became increasingly desperate and distraught. Her husband hated her, she wrote to Ottoline, and she did not know what to do. At dinner parties and other social occasions, she embarrassed Eliot by picking arguments, making accusations and generally causing a scene. His friends were becoming convinced she was deranged, while he was drinking heavily and searching his conscience as to whether he should or should not abandon her. That Eliot (as he showed in some of his correspondence) partially blamed Russell for Vivien's condition fits ill with his description of Russell as a 'great psychologist', but that he also blamed himself for the hellish life that he and Vivien shared accords well with his sense of the importance of confession and the need for redemption. In such a desperate emotional and spiritual crisis, it is not difficult to imagine, from

Eliot's point of view, what a false note would have been sounded by Russell's blithe confidence in the mastery of mankind over its own nature.

The winter of 1926–7 was to be the last that the Russells spent in their Chelsea home. Russell discovered that his brother Frank wanted to let Telegraph House, his large country home in Sussex, and, as this seemed the ideal place in which to house both their own family and their new school, Russell and Dora decided to sell the house in Sydney Street and rent Frank's home. Actually, as became apparent in the negotiations, Frank did not *want* to let Telegraph House, but rather *needed* to. The house was his pride and joy, and he would have done almost anything to avoid moving out of it, but he had lost a lot of money in speculating on the Stock Exchange and could no longer afford to live there. 'He was compelled by poverty to accept my offer,' as Russell put it in his *Autobiography*. 'But he hated it, and ever after bore me a grudge for inhabiting his paradise.'

By 1927, Frank Russell was a sad, lonely and embittered man. His three marriages had all ended in acrimony and, though he was now a Labour peer in the House of Lords, he was not considered respectable enough to play a leading part in Labour Party politics. His third wife, the writer Elizabeth von Arnim, left him very soon after their wedding in 1916 to live in Switzerland. In 1921, she published a novel called *Vera*, the central character of which, 'Everard Wemyss', is an undisguised portrait of Frank. In his *Autobiography*, Russell calls the novel 'intolerably cruel' and says that it caused him to advise his children: 'Do not marry a novelist.'

It is, however, a very fine novel, presenting a psychologically acute analysis of a man who is emotionally paralysed by his inability, or refusal, to acknowledge the depth and complexity of his own – and other people's – feelings. Everard finds it 'morbid' to dwell on the past and likes to think that everything is, in reality, very simple. 'There is only one way of looking at things,' he is fond of saying, 'and that is the right way.' As a result, he goes through life without really understanding anything. He does not understand, for example, that his problems with servants are caused, not by their being obstinate and wicked, but by the unreasonable demands he makes upon them. Nor does he understand that the problems he has in his relations with women are not the result of their not loving him enough, but of his inability to love them. This makes life unbearable for those nearest to him, but also, the novel makes clear, it makes life unbearable for *him*.

The only character in the novel to see this, and therefore the only one able to extend towards Everard any real compassion, is Miss Entwhistle, the maiden aunt of his second wife, Lucy. Lucy marries Everard (a name surely chosen to suggest an impenetrable, 'ever hard' soul) soon after the death of his first wife, Vera, because she is charmed by his simplicity, which she mistakes for a healthy refusal to make life unnecessarily complicated. Though shocked at the speed with which he seems able to forget his first wife, Lucy trusts Everard and does not believe the stories she hears that Vera committed suicide because she found life with him unendurable. When she comes to live with him at 'The Willows' (Telegraph House), however, Lucy becomes puzzled and distressed at the way his moods swing quickly and violently from smothering sentimentality ('Who's my duddely-umpty little girl?') to brutal, unforgiving anger. He gets hurt quickly over silly, childish things, and seems incapable of seeing that he is hurting others. Nor will Everard ever admit that he is wrong about anything, so that, although he repeatedly demands apologies from her, he never apologises himself: he genuinely cannot see that he has anything to apologise for. She grows frightened of him and obsessed with the thought that she is destined to repeat Vera's fate. Her aunt, Miss Entwhistle, on the other hand, can see deeper into his character and is thus not frightened of him. She sees Everard, not just as the boorish, insensitive bully he appears to others to be, but as 'a pathetic human being, blindly bent on ruining his own happiness'. 'Poor Everard', she reflects, has a loving, trusting wife, but he 'would spoil it all, inevitably smash it all sooner or later, if he wasn't able to see, wasn't able to understand'. The novel ends with Miss Entwhistle being ordered out of both Everard's house and Lucy's life, after she has tried to make Everard understand himself.

Everard's attitude towards Miss Entwhistle ('a mere maiden lady, an aunt, an unmarried aunt, – weakest, and most negligible, surely, of all relatives') carries very strong echoes of the attitudes of both Frank and Bertrand Russell towards their maiden Aunt Agatha. As Frank once memorably remarked, Aunt Agatha was 'always a wife behind' in her dealings with her nephews. When Russell took Dora to meet her, for example, she put a photograph of Russell's first wife, Alys, on the mantelpiece and remarked to Dora: 'Ah, when I look at you, I think of poor dear Alys.' Similarly, after Frank had once been to visit her, he reported to Russell that Agatha had been 'very sighful' about Alys, commenting on the fact that Alys still loved Russell and implying that she had been very badly treated. To Russell himself, Agatha was still more forthright. Replying to a letter in which Russell had rebuked her over the photograph of Alys, Agatha wrote rebuking him, in turn, for his callous forgetfulness of his first wife:

. . . you owe her everything since the separation. But for her, Dora would be Miss Black, and your children illegitimate – the slightest spark of gratitude in you would acknowledge what you owe to her since you left her, in so many ways that I cannot write of. Her conduct has been noble since the separation – I am very far from the only one who thinks this – and I feel her generosity intensely.

It would have been more manly and chivalrous of you to *write* me *not* to withdraw friendship from the woman *you* brought into the family, the woman you once loved and had forsaken, though *her* love was unchanged . . . You now in these later times always speak of 'pain to *me*', 'giving *me* pain' etc. – Do you ever think of Alys's suffering – from her love for you . . . Yet she always speaks beautifully of you, wishing only for *your* happiness. Do not imagine for a moment that I ever forget, and did not feel most acutely, your own unhappiness, which I know must have been very real and deep; – but to those who truly loved you, it is heart-breaking that you have not grown nobler, stronger, more loving and tender through suffering, but in every way the reverse.

Though Russell stopped loving her in 1902, and left her in 1910, Alys had never stopped loving him. In the 1920s she lived in Chelsea, just around the corner from Sydney Street, and would often walk up to the Russells' house and look in through the window at Russell, Dora, John and Kate, enviously and wistfully watching the family life that ought to have been hers. She followed Russell's public activities closely and kept a scrapbook of press cuttings about him. Russell, as far as one can tell, scarcely gave her a thought. As far as he was concerned, she was a part of the past that was as dead in him as the 'religion of contemplation' that he had developed while married to her, and he was evidently rather annoyed with Agatha for keeping up with Alys.

Dora dismissed Agatha as 'a malicious old lady', and Frank as an 'acid old spinster', while Russell himself hardly deigned to notice his aunt at all. But it is possible to see in her letter something other than maliciousness, something that shows an understanding of the kind of emotional hardness, the inability to feel another's suffering, that is so brilliantly dissected in *Vera*. At the start of the novel, the recently bereaved Everard talks piteously about the loss of his wife, but, after a while, one begins to notice that he regards her death solely as something terrible that happened to *him*. He talks repeatedly about *his* suffering. He reflects on how 'Vera had never understood him', of her 'disregard for others' and even on how, with regard to the manner of her death, 'if one looked at the thing dispassionately it would be difficult to find indifference to the wishes and feelings of others going further'. Never once does it occur to him to think of *her* suffering.

One of the things illustrated by the novel is that, if one lets one's feelings for others die, then something in oneself dies; to be emotionally forgetful is to be emotionally impoverished.[6] And this is the point made by Aunt Agatha to Russell: in closing himself off completely from the suffering of his first wife, he was allowing himself to become harder, less loving and tender. 'You do not realise how you have changed,' Agatha told him. 'We ought all to change and grow as life goes on; but it should be upwards, not downwards. For a long time I have seen that what you ask for is not love, but flattery.' In the face of this painful home-truth, Russell did figuratively what Everard in *Vera* does literally: he shut Agatha out.

During the summer, while Dora stayed up in London to arrange the transfer of the household to Telegraph House and see to the arrangements for opening the school (called Beacon Hill School, after the hill behind

---

[6] It is a plausible guess – hinted at in the Introduction to the Virago Modern Classics edition of *Vera* – that Elizabeth had been powerfully struck by an entry in Frank Russell's diary (written when he was ten) that reads: 'Father died in the morning. Went sliding in the afternoon.' In his autobiography, *My Life and Adventures*, Frank says about losing his mother at the age of eight: 'I have no recollection of my personal feelings at the time.' This tendency to ignore that which was painful is also illustrated by the fact that, in his autobiography, written after he and Elizabeth had separated, there is no mention of her whatsoever.

Telegraph House), Russell went to Cornwall in September with John and Kate. The summer of 1927 is remembered by Russell's daughter, Kate, as analogous to the time Adam and Eve spent in the Garden of Eden before the Fall. It was the last summer before the school opened, and at school, she says, she and John 'lost our childhood happiness'. Her memories of the 'Garden of Eden' are dominated by her father, so much so that 'he seems about the only real live person of my early years'. She remembers him amusing them by throwing a ball right over the house, something she later learnt was actually not very difficult: 'my father's skill at throwing was somewhat less than I supposed, though his skill as an entertainer was tremendous'. She remembers also that he told her that Hungary used to be called 'Yumyum' and that the Duke of Wellington had a tail, which necessitated a hole being cut into his saddle in order that he could ride comfortably. She believed him unquestioningly; he told her so many things, most of them true: 'My father was such a learned man in so many fields and so interested in everything that he couldn't help teaching us something in almost everything we did, from how to choose a safe branch when climbing a tree to the origins of Indo-European.' She also, of course, remembers him on the beach:

> He stands on the sand with his feet turned out like a dancing master, wearing a long white shirt, whose tails reach almost to his knees, and a Panama hat. He looks a little like a cockatoo, with his great red nose, always peeling in summer, his white hair and his sharply twinkling eyes. He is holding a pipe in his hand and telling a witty story, which he finishes with a deafening burst of hearty laughter, looking quizzically at his listeners to see if they share his amusement.

Kate, at three and a half, was revealing herself to have all the qualities that Russell had wished to see in John. 'Kate is proving amazingly intelligent,' he wrote to Ottoline that summer, 'a good deal more so than John. As far as I can judge, she is really remarkable. She reads and writes pretty well . . . and can do easy sums – but she has learnt everything by her own choice, and apparently without effort. She also has great courage: she stands in the waves and insists on letting them roll over her head.' Kate's abilities proved something of a challenge to Russell's long-held conviction that (as he was later to put it in *Marriage and Morals*) 'women are on the average, stupider than men'. John was as *charming* as ever, he told Ottoline, 'but I am afraid charm and intellect have been wrongly apportioned between the sexes'. As Kate sensed, and resented, John remained his favourite. When, some months later, Russell wrote to Dora trying to reassure her that he still loved her, he told her: 'I love you far more than you imagine – more than anything on earth except perhaps John.'

Kate's early memories of her mother are less vivid than those of her father. Indeed, 'in my memory of those early years she remains little more than one among a number of shadows in the bright light cast by my father'. One reason for this, no doubt, was that Dora was away from Carn Voel more often than Russell was. Usually this was because she was attending political meetings, but that summer she had the unenviable task of negotiating with the reluctant Frank the handover of his beloved house. This involved endless petty squabbles with Frank, meetings with his solicitors, the occasional threat of a law suit and many trips to Telegraph House to see to the delivery of furniture, and so on. She was helped in all this by Roy Randall, with whom she now began an affair that was to have a disastrous effect on her relations with Russell. In theory, Russell tolerated such things; in practice, he found them intolerable and reacted with all the hurt, jealousy and cold anger with which he had earlier reacted to Colette's infidelities. 'Dora speaks of the spiritual relation between her and me,' he wrote a few years later. 'She destroyed this in 1927. Since then I have not liked her, and I stuck to her only for the sake of John and Kate.'

For some time Russell had been attracted to Alice Stücki, the Swiss governess he had employed to teach John French. Now that Dora was involved with Randall, he felt free to seduce Alice, and the two of them began sleeping together at Carn Voel, much to the disgust of Hannah the cook, who was fiercely loyal to Dora. Furious with both Alice and Russell, Hannah wrote to Dora to tell her to come to Carn Voel at once. Russell also wrote to Dora to tell her about the affair and to inform her that, as Hannah was so 'profoundly shocked' by it, 'she can of course no longer stay with us'. The next day, he wrote again, saying that Hannah would not accept the month's wages and train fare to London that he had offered her in order to 'pay her off', so Dora herself would have to sack her. When Dora arrived at Carn Voel, she found Hannah standing guard over the children, refusing to let the governess near them. 'To a Hannah weeping on my shoulder', Dora recalls, 'I had to explain that, though I loved her for her loyalty, we did not feel quite the same way about these things.' The result was that Hannah was dismissed and the holiday in Cornwall was cut short, the Russells moving earlier than planned into Telegraph House, taking Alice with them to be the French teacher at the new school.

At Telegraph House, with just a few weeks to go before the school opened and Russell had to leave for America, Russell received an extraordinary letter from Roy Randall. 'For some weeks', it began, 'I have wished to express my gratitude for your generous conduct since you have known that Dora and I love each other':

> It is now three years since I knew that I loved her ... I am sure that Dora's love for me has not in the least diminished her love for you ... It is my great wish that by being frank and kind to each other we may turn this situation into a source of great happiness for us all.

Two weeks later, on the day Russell set sail and two days before the first term of school, Randall wrote again, this time to Dora. He enclosed a recently published article by the Rev. Inge, the Dean of St Paul's, on 'The Future of Marriage'. 'In my anger', Randall wrote, 'I've underlined part of it.' In one passage that he had underlined Inge remarked that 'For the

Christian, the marriage vow is not a declaration of passionate love, but a promise of life-long faithfulness . . . It involves a definite pledge of sexual fidelity, and of mutual affection and help in health and sickness, in prosperity and adversity.' Fidelity is crucial, Inge argued, since 'it is the knowledge that both parties may trust each other absolutely to keep troth that makes marriage happy. Under any other conditions any tiff may lead to a rupture, and any outside friendship may be a cause of suspicion and jealousy.' 'The institution of monogamous marriage is everywhere assailed,' Inge thundered; it was the duty of Christians to withstand the assault.

In the light of such statements, the question of whether Russell and Dora could save their marriage became not just a matter of their personal happiness but also a test of the 'new philosophy'. As Dora put it in a letter to Russell:

I have a silly kind of feeling that you & I are born to set the world right for the coming generation to give them some idea of how men & women can come together & build society instead of having this bitter sex war all the time & those confounded silly jealousies.

Russell, too, wanted to believe that a marriage could survive without monogamy, and he was prepared to do battle on the issue with defenders of conventional sexual ethics. But the real problem for him was more personal. The strongest emotion he felt was his love for John and Kate, and he was determined to do everything he could to ensure for them a happy life. This meant staying with Dora, a woman to whom he had not been able to make love for many years, whom he did not now even like, and by whom he felt hurt and even rather threatened. For the sake of John and Kate, he could not bear to leave Dora, but, equally, how could he possibly bear to stay with her?

As he sailed to New York in the last week of September, and throughout the following two months, as he travelled around the States giving lectures on education, Russell pondered this question and, in letter after letter to Dora, tried to analyse the situation in such a way as to find some hope in it. What emerged from this analysis was that Dora's affair with Randall was, from Russell's point of view, but the culmination of years of feeling hurt and undermined by her. What his Aunt Agatha saw more clearly than Dora ever did was Russell's need for admiration and flattery. Dora had such respect for Russell's brilliance and eminence that it rarely occurred to her to think of him as needing her attention and approval. With her mind taken up with her political work, her own writing and preparations for the school – not to mention the bringing up of John and Kate – she had little time for showing an interest in Russell's work. Besides, apart from *On Education*, she was not, in truth, very interested in it. Some indication of this is apparent in her autobiography, in which she repeatedly says that Russell was 'writing his book on education' during the summer of 1926 and even, on one occasion, during the summer of 1927. That the book had, in fact, been published at the beginning of 1926, and that during these later summers he was writing a host of other things, seems to have passed her by.

Nor does she ever seem to have realised that Russell was as vulnerable as a small child to this lack of attention, despite his trying to spell it out repeatedly in his letters from America. 'I am afraid you may need patience & kindness to restore my self-respect,' he told her:

I have often been hurt by little tiny things. I love to hear you read anything you have written, but if I ask you to hear anything I have written you have an air of patient endurance which makes me wish I hadn't asked you . . . I should like to revive your love if I could, by doing things you would admire, but I have no chance . . . I won you back again after Russia; I wonder if I could do it again?

In another letter, he told her: 'I feel you despise me, & I feel sexually worn out . . . I have felt hurt too for years, but I could never manage to tell you, because you always were either angry or patronising before I had come to the point . . . The chief thing, for me, is that you should be kind & gentle, not fierce & fault-finding. That terrifies me so that I become dumb.'

Dora paid no heed to this plaintive tone. 'You do me a wrong,' she insisted, 'if I am to pay for every moment of innocent gaiety with Roy by having to coax and reassure you.' She herself wanted reassurance; she felt that Russell no longer wanted her: 'you want the children & are happy with them & Alice'. She had been invited to visit America on a lecture tour in the New Year, in response to the interest generated by *The Right to be Happy*, and Russell encouraged her to accept. It would help her career as a writer, he argued, and (speaking from experience): 'It would give you a pleasant sense of being an important person.' But Dora worried that he wanted her out of the way, so that he could enjoy life at Telegraph House with Alice. Not that she wanted to get rid of Alice, nor even that Russell should end his affair with her. From her point of view, the ideal solution would be for all four of them to live together and to overcome the 'silly jealousies' that hindered such a thing. Roy, she told Russell, 'is really desperately in love with me' and, she added, with words that one knows would have wounded Russell to the quick: 'I do love him, as you know.' 'I wish', she implored Russell, 'you could appreciate Roy as I do Alice.' She had, in Russell's absence, re-employed Hannah, but, she claimed, Russell could rely on her to protect Alice from Hannah's wrath. 'There is absolutely no doubt', she wrote, 'that Hannah loved you & me & the children as genuinely as only her type of person can – like an old dog that growls at the least approach of danger.'

Less committed than Dora to the 'new philosophy', Russell could not feel as optimistic as she appeared to be that jealousy *could* be overcome. He knew that, whatever the principles of the 'new morality' might dictate, if she found happiness in sleeping with Roy, he *would* feel jealous and rejected. His preferred solution was for him to give up Alice in return for Dora giving up Roy. 'It was all a folly,' he wrote. 'And here we are landed with each a lover, & no possibility of happiness till that state of affairs is over . . . I wish we had never landed ourselves with lovers.' He would tell Alice that she had to leave at the end of the school year, and 'When she goes away, I shall not take up with any one else, whatever you may be doing. I find I can't bear having different people pulling different ways – I try to give everybody what they want, & I can't do it.' 'I should be infinitely happier', he told Dora, 'if we could get back to having only each other.' Of course, for that to work, there was 'no hope unless I can satisfy you sexually', but, he promised, for that he would see any doctor that Dr Newfield (their school doctor) could recommend. Dora never considered accepting such a compromise. From her point of view, they were sexual as well as educational pioneers, and to embrace monogamy now would be a faint-hearted capitulation to the forces of reaction and conventionality. They either believed in the 'new morality' or they did not, and, if they did, they would *have* to live with its consequences.

Russell conducted this correspondence about the future of his marriage while travelling from city to city on a lecture tour that was every bit as exhausting as his 1924 tour had been. For the most part, his lectures dealt with educational themes; indeed, the tour might be regarded as a promotional exercise, both for his book *On Education* (called in the US *Education and the Good Life*) and for his school. One or two parents promised to send their children to Beacon Hill the following autumn, and Russell's views on education were reported respectfully in the American Press, from which one gathers that their controversial aspects – the emphasis on the value of behaviouristic conditioning and the overthrow of conventional morality – were rather played down. In addition to his lectures, Russell also took part in public debates: with Will Durant on 'Is Democracy a Failure?' (Russell argued not), and with Max Eastman (then a Marxist) on 'The Road to Freedom'. Russell's attitude to these occasions was perfunctory and even cynical. He shocked Eastman (who at that time considered Russell's political opinions to be 'as trivial and superficial as his philosophic speculations were profound') with his comment, quoted earlier, that only an idiot would take these debates seriously. This comment, Eastman has recalled, 'roused my democratic indignation', since Russell was then 'making an enviable income out of these debates and lectures, gratifying the eagerness of a half-baked American intelligentsia to gaze upon, and gather pearls of wisdom from, a great British philosopher'.

In New York, Russell was taken to a Harlem jazz club, an experience to which he reacted with violent distaste. As he described it to Dora:

I wanted to enjoy myself, but when we got there they invited black ladies to our table & one was expected to dance & flirt with them. To my surprise, the mere idea was unspeakably revolting to me, & I left the place & went home. I couldn't bear the jazz music or the futurist walls or the negro ladies got up like Americans or anything about the place. I just felt jungle poison invading all our souls – I believe you would have liked it. I am too old.

That Russell thought Dora would enjoy something he considered to be 'unspeakably revolting' says much, I think, about his attitude towards her at this time.

As in 1924, Russell saved his most controversial talk until last. This time, it was his contribution to a debate on 'Is trial-marriage moral or immoral?' held at the American Public Forum in New York on 3 December. The background to the debate was the controversy surrounding the views of Judge Ben B. Lindsey, who had been ousted from office for advocating trial-marriages. 'I am much disgusted by the injustice and persecution to which you have been subjected,' Russell once wrote to Lindsey. 'I continue to be surprised by the fact that America persecutes Americans for the opinions which it hires foreigners at great expense to express.' Russell, naturally, supported 'companionate marriage' on this occasion, arguing that it enabled young people to satisfy their sexual desire for each other in a way that was 'immeasurably better than prostitution' and that would not entail the financial and social burden of legal marriage. 'The crew of traditional moralists on this whole matter are not rational,' Russell declared:

> Their explicit basis is texts of Scripture and theological dogma; their real basis is envy, cruelty, and love of interference. I hope and believe that the greater sexual freedom now prevailing among the young is bringing into existence a generation less cruel than that which is now old, and that a rational ethic in sex matters will, therefore, during the next twenty years, more and more prevail over the doctrines of taboo and human sacrifice which pass traditionally as 'virtue'.

On this occasion Russell stressed that he was talking only of 'childless unions', but, even so, one cannot help wondering whether, and to what extent, he felt the irony of extolling 'greater sexual freedom' as an antidote to cruelty at a time when he was experiencing Dora's insistence on sexual freedom as a species of cruelty.

A few days after this lecture, Russell sailed back to England (10,000 dollars richer) in time to spend Christmas at Telegraph House with Dora, John and Kate – and Hannah, Alice and Roy. Given the tensions that existed between this particular collection of people, it is hard to take at face value Dora's claim that: 'The first Christmas at Telegraph House – or Beacon Hill School – was very happy.' Dora herself was busy preparing to leave for her own American lecture tour in the New Year, and Russell had to steel himself for the onerous task of running the school in Dora's absence.

It is hard to know with what degree of enthusiasm Russell approached this task or how closely involved he really was in the day-to-day activities of the school. He had, to be sure, played a central role in establishing the general principles on which the school was run. These were largely borrowed from Margaret McMillan's nursery school, with its emphasis on a healthy diet, outdoor exercise and as much educational freedom as possible. To this the Russells added an uninhibited attitude to nudity (in warm weather the children danced naked outside), a determination to avoid religious or political indoctrination and an emphasis upon academic achievement. Russell himself taught history and geography and, later, mathematics, and Dora (after Alice had been dismissed at the end of the first year) taught languages. Both of them were born teachers and their lessons are remembered fondly by all who attended them. Most of the rest of the teaching was done by other people, whom the Russells hired on the basis of their commitment to progressive methods. In the first year, the bulk of the teaching fell to Beatrix Tudor Hart, who, however, fell out with the Russells over teaching methods and left Beacon Hill, eventually to found her own school. After she left, most of the teaching was done by Betty Cross, whom Kate remembers as a rather severe character ('Cross' by name, cross by nature, as she and the other children noted), but an excellent teacher. In general, the academic standards were fairly high, and children, like Kate, with a natural aptitude for learning received a rather good education. The school was 'free', in the sense that the children were at liberty not to attend lessons if they so chose, but most of them did choose to attend, because the lessons were lively and fun; besides, there was little to do if they did not.

One of the greatest assets of the school was its location. Telegraph House, though not especially elegant, offered plenty of accommodation for a family of four and a school of twelve, including several outlying buildings that could readily be converted into extra classrooms and living space for domestic and teaching staff. Its most distinctive feature was a large, square tower at the side of the house, at the top of which Russell had his study. There, among his 'Chinoiseries', he could sit and write in peace and gaze out of the large windows at a marvellous view over the Sussex Downs. But what made Frank's beloved house ideal for a boarding school was that it stood in some two hundred acres of private woodland, where there were stoats, foxes, rabbits and deer to be seen, and the children could play on the trees and look out for snowdrops in February, primroses in spring and hazelnuts in autumn. Russell knew this part of the country well ('The Millhangar', the cottage in which he had lived with Alys at the turn of the century, was not very far away), and sometimes he would take the children on afternoon walks, sharing both his detailed knowledge of plants and wildlife and his great love of nature. These occasions were regarded by the children as special treats, as were Russell's history lessons, in which, in his tower study, he would tell them about Alexander the Great, or Henry VIII, not by reading from textbooks, but by telling them stories: 'Well, it was like this . . .'

In the memories of the children who went to the school, Russell appears as a sort of benevolent uncle, a bestrewer of occasional treats, rather than as a headmaster. They were fond of him and conscious of the privilege of being taught by him, but none of them got very close to him and, for the most part, their affection towards him was not reciprocated. When he was with them he was lively and full of fun, but his remarks about them suggest, at first, a certain distance and, later, a definite recoil, speaking of them, for example, as 'sinister', 'cruel' and 'destructive'. The dozen or so children with whom the school opened were mostly about John's age (he was then almost six) and mostly from America. Of these, three were brothers whose mother had died, and one was adopted, prompting Russell to remark to Dora: 'Shall we say in the prospectus "For Bastards only"? I see we shall get lots.' For him, the primary purpose of the school was to provide fellow-pupils for John and Kate, and he was, from this point of view, rather disappointed with the kind of children the school attracted. As he put it in his *Autobiography*: 'The parents who were most inclined to try new methods were those who had difficulties with their children'; as a result: 'we got an undue proportion of problem children'. To let such children go free, he says, 'was to establish a reign of terror, in which the strong kept the weak trembling and miserable'.

One of the 'weak' was John himself, who, according to Kate's account, 'was teased unmercifully and incessantly by many of the boys, for he was little and excitable and fun to tease – he was easily brought to the verge of hysterics – and he was a readily available stand-in for his parents, the authorities of the school. I do not see how John endured it as he did; my blood used to boil, just listening, and I would have done anything in the world to stop it.' For John, the school was an almost unmitigated misfortune. Not only was he bullied by the other children, but he also, in a sense, lost his parents, who were reluctant to appear to be favouring him in front of the other pupils, leaving him feeling abandoned and hurt. He grew increasingly withdrawn and nervous, and struck many of the other children as a little 'strange'. Writing of the 'free' atmosphere of the school, Kate recalls it as being a peculiarly intellectual kind of freedom, which, emotionally, felt like a prison:

> ... no topic was ever forbidden ... We could talk about anything to anybody at any time, but only if we could put our feelings into words. Thought and its expression were free, bad language and rebelliousness were calmly tolerated, and we were allowed to say anything we *could* say. But the fears we were ashamed to acknowledge and the anxieties we could not put into words had no outlet. For night terrors and loneliness, for homesickness and fear of bigger children, there was little that could be done. Even the youngest of us had to manage our emotional lives pretty much alone, without any close and sympathetic comforter. I learned to get along inside a shell, fending off physical and emotional assaults from others, and trusting nobody. So did John, and so, I think, did the other children.

Russell's educational philosophy had as its basis the belief that education could, if done properly, eliminate fear. It is one of the most horrible and tragic ironies of his life that his attempt to achieve this for the two people he loved most achieved exactly the opposite. 'John and I', Kate says, 'felt turned adrift in a hostile world, unable to go to our parents for help, and that feeling remained with us always. John had been a very open little boy, ready to talk anybody's ear off, but he changed; lacking a friendly audience, he became wary and self-contained. He and I learned to live in the middle, between parents and children, slightly detached, keeping our own counsel, cautious and unwilling to commit ourselves.' Russell himself has said: 'The complete happiness that had existed in our relations to John and Kate was . . . destroyed, and was replaced by awkwardness and embarrassment.' Kate puts it more strongly. Describing the effect of the school upon her family, she writes:

> Those years shattered the crystal of our happiness and left us like jagged splinters, unable to touch one another without wounding. All of us longed for a give and take of love not possible in that public environment. Old pictures of my father with me on his knee, holding my hand or putting an arm around me, strike me as fakes. That is not the way I remember the school years; they were all duty and loneliness and being just one of the children, while all the time my father and mother kept working, night and day, to preserve the school and their separation from us.

In his first term of taking charge of the school during the early months of 1928, while Dora was away in America, Russell struggled to cope. 'Life here is arduous,' he wrote to Miriam Brudno, 'much more so than a lecture-tour of America.' The administrative tasks involved in running a school were uncongenial and time-consuming: he had to oversee the staff, plan the menus, pay the bills, collect fees, order supplies and solve the many problems that came up from day to day. He had an especial problem with Hannah, of course, who had still not forgiven either him or Alice for their transgressions the previous summer, and it cannot have been easy either to have Roy Randall – whom Dora had hired to help run the school – living on the premises. The financial obligation, too, was an anxiety. Partly because some of the parents were not very well off, the fees collected by the school fell a long way short of the money required to keep it going. The money Russell had earnt from his lecture tour was soon used up and, to keep more money coming in, he had to keep accepting commissions for journalistic articles and popular books. He also agreed to arrange yet another lecture tour of the States for the following year.

From this time onwards, in fact, his life became increasingly nightmarish. His love for Dora was gone, his relationship with his children was being ruined, he had no time to write anything in which he could take any pride, and the money he earnt – from doing things in which he took no intrinsic pleasure – was being used to pay for the education of a group of children who were making his son's life a misery. The one consolation he had was his relationship with Alice, but she would be gone when school finished in the summer, and the time they could spend together at Telegraph House in the meantime was being spoiled by the attentions they received from the disapproving Hannah.

Russell's journalism during these months strikes a less strident note than his writing of the previous year. Instead of writing of the 'new philosophy' as something already formed and ready to win an irresistible victory over the remnants of European monasticism, Russell now writes of the need to *construct* a new philosophy and, particularly, a new morality. 'The creation of a rationalist ethic is the great need of our time,' as he put it in one of his articles, emphasising that the young, in rejecting conventional morality, had nothing *as yet* with which to replace it. This note was struck most poignantly in a piece he published in March 1928 called 'My Own View of Marriage'. 'The old-fashioned morality had a basis which was not rational,' he writes, 'while the newer absence of morality tends to sweep away all that has real value in the relations of men and women; to preserve this we need a new morality, not less serious than the old, but based upon a truer psychology and a just appreciation of human needs.'

The human need he is thinking of here is not sexual but parental. The essence of marriage, he insists, is the desire to produce children. Marriage, when its 'importance and dignity' are properly understood, offers an open gate through which one can 'leave the prison of the self', but it does this, not by satisfying the desire to have sex, but through parenthood. The desire of parents to co-operate for the sake of their children, he writes, survives 'in decent people ... when mere pleasure has lost its vividness, or when perhaps some psychological strain has introduced difficulties into the merely personal aspects of the relation'. So far, this sounds rather similar to the old morality, but where it differs is in its attitude towards unfaithfulness. 'Occasional adultery', Russell insists, 'is quite compatible with deep and lasting affection and if this were generally realised, jealousy would not nearly so often wreck the happiness of married people, as it does at present.' 'I am not, however, advocating unfaithfulness,' he stresses, 'I am merely advocating a tolerant attitude to it when it occurs.' The article confirmed Russell's reputation as an 'apostle of adultery', but reading it now, in the context of his plea to Dora a few months earlier to resume a monogamous life, the emphasis seems to fall more naturally on his attempt to hold on to the dignity and seriousness of marriage – for the sake of the children – in the face of the emotional problems caused by infidelity.

While Russell was writing this, Dora was in New York, putting into practice her somewhat different conception of the new morality, according to which 'unfaithfulness' was not a difficulty to be tolerated; rather, 'sexual freedom' was a liberty to be enjoyed. At the very time that Russell was publishing an article on the 'importance and dignity' of marriage, Dora was telling her American audiences that 'the whole institution of marriage had been devised by men for their own protection, in order that they might be certain of the paternity of their children'. She had never wanted to marry Russell in the first place, and even now did not consider herself married 'in the conventional sense', an attitude that she appeared to believe was shared by Russell. In New York, she was introduced (by two of Helen Dudley's sisters) to Griffin Barry, an Irish-American left-wing journalist with a reputation (according to his friend, John Dos Passos) for knowing everybody and sleeping with everybody, male or female. He had been in Paris at the end of the war, reporting on the Versailles negotiations, and had then gone to Russia to report on the situation there. In Russia, he, like Dora, had become a friend of John Reed and had been very impressed with the Soviet system. By 1928 he was leading the life of an itinerant freelance writer and full-time sexual adventurer.

Dora took to him straight away, seduced by his blue-grey eyes, his handsome face and 'that voice [which] had the charm of one who might have kissed the famous Blarney stone'. They began a love affair, which, as Dora says, 'was to have far-reaching consequences for ourselves and others'. But, she adds: 'Both of us were romantic devotees of the free love code and did not at this time attach special importance to this encounter.' In her letters home, she did not mention her affair with Griffin, but continued to discuss with Russell the problems of their relationships with Alice, Roy and Hannah. In April, however, a month after arriving back in England, she told Russell that she was miserable because she had not heard from Griffin: 'I'm afraid I am rather badly in love with him. But I had not written myself, thinking I had better not write too often.' Roy was not told about the affair until August, when Dora wrote to Russell that Roy 'has got over the shock, but seems to think it makes no difference to him & me . . . people do try to live upon my energy & vitality & I'm rather reaching my limit of strength. This is what makes me tug at the leash so all the time.'

Dora eventually did write to Griffin, and the two of them planned a holiday in France together at the end of the summer. Russell's dream of living a monogamous life with Dora after Alice had returned to Switzerland and Roy was dismissed from Telegraph House therefore had to be abandoned. Even now, however, Russell abandoned it only very reluctantly. When school finished for the summer, John and Kate were sent to Switzerland to be looked after by Alice, while Russell and Dora – evidently in an effort to recover their marriage – took a holiday on their own in Locarno. The holiday was cut short by a telephone call saying that John had become gravely ill, with suspected meningitis. This produced in Russell, according to Dora's account, 'a night of such agonised anxiety that he was almost incapable of dealing with practical details'. When they arrived in Switzerland, John 'looked ghastly pale and ate nothing'. It turned out, however, to be a false alarm. John was suffering from nothing worse than food poisoning from a bad peach, and he quickly recovered.

A few weeks later, Dora set off on her holiday in France with Griffin. They stayed for two weeks on the French Riviera, where they fell in with a group of artists and writers who were friends of the *Daily Herald* writer, George Slocombe. Her letters to Russell during these two weeks paint a picture of a carefree Bohemian life: 'Living as an artist is quite good for me just now. Griffin will not tolerate my being executive . . . Griffin sunburnt & can't move, just stays in bed the whole time'. Russell's response was to try to find some sort of solace with whoever came his way. After the autumn term started at school, he told Dora: 'I contemplate going away for a weekend with that girl who wrote to me, whose letter I showed you. I had lunch with her on Saturday & the possibility came up. It would be on both sides quite light . . . I have often felt a desire to go with some one I scarcely know, just for a week-end.' During the weekend in question, he declared himself to be 'bored to extinction, as I knew I would be – indeed I now realise that subjectively that was my intention, so as to be all the more happy at home'. Meanwhile, he and Alice were exchanging love letters and discussing the possibility of his leaving Dora for good.

Dora claims that at this time she and Russell still hoped to produce another child. 'My love for Bertie had never wavered or altered,' she writes. 'I believed, and I think rightly, that at that time he was as devoted to me.' That Russell was unable to make love to her she regarded, not as a reflection of his feelings towards her, but as a symptom of a quite general 'disability':

> Bertie's severe Victorian upbringing and the intensity of his intellectual concentration had inhibited him sexually . . . Gossip has put upon his alleged numerous love affairs an entirely false interpretation. I believe that he always hoped that a sufficiently strong attraction to some woman would overcome his disability by spontaneous, natural means.

What Dora seems to be implying here is that Russell was promiscuous, not because he was oversexed, but rather because he was ever hopeful of overcoming his impotence. This may be right (though the evidence, I think, is rather against it), but she was manifestly mistaken about Russell's devotion to her. Dora may have been committed to their 'open' marriage and their school as twin aspects of the 'new philosophy', but Russell, by 1929, evidently persisted in both for the same, single reason: he thought it would be good for John and Kate to do so.

That John appeared to be suffering at school did nothing, at first, to undermine Russell's belief that, on the whole, it was doing him good. An article that he published in December 1928 called 'Science and Education' gives some hint as to how he then regarded John's plight. The modern child, he writes, 'has become accustomed to thinking of himself as the centre of the universe and to expecting from the world at large a degree of solicitude which only parents are likely to feel':

> This is a bad preparation for the world and is best remedied by association with contemporaries. A child is on the whole better fighting with other children than being coddled by grown-up people.

If his contemporaries treated him roughly, the implication went, then John had better get used to it – for that is the treatment he could expect from the world at large.

In the New Year of 1929, a dangerous flu virus spread throughout Beacon Hill School. Everybody recovered except John and Kate. John was particularly badly affected and had to have a double mastoid operation. 'As I comforted John with the promise that the germs would be conquered,' Dora recalls, 'he looked at me with his big, serious brown eyes and asked: "What happens if the germs win?" '

On a freezing night we drove down to Petersfield for his operation, John in my arms. Looking up at a brilliant starry sky he said: 'I have been thinking how poor people are', by which I knew he meant the frailty and insignificance of human life.

This 'terrifying experience', she adds, put a strain on both her and Russell. Its effect on Russell can be measured from a letter he wrote Ottoline at the time, in which he mentions that, on the day of John's operation, he had to take part in a debate on Christianity with Bishop Gore: 'I was told that suffering is sent as a purification from sin. Poor little John never sinned in his life. I wanted to spit in their faces – they were so cold & abstract, with a sadistic pleasure in the torture their God inflicts.'

No doubt partly prompted by this experience, Russell published an article a few weeks later on 'Your Child and the Fear of Death', in which he asks: 'What . . . shall we do with young people to adapt them to a world in which death exists?' His answer is the unexceptional and sensible one that we must neither avoid the subject, nor dwell on it, nor tell comforting lies about the after-life to pretend that death is less terrible than it is. But in making this case, he makes some interesting remarks about protecting a child from its own affections, in case the object of those affections – a parent, say – should die. 'I think that very intense affection for some one individual, in a child, is not infrequently a mark of something amiss,' he maintains:

> Affection of this kind, in childhood, is not wholesome. Where it exists the death of the person loved may shatter the child's life. Even if all seems well outwardly, every subsequent love will be filled with terror. Husband (or wife) and children will be plagued by undue solicitude, and will be thought heartless when they are merely living their own lives. A parent ought not, therefore, to feel pleased at being the object of this kind of affection. If the child has a generally friendly environment and is happy, he will without much trouble get over the pain of any one loss that may happen to him.

When read against the background of Russell's life up until that point, this is a deeply moving passage. For as a child, he had suffered the death of the people he loved most, and one can see in his letters to Dora and his previous lovers the 'terror' of which he speaks, the fear of losing their love, and his consequent feeling that Dora was being heartless when, from her point of view, she was merely living her own life. One sees also in this passage Russell's concern for John, lest he, too, should suffer the kind of effects that bereavement had had on Russell himself and on his brother, Frank. Again, as in *On Education* and in much of his writing on parenthood, one feels Russell's anxiety that, in loving John too much, he may be storing up trouble for him. Again the moral is: show your love for your child by *not* showing it. 'Whoever has to deal with young children', he writes in this article, 'soon learns that too much sympathy is a mistake . . . A child that invariably receives sympathy will continue to cry over every tiny mishap; the ordinary self-control of the average adult is only achieved through knowledge that no sympathy will be won by making a fuss. Children readily understand that an adult who is sometimes a little stern is best for them; their instinct tells them whether they are loved or not.' As emerges from Kate's memoir, however, her instincts and, especially, John's could have done with a little more reassurance on this point.

The stoicism preached in 'Your Child and the Fear of Death' (it was later reprinted as 'Stoicism and Mental Health' in his collection of essays, *In Praise of Idleness*) is, in some ways, a conscious corrective to the scientific optimism that Russell had expressed a few years earlier. In his present mood, in the spring of 1929, one feels, he could not have written an article like 'The New Philosophy of America', for, after his difficulties with Dora and with the school, he was now inclined to regard the 'modern view of life' as a problem, as much as a solution. In April, he reviewed *The Modern Temper* by Joseph Wood Krutch, a pessimistic analysis of twentieth-century life that identified its malaise as being due to the trivialisation of human affairs that, Krutch argues, is an inescapable consequence of seeing ourselves through the eyes of modern science. Though Russell dismisses this disenchantment as a 'passing malady', he says enough to show that he, in part, shares it. 'I think Mr Krutch is right', he says, 'in holding that religion, tragedy, and love have all decayed through a similar reason, namely a diminution in our estimate of the stature of human beings. We cannot any longer take ourselves quite so seriously as we formerly did.' The loss of religion and tragedy Russell can bear with equanimity, but the trivialisation of love is clearly an aspect of modern life that he finds hard to accept. Krutch's chapter on love, he writes, is the most important in the book, and what one learns from it is that, in the modern age, 'enthusiastic persons set to work to free love from the shackles of convention; in so doing, unwittingly and unintentionally they lessened its value'.

No one was more enthusiastic in this respect, of course, than Dora, who, at around this time, was arranging with Griffin Barry for the two of them to visit Russia together in the summer. 'It seems to me now, you and I together there, a divine plan,' Griffin wrote to her in May. 'You're going to have an amazing moment when you see touch hear and feel what's happening in Russia since you put to sea in a row boat and landed in Murmansk. I'm going to be happy watching you. I'm always happiest when the one I love is lit up.' Did Dora not realise that spending a month away from her family in order to be with her lover – in Russia of all places, the country about which she and Russell had argued so vehemently – would hurt Russell and put an almost intolerable strain on their marriage? It is as if she were testing him to see how far she could go before he said: 'Enough is enough.' Of course, such a thing was in fact far from Dora's mind. Her wilful blindness towards Russell's feelings – despite his having tried to express them to her – was typical of an aspect of her character that would infuriate members of her family for the rest of her life. So committed was she to the view that love need not be monogamous, and so implacable was her faith that Russell shared this view, that she did not even consider the idea that her going to

Russia with Griffin would be felt by Russell as a sign that she no longer cared about him.

While Dora was thus pushing him to the very limits of his tolerance, and his marriage was in very grave danger of collapse, Russell set to work on *Marriage and Morals*, the book he had planned two years earlier under the provisional title of *Sex Freedom*. Then, he had perhaps intended to write the tract on sexual liberty that many people mistakenly believe *Marriage and Morals* to be. In fact, despite its reputation, *Marriage and Morals* does not present, like Dora's *The Right to be Happy*, a plea for the release of hitherto restrained impulses. On the contrary, like 'Your Child and the Fear of Death', it presents an argument for stoic self-control, only the impulses that he argues should be controlled are not sexual ones, but rather 'impulses to jealousy, ill-temper, masterfulness, and so on'. Russell's argument is that the conventional morality that seeks to control sexual impulses is based on Christianity – and, in particular, the Christian abhorrence of sex itself – and, as such, cannot survive the loss of faith that is the inevitable outcome of the scientific or rational outlook. In any case, he argues, this abhorrence of sex, whatever its basis, does more harm than good. But Russell does not present sexual liberty as, in itself, a good thing; rather, he describes it as presenting a problem, the problem of how to preserve marriage in the face of it.

The theme that dominates the book is the importance of keeping a marriage together for the sake of the children it has produced. A marriage that does not produce any children is, for Russell, scarcely a marriage at all. 'Children are the purpose of marriage,' he declares unequivocally (and repeatedly throughout the book), 'and to hold people to a childless marriage is a cruel cheat.' The desire to have children, he maintains, is 'felt by the great majority of men . . . It is for this reason, rather than for the sake of sex, that men marry, for it is not difficult to obtain sexual satisfaction without marriage.' This being so, the question of the *morality* of marriage is primarily one of the moral responsibilities of parenthood, for 'A man who desires a child desires the responsibilities it entails.' Chief among these is that of preserving, wherever possible, some kind of harmony between the two parents:

> A child who has been used to two parents and has become attached to them both finds a divorce between them destructive of his whole sense of security. Indeed, he is likely in these circumstances to develop phobias and other nervous disorders. When once a child has become attached to both his parents, they take a very grave responsibility if they separate.
> . . . Marriage should be a partnership intended by both parties to last at least as long as the youth of their children.

Adultery, he says, 'should not, to my mind, be a ground of divorce', because 'There may still be ardent affection between husband and wife, even every desire that the marriage should continue.' Indeed, even when that affection is not so 'ardent', 'even after passionate love has decayed', it is 'by no means a superhuman task for sensible people who are capable of the natural affections' to co-operate in rearing their children. Without quite admitting that he is here speaking from his own experience, Russell adds:

> To this I can testify from a large number of cases personally known to me. To say that such parents will be 'merely dutiful' is to ignore the emotion of parental affection – an emotion which, where it is genuine and strong, preserves an unbreakable tie between husband and wife long after physical passion has decayed.

To overcome one's jealousy in the face of infidelity, to preserve harmonious relations with someone for whom one no longer feels any 'passionate love', requires a degree of stoicism, but these are nevertheless the moral duties of a parent. Sounding every bit as stern a moralist as those who would later attack him for his moral laxity, Russell remarks:

> The obligations of parents towards children are treated far more lightly than seems to me right by many persons who consider themselves virtuous. Given the present system of the bi-parental family, as soon as there are children it is the duty of both parties to a marriage to do everything they can to preserve harmonious relations, even if this requires considerable self-control.

He does not, of course, rule out divorce altogether. The really important thing, Russell suggests, is that parents should not quarrel, for: 'There can be no doubt that serious quarrels between parents are a very frequent cause of nervous disorders in children.' If one or both partners in a marriage 'has not sufficient self-control to prevent disagreements from coming to the knowledge of the children', then 'it may be better that the marriage be dissolved'. Worse even than divorce for children is 'the spectacle of raised voices, furious accusations, perhaps even violence, to which many children are exposed in bad homes'.

In what turned out to be a rather poignant anticipation of the dilemma he himself would soon face, Russell also discussed the possibility of a wife's infidelity leading to children:

> Where illegitimate children come in, the issue is much more complicated. This is especially the case if the children are those of the wife, for in that case, if the marriage persists, the husband is faced with the necessity of having another man's child brought up with his own, and (if scandal is to be avoided) even as his own. This goes against the biological basis of marriage, and will also involve an almost intolerable instinctive strain.

In yet another anticipation of a dilemma in which he would become involved later in life, Russell discusses the possibility of one or other of the partners in a marriage becoming insane. In this case, he thinks, separation is not only acceptable, but a positive duty:

... it is in this case not desirable that further children should spring from an insane stock, nor yet that any children who may already be born should be brought into contact with insanity. Complete separation of the parents, even supposing that the one who is insane has longer or shorter lucid intervals, is therefore desirable in the interests of the children.

Indeed, as the repeated references to 'nervous disorders' in children illustrate, the fear of insanity haunts the whole book. In his chapter on 'The Family in Individual Psychology', he discusses the theories of Freud, which he summarises, somewhat inaccurately, as follows:

A boy hates his father, whom he regards as a sexual rival. He feels, in regard to his mother, emotions which are viewed with the utmost abhorrence by traditional morality. He hates his brothers and sisters because they absorb some part of the parental attention, of which he would like the whole to be concentrated upon himself. In later life, the effects of these turbulent passions are of the most diverse and terrible kinds, varying from homosexuality at best to mania at worst.

Alluding to his experiences at Beacon Hill, he adds: 'considerable experience of young children during recent years has led me to the view that there is much more truth in Freud's theories than I had formerly supposed'. Nevertheless, he maintains, what Freud has identified are dangers rather than inevitabilities. Rather curiously, he then concentrates on the possibility that a sexually frustrated mother will unintentionally seek to 'centre the heterosexual feelings of a young son upon herself', and, if this happens, Russell remarks darkly, 'the evil consequences pointed out by Freud will probably ensue'. The answer, of course, is to ensure that a mother is sexually satisfied, for 'if a woman is happy in her sexual life she will abstain spontaneously from all improper demands for emotional response from her child'. This view, odd in itself, becomes even odder when one considers the circumstances of the Russell family between 1924 and 1927. For, until she started taking other lovers, Dora was not 'happy in her sexual life'. Did Russell think that, during those three years, she therefore made 'improper demands for emotional response' from John? And did he then expect 'the evil consequences pointed out by Freud' to ensue? Did Russell expect John to view him as a rival for Dora's affections, and to become, in consequence, homosexual 'at best' and 'at worst' a maniac?

Marriage and Morals contains, perhaps, more eccentric views than any other book Russell wrote. Granted, the casual racism and sexism of some of his remarks – 'It seems on the whole fair to regard negroes as on the average inferior to white men', 'women are on the average stupider than men' – would not have shocked a liberal audience of the 1920s to quite the extent that they would today, but they still fit uneasily with the conception of Russell as a 'progressive'. In later editions of the book he changed the remark about Negroes, replacing the phrase 'It seems on the whole fair to . . .' with 'There is no sound reason to . . .', but, as he left everything else as it was, this produced the rather odd sentence:

> There is no sound reason to regard negroes as on the average inferior to white men, although for work in the tropics they are indispensable, so that their extermination (apart from questions of humanity) would be highly undesirable.

Significantly, Russell never did change the remark about women. When asked to do so (for the *first* edition), he refused, saying: 'The habit of flattering women does a lot of harm.'

Russell's sexist and racist prejudices may have been widely shared in the 1920s, but surely his conviction that 'one can generally tell whether a man is a clever man or a fool by the shape of his head' would have seemed as eccentric then as it does now. Oddest of all, though, are the somewhat sinister opinions he expresses in his chapter on 'Eugenics', which again illustrate the depth of his fear of insanity. 'The sterilisation of the unfit', he insists, 'is within the scope of immediate practical politics in England':

> The objections to such a measure which one naturally feels are, I believe, not justified. Feeble-minded women, as everyone knows, are apt to have enormous numbers of illegitimate children, all, as a rule, wholly worthless to the community. These women would themselves be happier if they were sterilised . . . The same thing, of course, applies to feeble-minded men. There are, it is true, grave dangers in the system, since the authorities may easily come to consider any unusual opinion or any opposition to themselves a mark of feeble-mindedness. These dangers, however, are probably worth incurring, since it is quite clear that the number of idiots, imbeciles and feeble-minded could, by such measures, be enormously diminished.

These measures, he stresses, should 'be very definitely confined to persons who are *mentally* defective'; they should not, as yet, be extended to those who are considered *morally* degenerate. This is because mental deficiency 'can be decided in an objective manner which authorities would not disagree'.

Given his reputation as a defender of individual liberties against the power of the State, one almost struggles to take in what Russell is here proposing: that the State should be empowered forcibly to sterilise all those designated as 'mentally deficient' by experts, and that this measure should be introduced in full knowledge of the misuses to which it might be liable, because reducing the number of 'idiots, imbeciles and feeble-minded' people is a benefit to society that outweighs the dangers of such misuse. One does not know what to be more staggered by here: the extreme horror of insanity, the faith in psychiatric definitions and diagnoses, or the indifference to civil liberties. In any case, it confirms the impression of Russell's previous remarks that he did not regard mentally ill people as having any value to society or of deserving any rights or consideration. As far as he was concerned, to become insane was virtually to lose one's status as a person. This is presumably why he attached such colossal weight to the duty of doing anything to prevent the development of 'nervous disorders' in one's children.

Despite its eccentricities, *Marriage and Morals* is the most serious, and the most personal, book that Russell published in the 1920s. In its implied advice to himself, it is in some ways reminiscent of the 'stoic religion' that he had formulated in 'The Free Man's Worship' and 'The Pilgrimage of Life' during the first few years of the century. Then, trapped in a desperately unhappy marriage to a woman he no longer loved, he pronounced that happiness was unattainable, and that the noblest thing was to renounce the search for it and to concentrate instead on the search for truth. Now, similarly trapped, he announces a moral duty to restrain one's impulses of jealousy, anger and hurt towards a wife one no longer loves and to concentrate instead on the psychological well-being of one's children. The book is a personal testament through and through. From it one learns why, even after living with her had become a source of great suffering to him, Russell allowed Dora to believe that he was still devoted to her: he felt that to lose his self-control and disrupt the 'harmonious relations' between him and Dora would be to risk the *most* awful thing he could imagine – the mental illness of his children.

Even when the book is at its apparently most abstract and theoretical, autobiography is never very far from the surface. Why, for example, does he devote a chapter to eugenics? What do eugenics have to do with marriage? Ostensibly, the point is to speculate about the future of sexual ethics in the light of forthcoming advances in science. But when one looks at those speculations, one finds something altogether more personal. 'From the standpoint of private morals,' he writes, 'sexual ethics, if scientific and unsuperstitious, would accord the first place to eugenic considerations':

> That is to say that, however the existing restraints upon sexual intercourse might be relaxed, a conscientious man and woman would not enter upon procreation without the most serious considerations as to the probable value of their progeny ... There will therefore be no very cogent reason why a woman should choose as the father of her child the man whom she prefers as a lover or a companion. It may become quite easily possible for women of the future, without any serious sacrifice of happiness, to select the fathers of their children by eugenic considerations, while allowing their private feelings free sway as regards ordinary sexual companionship.

It follows that, in choosing to have children by Russell, but preferring the love and companionship of Griffin Barry, Dora was the very prototype of the 'woman of the future', and their marriage the very model of 'the morality of the future'.

Another recurring theme of the book – apparently impersonal, but in reality deeply personal – is the importance of fatherhood. Several times Russell raises the possibility that the State will, in future, help to take care of children, so that women have no financial need to marry in order to have children, and the importance of the father to a family is thus undermined. What would be the effects of such a system? How, in particular, would it affect men, if, as Russell puts it, they were to have 'no property' in their children, or 'if law and custom were adapted to the view that children belong to the mother alone'? Russell's answer is bleak:

> It would, I believe, immensely diminish the seriousness of men's relations to women, making them more and more a matter of mere pleasure, not an intimate union of heart and mind and body. It would tend towards a certain triviality in all personal relations, so that a man's serious emotions would be concerned with his career, his country, or some quite impersonal subject . . . the elimination of paternity as a recognised social relation would tend to make men's emotional life trivial and thin, causing in the end a slowly growing boredom and despair.

The implication is that the *only* thing that prevented Russell himself from concentrating solely on his career 'or some impersonal subject', that prevented his emotional life from becoming trivial and that held back boredom and despair was his relations with John and Kate. Another point that emerges from this passage, of course – and Dora might have taken warning from this – is Russell's vehement refusal to accept that, in 'law and custom', John and Kate belonged to Dora alone. This refers back to one of the very first conversations he had with Dora, when he got to know her in 1919. As Dora remembers it, Russell asked her about her views on matrimony:

> On this subject by now I felt very sure of myself. I explained my disapproval of conventional legal marriage, my belief in free love. He put a question as to what, in that event, should be done about children, to which I replied that they were entirely the concern of the mother, and fathers should not have primary rights over them. Russell gave one of his huge laughs, with his free hand slapped his knee in a very characteristic gesture and exclaimed: 'Well, whoever I have children with it won't be you!'

To a large extent, *Marriage and Morals* might be regarded as a continuation of this argument, with Russell presenting a well-worked out defence of conventional legal marriage against Dora's attack. Of course, the kind of marriage Russell defends is unconventional with regard to its attitude to sexual fidelity, but marriage, in Russell's understanding, is not centrally to do with sex. Its point, rather, is to preserve the rights and responsibilities of fathers.

If Dora read the book, she shows no sign of having understood this crucially important aspect of it, nor does she seem to have read very carefully the letters Russell wrote to her during his lecture tour of 1927, in which he tried to explain the various ways in which he felt hurt and neglected by her. Writing of his 'courtly behaviour towards his wife which disdained marital bickering', Dora says:

> We never had rows and reconciliations. But how much, if he could have given me a hint of a deep hurt, I would have wished and been able to comfort him with a warmth of love and, indeed, gratitude. For I certainly loved and honoured him more than ever. I hated to hurt him, but I could do nothing to comfort, or try to dispel a hurt which his pride forbade him to let me see. Nor do I think that he realised that I loved him more, not less, for masculine pride seems always to assume that when a loved woman takes an interest in another man, it must inevitably follow that she cares less for him.

From his published work alone, Dora might have realised the degree of self-control required for Russell to maintain the 'courtly behaviour' she describes, and it would not, surely, have taken much imagination to appreciate how he might have felt about her spending a month in Russia with a man with whom she had described herself as being 'badly in love'.

She seemed surprised, too, that Griffin Barry expected their love for each other to develop into something stable and permanent. During their visit to Russia in the summer of 1929, she writes, 'Griffin and I were pretty tired and quarrelled endlessly about our relationship.' Things were presumably made more difficult by the fact that they were rarely alone. They went with a group of tourists, whom Griffin had been employed to lead around the various showpieces of the Soviet Union. In Leningrad, they visited the Pavlov Institute, where they were shown a dissection of a dog's brain ('This is what he dances with, this makes him angry', and so on), and in Moscow, as Dora put it, 'we had those interminable sessions on education, social welfare, the marriage laws, with which so many delegations to the Soviet Union have become familiar over the years'. Despite the boredom apparent in this description, she returned with her enthusiasm for Soviet Russia intact, if very slightly dimmed.

Russell wrote to her to say that he wanted to 'hear all you have to say about Russia, which sounds very exciting', but there was little time for that. Just before school started in September, Dora took part in a week-long Congress for Sexual Reform in London, which she had helped to organise under the auspices of 'The World League for Sexual Reform on a Scientific Basis'. Papers were delivered by delegates from all over the world, including Bernard Shaw, Cyril Joad, Marie Stopes and Magnus Hirschfeld. Russell gave a paper on 'The Taboo on Sex Knowledge' (one of the chapters of *Marriage and Morals*), but otherwise stayed in Cornwall with John and Kate. Almost as soon as the congress finished, Russell set sail to New York for his third lecture tour in five years, while Dora returned with John and Kate to Telegraph House. Griffin Barry, meanwhile – having, as Dora says, 'put by and invested enough for him to live mostly in Europe freelancing' – stayed in London, where he lived in a flat in Bloomsbury that Dora had acquired for their joint use. During the three months that Russell was away, whenever she could spare the time from school, Dora came up to London to be with Griffin.

Largely because it was misunderstood to be about sexual freedom rather than the moral responsibilities of parents, *Marriage and Morals* sold extremely well and created a great deal of controversy. 'So long as it doesn't spoil my tour from a financial point of view, I don't mind,' Russell wrote to Ottoline on his way to New York. Of course, as he realised it would, the controversy only helped to sell tickets for his lectures. A controversy of a less welcome kind, however, was sparked immediately on his arrival by the comments he made to journalists about women teachers. The scarcity of men teachers, he was reported as saying, tends to 'feminise' boy pupils: 'Women do not take the same interest in hard facts . . . The scientific attitude toward life can scarcely be learnt from women.' The people likely to be offended by such remarks, of course, were precisely those who were disposed to agree with him on other issues, but one has the impression that, this time, Russell did not much care who he offended. When asked by American interviewers what he thought of American interviewers, he replied: 'Well, they're not quite as bad as the Japs, but that's as much as I can say for them.' 'We smiled in agreement,' wrote one of the reporters in question, 'blissfully forgetting that we were included in his generality.' Russell was also careless in showing his contempt for his audiences. 'If the American people wanted to find out what I thought,' he told a journalist, 'they wouldn't ask me questions or come to my lectures. They would read my books.' Fortunately, he added, they did *buy* his books, as he could see by the numbers he was asked to sign, but these 'were obviously all unread'.

None of this affected the size of his audiences or the commercial success of his tour, both of which were greater than ever. This time, however, he insisted that most of the money he made ought to be put in trust for John and Kate, rather than be swallowed up by the school. The tour was busier than ever and, for the first time, Russell travelled to the west coast as well as throughout the east, the south and the mid west. The lectures he gave, however, seem to have been rather uninspired. At many of the places he lectured, he gave a paper called 'The Outlook for Civilisation', which, as far as one can gather from the Press reports of it, repeated the view he had expressed many years earlier that, as the next war could destroy civilisation altogether, a world government was needed to keep the peace. This was hardly a new thought; nor does Russell seem to have adapted it to recent political events. Indeed, there is surprisingly little in his articles or lectures during this time to suggest any great interest in either British or world politics.

A few months before he left for the States, a British general election was held, the first since 1918 in which neither of the Russells had stood as a candidate. Russell took no active part in the election, or in the machinations within the Labour Party in the months leading up to it, which resulted in Labour dropping the word 'Socialism' from its manifesto. After Labour had won and Ramsey MacDonald formed his second minority Government, Russell wrote a short piece for the *Jewish Daily Forward*, in which he gave a lukewarm welcome to the new Government, but stressed that nothing much could be expected from it. In a second article a few months later, he conceded that political expediency was on the side of the MacDonald Government in its abandonment of Socialist aims, but whether the Labour Party, or Britain, *ought* to embrace Socialism was evidently not an issue on which he was prepared to write with any great passion. Similarly, in his American lectures, he seemed content to deliver platitudes about the danger of war, rather than comment more specifically on political developments or the desirability of Socialist goals. His days as a political agitator were, temporarily at least, evidently over.

Sounding equally platitudinous, from the newspaper reports of it, was the paper Russell delivered called 'My Philosophy of Life', in which, it seems, he came down on the side of a happy life in preference to an unhappy one. When he gave this talk in Oakland, California, the local reporter caught nicely his probable attitude to the occasion:

Rabbi Louis Newman, introducing him, said: 'If anybody doubts whether America is genuinely interested in philosophy, let him gaze at this assemblage here tonight.' Dowagers beamed inwardly, drew themselves up in their fur coats and felt that they had received their dollar's worth of satisfaction. Russell did not smile, but I detected a slight tightening of the upper lip.

California, Russell reported to Dora, 'has scenery & a perfect climate; everybody is rich & almost everybody is dull'. Texas, he claimed, rather implausibly, was 'full of people who have read all three vols of *Principia Mathematica*'. Generally, though, what struck him about America was that, wherever he went, the people were the same – an impression he later spun out into a magazine article called 'Homogeneous America'. Wherever he went, Russell took advantage of whatever 'one-night stands' (as he had learnt to call them) were available to him, sometimes writing to Dora about the various women he had slept with. Some of these women agreed to donate money to the school; others agreed to send their children there. Occasionally, these encounters became the basis of a valuable, long-lasting friendship, but it is hard not to believe that, in general, they were associated in Russell's mind with the triviality of human relations that, he remarked repeatedly on this trip, was characteristic of America. He dwelt particularly on the loneliness and sexual frustration of American women, which, he told Dora, he thought was the origin of their religious faith: ' "Thou God seest me" must comfort lots of women who are not seen by any interesting male.' 'There is something incredibly wrong with human relations in your country,' he wrote to Dora's friend Rachel Brooks. 'The fount of affection seems to have dried up.' He was thinking in particular of the lack of affection that American mothers showed towards their children.

Towards the middle of November, Russell received a letter from Dora that contained devastating news: she had become pregnant by Griffin Barry. 'Shall I just let it be, or what?' Dora asked. 'If you cable me "Please no" I will do what I can about it – if "all right" or nothing I will let it alone . . . I feel I would sooner have a baby than not have one, but deep in me I want *your* baby more than anything else in the world.'

What was Russell to do? The issue between his conception of marriage and Dora's, between her insistence that children were the mother's responsibility only and his insistence that fathers had rights too, was now being forced in the most acute way imaginable. He was in print as saying that, in a case like this, the only way in which the marriage could persist was if the child was brought up as if it were the husband's, but also that such an arrangement went 'against the biological basis of marriage' and that it would 'involve an almost intolerable instinctive strain'. But he was also in print as saying that divorce threatened the development of 'nervous disorders' in the children of a marriage. On his prior analysis of the situation that now faced him, therefore, Dora had presented him with a terrible choice: he must either accept an 'intolerable instinctive strain' upon himself or risk damaging the psychological health of his own children. The only other alternative was to insist that Dora have an abortion, but, as Dora had indicated a wish to keep the child, he might well have reasoned that such an insistence would inevitably lead to the kind of quarrels and recriminations between parents that he had identified as the worst possible thing for the mental health of children.

He was forced to take the only alternative that, on his previous analysis, did not threaten the psychological well-being of his children, and accordingly cabled 'ALL RIGHT LOVE BERTIE', following it with a reassuring and generous letter:

> My Darling Love,
>   I got your letter this morning saying your period was late, and I cabled at once. I should not at all like you to do anything about it – if it is so, much better let nature take its course. Since I cannot do my part, it is better someone else should, as you ought to have more children. But I dare say it was a false alarm. In any case there is no need to worry, you won't find me tiresome about it.

A few days later, on 17 November, he wrote again saying that he wanted the child to be regarded as his: 'Legally it will be mine in any case. I shan't mind much.' As for Griffin Barry's paternal rights: 'I do not see why Barry should not be about the place as much as he has leisure for. The troubles we had over Roy & Alice need not recur; but there is no reason why Barry should suffer unnecessary deprivation on that account.' In her autobiography, Dora attributes this generous attitude to the 'courtly behaviour' that was typical of Russell in his relations with her, and remarks: 'I have reason to believe that this decision [to bring the baby up as his own] cost Bertie much more distress than he was ever willing to reveal.'

This, surely, is disingenuous. That this situation would cause Russell great distress is not only dictated by common sense, but is evident from everything he said and wrote about the importance of fatherhood. It is also apparent in the letter he wrote her on 19 November, in which he told her that, having lain awake for many hours thinking about it, he had 'begun to know what I feel about your being pregnant':

> Over Roy, you seemed vexed because I had tried to conceal the less agreeable parts of my feelings, so I suppose I had better tell the whole truth. I do not feel the slightest anger, & I should be profoundly shocked if you did anything to stop it: my biological instinct couldn't stand that. At the same time it increases the feeling that you do not love me; I feel aloof, though friendly. It causes a diminution of love, though not of goodwill. And it causes me to feel less willing to forgo my own pleasures – especially Cornwall – to please you . . . Please don't think I feel less well of you, because I don't. It is only that the instinctive tie of common parenthood is loosened.

A week later, he set out, in an analytical and legal manner, an argument as to why he and Dora, not Griffin Barry, should have responsibility for the child. 'Barry has no legal rights', he insisted. 'I have both rights and responsibilities.' Given this, he was prepared to use his rights on behalf of the child, to see that it had the best possible future. This meant that Dora should keep it, that Russell should pay for it and that Barry should have the opportunity to see it whenever possible: 'Barry can come whenever he is free; you can go to him with the child in the summers.' If Barry wanted a closer tie with his own children, then he 'should seek out a woman without responsibilities & affections towards the children of another man'. Russell's chain of reasoning in support of these conclusions went like this: Dora would be bitter and unhappy if the child were taken away from her; John and Kate would suffer if Dora were embittered; therefore the child should remain with Dora.

Stung by the fact that in all this deliberation of Russell's there was no mention of his love for and devotion to *her*, and finally sensing, perhaps, that Russell's attitude to her and their marriage was not what she had imagined it to be, Dora responded with a fierce rebuke:

> I don't believe you are nearly as loyal to me in thought & word as I am to you & that breaks my heart – You value John & Kate, the school, your work – your wife as a person needing happiness has rather escaped your notice the last few years – I sometimes think you don't really love with the kind of abandoned love that sticks through everything – your love has so much pride in it – kind of stops & halts when your pride is hurt & never quite recovers.
>
>   O I do believe that the work & flattery of America has changed you for the moment.

Russell never responded to this letter, and there seems reason to believe it was the final nail in the coffin of his affection for her. After this, for a year at least, he wrote Dora only short, curt and, for the most part, unaffectionate letters.

Against the background of the fearful emotional turmoil caused by the news of Dora's pregnancy, Russell had to finish his lecture tour with a debate in New York on 13 December on the question 'Is Modern Marriage a Failure?', with John Cowper Powys as his opponent. Russell defended the view that modern (which, perhaps rather strangely, he interpreted to mean 'sexually faithful') marriage *was* a failure, on the familiar grounds that sexual fidelity bred boredom, resentment and strife. As having quarrelsome parents was bad for children and rearing children well was the true purpose of marriage, Russell argued (repeating the views expressed in his book), it would be better to adopt a custom in which married partners sought sexual satisfaction *outside* their marriage, and sought to control their jealousy, rather than 'the passion of illicit love'.

In his reply, Powys noted what Dora had belatedly realised: that in Russell's conception of marriage there was curiously little emphasis on the love, loyalty and mutual enjoyment of each other's company that could, and should, exist between a man and his wife. Russell had argued that after three years or so, man and wife inevitably come to find each other's company intolerably dull. On the contrary, Powys claimed, in a happy marriage 'five, ten, fifteen years, twenty years after marriage, they are conscious of the piquant, the provocative, the mysterious difference spiritually, mentally, aesthetically, morally and above all nervously, between the man and the woman. This, I contend, is the great, the grand purpose of marriage, whose end both at first and now is to intensify our interest in life.' Husband and wife might quarrel, Powys conceded, but, after all, what is so very bad about that?

> Children looking back upon their childhood, for children are much wiser than many of us philosophers, children looking back upon their childhood, forget the absurd quarrels of their parents, and even when they remember them, they remember them with a kind of humorous enjoyment. Their quarrels endear their parents to them; their quarrels prove that their parents are weak and human and fallible like themselves.

The instinct to swear eternal fidelity 'before man and God' is, Powys maintained, 'a deep, irrevocable human instinct'. This does not lead to boredom, but to 'a day by day struggle to retain a loyalty that is not easy in the face of a corrosive world', and this makes husband and wife respect one another and be tender to each other. 'The coming together of a man and a woman', Powys insisted, 'is worthy of more careful consideration than its opponent gives it.' Jealousy ought *not* to be overcome, for it is in its way a compliment: 'If you are really indifferent, why, you do not care.' The true purpose of marriage is this coming together of man and woman, which, 'quite apart from children', is, of all great institutions, 'the most fulfilling of the nobler nature, the subtler nature, the more imaginative nature . . . and the more *rational* nature of human beings'. Out of a *real* marriage, Powys concluded, emerges 'that human virtue, the greatest and the last of all, that used to be called pity'.

The exalted conception of the love between man and woman that Powys expressed was not, of course, entirely unfamiliar to Russell. He had embraced an even more exalted conception in his love for Ottoline, and he had entertained hopes of sharing such a marriage as Powys described with Colette and even, at first, with Dora. But he was now, in this respect, a broken man, hoping from his relations with women for no more than a few nights, or, at most, a few years of sexual enjoyment. His love for Dora had turned to cold anger, which he felt a duty to disguise for the sake of his children, while his sense of comradeship with her, which he had hoped to preserve even after his love for her had died, was now lost. As a last refuge in trying to see some value in his relations with Dora, Russell had tried to convince himself that, in rearing children together but loving other people, they were harbingers of a new morality – a morality more scientific than the old one in recognising the importance of eugenic considerations in choosing the person with whom one has children; in recognising, too, that having children was a far deeper, more serious matter than simply having sex and falling in love. By becoming pregnant with Griffin Barry, Dora had torn apart even this conception of the value of their marriage. Russell said many times afterwards that he wished he had divorced Dora as soon as he learnt of her pregnancy. Instead, he returned home determined to demonstrate the self-control he had advocated in *Marriage and Morals*.

The strain began to show as soon as Russell was back in England, when, emotionally exhausted, he fell ill with bronchitis and had to retire to bed. Griffin Barry fell ill at about the same time. The Stock Market Crash of 1929 had wiped out the investments he had hoped would provide an income for himself, Dora and the coming baby, and, in his anxiety for the future, he developed a perforated duodenal ulcer. He was sent to a private nursing home, where a speedy operation saved his life. Meanwhile, at Beacon Hill School, a combined epidemic of measles and chickenpox broke out. When the family retired to Cornwall for the Easter holiday of 1930, Dora was six months pregnant, John had measles, Kate had chickenpox and Russell was enduring what he later described as an emotional strain 'that introduced an intolerable tension into every moment of daily life'. It was in these circumstances that Russell decided to write a book telling people how to be happy.

Before he could begin *The Conquest of Happiness*, however, he had a not entirely welcome visit from Wittgenstein. For a year, Wittgenstein, having abandoned his career as a schoolteacher, had been back at Cambridge resuming work on philosophy in collaboration with Frank Ramsey. Trinity College authorities now wanted an opinion on his latest work in order to decide whether to continue supporting him. For this they turned to Russell, who was hardly very enthusiastic to take on the job, but felt unable to refuse. 'Since it involves arguing with him,' he wrote to G. E. Moore, 'you are right that it will require a great deal of work. I do not know anything more fatiguing than disagreeing with him in an argument.' Wittgenstein spent two days at Telegraph House before the end of term and then travelled down to Cornwall with the manuscript of what has now been published as *Philosophical Remarks*. He spent a further day and a half at Carn Voel, trying to explain his new work to Russell, after which Russell wrote Moore a rather half-hearted attempt to summarise Wittgenstein's work, which, after struggling briefly to make sense of his new conception of 'logical grammar', concluded: 'His theories are certainly important and certainly very original. Whether they are true, I do not know; I devoutly hope not, as they make mathematics and logic almost incredibly difficult.' Would that do? he asked Moore: 'Reading Wittgenstein's stuff thoroughly is almost more than I can face.' Moore asked only that it be rewritten in a more formal style, and Russell was spared further effort. 'I find I can only understand Wittgenstein when I am good health,' he explained, 'which I am not at the present moment.'

With Wittgenstein out of the way, Russell got down to writing *The Conquest of Happiness*, arguably the most superficial and dishonest book he ever wrote. 'The book was written', he says in his *Autobiography*, 'at a time when I needed much self-command and much that I had learned by painful experience if I was to maintain any endurable level of happiness.' In the book itself, however, he gives the impression of having conquered happiness without very much of a struggle. His *childhood* was unhappy, he confesses, but:

> Now, on the contrary, I enjoy life; I might almost say that with every year that passes I enjoy it more. This is due partly to having discovered what were the things I most desired and having gradually acquired many of those things. Partly it is due to having successfully dismissed certain objects of desire – such as the acquisition of indubitable knowledge about something or other – as essentially unobtainable. But very largely it is due to a diminishing preoccupation with myself.

One is reminded here of the comment Wittgenstein once made when asked for his opinion of Russell's views on marriage, sex and free love: 'If a person tells me he has been to the worst places I have no right to judge him, but if he tells me it was his superior wisdom that enabled him to go there, then I know that he is a fraud.'

The Conquest of Happiness is divided into two parts: 'Causes of Unhappiness' and 'Causes of Happiness'. In the former, Russell attacks what he describes as 'Byronic Unhappiness', the modern spokesman of which he names as Joseph Wood Krutch. Hoping, perhaps, that no one would remember that just a year earlier he had described Krutch's chapter on love as important and correct, here he says: 'One of Mr Krutch's most pathetic chapters deals with the subject of love.' 'I have by no means lost my belief in love,' Russell declares, 'but the kind of love that I can believe in is not the kind that the Victorians admired; it is adventurous and open-eyed, and, while it gives knowledge of good, it does not involve forgetfulness of evil, nor does it pretend to be sanctified and holy.'

Contradicting what he had said in his review of *The Modern Temper*, Russell now declares that the cure for the modern *Angst* about love lies 'in a more courageous acceptance of the modern outlook'. People are unhappy, Russell maintains, because they think too much of themselves; if they could find a purpose in life *outside* themselves they would be happy. Such a purpose is provided by parenthood, which is 'capable of providing the greatest and most enduring happiness that life has to offer ... speaking personally, I have found the happiness of parenthood greater than any other that I have experienced'. Perhaps with the arrival of Dora's new baby in mind, Russell emphasises that 'parents feel a special kind of affection towards their own children, different from that which they feel towards each other or towards other children ... parental affection is a special kind of feeling which the normal human being experiences towards his or her children, but not towards any other human being'. Somewhat against the general theme of the book – which is the importance of finding reasons for living *outside* one's Self – the reason that Russell gives for regarding one's own children as special is curiously egocentric. The pleasure of parenthood, he says, is largely bound up with 'the feeling of part of one's own body externalised, prolonging its life beyond the death of the rest of one's body'.

On the subject of how one should bring up one's children, Russell becomes enmeshed in what looks like an inconsistency. After discussing the anxieties parents feel in the face of conflicting scientific advice, he counsels: 'The parent who genuinely desires the child's welfare more than his or her power over the child will not need textbooks on psycho-analysis to say what should and what should not be done, but will be guided aright by impulse.' A few pages later, he declares: 'There is no heaven-sent instinct which teaches women the right thing to do by their children ... Many a child is psychologically ruined by ignorant and sentimental handling on the part of its mother.' The apparent contradiction is resolved when he remarks: 'children are as apt to love their fathers as to love their mothers. The relation of the mother to the child will have in future to resemble more and more that which at present the father has.' The 'impulses' that are to be trusted, then, are those shared by mother and father; the 'instincts' to be distrusted are those of the mother alone.

Despite the fact that the book was written at a time when Russell was exercising 'self-command' to the utmost, its concluding message is that such self-control is a cause of, rather than a solution to, unhappiness:

Professional moralists have made too much of self-denial, and in so doing have put the emphasis in the wrong place. Conscious self-denial leaves a man self-absorbed and vividly aware of what he has sacrificed ... What is needed is not self-denial, but that kind of direction of interest outward which will lead spontaneously and naturally to the same acts that a person absorbed in the pursuit of his own virtue could only perform by means of conscious self-denial.

The moral of the book, then, is that unhappiness is a kind of selfishness, and so is self-denial. One must not think of oneself *at all*. To seek to control or deny oneself *is* to think of oneself; therefore, one should seek instead simply to *forget* oneself: 'a man should be able to achieve happiness, provided that his passions and interests are directed outward, not inward ... So long as he continues to think about the causes of his unhappiness, he continues to be self-centred and therefore does not get outside the vicious circle.'

Applied to himself, this would seem to suggest that he should not think of Dora's love for Griffin, or her forthcoming child, but should concentrate solely on the well-being of John and Kate. And this is what he tried to do. When the school summer term started, he returned to Telegraph House with John and Kate, Dora went to live in London with Griffin while she awaited the 'event', which was due in July. At this point, the developing nightmare of the Russells' marriage took another turn for the worse, as Dora and Griffin, deciding that sitting at home in their flat waiting for the baby to arrive was just too tedious to tolerate, started spending much of their time in Kleinfeldt's, a pub in Bloomsbury fashionable among the Bohemian and left-wing élite. There they would meet, among others, the artists Nina Hamnett and Augustus John, and the Communist scientist J. B. S. Haldane. There Dora also met the man who would exert a profound, if inexplicable, influence on her life: Paul Gillard.

Gillard was a handsome and feckless unemployed young man, then twenty-six years old, who, having trained as a bank clerk in his native Plymouth, had been transferred to a bank in London. Shortly before Dora met him, he had lost his job at the bank due to his involvement with the National Unemployed Workers' Movement, a Communist organisation led by the charismatic Wal Hannington, which was responsible for the famous Hunger Marches that drew attention to the plight of the unemployed throughout the 1930s. Gillard was homosexual, and he had been drawn into working for the NUWM through his attachment to one of its officers, who subsequently left London to agitate among the unemployed in the North of England. What Gillard actually did for the NUWM is unclear, though he gave the impression to his friends that he was involved in illegal, clandestine work on behalf of the Communist Party. Like almost everything else about Gillard, it is uncertain how much of this was his fantasy and how much reality. What is clear is that he enjoyed the company of the writers and artists who frequented Kleinfeldt's, and that he was accepted and admired by that company primarily because of his charm and good looks.

Griffin had met Gillard in the autumn of 1929, and it seems likely that the two had some kind of affair. If this is so, Dora remained oblivious to it. When she met Gillard in the summer of 1930, she fell in love with him at once, and immediately conceived a romantic picture of him as a gallant, sensitive and artistic class-warrior, dedicated to the cause of Socialism and unswervingly loyal to his working-class roots. This was a fantasy: Gillard was from a middle-class family (his father was a teacher), had rather a contemptuous attitude towards the working-class people with whom he had gone to school and was only too pleased to leave them behind in preference for the middle-class Bohemians with whom he mixed in Bloomsbury. Nor, as far as one can tell from his surviving papers, was he especially interested in politics; he liked the sense of intrigue that went with working clandestinely for 'the Movement', but otherwise had little sympathy for the ideology of his Communist friend and lover. It even seems possible that he was spying *on* the Communist Party and the NUWM, rather than for them. Such, at least, were the suspicions of many people involved – fuelled, in part, by his close associations with homosexual Fascists who frequented the gymnasium to which he belonged. The truth about him will probably never be known, but Dora became, and remained, completely besotted with him.

By the time Dora's baby was born on 8 July, the school term had finished and Russell was down in Cornwall again with John and Kate. The baby was a girl, whom Dora and Griffin named Harriet, after Griffin's mother. Acting in accordance with what Russell had written from America, Dora registered Harriet as Russell's daughter. She, Griffin and baby Harriet then set off for Cornwall. Within hours of their arrival at Carn Voel, Russell told Dora that he had transferred his affections to Patricia Spence, the governess whom Dora had hired to look after John and Kate. 'I felt sick and shrivelled inside,' Dora wrote. 'All I could do was to hope that it might end with the summer. But something was gone that I feared might now never return.'

Patricia Spence was then a twenty-year-old Oxford undergraduate student of history. As her parents had always wanted a boy, she was known as 'Peter', although she was anything but boyish. Kate remembers her as 'one the most beautiful women I have ever seen . . . full of fun and zest for life. It is no wonder that my father fell in love with her. I loved her too, for her elegance, her femininity and her kindness towards me.' As Russell remembers the weeks they spent in Cornwall before Dora arrived, he and Peter 'were left tête-à-tête every evening after the children were in bed and in the course of conversation we soon came to know a good deal about each other.' He was, he says, feeling unhappy, and found comfort in talking to her. After Dora, Griffin and Harriet arrived, a pattern developed of Russell and Peter spending the days in taking John and Kate to the beach, returning to Carn Voel for tea, after which Dora would wash the baby while Griffin looked on. 'Anyone would think he was the child's father,' the maids remarked.

At this time, Griffin hoped to revive his writing career by securing a job on the new magazine, *Fortune*, that Henry Luce was then setting up in Paris. Accordingly, towards the end of August, he left Carn Voel for Plymouth, from where he hoped to sail to Cherbourg on his way to Paris. Before he left, Dora remarked jokingly that he might see Paul Gillard in Plymouth. In the event, Griffin *did* meet Gillard there, though it stretches credulity to imagine that this was by accident. From an unpublished autobiographical novel that Gillard wrote two years later, one gathers that he and Griffin intended to leave for Paris together. What happened to prevent this is, however, shrouded in the mystery that surrounds almost every aspect of Gillard's life. In Cornwall, Dora received a telegram from Griffin saying that he had been arrested and was being held in Exeter prison for £1,000 bail. Then she got a letter from Gillard, explaining that Griffin had been imprisoned because he had failed to register as an alien. Dora at once telegraphed the Devonshire police, offering bail, and set off for Plymouth, taking baby Harriet with her. In Plymouth, she was met by Gillard, who had hired a solicitor to act for Griffin and had also contacted the American Consul. At court the next morning, Dora was told by the police inspector that Griffin had been arrested, not only because he had failed to register, but also because he had Soviet visas in his passport, had 'popped to and fro' across the Channel several times and had come down to the boat with a 'known Communist'. Dora, the police inspector added grimly, could not be aware of all this man had been up to. Griffin was fined £5 for his failure to register, but the consequences of this odd affair did not end there. According to Dora, his diary was taken from him on his arrest, and, after his trial: 'We soon learned that every person whose address or phone number appeared in his diary had been visited by plain-clothes men, asking about his movements, contacts and character.' Fearing that if he left Britain he would not be allowed back in, Griffin abandoned the idea of going to Paris, and, taking Paul Gillard with them, he and Dora returned to Carn Voel.

In describing the rest of the summer at Carn Voel in his 'Private Memoirs', Russell remarks that it is difficult to imagine anything more insane. He took a violent dislike to Gillard, whom he described as a 'drunken homosexual spy'. He found Gillard so repellent, he says, that he aroused murderous impulses in him. As Russell remembers the routine that developed, Griffin and Gillard would go pub-crawling and come back late for dinner to face angry looks from Dora who was jealous of both of them, each on account of the other. When Russell's friend Freda Utley, then still an ardent Communist, turned up unexpectedly, she shrank back from Gillard as if he were a snake and whispered to Russell that she had been warned about him by friends in Russia. The only thing that alleviated the nightmare, Russell recalls, was the task of keeping John and Kate from feeling abandoned by their mother.

Either Russell was extraordinarily good at disguising these feelings from Dora, or Dora was, by this time, entirely blind as far as Russell's feelings were concerned. In her autobiography, she gives no hint of Russell's fierce detestation of Gillard – of which she seems to have remained entirely unaware – and indeed implies that Russell was sympathetic and helpful towards both Gillard and Griffin. She also suggests that, when the summer ended, and Griffin returned to London and Peter to Oxford (she does not say where Gillard went), she and Russell enjoyed a pleasant and harmonious married life. 'There was every sign', she writes, 'that we were both happy and united in our joint work. There was now in the school no one to distract either of us from enjoyment of each other's company; we discussed staff, children, politics, often in joking and laughter and in full reliance on one another.' This is not how Russell remembers it. In the first draft of his

Autobiography, he wrote that he was at this time on the verge of 'some kind of breakdown', caused mainly by the effort of trying to preserve a normal family life in the face of the arrival of Harriet. 'I tried to accept the new child and treat as if she were my own,' he writes:

> This proved to be beyond my strength. I did not at all dislike her, and I felt strongly that it would be unjust and bad for her if, so long as we were nominally all one family, I allowed any preference for my own children to appear. But the resulting strain of daily and hourly insincerity was intolerable, and made family life a torture.

Towards the end of 1930, Russell was asked by a journalist called Hayden Church: 'When you look back on your life from your death-bed, by what facts will you determine whether you succeeded or failed?' In his reply, Russell listed four factors by which he would judge the success of his life: 1. work in philosophy and mathematical logic; 2. work on social questions; 3. the success or otherwise of his children; 4. his personal influence on people he had known. With regard to his children, he wrote: 'I shall be satisfied if they turn out to be happy, intelligent, and decent individuals.' As for his influence on others, he singled out an interesting and significant example: 'I once persuaded a young man to be a philosopher rather than an aeronaut, and he became a first-rate philosopher. I shall think of this with satisfaction on my death-bed.' When his replies were published in the *Sunday Express*, this last sentence was left out – presumably the editor did not recognise the reference to Wittgenstein and did not think that his readers would understand the importance Russell attached to having persuaded Wittgenstein to stick at philosophy. What seems most striking about Russell's replies, however, is that, at a time when he was associated in the public mind above all with *Marriage and Morals*, there is no suggestion whatsoever that he considered success or failure in marriage as an important factor by which to measure his life. Nor, indeed, is there any mention at all of love. To be happy in love was, for the moment, a discarded ambition. He continued to see Peter at Oxford whenever he could, but, at this stage, he had no great hopes for his relationship with her, being convinced that she would tire of him and find at Oxford someone more suitable, someone nearer her own age.

Despairing of the daily torture that his married life had become, Russell was ready for an abrupt and drastic change in his life. Hope of some kind of change arrived on 3 March 1931 with the news of Frank's sudden death in Marseilles. As Frank had died childless, Russell inherited his title, becoming the third Earl Russell. This made Dora a Countess, nine-year-old John a Viscount and seven-year-old Kate and baby Harriet 'Honourable Ladies'. It also meant that, if Dora had another child by Griffin that was registered as Russell's, and, if that child was a boy and John died childless, that child might in future become an Earl. That Russell attached any importance to such things did not, at first, occur to Dora. She at once issued a statement to the Press that neither of them wished to use their titles except on the rare occasions that formal protocol demanded it. 'Looking back now,' she later confessed, 'I am not sure if this is what Bertie would really have intended.' In fact, though Russell wrote to his publishers, saying that he did not want his title to be used on his books, he took an enormous pride in his family history and in his own aristocratic status and title. He found it intolerable when he later discovered that Harriet was listed in *Burke's Peerage* and *Debrett's* and campaigned for years to persuade them that, whatever it said on her birth certificate, he was *not* her father. When, in his old age, someone remarked with surprise that only *Debrett's* listed his second daughter, he responded angrily: 'I have no second daughter. That was my wife's child. It took me ten years to get the bastard out of Burke.' He did not let the matter rest until many years after that, when he finally persuaded *Debrett's* to drop Harriet's name. Given all this, one can see how horrifying the prospect was for him that Dora and Griffin might have a son who would inherit the proud Russell name and heritage under false pretences.

Soon after he inherited the title, Russell was invited by the Webbs to their home at Passfield Corner, to 'talk over his new role as a Labour peer', as Beatrice Webb put it in her diary. 'My wife was so sorry she could not come,' Russell told the Webbs, 'but she has the infant to attend to.' Beatrice Webb, still loyal to Alys, had always disliked Dora and had now, shocked by Dora's open acknowledgement of Harriet as another man's child, decided 'to withdraw as Dora's acquaintance'. Ever perceptive of Russell's moods, it took just this one afternoon for Beatrice to see what Dora apparently could not: that Russell was desperately unhappy in his marriage and with his entire life:

> What interested me was the change in Bertrand; he looked wretched. I watched his expression and tried to describe it in words. Is it sheer disgust, a sort of savage resentment? He has lost the sardonic liveliness, the cheerful and witty cynicism of the first years of his marriage . . . Poor Bertie; he had made a mess of his life and he knows it. He said drearily, when I asked him if he was going back to his old love – mathematical metaphysics – 'I am too old to write anything but pot boilers'.

Later, Dora accused Russell of meeting the Webbs to discuss his position in the House of Lords because 'he had become convinced that he could make a greater contribution to public life and politics; like Caesar, he was ambitious'.

This is quite absurd, and another indication of how far Dora was from understanding her husband during this fraught time. Russell, at this time, had no intention of playing a very active part in Labour Party politics (though, for a brief time a year or so later, this changed). He did not expect to attend the House of Lords regularly, he wrote to the Labour Lords Whip, Lord Marley, 'or to give a very great deal of time to politics'. To Fenner Brockway at the same time, he complained about the attention he was receiving from Marley. He would take up his seat in the Lords, he told

Brockway, and speak on unpopular issues 'such as divorce and obscene literature' every once in a while. 'But I do not intend to be turned aside by an accident from writing, which is clearly my proper job.' He could not, in any case, be a very loyal Labour peer, he explained to Gilbert Murray, since he was too dissatisfied with the MacDonald Government: 'I like their conduct of foreign policy, and their concordat with Gandhi, but not their complete inaction at home.' The Labour Government was at this time facing a crisis that would, over the next few months, transform British party politics. The economic crash of 1929 had resulted in greater levels of unemployment than ever, and the question of what to do about it was dividing both the Labour Party and the country. Oswald Mosley, having failed to persuade the Cabinet to support a spending programme designed to reduce unemployment, had left the Government and the Labour Party and, in February, had announced the formation of his own 'New Party', which later evolved into the British Union of Fascists. Meanwhile, the Communist Party was gaining new adherents among the unemployed, through the NUWM, and was becoming increasingly fashionable among students at both Oxford and Cambridge. A climate of opinion was developing that regarded both capitalism and liberalism to be dead and which accepted the dichotomy: Fascism or Communism. The 'creed wars' of which Russell had warned in 1926 were breaking out (albeit on slightly different lines from those he had anticipated), and Russell, like Erasmus, wanted no part in them.

He turned instead, as he had in 1926, to writing about science: not, this time, a technical analysis of the philosophy of physics, but a polemical attack on the popular scientific writing of the physicists Arthur Eddington and James Jeans. The result, *The Scientific Outlook*, shows Russell at his most irascible. The point of the book, he wrote to Stanley Unwin, was to pillory the 'hogwash in which Eddington and Jeans . . . are causing the public to wallow'. Having recently reviewed Jeans's *The Mysterious Universe*, Russell had become convinced that Jeans and Eddington, in arguing for the consistency of modern physics with religion, were motivated by ulterior political considerations. Making great play of the fact that both men were knighted (he refers repeatedly to 'Sir Arthur' and 'Sir James'), Russell portrays them as, consciously or unconsciously, undermining the threat previously posed by the scientific outlook to established religion, in reward for social distinctions and honours. 'In return, the established order showers knighthoods and fortunes upon the men of science, who become more and more determined supporters of the injustice and obscurantism upon which our social system is based.'

These eminent physicists, he alleges, have placed themselves at the service of theologians by 'stating that recent advances in science have disproved the older materialism, and have tended to re-establish the truths of religion'. In this way, 'the general public has derived the impression that physics confirms practically the whole of the Book of Genesis'. But, Russell insists, 'what they have said in the way of support for traditional religious beliefs has been said by them not in their cautious, scientific capacity, but rather in their capacity of good citizens, anxious to defend virtue and property'. Putting the point in such an extreme way it becomes ridiculous, Russell claims:

> The reconciliation of religion and science which professors proclaim and Bishops acclaim rests, in fact, though subconsciously, on grounds of quite another sort, and might be set forth in the following practical syllogism: science depends upon endowments, and endowments are threatened by Bolshevism; therefore science is threatened by Bolshevism; but religion is also threatened by Bolshevism; therefore religion and science are allies.

This claim to have access to the subconscious motivations of Jeans and Eddington is bizarre, as is Russell's entire attempt to blacken them by portraying them as lackeys of the established order. Neither had made any public pronouncement in favour of the established Church or of the capitalist system. Clearly, though, what annoyed Russell about their popularisations of science was that they threatened his own view that science was inherently on the side of progress; among other things, this meant that it was, necessarily, antithetical to religious faith. If Jeans and Eddington thought otherwise, Russell seems to have reasoned, it could only be because they had been pressed into the service of the reactionary forces of society.

The Scientific Outlook distinguishes two very different motivations for scientific inquiry: 1. the disinterested quest for truth; and 2. the desire for power. Of the first, Russell writes that: 'It belongs with religion and art and love, with the pursuit of the beatific vision, with the Promethean madness that leads the greatest men to strive to become gods. Perhaps the only ultimate value of human life is to be found in this Promethean madness. But it is a value that is religious, not political, or even moral.' This might seem as if it put Russell on the side of those who would link science and religion, but Russell argues that, pursued with honesty and integrity, the search for truth leads to 'the cold breath of scepticism':

> That this is a misfortune is undeniable, but I cannot admit that the substitution of superstition for scepticism advocated by many of our leading men of science would be an improvement. Scepticism may be painful, and may be barren, but at least it is honest and an outcome of the quest for truth. Perhaps it is a temporary phase, but no real escape is possible by returning to the discarded beliefs of a stupider age.

With regard to science as the pursuit of power, Russell, as he had in *Icarus*, paints a grim picture of a future society shaped by the advances in technology due to scientific progress. Essentially, this is the society described in Aldous Huxley's *Brave New World*, which, Russell alleged, was plagiarised from *The Scientific Outlook*. In contradiction to the optimism of his earlier writings, such as 'The New Philosophy of America', Russell now argues that there is something *inherently* destructive about regarding science 'as a technique for the transformation of ourselves and our environment'.

His argument for this is a variation on the view of Joseph Wood Krutch in *The Modern Temper* that the scientific outlook has trivialised religion, tragedy and love. Essentially, Russell now agrees with this, so long as it is understood to apply only to science as the pursuit of power. Science as the pursuit of truth, the 'Promethean madness' he had described, is, he thinks, quite separable from science as the quest for power; indeed, it belongs, like 'religion and art and love', to the things that have been trivialised in the modern world. We pursue the truth about the world, Russell now argues, because we *love* it; if, on the other hand, we seek power over the world, we cannot do so with the attitude of a lover:

> Thus it is only in so far as we renounce the world as its lovers that we can conquer it as its technicians. But this division in the soul is fatal to what is best in man. As soon as the failure of science considered as metaphysics is realised, the power conferred by science as a technique is only obtainable by something analogous to the worship of Satan, that is to say, by the renunciation of love.

So, science as metaphysics and science as the pursuit of power are, in fact, antagonistic forces, the one driven by love and doomed to failure (because the search for truth has ended, at least for the time being, in scepticism), the other driven by the renunciation of love and also, it seems, doomed to failure, since 'the seeker after power must be perpetually engaged in some fresh manipulation if he is not to suffer from a sense of emptiness'. Against the spirit of his earlier articles, which celebrated the triumph of science over mysticism precisely because it gave us power over nature, Russell now declares himself in favour of 'the lover, the poet and the mystic', who 'can find a fuller satisfaction than the seeker after power can ever know, since they can rest in the object of their love'. In more optimistic times, Russell had declared the awed reverence for nature to be a dead sentiment; now, he reveals it to be alive and well in his own heart:

> When I come to die I shall not feel that I have lived in vain. I have seen the earth turn red at evening, the dew sparkling in the morning, and the snow shining under a frosty sun; I have smelt rain after drought, and have heard the stormy Atlantic beat upon the granite shores of Cornwall.

Far from celebrating the power over nature that science brings as the harbinger of a triumphant 'new philosophy', Russell now urges us to remember the wisdom of the past: 'men should not be so intoxicated by new power as to forget the truths that were familiar to every previous generation. Not all wisdom is new, nor is all folly out of date.'

The tone of disillusionment and despair that pervades *The Scientific Outlook* is evident also in the autobiography that Russell wrote at this time. Despite the advice he had offered in *The Conquest of Happiness*, it is clear that, in his unhappiness, Russell could not overcome his natural tendency to turn his attention *inward* and to review his past life. In so doing he produced a literary masterpiece. The autobiography he wrote at this time (which ended in 1921) was not published until thirty years later, by which time he had added to it the much inferior material that describes his life after 1921 and had divided the whole into three volumes. What he wrote in 1931 thus forms the basis for Volume I and the first three chapters of Volume II of the published version. From a literary point of view, it is arguably his finest piece of writing, and it is certainly the most penetratingly self-searching. In his desire to understand what had gone wrong in his life, Russell subjected his early emotional life and romantic attachments to a scrutiny more honest and ruthless with himself than he would ever manage again. When he came to analyse the despair that gripped him at the time of writing the autobiography, however, the honesty and desire to understand, which drive the rest of the book, were compromised by what he later acknowledged as a refusal to admit the true causes of his unhappiness.

In this original 1931 version, the *Autobiography* ends with an 'Epilogue', the theme of which is that, emotionally, intellectually and politically, his life had been a failure. 'My activities continue from force of habit,' he wrote, 'and in the company of others I forget the despair which underlies my daily pursuits and pleasures':

> But when I am alone and idle, I cannot conceal from myself that my life had no purpose, and that I know of no new purpose to which to devote my remaining years. I find myself involved in a vast mist of solitude both emotional and metaphysical, from which I can see no issue.

Rather characteristically, it is the metaphysical rather than the emotional solitude that he concentrates on in this 'Epilogue', and here his autobiography becomes recognisably of a piece with *The Scientific Outlook*. Despite his anger with Jeans and Eddington for giving succour to religious believers, there was one important aspect of their view of physics that Russell felt compelled to accept, and that was its emphasis on the laws of physics being constructions of the human mind rather than part of a mind-independent reality. Several times in *The Scientific Outlook*, he expresses this by saying that the work of modern physics drives us to accept a metaphysical point of view like that of the eighteenth-century philosopher, Bishop Berkeley, who famously denied the reality of matter and insisted, as Russell puts it, that 'only thoughts exist'. 'Berkeley saved the universe and the permanence of bodies by regarding them as God's thoughts,' Russell adds, 'but this was only a wish-fulfilment, not logical thinking.' It is this Berkelian immaterialism minus Berkeley's God that Russell had in mind when he spoke of the scientific quest for truth ending in 'scepticism'. In his autobiography, he describes the same quest leading to the same conclusion, only this time as a description of what he saw as the failure of his own intellectual life:

> And what of philosophy? The best years of my life were given to the Principles of Mathematics, in the hope of finding somewhere some certain knowledge. The whole of this effort, in spite of three big volumes,

ended inwardly in doubt and bewilderment. As regards metaphysics, when, under the influence of Moore, I first threw off the belief in German idealism, I experienced the delight of believing that the sensible world is real. Bit by bit, chiefly under the influence of physics, this delight has faded, and I have been driven to a position not unlike that of Berkeley, without his God and his Anglican complacency.

'When I survey my life,' he says grimly, 'it seems to me to be a useless one, devoted to impossible ideals.' This is as true in politics, he implies, as it is in philosophy: 'I have not found in the post-war world any attainable ideals to replace those I have come to think attainable. So far as the things I have cared for are concerned, the world seems to me to be entering upon a period of darkness.' He is depressed, he writes, 'by the downfall of England . . . The history of England for the last four hundred years is in my blood, and I should have wished to hand on to my son the tradition of public spirit which has in the past been valuable. . . . [but] The feeling of impending doom gives a kind of futility to all activities whose field is in England.' He compares it to the fall of Rome, when 'St Augustine, a Bolshevik of the period, could console himself with a new hope'; but, for him, there is no such consolation: 'I find in the most modern thought a corrosive solvent of the great systems of even the recent past, and I do not believe the constructive efforts of present-day philosophers and men of science have anything approaching the validity that attaches to their destructive criticism.'

The contrast between the point of view expressed in this 'Epilogue' and that expressed in *The Conquest of Happiness* could not be more complete. In the latter, he had emphasised that unhappiness is generally caused by looking inward, and that finding an *external*, impersonal purpose in life is the route to happiness. In the 'Epilogue' he paints a bleak and unrelieved picture of his own unhappiness, which, however, he attributes to entirely *impersonal* causes, and further claims that it is only when he averts his gaze *away* from the outside world that he finds happiness. 'My personal life since I returned from China has been happy and peaceful,' he claims:

I have derived from my children at least as much instinctive satisfaction as I anticipated, and have in the main regulated my life with reference to them. But while my personal life has been satisfying, my impersonal outlook has become increasingly sombre . . . I have endeavoured, by concerning myself with the education of my children and with making money for their benefit, to shut out from my thoughts the impersonal despairs which tend to settle upon me.

Russell was a master of disguising and misrepresenting his own feelings, and, in the contrast between what he says in this 'Epilogue' and what he had said in *The Conquest of Happiness*, one gets a glimpse of how Dora could have lived and worked with him, day after day for many years, under a completely false impression of how he felt towards her, their marriage and their school. For though both works present plausible, if contradictory, descriptions of how he felt, they are both untrue: he did not feel happy, as he claimed in *The Conquest of Happiness*, and his unhappiness was not, as he claims in the 'Epilogue', chiefly to do with the fall of England, the unattainability of certain knowledge and the abandonment by physicists of metaphysical realism. What both pieces of writing serve to disguise is precisely what he successfully concealed from Dora: that he was desperately unhappy in his personal life.

Russell did not write his autobiography for immediate publication – he wrote it primarily in order to try to understand his life – and, when it was finished, he stored it away, intending it to be published only after his death. He did not know, of course, that he would live for nearly forty more years, and it may well have seemed in the summer of 1931, at the age of fifty-nine, that his life had reached some sort of terminus. Certainly, the impression he gives in the 'Epilogue' is that he could see nowhere left to go and regarded his creative life as all but finished. He felt washed up, with no ambitions, for the time being, of returning to philosophy, of having any political influence or, indeed, of writing anything serious at all.

In July 1931, soon after finishing his autobiography, Russell started a syndicated weekly column for the Hearst chain of American newspapers (this included, among others, the *New York American*, the *Washington Herald*, the *San Francisco Examiner* and the *Chicago Herald and Examiner*), and for the next two or three years he published little else. These slight and ephemeral pieces represent the nadir in Russell's writing career, and show, I think, how earnestly he felt the despair, expressed at the end of his autobiography, of accomplishing any more serious tasks. Each of these essays (of about 700 words) took about an hour to write, and often, immediately before sitting down to write them, Russell would ask whoever happened to be with him at the time to come up with suggestions for a topic. One week it might be jealousy, the next snobbery, and the next 'Who may use lipstick?' Whatever the topic, it was given the same witty but glib treatment. They were all very polished pieces of writing, of course – this sort of thing came so easily to Russell – but they rarely contained any original thought, or even any serious attempt to grapple with the topic under discussion.

They were written to amuse and entertain, not, like some of his journalism of the 1920s, to influence public opinion or to express his considered political and social views. Sometimes, they contain an inspired phrase or witty epigram ('Mankind is divided into two classes: those who, being artificial, praise nature, and those who, being natural, praise art'), but equally often they are simply dishonest. For example, in a piece on 'Marriage', he quotes a New York cab driver as saying: 'Now I am a married man and have ceased to be a person.' 'Why should marriage,' Russell asks, 'which ought to be the fulfilment of personality, be felt as quite the opposite? . . . I never myself experienced any such result of being married.' By the time he wrote this, he had experienced *two* marriages that were anything but the 'fulfilment of personality'. In the normal course of events, these lightweight pieces – like thousands of others like them – would have been long forgotten, but, because they were written by Russell, they have been collected in a book, *Mortals and Others*, published in 1975, the editor of which, Harry Ruja, makes extravagant claims for their merits:

> Though unostentatious and sometimes even casual, the essays reveal Russell's genius: his wit, his irony, his perspicuousness, his erudition, his moral sensitivity, his boldness – why not say it? – his wisdom. Our generation has as much urgent need for his rational clarity and his sense of concern for mankind as that generation that first read the essays forty years ago. Moreover, they are a delight to read, for Russell's love of fun keeps bubbling over in them all.

Where Ruja sees a 'love of fun' and a 'concern for mankind', it is possible to discern instead the bitterly ironic contempt and savage resentment that Beatrice Webb saw in Russell at this time. However, though Ruja is surely in a minority in seeing genius in these consciously superficial little essays, he is clearly not alone in his enjoyment of them. Russell continued writing them for four years (earning thereby, at first, $1,000 a year), and they were evidently very popular. Taken out of their context and read more than sixty years after they were written, however, they do not stand up to much scrutiny. Their tone is so dominantly ironic that it is often difficult to know whether Russell believes what he is saying or not. In 'On Being Edifying', for example, he writes that the 'morality of the heart', which he defines as 'kindly feelings and good nature', is produced, not by moralising, but by 'good digestion, sound glands and fortunate circumstances'; thus an 'edifying' appeal to people to do their duty is of no use (save to satisfy our 'sadistic instincts'), while an effective, but unedifying, 'scientific' morality would take the form of saying: 'Eat more green vegetables, and you will hate your neighbours less.' Clearly, most of this is tongue-in-cheek, but does Russell also, somewhere in it all, intend to make a serious point?

Sometimes the superficiality is revealing. For example, in 'On Feeling Ashamed', Russell writes:

> I think remorse is essentially a social phenomenon, which occurs when we realise that, owing to something we have done, we cannot make other people take that favourable view of ourselves that we should wish them to entertain.

Feeling ashamed of something is, in other words, a kind of vanity and depends crucially upon fearing that one's misdemeanours will be discovered. 'Those who commit a murder', Russell claims (and in another one of these essays he remarks that many people 'would like to commit murders but dare not' – which is why we read about crime), 'feel little remorse so long as they are sure that they will not be found out.' Behind the flippancy of such remarks it is possible to identify a rather grim view of human nature; whether one regards this as 'moral sensitivity' will, I suppose, depend upon whether one regards this view as correct. Even one who shares Russell's view, however, will not be satisfied for very long with its expression in these essays.

The great advantage to Russell of writing these pieces was that they enabled him to earn substantial amounts of money for very little effort. They also could be dashed off wherever he happened to be. The first few of them, for example, were written while he was on a family holiday in Hendaye, on the border between France and Spain. The 'family' was now an extended one that included Peter, Griffin, Dora, John, Kate and Harriet. In effect, it was two families and, while Russell, Peter, John and Kate went out walking the Pyrenees, Griffin and Dora took Harriet to the beach. Russell later wrote bitterly about the holiday, accusing Dora of neglecting Kate and, especially, John, but at the time he evidently gave Dora the impression that he was enjoying himself and was content to regard the four adults and three children as one happy family. Even after Russell had tried, in as brutal a fashion as he knew how, to disabuse Dora of the notion that he was content with this arrangement, she could write of the 'harmony' of the Hendaye household and claim that Russell was as committed as she was to the idea that such harmony was living proof of the success of the new morality. 'The foundation of it all was love for people and especially children,' she wrote. 'In such exchanges as took place between Bertie and myself during the holiday at Hendaye, it was clear that we both felt that our partnership was the stable element.'

Both Peter and Dora became pregnant at Hendaye. According to Dora, they all talked about the desirability of having more children and there emerged an agreement between the four of them, subsequently referred to by her as the 'pact of Hendaye', according to which: 'any child that might be born would not be let down by any of us and could be cared for in the school if desired'. Dora seems to have understood this to imply a binding agreement between her and Peter that they would not abort their pregnancies, and an understanding that both her child and Peter's would be raised at Telegraph House as additions to the extended family and treated by the outside world as Russell's. As so often during these years, it is difficult to know whether this is an example of Dora's tendency to delude herself or of Russell's to deceive her, but there is no sign that he ever considered himself or Peter to be bound by any such agreement, and the whole idea was obviously repugnant to him. He had gone to great lengths to legitimise John in 1921, and had suffered deeply from the arrival of Harriet, and it is scarcely likely that he would commit himself happily to producing an illegitimate child by Peter and welcoming into his proud family line another 'bastard' of Griffin's. If there was such a pact as Dora describes (and it seems unlikely that she just made it up), one cannot imagine Russell entering into it with the confident and joyful pioneering spirit that Dora implies; he must either have entered into it with no intention of honouring it, or else have agreed to it with a very heavy heart and stoic resignation. It is possible, indeed, that this pact is part of what Russell had in mind when he wrote later in his *Autobiography*:

> In my second marriage, I had tried to preserve that respect for my wife's liberty which I thought that my creed enjoined. I found, however, that my capacity for forgiveness and what may be called Christian love was not equal to the demands that I was making on it, and that persistence in a hopeless endeavour would do much harm to me, while not achieving the intended good to others. Anybody else could have told me this in advance, but I was blinded by theory.

In his 'Private Memoirs', Russell remembers both the holiday and the decision to have more babies very differently from Dora. According to him, the 'temporary ménage' they attempted at Hendeye was hardly likely to be a success, and Peter's pregnancy was not felt by him to be a cause for celebration but rather something he had been tricked into. He had, he claims, told Peter emphatically that he did not want her to become pregnant and she had promised to take precautions. When, however, she became pregnant, she confessed, according to him, that she had deliberately refrained from taking precautions. Because of his opposition to the pregnancy, the 'Private Memoirs' state, Peter tried to miscarry, and, when that failed, they agreed to let her pregnancy go forward'.

Meanwhile, Dora was considering what to do about her own pregnancy. She, Griffin and Harriet left Hendaye before the others, Griffin to go to Paris looking for work and Dora to return to Telegraph House to prepare for the start of term. Despite the pact, she considered having an abortion. 'I have often thought', she later wrote, 'things might have been different had I brought myself to sacrifice that baby.' The decision not to abort was, she says, one of the most difficult of her whole life. This does not quite square with her apparent conviction that everybody was in agreement that they *wanted* more children; nor does the letter to Russell she wrote at this time quite tally with the impression she gives that she and he were in close harmony during this period. 'I had wanted to talk to you about very many things,' she told him, 'but it is not easy, because you have built up a very complete barrier . . . I have felt very lonely since I came back & as if sometimes you wished me to feel I no longer belonged in our house . . . I do think that you no longer care for me, & therefore do not see me with tender eyes.' In the end, she 'simply could not bring myself to do away with this child' and resigned herself to her pregnancy. She was influenced in this, she later said, by Peter's decision to keep *her* child.

When Russell, Peter, John and Kate returned from Hendaye, Peter went back to Oxford to face the prospect of having a baby during her final year as an undergraduate, and Russell prepared to leave for yet another lecture tour of the United States. On 22 October 1931, a few days after he left, Dora wrote him a tender letter, telling him that Peter had, after all, had a miscarriage:

I cried so bitterly when I heard from her, & fussed so for the grief & shock to you all alone in America. O my darling, I wish it had been me instead. You had begun to feel so happy in the thought of a new baby, & all the comfortable respectable thoughts about Peter's degree etc. – won't make up for it. I realised how deeply happy I'd been for you both when the shock of the news came. Please darling, do plan for the future, if you both want a baby, because you see if it happened once now, it can happen again, & you've no need to fear that you have more children.

Dora later told people that Peter's 'miscarriage' had, in fact, been an abortion and thus a contravention of the 'pact of Hendaye'. She felt bitterly let down by what she regarded as Peter's betrayal of their agreement. Russell, on the other hand, referring always to it as a 'miscarriage', says in his 'Private Memoirs' that Peter was bitterly disappointed by the loss of her baby and from that time onwards she was liable to hysterical outbursts in which she expressed hatred of him, though still passionately in love with him. The one person who did *not* seem bitter about the loss of Peter's baby was Russell himself, who, before he received Dora's letter about it, wrote insouciantly: 'Did Peter tell you she had miscarried? I am sorry, but in many ways it simplifies things. She will now stay out her time at Oxford, as she has managed to avoid scandal.' Later, he added: 'I don't mind so *very* much about Peter's mishap, because the financial worry would have been very great, & it is a good thing she can finish her Oxford career.' It seems Dora was mistaken to believe that Russell wanted this baby, and her extraordinarily kind expressions of sympathy were misplaced. Indeed, given Russell's firm statements that he had *not* wanted the baby, his calmness in the face of Peter's 'mishap', Peter's anger towards him and his later expressions of guilt over Peter's 'miscarriage', it appears most likely that Dora was right to believe that Peter had had an abortion, but wrong to blame her for the decision. Russell, it seems most reasonable to assume, had urged Peter to abort the baby, partly because he did not want the expense of looking after her and the child, and partly because he did not want the scandal of producing an illegitimate child with a girl who had not yet finished university.

Russell had, in any case, come to believe that it would be better to end his relationship with Peter. He wanted her to complete her degree and start a life of her own without him. Meanwhile, he would do his best to repair his marriage to Dora. Accordingly, he wrote to Dora reassuring her that he was happy to have her new child recognised as his own, that he was as devoted to her as he had ever been and that they should resist the pressures that threatened their marriage:

I feel that with Griffin & Peter pulling us opposite ways, there is a danger that you & I may get more separated than we wish. You know, Darling, that I have a profound affection for you, & an immense respect. I never remain physically attracted to any woman for more than about seven years, so I cannot build any permanent relation on physical attraction.

But I want my relation to you to be permanent. I want to grow old with you about, & I want John & Kate to have the example of your courage & indomitableness. And I want the stimulus of your mind. I had grievances some time back, but I have none now. I don't want to restrain you from anything you want to do, & clearly you will want to be with Griffin a good deal, but I do want you to know that I value, & should feel maimed if I lost you.

It sounded sincere, and it is scarcely any wonder that Dora took it as such. But it was, as ever, motivated by Russell's feelings for his children, especially his son. He could not bear to risk losing John, however much the thought of leaving Dora for Peter might appeal to him (and, as Peter became more shrill in her bitterness towards him, this thought grew less appealing). On 15 November, the day before John's birthday, Russell wrote: 'I think of little John being 10 tomorrow. It seems a long time since that morning in Sydney St. How happy I was!'

Russell loathed the lecture tour, which lasted for two months, more than ever. He hated being away from his children; he had more or less decided to close the school and therefore could not feel the sacrifices he was making to finance it were justifiable; and, in any case, after the recession, there was less money to be made from these tours than he had become used to. All in all, he told Dora: 'I hate, *hate*, *hate* this tour. Formerly I have been cheered by the cheques, but this year they are poor.' He resolved *never* to go back, if he could possibly avoid it. This time, to make things worse, he did not get home in time for Christmas. On Christmas Day, he was alone on the SS Bremen half-way across the Atlantic. It was then that he wrote 'Christmas at Sea', the most remarkable of his Hearst articles, and the one in which glibness and flippancy are brushed aside in favour of the deep earnestness and fine writing that characterise the autobiography he had written earlier in the year. He began by remarking that this was the second time he had spent Christmas Day on the Atlantic, the previous occasion being in 1896, when 'I was lately married, childless, very happy, and beginning to taste the joys of success':

Family appeared to me as an external power hampering to freedom: the world, to me, was a world of individual adventure. I wanted to think my own thoughts, find my own friends, and choose my own abode, without regard to tradition or elders or anything but my own tastes. I felt strong enough to stand alone, without the need of buttresses.

Now, however, standing alone was oppressive rather than liberating, for 'Time makes a man afraid . . . And with fear comes the need of affection, of some human warmth to keep away the chill of the cold universe':

To stand alone may still be possible as a moral effort, but it is no longer pleasant as an adventure. I want the companionship of my children, the warmth of the family fire-side, the support of historic continuity and of membership of a great nation. These are very ordinary human joys, which most middle-aged persons enjoy at Christmas. There is nothing about them to distinguish the philosopher from other men; on the contrary, their very ordinariness makes them the more effective in mitigating the sense of sombre solitude.

'And so', he concluded, 'Christmas at sea, which was once a pleasant adventure, has become painful. It seems to symbolise the loneliness of the man who chooses to stand alone, using his own judgment rather than the judgment of the herd. A mood of melancholy is, in these circumstances, inevitable, and should not be shirked.'

Russell returned from America, he said later, 'resolved to break off relations' with Peter, who had spent Christmas with Dora and Griffin at Telegraph House. Peter, however, was determined not to be shaken off. After her 'miscarriage' she had lost all interest in her studies at Oxford, and wanted only to be with Russell and, if possible, have a baby with him. Because (he says in his 'Private Memoir') of the guilt he felt over the loss of Peter's baby, and also because 'I was still in love with her', Russell abandoned his resolve to leave her. But, since he would never consent to having an illegitimate child, if he was to accede to Peter's desire for a baby, divorce from Dora became at this point inevitable.

In the New Year, Griffin left for Majorca to stay with some literary friends, hoping that the now heavily pregnant Dora would join him there. With some misgivings at leaving Russell and Peter alone together at Telegraph House, Dora agreed and set off for Majorca in mid-January 1932, remaining there until March, shortly before she was due to give birth. 'I now think', she wrote later, 'that, had I remained at home, Bertie and I would have found some way round our difficulties and stayed together. We missed each other terribly: I wrote to him twice from the train en route and telegraphed my safe arrival in Palma; in some ways we had never been closer than at this time.' Russell, however, resented her leaving him in charge of a school in which he, by this time, had little interest. While Dora was in Majorca, he wrote to her that he had, reluctantly, decided to give up the school and concentrate on politics: 'I want to spend more time in London & try to stir people up to think out a programme to urge on the Labour Party . . . The world is going to the devil faster & faster. I see no hope anywhere but in Russia.' A week later, he had changed his mind and told her: 'I wish very much to go on with the school.' When Peter left Oxford, he said, he would employ her at the school and build a bungalow for her at Telegraph House: 'I know you will hate having Peter here as a teacher, but I don't see how else I can fulfil my responsibilities to her . . . My belief is that she will ultimately marry a man nearer her own age. I think you & I can still work together over the school, & that ultimately our troubles will grow less . . . Dearest, don't doubt the depth of my affection.'

Dora replied that she would prefer to dissolve the school than have Peter employed there, since she did not want a repetition of the problems they had had in 1927, when 'we tried bringing in Roy & Alice'. 'About our whole life the last five years', she told Russell, 'I think we have made lots of muddles through impatience':

> We had cast our lives in so very monogamous a mould that it made it much more difficult both for us, & for the other people concerned, to change it . . . I have always loved you best & no other relationship would ever replace the one with you for me . . . Perhaps I shouldn't have tried to live in patriarchal monogamy – or perhaps if I did I should have done it thoroughly . . . It was of course very stupid of me not to have known that Harriet would make all the difference to your feelings, stupid perhaps, not to have foreseen that they would change anyhow, Harriet or not. But I have certainly never recovered from it, & I could not bear listening to the story of your first marriage, because of that.

In reply, Russell assured her that he had 'a deep & indestructible affection' for her, and would 'be very unhappy if we became estranged'. He did not imagine his sexual feelings for her would revive, but 'I want to grow old with you'. His reasons for wanting Peter at the school, he claimed, were 'practical rather than emotional', and in the same practical spirit he offered to pay Dora £200 a year, since 'I have felt for a long time uncomfortable because you were so poor.' Dora remained unconvinced. At Christmas, she told Russell, she had felt Peter's attitude towards her change, '& it naturally frightened & worried me . . . I feared Peter's possessiveness . . . as though she would take away if she could even what I had left to me of you . . . I wish we could get some time to ourselves, you & I.' 'Don't take Peter's mood at Xmas as normal,' Russell tried to reassure her. 'She was furious with me for having made her lose her child, & some of this fury went to you . . . She knows that in no circumstances should I wish for a breach with you.'

A month later, when Dora and Griffin, having returned from Majorca, were in London awaiting the birth of their baby, Russell wrote: 'The things that had been troubling me in regard to Peter turned out to be not very grave, & I find myself more fond of her than I have ever been before. We both wish to live together . . . I want to live with her openly & domestically.' The school, he assumed, would have to close. The next day Dora gave birth to a baby boy, whom she and Griffin called Roderick. This time, it was registered in Griffin's name. Whatever else happened, it would never grow up to become the fifth Earl Russell. Within a few days, Russell had consulted his old friend and solicitor, Crompton Llewelyn Davies, about arranging a divorce. 'He is not sure whether it is possible,' Russell told Dora, 'but if it is to be attempted, he says I must be the guilty party.' He wanted the divorce, he said, only 'in order the children might be legitimate, not from any unfriendliness. You will remember from the time when John was coming that I think legitimacy important.' He and Peter had decided to live at Carn Voel, he announced, at least for the summer, and possibly, if Dora was willing, for the rest of his life.

By the time Dora got back to Telegraph House at the end of March, Russell and Peter were in Cornwall, and the staff at Beacon Hill were under the impression that the school was to close. She was in a state of shock, bewildered that, within a few months, Russell could change from declaring an 'indestructible affection' for her, and a wish to grow old with her, to leaving her and consulting lawyers to arrange a divorce. How could the 'pact of Hendaye', the new morality, their school, their marriage and everything they had fought for together over the years suddenly mean so little to him? She decided that he simply could not have changed so drastically. The man she had known and loved was the real Bertrand Russell, and his present behaviour was 'entirely out of character'. The ruthlessness, lack of concern for her feelings and indifference to their joint work had to be due to Peter, not to Russell. Russell was still devoted to her – had he not said so in his letters of February? His departure hurt her, but, Dora insisted on believing, it 'must also have been very painful for him'. After all: 'We were never closer in love and tenderness than in those last months before the break was made.'

In a letter of 15 April, Russell tried to disabuse Dora of this comforting delusion. 'I suppose you imagine that my present attitude is due to Peter,' he told her, 'but in this you are mistaken':

> I don't think you realise what my feelings about our marriage have been for a long time past. My love for you was killed by your behaviour about Hannah, but for the sake of the children I tried to revive it, & hoped to succeed. I failed; but again for the sake of the children I made the best of things, even after Harriet was born. I do not think you were acting rightly by me in having Harriet & Roderick if you wished our marriage to continue, or by Griffin if I meant more to you than he did. Having at last a chance of happiness, which I have not had with you since 1927, I consider that I have a right to it, & I also have a right to do what I can for Peter & for any children she may have ... I am afraid this letter must hurt you, but there are misconceptions which ought to be cleared away, & I do not see how to do it more kindly ... I think we must make up our minds to give up the school at the end of this term.

It is hard to imagine the truth being spelt out more directly and brutally than this, but Dora simply could not believe it. Her sense of herself and Russell as comrades in a struggle against orthodoxy, as educators in the 'right to be happy', and as pioneers in the new sexual morality was too deep for her to admit that, for Russell, it had led only to deceit and unhappiness. They *had* loved each other deeply, and they had done so in a way that was more expansive, more liberating and *happier* than that which demands monogamy. And in doing this they had shown the world the way forward.

Russell felt no such thing. Having taken the step of leaving Dora, he felt able, not only to admit that he had been deeply unhappy in their marriage, but also to repudiate completely the ideals upon which it had been based and which he and Dora had publicly advocated. In an affidavit he submitted to court in connection with his divorce, he stated:

> I am persuaded that infidelities are undesirable so long as the marriage has any reality, and that they tend to cause trouble which a little self-control would avoid ... it was at Dora's initiative that I accepted an unusual basis for our marriage, and experience has not shown that this was wise.

As far as he was concerned, the 'new morality' had simply been a mistake – Dora's mistake.

5
DIVORCE

In his 'Private Memoirs', Russell describes his divorce from Dora, which dominated his life for two years from 1932 to 1934, as painful, sordid and altogether horrible. Divorces are rarely pleasant, but this one was especially vicious – and extremely complicated. Undoing the tangled knots that had been tied by Russell, Dora and Griffin required very subtle legal manoeuvres and a great deal of heartbreaking ruthlessness. The legal process was grotesquely complex and the patterns of emotional torment that it inflicted scarcely less so. It damaged everybody involved, but especially Dora, Griffin, John and Kate, and the fierce acrimony aroused by it would have dire consequences for those – most notably John's children – as yet unborn. Russell seems never to have understood, or to have cared about, the devastating effect of the divorce on Dora's life (and the ruin of Griffin's life was an effect of the 'war' between Dora and Russell that both combatants regarded as something of a side-show), but, in a passage he wrote for the second volume of his *Autobiography* but deleted from the published version, he conceded that: 'The effect upon John and Kate was as bad as I feared':

> Both, especially John, suffered deep psychological damage. I cannot, however, see that I should have done better to stay with Dora. I should soon have had some kind of breakdown, and should have become useless both as a father and as a breadwinner. I think, in fact, that I made a mistake in enduring such a mockery of marriage as long as I did.
>
> Until I made up my mind to the breach, my state of mind was confused, and, in a sense, insincere. I did not wish to admit to myself how profound was my unhappiness.

Now that Russell felt able to admit the unhappiness he had felt for years in his marriage to Dora, there was nothing holding him back from expressing also the hurt, anger and resentment that he felt towards her. And, just as Dora never believed that he *was* unhappy with her, so she now could not believe the extent of his bitterness towards her. One of the things that makes the papers relating to their divorce so heartbreaking to read (papers that now fill five large boxes at the Russell Archives) is that Dora never appreciated the depth of Russell's hatred of her and kept acting on the assumption that, somehow, there was still goodwill between them. Russell claims in his 'Private Memoirs' that, in the course of the divorce, Dora and he came to hate each other deeply, but this is not true; Dora, like Alys before her, continued to both love and respect Russell and to hope that his love for her would one day revive.

This was one reason why the divorce dragged on for so long. Moreover, Dora deeply disliked settling their affairs through the process of law. As far as she was concerned, all of them – herself, Russell, Griffin and Peter – had lived outside the law, according to their own morality and in defiance of conventional, respectable society. To involve the law now, with its inbuilt assumption that adultery was immoral, seemed to her hypocritical and a betrayal of the values by which they had tried to live. She had never wanted a legal marriage, and she resented now having to be put through the ordeal of a legal divorce.

Dora's attitude would not have mattered to Russell so much if the divorce procedure had been as straightforward then as it is now. In the 1930s, a divorce could not be granted simply because the partners in a marriage wished it; a wrong had to be committed by either side, and, given that neither Dora nor Russell could be accused of cruelty (and neither had become certifiably insane), this meant that one or other of them had to be accused of adultery. As both were on record as arguing that adultery was not either immoral or an insuperable obstacle to a happy marriage, it was clearly going to be difficult to present themselves as having been 'wronged' in this respect. Russell evidently considered suing Dora for divorce, using as evidence of her adultery the existence of Harriet and Roderick. He was talked out of this by Crompton Llewelyn Davies, who assured him that it would never work and that Dora, not Russell, had to be the 'wronged' party. Quite what the reasoning was behind this decision is not entirely clear. Russell, to be sure, had famously condoned adultery, but then so had Dora. Dora was inclined to attribute it to Russell's generally 'courtly' attitudes, which demanded that 'gentlemen' did not divorce their wives. It seems more likely, however, that it was based on the pragmatic judgment that a divorce court would never swallow the idea of a notorious philanderer like Russell – who had, after all, been successfully sued by his previous wife for adultery – seeking legal redress against his wife's lack of virtue.

Whatever the reasons, the decision was final, and it thus fell to Dora to divorce Russell for *his* lack of virtue, in spite of the facts that (a) she did not want to divorce him, and (b) she did not object to his lack of virtue. Her only possible reason for doing this was that it was what Russell wanted, but, given the divorce laws at the time, this too had to be concealed, for 'collusion' was not allowed and, if suspected, would jeopardise the divorce. There was also the problem of Dora's children by Griffin: how could she pretend to be a virtuous wife shocked by her husband's infidelities when she herself had two children by another man? The solution was as ingenious as it was dishonest: she and Russell would sign a 'Deed of Separation' in which she disclosed her adulterous offspring, but promised to remain 'chaste' in future, and they both agreed to 'forgive' each other for past misdemeanours but not for future ones. Meanwhile, Russell would continue to live with Peter; then, after a decent interval, Dora, having kept her promise of chastity, would divorce him for the adulterous behaviour he had committed *after* the deed was signed.

The advantages to Russell of this arrangement are obvious: he would get the divorce from Dora he wanted and, in the meantime, would live with Peter. But what of Dora? Why should she have gone along with a plan that not only made a mockery of the sexual morality in which she passionately believed, but also placed her under a legal obligation not to sleep with Griffin or anybody else for a year or two, in order to achieve a divorce that she did not want? To understand the course of the divorce, and why it became so messy and horrible, it is necessary to understand Dora's shifting attitudes to this question, and the complications of her own emotional life in the years leading up to the divorce; complications caused, in the main, by her despair at having been abandoned by Russell – not to mention her disillusionment at realising that he did not, after all, believe in the 'new morality' they had championed together.

Russell's attitude was quite straightforward and was held resolutely and consistently throughout the proceedings: he wanted to divorce Dora and marry Peter as quickly as possible, and he wanted the custody of John and Kate to be held jointly by Dora and himself. In his mind, the matter was quite simple. Not so in Dora's. To begin with, however, she did, reluctantly, go along with the plan and, in a letter to her solicitor, Mr Maw, of 20 April 1932, she explained why: she felt obliged to do so for the sake of preserving tolerably decent relationships with Russell, Peter and Griffin. She did not want, she said, to 'incur the resentment of the two men I care deeply about, and of the woman who will have a relation to my older children and an increasingly close influence with my husband'. Besides: 'The tacit assumptions on which the arrangement of my life has been built fall to the ground. It seems to me therefore that I must go as far as ever I possibly can towards making the divorce possible.'

But her reasons were not entirely selfless. There were also some advantages to her in signing the Deed of Separation, not the least of which was that it gave her a much better chance of keeping Beacon Hill School going. When Russell left Telegraph House in the spring of 1932, he assumed that the school would close, but in this, as in much else, he underestimated the strength of Dora's resolve. Dora's belief in the school was as passionate as her belief in free love and she was determined, if at all possible, that it would survive Russell's departure. In this, she had the support of the staff and of the parents, and, as the school had now expanded somewhat (by 1932 it had grown to about thirty pupils), she thought she stood a good chance of making it a profitable business. The loss of Russell's name would be a serious blow to the school's prestige, but, if she could keep Russell's children there, that blow would be softened somewhat. Moreover, under the terms of the Deed of Separation, Russell was prepared to give her an annuity of £400 a year, to pay the school fees of John and Kate and to pay her rent while he lived with Peter at Carn Voel (which had always legally been Dora's). He was also prepared to allow the school to stay, free of rent, at Telegraph House for at least a year (which, of course, he was under no legal obligation to do).

There was also the question of the custody of John and Kate. As things stood, until Russell and Dora were divorced, Russell, as father, had legal custody of his children. This meant that he could, if he so chose, not only remove them from the school, but also insist that they live with him. In a letter to Dora of 4 June 1932, Russell argued that his having custody of the children was not only legally, but also morally, right. After all:

> you have two other children, therefore John & Kate are relatively of more emotional importance to me than to you; and I have to find the money for them. Therefore it seems just that, since one of us must have the ultimate decisions, it should be me.

However, in the face of Dora's implacable opposition to this and in return for the advantages that the Deed of Separation would give him, Russell was prepared to add a clause to it giving Dora equal legal rights over the children. He was also willing to allow them to remain at Beacon Hill at least for the next year, so long as they spent the school holidays with him and Peter. When they left Beacon Hill, the clause stated, they would divide their time equally between his home and Dora's. Though Dora did not quite see it like this, these concessions amounted, in effect, to a surrender by Russell of part of the rights that were his by law, and he was irritated by Dora's refusal to regard them as such. For months he and Dora haggled through their respective solicitors over the wording of this clause, with Dora wanting it to say that she had 'physical care and control' over John and Kate, and Russell wanting it merely to say that they had 'equal rights'. Finally, after Russell had threatened to break off negotiations, Dora capitulated and signed the deed, worded as he wished, at the end of December 1932.

Throughout these negotiations, one can see in Dora's side of the correspondence her bewildered attempts to come to terms with the new, hard tone that Russell now used to address her. To Russell's increasing exasperation, she kept writing to him and their solicitors, not just about the legal points under discussion, but also about her *feelings* – towards him, Peter, John and Kate, their marriage, and so on – as if these still mattered in some way to Russell. In a letter of 28 May 1932, she pleaded with him to deal with her as a *person* and not just as a co-respondent in a law case. She wanted to continue with the divorce, she told him, only 'if I could be confident that we would try & preserve an imaginative picture of each other's needs, & not take a stand on merely legal rights'. She had, to begin with, felt that this was the case: 'But then came a tone in your letters that made me feel you had ceased to think at all about my life or work, except in so far as it might affect you.' In a later letter, she tried to explain how she felt about the children. Her objection to Russell having sole custody of them, she said, was that Peter, whom by now she loathed deeply, would replace her as their mother:

And this is the thing that I face, and that worries me desperately and keeps me awake night after night, that your instinct is to make Peter into a new mother for them and she, for various psychological reasons that are also clear, wants this to happen too. Naturally I can't tolerate that.

. . . Peter's relation to the children was acquired by my sharing everything I had with her. She has replied by getting comfort and leisure and security for herself by taking John and Kate's home away, and my home also, for which and in which I had worked twelve years, robbing me of the last years of my youth.

. . . I can't find any code by which I can endorse her attitude. She hasn't really worked as you and I have all our lives, she shares no burdens or responsibilities, but only imposes them on others. If she had even taken her finals I could have respected her more.

Though it clearly tested his patience to do so, Russell replied to these charges on Peter's behalf. She did not impose a burden, he argued; on the contrary, 'she has worked hard as my secretary . . . her help with my work is of great value to me'. (Working as his secretary, of course, was what Russell had originally suggested to Dora when he first met her in 1918 – she had refused on the ground that the suggestion gave no respect to *her* work.) With regard to Dora's implicit suggestion that she, not Peter, was a proper wife for him, Russell told her:

You seem to forget that the two acts which, with their attendant circumstances, made our marriage one in name only, were both yours: first, when, without any provocation from me, you decided to have an affair with Randall; second, when you had children by Barry. It is obvious that, for me, our marriage could no longer be a source of anything but great unhappiness.

If Russell really believed that the first of these had made their marriage 'one in name only', then he could not have meant what he had said in *Marriage and Morals* and elsewhere about the necessity of married partners tolerating adultery. And it was crucially important to Dora to think that he *had* meant it. The view he was expressing here, she insisted on believing, *could not* have been his view while they were married; it was a change of view, a loss of heart, brought about by the influence of Peter. So, no matter how many times Russell denied it, Dora could not be shaken from believing that he had been happy with her, that they had had a marriage that was deeper and more worthy than anything Russell could expect with Peter. After she had signed the deed, she wrote to him saying that she thought Peter was jealous of what she and Russell had shared and continued to share, jealous of 'what I have left in your respect and affection for me as an individual and John and Kate's mother', and that Peter was determined, not only to possess Russell herself, but also to change him:

Peter is from now on your wife, as far as I'm concerned, I'm a free woman on my own, for I'll never bind Griffin or bind myself again – we are going to live free and make no claims upon each other, only try and see that each is realised as a person. I have come to love people, and to love real things in them and life through this new way of living, – and I'll never give it up. I learned it from what Griffin calls the 'ineffable Bertie' whom I married, and who I feel Peter does not want to exist any longer. For that is what I mind most, that she wants to make you into someone different. You want and need what she can give now, I know, but it isn't all you want, and I shall measure her by how she sets about making you happy. Your relation to me is still unresolved, whatever the legal situation may be, or whatever you may think with your head about it, because John and Kate are between us and will always be there. More than that, you and I were deeply married, and I can see that, while you think you are free of me, you do not really treat me as at liberty so far as you are concerned.

None of this made any impression on Russell at all, except perhaps to harden him still further against Dora. He was, for the moment, in love with Peter and delighted to be living with her in Cornwall, away from the strain of Beacon Hill School, of his marriage to Dora and of having to pretend not to mind about sharing his home with illegitimate children. When John and Kate came to join him at Carn Voel for the summer, they noticed the change in him. Kate remembers it as a time of 'jokes and folly and lightheartedness'. A running joke was that Peter was a witch, exerting her spell of 'miching mallecho'[7] all around her. The joke started when the four of them – Russell, Peter, John and Kate – were standing over a hole in the rocks that looked down to the sea. A gust of wind blew Peter's hat off and took it into the hole and then, to everyone's amazement, back out again. Peter at once claimed magic powers, and began throwing other things down the hole – grass, leaves, handkerchiefs – until, overreaching herself, she threw down a silver cigarette case, which, however, never returned. She was, she explained, a young and relatively inexperienced witch.

Dora's fears of being supplanted by Peter in the affections of John and Kate were well founded, and Kate in particular, who had always favoured her father over her mother, now began to compare Dora unfavourably with Peter. Peter, at twenty-three, was so much younger and prettier and altogether more charming. Moreover, she made a special effort with Kate in ways that Dora, busy with the school, her writing, her politics and her other children, had never bothered with. 'She listened to my stories,' Kate remembers, 'co-operated in my games and introduced me to the feminine mysteries of perfume and powder, nail files and cold cream. My mother used such things too and could have taught me had I asked, but Peter *invited* me to learn and made me feel I was being initiated into the art of being a

---

[7] The phrase (which Kate remembers cropping up often in the lighthearted banter of that summer) comes from Hamlet: 'Why, tis miching mallecho, my Lord, that means mischief.' Russell surely had this phrase in mind when he called the villain of 'Satan in the Suburbs' 'Dr Mallako'.

woman.' John's sympathies were more evenly divided – if anything, he was more loyal to Dora than to Russell – and the process that had begun at Beacon Hill School of his withdrawal from the world was accelerated as he grew ever more introverted and distrustful of the people around him.

At this stage, both Russell and Dora were sensitive to the potential dangers to John and Kate of appearing to be bitter about one another, and, on the whole, resisted the temptation to use them directly in their battles. Behind the scenes, however, things were different. When Russell left Telegraph House for Cornwall, he took care to take with him the children's passports, lest Dora should decide to take them out of the country. After the children had returned to Telegraph House for the autumn term, he wrote to Crompton that he would *never* concede that Dora should have 'physical care and control' of them. Crompton's reply was chilling: 'I suppose you could not get possession of John and Kate, as the strength of Dora's position is that she has them now?'

Russell's fear that Dora would take John and Kate abroad was based on an idea she had considered, soon after Russell left her, of moving to the United States to make a career as a writer. She abandoned this idea precisely because she could not take John and Kate with her (among other reasons, because Russell had taken their passports), nor could she afford to pay for them to visit her during their holidays if she left and they stayed in England. She tried, in the negotiations leading up to the Deed of Separation, to persuade Russell to agree to pay their transatlantic fares himself if she moved to the States, but he was having none of it. Thus, as she put it to Russell, the idea 'to clear out for America' – though 'the only chance of personal happiness' that she could envisage for herself – had to be abandoned because it 'involved a desertion of John and Kate at this juncture that I did not care to inflict on them'. Instead she decided to make a go of keeping the school open.

Adding to her sense of isolation, Griffin Barry left for the States shortly before the deed was signed, leaving Harriet and Roderick in Dora's care. Prevented by the deed from living with Dora, there was little to keep Griffin in England, and he thus went to New York, where there was a greater chance of finding work. There he shared a house on East 53rd Street with the famous literary critic, Edmund Wilson (Wilson's fame was not so great then as it became later, though *Axel's Castle*, the book that established his reputation, had been published in 1931). In his diaries of the period, Wilson complains that Griffin 'drove me crazy' with his incessant talk of Dora and his 'unctuous old woman's voice'. Griffin was, Wilson thought: 'Exactly like a woman, and yet not exactly like a fairy.' He was also shocked when Griffin once remarked that 'when a Jew insulted you at the opera in Russia, you understood Hitler's anti-Semitism'. However, in a letter to their mutual friend, John Dos Passos, Wilson spoke more kindly of his housemate, reporting that 'Griffin and I are quietly working along here toward a better understanding between classes and nations, but with results increasingly disappointing', and that they thought seriously of turning their flat into a 'home for unmarried fathers – one of the most pathetic and helpless types produced by our modern civilisation and one for whom society has yet done nothing to provide'.

While he canvassed all the old friends he could think of for a job on a newspaper or magazine, Griffin wrote regularly to Dora, asking after Harriet and Roderick and giving her sympathetic advice on how to deal with Russell. On the whole, his advice was perceptive. For example, warning Dora not to keep attacking Peter in her letters to Russell, he counselled that, though 'it may, just possibly, give him some clue to your motives he hasn't thought of already or appeal to his odd sense of justice', such a thing was really unlikely:

> because the whole delicate shaky structure of his self-respect and his daily happiness depends on not thinking her a bitch. I'm sure the outburst shouldn't be repeated because it would be set down to female jealousy; and B will recast again in his mind his own version of his relations with you, and be cruel, under the subtle disguises of which he is capable.

Griffin annoyed Dora by encouraging her to go ahead with the divorce and by assuming that, if she did, he, she, Harriet and Roderick would live together as a family. In Dora's mind, this meant that Griffin, along with Russell and Peter, had reneged on the new morality and the 'pact of Hendaye'. Somewhat unfairly, she tended to treat him as if he were involved in some sort of conspiracy with Russell and Peter to rob her of John and Kate. In his letters, Griffin thus had to reassure her that he *knew* that 'you never meant to break your marriage and that you love him' and that Dora must not get the divorce 'or anything at the price of abandoning John and Kate'. 'More than you think', he told her, 'I know what you are going through, and have all along.' Of course, he added, he was sorry for Russell as well: 'poor fellow; he has looked bleakly into so bleak a world so long. Ours is as painful as spikes, but not so bleak. Think of having to rely seriously on Peter.'

Because Griffin's attitude towards her was more understanding and sympathetic than Russell's, Dora felt able to express to him the full force of the anger she was experiencing at the betrayal of her principles, represented by the legal manoeuvres in which she had now become reluctantly embroiled. On 20 January 1933, she sent him a stinging letter – 'a magnificent letter, full of temper and hate and love', as Griffin described it – attacking him, Russell, Peter and the whole rotten situation. 'I'd rather do it by love than by law on both sides,' Dora wrote, '& that's my whole case – that the way of love has been discarded . . . Don't see why we shouldn't sleep & copulate as we damn well please without economic and emotional slavery to follow.' So impressed was he by this letter that Griffin had extracts of it typed out and sent them to Russell, 'for', he explained, 'it seems to me that you cannot be aware of how she is feeling'. He urged Russell to take a different attitude and to try to understand, not only what Dora wanted in law, but how she *felt*:

With the attempt last year to take away from Dora mutual control with you of John and Kate, an incurable (as she thinks now) antagonism to Peter began . . . Loneliness, overwork and grief over the spiritual breach with you have done the rest. Now our relation seems drifting toward bitterness, for all I can do. It always depended very greatly on her not thinking her marriage with you a failure. Or on your affection and esteem for her, quite simply.

In all this I think you have a responsibility, undertaken in 1920 toward Dora herself . . . Certainly I . . . had reason to believe your notion of responsibility very different from all I can gather of it since I talked with you last.

. . . As to Dora's central attitude, I would care far, far less than I do for her if her continuity of feeling from you and your children to me and mine could be broken easily; and anyhow it can't. I've never tried, either.

It was in reply to this letter that Russell wrote the icy remark quoted earlier: 'Dora speaks of the spiritual relation between her and me. She destroyed this in 1927. Since then I have not liked her, and I stuck to her only for the sake of John and Kate.' His life with Dora, he told Griffin, had been 'intolerably unhappy' since then, and, now that he wished to have children with Peter:

I could not put up with a situation in which our children would be bastards while hers would be legally mine. (You can do nothing to prevent Roderick sitting in the House of Lords if he wishes to and if John dies childless.) What Dora calls her 'higher morality' is one that gave her all she wanted at the cost of misery for you and Peter and me.

Somewhat tactlessly, Griffin forwarded this letter to Dora, interpreting Russell's 'dislike' for her as having to do, not with Roy Randall, but with himself. The main cause of it, he felt sure, was Dora's decision to have children with him, which Russell 'by reason of his peculiar pride, which is ancestral and hag-ridden but real and quite evident . . . simply couldn't bear':

He *was like that*; you had loved him for seven years and slept with him nightly and been honoured as his wife and been glad to have his children; and I think you knew in your heart how you could hurt him most, and did. Well, he 'dislikes' you for it. What he really 'dislikes' was the end of your love for him; he knew it was the end of love because you were using recklessly your capacity to hurt him – not to hurt the sort of man he ought to have been, but the man he was. If you didn't know the latter, who should? And what right had you to hurt him for not being the man he ought to be? We're all dependent, in the beloved, on an image of ourselves better than the reality.

To Russell himself, Griffin wrote that his stated 'dislike' of Dora was something 'I simply cannot comprehend a serious man continuing who ever cared enough about a woman to marry her and want her to have his children.' He also reminded Russell that, with regard to Dora, 'you are still deepest in her heart'. Dora, he insisted, had both Russell's interests and those of John and Kate at heart, and, if Russell wanted a mutual arrangement rather than revenge, he could get it by discussing the situation with Dora, rather than through the law. 'Otherwise, of course she will fight, to the degradation of us all. If she has to fight, I hope she wins.'

Russell professed himself baffled by this. Had he not handed over a part-share of the legal rights over John and Kate that were his alone in law? Had he not treated Dora fairly over finance? The root cause of Dora's complaint, of course, was that Russell no longer treated her as a person, that he refused to meet her to discuss the development and future of their children, that he suddenly seemed entirely indifferent to her happiness and well-being. On these things, however, Russell was immovable: Dora had caused him great misery for years, and now that he had found happiness with Peter, he wanted as little to do with Dora as possible. Increasingly, his only contact with her was through his lawyers, who sent Dora letter after letter demanding to know when she was willing to vacate Telegraph House, what plans she had made about John and Kate leaving Beacon Hill and attending another school, and so on. Dora became increasingly hostile to the whole business and either refused to answer these letters or gave evasive replies to them. At every turn she thus angered and exasperated Russell and Crompton by her refusal to discuss things in a level-headed, legal fashion. Several times she considered abandoning altogether the plan to give Russell the divorce he wanted. She stuck to it mainly because she was advised by her solicitor, Mr Maw, that if she were granted a divorce from Russell she would most likely also be given custody of John and Kate. Russell, meanwhile, assumed that the 'equal rights' clause in the Deed of Separation meant that, when Dora filed for divorce, she would ask only for joint custody.

Things might have gone Dora's way on this question had she not, in 1933, developed an inexplicable and, as it turned out, self-destructive passion for the enigmatic Paul Gillard, who, shadowy and mysterious though he remains, played a decisive role in the way the divorce was conducted. Gillard had a habit of turning up at critical moments. In April 1932, for example, when Russell had just left Telegraph House, he appeared there unannounced and, according to Dora, seemed shocked at the arrival of Roderick. Dora interpreted this as a sign of what she imagined to be Gillard's love for her, though it seems equally likely that it had to do with his feelings for Griffin and his erstwhile hopes that he and Griffin would escape to Paris together. Then, the following September, Gillard turned up at Carn Voel, apparently under the impression that he would find Dora and Griffin there. Instead, he found Russell, Peter, John and Kate. 'Bertie was very charming,' he reported to Dora, both of them still clearly oblivious of Russell's detestation of him.

Gillard had recently lost his job as an accountant with Russian Oil

Products, and he was now living with his parents in Plymouth, writing an autobiographical novel called *One May Smile*, having given up any further attempts to find work as a bank clerk or accountant. Dora's claim that Gillard had a 'deep reverence for Bertie' is to some extent confirmed by the novel, from which more can be gleaned about Gillard's personality and opinions than from any other surviving record. Russell appears in the novel as 'Basil Hoare' (a name chosen, one supposes, for its allusion to Sir Samuel Hoare, the MP who defeated Russell twice at the polls, but perhaps also a pun on 'whore' was intended). The central character of the novel, the Gillard figure, George Burnell, is introduced to Basil Hoare by Ruth Warne, a character modelled on Dora. 'Poor old Basil!' Ruth remarks. 'He's cracking up I'm afraid . . . he really is disillusioned. Everything seems to have been as much against him personally as against his opinions. He spent the greater part of his private money on the various movements with which he is connected; so that, now, he has to live on about two pounds a week and whatever he can rake in by hack-work of one kind and another.' George, however, admires Hoare, chiefly for his intellectual integrity, which, he sees, is achieved at the price of political and personal isolation:

> George could divine how Basil had lost friends. The ordinary mildness of his manners gave no indication of the trenchant bitterness of which he was capable when analysing the motives of political turncoats. For all his gloom and disillusionment, cynicism of the time-serving kind had always been hateful to Basil – as hateful as the intellectual dishonesty which he regarded as the sovereign crime.
>
> Basil was no more popular with the younger generation than he was with the renegades. There was no doubt that he could be very depressing company, but George was of the opinion that his unpopularity was mainly due to the manifest delight that he took in destroying easy optimism or shallow enthusiasm.

Gillard then puts some authentic-sounding phrases in the mouth of his Russell character, phrases that may have come directly from his conversations with Russell in Cornwall. 'To my mind,' Basil tells George, 'the raucous optimism and "out to win" hysteria of these times is a recrudescence of barbarism. It is obvious to me that the great achievement of civilisation on the intellectual plane was philosophical pessimism. Optimism in the crude sense became irreconcilable with the extended knowledge of the universe. The sublimity of human destiny was a belief which could no longer be held by intelligent men; and with it went all the extravagant hopes for the eventual triumph of the human race.' George, Gillard writes, 'could not but admire the way in which Basil faced up to the barren conclusion to which his own pitiless logic led him; for he guessed what renunciations were implied in his abandonment of comfortable illusions'. Rather perceptively, he describes Russell/Hoare as 'thrown back against the steel grille of the future':

in actual fact sick at heart, but trying bravely to overcome his dread of its coldness and hardness, to create a new Utopia, in which godlike creatures – culminations of the study of Eugenics, Vitamins and Behaviourism – would move gracefully against a background of gleaming, beautifully-proportioned metal shapes.

Most of this might have been obtained from reading Russell's published work, but Gillard also puts into Hoare's mouth a remark about economics that, though it sounds as if it *should* be an actual quote from Russell, does not, as far as I know, appear in any of his work. Economics, Hoare says, 'has the same kind of claim to exactitude as heraldry... The science of economics is like a short-sighted geologist who, finding a Greek statue in a cave, mistakes it for a stalagmite, and attempts to find a reason for its curious shape in a peculiar quality of the local Jurassic formation.'

Dora, in describing Gillard's novel, says that it tells 'something of his relation with the Communist Party'. What she does not say is that the novel describes 'George' becoming involved in Communist Party intrigues, not because he was committed to the cause, but because he liked intrigue for its own sake and because he fell in love with a fiery Communist Party activist called 'Albert'. George in the novel, like Gillard in real life, *hated* being ordinary. He is described as being 'only happy when he was playing a game of make-believe with himself'. Usually these games involved pretending to be grander than he was, convincing people that he was not a mere bank clerk, but, say, a member of the landed gentry. His involvement in the Communist Party was an extension of these games.

In a passage that might reveal something of what Gillard and Russell talked about at Carn Voel – and also throw some light on why Russell despised him so much – *One May Smile* contains this intriguing account of George's frustrated attempt to get Hoare to discuss matters of sexual intimacy:

Basil was a man who lived entirely in books... A similar inconsequence characterised his emotional and sexual life. One of the first to acclaim the psycho-analysts and the behaviourists, he had never conquered a Victorian bashfulness in speaking of his own, most innocent, psychological experiences, although some of his objective writing on these subjects had caused storms of protest from the supporters of conventional morality. George had discovered this strange cleavage when, thinking that Basil might be a sympathetic counsellor, he had started to ask his advice on certain personal problems. Basil's discomfiture, his blushing, and his haste to change the subject surprised George beyond measure and he had been careful, since, to avoid topics which might cause such embarrassment.

The novel is one of self-discovery, chronicling George's gradual acceptance of the fact that he is homosexual. An early scene has him getting drunk in a pub 'which, in a less exalted mood, he would have found merely squalid' and achieving with a sailor 'the intimacy which is only possible between entire strangers'. His brief affair with Ruth Warne (Dora) is dealt with as one stage towards his realisation that it is with men – and, in particular, with 'Gregory' (Griffin Barry) – that George finds romantic fulfilment. It is surely in connection with this realisation that we are to imagine George raising 'personal problems' in his conversation with Hoare, and one can easily imagine the blushing, discomfort and haste to change the subject that would have met Gillard if he had, similarly, tried to discuss his homosexuality with Russell.

At the beginning of March 1933, after he had finished the novel, Gillard once more got in touch with Dora, asking her advice on launching a literary career for himself and sending her an essay he had written called 'The New Honesty'. 'Quite frankly,' he asked her, 'do you think that I can make the grade?' Dora thought he might, and, on her advice, he sent his novel to the Woolfs' Hogarth Press. It was evidently turned down, however, and he seems to have made no further efforts to publish it. For the moment, he abandoned his literary ambitions, but his approach to Dora was to change both their lives. His letter arrived just as Dora was about to leave for Cornwall for the Easter holidays. Russell and Peter had decided that they did not, after all, want to live permanently at Carn Voel ('since the Cornish climate gives Peter rheumatism,' Russell explained to Dora), and had moved out at the end of 1932 to live in a flat in Emperor's Gate, London, where John and Kate spent that Easter holiday. Harriet and Roderick, meanwhile, went to New York – accompanied by Dora's housekeeper and faithful servant, Lily Howell ('Our Lil') – to stay with Griffin. It seemed an opportune moment for Dora to pursue her long-standing interest in Gillard, and she invited him to spend the holiday with her at Carn Voel.

In Cornwall, Dora says, she was able to talk to Gillard 'about Griffin and all my personal affairs, my doubts about the divorce, my indecision as to the whole future'. 'This is what I badly needed,' she recalled, 'someone who saw eye to eye with me about moral issues and human values and thus could really help with advice.' Gillard's advice was for her to forget the divorce and try to get back with Russell, advice that Dora interpreted as arising out of Gillard's reverence for Russell and 'a romantic idea that we ought to save Bertie from himself and for the world'. One might also imagine that it arose out of Gillard's desire to separate Dora from Griffin, and, certainly, that was its effect. After the holiday, Dora invited Gillard to work as her secretary at the school. After some hesitation on his part and further persuasion from her, he accepted and spent the summer term at Telegraph House. During this time, Dora's attitude to Griffin hardened considerably, and she did, in fact, make some attempt to call the divorce off and persuade Russell to come back to her.

Griffin, meanwhile, having given nothing but support and sympathy to Dora, was rather puzzled by her new attitude. Since the New Year of 1933, things had been going well for him in New York. In January, he was appointed foreign editor of the recently established magazine *Newsweek*, and, momentarily, he regained his belief in himself, his relationship with

Dora and his ability to provide for Harriet and Roderick. Having his children with him for Easter was a great pleasure for him, and he imagined that it would be a taste of things to come after Dora's divorce from Russell. For a while, all looked well. It was an exciting time to be a foreign editor, and, living with Wilson, he was mixing with the élite of New York's literary society. In May, he recorded an odd and intriguing encounter with T. S. Eliot, who, while lecturing in New York, was staying with Wilson. 'I have been talking to him about Bertie,' Griffin wrote to Dora. 'His tone was a tone I've heard you use – great affection, but he thinks B a tragic divided person.' Eliot knew nothing about Griffin's relationship with Dora, and Griffin knew nothing about Russell's past affair with Vivien. Nor, while discussing Russell's marital problems, did Eliot tell Griffin that he was then separated from Vivien and intended to leave her for good. 'I told him you and B are separated,' Griffin told Dora, 'to which he said reflectively "Well, it's probably Bertie's fault. I think of him as the most sadly frustrated man I know. But very highly endowed – so much more so than Whitehead who has made a better career. As he grows older I observe inherited family patterns are taking the place of the clear flashes of insight he used to have. What a waste." Eliot is a gentle reactionary himself.'

A month later, Griffin lost his job, and Dora began writing to him that she had lost faith in him as a husband and as a provider for their children. She was, she told him brutally, 'through' with him and was looking elsewhere. Griffin was as bewildered as he was hurt. 'You intimate you are looking for another man,' he wrote. 'If he lives with you, this means another father for my children . . . It is all a queer, queer history. I don't understand you . . . Whatever course you take I am going to England as soon as I can.'

Dora was by this time – to the dismay of many of her staff at Beacon Hill – deeply (perhaps, in a literal sense, madly) in love with Gillard, whom she idealised as 'a man in whom mind and body were in harmony, a whole man, such as I had dreamed and written about and who was, in my knowledge, rare in our world of false masculine values'. As the term wore on, she writes, 'and we did the work that we shared side by side, there grew between us a new companionship, a certainty that neither of us was any longer alone'. She told Griffin that she had employed Gillard, but not that she had fallen in love with him. 'Darling,' Griffin wrote, 'I'm glad Paul stayed with you and was of help. How funny that you think I might be jealous':

> I have so identified you with myself, feel so married and at one with you . . . that I would not suspect you of infidelities unless I had committed them myself and I have committed none, nor could (of course I'm not talking about mere copulation, but with me that temptation is lacking too). I liked Paul at first because I thought he might be a brave fellow trying to write and think his way out of the fate of young Englishmen in his situation but I didn't like his hysteria later nor his feeble attempt to make trouble between you and me.

Some months later, still in ignorance of Dora's love for Gillard, but

distraught at her tendency to write to him only of what *she* intended to do in
the future, and never of their plans together, Griffin hit out: 'As a free lover
you seemed familiar to me and got children from me because I was at home
with you. But as a creature now willing to destroy all between us, including
depriving the children of me and me of them for the sake of a marriage that
is dead, you are a stranger and a little hideous.'

Paul Gillard was the one person in the world, apart from Dora herself,
who could not see that her marriage to Russell *was* dead, and this no doubt
was part of the comfort she took in his company. Encouraged by Gillard, by
the summer of 1933, Dora had begun to persuade herself that her marriage
to Russell might be rescued after all. She had already extracted from him,
somewhat against his better wishes, a promise that John and Kate could stay
at Beacon Hill for another year, and that the school could continue to use
Telegraph House for that year (albeit at a rent – £400 – that was exactly
equal to the annuity Russell paid her). The summer term ended with an
Open Day for the parents, which Russell, much to Dora's delight, attended.
Gillard played a prominent part in the event, helping Dora to meet the
parents and show them around the school. He also marked the occasion with
an odd 'prank'. Up in the tower room, Russell's former study, Dora found
that Gillard had turned all the pictures of Russell's 'spiritual and temporal
ancestors' round to face the wall. 'I thought that you admired and respected
the great philosopher,' she said to him. 'So I do, indeed,' Gillard said, and
went away laughing.

Shortly afterwards, John and Kate went to stay with Russell, while
Harriet and Roderick again left for New York to stay with Griffin, leaving
Dora alone for a few days with Gillard, before he left for Plymouth and she
for Cornwall. During this time, encouraged by Gillard, Dora made a
desperate and, under the circumstances, rather bizarre attempt to woo
Russell back. On 18 July, she wrote telling him: 'I hate this whole
performance more every day.' At the Open Day, she said, she thought
Russell had looked 'ill and unhappy, too':

> It's very bad for John to have us apart. I wish you'd come back again. We
> could practically live by the school now, or else close it and get on very
> simply here. I shall never be able to think of either of us in any serious
> relation to anyone else, and indeed I never have.

When Russell replied that he had no intention of putting himself through
yet more misery by returning to her, Dora tried another tack: if he would
not do it for himself, would he not do it for the sake of her, John and Kate?

> I can understand that now you can feel no advantage to yourself in
> coming back to live with me. The only reason for it could be that you
> cared somewhat for my happiness and welfare and that of the children. It
> is very strange to me that you should look at everything from the point of
> view of your own immediate happiness, I have never looked upon love
> relations in this way.

Besides, Dora added, was Russell really expecting her to believe that everything he had told her about his beliefs and his attitude to her during the last five years of their marriage had been untrue?

You complain that you were unhappy with me, but you always led me to suppose that the liberty you had and the way we lived was what you wanted and believed in, and that our relation should always come first. Three weeks before you went away with Peter, you wrote to me that you looked on her only as an economic and emotional liability.

'Nobody has ever mattered to me as you and John and Kate do,' Dora insisted. 'To me love is not only sex and enjoyment, it is something more abiding and enduring. In this sense I have loved only you, and cannot love anyone else.' His relationship with Peter could not last, she told him: 'because she is too young; and I love you and want to take care of you. This fact has put me at a disadvantage all the while in our negotiations. I tried to think of life alone or a relation to someone else, but both are impossible':

I want our life together and for me it is not too late for that. The loss of it gets worse instead of better as time goes on. Otherwise I have nothing but the school, and to that you are hostile, apparently, except in so far as it pays your rent and rates and upkeep here ... You have become my enemy, whom I looked upon as forever my dearest friend. I do not see how either of us can be happy in this situation. I cannot, and can only wish I were not healthy, so that I might soon be dead, for that would resolve things for everyone.

When this plea fell, as it was bound to, on deaf ears, Dora – desperate for *someone* to love and cherish her – became fixated with the idea that Paul Gillard was her ideal companion and even that, after she had divorced Russell, she and Gillard might get married. She had always idealised Gillard; now she began to mythologise him, and built around him and their relationship a romantic picture that was, as far as one can judge, almost entirely at variance with the facts. In her eyes, Gillard now became the equal of Russell, a hero of the working-class movement, a man who 'fully expected to die through his involvement in the political struggle', heroically engaged in some kind of dangerous and covert activity, the details of which he was too gallant to disclose to her.

Whether this was a *complete* fantasy or not is difficult to tell. Gillard's novel suggests no great love of either the working class or Communism, and both it and his letters to Dora suggest that he was really not very interested in politics at all. What he was interested in was *intrigue* and, most of all perhaps, in being considered intriguing. The indications are that Gillard had been, in the late 1920s, involved in some kind of undercover work for the Communist Party, and, given that he had been employed in Plymouth, London and Bristol – all important military ports – the best guess as to what this might have been is that he kept an eye on the movements of military ships. Other than this, it is difficult to see how he could have had access to any information likely to be of interest to the Third International. On the other hand, it is very easy to see how he might have been of some use to the British secret service. The National Unemployed Workers' Movement, with which he had been involved before he met Dora, was an organisation obsessed with espionage. As a movement led by the Communists, it was kept under extensive surveillance by the British security services – which is why, presumably, Gillard was a 'known Communist' at the time of Griffin's attempted departure for Paris in the summer of 1930 – and its leaders became intensely, and justifiably, suspicious of having spies in their midst. People suspected of spying were labelled 'unreliable', and, as Wal Hannington grimly records in his autobiography, the consequences of being thought 'unreliable' by the NUWM were often dire. Gillard was suspected of unreliability in this respect, and it seems possible that – perhaps frightened by his experiences of 1930 – he was acting for the British Government as an inside informant on the leadership and activities of the NUWM.

All this, of course, is highly speculative, but where Gillard is concerned, speculation becomes unavoidable. The picture Dora painted of him – for which there is no evidence whatever, other than Gillard's strange behaviour while with her – is that he was the target of a concerted effort by Fascists to hunt him down and kill him. Why this should have been so, Dora does not explain, other than by saying: 'I guessed that he was involved in keeping a watch on fascist activity in Plymouth – they had a centre there in Lockyer Street.' In any case, Gillard dropped many dark hints that he might die soon, and appeared to be suspicious and anxious of any strangers who approached Telegraph House. The myth of Gillard as a martyr in the struggle against Fascism received strong confirmation in Dora's mind by an odd event that occurred towards the end of July 1933, just before Gillard was due to leave for Plymouth. One morning, Dora was told by Gillard that there had been a 'Fascist raid' on the school during the night. The red flag that Dora had earlier hung up on the flagpole was gone, and in its place was a Union Jack. Moreover, the front door and steps of Telegraph House were daubed with anti-Communist slogans, such as: 'Down with Zozo [Stalin], we have taken your bloody flag and left you ours'.

The most natural interpretation of this event is that it was the action of local right-wing patriots, incensed at the sight of the red flag flying over Telegraph House, but Gillard persuaded Dora that he, not the school, was the target of the attack. Dora accepted this, and 'wondered in what and how deeply Paul was involved, and whether the raid on the school might have been designed by his enemies to winkle him out'. The night after the 'raid', Gillard put broken glass on the back lane to Telegraph House and cut himself a stout stick, which he took with him to bed. A day or two later, he left for Plymouth, saying that it would be 'safer' for Dora if he was not with her. In a statement that she typed out after Gillard's death, Dora attributed this to his heroism: 'As I knew the high regard he had for the school and myself, and that he was a man of great courage, I can only suppose that he thought his departure was what would bring us immunity from further disturbance.'

One cannot help feeling that there is something phoney about Gillard's melodramatic reaction to this incident, something that resonates with his love of make-believe and his desire to appear to be something – anything – other than the obscure, unemployed bank clerk he was. When he returned to Plymouth, he played up to the hilt Dora's image of him as a Fascist-watcher, dwelling on the Fascist activity evident on the streets of the town, which was, he said, 'led by a rather good-looking obviously ex-army bloke'. His only claim to inside information, however, was the rather ludicrous allegation that Dartington School had fallen into the hands of Fascists. Dartington, a progressive school run by Dorothy and Leonard Elmhirst, had opened in 1932, financed by Dorothy Elmhirst's vast inherited wealth. In Russell's opinion, the competition from Dartington made it fruitless for Dora to continue with Beacon Hill, and he had already indicated his wish that John and Kate, when they left Beacon Hill in the summer of 1934, should transfer to Dartington. To advise Dora on this question, Gillard reported: 'I have fairly definite proof that Dartington is being run by a Fascist nucleus – which boasts of putting across Fascist teaching in the School. This I think is the ground on which BR should be opposed in [his] project of sending kids there.' His 'definite proof' turned out to be the word of 'one of the chief blokes in the Plymouth blackshirt stunt', who was 'an ex-employee of Staveston Builders (the subsidiary of DH)' and who 'says that the whole concern is F[ascist] & that the Elmhirsts themselves are not unsympathetic'. In letters to Russell, Dora repeated these charges (without giving their source) and, as Gillard suggested, made them the basis of her opposition to the transfer of John and Kate to Dartington. To Russell, this simply provided further evidence that Dora was going insane.

There is indeed something deeply delusional about Dora's state of mind during this time. Gillard's letters to her are *not* love letters, and there is no indication whatever that he was interested in Dora romantically. On the contrary, there are plenty of indications that he wanted to shake her off. Having used the 'raid' on Telegraph House as a respectable, even glamorous, reason for leaving her, he could not be persuaded to come back to the school for the following term, nor did he invite her to his home in Plymouth. Nevertheless, within a few days of his departure, Dora – who could hardly drive at this time – got in her Austin Seven and made the 'terrifying journey' down to Plymouth, in order, she implies, to rescue him from the Fascist threat that hung over him. She remained there for three weeks, staying at a hotel and seeing Gillard every day. They talked about the school, and about Griffin. 'He was convinced', Dora recalls, 'that I could never settle down to a partnership with Griffin, he wondered if it would not have been better for Griffin himself if he had died when he was so ill, "he would have made a good exit, then".' Gillard also dwelt on the imminence of his own death, and added to the mystery of his covert activities by telling Dora that two young workers who passed them on the street and smiled at him were his 'bodyguard'.

Dora could not get him off her mind, and, when she returned to school for the autumn term, she urged him to come back with her. Several times he refused. Then, towards the end of October, Dora once more invited herself down to Plymouth. This time she stayed for a few days with Gillard's family, and remembers Gillard as being edgy and uncommunicative. He did not respond to her suggestion that they go abroad together and seemed altogether remote. 'I could not seem to get near him,' Dora wrote. 'I did not believe that he was the kind of person to retreat from his declared love for me; I inferred that perhaps he was scared of committing himself irrevocably to intimate love with a woman.' Once, when they were in a pub, Gillard got up suddenly as two men walked in and, urging Dora to come along, left the pub quickly. Dora thought they might be part of a police surveillance operation against Gillard, but 'he did not confide in me, I felt helpless'. She again tried to get Gillard to return to Beacon Hill, and again he refused. A few days after she returned to Telegraph House, she received a letter from his father saying that Paul had been found dead by the side of a railway line.

If Dora was half-crazy in her love for Gillard, in her grief for him she went completely over the edge and suffered what she herself later described as a 'nervous breakdown' from which she did not recover for about six months, by which time she discovered that the tables had been turned against her in her hopes of getting custody of John and Kate. During those months she was in a state of delirium in which nothing mattered to her, except her sorrow and anger at the death of the man she loved. Neglecting her family and her school, she could think only of her beloved Paul, about how and why he had died, whether she could have saved him, how happy she would have been had he not died, and so on. Her first reaction on hearing of his death was to head for Plymouth, where she was told that he had met an accidental death. The medical cause of death was suffocation, and the verdict of the inquest was that, coming home from drinking in a local pub, he had sat on a wall on a bridge over the railway, and, perhaps drunk, had fallen on to the embankment below, where he landed awkwardly and suffocated himself.

Dora did not believe it. She was convinced he had been murdered by Fascists. She went to see the body and saw cuts on Paul's face that had not been reported at the inquest. Then she made further inquiries and discovered contradictions in the statements of witnesses who had seen Paul on the night of his death. What everyone agreed was that he had been to the local gymnasium, which he used to frequent regularly, met some friends of his there – who were both homosexual and Fascist – and had then gone for a drink with them. Accounts differ as to what happened after he had left the pub. The landlord of the pub said that Gillard left sober, having had only one drink. One of his drinking partners said that he was incapably drunk. One passer-by saw him running away from his friends at great speed, obviously frightened. Another said she saw him staggering towards the railway bridge, so drunk he could hardly stand up. The policeman who was called first to the scene said that he was lying face down with his arms under him and that out of his mouth came liquid smelling strongly of alcohol. The local woman who, after seeing his dead body, had called the police said that his right arm was bent behind his back, and the doctor who examined him found no trace of alcohol. Gillard's father, evidently fearing that, if Dora made more investigations she would uncover some unsavoury details of his son's way of life, pleaded with her to accept the official verdict and to inquire no more. The cuts she had seen on Gillard's face, however, persuaded Dora that the official verdict was wrong, and, after discounting the idea that Gillard had committed suicide,[8] she remained convinced that he had been the victim of a political killing.

Gillard's death remained a haunting mystery for the rest of Dora's life. At various times she tried to find evidence that he had been murdered, but found only more contradictions and more mysteries. In her imagination, her brief affair with Gillard – which, in truth, had hardly begun and which Gillard had shown no sign of wanting to continue – became the great love of her life. When she returned to Telegraph House, the staff became worried that she *had*, finally, gone mad. The anguished cry 'My darling Paul!' was heard day and night, and Dora took little interest in the running of the school or in anything else. When Roderick fell out of a window, Dora scarcely bothered to inquire whether he was all right. John became distressed at his mother's state and, at the age of twelve, alarmed his teachers by lapsing into baby-talk. 'Night after night', Dora recalled, 'I lay awake talking to Paul in a kind of delirium.' She took to spending most of her time in London – 'the school was certainly better without me' – where she met with friends who were able to comfort her in her grief.

Dora says she has no recollection at all of that Christmas, and it is possible that she had no recollection either of writing a long, anguished

---

[8] It is tempting to imagine that Gillard intended to kill himself by throwing himself under a train, but, if so, he chose the wrong line. The railway beside which his body was found was a tiny goods-only line on which trains ran only during the day, and even then too slowly to kill anyone. Gillard's house – near where he died – stood right next to the main Plymouth–London line, where high-speed trains ran all night. If he had wanted to throw himself under a train, he would have done better to wait until he got home. One possibility that Dora did not consider is that Gillard had been the victim of a political killing by the left rather than the right. There is, however, much to be said for this theory. Gillard was deeply distrusted by his former colleagues in the Communist Party, and, in the years immediately before his death, mixed much more with Fascists than with Communists. In a letter to Dora a few weeks before he died, Gillard recounts a visit he had from Wal Hannington himself. He and Hannington, he said, had a 'nearly night-long argument', in which Hannington had urged him to return to the Communist Party, offering him, as an inducement, a job in the Soviet Union. Gillard had refused, and said that Hannington was 'obviously shocked . . . when I went on to explain how I felt about things. He will probably tell everybody now that I am definitely a renegade &, even if I wanted to rejoin the CP, they probably wouldn't have me.' Why did Hannington – a powerful figure on the extreme left of British politics – think it worth his while to journey down to Plymouth and spend all night talking to Gillard? One possibility, I think, is that Hannington suspected Gillard of being the 'mole' in the NUWM that the organisation at this time was convinced existed and was determined to uncover. The fact that Gillard spent so much time in Plymouth in the company of Fascists suggests that he had little to fear from them, and it seems possible that his fear of being followed, and his conviction that he would be killed, arose out of the evident suspicion in which he was held by the NUWM and the Communist Party. However, Gillard's life and death are so enmeshed in mystery and contradiction that one feels almost *anything* is possible – including the truth of the official verdict on his death.

letter to Russell dated 4 November, just three days after she heard of Gillard's death and immediately after she returned to Telegraph House from Plymouth. That letter, however, was a critical turning point in the divorce and might well have cost her the custody of her children, which she had hoped to obtain from it. The letter is a passionate and moving cry of pain and grief, obviously written without regard to the consequences and in ignorance of Russell's fierce dislike of Gillard. Paul's death, she told Russell, may have been suicide or 'It may have been a political attack, or a sex crime against him.' With astonishing recklessness and confidence in Russell's goodwill, she went on:

> You will wonder why I write all this to you. It is because I loved Paul, and either directly or indirectly by unconscious failure to save himself, he died for me. And for you, too, because he always hoped we would come together again. In his wallet were some old letters of yours he must have got when here.[9]
>
> ... I loved Paul when I first saw him, before Harriet was born. But I had heard he was homosexual and devoted to communism and a free bohemian life and I did not suppose I could have any meaning for him. As you know I believed him attracted to Griffin. But I did not know until this summer term that he loved me better than anything in the world ... He would not try living with me, because of the legal situation and in no other way could he have found out whether his homosexuality was permanent – I am quite clear that it was not, and that Paul and I were made for each other. But he would neither let me divorce you nor live with him, because he had no money to protect me from the consequences of the divorce, or the possible consequences of breaking the terms of the deed of separation – But chiefly he believed that I loved you still, that our separation was a calamity to ourselves and the public and that a divorce would create more despair and fascism and turn you into a reactionary ... He always said 'Give it time'.
>
> ... Do not think this was a momentary thing – I had the same sort of fatalistic feeling towards Paul when I first saw him four years ago, as I had towards you two years before you thought of marrying me ... Paul was you young, as you might have been if born of his generation. I think he knew this and he identified himself with you, feeling he could never supplant you until after your death.

Dora had still not learnt, apparently, what cold anger and jealousy she aroused in Russell by writing to him that she was in love with other men. As soon as he received Dora's letter, Russell, without answering it, had it typed

---

[9] One of the oddest things about Gillard's death is that in his jacket when he died were found some letters from Joseph Conrad to Russell that he obviously stole from the tower room in Telegraph House. Why did he steal them? Dora interpreted it as a sign of his 'reverence' for Russell; Russell thought that Gillard hoped to sell them. Either or both might be possible. Certainly, Gillard would have known of Russell's reverence for Conrad and that these letters were among his most prized possessions – and not for their monetary value.

by Peter and then sent the typed copy and the original to Crompton, together with a terse letter, saying: 'Please keep the original, which may some day be useful to us . . . I want your advice as to how to answer it, as I do not wish to lose any advantages to be derived from it.'

Crompton's advice was to 'take no notice of Dora's outburst' and to reply only to the parts of the letter that mentioned John and Kate. 'I think your advice is excellent,' Russell told him. 'I am glad you are hopeful about ultimate control of the children.' In a later letter, Crompton indicated one use to which Dora's letter could be put. 'If there is a breakdown of the equal rights agreement,' he advised, 'and if she were to ask any tribunal to hand over the children to her at some new school, we would produce her recent letter.'

Heedless of the hole she was digging for herself, but conscious of a new, firmer line from Crompton and Russell with regard to the children's schooling, Dora wrote to both of them on 11 January 1934 in the same uninhibited way about her feelings towards Gillard. 'I have never pretended to objectivity in my views on this question of the children,' she told them. 'I love them and want them with me.' Russell ought to care less about the children; after all 'He no longer cared much for the school work, and he has made a life which he finds happiness in, at the same time placing me in a situation in which it was not possible for me to do the same.' Her only chance of happiness was gone:

> Paul Gillard, who loved me hopelessly for four years, and is the only man I have ever completely loved or with whom I had a real chance of the full happiness of marriage, felt chivalrously towards Bertie as I and others did. His death is chargeable to Bertie's ruthlessness and present lack of understanding of the problems or needs of younger people than himself. Bertie used to belong in our world and this is why we loved him. But he has robbed me of everything.
>
> . . . I have lost the only human being who was seriously concerned for my happiness, but I cannot die, since I have the younger children. I explain my position, in order that it should be clear to you that I cannot now act except in regard to my own interests and those of the children. And I have little faith in Bertie's judgment in regard to them, especially as regards the problems that may arise in their adolescence, after what I have seen of his character in the past year.

Blinding themselves to the palpable hurt, disillusion and grief in these letters, Crompton and Russell saw in them only some careless confessions and the manifest contradiction between Dora's claim now that Gillard was the only man she had ever completely loved and her declaration of July that *Russell* was the only man she could ever love. In a letter to Crompton of 25 January, Dora tried to explain. 'The tragedy that envelops this whole business is beyond words,' she began, admitting that it was, in a way, pointless even to try to make herself understood: 'You are Bertie's old friend and his lawyer, for you to understand my position was never easy, nor was it, since you were acting for him, I presume, correct. But it would have been humanly wise':

> As a person I loved my husband profoundly, he remained a sort of god to me up to the very day that he left me. His indifference to my own pain . . . was terribly hard to bear, especially as everything in our marriage had been a matter of mutual agreement, and on my side at least of the plainest honesty about my feelings.
>
> . . . I had endured a good deal previously, and was now asked by everyone to endure more and worse, for values that I felt were false ones, and likely to kill realities. All this has happened. But the worst thing of all happened to me, since the love I had for Paul who is dead was the supreme thing of my life, a companionship of thought and feeling unbelievably lovely to us both. And he died through my trying to go on fulfilling obligations to people who do not care for me at all. He was so tender of the children and of Bertie that it was he who wished me to ask Bertie once more to return, as he thought Bertie was not happy when he saw him here.
>
> . . . My own way out was perfectly clear this summer, but I did not take it because of the obligations I had undertaken. Had friendliness remained between Bertie and me it would have been possible to explain. But he has been revengeful and utterly unwilling to consider my position at all.

Even now Dora did not understand just how indifferent Russell was to her suffering, nor how devious he was prepared to be in dealing with her. In their disputes about transferring John and Kate from Beacon Hill to Dartington, Russell asked her to spell out exactly what her objection to Dartington was. This she did in a letter of 12 February 1934. Sensibly leaving aside Gillard's claim to have uncovered a Fascist nucleus at Dartington, Dora centred her objections on what she perceived to be the school's overly restrictive sexual morality. 'In later adolescence', she wrote, 'I think the children may be under some strain, for boys and girls will be living at close quarters; while the general tone of the school will be against sexual encounters . . . I think John and Kate will need care in adolescence, as they are both of them of rather indeterminate sex, and certain circumstances might tip them into actual or psychological abnormality.' Besides, she added, Dartington was too upper-class, and she would prefer John and Kate 'to be in contact with ordinary types of children'. She therefore favoured sending them to an ordinary day-school, while she looked after them at home. In this way, she would 'be able to make some sort of home for them in the years when they are passing examinations and arriving at sexual awakening, so that I could help relieve strain and really know what was going on'.

Russell was delighted by this, especially the part about sexual morality. 'In asking Dora to say why she thought Dartington bad for adolescents,' he told Crompton, 'I had a definite purpose, which was achieved. Her objections, as they stood, sounded very respectable and I did not wish to leave them unexplained. She now says (in the letter you have) that what is bad about it is not allowing sexual freedom. This would not be a good argument to put before a judge.' Russell now felt in a position to *insist* that John and Kate leave Beacon Hill and transfer to Dartington in the summer of 1934, and Dora, once more, had no option but to agree.

At the end of March, Dora finally filed her petition for divorce. As Crompton and Russell had long suspected, it included an appeal for custody of John and Kate. From this point the proceedings became extremely unpleasant. As Russell had told Crompton before the petition was filed: 'I will stick at nothing to prevent her getting sole custody.' Dora, he wrote, 'is slippery, & very wicked; we must be careful'. Because of their suspicions that she would ask for custody, Russell and Crompton had John and Kate made Wards of chancery court immediately *before* they received Dora's petition. This meant that any decision as to the custody of the children would be a matter, not just for the divorce court, but also for the chancery court. It thereby increased Russell's options, by allowing him to present to the chancery court evidence that Dora was not fit to have custody of the children without, in the process, jeopardising the divorce he badly wanted. Russell was in a difficult position: he wanted the divorce court to accept that Dora was a blameless wife who had been 'wronged' by her husband's adultery and so grant her a divorce from him. At the same time, he wanted the chancery court to hear all about Dora's past adulteries, her children by Griffin Barry and her strange affair with Paul Gillard, in order to decide that she was not fit to have sole custody of John and Kate. It says much for Crompton's abilities as a lawyer that he was able to steer this extremely complicated situation to the conclusion that Russell desired.

Crompton's success in this was achieved by adopting a relentlessly ruthless attitude towards Dora. In the process, Russell gave up treating her with even minimal courtesy. When writing to her, he did not begin 'Dear Dora', but 'Dear Madam', and when Dora delivered the children to him during the Easter holidays, she and he pretended not to see each other. Russell abandoned, too, any compunction about using John and Kate in his war against Dora. While they were with him over Easter he urged them to tell him anything that could be used against Dora in court. On 13 April, he wrote to Crompton that he had succeeded in getting 'a sudden burst of confidences' out of the children:

> They are both, but especially John, acutely unhappy at School. 'Betty' [Cross] . . . bosses the place and eggs on the bigger boys (whom she vamps) to make his life a misery. She also frequently says nasty things about both Peter and me, whom she calls 'some people whom I won't name' . . . Kate spoke on John's behalf almost more vehemently than he spoke for himself. They were both so wretched at the thought of returning that we invented a scheme for keeping them another fortnight.

Russell suggested to the children that they put their complaints about the school in writing in the form of letters to Dora, which they did, apparently without realising Russell's motives.

After the children had returned for what would be their last term at

Beacon Hill, Russell discovered that a number of employees and ex-employees of the school had become disenchanted with the place since Dora had brought Gillard there the previous year. Would it not be a good idea, he suggested to Crompton, to get statements from these people to add to Dora's own letters about Gillard, as evidence of her unfitness as a mother? Crompton agreed and at once secured a particularly poisonous statement from Mary Bailey, the ex-art teacher at the school. 'I took a dislike to Gillard immediately,' she wrote. 'He was tall and dark and Jew-like, with an effeminate appearance.' During the Christmas holidays of 1931, she revealed, while Russell was still away on his last US lecture tour, Gillard had visited the school and had taken Griffin out drinking, leaving Dora behind. After the Deed of Separation was signed, she said, Dora 'talked freely about her position. I understood that she valued the prestige of being Bertrand's wife, and she wanted to keep on the School, which was run on the money earned by him. She wanted to have all the advantages of being his wife, together with freedom to indulge her own sexual inclinations, and breed children. She spent money on Barry and Gillard, who had no means themselves.' When Gillard arrived at the school, he slept in the Cottage in the ground-floor room. Dora then moved out of the house and into the bedroom directly above Gillard's:

> While Dora and Gillard were occupying bedrooms in the Cottage they went out every evening, sometimes to a public house, the Royal Oak close to the School, and sometimes to the 'Ship' at Harting. On returning, Dora used to stay late in Gillard's ground floor room in the Cottage. They used to bring drink home, and we could hear them come home late and saw the beer bottles in the morning ... Towards the end of the Summer Term all the children were aware that something was going on between Dora and Gillard, and were grinning at them. One evening they gave a party at the Bungalow, which adjoins the House and is used for class rooms. Children got out of the House during the night and found drink in the Bungalow and drank it and were the worse for it. All the children, including John and Kate, knew that there was something up.

When Gillard died, Mary Bailey went on, 'Dora became hysterical, saying that Paul was the only man she had ever loved. She went about screaming up the stairs, crying out "My lovely Paul".' She had even heard gossip that Dora had become pregnant and had had an abortion, 'but what Betty says is not always to be believed'. Dora blamed the School staff for Gillard's death 'because our dislike of him had kept him from returning ... she brought back his mackintosh and hung it up in the hall with the gloves sticking out, and she wore his old sweaters, and said that she was keeping the rest of his clothes for John'. Mary Bailey and her fiancé (who also worked at the school) had given notice to leave Beacon Hill 'because Gillard was having such a bad effect on the place, causing Dora to be unpleasant to the servants and visitors, and because of the excessive drinking and the late hours which she kept and which gave her a bad temper'. The art teacher ended her statement with the fact that she and her fiancé 'have never been able to endure Gillard'.

In its venom towards Dora and Gillard, this statement exceeded the expectations of Crompton and Russell and, for a while, they considered using it as the basis for a counter-petition, in which Russell would sue Dora for *her* adulterous behaviour after the Deed of Separation had been signed. In the end, however, they decided against it. 'I should of course be glad if I could divorce Dora, instead of the other way round,' Russell told Crompton. 'But I should have thought that difficult. There is no evidence that Gillard liked her, so far as I can see; the advances seem to have been all on her side. Mary Bailey's statement is admirable as showing that Dora is not fit to have custody of the children, but seems barely adequate to prove adultery. Moreover, would it not be difficult for me, at this date, to begin to seem sufficiently virtuous?'

Instead they concentrated on gathering more dirt on Dora. From two more disaffected members of staff they got statements to back up Mary Bailey's claims that the school had become a centre of licentiousness and drunkenness. To these was added a long statement by Russell himself, detailing his grievances against Dora and claiming that 'The last time I visited the School (February 1934) I found everything incredibly dirty. The WC had an insanitary smell, which the children tell me it always has. The floor and walls everywhere were disgusting.' When this statement was later expanded into a formal affidavit for the chancery court, Russell dwelt further on Dora's infatuation with Paul Gillard, quoting from her letters to him, drawing attention to the contradiction between them and the letter she had written him the previous summer, and commenting: 'What disturbed me, however, far more than the knowledge that she had deceived me as to her attitude towards myself was my realisation of the state of affairs in which the children were and had been living at Beacon Hill.' On the basis of the evidence he had collected, Russell stated: 'I do not think . . . that Dora is or has been for the past year a fit person to look after the children, or that her influence upon them can be anything but detrimental.' In June, Russell and Crompton heard that Griffin Barry was back in England (he had come on a fruitless mission to rescue his relationship with Dora), and a private detective was despatched to Telegraph House to gather further evidence that Dora had broken her vow of chastity.

Of course, word reached Dora that these statements had been made, that detectives were snooping about asking questions about her, Gillard and Griffin, and, at first, she resolved to fight the chancery action and to stick to her claim for custody of John and Kate. She began gathering affidavits from members of staff loyal to her, but the legal expenses involved in carrying on this fight were beyond her, and she could see that she was fighting a losing battle. In a desperate attempt to find a sympathetic intermediary, Dora called unexpectedly on Ottoline Morrell at her home in Gower Street. Ottoline was out, so Dora wrote a short note asking for help and returned home. Ottoline at once wrote to Crompton asking for his advice on how to answer Dora's note. Her 'faithful maid Nelly', she told Crompton, had seen

Dora walking up and down Gower Street all day: 'Nelly said she looked "awful", very dirty. She thought she was a charwoman. Do tell me what is she up to? Poor woman.' Presumably following Crompton's advice, Ottoline wrote to Dora saying that in her view Russell should be given custody of John and Kate.

The threat facing Dora was this: if she went ahead with her divorce petition claiming custody, Russell would go ahead with his chancery action. Her letters about Gillard, and all the other damaging material that Russell and Crompton had gathered about her life at the school, would then be brought into the open and reported in the Press, and both she and Beacon Hill would face humiliation and ruin. This Russell spelt out in a letter of 20 June to Ted Lloyd, one of the trustees of the fund that Russell had set up for John and Kate with the money he had earnt in America. 'By a great expenditure of time and money and worry,' Russell explained, 'I am now in a position to combat her petition and expose its dishonest trickery. If she proceeds with it, she will be utterly discredited and disgraced, and in all likelihood the children will no longer be in any degree under her control. This, obviously, would be the best issue for the children, but the worst for her.' 'Before you condemn my attitude as harsh,' he added, 'please try living with her for 12 years . . . For the past seven years, I have found Dora treacherous, deceitful, hypocritical, dishonourable and cruel.'

Faced with this threat, Dora once more capitulated. She withdrew her petition for divorce appealing for custody and filed an amended petition asking only for the discretion of the court with regard to the children. In return Russell withdrew his chancery action, and the damaging material he had gathered to blacken Dora's reputation was not submitted as evidence to either the divorce or the chancery court. When Dora's amended petition was heard, unopposed, on 22 November 1934, however, a further twist was added to what had already become a horribly tangled case: the judge declared himself unhappy with the Deed of Separation and refused to accept it as evidence of Dora's claim to have been 'wronged' by Russell's adultery with Peter. He thus ruled that the deed should be considered irrelevant to the case and that a decision about the divorce and the future of the children should be made on the basis of a consideration of *all* the facts and documents relating to the case. It was thus not until December that a divorce was granted and not until 1 July 1935 that the marriage was finally dissolved, when the decree nisi was made absolute.

The courts awarded neither Dora nor Russell custody of John and Kate. Instead, their affairs were to be handled by a Board of Trustees that included, apart from Russell and Dora, Ted Lloyd and Francis Meynell. From Russell's point of view, this had the huge disadvantage of obliging him to meet Dora to discuss the children's affairs ('Two days ago we had a meeting of the children's trustees,' he reported to Ottoline after one such occasion. 'Dora seemed much more insane than before. I hate the children having to associate with her. Perhaps in time she will be certified'). However, it had the inestimable advantage that Dora could do nothing with regard to the children without the permission of the other three trustees.

After a long hard battle, he had won: he was now legally free to marry Peter, and had not had to pay the price of losing thirteen-year-old John and eleven-year-old Kate to Dora. The price of his victory, however, was extremely high. As Kate has said, 'all involved, including the children, emerged hurt, angry, bitter and desperately defensive'.

6
FORWARD TO THE PAST

When Russell left Dora for Peter in the spring of 1932, what drove him was not just a desire to escape from a dreadfully unhappy marriage, or even simply the desire to share his life with a young, pretty woman who was willing to work as his secretary and personal assistant. In addition to these things, he felt powerfully the need to put his entire life on a different footing. It was not only Dora he was leaving behind, but also the hopes, beliefs and values that he had shared with her, the conviction that together they would help create a new generation, free from fear, and usher in a new world, free from religion and repressive morality. He had lost faith in their school as a model for the education of the future, in their marriage as the sexual morality of the future, and in Dora as the woman of the future. Moreover, he was tired of writing hack-journalism and pot-boiling books to pay for what he now regarded as their failed experiments and lost hopes. What he wanted most of all was a new direction, a new purpose: something that would prove the pessimism with which he had ended his autobiography to be unfounded, something that would show that he *was*, after all, still capable of achieving something important.

For a short while, he considered that this 'something' might be in politics. As a new Labour peer, he felt, he might have an important role to play in shaping Labour Party politics. It is not entirely clear why he abandoned this ambition, but it seems to have lasted no more than a few months. On 20 February 1932, two months before he left Dora and a few weeks before he took up his seat in the Lords, he visited the Webbs at Passfield Corner to discuss his possible role in the party, but the meeting does not seem to have led to anything. Before the meeting he told Dora that he wanted to 'spend more time in London & try to stir up people to think out a programme to urge on the Labour Party . . . The world is going to the devil faster & faster. I see no hope anywhere but in Russia.' At the meeting itself, however, he told Beatrice Webb that his hopes for the future lay in the USA, 'in spite of all the corruption and the violence', a view that is, indeed, more consistent with his published work over the previous ten years. With regard to the Labour Party, Beatrice Webb records little of Russell's opinions other than his violent indignation at the 'flunkeyism and treachery of J.R.M. and Snowden'.

This was a reference to the events of the previous year, which saw Ramsay MacDonald leave the Labour Party and head a 'National Government', with Cabinet members drawn mainly from the Conservative and Liberal Parties (with the isolated exception of Philip Snowden, who remained as Chancellor of the Exchequer). This followed the belated realisation by the Labour Government of the extent of the financial crisis in which Britain found itself after the Wall Street Crash of 1929. By 1931, the national debt, the budget deficit and unemployment were all increasing at a rate that created an atmosphere of national emergency, and MacDonald and Snowden felt that cuts in Government spending, including unemployment pay, were essential to the survival of the British economy. In this they were supported by the majority of Conservatives and Liberals in the House, but not by their own party, and thus the National Government was born. In October 1931, MacDonald called a general election over his handling of the economy, and his National Government achieved a landslide victory. The new Government was, however, in all but name a Conservative one, albeit with MacDonald at its head; of the 554 seats won by the National Coalition, only thirteen were Labour, with the vast majority (470) filled by Conservatives. The Labour Party outside the coalition, now led by George Lansbury, was reduced to fewer than fifty seats.

Russell's outrage against MacDonald for his betrayal of the Labour movement was widely – almost universally – shared among Labour supporters, and the party was, at this time, in a state of disarray and demoralisation. Some of its leading intellectuals became convinced that the financial crisis of the Great Depression represented the collapse of capitalism itself and that the only viable political options were Communism or Fascism. This was not a view widely shared among the general public, however; both extreme parties remained small and uninfluential in the country at large, while the Conservatives continued to dominate the polls throughout the decade. Among those previously hostile to the Soviet Union, but who now looked to it to provide leadership, were the Webbs themselves, who, after their visit there in the summer of 1932, announced that the Soviets were building a 'new civilisation' for others to emulate. Though this was a view endorsed by, among others, H. G. Wells and George Bernard Shaw – not to mention a good proportion of the new generation of bright undergraduates at Oxford and Cambridge – it was one that Russell steadfastly resisted.

But, in adhering to Socialism while rejecting Soviet Communism, Russell was not as isolated as he often portrayed himself as being. The Labour Party, after the débâcle of 1931, had became more stridently and unashamedly Socialist than it had been under MacDonald, while remaining as hostile to Communism as ever. The party was open to, and indeed positively searching for, new ideas, and it would have been an opportune moment to urge a new programme upon it. The challenge facing the party was to find a credible alternative to both Communism and the budgetary caution advocated by MacDonald, Snowden and the Conservatives – a set of economic measures that would do something to help the growing number of unemployed workers without sinking the nation into financial ruin. Nor was there any shortage of people prepared to take up this challenge, one of the most notable being G. D. H. Cole, whose *Intelligent Man's Guide Through World Chaos*, published in 1932, proved to be a best-seller and introduced the perplexities of economic policy to a wide audience. A few years later, J. M. Keynes's *General Theory of Employment, Interest and Money* came to be regarded as providing a definitive solution to the problem.

There is no way of knowing whether the programme that Russell wanted to stir people up to think out and urge upon the Labour Party was centred on economic policy, but it is striking that at this time of economic crisis, when everyone, it seemed, was talking about such things as inflation, the gold standard, the budget deficit, and so on, Russell published almost nothing on economics. In the few articles he did publish on the subject, his perspective is so resolutely international that the lessons he wishes to draw for British policy are rather obscure. In 'The Modern Midas', for example, which he published in *Harpers* in February 1933, he explains in a very witty and accessible way the issues raised by the gold standard, national debt and international financial instability, but, typically, his proposed solution to the problem of securing a stable currency is to have 'a single world Government, possessed of the sole effective armed forces . . . This is the only true stability, and gold does not possess it.' He goes on to argue that there should be in the world just one central bank and one currency. In themselves, these may be sensible suggestions, but one wants to ask: in the world as it is, rather than as it should be – that is, in the face of the reality of many competing nation states, national armed forces, banks and currencies – what ought Britain's economic policy to be? Russell, apparently, had no answer to this question, and seems to have shown surprisingly little interest in it.

Indeed, other than objecting to MacDonald's 'flunkeyism', it is difficult to know what Russell's views were on the issues that dominated British politics at this time. The political subjects that moved him to eloquence and action – free speech, world peace, the threat to civilisation, the need for international government – did not include the intricate and baffling issues involved in the construction of domestic economic policy. Therefore he had little to say that was relevant to the problems facing Britain in the 1930s. One searches in vain in Russell's published writings of the early 1930s for any sign of his opinions on the questions that loomed large in political discussions in Britain at that time, particularly on the question that loomed largest: what could be done about unemployment?

And perhaps in this lies the answer to the question of why he withdrew from politics after announcing his intention of becoming more involved: he had no firm convictions one way or the other on the questions being debated in the Houses of Parliament during this period; no clear idea of what the Labour Party should be urging the Government to do about the problems that beset it; or indeed of what policies the Socialist left ought to be urging upon the Labour Party. Russell had adopted Socialism as an answer to the world's problems, not Britain's. His argument in the 1920s, that Britain

could never become Socialist until the United States did, had its analogue in
the 1930s, at a time when Britain was dependent upon loans from the
United States which it could secure only if it adopted a 'tough' policy on
Government spending. And, just as then he was reluctant to advocate
measures which he thought likely to lead to an American blockade of
Britain, so now, presumably (he never spelt this out), he was reluctant to
urge upon it a course likely to lead to the severance of its economic lifeline.
But, then, what course of action *ought* a Socialist to be urging upon the
British Government? As in the 1920s, so in the 1930s Russell had little to
say on the subject.

But, if he was not to write anything or do anything that would help solve
Britain's political and economic problems, what was he to do? In the
summer of 1932, he wrote *Education and the Social Order*, but this was, as he
himself freely admitted, a very dull book. Towards the end there is some
impassioned rhetoric about the madness of a world in which 'the forces of
the State are devoted to producing in the young insanity, readiness for
homicide, economic injustice and ruthlessness', and about the cure to this
problem being 'to make men sane' (that is, to educate them properly). But
there is something rather tired and formulaic about this rhetoric, especially
as the book, unlike his earlier *On Education*, contains no great faith that
education *can* 'make men sane'. Indeed, it is, to a large extent, a corrective to
the optimism of that earlier book, warning that 'The powers of education
have been exaggerated', especially by behaviourists (he does not own up to
having exaggerated them himself, but, if this book is read alongside the
earlier one, that is surely implicit). This time, the emphasis is on social,
rather than psychological, aspects of education, urging a diminution of
propaganda, religious instruction and snobbery in the classroom, and
recommending instead honesty about sexual matters, a respect for democracy and the encouragement of scientific inquiry. On the subject of eugenics,
Russell is notably more circumspect than he had been in *Marriage and
Morals*, and now dismisses the belief that 'Negroes are congenitally inferior
to white men' as an unwarranted assumption of right-wing eugenicists
(again, without confessing to having held – and published – the view himself
just three years previously). The book is free from many of the wildly
exaggerated claims of *On Education*, but, as his evangelical fervour for the
subject had been largely based on his belief in those claims, the result is a
rather bland, devitalised and uninspired work.

After writing *Education and the Social Order*, Russell says in his
Autobiography, 'I gave up writing pot-boilers. And having failed as a parent,
I found that my ambition to write books that might be important revived.'
The implication that he considered *Education and the Social Order* to be a
pot-boiler is unsurprising. But why should he have thought that he had
failed as a parent? And what does his failure as a parent have to do with his
revived ambition to write important books? The answer, I think, lies in his
sense that, by 1932, the life that he had made for himself since 1921 had
collapsed, a life in which everything he did – his journalism, lecture tours,
popular writing, and so on – was done for the sake of his children. He had

'failed as a parent' in the sense that he had failed to make a success of that life. Having decided that he could no longer put up with Dora for the sake of John and Kate, he had to accept that not *everything* in his life could take second place to his children's happiness; some things – his own sanity, for example – had to be given a higher priority even than that. This meant that, in place of the 'new emotional centre' that he described parenthood as providing, there was now a void that had to be filled with something else that he regarded as of paramount, intrinsic importance. Writing of his experience of fatherhood, he says that, after John was born, 'during the next ten years my main purposes were parental'. What is implied is that *after* that time, they were not. His 'main purpose', his justification for living, as it were, had to lie elsewhere.

Dissuaded (by what or whom, exactly, we do not quite know) from making politics the centre of his life, and convinced, for the moment, that he had nothing left to achieve in philosophy, Russell turned to history. In keeping with his desire to make this work the very centre of his life – having the same importance to him as *Principia Mathematica* or the birth of his children – Russell conceived of writing an extremely ambitious work on which, he told Stanley Unwin, 'if I could afford it, I should be glad to spend ten years'. His plan was to write a large-scale history of Europe between 1814 and 1914 that would include analysis of both the intellectual ideas that had shaped the events of that hundred years and the psychology of the individuals who had given birth to those ideas. 'I do not want to write an ordinary history,' he explained to Unwin, 'what I want to do is to bring out the part played by beliefs in causing political events, the part which, I believe, Marxists unduly minimise.' His plan was 'to take important individuals, portraying the world as they saw it':

I want to bring out the extraordinary subjectivity of each man's cosmos. Consider, say, Marx and Disraeli, almost exact contemporaries, both Jews, and living in London within a stone's throw of each other. I suppose that Disraeli never heard of Marx, unless possibly in Scotland Yard dossiers. The interests, the knowledge, the whole universe of either was alien to that of the other.

He saw the period, he told Unwin, as framed by two emperors, Alexander I and William II, 'both completely silly, but both possessed of more influence upon the events of their own period than fell to the lot of many able men, with the exception of Bismarck'. Other individuals – each with their own 'cosmos' – that he wanted to include were: 'Bentham, Malthus, Cobden, Robert Owen, Marx, Mazzini, Napoleon III, Disraeli, Darwin, Pasteur, perhaps Stevenson, Carnegie, Rockefeller, and as the grand finale of so much intellect, the Emperor William II'.

The result, *Freedom and Organization 1814–1914*, took just over a year to write and, in many ways, does not quite live up to this billing. The theme of 'the extraordinary subjectivity of each man's cosmos' is barely explored at all, and in its place is what Russell says in the Preface is the purpose of the book, namely: 'to trace the opposition and interaction of the two main causes of change in the nineteenth century: the belief in FREEDOM which was common to Liberals and Radicals, and the necessity for ORGANIZATION which arose through industrial and scientific technique'. Even this theme, however, does not pervade the book to quite the extent that Russell suggests. For the most part, the book is filled with lighthearted, even gossipy, accounts of the lives and work of the individuals in whom Russell is interested and whom he regards as having had a decisive influence on the century he is writing about. As a work of scholarly history, it is amateurish and displays many of the idiosyncrasies that would later infuriate academic philosophers about his *History of Western Philosophy*. In particular, Russell is uninhibited about giving free rein to his personal prejudices ('the Tories were, on the whole, less intelligent than the Whigs') and about giving short, confident summaries of the characters of the people he writes about (Ricardo was 'a lovable man', Malthus 'a pleasant old gentleman, with the comfortable eighteenth-century characteristic of holding no doctrine more firmly than a gentleman should', and so on). Like *History of Western Philosophy*, it is fun to read, but it is not a serious contribution to the historical literature of its period (it does not, for example, contain any original research – all its sources are published texts), and it has been, by and large, ignored by subsequent historians.

Part of Russell's purpose in writing the book, one feels, was to analyse the forces that led to the First World War and to show that those forces, though powerful, were *not* irresistible. 'The Great War was made probable by large causes,' he writes, 'but not inevitable. Down to the last moment, it might have been postponed . . . and if it had been postponed, the forces making for peace might have been predominant.' The 'forces making for peace', he makes clear in the Conclusion to the book, are those that lead to increased organisation between nation states, while allowing freedom for individuals within states. The 'large causes' that made the war probable, on the other hand, are those that lead to increased organisation *within* states, while allowing freedom, competition and anarchy to prevail internationally. As a framework within which to describe a hundred years of political, social and intellectual history, this is far too neat, but the moral Russell wishes to draw from it for the world of the 1930s is clear:

> The same causes that produced war in 1914 are still operative, and, unless checked by international control of investment and of raw material, they will inevitably produce the same effect, but on a larger scale. It is not by pacifist sentiment, but by world-wide economic organisation, that civilised mankind is to be saved from collective suicide.

In his 1931 article 'Christmas at Sea', Russell had mentioned 'the support of historic continuity and of membership of a great nation' as one of the things he wanted to allay the fears of solitude, and one can see this desire at work in *Freedom and Organization*. The period with which he begins the book is that in which his grandfather, Lord John Russell, was one of the most influential politicians of the day, and Lord John appears frequently throughout the book. But, more than that, the book recapitulates a very Whiggish theme, a theme that was, indeed, very close to Lord John's heart. In 1823, Lord John published a history of England called *An Essay on the History of the English Government and Constitution from the reign of Henry VIII to the present time*, which is in many ways similar to *Freedom and Organization*, describing the development of the English constitution in terms of the twin virtues of 'liberty' and 'order'. 'The history of society', Lord John writes, 'may be divided into four different stages of civilisation.' The first stage is that of the savage ('exemplified to this day in the North American'); the second is that in which property rights are established, but Government is weak; the third – the stage reached by despotic European countries such as Russia and Prussia – is that in which a state of order exists without liberty; and the fourth is that perfect union between liberty and order that only the most civilised nation on earth, England, has reached. This conception of civilisation as a harmony, a compromise even, between liberty and order, freedom and organisation ('authority and the individual', as it appeared in Russell's writings of the 1940s), is one that informs much of Russell's thinking about history and politics and shows the extent to which he remained, as he himself frequently said in the 1930s, 'a British Whig'.

In his marriage to Dora, Russell had strained to overcome the past and to present himself as the very epitome of the modern, forward-looking man. With Peter, however, he reclaimed his past, placing himself, the third Earl Russell, squarely in the long and proud tradition of his forebears. In this, it helped that Peter was both a snob, eagerly looking forward to becoming Countess Russell, and passionately interested in history, the subject she had studied at Oxford. This meant that she could not only give Russell encouragement, but also much practical assistance. She was, in effect, his full-time research assistant on *Freedom and Organization*, and, though Russell did not go as far as he had done with Dora, when he gave her a joint-writing credit for *Principles of Social Reconstruction*, he did add to the Preface of the book a fulsome acknowledgement of Peter's help:

> Throughout the writing of this book, the work has been shared by my collaborator, Peter Spence, who has done half the research, a large part of the planning, and small portions of the actual writing, besides making innumerable valuable suggestions.

That Peter was a trained historian is not coincidental to the fact that, while he was with her, Russell published more works of history than he had done before or would do afterwards.

While Russell and Peter worked on *Freedom and Organization*, they lived together at Deudaeth Castle on the Portmeirion Estate in North Wales. Portmeirion, which has since become famous as the setting for the 1960s' television series, *The Prisoner*, is a whimsical and strange 'village' designed by the architect Clough Williams-Ellis, who bought the estate from a relative in the 1920s and began building on it soon afterwards. It is difficult to know how and when Russell met Willliams-Ellis, but they had moved in the same circles for years. A little younger than Russell, Williams-Ellis had been educated at Trinity, Cambridge, during the first few years of the century and, by the 1920s, was a successful and fashionable architect. His wife, Amabel, was a Strachey, the daughter of St Loe Strachey, the editor of the *Spectator*, brother of John Strachey, the Labour MP, and a cousin of Lytton. Amabel, as well as writing children's stories, had been politically active in the Independent Labour Party and had taken part in some of the same campaigns as Dora. Their sympathies, however, seem to have been primarily with Russell, whom they invited to their 'castle' (a nineteenth-century curio, built as a home and, by 1933, pressed into service as an annexe of Portmeirion Hotel) to sit out the troubled time of his divorce.

Russell and Peter were at Portmeirion for just over a year, from the early summer of 1933 to the late summer of 1934. When John and Kate came to stay, they were taken on walks in the glorious mountainous countryside of Snowdonia in which Portmeirion is set and introduced to the Williams-Ellis family, the children of which – Christopher, Susan and Charlotte – all attended Dartington. Susan became a close friend of John's and remained devoted to him throughout his life, but Kate remembers Clough and Amabel as tall, loud and rather alarming: 'I was quite frightened of both of them, though they were truly kind people.'

Throughout this time, Russell, as well as writing *Freedom and Organization*, was fighting his battles with Dora to get John and Kate out of Beacon Hill School and to persuade her to drop her appeal for sole custody of them. He also refused to renew Dora's lease on Telegraph House. Determined to carry on the school in the face of Russell's hostility and without its most valued pupils, Dora relocated both her family and Beacon Hill School to a house called Boyle's Court, near Brentford in Essex. With Dora out of the way, Russell now had Telegraph House restored to its former state, and, with all traces of its use as a school removed, he and Peter could finally move there in August 1934. 'Peter went to work on the house with energy and skill', Kate recalls, 'and by the time she had finished it was altogether delightful . . . The orderly beauty of Telegraph House was due to Peter, who set the stage and managed the proceedings with great skill . . . After the chaotic, demanding, uncomfortable years of the school, it was restful for him [Russell] to sink back into a quiet private life, cared for by a young, beautiful and devoted wife who appeared to put his interests before her own.'

For John and Kate, the move to Dartington provided a welcome escape from *both* their parents. During their holidays, the rule of spending equal time with Russell and Dora was strictly enforced; if the holiday had an odd number of days, then precisely half of one of them was spent with each parent. When the end of term came, Kate remembers, all the other children got excited and began to long for home: 'I, however, began to think anxiously of the tensions awaiting John and me in both our homes.' During the holiday, 'we moved from one house to another like pawns, pretending to have no feelings':

Even now, I cannot write about those years with detachment. The old bitterness rises and flows out of my pen as I recall the anxiety and unhappiness John and I felt whenever we stayed in either home . . . We, who had been the field of their joint endeavours at human reform, became the battleground for their now opposing theories of child welfare . . .

A word from us of what the other parent thought could bring on an endless explanation from the one to whom we spoke. I can remember still the sick, trapped feeling I used to get when some careless word of mine brought on a speech of self-justification, which could be ended only by assent, whether genuine or feigned.

For Dora, the contrast between her chaotic, untidy home and the beautiful orderliness of Telegraph House had a political as well as a personal significance. While Russell and Peter seemed determined, as Dora saw it, to live the life of the pampered aristocracy, she identified herself more and more with the working class, a sympathy that she announced to the world in her appearance and her behaviour, especially (much to Kate's embarrassment) when she came to Dartington Hall. Though admitting that she is now 'ashamed of my unfairness', Kate recalls that: 'All through the Dartington years I disliked and despised my mother':

I cringed when she came to visit us and tried to hide her from my friends. She used to buy old secondhand cars for ten pounds or so and drive them till they died, sitting at the wheel in her shabby and eccentric clothes, squinting through the smoke of a lipstick-stained cigarette whose ashes dropped into her lap as she drove, and laughing her hearty, raucous laugh as she made light of conventional manners and morals. She would sit through 'God Save the King' in cinemas, sing the 'Internationale' in public places, march in Communist demonstrations, while I shrank into myself and tried to pretend I didn't know her. With the harsh intolerance of childhood, I despised her and shut her out of my life, which was happily filled by my love and admiration for Peter and my father.

Providing her with the opportunity to offend the sensibilities of the rich and conventional was one of the few things Dora had to be thankful to Dartington for. She loathed the place for taking her children away from her and – at a time when she was permanently struggling to avoid bankruptcy – for being so infuriatingly well provided for. To Griffin, she expressed the fear that Dartington would turn John into a homosexual: 'If that happens to him I think I'll murder Francis & Lloyd & BR for their obtuseness & brutality.'

The remark was made with deliberate tactlessness, for Dora had by now learnt that Griffin and her beloved Paul Gillard had enjoyed a homosexual affair. Along with Russell, Dora was inclined to believe that homosexuality was caused by 'sentimental' mothers. 'I swear', she told Griffin, 'I will never do to John & Rod. what Paul's & your mother did to you two men.' The aggressive tone is typical of the way in which she wrote to him, and, eventually, the blasts of anger she sent to him across the Atlantic had the effect of killing their relationship. Like Kate, she later became ashamed of her unfairness. 'I have much regretted', she says in her autobiography, 'the injustice of some of my behaviour towards Griffin.' The surviving correspondence shows just how unfair she was.

When Gillard died, Dora wrote Griffin a letter similar to the one she penned to Russell that had such dire consequences for her in her battle for the custody of John and Kate. Like Russell, Griffin was shocked to be told that Dora had been in love with Gillard and hurt by her previous deception, but, unlike Russell, he responded with warmth and humanity:

> It is terribly shocking. I had thought you had a lover, but put the thought out of my mind. Couldn't face any more agony. Now suddenly I have only pity and love for you, my own dearest, and a desire to protect you from further sorrow, if I could.

About Paul, he wrote: 'I did make gay homosexual proposals (which didn't mean much in themselves to me) because his quality was irresistible as a person. When he conveyed them understandably to you I ceased to like him.'

For months afterwards, Dora sent Griffin letter after letter about her love for Paul, even after he pleaded several times with her to drop the subject. 'Your rehearsals of your transports with Paul', he tried to explain to her, were breaking his heart: 'Evidently you think of them as cruel but necessary measures to break an attachment, but the cure kills not only the loves but the man . . . I was in a frenzy of despair all day.' Throughout the later stages of the divorce, Griffin kept writing soothing and supportive letters to Dora, hoping that she would soften towards him and that they might, after all, be able to build a life together around their joint children. These hopes were dashed in a letter Dora wrote to him in February 1935, in which she told him brutally: 'I can love a comrade or a partner. Never had such – except Paul. But I can't love a tyrant or a whining child – unless it's a *real* child in whom I can hope to build some courage. Let your mother carry on with her job, my dear, she made you – & she had better look after her handiwork now.' After this, Griffin stayed in touch, and saw Harriet and Roddy whenever he could, but he gave up any hope of ever reviving the love between him and Dora. He remained, however, in the background of what was becoming a complex, extended family, and, at various times during the following two decades, he was to play an important part in John's life and indirectly, therefore, in Russell's.

Towards the end of 1934, Dora added another member to this family, when she took up with an old friend of Paul Gillard's called Pat Grace. Grace, then twenty-four years old and described by Dora as looking 'haggard, dishevelled and distraught', introduced himself to Dora when she gave a talk in London to the Rationalist Press Association. He approached with the words: 'I think that you knew a friend of mine, Paul Gillard', an introduction that immediately guaranteed him an invitation to come and live with Dora at Boyle's Court ('I took Pat Grace . . . back with me and put him straight to bed,' as Dora puts it in her autobiography). Grace, like Gillard, had been a member of the Communist Party and the NUWM, and had taken part in the Hunger Marches from Plymouth to London. Like Dora, he seemed convinced that Gillard had been killed by Fascists. Since Gillard's death, according to Dora, Pat 'had been living from hand to mouth, unable to sleep, in a state of grief and remorse and anger that I was well able to understand'. After providing Pat with the rest and food she perceived him to need, Dora insisted on his staying at Boyle's Court to work as her secretary and 'right-hand man'. One reason for this, she says, was that she was convinced that Pat, having worked alongside Gillard and been involved, like him, 'in some kind of espionage that spelt danger' lived under the same mysterious threat that had been responsible for Gillard's death: 'there should not, if I could prevent it, be another "accidental death" '.

Dora seems never to have been quite in love with Pat Grace, but she valued him for the support he offered her at the school and, above all, for comforting her in her grief for Gillard. Eventually, after living with him for six years, she married him. All four of her children, but especially the girls, were puzzled and dismayed by her choice. Kate describes him as being 'like a stray animal' that her mother brought into the house, and, though conceding that he was 'funny and kind and inventive', found him embarrassing; he was 'vulgar and ugly and utterly unreliable'. Harriet disliked him intensely, considering him no match for her handsome and gifted father. John, however, seems to have rather liked Grace and to have accepted him as part of a family that, from John's point of view, now included two fathers, two mothers, a sister, two half-siblings, and an ex-lover of his mother's waiting in the wings. At every turn in the growth of this family, the potential for divided loyalties grew exponentially.

After he and Peter had moved into Telegraph House, Russell continued the search for the large, ambitious writing project that would fill the void in his life created by the 'failure' of parenthood, continuing, for a while, to regard himself as a serious historian. 'I enjoy writing history so much', he wrote to his American publisher, Warder Norton, 'that I feel prepared to continue doing it for the rest of my natural life.' Before *Freedom and Organization* was finished, he conceived what he described to Unwin as 'another big book', to which he gave the provisional title *The Cult of Feeling*, which would attempt to describe the 'break up of 18th century rationalism'. Russell's starting point for this project was his conviction that the 1930s were an 'irrational age', and his intention was to describe the intellectual and social forces that had made it so. Hitler's pogroms against political opponents and Jews, he told Unwin, 'spring from the cult of the heart as opposed to the head', and, as such, were the latest development in an unhappy progression of irrationalism that began with Methodism and the Romantic Movement and continued through the philosophy of Carlyle, Nietzsche, William James and Bergson to find its culmination in *Mein Kampf*. In this way, the philosophers against whose work he had campaigned since the beginning of the century could be seen by Russell as the 'ancestors of Fascism'.

The Cult of Feeling (or *The Revolt against Reason*, as Russell soon began calling it), was never written, perhaps because *Freedom and Organization* was neither a critical nor a commercial success, or perhaps because Russell's thoughts on the subject could never quite cohere sufficiently for him to make them the theme of a large book. His preliminary notes for the book show him experimenting with different explanations as to the *cause* of unreason:

> Unreason is a means of inducing people to act against their own interests, but in the interests of others. Heroism, self-sacrifice, etc. Supporters of unreason are those whose interests, on calm reflection, are seen to be opposed to the general interest; ages of unreason are those in which such men control propaganda. Fear of socialism is the chief cause of unreason in the present age.
>
> Reason depends on the state of the art of war; it flourishes when the defence is stronger than the attack. *Or* Reason flourishes when the means by which I grow rich enrich others; unreason, when I can only grow rich by impoverishing others.

In a Fabian lecture he delivered in October 1934 called 'The Revolt against Reason' (later reprinted in *In Praise of Idleness* as 'The Ancestry of Fascism'), Russell did not commit himself to any of these formulae. Instead, perhaps rather bizarrely, he traced the 'revolt against reason' to the scepticism of the eighteenth-century British empiricist, David Hume. In demonstrating that 'induction is a habit without logical foundation', Russell claims, Hume had shown that 'science, along with theology, should be relegated to the limbo of delusive hopes and irrational convictions' and had thereby undermined the faith in scientific reasoning that had provided the intellectual foundation of the 'Age of Reason'. Thus: 'among all the successors of Hume, sanity has meant superficiality, and profundity has meant some degree of madness'. Briskly dismissing Kant's attempts to answer Hume's scepticism as an obvious sophistry, Russell then charts the rise of a kind of philosophy that exalts intuition and the pursuit of power and disdains the concern for rationality and truth that had characterised the philosophers of the Enlightenment. Fichte, Carlyle, Mazzini and Nietzsche are named as the 'ancestors' of Fascism, the intellectual root of which is finally identified as the denial of objective standards of truth and the adoption of the view that 'there is English truth, French truth, German truth, Montenegran truth, and truth for the principality of Monaco'. In his conclusion, Russell seems to imply that it is the adoption of this view of truth that prevents international disputes from being decided by negotiation rather than by war:

> Between these different 'truths', if rational persuasion is despaired of, the only possible decision is by means of war and rivalry in propagandist

insanity . . . while reason, being impersonal, makes universal co-operation possible, unreason, since it represents private passions, makes strife inevitable. It is for this reason that rationality, in the sense of an appeal to a universal and impersonal standard of truth, is of supreme importance to the well-being of the human species, not only in ages in which it easily prevails but also, and even more, in those less fortunate times in which it is despised and rejected as the vain dream of men who lack the virility to kill where they cannot agree.

It is in passages like this that one sees the justice of John Maynard Keynes's famously wicked barb: 'Bertie held two ludicrously incompatible beliefs: on the one hand he believed that all the problems of the world stemmed from conducting human affairs in a most irrational way; on the other that the solution was simple, since all we had to do was to behave rationally.'

Seeking the intellectual roots of Fascism in the adoption of a pragmatist theory of truth seems almost breathtakingly naive and implausible. *Mein Kampf* does not commit itself to any particular theory of truth, and the idea that Hitler's ruthless suppression of political opposition, his contempt for democracy, his poisonous hatred of Jews and his obsessive desire for military conquest arise out of a rejection of an objective standard of truth, and might be countered by an appeal to properly conducted rational inquiry, seems astonishingly out of touch with political reality. In seeking to explain the irrationalism of Nazism, one feels, Russell was overly determined to hark back to the arguments he had had in the past with Willliam James. James, Russell writes, 'who invented this point of view [pragmatism], would be horrified at the use which is made of it; but when once the conception of objective truth is abandoned, it is clear that the question "what shall I believe?" is one to be settled, as I wrote in 1907, by "the appeal to force and the arbitrament of the big battalions" '.

Russell is on much more secure ground when he seeks psychological, rather than intellectual grounds for Nazism, when he remarks:

the Hitlerite madness of our time is a mantle of myth in which the German ego keeps itself warm against the cold blasts of Versailles. No man thinks sanely when his self-esteem has suffered a mortal wound, and those who deliberately humiliate a nation have only themselves to thank if it becomes a nation of lunatics.

However, when he extends this analysis to suburban England, claiming that 'a Fascist movement may well appear as a deliverance' to the alienated inhabitants of the prosperous suburbs around London, he again appears out of touch. Fascism had no great appeal among the British suburban middle class, nor is it clear why it should have done. The British Union of Fascists remained a tiny and uninfluential party right up until the outbreak of the war, and what support it did have was restricted to the urban, unemployed working class and a handful of eccentric aristocrats. Russell's psychopathology of the suburban middle class was thus not only unconvincing, but also irrelevant.

In a slightly earlier article, 'Why I am neither a Communist nor a Fascist', published in *New Britain* in January 1934, Russell had claimed that 'there is no philosophy of Fascism, but only a psycho-analysis'. Fascism and Communism are to be rejected, he writes there, because both neglect the freedom of the individual that is essential to a civilised society: 'an element of free growth, of go as you please and untrained natural living, is essential if men are not to become misshapen monsters'. The article was written to counter the view – which Russell saw as characteristic of the time – 'that Communism and Fascism are the only practical alternatives in politics, and that whoever does not support the one in effect supports the other'. It was, as it were, a statement of neutrality in the 'creed war' that had gripped Europe in the 1930s.

Though there is little enough with which to disagree in this article, the premise upon which it was based seems again to show that Russell was not fully engaged with British politics, nor fully aware of the mood of the British electorate. The view that one had to choose between Communism and Fascism because liberal democracy was a thing of the past *was* one that was heard repeatedly among what would later be called the 'chattering classes', but in the country at large it held no sway whatever. Both extremist parties failed to make any great impact at all on British politics during the 1930s; their membership remained small and their influence upon public opinion and Government policy was almost insignificant. The National Government that had been created in 1931 scored decisive victories in both the 1931 and the 1935 general elections, which meant, in effect, that British politics at this time was dominated by the Conservative Party. The Labour Party recovered somewhat in the 1935 election, and, although it moved sharply to the left, its hostility to Communism remained as implacable as ever. Neither the British Commuunist Party nor the British Union of Fascists had any MPs throughout this period (indeed, the Fascists did not even put up any candidates in the 1935 election, settling instead for the slogan 'Fascism next time'), the activities of both being more or less confined to fighting each other, fights that the overwhelming majority of people in Britain regarded with a distant distaste.

As the nature of Hitler's regime in Germany became increasingly apparent, the chances of the British Union of Fascists making any headway among the British electorate dwindled to nothing. The chief hope of the Communist Party having some influence was through the Labour Party, but, though they tried several times to persuade the Labour Party to form a 'United Front' against Fascism, the Labour Party steadfastly refused to work with them. Thus, Russell's repeated appeals to preserve liberal democracy in the face of the twin threats of Communism and Fascism were, in the context of British politics, largely an exercise in pushing at an open door. As evidence mounted of the brutality of the Nazis and of their alarmingly rapid programme of rearmament, the question that dominated

British politics was not whether liberal democracy was worth preserving, but *how* to preserve it in the face of the Nazi threat to Europe.

In the early years of Hitler's rule, Russell had surprisingly little to say on this question. He made repeated pleas for peace, rationality, Socialism and the formation of an international government, but these were all couched in terms too general to identify any specific policy recommendations relating to how the British Government was to react to the growing menace of a heavily armed Nazi Germany. Though Russell continued to publish regular journalistic articles, these tended to avoid the momentous political events of the day. This was especially striking in 1934, the first year of his return to Telegraph House. It was towards the end of November of that year that Churchill made his famous speech in the House of Commons imploring the Government to tell the truth about the extent of German rearmament and urging them to take seriously the threat to Britain's defence that Hitler's armed forces posed. In the summer, Hitler had demonstrated his ruthless way with political opponents in the 'Night of the Long Knives'; in August he had become Chancellor following the death of Hindenberg; and at the Nuremberg rally in September he had announced his vision of a glorious 1,000-year Reich. Meanwhile, his army, navy and air force continued to expand at an alarming rate, and his public statements of foreign policy grew ever more bellicose.

In the face of these events, one might have expected Russell's journalism to be devoted to an analysis of the threat to peace posed by German rearmament and the options open to the British Government and the League of Nations to deal with it. Instead, one finds him concerned with the subject of good manners, a topic to which he devoted no fewer than three articles at the end of 1934, all of them arguing that 'the decay of formality marks an advance in civilisation' and that 'good manners are a form of hypocrisy'. At the end of year, he finally addressed the question of the threat of Nazi Germany in an article in the *Sunday Referee*, but only to offer the rather lame and unpersuasive reassurance that 'peace will come to Europe if Germany tires of Hitler'.

One reason, perhaps the main one, that Russell seemed curiously out of touch with political events during this time was that he was emotionally exhausted and under a great deal of strain. It was in November 1934 that his divorce from Dora finally reached the courts, and, as it did so, cracks in his relationship with Peter began to show. Russell later claimed that the effort of restoring Telegraph House exhausted Peter so much that she attempted suicide when the work was finished. There are signs that she had already become disillusioned with Russell and was beginning to regret having decided to live with him. As Russell legally rid himself of Dora, it began to look as if he might lose Peter too. She fell in love with Richard Llewelyn Davies, Crompton's son, and seemed prepared to leave Russell for him. In his 'Private Memoirs', Russell says that he was at this time still sufficiently fond of Peter to mind and that he came near to having a nervous breakdown. Richard Llewelyn Davies, however, he claims, did not want to live with Peter, and so he and Peter went away on holiday together to the Canary Islands, where their relationship settled down as before. In several letters written at the time, Russell refers to his 'nervous breakdown', and there is no doubt that his decision to take two months' break at the beginning of 1935 was motivated by a desire to restore his mental health. His relations with Peter, however, never really recovered and she began, from this time on, to display the ferocious and frequent bouts of bad temper that Russell, Kate and John complained of later on.

The partial breakdown of his relations with Peter perhaps goes some way to explaining why *The Revolt against Reason* was never written. He had depended upon her historical research in writing *Freedom and Organization*, and no doubt had intended to work on this new history book in the same manner. In any case, when he and Peter returned from the Canary Islands, he wrote a book that required little or no help from Peter: *Religion and Science*. The theme of this was the familiar one that science had undermined faith in Christianity and that: 'The spread of the scientific outlook, as opposed to the theological, has indisputably made, hitherto, for happiness.' To this well-worn theme was added the thought that Communism and Fascism were, in effect, new religions and, as such, needed to be resisted by men of science. 'The threat to intellectual freedom', Russell announced, 'is greater in our day than at any time since 1660' (the date of the restoration of the monarchy):

> It is the clear duty of men of science, and of all who value scientific knowledge, to protest against the new forms of persecution rather than to congratulate themselves complacently upon the decay of the older forms.

If these new forms of religion prevent men of science from doing their work, Russell says, 'the human race will stagnate, and a new Dark Age will succeed, as the earlier Dark Age succeeded the brilliant period of antiquity'.

Religion and Science was published in October 1935. The following month, Stanley Baldwin, who some months earlier had replaced the ailing Ramsey MacDonald as Prime Minister, called a general election. Foreign policy, naturally, dominated the election, though there was no great difference of opinion on the subject between the Labour and Conservative Parties; both invoked the 'collective security' of the League of Nations as a means of dealing with the threat of Fascism, exemplified not only by German rearmament but also by the Italian invasion of Abyssinia. As in 1931, Russell took no public part in the election. His sympathies, no doubt, lay with the Labour Party, but his speeches, articles and interviews of the period show him taking a much more pacific line on international relations than the Labour Party, which, by the time of the election, had replaced George Lansbury as its leader with Clement Attlee. Lansbury was, on religious grounds, an absolute pacifist, and believed that Britain ought to continue unilaterally with a programme of disarmament, even in the face of the massive rearmament taking place in Germany. He also opposed sanctions against Italy on the grounds that this might lead to war. On both questions, Lansbury was defeated at the Labour Party conference, and the party adopted the tougher line proposed by Attlee.

On these questions Russell's sympathies were with Lansbury. Britain, he argued, ought to give up its colonies and withdraw from any international and European commitments. Above all, it must not do anything that might involve it in another war. Thus it must not intervene in the Abyssinian or in any other crisis, but must instead declare its neutrality in *any* dispute involving other nations. To rearm, Russell insisted, would be to make war more likely, not less. Britain must therefore resist the 'war-mongering' of people like Winston Churchill and pledge itself instead to disarmament and peace. Immediately before the election, Russell published a collection of essays called *In Praise of Idleness*, which, as well as 'The Ancestry of Fascism' and 'Why I am neither a Communist nor a Fascist', contained a new essay called 'The Case for Socialism'. To a large extent, this simply repeats what he had been saying on the subject since 1921: Socialism is still defined by him as consisting of 'State ownership of ultimate economic power, which involves, as a minimum, land and minerals, capital, banking, credit and foreign trade', and he still insists that, so defined, it is so obviously in the interests of the vast majority of people that all that is required to bring it about is open debate and democracy (though, once established, he admits that some force may be necessary for 'the defeat of small bands of malcontents').

However, now more than ever he insists that the 'strongest argument for Socialism' is that it is the best means of preventing war. 'The world', Russell writes, 'is in the condition of a drunkard anxious to reform, but surrounded by kind friends offering him drinks.' The 'drunks' are those intoxicated by notions of patriotism and national honour who actually *want* to wage war against their neighbours; the 'kind friends' are the capitalists – principally steel magnates – who stand to make money from war and therefore encourage the consumption of these dangerous intoxicants. Thus, if capitalism were defeated, 'the absence of this stimulus would quickly cause men to see the absurdity of war, and to enter upon such equitable agreements as would make its future occurrence improbable'. Of course, the final solution to war, in Russell's opinion, is *international* Socialism, but, he claims, 'nationalisation in each of the leading industrial countries would probably suffice to remove the pressing danger of war', and thus 'it may be safely assumed that each country which adopts Socialism will cease to be aggressively militaristic'. If Britain were to adopt Socialism, therefore, and, particularly, if it were to nationalise its steel industry, the chief obstacle to treating the Germans fairly would be removed and peace with Germany would become a much more likely prospect.

The idea that Britain should respond to the Nazi threat by nationalising its steel industry has about it as much plausibility as Russell's earlier suggestion that Nazism should be met by a rejection of the pragmatist theory of truth. It seems to reinforce the suspicion that Russell was, by this time, woefully out of touch with political realities. Russell's argument in 'The Case for Socialism' contains many weaknesses, but perhaps the most glaring is its implicit assumption that, if Hitler were treated fairly and the injustices of the Versailles Treaty remedied, he would lose his desire for military conquest. Related to this is a feature of Russell's political rhetoric that would figure ever more largely in his subsequent public utterances: his tendency to misrepresent grotesquely the views of his opponents. Those people – like Churchill and Duff Cooper among the Conservatives, Hugh Dalton and Ernest Bevin in the Labour Party, and Robert Vansittart, a leading civil servant at the Foreign Office – who urged the British Government to rearm in defence against Nazi Germany were not motivated, as Russell repeatedly implied, by a *desire* for war; rather they were convinced (on entirely reasonable grounds) that the only thing that would stop Hitler's Germany from embarking on a programme of aggression and annexation was military force.

The strength of this view – and the weakness of Russell's – became increasingly apparent in the years following the publication of *In Praise of Idleness*. However, as it became manifestly clear that nothing but armed force would deter Hitler's aggressive intentions, Russell did not abandon his pacifist position, but rather resorted to publishing ever less convincing proposals for preserving peace. This culminated in October 1936 in the publication of *Which Way to Peace?*, in which he suggested that Britain should respond to the increasingly threatening international situation by giving up its colonies, disbanding completely all its armed forces and announcing that it would not, under any circumstances, be drawn into a war. In defence of this manifestly suicidal policy, Russell indulged in some fantastic flights of wishful thinking. 'Suppose England and France were both to disarm,' he claimed:

> If the Nazis endeavoured to continue their military parades and their glorification of war they would cease to look heroic and would become ridiculous; their own compatriots would begin to laugh at them, and to reflect that so much strenuousness was no longer called for. Is it not clear that this is the really effective way of fighting militarism?

Lest it might *not* be clear to his readers that ridicule was the most effective weapon against a murderous and ruthless Fascist dictatorship intent on military expansion, Russell produced more arguments of equally startling naïvety. Look at Denmark, he urged:

> Because the Danes have almost no armed forces, it does not matter to the Germans what their opinions are; and as they have no Empire, they have no possessions that might afford a field for the investment of German capital. In this way they are defended by their own defencelessness.

Thus the way forward for Britain, Russell suggests (without a trace of irony), is to imitate Denmark, for then 'Having no longer large armed forces, we should threaten no one, and no one would have any motive to make war on us.'

'When disarmament is suggested,' Russell goes on, 'it is natural to imagine that foreign conquest would inevitably follow, and would be accompanied by all the horrors that characterise warlike invasions. This is a mistake, as the example of Denmark shows':

> Probably, if we had neither armaments nor Empire, foreign States would let us alone. If they did not, we should have to yield without fighting, and we should therefore not arouse their ferocity. The consequences, both to ourselves and to the world, would be infinitely less terrible than the consequences of a war, even if it ended in victory.

Nazi Germany, then, Russell would have his readers believe, would not attack a defenceless nation, or, if it did, it would treat its inhabitants well so long as they offered no resistance. His faith in this, it appears, rested on a quite general thesis about the behaviour of nations towards one another. If one nation prepares itself for war against another, he claims, then the other will learn to hate and fear it, and will attack it; but 'if, suddenly, you declare that the whole thing has been a folly, and that you prepared to be defenceless and trust to luck, the other people, having no longer any reason to fear you, will cease to hate you, and will lose all incentive to attack you'.

And if this defence by defencelessness does not work and Nazi Germany *does* invade Britain, well, Russell urges, we could expect to overcome 'what is harsh and silly in the Nazi philosophy' by succumbing without any resistance whatever. He was not, as is often said, urging a policy of Gandhian passive resistance; rather, his claim was that, if we did nothing to arouse the 'ferocity' of the Nazis, then life under Nazi occupation would not be so bad. Political opponents to Nazism, he implied, had little to fear: 'There would be little objection to British Communists, Socialists, or pacifists, since they would be regarded as having caused the military weakness of Germany's former enemies.' However, he concedes, there would be certain restrictions on freedom of speech, 'and, at first, the situation might be unpleasant and very galling to our pride'. But 'if we refrained from force and violence, I do not think it can be doubted that the mood of the Germans would change':

> It is difficult to remain fierce when there is no occasion of fear or envy, and when pride has been fully gratified. A great civilised nation, in the absence of all stimulus to hatred, cannot long remain in the mood that has put the Nazis in power. With the fear of war removed, bullying would soon lose its charm, and a liberal outlook would become common.

Russell was later embarrassed by the obvious stupidities of *Which Way to Peace?* and claimed that he had been 'unconsciously insincere' in writing it. Unconscious insincerity is a problematic concept; what Russell seems to have been implying is that, though what he had said about the threat of Nazi invasion was extremely foolish, he could not possibly, for that very reason, have actually *meant* it.

Of course, to some extent *Which Way to Peace?* reflects the general mood in Britain at this time. Memories of the First World War were still strong, and many people were prepared to believe *anything* rather than face the prospect of another war. Aldous Huxley, John Middleton Murry and many others published pacifist statements about Nazi Germany every bit as naïve as Russell's. Moreover, the British Government, though not in the slightest bit tempted to adopt the policy recommended by Russell, did everything it could to avoid war, resisting appeals from the French to stand firm against the Nazi occupation of the Rhineland in March 1936, lying to the House of Commons about the extent of German rearmament and taking false comfort in the belief that Nazi Germany, in preparing for a war against the Soviet Union, posed no threat to Western Europe.

However, though *Which Way to Peace?* is in some ways typical of the pacifist literature of the 1930s, in other ways it is unique. Other prominent pacifists, such as George Lansbury, John Middleton Murry and the Reverend Dick Sheppard, the leader of the Peace Pledge Union, were opposed to war on absolute, religious grounds. Murry, for example, wrote that to commit oneself to pacifism was 'to pass out of the realm of rationality into that of religious faith'. 'This movement from rationality to religion', he added, 'I believe to be inevitable, in so far as the Pacifist movement in this country means business.' Signing Dick Sheppard's Peace Pledge, Murry claimed, 'has meant for me a gradual passing into an entirely new sense of the reality of Christian Communion'. Clearly, such a view was not open to Russell, who had to defend the pacifist view, not on the basis of an unshakeable, categorical principle, but rather as the outcome of an entirely rational calculation of foreseeable consequences. This is presumably why he felt obliged to present utterly incredible assessments of the likely behaviour of the Nazi regime when faced with defenceless people. The consequences of facing the Nazis unarmed, he had to pretend, were really not as bad as people feared; given time, the worst that could happen was that we would find ourselves living under a liberal democracy governed by the Germans rather than the British, so that, 'if we could educate our pride', there would be nothing to prevent us accepting the consequences of pacifism.

In order to make this even the slightest bit plausible, Russell was forced to emphasise the essentially *civilised* nature of the German people. 'Admiration of the Germans as a nation is entirely justified,' he writes:

> In intelligence, courage, and public spirit they surpass all other nations. At the moment, it is true, they have an abominable government, but so should we have if we had suffered as they have since 1918. Governments are not eternal, but the merits of the Germans are important to mankind, and may soon again be liberated from their present bondage to cruelty and war. The German nation must not be identified with Hitler, Goebbels and Göring, and it will be a misfortune to mankind if these men compel the world to inflict another defeat upon compatriots.

The odd thing about this is that elsewhere in the book Russell demonstrates a realistic appreciation of the nature of the Nazi regime:

In the present temper of the Nazi rulers, it is not to be supposed that any obstacle except fear would prevent them from embarking upon a war of conquest.

. . . it is argued that, if all Germany's just claims are met in a friendly spirit, the militaristic temper which is now dominant will gradually become softened . . . This may, of course, be true, but I confess that I think it very improbable. The treatment of the defenceless opponents within the Reich suggests the mentality of the bully, who grows worse, not better, with success.

. . . the probability, upon which we have to act, seems to be that Germany will engage in aggressive war whenever the chance of victory is judged to be good.

How these observations are compatible with the claims he makes elsewhere in the book, that the Nazis will give up their army rather than face being laughed at, that they will not attack an unarmed nation and that they will refrain from persecuting political opponents in the countries they occupy, is not explained.

Indeed, unlike the publications of other pacifists, Russell's book is a curious mixture of startling naïvety and cold-blooded *realpolitik*. Thus, he admits that 'The Germans would like to be let alone while they attack Russia', and does nothing to suggest that they would be deterred from this by the Russians adopting the pacifist policies he urges upon Britain. That is, there is no suggestion that, if Russia imitated Denmark, it would be safe from Nazi attack. On the contrary, Russell seems to regard a German attack upon Russia as almost an inevitability. He also seems to think it extremely likely that Germany would defeat Russia, a prospect that he shows no sign of either regretting in itself or thinking would be disastrous for Britain. Recalling the situation in 1914, he writes: 'If Russia had not been allied with France, or France with England, Germany and Austria could have defeated Russia in half a year. But, owing to the system of alliances, all Europe, almost, had to fight for over four years.' This time, he seems to think, it would be in the interests of 'humanity and the progress of civilisation' if Britain and France granted Germany its wish to defeat Russia. The obvious objection to such a policy is that France and Britain would then be faced with a Nazi German Reich occupying almost the whole of Europe east of the Rhine. What would then be to stop such a monster marching west? Russell did not deny that such a danger existed, but argued that it *might* not happen: perhaps Hitler would, like Napoleon, find it disastrous to march into Russia; perhaps 'after a successful campaign against Russia, the Germans would feel satisfied and grow less warlike'; or perhaps 'the United States might be roused to prevent further conquests'. Even at the very worst, he argued, 'it would be less disastrous to permit German domination than to destroy Germany, France and England in a really scientific war'.

Russell continued to support the pacifist position right up until the outbreak of hostilities. In February 1937, he made isolationism the theme of his maiden speech in the House of Lords when he supported Lord Arnold's resolution in favour of British neutrality in the next war. The general assumption was that this would be between Germany and the Soviet Union, but, as Russell made clear in a letter to Gilbert Murray soon after his speech, he was in favour of British neutrality even in a war between Germany and France. 'Having remained a pacifist while the Germans were invading France & Belgium in 1914,' he told Murray, 'I do not see why I should cease to be one if they do it again.' He maintained this position throughout the German *Anschluss* with Austria, the Munich crisis and the invasions of Czechoslovakia and Poland. Only in the spring of 1940, when, after the 'phoney war', British troops were finally enagaged with the German army, did Russell finally abandon his pacifist stance. 'If I were young enough to fight myself I should do so,' he then wrote to Kingsley Martin, the editor of the *New Statesman*, 'but it is more difficult to urge others. Now, however, I feel that I ought to announce that I have changed my mind, and I would be glad if you could find an opportunity to mention in the *New Statesman* that you have heard from me to this effect.' In his *Autobiography*, Russell attributes this change of mind to the fact, whereas in the First World War, he had 'never seriously envisaged the possibility of utter defeat' for Britain, in 1940 this possibility was all too easily envisaged and 'I found the possibility unbearable'. Moreover, though the 'supremacy of the Kaiser's Germany' was something he 'had been able to view with reluctant acquiescence', 'Hitler's Germany was a different matter'. Of course, it had been a 'different matter' ever since 1933, and Russell says nothing to explain why, from then until 1940, he *had*, apparently, been able to bear the thought of both British defeat and Nazi domination.

One interesting aspect of Russell's vacillating views on the threat of Nazism, which prefigures the views he was to express later, is that he never seemed to take quite seriously the idea that military conflict might be *deterred*, rather than promoted, by military force. 'The hope of preserving peace by an increase of armaments', he writes in *Which Way to Peace?*, 'has always proved fallacious in the past, and is likely to prove so on this occasion also.' He was thinking, of course, of the idea that the First World War was *caused* by the arms race that preceded it. Again, this sits oddly with his admission that 'Germany will engage in aggressive war whenever the chance of victory is judged to be good', the natural inference from which, one might have thought, is that it was in the interests of Britain, France and the Soviet Union to persuade Germany that its chances of victory were *not* good.

The only concession Russell makes in *Which Way to Peace?* to the theory of deterrence is in relation to the United States. 'When the weight of America comes to be added on the side that is opposed to aggressive adventures,' he writes, 'the reasons against aggression will become so overwhelmingly obvious that the danger of war may rapidly diminish.' However, he says, elsewhere in the book, 'if I were an American I do not think I should advocate departure from the policy of neutrality. Europe has no right to expect America to make immense sacrifices to save it from the consequences of its own folly.' In several articles up to and including March 1939, when he published 'The Case for US Neutrality' in the *Common Sense*

Magazine, Russell urged the US to stay out of the coming European war, on the grounds that, if America became one of the belligerents, it would become 'inflamed by war passions' and would therefore be unable to play the role that Russell envisaged for it *after* the war – namely that of overseeing a sane and peaceful reconstruction of life in war-torn Europe. The following month, however, Russell urged the US to declare itself on the side of Britain and France, arguing that 'Fear of America is the only force able to avert a general war.'

The general impression one has of Russell's political writings of the 1930s is of a man who, convinced that the world around him has gone mad, is unable to make sense of what is happening. This impression is reinforced by the 'auto-obituary' he published in *The Listener* in the summer of 1936 under the title 'The Last Survivor of a Dead Epoch'. Here, he presents himself as an unapologetic defender of an 'antiquated rationalism' that leaves him 'politically, . . . as isolated as Milton after the Restoration'. Imagining his obituary to be written after the war that was then looming, he writes of himself:

In the second World War he took no public part, having escaped to a neutral country just before its outbreak. In private conversation he was wont to say that homicidal lunatics were well-employed killing each other, but that sensible men would keep out of their way while they were doing it.

'His life,' he goes on, 'for all its waywardness, had a certain anachronistic consistency, reminiscent of that of the aristocratic rebels of the early nineteenth century.' What he meant by this was, to some extent, expanded upon in an article he published in 1938 called 'Aristocratic Rebels'. His model of an early nineteenth-century aristocratic rebel, it appears there, was Lord Byron. The aristocratic rebel, Russell writes, 'is a very different type from the leader of a peasant or proletarian revolt'. The latter, being hungry men, have simple and primitive values, according to which the good life is one in which there is enough to eat. On the other hand:

The aristocratic rebel, since he has enough to eat, must have other causes of discontent . . . It may be that love of power is the underground source of their discontent, but in their conscious thought there is criticism of the government of the world, which, when it goes deep enough, takes the form of Titanic cosmic self-assertion or, in those who retain some superstition, of Satanism.

Russell's image of himself as the 'last survivor of a bygone age', the last representative of the tradition of aristocratic rebelliousness, recurs in much of his writing, conversation and correspondence of this period, sometimes leading him to even less likely comparisons than that with Lord Byron. 'Did you ever read the life of Averroës?' he asked Gilbert Murray. 'He was protected by kings, but hated by the mob, which was fanatical. In the end, the mob won. Free thought has always been a perquisite of aristocracy':

> The eighteenth & nineteenth centuries were a brief interlude in the normal savagery of man; now the world has reverted to its usual condition. For us, who imagined ourselves democrats, but were in fact the pampered products of aristocracy, it is unpleasant.

A free-thinker in an age of dogmatism, a rationalist in an age of unreason and an aristocrat in an age ruled by the mob; Russell had always been prone to feelings of emotional isolation, but now he felt that, in his separation from the world around him, it was the world, not he, that was at fault.

Russell had never shared Dora's sentimental admiration for manual labour and the working class ('Moving matter about,' he wrote in 1932, 'while a certain amount of it is necessary to our existence, is emphatically not one of the ends of human life. If it were, we should have to consider every navvy superior to Shakespeare'), but now he went out of his way to distance himself publicly from such sentiments. In the summer of 1937, he published a piece in *The Nation* called 'The Superior Virtue of the Oppressed', in which he diagnosed a particular kind of sentimentality to which oppressors are liable. This takes the form of attributing to oppressed people (his examples are subject nations, women, children and the working class) a superior kind of virtue, which they are held to possess precisely *because* they are oppressed. Thus the Greeks and the Poles, while fighting for liberation, were held to be 'poetic'; women were said to be 'angelic', while denied economic and political equality; and children, who had no rights at all, were regarded by pious Victorians as heavenly creatures. Freud, Russell claims, has disabused us of this particular piece of Victorian humbug by convincing us that children actually display 'an ingenuity and persistence in sinful imaginings to which in the past there was nothing comparable except St Anthony'. With regard to the proletariat, however, Russell alleges, we are still at the sentimental stage:

> Admiration of the proletariat, like that of dams, power stations, and aeroplanes, is part of the ideology of the machine age. Considered in human terms, it has as little in its favour as belief in Celtic magic, the Slav soul, women's intuition, and children's innocence. If it were indeed the case that bad nourishment, little education, lack of air and sunshine, unhealthy housing conditions, and overwork produce better people than are produced by good nourishment, open air, adequate education and housing, and a reasonable amount of leisure, the whole case for economic reconstruction would collapse, and we could rejoice that such a large percentage of the population enjoys the conditions that make for virtue. But obvious as this argument is, many Socialist and Communist intellectuals consider it *de rigueur* to pretend to find the proletariat more amiable than other people, while professing a desire to abolish the conditions which, according to them, alone produce good human beings.

Children were idealised by Wordsworth and unidealised by Freud. Marx was the Wordsworth of the proletariat; its Freud is still to come.

Again and again in his journalism of the 1930s, Russell reiterated the point that he felt estranged from the age in which he was living. The picture is drawn of a world becoming increasingly mechanised, homogenous, intolerant of the individual and dominated by the unthinking herd, to which conformity is enforced by the pressures of a society indifferent to the virtues of the 'aristocratic rebel'. In the 1920s, Russell had endeavoured to overcome his sense of isolation by presenting himself as the spokesman for the 'modern age'; now, he sought to distance himself from contemporary currents of thought and action and to present himself as an unheeded prophet of neglected values. In 'On Being Modern-minded', he poured scorn on the modern man, who 'suppresses what is individual in himself for the sake of the admiration of the herd'. In what looks almost like a confession, Russell analyses the temptations placed in the way of 'able men' by the 'money rewards and widespread though ephemeral fame' available to those who are prepared to give the crowds what they want, rather than pursuing, like Copernicus, Spinoza and Milton, a 'mentally solitary life':

To be pointed out, admired, mentioned constantly in the press, and offered easy ways of earning money is highly agreeable; and when all this is open to a man, he finds it difficult to go on doing the work that he himself thinks best and is inclined to subordinate his judgment to the general opinion.

The isolation he feels from the rest of mankind is thus seen as a prerequisite of worthwhile work:

A certain degree of isolation both in space and time is essential to generate the independence required for the most important work; there must be something which is felt to be of more importance than the admiration of the contemporary crowd. We are suffering not from the decay of theological beliefs but from the loss of solitude.

Or rather, perhaps he should have said, *he* had been suffering – since his abandonment of philosophy and the contemplative life – from the loss of solitude.

Russell's feeling of estrangement from the present and identification with the past found partial expression in *The Amberley Papers*, a two-volume collection of his parents' letters and diaries that he and Peter edited together and which was published by Woolfs' Hogarth Press. Leonard Woolf described it at the time as 'one of the most fascinating books I've read for a long time', but a more common reaction, I think, is to find it almost unreadably tedious. The lives of Russell's parents, Lord and Lady Amberley, were short and, for the most part, uneventful, and their letters and journals do not show them to have been especially remarkable people or particularly gifted writers. Nor, despite Russell's grandfather being one of the leading statesmen of the time, were they at the centre of political life. What one gets from the book is a detailed picture of the domestic life of a couple of thoroughly decent, if rather dull, people, whose reasoned political radicalism sat comfortably with the inherited privileges of aristocracy. The world depicted in it – a world innocent of the horrors of the First World War and of the even greater horrors promised by the impending 'creed war' between Nazism and Communism, a world in which the superiority of the British over the rest of mankind was safely assumed and the virtues of reason, moderation and aristocratic leisure accorded their proper respect – was, one suspects, a world to which Russell yearned to belong.

Apart from two entertaining introductory chapters describing the idiosyncrasies of the Russells and the Stanleys (his mother's family), Russell and Peter kept their editorial comments to a minimum, Russell allowing himself to be expansive only on the subjects of his grandmother's damaging piety ('she had a Puritan dislike of vitality and of many innocent forms of enjoyment . . . She never for one moment doubted her own rightness, and met disagreement with ridicule that pretended to be playful') and the relevance of his father's opinions to the world of the 1930s. Echoing the themes of his journalism, Russell underlines the importance of his father's publicly stated objections to the doctrinal declarations required of Anglican clergymen (who, in the nineteenth century, were required to swear assent to both the articles of faith and the Book of Common Prayer, despite the fact that these were arguably inconsistent with each other). Though the issue, Russell says, may seem 'no longer important':

> We cannot agree. The issue, to my mind, is more important than in Amberley's day, since doctrinal declarations are now required, not only by Churches, but also by political parties. Intellectual integrity is a personal virtue, not always easy to combine with co-operation in a collective enterprise. But on a long view its social utility is very great, and Amberley deserves to be honoured for having practised it fearlessly in spite of all the specious arguments of ambition and Party.

His father, in other words, is to be regarded as a paradigm of the virtues Russell felt to be disappearing in the 'machine age' of the 1930s.

Lord Amberley's political career, brief and undistinguished as it was, is dwelt upon at great length in *The Amberley Papers*. He fought and lost the constituency of Leeds in 1865, was elected as MP for Nottingham in 1866 and unsuccessfully contested South Devon in 1868, after which he retired from public life altogether. 'In Amberley,' Peter writes (many of the editorial notes are initialled individually), 'as in many Russells, the desire to study and philosophise fought with an inherited desire for power, and with the moral conviction – for it was no less – that he must do a Russell's duty to the State.' In this struggle, the 'desire to study and philosophise' won out, and Amberley spent his last years writing *An Analysis of Religious Belief*, which, Russell concedes, is 'flat and dull'. The book ends with the appalling story of the deaths of Russell's sister, Rachel, and his mother, Kate, from diphtheria, and the subsequent loss of his heartbroken father's will to live. As throughout, Russell and Peter allow the documents to speak for themselves and, for once, they do so eloquently and movingly.

The story of the Amberleys would, one suspects, have struck a familiar chord in the minds of Russell and Peter, their own quiet and isolated existence at Telegraph House being reminiscent of the life shared by the Amberleys in semi-retirement at Ravenscroft, their home in the Wye Valley. Replacing the chaotic hustle and bustle of the socially and politically active life that Russell had shared with Dora with the ordered calm of life with Peter was not all gain. The younger, more active people with whom he had mixed during his marriage to Dora had largely stayed loyal to her, and, for the most part, Russell was thrown back, after his divorce, to his friends of an earlier era. They, however, were getting old and, in many cases, reaching the end of their lives. Ottoline – now, like Russell, in her sixties – had sold Garsington Manor and was leading a quiet life in her London home in Gower Street. Plagued by increasingly severe illness, she had not long to live (she died in April 1938) and rarely went out. The members of the Bloomsbury Group, too, were reaching the twilight of their lives and feeling, like Russell, survivors from an earlier age. Lytton Strachey died in 1932 and John Maynard Keynes in 1937. Virginia Woolf, consumed with anxiety and mental illness, took her own life in 1941. Crompton Llewellyn Davies died in November 1935. Other important figures from Russell's past were either long dead (Joseph Conrad in 1922, D. H. Lawrence in 1930) or, like Wittgenstein, Whitehead and T. S. Eliot, long estranged from him.

The Webbs were still active and still friends, though their enthusiasm for the Soviet Union after their visit there in 1935 – announced in *The Soviet Union – A New Civilization?*[10] – presented something of a barrier between them and Russell. Perhaps because she had always disliked Dora intensely, Beatrice Webb was immediately well disposed towards Peter. After visiting Telegraph House in 1936, she described her as an 'attractive vision', who, though suffering from 'the inferiority complex, alike in social origin and conventional ethics', was nevertheless 'devoted to her great man'. 'Will this coupling of elderly genius (sixty-five) with youthful charm (twenty-five) endure to the end of the road?' Webb wondered. She was inclined to think it might, so long as the road was fairly short: 'It is to be hoped that Bertie will die suddenly, while still a brilliant talker and a successful writer and lecturer, otherwise I should fear a solitary end for this ageing adventurer in matrimony.' A month later, Russell and Peter visited the Webbs at Passfield Corner, with Russell in wistful mood, saying that if he had to live his life over again, he would devote it to physics or biochemistry. 'I have largely wasted it on philosophy,' he remarked ('dabbling in economic and political problems, he ought to have added,' Beatrice Webb commented in her diary: ' "Wasted gifts" is writ large over Bertrand Russell's life').

The 'inferiority complex' that Beatrice Webb detected in Peter revealed

---

[10] In subsequent editions, the title lost its questionmark.

itself to others as well. Dora had commented on how intimidating it was to be the younger wife of Bertrand Russell, accompanying him to dinner parties where she was expected to make intelligent conversation with such people as Virginia Woolf and Beatrice Webb. How much more daunting must it have been for Peter, nearly twenty years younger than Dora and without the latter's natural and inherited self-assurance? Dora, after all, while in no way an aristocrat, came from an established, upper middle-class family. Her father, Sir Frederick Black, was a distinguished senior civil servant, whereas Peter's was a postmaster (hence Beatrice Webb's remark about 'social origins'). And, while Peter had left Oxford without a degree, Dora had graduated from Cambridge with a First and had been elected a Fellow of Girton College. Thus, where Dora had felt able to be openly defiant against conventional expectations, Peter, feeling more insecure, was often merely prickly, overly sensitive to signs of being slighted.

When, for example, Leonard Woolf asked Russell to sign copies of *The Amberley Papers* to be sold at a fund-raising fair, he received a sharp rebuke from Peter, angry that she had not also been asked. 'Would you', she wrote to Woolf, 'at a party confine your polite attentions to those who were old friends, rich, famous, popular, and already overwhelmed with attentions, ignoring altogether poor, shabby, young, shy and generally insignificant newcomers?' From Woolf's point of view, of course, it was a silly fuss to make about such a little thing, and he responded with magisterial bluntness: 'I really don't think any the better of Bertie because I know that at a bazaar some snob will probably pay more than the published price for his book if it is signed by him, nor do I think the worse of you if I doubt whether in your case the snob would.' From Peter's point of view, however, the issue was rather deeper: was she content to be seen as nothing more than the 'young, pretty, charming and devoted' wife of Bertrand Russell or was she to insist on some recognition for her own achievements?

On 18 January 1936, Russell and Peter were married at Midhurst register office in Sussex (not far from Telegraph House). Russell told Kate that Peter had agreed to marry him 'as a result of my weekly proposals, which she saw no other way of stopping', though, surely, the real reason was the familiar one of legitimising any children they might have. Peter explained her reluctance to accept Russell's proposals on the grounds that, as the only possible reason to get married was to be able to secure the services of a cook in order to hold dinner parties, and as they were now too poor to entertain or to employ a cook, there was no point in marrying. It seems likely, however, given her affair with Richard Llewllyn Davies and Russell's subsequent 'nervous breakdown', that she had other misgivings about entering into marriage with a man forty years her senior.

Soon after the wedding, Russell and Peter went on holiday to Spain for a month. There they stayed with Gerald and Gamel Brenan at their beautiful home in Churriana, near Malaga. Gerald Brenan was a writer, who, in the 1920s, had been one of the links in a subsequently much-discussed chain of Bloomsbury romantic entanglements: he was in love with Dora Carrington, who, while married to Ralph Partridge, was in love with Lytton Strachey;

Strachey, meanwhile, was besotted with Partridge, who, in turn, was in love with Frances Marshall, whom – after Carrington had committed suicide – he eventually married. Since 1920, when he had bought a house in the Spanish village of Yegan, Brenan had divided his time between England and Spain, and by 1936 he was living mostly in Spain. At Yegan, he had caused a scandal by living with a fifteen-year-old local servant girl called Julianna, with whom he had a child. In 1930, while staying in Dorset, he met Gamel Woolsey, a beautiful and cultured American poetess from South Carolina, who was then forlornly in love with the already married Llewelyn Powys (the brother of John Cowper Powys, with whom Russell had debated the subject of marriage on one of his American lecture tours). Brenan at once fell in love with Gamel, married her and brought her back to Spain, where the two of them adopted his daughter by Julianna and moved to Churriana.

On Roger Fry's recommendation, Russell and Peter had been to stay with the Brenans at Yegan in 1933, and, subsequently, the Brenans had been to stay at Telegraph House. The two couples had also spent some time together in Lulworth, Dorset. By the time of their visit to Churriana in 1936, Russell and Peter (despite having met them on only three occasions) had come to regard the Brenans as their closest friends. It is a mark of how important the friendship was to them – and, perhaps, also of how few friends and other ties they had in England at this time – that Russell and Peter seriously considered selling Telegraph House and moving to Churriana (they were prevented from doing so by the outbreak of the Spanish civil war in the summer of 1936). The feeling was not entirely mutual. 'I used to enjoy his company very much,' Brenan wrote to Frances Partridge after Russell's death, 'but I never cared for him as a man. Like Milton he was unloveable because he had no warmth in his personal feelings and too much hatred and rancour.'

In his autobiography, *Personal Record*, Brenan devotes a chapter to Russell, which, though generally admiring, shows a keen eye for his faults, dwelling in particular on Russell's 'violent vituperation of those whose views he disliked'. Russell, he records, often said in conversation how much he *despised* people. About Clive Bell, for example, Russell remarked: 'I like him, as one likes people who flatter one, but I despise him.' This, thought Brenan, was unfair on Bell. Indeed, he says of Russell: 'outside his philosophy, of which I was no judge, his great quality was his unfairness'. Russell told Brenan, as he told many others, that he regretted having devoted himself to philosophy; his vanity, he said, suffered deeply because he was not as well known as H. G. Wells or Albert Einstein (Russell was, Brenan recalls, 'deeply impressed' by Bismarck's aphorism that the measure of a man is his intelligence after his vanity has been deducted from it).

Yet, Brenan claims, the men whom Russell most wished to resemble were not men of intellect, but those who had exposed some great barbarity or injustice: 'What he really wanted was that his great superiority of mind should be generally recognised so that he should be in a position to exert a useful influence on human affairs.' In this respect, however, Brenan considered Russell to be hampered by the excessively intellectual caste of his mind, which prompted him to form judgments that were too hasty and too rigid to deal with the complexities of political realities:

> Outside his philosophical works he could only turn out propaganda because he wished to influence the world *at once*.
>   . . . his mind and his work can be seen as split into two separate compartments. In one he is the logician and philosopher, the man of pure intellect who is completely cut off from all feelings. In the other he is the political writer, educationalist, teacher, prophet, moved by generous indignation at the follies and cruelties of the world, but also by a hankering for public esteem and applause . . . But when engaged in this way he was severely handicapped. Pure reason is not a good instrument for plotting a course in politics . . . though he was not lacking in the faculty of intuition he rarely gave it full play but drove his logical judgment through the maze of inter-related circumstances, simplifying everything that lay in its path till his conclusions no longer corresponded to reality. Then he was a man who, whenever his moral indignation was aroused, became blinded by passion. As is so often the case with pacifists, there was a strong streak of aggressiveness in his nature. The result was that, although in the course of his political and propagandist writings he has said many wise and just things, in the end he has generally lost his head and come out with foolish and desperate ones.

Russell was anxious for Brenan's approval of his published work, but, on the whole, did not receive it. When the Brenans stayed at Telegraph House, Russell insisted on reading out extracts from *The Amberley Papers*, but, Brenan remarks: 'I found them rather dull.' At Churriana, Russell and Brenan argued about the impending war with Nazi Germany, and, when, later in the year, Russell sent Brenan a copy of *Which Way to Peace?*, Brenan replied with some trenchant criticisms, not only of the book itself but of Russell's political and social writing generally. 'I regret', he told Russell, 'you shd have such a desire to counsel & improve mankind: you use only half your powers when you write homilies.'

His wife, Gamel, was still more critical. In April 1936, after the Russells had left, she wrote to Llewelyn Powys:

> I am so tired of seeing people – it sounds strange to say so here, but so many people seem to come, and the Russells stayed such a *long* time. And I only half like him. It's queer that I can never really like him. My heart never warms to him at all. His guiding forces are vanity and love of power, and to gratify them he wasted his amazing talent for Mathematics and took to writing books on happiness and marriage, and all the subjects about which he so evidently knows nothing worth saying. But in many things he shows great integrity of thought and character. And I *admire* him, only I can't really like him. I never quite know why.

Russell found Gamel deeply attractive. 'From the first,' he later wrote to

her, 'I have loved your strange eyes, expressing a kind of gentle mockery and
the wisdom of old pain assimilated . . . Gradually your beauty invaded my
inmost being.' She, he thought, lived – like him – 'in an alien world, whose
manners and customs and assumptions are not what seem deeply natural to
you. This has caused us both to have a secret inner life of memory . . .
Those with whom we associate, even in apparent intimacy, cannot share this
inner life, and are even likely to be jealous of it. And so I came to look to you
for a companionship I had no longer hoped to find.' The Conradian image
of a 'secret sharer' was one that held a powerful sway over Russell's
imagination; he liked to imagine when he fell in love with a woman that he,
and only he, could see into her soul and that she, and only she, could see
into his. Gamel Brenan, like many others, was very flattered that he should
regard her in this light, and, in time, she came to feel fondly towards him,
and even (as she told her friend, Alyse Gregory) to find his vanity *touching*.
But, like her husband, she was inclined to feel that the key to his character
was the hostility he felt towards other people:

> it was very hard for him to get over this – I saw how much it explained in
> his character and manner. The brilliance, the instinctive attack with the
> sharpest weapons because he expects attack – But what do such feelings
> come from? – Something far away and long ago I am sure – deeply
> hidden and deeply rooted. What maimed and halting creatures we all are.

She seems never to have reciprocated Russell's sexual feelings for her.
After she had grown fond of him, she said that, though she wanted very
much to see more of him, 'it leads to such difficulties – and then I feel
despondent and will not try'. In 1936, however, Russell's undisguised
attraction towards Gamel was felt merely as a source of irritation by both
her and her husband.

The desire felt by Russell and Peter to sell up in England and move to
Spain to be with the Brenans was part of a more general desire to make a
fresh start that showed itself in other ways too. Soon after their return from
Spain, it was discovered that Peter was pregnant, and when, in April 1937,
she gave birth to a son, Russell gave him the name Conrad. It was a name
very dear to him – perhaps the name dearest to him above all others – and
he had already used it as the middle name for his first son. Calling *this* child
Conrad seemed symbolic of a wish to erase the past and start again. Russell
and Peter wanted Conrad to have little to do with the rest of their respective
families. Soon after the birth, Russell wrote to the Brenans saying that, if
anything happened to him and Peter, he wanted them to take charge of
Conrad: 'We do not know anyone else whose atmosphere and way of life and
general outlook is so completely what we like.' All their relatives, Russell
emphasised, were unsuitable for the task.

While Russell planned a new life for himself, Peter and their new baby,
his relations with Kate and, especially, John deteriorated somewhat. Kate,
now thirteen, remained as devoted to him as ever, but even she became
increasingly embarrassed and indignant at the petty vindictiveness that

characterised his treatment of her mother. In his negotiations with the children's trustees over such things as holiday and travel arrangements, Russell did everything he could to make life difficult for Dora. When, for example, Dora asked John and Kate to come to her school on the first day of the Easter holiday of 1936 to attend the school play, Kate wrote to Russell requesting his permission to do so and received in reply a coldly correct statement that 'the rule is that you come first to us, and she should have spoken sooner and [here Russell had crossed out the phrase 'let us stay longer abroad'] not ask us to bear the disappointment of not seeing you after so long'. 'What upsets me', Kate said, after reading this correspondence through many years later, 'is his dishonesty and his unkindness . . . During the thirties he treated my mother ruthlessly and was regrettably devious in attempting to prove to us that what he wanted was best. I say this with sorrow, because I have always loved my father, never been able to love my mother, do not like to admit that he behaved badly.'

Faced with the continued and, as it seemed to them, unnecessary warfare between their parents, Kate and John became ever more depressed, disturbed and disillusioned. Russell noticed the change in their behaviour, but failed to see the obvious cause of it. 'When you were here, you seemed unhappy,' he wrote to Kate in May 1936, 'and I should have liked to know what was troubling you, and if possible put it right – I rather think you and John don't know how fond I am of you both and how much I think about you and plan for you.' It was clearly intended as sympathy, but it was felt as criticism, the more so as, at the same time, Russell wrote to Curry, Kate's headmaster at Dartington, to say that Kate had been grumpy and conceited during the holiday. Some weeks later, Peter wrote to Kate, explaining that she had not come to Dartington for the weekend for fear that Kate should be as disagreeable as she had been over Easter. 'I was just beginning to move out of childhood,' Kate said later, 'into a world of conflict and uncertainty, both personal and public, and I was sick and tired of diplomacy and message-running.'

Less spirited than his sister, John, at fifteen, reacted not with open expressions of anger and dissatisfaction, but with silent withdrawal. To Dora and Russell he said whatever he felt they wanted him to say (though, throughout this period, Russell complains repeatedly in his letters to Kate that John does not write to him often enough), but his teachers and fellow-pupils at Dartington saw him becoming increasingly disturbed. In adulthood he wrote a short story that is clearly an allegory of the strain placed upon him by the incessant need for the 'diplomacy' of which Kate complains. Called 'Mr von Sohn's Reputation', it concerns the plight of a young diplomat called upon to mediate in a dispute between the quarrelling nations of Madagascar and Timor. Despairing of ever getting either side to forgive the other's trangressions, the diplomat hits upon the idea of sending out a memorandum declaring both governments to be entirely blameless and taking upon *himself* full responsibility for the misdemeanours that lie at the heart of their dispute. With that, he retires from his job, goes into hiding and pledges, in the interests of peace, for ever to hold his tongue about all things related to the dispute. Such was John's strategy in dealing with Dora and Russell, a strategy that helped to keep the peace but in the long run cost John dear, forcing him – just as the central character in his story was forced – to retire, not only from his post as diplomat, but also from the world. In John's case, the 'retirement' took the form of withdrawal into himself. His friend, Susan Williams-Ellis, remembers him at Dartington repeatedly enacting a mad ritual in which he would put a black, woollen balaclava helmet over his face so that it covered his eyes and then cycle round and round in circles, oblivious to everything and everyone around him. To those who chose to see, it was clear that John was living in a solitary, dark and private hell in which everything seemed pointless.

That Russell, too, was to some extent aware of the distance between himself and his two children by Dora is suggested by a dream he recounted in a letter to Kate of September 1936: 'I dreamed last night that we were playing a game in which you both tried to escape, and you got sheep's fleeces and joined a flock of sheep, hoping I shouldn't notice that two of the sheep were children.' The dream resonates with the image that repeatedly crops up in Russell's journalism at this time of the mass of mankind as an unthinking and conformist herd, to which he himself does not belong. His children, the dream suggests, have succeeded in getting away from him and joining the world outside – hence, presumably, his concern to reassure Kate of how fond he really is of them and how much he thinks of them.

In the summer of 1936, Dora took John and Kate on a holiday to Paris. As she did so without Russell's permission, the trip was made the occasion for even more recriminations. 'What fun to have gone to Paris!' Russell wrote to Kate, adding: 'Your mother and I are supposed to consult each other and the Court of Chancery before taking you abroad; she could easily have done so and got consent, but she didn't. It would be a pity if she took you abroad, and then refused to bring you back so as to keep you away from Dartington.' 'This seems a very gentle criticism of my mother's actions,' Kate commented, 'but every word bit like acid in my mind. I knew it was the beginning of another flurry of lawyer's letters and reproaches and justifications, by letters during the term, by mouth during the holidays.'

John and Kate were alarmed too by the suggestion that Russell should sell Telegraph House. It was, Kate said, a house 'I had known and loved since I was four, and so another security was departing from my life'. After Dora was forced to move Beacon Hill School out of Telegraph House, she, her family and her school led an unsettled existence, occupying three different premises in as many years. Forced to leave Boyle's Court in Essex for financial reasons, Dora temporarily joined forces with another school in Northiam, Kent, called 'Brickwall'. This lasted no more than a year and, by the summer of 1937, Beacon Hill School had transferred yet again, this time to Kingwell Hall, near Bath. Here, at last, it settled and, for the two years before the outbreak of war, the school enjoyed what Dora remembers as the best period in its history. Despite the best efforts of Dora and Pat Grace, Kate refused to regard any of these places as her home. Her home, she insisted on believing, was Telegraph House, or, in any case, with her father.

7
BACK TO PHILOSOPHY

The decision to sell Telegraph House had been forced upon Russell by financial considerations. Since he stopped writing for the Hearst Press, his earnings from journalism had dwindled dramatically, and the books that he had written since his divorce – *Education and the Social Order*, *Freedom and Organization*, *Religion and Science*, *Which Way to Peace?* and *The Amberley Papers* – had not sold as well as his 'pot-boilers' of the 1920s. Moreover, he was obliged by the divorce settlement to pay Dora one-third of all his earnings, and was legally bound to continue paying alimony to Frank's widow, Mollie. 'I see ruin staring me in the face,' he wrote to one correspondent.

In the past he had solved such problems by embarking on an American lecture tour, publishing a popular book or increasing his output of journalism. But now that he had decided to write only *serious* books, what was he to do? *The Revolt against Reason*, his planned history of irrationalism, was, if the sales of *Freedom and Organization* were anything to go by, hardly likely to earn him a fortune. In any case, as the Webbs, the Brenans and others had been at pains to tell him, his *real* talent lay in philosophy, not in the analysis of politics and society. But, unless he found an academic position, writing philosophy was not likely to improve his financial situation.

Despite the fact that he repeatedly expressed the feeling that he had wasted his life on philosophy, Russell had to accept that, if he stood any chance at all of a professorship, it would not be in history, politics or physics. Whether he liked it or not, his greatest work had been done in the philosophy of mathematics, and if he was, at this late date, to begin anew his academic career, then it would have to be in philosophy. With this in mind, and perhaps also urged on by the insistence of his friends that outside philosophy he had little of any great importance to say, Russell had been laying the foundations for a return to academic philosophy ever since his 'nervous breakdown' in 1935. In the late summer of that year, he attended the International Congress of Scientific Philosophy in Paris – the first academic conference he had attended since before his marriage to Dora – and immediately afterwards wrote a formidably technical paper called 'On Order in Time', written largely in the symbolism of *Principia Mathematica*. At the age of sixty-three, and after a break of more than a decade (since he had worked on the second edition of *Principia Mathematica*), the effort required to return to the abstruse issues of mathematical logic must have been colossal, especially as he had come to believe that his work in that field had been more or less fruitless.

What motivated him to make such an enormous effort? First, after the emotional upheaval of his divorce and having been brought, so he thought, to the edge of insanity, he wanted more than anything to return to the tranquillity of the contemplative life he had known in his youth. One is reminded of his urge to return to philosophy in 1917, after having been brought to the brink of suicide by the attack upon his character by D. H. Lawrence, thrown into a deep depression by the conviction that his work for peace had all been for nothing, and shocked by the violence of the mob at the demonstration against the Socialist meeting he had attended in East London. Then he had written to Ottoline: 'it is an extraordinary rest to turn my thoughts to abstract things'. So, in the summer of 1935, after returning from his holiday in the Canary Islands, he found his thoughts turning to comfortingly remote subjects. For two months, he says in his *Autobiography*, he 'worked on the problem of the twenty-seven straight lines on a cubic surface'. This was a return to the thoughts that had occupied him in the 1890s, when he had studied topology and projective geometry – an attempt, perhaps, to rediscover the joy he had taken in pure mathematics as a young man, before the corrosive influence of philosophical scepticism had persuaded him that there was not, as he had first thought, a realm of objective, eternal truths to which the study of mathematics might provide access.

Concentrating on such a problem provided a welcome refuge from the traumas of his divorce and the discovery that Peter had had an affair with Richard Llewlyn Davies, but, Russell says, it 'would never do, as it was totally useless and I was living on capital saved during the successful years that ended in 1932'. His paper, 'On Order in Time', sent to the journal *Proceedings of the Cambridge Philosophical Society* at the end of September 1935, could be seen as an attempt to address his financial problems only if it was regarded as the opening shot in a campaign to convince people that he was still capable of working on technical philosophy and therefore still eligible for a university professorship – and this, surely, was its primary purpose. It is possible, I think, that he was partially inspired to return to mathematical logic by the Harvard logician and philosopher, Willard van Orman Quine, who, in the summer of 1935, sent Russell a copy of his book, *A System of Logistic*. Quine, who subsequently became one of the most influential philosophers of the twentieth century, was then just starting out on his career. In his style of writing, his grasp of mathematical technicalities and his concern with the logical foundations of mathematics, Quine might be regarded as a disciple of Russell's, and it must have pleased Russell greatly to see the influence that his earlier works had exerted on so obviously an able mind. Perhaps it even convinced him that his early work on mathematical philosophy had not, after all, been a waste of his talents. Writing to thank Quine for the book, Russell was fulsome in his praise of it.

'I think you have done a beautiful piece of work', he wrote; 'it is a long time since I have had as much intellectual pleasure as in reading you'.

Quine repaid the compliment by publishing a laudatory review of 'On Order in Time' in *The Journal of Symbolic Logic* in the summer of 1936. Despite Quine's praise, however, the paper has been largely ignored by mathematicians and philosophers alike.[11] The issue it deals with is the peculiarly recherché one of providing a mathematical definition of the notion of an 'instant' of time. Russell assumes that the definition must be made in terms of classes; that an instant must be defined as a class of physical events (that is, those events that 'all happen at the same time'). Then, using the theory of classes that he and Whitehead had developed in *Principia Mathematica*, he shows that such a definition will not work unless one has a method of 'well-ordering' the whole class of physical events. As no such method exists, he concludes that it is impossible to prove the existence of temporal instants; a conclusion, he says, 'which may be not without importance in physics'. In fact, Russell's argument has not troubled physicists one bit, for – as Russell would have known very well – the 'order in time' of which he painstakingly attempts to provide a rigorous mathematical definition is one that physicists abandoned when they accepted Einstein's Theory of Relativity. The 'relativity of simultaneity' that forms a central part of Einstein's theory dispenses with the notion of time as a single, sequential ordering of events, and so the conclusion that 'instants', in Russell's sense, cannot be rigorously defined is of very little conseqence.

The impression created by 'On Order in Time' is that of an ageing mental gymnast putting himself through his paces for no other purpose than to show that he can still do it. The signal it sends out is that, in his sixties, Russell could still juggle with abstract ideas and logical formulae as well as anyone. What remained to be shown, if he was to convince anyone to employ him as a philosophy professor, was that he still had something interesting and important to say. Taking up this challenge with impressive vigour, Russell wrote, soon after 'On Order in Time', a paper called 'The Limits of Empiricism', which he read to the Moral Science Club in Cambridge at the end of November 1935 and which is arguably his most serious contribution to philosophical debate since the First World War.

'The Limits of Empiricism' shows Russell determined to engage with the work of the philosophers of the 1930s, rather than (as had been his wont for a long time) rehashing the debates he had had at the turn of the century with such figures as Henri Bergson and William James. In particular, it might be read as an indirect attempt to engage with the later work of Wittgenstein, which, as Russell would have known, had by this time become the centre of much discussion among philosophers at Oxford and Cambridge. Wittgenstein had been lecturing at Cambridge since 1929, and, though he had not published any of his later work, it was becoming well known that he had

---

[11] However, it has been made the subject of an intelligent and sympathetic analysis by C. Anthony Anderson – see 'Russell on Order in Time' in *Rereading Russell: Essays in Bertrand Russell's Metaphysics and Epistemology*, edited by C. Wade Savage and C. Anthony Anderson.

come to reject many of the views that he had expressed in *Tractatus Logico-Philosophicus* and was developing an entirely fresh approach to philosophical problems. Knowledge of Wittgenstein's new views spread, partly through the reports of people who had attended his lectures, and partly from clandestine reproductions of the 'Blue Book', a typescript he had handed out to his students during the academic year, 1933–4. In the autumn of 1935, just when Russell was writing 'The Limits of Empiricism', Wittgenstein sent him a copy of the Blue Book, describing it as 'some notes' he had dictated to his students 'so that they might have something to carry home with them, in their hands if not in their brains'.

When Wittgenstein heard that Russell was to come to Cambridge in November 1935 to read 'The Limits of Empiricism' to the Moral Science Club, he wrote a characteristically tortuous explanation of the difficulty that this presented to him. He had, he explained, stopped going to the club, because of complaints made by C. D. Broad and others that he dominated the discussions too much. But, if Russell wished him to attend, he would do so, 'Broad or no Broad'. In any case, he suggested, perhaps he and Russell could take the opportunity to have a philosophical discussion in his rooms the day after the meeting. 'I am pleased that you're reading my MS,' Wittgenstein told Russell. 'But please don't think it's in any way necessary. You need neither write nor speak a review about it.'

Wittgenstein evidently anticipated Russell's visit with an intense sense of occasion, expecting perhaps that Russell's paper would consist at least partly in a response to the Blue Book, or, at the very least, that Russell would in private conversation respond to his latest work. Russell's reply to Wittgenstein's letter has not survived, but it seems that he did not react to these overtures with the reassurance that Wittgenstein was looking for, since Wittgenstein did not, after all, attend Russell's lecture, nor, apparently, did the two of them engage in private philosophical debate. Wittgenstein's friend Rush Rhees, however, remembers that Wittgenstein was very anxious to know what Russell said and asked Rhees to attend the lecture and give him a full report of it.

Russell, too, approached the occasion with great anticipation. The preliminary notes and drafts that survive show that he lavished more care upon the writing of 'The Limits of Empiricism' than he had done on anything he had written since *The Analysis of Mind*. He evidently wanted this paper to make an impression; it was to mark his re-entry into the world of academic philosophy. More than that, it was to be his attempt to recapture the attention of a Cambridge now in thrall to his erstwhile student.

The theme of the paper does not at first appear to be very Wittgensteinian. Whereas Wittgenstein had inaugurated a conception of philosophy that eschewed traditional questions of knowledge in favour of questions of meaning, Russell takes as his starting point the time-honoured question: what are the foundations of knowledge? In his 'logicist' days of the beginning of the century, Russell had believed that one secure foundation upon which knowledge might be built was logic, but, since his adoption of a

Wittgensteinian 'linguistic' view of logic, he now believed that logic by itself gave us no knowledge at all; it just enabled us to infer one thing from another, which, when properly understood, amounted simply to restating the same thing in different words. Knowledge had to start, not from logic, but from sense-experience. It had to be built, not from the kind of logical axioms with which *Principia Mathematica* begins, but from what Russell had for a long time called 'sense-data', the information received from immediate experience – what Russell, in his epistemological work of 1912–14, had called 'direct acquaintance'.

Accepting this view placed Russell firmly in the tradition of British empiricism that included Locke, Berkeley, Hume and Mill, a central tenet of which was that all knowledge derived from experience. In 'The Limits of Empiricism', however, Russell subjected this view to searching and perceptive doubts, centred on the problem of saying what, exactly, sense-data *are*. Is it possible to identify the objects of our immediate experience? Can we isolate the immediate from the mediated, what we see from what we infer? Say, for example, that someone is hurt and cries out: do we hear the cry and *infer* that the person is hurt? As Russell says: 'The pain and the cry are within one specious present, and we seem to *see* a connection between the two.' But what is it to *see* a connection? A connection is not, after all, an object. If you look at a photograph of a mother and another of her daughter and you see a likeness between the two, that likeness is not some third object that you see in addition to the two photographs. A connection is a relation, and relations are what Russell calls *universals*, rather than particulars.

The 'limits of empiricism', then, are reached when we are forced to admit that the notion of 'sense-experience' is a good deal more complicated than traditional empiricists thought. For once we acknowledge that, among the objects of immediate perception, are universals as well as particulars, the doctrine that all our knowledge comes from our senses loses much of its simplicity and becomes, indeed, rather mysterious. In his preliminary notes for the paper, Russell was even prepared to draw the Kantian moral that 'knowledge is not derived solely from pure logic and pure sense, but also from synthetic knowledge concerning universals'. In the same set of notes, he also outlined the similarity between the line of thought he was developing and that which Wittgenstein had been developing in his Cambridge lectures since 1930. Having listed some of the ways in which we might be said to *see* universals – the relations between colours, the musical intervals between different notes, and so on – Russell remarks: 'These are the things that Wittgenstein calls "grammar".'

Thus, beginning from a set of problems inherited from Locke and Berkeley, Russell had ended up, consciously, in Wittgensteinian territory. The idea that we can *see* connections is central to Wittgenstein's later philosophy, and he had wrestled intensely with precisely the problem Russell was addressing in 'The Limits of Empiricism' – the problem of describing *how* we can see connections when connections are not a kind of object. The problem has echoes, too, of the work Russell had written during the year 1912–13, when he and Wittgenstein had worked closely together.

Then, in his unfinished paper 'What is Logic?' and again in his abandoned manuscript, *The Theory of Knowledge*, Russell had struggled inconclusively with the problem of what logical form was. Convinced by Wittgenstein that logical forms were not objects, he nevertheless wanted to insist that, in thinking about logic and mathematics, we had 'direct acquaintance' of them. As direct acquaintance was then understood by him to be a relation between a mind and an object, Russell seemed locked into a contradiction, from which he could not free himself. In *Tractatus Logico-Philosophicus*, Wittgenstein had avoided this and similar difficulties by appealing to the difference between what can be said and what has to be shown (seen); the truths of logic, for example, can be *seen*, but they cannot, without contradiction, be stated. Wittgenstein's emphasis on 'the kind of understanding that consists in seeing connections' in his later work was the direct descendant of this point of view.

Russell always regarded Wittgenstein's use of the distinction between what can be said and what has to be shown as an unacceptable kind of mysticism, and 'The Limits of Empiricism' does nothing to bring him closer to Wittgenstein on this point. The insistence that we can 'see connections' did not send Russell in the direction of stressing the limits of what can be said, but only of recognising the limits of traditional empiricism. His preferred method of overcoming those limits was through an analysis of what he would later call 'non-demonstrative inference' – the kind of inference that, unlike strictly logical, *demonstrative* inference, might provide the foundations for knowledge. In this way, 'The Limits of Empiricism' provides the agenda for much of the philosophical work that Russell was to write during the rest of his life; its call to 'seek a theory of knowledge other than pure empiricism' being answered by his very last philosophical book, *Human Knowledge*, which he published in 1948.

One respect in which 'The Limits of Empiricism' engaged with the concerns of the philosophers of the 1930s was in connection with Russell's insistence that a proper theory of knowledge must acknowledge that 'we can understand a form of words, and know that it expresses a truth or falsehood, even when we know of no method of deciding the alternative'. This insistence presented a direct challenge to the doctrine of verificationism that was, in the 1930s (partly under Wittgenstein's influence), becoming fashionable among analytic philosophers. Verificationism asserts that a proposition has meaning only if there is a method of establishing whether it is true or false. This doctrine was associated with a group of philosophers led by Moritz Schlick, known as the Vienna Circle of Logical Positivists, with whom Wittgenstein used to have regular meetings. Inspired by the mathematical logic developed by Russell and Frege and by the theory of meaning outlined in Wittgenstein's *Tractatus Logico-Philosophicus*, the Vienna Circle took a robustly scientific view of the world and hoped that, by using the tools bequeathed to them by Russell, Frege and Wittgenstein, they might put philosophy itself on a scientific footing. The purpose of the Verification Principle, from their point of view, was to distinguish meaningful, scientific discourse from meaningless 'metaphysics'. Wittgenstein was, in spirit, far removed from this conception of philosophy, but, for a while at least, he was regarded by the circle as an ally, and it was quite common in the 1930s to hear philosophers speaking of *Wittgenstein's* Verification Principle.

As Wittgenstein had not published any of his later philosophy, Russell's challenge to it in 'The Limits of Empiricism' had necessarily to be indirect. Instead of discussing Wittgenstein's own views, he chose to attack an article published in *Mind* by one of Wittgenstein's students, Alice Ambrose. The article, called 'Finitism in Mathematics', was widely understood to be an exposition of Wittgenstein's latest opinions, though Wittgenstein himself disowned it and, indeed, was furious with Ambrose for having published it. Its central claim is that mathematical propositions that purport to say something about an infinite collection ('all even numbers are the sum of two primes', for example) have either to be recast so as to limit themselves to finite collections or be condemned as meaningless. Her argument for this rests on an application of verificationism to the philosophy of mathematics. 'The finitist', she writes, 'demands that we should be certain of being able to verify or to prove false a verbal form before we hold it to be either true or false.'

Taking Ambrose's formulation of finitism as his text, Russell argues against both the Verification Principle itself and its application to mathematics. With regard to mathematics, Russell argues, the finitist is forced to deny something that is obviously true, namely that, for every number N, there is a greater number, N + 1. The finitist is forced to deny this, since the word 'every' here refers to an *infinite* totality, and the finitist is therefore compelled to say that the phrase makes no sense. More generally, Russell says: 'we can understand a form of words, and know that it expresses either a truth or a falsehood, even when we know of no method of deciding the alternative'.

Wittgenstein did not pick up the cudgels laid down by the challenge of 'The Limits of Empiricism', and the paper, even now, is not as well known among academic philosophers as it deserves to be. It nevertheless succeeded in what was presumably its main purpose: of announcing Russell's return to the world of academic philosophy. After it was delivered at Cambridge in November 1935, Russell was invited to give it at the Aristotelian Society the following April. In the meantime, he had another opportunity of engaging with the important currents of contemporary philosophy when he was asked to review A. J. Ayer's combative first book, *Language, Truth and Logic* for the *The London Mercury*. Ayer wrote the book after a spell in Vienna, learning logical positivism from the Vienna Circle, and it might be regarded as a popularisation of verificationism, introducing it to an English-speaking audience. As soon as it was published, *Language, Truth and Logic* caused a sensation, largely because of the strident way in which Ayer dismissed the work of earlier philosophers, such as F. H. Bradley, and because of the emphasis he gave to the implications of logical positivism for ethics, aesthetics and religion (the propositions of all of which, Ayer confidently asserted, were nonsense).

Safe in the knowledge that he was not one of the earlier philosophers dismissed by Ayer, Russell welcomed the book as representative of 'the youngest and most vigorous off-spring of the marriage of empiricism and mathematical logic which took place at the beginning of the present century'. Expressing again his dissent from the verificationism at the heart of logical positivism, however, Russell chose for his example the proposition 'God exists'. For Ayer, this proposition is meaningless, as no method exists of proving it true or false. This, of course, means that its denial is also meaningless, so that atheism is rejected by Ayer as much as theism. As Russell puts it, Ayer is 'led to a view which is opposed equally to the assertions of the orthodox and to the doubts or denials of the sceptics'. To this, Russell responds that 'the word "God" is one which arouses certain emotions, and the question in people's minds is whether there is an object to which these emotions are appropriate'. This question, Russell insists, 'is not disposed of by Mr Ayer's arguments'.

Shortly before his review of Ayer appeared, Russell was given a further opportunity to announce his intention of returning to academic philosophy when he was invited to deliver a public lecture by the Philosophical Society of the University of Durham. He chose to deliver a paper on 'Determinism and Physics', a theme that allowed him both to continue his polemic against Eddington's interpretation of physics and to develop the themes of 'The Limits of Empiricism'. Russell's argument in 'The Limits of Empiricism' seemed to demand that, in addition to formal logical principles and sense-data, we recognise the need for 'non-demonstrative' principles of reason upon which to build our knowledge of the world. An example of such a principle would be the Law of Causality, the assumption that everything that happens in the world can be attributed to a causal law (a law linking cause and effect) that is, in theory, discoverable. Eddington, in his reflections upon quantum physics, had (in common with many other scientists) advanced the idea that modern science had, in effect, given up the Law of Causality. The behaviour of subatomic particles cannot be brought under deterministic causal laws. And this, argued Eddington, is not because we do not yet know *what* causal laws apply to these particles; rather, it is that their behaviour is *in fact* non-deterministic.

In 'Determinism and Physics', Russell rejects Eddington's interpretation of the philosophical significance of quantum physics, arguing that determinism is *still* the 'best working hypothesis' about the nature of the world. Indeed, Russell argues, causality is an 'unavoidable working hypothesis in all scientific investigations'; where determinism fails, he insists, 'scientific knowledge fails'. It follows that, if Eddington is right about the behaviour of particles at a quantum level, then no scientific knowledge at that level is even possible – a conclusion that can be avoided, Russell suggests, if we assume that the *apparent* refusal of subatomic particles to behave in accordance with the laws of classical mechanics is due, not to their inherent nature, but rather to our imperfect and incomplete knowledge. And, if we are too quick to abandon belief in a deterministic physical world, he implies, we will *never* discover what causal laws *do* operate at the quantum level.

During 1936, then, Russell had three articles published in impeccably academic journals – 'Determinism and Physics' in the *Proceedings of the University of Durham*, 'On Order in Time' in the *Proceedings of the Cambridge Philosophical Society*, and 'The Limits of Empiricism' in the *Proceedings of the Aristotelian Society* – and by the end of the year he felt ready to make approaches towards securing an academic appointment.

His first move in this direction was a letter to his American publisher, Warder Norton, written on 30 November 1936, putting out feelers for a job in an American university. He would, he told Norton, 'like to live in America if it were financially feasible'. His chief reason for this, he said in a subsequent letter, was that 'Europe is no place for children, with the imminent risk of war – particularly England, which is likely to suffer most in the next war'. This seems to imply that he was planning to take John and Kate with him, though it is hard to see how he imagined Dora falling in with that plan. Peter was then two months pregnant (Conrad was born the following April), so perhaps he was thinking of the children he might have with Peter, rather than those he already had. In any case, it seems of a piece with his desire in the spring of 1936 to move to Spain and his later suggestion that the Brenans should adopt Conrad if anything happened to him and Peter. Evidently, he did not want to bring Conrad up in an England that was heading for war with Germany.

Russell's intention in writing to Norton was to ask him to sound out the possibility of a Research Chair at Princeton's Institute of Advanced Study, a prestigious and highly desirable honour awarded to many distinguished European intellectuals, most notably Einstein. The trouble was, he could remember neither the name of the institute nor the university that housed it. Thus he was forced to write to Norton in vague terms: 'I gather there is a university somewhere in America which has given Einstein and many others purely research jobs. Do you know which it is? If I had any chance of such a job I should apply for it.' Norton, of course, knew which institute Russell had in mind, and replied that he had been 'pulling wires and otherwise wangling for that Princeton post'. Norton's 'wangling', however, proved ineffective. The Director of the institute, Abraham Flexner, wrote to Russell to say that his application had been rejected. No reason was given, but it seems possible that personal matters played a part: Flexner's brother, Simon, was the husband of Alys's cousin, Helen Thomas. It is equally possible, however, that the institute simply had no use for Russell. There are no Philosophy Chairs at the Institute for Advanced Study, so, if they had hired Russell, it would have had to have been as a mathematician or as a social scientist, and in neither field was it very plausible to imagine the sixty-five-year-old Russell conducting original research at the highest level.

Despite his desire to move to America, Russell next tried Cambridge. On 8 February 1937, he wrote to G. E. Moore asking for a job. 'I have become very desirous of returning to purely philosophic work,' he began:

[I]n particular, I want to develop the ideas in my paper on 'The Limits of Empiricism', & to investigate the relation of language to fact, as to which Carnap's ideas seem to me very inadequate. But I am in the unfortunate position of being legally bound to pay between £800 & £900 a year to other people, & having only £300 a year of unearned income. I cannot therefore work at philosophy unless I can get some academic job. I suppose there is no possibility at Cambridge? I should be very glad if there were, as my desire to get back to philosophy is very strong.

Moore's reply has not survived, but it was evidently not encouraging. 'It is hardly worth proceeding in the matter,' Russell told him in a subsequent letter, 'as the chance of success seems small, & there are other possibilities elsewhere.'

Were there other possibilities elsewhere? In his letter to Moore, Russell mentioned the possibility of a two-year Fellowship from the Leverhulme Foundation, but nothing seems to have come of that. Nor did anything come of an approach he made to Whitehead in Harvard. 'I should *very much* like to succeed Whitehead at Harvard,' he told Norton, 'but I have no reason to suppose that he contemplates retirement. Have you?'

When the Webbs visited Russell at Telegraph House in March 1937, they found him 'physically worn out and mentally worried', and, commented Beatrice, '[at] sixty five, with a young wife and a coming child, with little or no income beyond what he earns . . . well he may be':

He would like a Professorship, but he is past the age at which any British university could appoint him. His only hope is the USA. But his particular subject, the philosophy of mathematics, is off the modern curriculum: physical and sociological investigations are in the ascendant. Russell's wit and subtlety, his literary skill and personal charm, his particular obsessions in favour of freedom for the intellectual coupled with non-resistance, are all demoded in favour of factual (not philosophical) studies of how we can climb out of the terrible tragedy of international hostilities and decadent capitalism.

She and Sidney, she went on, had been thinking of how they could help Russell; after all, did they not owe him a debt of gratitude for his generosity in donating money to the London School of Economics in its early days? 'He ought to be given a Civil List pension,' she concluded, 'but what government would reward so distinguished a rebel against authority, human or divine?'

Gradually, word spread among Russell's old friends that he was in financial difficulties. Desmond MacCarthy wrote to sympathise with him about having to pay alimony to Molly and Dora, reminding him of the story of Schopenhauer, who, having injured an old woman by throwing her downstairs, was legally bound to pay her a certain sum every quarter for as long as she lived. When she died, Schopenhauer wrote in his diary: '*Obit anus, abit onus*' ('The old woman dies, the burden departs'). 'I look forward',

MacCarthy told Russell, 'to getting *two* postcards from you, soon, with these words on them.' 'Is it true', he added, 'that you could manage on £500 a year till you can write those post-cards? Your admirers ought to be able to raise that. Would you object to being pensioned?'

Indeed, Russell did not, and he was only too grateful when he heard through Ottoline that George Santayana was willing to help him out by giving him £1,000 a year. Only, he asked: 'Do you think Santayana would mind arrangements intended to prevent the money going to Dora?' For, he explained, 'if *I* am given capital, or a claim to an annual sum, Dora will get her share'. The solution arrived at was that the money should be given as an 'anonymous' gift, rather than as something Russell had a legal right to, and the first six-monthly £500 duly arrived in September 1937.

Throughout 1937, as he waited anxiously to find a buyer for Telegraph House, Russell steadfastly refused to return to the kind of popular writing that had earnt him so much money throughout the previous two decades, concentrating instead on work aimed at the academic community. Towards the end of the year he wrote a new Introduction to *The Principles of Mathematics*, the book – first published in 1903 – that was (and is) generally regarded as his greatest contribution to philosophy. The new Introduction provided Russell with an opportunity to respond to the huge amount of work that had been written on the philosophy of mathematics in the 1920s and 1930s, and, in particular, to put on record his views on the two rival schools that had arisen during that time: the formalists, led by David Hilbert, and the intuitionists, led by L. E. J. Brouwer. The formalists – officially, at any rate – regarded mathematics as a set of uninterpreted symbols, which were, in themselves, meaningless. They had forgotten, Russell charged, 'that numbers are needed, not only for doing sums, but for counting', and therefore they were unable to say what the word 'twelve' meant in such propositions as 'There were twelve apostles'. 'The formalists', Russell wrote, 'are like a watchmaker who is so absorbed in making his watches look pretty that he has forgotten their purpose of telling the time, and has therefore omitted to insert any works.'

So much for formalism. Intuitionism, Russell says, 'is a more serious matter'. Its proponents' view was that logicism – the point of view espoused by Russell in *The Principles of Mathematics*, as well as by Frege – had fundamentally misunderstood the relationship between logic and mathematics. Far from mathematics being a branch of logic, as Russell and Frege took it to be, the intuitionists regarded mathematics as an autonomous kind of thinking, one that was *more* basic even than logic. Logic, according to Brouwer, was essentially linguistic, whereas mathematics was founded on a set of pre-linguistic 'intuitions' about space and time. What Brouwer called the 'basal intuitions' – those upon which the whole of mathematics is ultimately founded – concerned only the natural numbers: 1,2,3 . . . , and a central tenet of intuitionism was that those parts of mathematics that cannot be constructed out of this initial base ought to be regarded as doubtful. Unless a 'constructive' method existed of proving a theorem, Brouwer held, it cannot be regarded as being either true or false; this meant that a basic law

Russell and Dora during the General Election of 1922.
'Living and working together day by day, very much in harmony about our
beliefs and purposes, we had become almost part of each other'
(Dora Russell, *The Tamarisk Tree*)

Dora with baby John
and (inset) Dora in Cornwall in the early 1920s

Russell, John and Dora on holiday in 1924

The family in Cornwall,
the 'Garden of Eden', summer 1925

(right) Alice Stücki and Russell with John
and Kate, summer 1926

Telegraph House

(left and below) Dora with the children
at Beacon Hill School

'Anyone would think he was the child's father': Griffin Barry and Dora with baby Harriet, 1930

(above) Dora, John, Kate, Harriet and baby Roddy, 1932

(from left) Griffin Barry, Harriet, Peter and Russell, Hendaye, 1932

Kate, Peter and John at Hendaye

Griffin Barry and John at Hendaye

(right) Paul Gillard

Patricia (Peter) Russell at Telegraph House, c. 1936

Russell lecturing at UCLA, 1939 and
(inset) Peter and Conrad in Chicago, 1938

'As I stood high on the deck watching Southampton dock receding into the distance,
I felt I was escaping from a nightmare'. As she sails for America in August 1939,
Kate leaves behind: Pat Grace (cigarette in mouth), Dora (to the right of him),
Harriet (in front of Pat) and Roddy (in front of Dora)

John and Kate in Los Angeles,
c. 1940

Russell, Peter, Conrad and Kate in front
of a giant Californian Redwood tree,
summer 1939

Russell and Dr Albert C. Barnes, 3 January 1941,
Russell's first day at the Barnes Foundation

Russell, Conrad and Peter in the grounds of Trinity College, Cambridge, 1944

John (second from left) in Washington, 1945

Kate as a graduate student at Radcliffe, 1947

John and Susan at the time of their wedding in August, 1946

Susan Russell, c. 1951

(left) Plas Penrhyn

Russell in his study
at Plas Penrhyn,
1957

Ralph Schoenman,
Russell and Edith
on their way to
Bow Street Court,
12 September 1961

Ralph Schoenman
celebrates 'the
beauty of Bertie',
Royal Festival Hall,
London, 1962

(from left) Sarah, Russell, Anne, Edith and Lucy, 1956

Lucy Russell, 1968

of logic, the so-called 'Law of Excluded Middle' (which says that *every* proposition is either true or false), cannot be used in mathematical proofs. This in turn meant that large parts of standard analysis – including the work that had inspired Russell's philosophy of mathematics – had to be abandoned until 'constructive' proofs could be found for the theorems in question.

In objecting to this point of view in his new Introduction to *The Principles of Mathematics*, Russell rehearsed the arguments he had used in 'The Limits of Empiricism' against Alice Ambrose's 'finitism'. The idea that we cannot know that a proposition is either true or false, until we have a method for deciding which, has, Russell says, 'consequences even more destructive than those that are recognised by its advocates'. It would prevent us from making *any* general statement – such as 'All men are mortal' – about a collection defined by its properties, and thus 'would make a clean sweep of all science and of all mathematics, not only of the parts which the intuitionists consider questionable'. Such a doctrine could be challenged, Russell insists, only by a 'complete theory of knowledge', one that showed such 'thorough-going empiricism' to be false. It was such a 'complete theory' that Russell hoped to provide, if only he were able to secure an academic appointment.

In September 1937, Russell was able, at last, to sell Telegraph House and move to somewhere cheaper. He decided to move to Oxford, having in the summer been invited to give a series of lectures there on 'Words and Facts'. This, he hoped, would in time lead to an offer of a permanent job. He and Peter found a suitable house in Kidlington, just north of Oxford, which they called 'Amberley House'. It was a small house, too small even to put up John and Kate during the holidays, but they converted two tiny outhouses into guest rooms. Soon after moving in, Russell wrote to Ottoline:

> I have gone back to philosophy & I want people to talk about it. I am lecturing (at Oxford) & shall get to know all the people in my line, of whom, among the younger dons, there are now quite a number. In Cambridge I am an ossified orthodoxy: in Oxford, still a revolutionary novelty.

Russell's lectures at Oxford did not lead to a job, and he was to complain later that he was excluded from Oxford society ('only one Oxford lady called,' he wrote in his *Autobiography*. 'We were not respectable'). A. J. Ayer, however, who was then still at Christ Church, maintains that Russell 'was certainly not neglected by the younger philosophers, many of whom attended his lectures and discussed them with him afterwards', and one of those younger philosophers, James Urmson, recalls that so many students turned up to Russell's lectures that the largest lecture room in Examination Schools overflowed.

Though he still had no academic position, Russell had succeeded in his aim of getting people to talk about his latest work and to recognise his intention of re-entering the philosophical profession. In 1938, A. J. Ayer published an article, 'On the Scope of Empirical Knowledge', that dealt respectfully – albeit critically – with Russell's argument in 'The Limits of Empiricism', and for the academic year 1937–8 Russell was elected President of the Aristotelian Society. His presidential address, given on 8 November 1937, was 'On Verification', which renewed his engagement with the views of Ayer and the positivists.

Though Russell's intention in 'On Verification' was clearly to contribute to the issues that dominated philosophical debate in the 1930s, in some ways the paper served to highlight the fundamental difference between himself and the younger philosophers with whom he sought to engage. Amongst these younger philosophers, interest in the Verification Principle centred on its application to questions of *meaning*, but Russell scarcely discusses this aspect of verificationism in his paper, concentrating instead – as he had in all the papers he had written since returning to philosophy – on questions of *knowledge*. The central theme of 'On Verification' is the tenability of the notion, employed by Ayer and others, of a 'basic proposition', that is, a proposition that is derived not from other propositions but from direct experience. Russell's view is that there have to be such propositions in order for there to be any knowledge at all. However, perhaps rather curiously, he analyses these propositions, not from the point of view of logic, nor even of epistemology, but rather from that of psychology. A 'basic proposition', in Russell's analysis, is not one that is *true*, but one that, psychologically, we cannot help believing.

This psychologistic point of view Russell contrasts with the more linguistic conception of basic propositions held by the logical positivists, Rudolf Carnap and Otto Neurath. For these latter two philosophers, basic propositions – what they call 'protocol sentences' – are accepted, 'verified', not by experience of reality, but by their consonance with other sentences, particularly those of the physical sciences. 'The logical tendency of this theory', Russell objects, 'is towards a Platonic idealism: The Real World will be that of words, while the world of sense will be condemned as illusory.' In Russell's understanding, 'verification' does not take the form of measuring it against what scientists of the day tell us, but rather of measuring a proposition against certain psychological states: expectation, surprise, and so on. Words produce expectations ('Look, there is a dog' produces the expectation of seeing a dog), and where those expectations are fulfilled, the proposition expressed by the words has been 'verified'; where they are not, the proposition is shown to be false. 'Verification', therefore, Russell claims, 'is emotional rather than intellectual; we prefer what we consider "truth" to what we consider "falsehood" partly because we cannot help it, and partly because surprise, which is the mark of falsehood, is usually unpleasant.'

This tendency to look at philosophical problems from the point of view of empirical psychology surprised many of the philosophers within the analytic tradition, who regarded Russell as one of the pioneers of the view that sharply differentiated logical from psychological problems. At the Joint Session of the Mind and Aristotelian Societies held in Oxford in the summer of 1938, the Cambridge philosopher Richard Braithwaite took Russell to task on this point in a paper called 'The Relevance of Psychology to Logic'. Quoting extensively from both 'The Limits of Empiricism' and 'On Verification', Braithwaite argued that Russell had confused the *meaning* of propositions with the *causes* that, on particular occasions, might make someone utter them; only the latter, he insisted, can be dealt with by naturalistic psychology, the former being the province of logic and philosophy (Wittgenstein made the same point by saying that, if I push you, causing you to fall over, your fall is not the *meaning* of my push). 'Problems of logic and theory of knowledge', Braithwaite declared, 'cannot be solved by considerations which belong to the science of psychology ... It should be the task of logicians, by taking account of the linguistic considerations, to strengthen Philosophy against the onslaught of the infidel psychologists.'

In his reply, Russell remarked that it was the problem of meaning 'which first led me, about twenty years ago, to abandon the anti-psychological opinions in which I had previously believed'. The meanings of words, he insisted, had to be understood in terms of the experiences, beliefs, expectations, and so on of the people using them, and that is why psychology is relevant. The emphasis in Russell's reply, however, as always, is not on the theory of meaning, but on the theory of knowledge. 'I hold', he states, 'that, in a critical scrutiny of what passes for knowledge, the ultimate point is one where doubt is psychologically impossible, whereas he [Braithwaite] holds that it is one where doubt is logically absurd.' Doubt, in Russell's view, is *never* logically absurd – scepticism is, to that extent, irrefutable – and thus the most secure foundation we can hope to achieve in philosophy will have to be built, not by logic (as he himself had once imagined possible) but by empirical matters of fact, including those of psychology.

At stake in this debate was the issue that would continue to divide Russell from the younger generation of analytic philosophers for the rest of his life. Whereas he sought in philosophy a foundation for *knowledge*, they sought a theory of meaning; whereas he thought of philosophy as continuous with the natural sciences, they thought of it as a separate, autonomous study. So, with regard to answering the sceptic – the person who challenges *any* claim to knowledge by finding reasons for doubt – they, the younger, Wittgensteinian philosophers, sought to show that the sceptical challenge was meaningless, while Russell's approach was to acknowledge that there was no *certain* knowledge and to look for the next best thing. Whatever the merits of each view, it must have become apparent to Russell during 1935–8 that he was swimming against the tide. The chairman of his debate with Braithwaite, Friedrich Waismann, was expressing the view of an entire generation of British philosophers when he announced that he was 'largely in agreement with Mr Braithwaite's views as to the relation between logic and psychology'.

By the time of his debate with Braithwaite, Russell had at last succeeded in securing an academic appointment, albeit a temporary post. In March 1938, he was offered a one-year contract as a visiting Professor of Philosophy at the University of Chicago. The salary was fairly high – $5,000 – and his duties were light. He had to give one seminar class on a subject of his choice and a few occasional lectures. Other than that, he was told, 'your time would be your own'. It was not quite what he was hoping for, but, as it was the best offer he was likely to get, he accepted immediately.

Before he left for the United States in September, Russell had to finish a book on power that he had agreed to write for Stanley Unwin. He wrote it during the summer of 1938 in the atmosphere of foreboding that pervaded England as, in the aftermath of the *Anschluss* between Germany and Austria, the European nations prepared for war. 'I have very little hope that a great war will be avoided,' Russell wrote to Ottoline on 10 April. 'Chamberlain is only talking peace till our re-armament is complete. No doubt he would like to preserve peace, but I don't believe he thinks it possible.'

Ottoline had for a long time been very ill, with a variety of symptoms that baffled her doctors, whose many diagnoses varied from diabetes to 'poisoning of the nervous system'. Exhausted, emaciated and so weak that she was unable to get up from bed, she was being treated at the Sherwood Park Clinic at Tunbridge Wells by a doctor called Cameron, who was at this time being investigated by the medical authorities because of his misuse of a new, powerful antibiotic called Prontosil, which, against expert advice, he administered to his patients through injections. Apparently believing that Prontosil could cure anything, Cameron prescribed it to Ottoline. On 21 April 1938, while receiving her morning injection, Ottoline died of heart failure. 'The news is a terrible blow,' Russell wrote to her husband, Philip. 'A great part of my life, stretching back into childhood, is gone dead with her. I do not know anything consoling to say.'

Inevitably, perhaps, *Power* reflects the sombre times in which it was written. Though conceived by Russell as a major contribution to sociological and political theory, the book reads more naturally as a response to the immediate political situation of the 1930s, a plea to the world to turn back from the madness that threatened it. Ostensibly, its chief concern is to argue that power, not wealth, should be the basic concept in social theory, a thesis that Russell regarded as an important challenge to both Marxism and classical economic theory. In his *Autobiography* he records his disappointment that this challenge was not taken more seriously by social and political theorists and that 'the book fell rather flat'. 'I still hold', he insists, 'that what it [*Power*] has to say is of very great importance, if the evils of totalitarianism are to be avoided, particularly under a Socialist regime.'

These remarks show the self-delusion to which Russell was prone whenever he wrote on social, political and historical subjects. For, just as *Freedom and Organization* can hardly be regarded as a serious work of scholarly history, so *Power* has few claims to be regarded as a weighty piece of political theory. Indeed, there is very little theoretical discussion in it. In its first chapter, Russell announces that he will 'be concerned to prove that the fundamental concept in social science is Power, in the same sense in which Energy is the fundamental concept in physics', but what follows does not live up to this apparently austere promise. Much of the book is taken up with a sketchy taxonomy of the forms of power: priestly power (exemplified by the popes of pre-Reformation Europe); kingly power (exemplified by the kings of European countries who opposed the power of the Catholic

Church); 'naked power' (defined as that which 'involves no acquiescence on the part of the subject'); revolutionary power (represented by early Christianity, the Reformation and the French and Russian Revolutions); economic power (banks and big business); power over opinion (the force of reasoned argument and propaganda); and, finally, the power of creeds.

After listing the forms of power, Russell then discusses the ethics of power and what he calls 'power philosophies' (the now familiar list of philosophical villains – Fichte, the pragmatists, Nietzsche, Bergson – whom he had earlier identified as the intellectual ancestors of Fascism), before ending with what, one feels, he is *really* interested in, namely the *taming* of power. Russell's suggested means of taming power, unsurprisingly, is through educating young people to love each other more than they love power, and training them to subject all creeds and propaganda to critical thought:

> . . . just as we teach children to avoid being destroyed by motor cars if they can, so we should teach them to avoid being destroyed by cruel fanatics, and to this end we should seek to produce independence of mind, somewhat sceptical and wholly scientific, and to preserve, as far as possible, the instinctive joy of life that is natural to healthy children. This is the task of a liberal education: to give a sense of the value of things other than dominion, to help to create wise citizens of a free community, and through the combination of citizenship with liberty in individual creativeness to enable men to give to human life that splendour which some few have shown that it can achieve.

Thus the book ends, reading more like a sermon than an attempt to redefine the basic concepts of a theoretical enterprise. As Gerald Brenan, Beatrice Webb and others had noted, Russell was almost unable to theorise about politics; what he wanted was to change the world, and to do so quickly and fundamentally. But saying 'war should be abolished' is not a contribution, either to the theory of war or to its abolition; nor is saying 'people should be more reasonable' a large step in making them so. Russell's purpose in writing *Power*, like his purpose in writing *Freedom and Organization*, was to persuade mankind to avoid the mistakes it seemed about to make. But his solutions are too pat to be convincing and, in place of theory, he offers, for the most part, rhetoric. 'If human life is to be, for the mass of mankind, anything better than a dull misery punctuated with moments of sharp horror,' runs a characteristic passage from *Power*, 'there must be as little naked power as possible':

> The exercise of power, if it is to be something better than the infliction of wanton torture, must be hedged round by safeguards of law and custom, permitted only after due deliberation, and entrusted to men who are closely supervised in the interests of those who are subjected to them.

'I do not pretend that this is easy,' he adds. 'It involves, for one thing, the elimination of war, for all war is an exercise of naked power. It involves a world free from those intolerable oppressions that give rise to rebellions. It involves the raising of the standard of life throughout the world, and particularly in India, China and Japan, to at least the level which had been reached in the United States before the depression.' And so on. The message of *Power*, then, is a very familiar one: if we educate children properly, they will reason correctly and love one another and the result will be that famine, war, hatred, poverty and oppression will be abolished. Under the guise of restructuring political, social and economic theory, it in fact merely repeats the prescriptions for a happy life that Russell had been retailing since *On Education*.

Meanwhile, Russell's relations with his first son, John, upon whom the burden of Russell's hopes for 'scientific' parenting and education had fallen since his birth, were going from bad to worse. The year Russell and Peter spent at Oxford, Kate recalls, 'was a time of bitter division for us all: faultfinding between our parents and cautious silence between John and me'. When John and Kate came to stay at Kidlington, they stayed in the adjoining cottages: Kate in the one nearest the house and John in the far one. While Kate spent her time with Russell, Peter and the infant Conrad, John would confine himself to his own cottage, 'like an animal at bay', as Kate put it: 'There he stayed much of the time, in untidy isolation, protecting himself from adult demands for loyalty and other assaults on his emotions.' Sometimes, Kate would try to talk to him about the family conflicts, but her liking for Peter and his sympathy for Dora made such conversations difficult. When she asked him about it, Kate remembers, 'his brief and noncommittal answers made me realise that he saw the situation differently and didn't want to discuss it'.

Russell, perhaps surprisingly, was more concerned about Kate's state of mind than John's. After the Christmas holiday of 1937, he wrote to Curry, the headmaster at Dartington, to say that Kate had seemed tired, listless and morose, symptoms that Russell interpreted as suggesting that she might have inherited the family madness. An eye should be kept out for signs of further mental deterioration, he demanded. In reply, Curry pointed out as delicately as he could that, without appealing to inherited traits of insanity, there was a perfectly adequate explanation for Kate's emotional disturbances. The animosity between Russell and Dora, Curry explained, was embarrassingly well known at the school and a source of great distress to Kate. When Kate heard about the correspondence, it only added to her embarrassment and pain:

> I can still remember, among all that I have forgotten, the rage and pain of those months of 1938, when my anguish was exposed and clumsy adults tried to 'do something about' an incurable wound.
>
> None of us had the insight (or perhaps the honesty) to face the real causes in our tangled family situation. Curry understood, of course, but there was a limit to what he could say to a parent who was also one of his heroes.

In an effort to 'do something about' Kate's depression, Russell and Peter came down to Dartington for a long visit, taking John and Kate on walks and expeditions and buying them cream teas, hoping, as Kate later put it, 'that this would put me right'. Meanwhile, Kate had to cope with long, angry, self-justifying letters from Dora, full of anger against Russell, Dartington, Curry and, most of all, Peter. Living in luxury at Dartington and in snobbish luxury with Peter, Dora argued, how could John and Kate learn to be like other people and to live as most people do? In Dora's mind, the split between her own 'proletarian' life and the 'aristocratic' life enjoyed by Russell and Peter was mixed with the political split between those left-wingers, like her, who thought that the Labour Party should join the Communists and the Soviet Union in a 'United Front' against Fascism, and the pacifists, like Russell, who still hoped for an avoidance of conflict. In this dispute, as in others, Curry, an active member of the Peace Pledge Union, was squarely on Russell's side, and Dora believed, perhaps with some justification, that an ideological barrier was being erected between her and her children: 'What your mother stands for, you are now for the time being, prevented from loving,' as Dora put it in a long letter to Kate. 'What really troubled her', Kate has claimed, 'was her own poverty and toil compared with Peter's elegant life, and the struggles of Beacon Hill compared with the American wealth of Dartington. She was extremely envious and had to dress it up as a matter of proletarian principle because envy is bad.'

In the summer of 1938, before Russell left for Chicago, he and Peter took John and Kate on holiday to Pembrokeshire. While Russell, Peter and Conrad slept in a caravan, John and Kate slept in tents. It was not a success. 'Peter was not used to doing all the meals for the family,' Kate remembers, 'let alone doing them in a tiny caravan, and she got very tired.' To make matters worse, the weather was dreadful, and one night Kate's tent fell down in the wind and rain and she had to wake up Russell and Peter to beg them to allow her into the caravan. Reluctantly, they agreed. 'We are not really a camping family,' Kate says, 'and it was a mistake; a mistake for which John and I felt guiltily responsible because we had recommended it on the basis of the more successful trip with Dora some years before.'

On 20 September, Russell, Peter and Conrad set sail for America. They were leaving an England in the grip of fear over the Czechoslovakian crisis, then at its height. To Gamel Brenan, Russell wrote that he was 'in despair at the thought of leaving John and Kate behind to face the horror without me'. If it had been legally possible, he told her in a subsequent letter, he would have taken them with him. When he arrived in New York on 26 September, he was greeted by newspaper reporters asking him what he thought of Neville Chamberlain's decision to meet Hitler in Munich to discuss the secession of the Sudetenland to Nazi Germany. Russell told them that he had never had a high opinion of Chamberlain as Prime Minister, but that, after his dramatic agreement to meet Hitler to try to avert war, he began to think better of him. He described his own views as those of 'an extreme pacifist', saying that, after the next great war, the world would become 'mad' whoever won: 'I am afraid war would do an extraordinary amount of harm to the world. Even if we win, after the war I am afraid we would be just as mad as Hitler is.'

It took Russell a year to change his mind about this and a further six months to make public his change of heart. In the meantime, he could take some comfort from the fact that at least he, Peter and Conrad were safe from the madness that was about to engulf Europe.

Part IV
1938–70

8
RUSSELL IN AMERICA

Russell's career as a college lecturer in the United States was brief, turbulent and unsuccessful, as, perhaps, it was bound to be. At the age of sixty-six he was attempting not so much to rekindle an academic career as to begin a new one. For over thirty years he had earnt his living as a freelance writer and journalist, and his previous experience as an academic – a five-year Fellowship at Trinity College, Cambridge, from 1896 to 1901 and a six-year spell as a lecturer at the same college from 1910 to 1916 – was a far cry from being a member of Faculty at an American university in 1938. At Cambridge, he had lectured to classes of six and had enjoyed the benefits of a collegiate life that was at once élitist and, in its own way, extraordinarily democratic. Fellows of a Cambridge college were considered, socially and intellectually, equals, and the Master of the college had little opportunity or desire to impose autocratic rule upon them. They wrote what they liked, taught what they liked and, at High Table, discussed whatever interested them in an atmosphere of learned and scholarly conviviality, untouched by the demands of the ways of business and commerce. It was a life that epitomised the monastic contemplation that Russell had, for a long time, alternately despised for its inertia and conservatism and envied for its peaceful seclusion from the hurly-burly of modern times. In any case, it was his model, for better or worse, of what academic life should be like. True, he had spent a term as a visiting lecturer at Harvard in 1914, but on that occasion he had enjoyed the experience so little that he had vowed never to return.

The University of Chicago, prestigious place of learning though it was and is, was even less like pre-war Cambridge than Harvard had been in 1914. In the demands it made on its staff it was far more like a present-day British provincial university. At Chicago, Russell was required to lecture to an undergraduate class of 150 registered students of widely varying ability, and to give seminars attended by (according to one participant) 'several hundred townspeople, including housewives and businessmen, as well as scholars from the University . . . and a sprinkling of physicists, chemists and biologists'. With thousands of students and hundreds of academic staff, the university had necessarily to be governed by a structure far more bureaucratic than that which made decisions at a Cambridge college. At its head was the autocratic and business-like President Hutchins, a man of whom Russell spoke dismissively as being 'occupied with the Hundred Best Books' and whose managerial style extended to trying to influence the kind of philosophy taught at the university. As his sympathies in that respect lay in the area of medieval Catholic philosophy, it was perhaps inevitable that he and Russell would not see eye to eye. Russell went to Chicago hoping that his one-year contract there would be extended. As it was, when his contract expired at the end of the winter session in March 1939, he was left once more to find a new job elsewhere. In his *Autobiography* he devotes a mere paragraph to his six months in Chicago, describing his time there as 'disagreeable': 'The town is beastly and the weather was vile.'

To begin with, however, things seemed to be going well. He, Peter and Conrad arrived in Chicago towards the end of September 1938 and moved into a residential hotel called the Plaisance, on the Midway, close to the university. Decades later, local residents were still vividly recalling their sightings of the great philosopher with his baby son. 'During a chilly fall day,' wrote one, 'with a biting wind sweeping down the Midway, Russell was pushing a baby buggy':

> His face was red from the wind, his pipe gripped between his teeth, his hat clamped firmly on top of his head, and his hands stuffed deep into the pockets of his topcoat. He occasionally gave the buggy a nudge with his stomach and the buggy rolled ahead until he caught up to give it another push. Apparently, it was his way of amusing the baby and enjoying the walk himself.

Russell's undergraduate course was a very standard series of weekly lectures on 'Problems of Philosophy', in which he took his students through the usual canon of philosophical classics – Plato's *Theaetetus*, Descartes's *Meditations*, Berkeley's *Three Dialogues*, Hume's *Treatise*, and so on – and asked them at the end to write a 2,000-word essay on causality.

Of much greater interest to Russell was the series of seminars he gave on 'Words and Facts', the subject that he had lectured on in Oxford. The students who took this course were, Russell judged, much better than those he had taught at Oxford, and included at least three who went on to become professional philosophers: Norman Dalkey, Abraham Kaplan and Irving Copi. But what made the seminars memorable for Russell was that, in addition to the registered students, they were attended by two well-known and established philosophers: Rudolf Carnap and Charles Morris. At each session, Russell would read out parts of the book that he was then preparing – published in 1940 as *An Inquiry into Meaning and Truth* – and then respond to the devil's advocate questions put to him by Carnap, Morris and the others. According to Morris: 'Russell was brilliant and masterly in reply and three of us [Carnap, Morris and Russell] had sufficient in common to make the discussion a genuine "inquiry" and not a "confrontation".' Carnap later recalled: 'Russell had the felicitous ability to create an atmosphere in which every participant did his best to contribute to the common task.'

Carnap, one of the leaders of the Vienna Circle of logical positivists, had been at Chicago since 1935, and had recently published an English edition of his influential work, *The Logical Syntax of Language*. Since being at Chicago, his interests had shifted from syntax to semantics, and in this and in many other respects he was the ideal discussion partner for Russell in 1938 – one with whom he could discuss both his critique of verificationism and his attempts to construct viable theories of meaning and knowledge. These discussions do not appear to have influenced the subsequent work of Carnap very noticeably, but their influence on Russell's *An Inquiry into Meaning and Truth* was, as Russell acknowledged in the Preface to the book, manifest throughout. Not that Russell became converted to logical positivism; nor was he persuaded to abandon the causal theory of meaning, which Braithwaite had criticised so acutely. Indeed, on most of the essential points, Russell's views remained unchanged, but his defence of them became, under the probing questions that he faced during these seminars in Chicago, strikingly more sophisticated.

'We used to have close arguments back and forth,' Russell remembered of his seminars at Chicago, 'and succeeded in genuinely clarifying points to our mutual satisfaction, which is rare in philosophical argument.' This recollection is to some extent challenged by that of Copi, who remembers having to reassure Russell of the great esteem and affection that Carnap had for him in order to 'eliminate or at least to diminish the tension between the two great men'. Carnap had told Copi that his most prized possession was a bound sheaf of papers on which Russell, twenty years earlier, had copied out in his own hand the major propositions of *Principia Mathematica*, after Carnap – then an unknown young man – had written to Russell to say that he could not find a copy of the book in Germany. 'I remember Russell being touched,' Copi later wrote, 'and reminiscing about the time at which he had prepared the material for Carnap.' 'Despite my best efforts, however,' Copi says, 'no real rapprochement took place, though each was unfailingly courteous to the other whenever their paths crossed.'

At the first meeting of the seminar, Dalkey, Kaplan and Copi had hoped to greet Russell with a limerick:

> Discouraged from saving the masses,
> Defamed for depraving the lasses,
>   He kicked off his traces,
>   Came here – of all places –
> Where he's teaching this class – of all classes!

which they wrote on the blackboard before Russell entered the class. When Russell came in, however, no doubt preoccupied with what he was going to say, he saw only that the board was not clear and, without reading what was on it, simply wiped it clean.

After the seminars, Russell and Peter would entertain the graduate students at the Plaisance Hotel. As one of them remembered it, the people attending these 'at homes' would divide into two groups: 'those clustered about Mr Russell, talking chiefly about logic, and those about his wife, a dashing tall redhead many decades his junior, who talked most of the time about relations between the sexes. It was a difference between propositions and propositioning.'

Apart from his regular university teaching, Russell accepted a great number of invitations to give public talks. The Chicago university newspaper, *The Pulse*, reported (surely exaggeratedly) that Russell 'has been delivering from ten to twenty speeches a week'. Russell, the report stated, 'always receives top billing' and showed himself willing to 'talk on anything, from pacifism and free love to symbolic logic'. Invited by the university's Sociology Club to talk on 'The Role of the Intellectual in the Modern World', Russell began:

> I have been speaking a fair amount and I have become quite adept at talking on subjects of which I am completely ignorant, and I gather that is what is expected of me tonight. I want, first of all, before I embark upon my remarks, to make it perfectly clear to you that I am not a social scientist, and I am speaking as an ignoramus. But now, having made this statement, I will assume the prophetic mantle.

This, it seems, was interpreted by those present as an example of Russell's famously acute sense of humour, though one might equally regard it as simply a candid statement of the truth.

At Northwestern University, also located in Chicago, Russell was invited by Paul Arthur Schilpp to give a talk on 'Can Democracy Survive?' The lecture was given on 29 November 1938 at Orchestra Hall, home of the Chicago Symphony Orchestra, and, though Russell seems to have pleased most of the capacity audience, Schilpp felt that the cheque for $1,000 that Russell received on this occasion 'was out of all proportion to what he gave his audience':

> I swear that he had never given that lecture a single thought until he got up on his feet. All the way through he played to the galleries, moving them to laughter or tears, as he pleased. But the audience just loved it and seemed sure that they had gotten much more than their money's worth. It was one of the best illustrations to me that even the great Lord Russell was not beyond stooping to conquer.

Schilpp, who died in 1993 at the age of ninety-six, is known primarily for his editorship of the 'Library of Living Philosophers', a series of books that honoured living philosophers by inviting contemporaries to write essays about their work, each collection rounded off by an autobiographical sketch and a section in which the philosopher in question replied to the essays. Russell's contact with Schilpp led, despite Schilpp's disappointment about the quality of his public lecture at Northwestern, to his being invited to contribute an essay to the very first volume in the series, devoted to the work of the American pragmatist philosopher John Dewey. Schilpp also raised the possibility of devoting a volume in the series to Russell himself. Half-expecting Russell to be bashful or reluctant about the idea (he evidently did not know his man), Schilpp was taken aback by the enthusiasm with which Russell greeted the idea. Russell, he recalled, 'agreed not only merely to fullest cooperation, but carried this cooperation out that very evening by discussion with me in considerable length about the philosophers around the world who might or should be invited to contribute essays to my projected Russell volume'.

The Russell volume was to be another five years in the making, but Russell's contribution to the Dewey volume was delivered promptly in March 1939. 'It has been done under difficult circumstances,' Russell wrote to Schilpp when he delivered the manuscript, 'and is much less good than I could wish.' Thirteen years older than Russell, Dewey was, by 1938, generally considered the most distinguished living American philosopher. He had first taught at the University of Chicago in 1894, and had returned there in 1930 as Professor Emeritus after his retirement from Columbia University in New York. He was, in many ways, the American Bertrand Russell, their lives having run strangely in parallel for many decades. Like Russell, Dewey had visited both Russia and China during the 1920s, and, like Russell, hated what he saw in Russia as much as he loved what he saw in China. Again like Russell, Dewey had formed a deep interest in the philosophy of education and had established at Chicago the University Elementary School (better known as the Laboratory School or the Dewey School), where his ideas on education – broadly similar to Russell's – were put into practice. Naturally perhaps, Dewey and Russell had crossed paths on several occasions. They first met in 1914, during Russell's stay at Harvard, when Russell described Dewey as having 'a large, slow-moving mind, very empirical and candid, with something of the impassivity and impartiality of a natural force'. When they met again in China in 1921, however, Russell was more critical, accusing Dewey of being 'unwilling to face any unpleasant facts' and announcing simply and brutally: 'I can't stand him.'

In Russell's writings of the 1930s, Dewey, as an exponent of that despised 'philosophy of power', pragmatism, appears regularly alongside William James, Henri Bergson and Friedrich Nietzsche as one of Russell's philosophical villains, one of the unwitting intellectual 'ancestors of Fascism'. Unsurprisingly, then, his essay on Dewey for Schilpp, 'Dewey's New *Logic*', was deeply critical, characterising – perhaps, more accurately, caricaturing – Dewey's 'instrumentalism' (the term Dewey preferred to 'pragmatism') as being at once a watered-down Hegelianism and an expression of 'industrialism and collective enterprise', which, like all 'philosophies of power', elevated action above thought and results above truth. In its determination to draw battle-lines along the axis of contemplation versus enterprise, Russell's essay recalls his 1924 article, 'The New Philosophy of America' – only now Russell had jumped sides once more, declaring himself a passionate adherent of the value of the contemplative life. Dewey's rejoinder consisted mainly of an account of the various ways in which he had been misrepresented by Russell, objecting especially to Russell's tendency to portray his philosophy as an expression of those aspects of modern life that Russell most loathed. 'Mr Russell's confirmed habit of connecting the pragmatist theory of knowing with obnoxious aspects of American industrialism', Dewey wrote, 'is much as if I were to link his philosophy to the interests of [the] English landed aristocracy instead of with [a] dominant interest in mathematics.'

There is a certain irony in Russell's contrast between his defence of academic contemplation and Dewey's exaltation of commerce, industrialism and action, since, during his time in Chicago, Russell himself was the very model of commercial enterprise, rarely refusing any opportunity that came his way to earn some money by giving public lectures. No matter what the subject or the occasion, he could be relied upon to fill an auditorium with some wittily expressed opinions. He spoke on education to the National Association of High School Principles at Cleveland, on the existence of God to the Student Religious Association at the University of Michigan, on physics and philosophy to the American Physical Society and the Physics Club of Chicago, on the Munich Agreement to the Council of Foreign Relations in Chicago, on 'the ethics of Fascism' to the Chapel Union at the University of Chicago, and so on. He also took part in a public debate with the Marxist historian, C. L. R. James on the question 'Can Democracy Be Defended?', and in at least two NBC radio discussions on political and economic themes in the 'University of Chicago Round Table' series. Wherever he went, he gave interviews to the newspapers on any aspect of international politics they wished him to discuss. Typical is the report of his visit to the University of Michigan in *The Michigan Daily*, which describes how, after spending the morning explaining the concept of space in modern physics and philosophy, in the evening Russell denied the existence of God to an audience of more than 2,000. In the meantime, he had given an interview on politics, reported under the heading: 'Munich May Lead to Downfall of Hitler, Lord Russell Declares'.

Many of these public lectures, of course, were turned into journalistic articles, and in addition he wrote articles specially for the Press on subjects such as 'Individual Freedom in England and America' and 'The Case for US Neutrality'. In the latter, published in *Common Sense Magazine* in March 1939, Russell reprised the argument of *Which Way to Peace?*, that the attempt to defeat Fascism through war was futile, since any nation that went to war would become Fascist itself. This applied to America as much as to the European nations, and thus the best thing America could do to save civilisation in Europe was to remain neutral and then, when the war was over and Europe in ruins, use its economic power to restore as much 'sanity and liberalism' as possible. 'If America becomes a belligerent,' Russell claimed, 'the first effect will be the complete eclipse (at least for the time being) of liberalism, democracy, and free thought in the United States. What will the world gain by the defeat of the fascist Powers if, in the

process, the fascist form of government becomes everywhere triumphant?'
Like almost everything Russell had said publicly about the threat of
Fascism, the article was politically blind and astonishingly oversimplified,
presenting only two alternatives for Europe, both of which led to the
triumph of Fascism: either Britain and France fought Nazi Germany and
became indistinguishable from Fascists themselves, or they surrendered to
every demand Hitler made and thus allowed Fascism to triumph without
war. Rightly believing that England and France would, eventually, refuse to
pay the price of avoiding war with Hitler, Russell announced that he now
believed war to be inevitable. That being so, the only hope for the survival
of civilisation was, he contended, the neutrality of the United States. The
idea of fighting to preserve civilised democracy was ruled out: 'A war for
democracy cannot but end with the disappearance of democracy in Europe.'

At the root of Russell's argument for US neutrality lay his assumption
that neither Britain nor France could fight a war against Germany without
imposing 'a severe military dictatorship' and his corresponding refusal to
admit any great moral difference in the outcome. Once war broke out, he
appeared to believe, it did not much matter who won, since each side would
be as bad as the other and the war would, whoever turned out to be 'the
nominal victors', destroy most of what was valuable in European civilisation.
This, anyway, was the view he expressed in public. In private, he admitted
that patriotism made it difficult for him to sustain such a view. Soon after he
arrived in Chicago, he wrote to a friend that, at the time of the Munich
Agreement, 'nine people out of ten think that we ought to have fought but
America ought to have remained neutral – an opinion which annoys me'.
And in a letter to Gamel Brenan of 1 February 1939, he told her: 'To me,
love of England (not the political entity but the place) is almost as strong as
love of my children, and very similar. I should find perpetual exile hardly
endurable.'

Despite these sentiments, however, Russell began, in the new year of
1939, to make strenuous efforts not only to stay in America himself for a few
more years, but also to bring John and Kate over. When his contract with
the University of Chicago ended in March, Russell discovered to his
disappointment that it would not be renewed. The official explanation was
that, according to the statutes of the university, no one could be employed
beyond the age of sixty-eight, the age Russell would reach in 1940.
Unofficially, however, Russell believed it had more to do with President
Hutchins's dislike of him. In any case, long before his contract expired, he
had begun negotiations with the University of California, Los Angeles, and,
by the beginning of March, had secured a three-year appointment there as a
lecturer in philosophy.

Before he left England in the summer of 1938, Russell had tried and
failed to get Dora's agreement to take John and Kate with him to America.
While in Chicago, he kept up the pressure by insisting on the superiority of
American universities to British ones and urging that it would be much
better for them to finish their education in the States. 'Even if there is no
war,' he wrote to Curry, the headmaster of Dartington, 'the atmosphere of

England is now bad for young people. Nothing is so depressing as despairing preparations for a war which inspires no-one with enthusiasm. England's great days are over & the young therefore tend to be listless and cynical. Here, on the other hand, they are full of energy and hope. I am quite sure that Chicago University is better than either Oxford or Cambridge.'

In letters to his children Russell pressed the same point of view. 'If you and John were living in America,' he wrote to Kate in April, 'I shouldn't have a care in the world.' Kate, now fifteen, was only too happy at the thought of leaving her untidy, argumentative and embarrassing mother to live with her beloved father and his attractive young wife, and replied saying how she hated Dora's home and that she considered wherever Russell lived to be her *real* home. John was harder to convince. 'I think I should rather stay here until I have been to the University,' he wrote to Russell on 3 February 1939, 'because I don't think American universities can be very good for history.' John wanted, with his mother's wholehearted approval, to study history at Cambridge. Though he had tried and failed to secure a scholarship to Trinity College in the autumn of 1938, he still entertained hopes of being admitted on a second attempt. Besides, he told Russell, 'I feel much more English than I would American, and it would seem very odd to go to an American university.' Throughout the spring, Russell kept pressing and John kept refusing. 'About going to America,' John wrote at Easter, 'it is obviously the most prudent and reasonable thing to do, and it is obvious that America is a safer, better and more hopeful place than England, but all the same, I do not feel very inclined to go.' By the summer, however, after Curry had weighed in on Russell's side and suggested that John go to America for a year and then think of reapplying for Cambridge, John's resistance had been worn down. 'It seems quite a good idea,' he wrote to Russell. 'I am beginning to feel, as you do, that America is the country of the future, and a better place than England.'

The background to this correspondence between Russell and his children was a sharp deterioration in Dora's affairs. Beacon Hill School, now housed at Kingwell Hall in Somerset, was not doing well financially, suffering from the loss of many of its American pupils, whose parents, understandably concerned about the political situation in Europe, had withdrawn them. Weighed down by work and anxiety, Dora fell ill with a particularly severe bout of eczema that forced her to spend some weeks in hospital. On 18 June 1939, Kate wrote to Russell that Dora 'has been in hospital with a skin disease and a general breakdown and has been brooding about things'. What Dora was brooding about was the thought of losing her children to the despised Peter Spence, as she explained in a long letter to Kate in which she gave, once again, her side of the story of the dreadful divorce. 'I am afraid', wrote Dora, 'that no one who knows the whole story could ever say other than that Peter Spence was ruthless and selfish and cruel.' Kate's admiration of Peter perhaps hurt Dora more than anything else. 'When someone comes and walks away with your husband,' she wrote bitterly, 'I shan't come and tell you how reasonable it all is, and isn't she charming.'

None of this, however, had any effect on Kate's loyalty, which remained firmly with her father, and every time Dora had an outburst against Peter, Kate wrote to Russell about it in a way that made plain where her sympathies lay. 'We had to listen to the story of Mummy's wrongs,' she wrote after a weekend at Kingwell, 'and from what *she* says, no saint's suffering is anything compared with what she has had to bear. I fear that we didn't tell her definitely enough that we wanted to go to America.' 'It is odd what different opinions people have about the same things,' she wrote in another letter, 'you think of America as the hope of civilisation and Mummy thinks of it as shallow and superficial and ruled by money. I expect you are right . . . Oh Lord it is beastly having one's life split in half and both halves thinking the other half is rather awful. My opinions and most of my love belong to you, but I still love Mummy and it annoys me that she says nasty things about you both.' Despite all the protestations and self-justifications, however, Kate reassured Russell: 'I don't think Mummy will be able to prevent us coming to America if we want to.'

And so it turned out. At a meeting of the chancery court that Dora attended, still suffering from eczema, it was decided that Kate and John should join their father in America, at least until the autumn, with the proviso that John would return if and when he was required to do so in order to serve his country in war. And so, on 2 August, John and Kate set sail from Southampton on the *Queen Mary*, seen off by Dora, Pat, Harriet and Roddy. 'As I stood high on the deck,' Kate later wrote, 'watching Southampton dock receding into the distance, I felt I was escaping from a nightmare.' To preserve this moment of glorious escape, she took a photograph, which, she says, became 'one of my most shameful secrets, yet I never threw it away':

> There on the dock stands my mother, smiling and crying and waving a handkerchief, plagued with worries, frantic with eczema. Next to her my half brother and half sister, looking sulky and bored and vaguely unhappy. Then her strange sister Mary, with whom we had been staying and some of Mary's awkward boys, in baggy English schoolboy raincoats. I kept the picture hidden for years.

In her autobiography Dora wrote: 'how glad I am now that I did not know at that moment what was passing through Kate's mind. It was thirty-seven years before I was to read it in her book.' For her part, Kate, some years after the publication of her own book, wrote:

> Dora was seriously ill at this time, and my lack of sympathy for her . . . is quite atrocious. She had eczema, which made her look unattractive, and I simply observed her from a distance with distaste. I do not want to excuse myself by saying 'Just like my father', but he did have the same capacity for withdrawing all feeling from a person who had disappointed him. I am still ashamed, though, of the way I treated my mother that year; I shall never get it off my conscience.

Though Russell's job in Chicago finished in March 1939, his three-year post at UCLA did not begin until the following September. After moving Peter and Conrad into a rented house in Santa Barbara, on the Californian coast, he filled the months in between by embarking on another lecture tour, organised, as ever, by William B. Feakins. Of this lecture tour, he said in his *Autobiography*, he could remember only two things: 'One is that the professors at the Louisiana State, where I lectured, all thought well of Huey Long,[12] on the ground that he had raised their salaries. The other recollection is more pleasant: in a purely rural region, I was taken to the top of the dykes that enclose the Mississippi. I was very tired with lecturing, long journeys, and heat. I lay in the grass, and watched the majestic river, and gazed, half-hypnotised, at water and sky. For some ten minutes I experienced peace, a thing which very rarely happened to me, and I think only in the presence of moving water.'

Newspaper reports of Russell's lectures during this tour suggest that his main theme was the role of America in the preservation of European civilisation, though his view on *how* it was to achieve this purpose seems to have undergone a major shift in the course of the tour. On 28 March 1939, the *Los Angeles Times* reports him in an interview, repeating the message of 'The Case for US Neutrality' and urging American isolationism as the best hope for civilisation. Just a few days later, however, on 4 April, the New Orleans *Times-Picayune* reports Russell arguing that, if America joined forces with the Allies, it could avert war by tipping the odds too far against Hitler for him to risk further invasions. On 9 April, the *New York Times* has Russell urging the United States to avert war, not by forming an alliance with Britain and France, but rather by adopting the role of a *de facto* world government, or a 'World Dictator' as the report puts it, a view that seems to have been repeated in Philadelphia in a lecture reported under the heading: 'Russell sees US as ruler in war: Neutrality would give nation world domination, peer predicts'. When, on 15 April, Roosevelt publicly urged Hitler to pledge himself against any future invasions, Russell wrote to him effusively, saying:

> I cannot resist expressing to you my profound gratitude and admiration for your peace plea to Hitler and Mussolini. In so far as a humble professor can, I have worked for peace before the Great War, during it, and ever since; to this cause I have sacrificed all conflicting loyalties. Never before have I felt moved to express such feelings as now master me to any possessor of power.

In reply, Roosevelt wrote: 'It was very kind of you to write me that fine letter approving the course which I took. I do appreciate it indeed.'

As indicated by Russell's recollection of his peaceful ten minutes by the River Mississippi – and by the fact, perhaps, that he could recollect almost

---

[12] A demagogic – some would say Fascist – politician, Long was Senator for Louisiana from 1931 until 1935, when he was shot dead in Baton Rouge.

nothing else about the tour – Russell, now in his late sixties, found the rigours of the tour exhausting. 'No wonder', Kate has written, that 'his speeches were sometimes superficial and his nights full of anxiety dreams in which he couldn't find the lecture hall, or arrived on the platform without his trousers'.

In May 1939, after the tour finished, Russell rejoined Peter and Conrad in Santa Barbara to prepare his lectures for the coming autumn. Understandably, the Russells found the Californian summer much more to their liking than the Chicago winter they had fled, and initially both Russell and Peter were delighted by the move west. In Santa Barbara they rented a comfortable creeper-covered cottage, set in a fine, green garden, and to explore the Californian countryside they bought a car, which Peter drove (Russell never learnt to drive). In August, when John and Kate arrived in San Francisco, Peter and Russell drove up to meet them and then took them on a holiday in the Yosemite mountains. 'Though my father was sixty-seven,' Kate remembers, 'we took it for granted that he would go with us, walking uphill all morning and down over rough rocks in the afternoon. If he ever got tired, he never showed it.'

Soon after the family returned to Santa Barbara, Russell injured his back and had to lie flat in great pain for several weeks. When the time came to move to Los Angeles for the start of term, therefore, he felt underprepared and was conscious, he later said, that his lectures throughout that term were 'inadequate'. He found it difficult, in any case, to concentrate on philosophy at a time when the news from Europe was so grim. A week before the Russells' move to Los Angeles, the Nazi-Soviet Pact was announced and on 1 September 1939, the day the Russells moved into their new house, the Germans marched into Poland. Two days later, Britain and France declared war. During these days, Kate remembers, everything in the Russell household 'was done between news broadcasts'. Russell and Peter 'sat by the radio with drawn faces, listening desperately for news, and getting only fragments interrupted by jolly commercials'. Russell's students, too, remember him being far more interested in news from Europe than he was in giving lectures, and more inclined to discuss the political situation than philosophy.

One student, Fenwick W. Holmes, recalls that Russell once broke off a lecture he was giving on the history of philosophy to make a statement about the threat to civilisation presented by the Hitler-Stalin axis. The combined forces of the Nazis and the Soviets, he said, stood a highly probable chance of military success, with the consequence that a 'great darkness' would engulf Europe. Interpreting Russell as arguing for American involvement, one student objected that Russell had not given him a single reason to 'spill his guts on a battlefield'. Russell devoted the beginning of the next class to answering the objection at length. At stake, he argued, was the entire liberal tradition and the possibility of free, scientific inquiry. Russell gave his students to understand that, faced with the threat of the defeat of this tradition, he was prepared to renounce his earlier pacifism. 'This decision',

Holmes later wrote, 'we were made to feel was Russell's particular Gethsemane.'

Outside his lectures, however, Russell said little about the war, hesitating, for the time being, either to renounce or to defend in public the pacifism he had repeatedly expressed throughout the 1930s. In an interview with Flora Lewis for the Los Angeles-based *California Daily Bruin* of 11 September, he did not commit himself one way or the other on the question of whether Britain and France were right to declare war on Germany, preferring to emphasise his view that the key to winning the war would be the preservation of adequate food supplies. In a letter to his old Cambridge friend Robert Trevelyan written three months into the war, Russell told him: 'I try to remain a pacifist, but the thought of Hitler and Stalin triumphant is hard to bear.'

His thoughts dominated by the war, Russell found it hard to settle at UCLA, which he found in any case 'much less agreeable' than the University of Chicago. His students were, he considered, less able and the administration even more autocratic. He formed in particular a deep dislike of UCLA's President, Robert Sproul, whom he likened to Hitler and later accused of dismissing any lecturers who published liberal views. In a letter to Lucy Donnelly of 22 December 1939, Russell wrote: 'It is the custom of this country to keep all intelligent people so harassed and hustled that they cease to be intelligent, and I have been suffering from this custom.' When he found time, he told her, he was writing a book on 'Words and Facts' ('or "Semantics", as it is vulgarly called'). This book was used the following year as the basis for Russell's William James Lectures at Harvard and was subsequently published as *An Inquiry into Meaning and Truth*.

The war, naturally, put an end to any thought there might have been of sending John and Kate back to England for the autumn, and the house that Russell and Peter rented in Los Angeles – a luxurious Spanish-style villa in the Westwood suburb – became their home. John, now almost eighteen, enrolled at UCLA, which, Russell told Lucy Donnelly, he did not find 'a satisfactory substitute for Cambridge'. Kate was fifteen, and, for a month, attended a local, private school for girls, which she found unbearable; the girls wore uniforms, asked permission for everything they did and history was taught from books that had big print and pictures. It was all a far cry from what she was used to. Sparing her any further ordeal, Russell withdrew from the school and educated her himself at home, taking her through Plutarch's *Lives* in English and Heine in German.

'We were all unhappy in Los Angeles,' Kate remembers, 'and we all *meant* to help each other, but what we understood by helping was not to complain about our personal troubles to others, whose griefs were as great or greater ... Since none of us felt free to express our grief, none of us was open to offers of sympathy from others. We lived alone, stoically bearing our burdens and refusing to inflict them on each other.' Kate's misery at being cut off from her friends at Dartington was compounded by her sense of alienation from the young ladies she had met at school. Having long admired Peter for her grace, composure and beauty, Kate turned to her for support, but found that Peter, consciously or unconsciously, exacerbated her sense of herself as being 'awkward and overweight'. Peter took Kate in hand by putting her on a diet, cutting her hair and buying her new clothes. 'I looked better when she was finished,' Kate wrote years later, 'but I still *felt* awkward. She had a way of emphasising the drawbacks she was showing me how to conceal.'

According to Russell's later (unpublished) recollection, his time in Los Angeles 'was rendered difficult by Peter's growing hysteria, and by her hatred of John'. In Chicago, his marriage to Peter had been put under strain by her infatuation with a man 'whose company she constantly inflicted upon me', and soon after moving to Los Angeles Russell announced to John and Kate that he and Peter were separating. Walking in suburban Westwood one afternoon, he told them: 'Peter has decided to leave us.' 'Would you like me to ask her to stay?' asked a stunned Kate. 'Well, I don't think it would do much good,' Russell replied – 'leaving', Kate recalls, 'the distinct impression that he would be quite relieved if she did go'. In the days that followed, however, John and Kate were surprised to find that life went on as before, and, somewhat awkwardly, Russell had to tell them that Peter had changed her mind. She stayed, but, patently angry and frustrated at the situation she found herself in, grew increasingly bad tempered until, Kate says, she and John 'feared to say or do anything that she did not command, lest we unwittingly offend and set off an explosion'.

Within a few months of being in Los Angeles, Russell was negotiating to find another job, preferably in the east. In the New Year of 1940, it was announced that he was to give the prestigious William James Lectures at Harvard the following autumn, and soon afterwards he was invited to take up a professorship at the College of the City of New York (CCNY). The appointment would run from 1 February 1941 until 30 June 1942, and Russell would receive a salary of $8,000 – an improvement on both Chicago and UCLA. Feeling that this was too good an opportunity to miss, Russell accepted immediately, and at once wrote to President Sproul to resign his UCLA post with effect from the summer of 1940. On 24 February 1940, CCNY issued a statement to the Press announcing with pride the fact that it had secured the services of such a well-renowned scholar as Bertrand Russell, and a few days later Russell received a letter from Ordway Tead, the Chairman of New York's Board of Higher Education, telling him: 'It is with a deep sense of privilege that I take this opportunity of notifying you of your appointment as Professor of Philosophy at the City College . . . I know that your acceptance of this appointment will add luster to the name and achievements of the Department and College and that it will deepen and extend the interest of the College in the philosophic bases of human living.'

This last phrase is a little odd, since the courses that Russell was being hired to teach were only remotely connected with 'the philosophic bases of human living': one was on logic and the other two on the philosophy of mathematics and science. If CCNY, in using such phrases, was attempting to exploit the popularity of Russell's journalism and lectures during the 1920s and 1930s, then the attempt was to backfire in spectacular fashion. In

New York, Russell had an implacable and influential enemy, with whom he had clashed earlier in connection with *Marriage and Morals*, but whom he had now no doubt forgotten. During Russell's lecture tour of 1929, when he was promoting *Marriage and Morals*, the Episcopal Bishop of New York, Dr William T. Manning, conducted a sustained campaign against him, focusing in particular on a condemnation of the invitations that Russell received from schools and colleges. An ominous indication of Manning's influence in New York on that occasion was that the most notable success he had was in persuading the President of Columbia University to withdraw an invitation for Russell to lecture there.

Outraged that Russell, 'a man who is a recognised propagandist against both religion and morality, and who specifically defends adultery', was being welcomed as a distinguished scholar by the publicly funded college of his own city, Manning now launched a vigorous and aggressive assault on CCNY for making the appointment. In a public letter of 1 March, which was reported in all the New York newspapers and many others throughout the States, Manning quoted Russell's offensive opinions on marriage and morals, and thundered: 'Can anyone who cares for the welfare of our country be willing to see such teaching disseminated with the countenance of our colleges and universities? How is it that the College of the City of New York makes such an appointment as this?'

Manning's attack put Russell in a difficult position. In the 1920s and early 1930s, he would have relished the opportunity to engage in a controversy over sexual morality with a reactionary bishop. But, since 1935, he had wanted to put such controversies behind him and to concentrate on technical philosophy. In 1940, he wanted to be known for his views on logic and language, not his views on adultery. When he was asked to comment on Manning's attack, therefore, he refused to rise to the bait and said little, other than that he attached no importance to Manning's views and still intended to assume his post at CCNY.

But Manning was determined not to be shrugged off. A few days after his first letter to the Press, Manning sent another, condemning those 'who are so confused morally and mentally' that they could see nothing wrong in appointing Russell. Within days, the newspapers were full of denunciations of Russell. In editorial columns, letters pages and reports of statements made by politicians, Russell was attacked with an astonishing ferocity. *The Tablet* described him as a 'professor of paganism' and demanded that his appointment be revoked. The Jesuit weekly, *America*, called him 'a desiccated, divorced and decadent advocate of sexual promiscuity', who was indoctrinating his students at UCLA 'in his libertarian rules for loose living'. The Chairman of the Catholic Affairs Committee of the New York State Council of the Knights of Columbus denounced the appointment as 'a disgrace to our city'. An open letter to Mayor LaGuardia, reproduced in *The Tablet*, urged him 'to protect our youth from the baneful influence of him of the poisoned pen'.

Within a week, this extraordinary campaign of vilification bore fruit. On 7 March, the Board of Higher Education announced that at its next meeting of 18 March it would review the question of Russell's appointment. In this, it was led by Charles H. Tuttle, a member of the board and a leading lay member of Manning's diocese. In urging the board to reconsider the appointment – in effect, to sack Russell even before he had taken up his post – Tuttle explained that when he, along with the rest of the board, had agreed to appoint Russell, he had been 'unaware of Earl Russell's views on religion and morality'.

In the week leading up to the board's meeting of 18 March, the campaign against Russell became ever more vitriolic. In the Hearst Press, he was denounced as a Communist, and in a speech to the New York Police Department by Monsignor Francis W. Walsh, Russell was alleged to advocate ideas that led to violent crime (the thinking – if one can call it that – behind this charge went like this: Russell advocates adultery, adultery creates 'matrimonial triangles', and matrimonial triangles sometimes result in the police 'finding one corner of the triangle in a pool of blood'). Religious groups of all kinds came forward to demand Russell's dismissal – and that of any members of the Board of Higher Education who supported his appointment. Feeling that they could not afford to ignore the strength of feeling on this issue, the City Council of New York joined in the witch-hunt, and, on 15 March – just three days before the crucial meeting of the Board of Higher Education – passed a resolution calling upon the board to revoke Russell's appointment.

Meanwhile, public support for it was expressed by, among others, members of the Philosophy Department at CCNY, the Committee for Cultural Freedom and the American Civil Liberties Union, together with various eminent intellectuals, such as Einstein, Whitehead, Dewey and several college presidents. By the time the board met to consider the question, Russell's appointment had become a *cause célèbre* of free speech and academic freedom. In a letter to the New York *Herald Tribune* of 9 March, Sidney Hook, Chairman of the Committee for Cultural Freedom, declared:

The hue and cry which has recently been raised in some quarters over the appointment of Bertrand Russell . . . carries with it a serious attack on hard-won principles of academic and cultural freedom. The ultimate implications of the organised campaign against Mr Russell's appointment menace the integrity of our intellectual life, which consists in the free and open consideration of alternatives honestly held and scientifically reasoned.

Amid this public furore, Russell himself – 3,000 miles away – remained silent. In private correspondence, however, it emerged that he was less concerned with the issue of free speech than with that of nationalism. Had he been asked to give an undertaking not to express to his students the opinions on adultery he had expressed in his lecture tour of 1929, he would no doubt have willingly agreed – if only because he no longer held those opinions. Having seen his second marriage destroyed through infidelity, and now tortured by Peter's unfaithfulness, he was not likely to go to the cross in the name of adultery; to anyone who would listen in 1940, he explained that he thought fidelity a *good* thing in a marriage. When, however, he was asked by CCNY to indicate his intention to apply for American citizenship (in order to counter the technical objection being made that, as a British citizen, he was not eligible for the post), he dug in his heels. In a telegram to Nelson Mead, the President of CCNY, of 12 March, he said: 'In other circumstances I might have applied for American citizenship but cannot contemplate doing so in deference to an illiberal and nationalistic law unworthy of a great democracy.'

Legal advice indicated that the technical objection had no force in law, but Russell's telegram alarmed his supporters at CCNY sufficiently for one of them, Professor Bronstein of the Philosophy Department, to write to him pleading to keep quiet in future about his thoughts on US citizenship. 'If you can find it consistent with the canons of scientific method to refrain at this time from making predictions about your own future intentions with regard to citizenship,' Bronstein wrote, 'it would greatly strengthen our case.' In reply, Russell told Bronstein: 'on hearing that my appointment might possibly be rescinded technically on grounds of nationality I thought, and still think, that this issue is even more important than that of religious opinions. The growth of national barriers is the greatest source of evil in the modern world':

> My objection to applying for American citizenship is not an objection to American citizenship but an inability to concede that the race or nationality to which a human being happens to belong is of any importance. If I were in England I should oppose with all my energy any proposal that professors from America or any other country should be asked to become British citizens.

Of course, it is not true that Russell's Britishness was of no importance to him, *especially* at this time, and behind these internationalist sentiments no doubt lurked a tenacious nationalism. At this time of crisis, with Britain facing defeat by Nazi Germany, the one thing Russell was *not* prepared to do was abandon his British nationality.

As the Board of Higher Education's meeting of 18 March approached, the fervour of both Russell's detractors and his defenders intensified. On 14 March a rally of his supporters at City College attracted more than 2,000 people, who heard Morris Cohen give a speech in which he claimed that, if New York revoked Russell's appointment, 'the fair name of our city will suffer as did Athens for condemning Socrates as a corrupter of its youth or Tennessee for finding Scopes guilty of teaching evolution'. Meanwhile, at a mass rally of Russell's opponents, emotional fever-pitch was reached. George V. Harvey, President of the Borough of Queens, argued that, if CCNY persisted with Russell's appointment, it should be deprived of its budget allocation of seven and a half million dollars. Councilman Charles E. Keegan called Russell a 'dog' and declared: 'If we had an adequate system of immigration, that bum could not land within a thousand miles.' Even these sentiments were outdone, however, by the Registrar of New York County, Miss Martha Byrnes, who shouted that Russell should be 'tarred and feathered and driven out of the country'.

Predictably, the board meeting itself was a long and highly charged affair, lasting well into the night. The motion to revoke Russell's appointment was put by Charles Tuttle, and was supported by a number of those board members who, just a month before, had voted in favour of offering Russell the Chair. Eventually, however, the majority of the board refused to buckle under the intense pressure put on them and Ordway Tead, its Chairman, emerged from the meeting to tell the Press that Tuttle's motion had been defeated by eleven votes to seven. Emphasising once again that Russell would be teaching logic, the philosophy of mathematics and the philosophy of science, and quoting from favourable reports of Russell's work by the Presidents of Chicago and UCLA, Tead confirmed that the decision of the board to appoint Russell still stood. Russell and his supporters had, it seemed, won a notable victory.

The day after the board's decision was announced, Russell sent a letter to the *New York Times* – his first public statement on the controversy. Announcing himself 'delighted by this victory both on public and private grounds', he took the opportunity to distance himself from the opinions on marriage and morals with which he was now apparently indelibly associated. 'It is ridiculous', he wrote, 'to say that I advocate infidelity in marriage, on the contrary, I think that fidelity in marriage is highly desirable.' In letters of thanks to staff, students and others who had supported him, Russell wrote that he doubted that the fight was yet finished. 'It still seems to me probable', he told the publisher, Warder Norton, 'that my enemies will find some way of ousting me; if necessary by some change in the law.'

He was right; the battle was far from over. An ominous note was sounded on the very day that the board announced its verdict. Emerging from the meeting, Charles Tuttle remarked: 'The issue now passes from the Board of Higher Education to the public.' What he meant became evident the following day, when a petition was presented to the State Supreme Court urging it to direct the Board of Higher Education to overturn its decision to hire Russell. The petitioner was a housewife called Mrs Jean Kay, a woman with no connection with CCNY, whose motives for wanting to hound him out of New York remain obscure. The impression was given that she was worried about the potential damage to her daughter, Gloria, of Russell's teaching, but in fact Gloria was not a student at CCNY and neither could she have enlisted in any of Russell's courses, which, like all arts courses at CCNY, were open only to men. The official grounds for Mrs Kay's petition were: 1. that as an alien, Russell had no legal right to be employed at CCNY; and 2. that his teachings 'constitute a danger and a menace to the health, morals and welfare of the students who attend the College of the City of New York'. It says much for the atmosphere surrounding the issue of Russell's appointment at this time that this petition even reached the court, let alone that it was successful.

In support of Mrs Kay's petition, her lawyer, Joseph Goldstein, filed an affidavit that was a piece of near-hysterical character assassination. Russell, Goldstein alleged, had run a 'nudist school', participated in a nudist colony and 'went about naked in the company of persons of both sexes who were exhibiting themselves naked in public'. Furthermore, he 'has gone in for salacious poetry' and 'winks at homosexuality'. Clearly seeking to portray Russell as a dangerous fanatic, Goldstein suggested that the philosopher's mental condition ought to be examined by an 'alienist'. In support of his claim that Russell was 'entirely bereft of moral fiber', Goldstein submitted four of his books to the court: *Marriage and Morals*, *On Education*, *What I Believe* and *Education and the Modern World*. Russell, Goldstein concluded (in a description that would later be repeated by Russell himself with obvious relish) was: 'lecherous, salacious, libidinous, lustful, venerous, erotomaniac, aphrodisiac, atheistic, irreverent, narrow-minded, bigoted and untruthful'. As for Russell's philosophy, Goldstein wrote, it was simply 'cheap, tawdry, worn-out, patched up fetishes and propositions, devised for the purpose of misleading the people'. Russell's great work on logic and the philosophy of mathematics, of course, was not mentioned in Goldstein's affidavit; nor was it pointed out, or even acknowledged, that it was to teach these subjects that Russell had been hired by CCNY. Instead the impression was created – as it had been throughout – that Russell was to lecture on sexual morality. Russell, Goldstein alleged, hoped to use his position at CCNY as a 'license to teach and be the purveyor of filth, obscenity, salaciousness and blasphemy'.

Mrs Kay's petition came before the Supreme Court on 27 March. The judge was an Irish Catholic called John E. McGeehan. The Board of Higher Education was represented by Nicholas Bucci, a lawyer employed by New York City Corporation, who restricted his defence to challenging the technical point that Russell, as an alien, had no right to teach at CCNY. The charges against Russell's character and morals made by Kay and Goldstein went unchallenged. Russell later alleged that the City Corporation 'was as anxious to lose the suit as the good lady [Mrs Kay] was to win it', though it seems possible that Bucci thought his best tactic was to argue for the case to be dismissed, rather than to reply to the grounds produced for it. Russell himself was not invited to appear in court to defend his good character – indeed, he was refused permission to do so, on the grounds that he had no 'legal interest' in the case. In his presentation to the court, Goldstein repeated the allegations against Russell made in his affidavit and supplemented them with some impassioned rhetoric against Russell's 'vicious, nasty lie' during the First World War that American soldiers would be used for strike-breaking. Continuing to insist that Russell's popular works on education and sexual morality *were* his philosophy, Goldstein asked the judge: 'Have we got to pay him $8,000 a year to have such philosophy taught in our schools?'

Justice McGeehan seemed to accept that Russell's fitness to teach logic and the philosophy of mathematics might be assessed by reading his popular writings, and called an adjournment to give him time to read the books submitted in evidence by Goldstein. 'If I find that these books sustain the allegations of the petition,' he declared, 'I will give the Appellate Division and the Court of Appeals something to think about.'

Three days later, Justice McGeehan announced his verdict, on Russell, his appointment at CCNY and his books. 'Mr Russell', he said, 'has taught in his books immoral and salacious doctrines', and the Board of Higher Education had 'acted arbitrarily, capriciously and in direct violation of the public health, safety and morals of the people' in appointing him to what would have amounted to 'a chair of indecency'. Thus, the board's appointment of Russell was revoked. Three grounds were given: 1. that, not being a citizen of the USA, Russell was ineligible for the post; 2. that the Board of Higher Education had failed to submit Russell to an examination or any competition for the job; and 3. that Russell was morally unfit to teach philosophy.

In a long statement to the court, McGeehan made clear that it was the third of these that he found 'most compelling'. Revealing himself unable to distinguish both Russell's popular writing from his philosophy, and mathematics from the philosophy of it, McGeehan argued:

It has been argued that the private life and writings of Mr Russell have nothing whatsoever to do with his appointment as a teacher of philosophy. It has also been argued that he is going to teach mathematics. His appointment, however, is to the department of philosophy in City College.

On this basis, McGeehan laid great emphasis on the views Russell had expressed in his popular writings, especially his views on sexual morality. From all four of the books submitted by Goldstein, McGeehan found ample evidence of Russell's 'immoral and salacious doctrines', and selected the following quotations to illustrate the 'filth' in which Russell peddled:

I am sure that university life would be better, both intellectually and morally, if most university students had temporary childless marriages. [from *Education and the Modern World*]

I should not hold it desirable that either a man or a woman should enter upon the serious business of a marriage intended to lead to children without having had previous sexual experience. [from *Marriage and Morals*]

The peculiar importance attached, at the present, to adultery is quite irrational. [from *What I Believe*]

I shall not teach that faithfulness to one partner through life is in any way desirable, or that a permanent marriage should be regarded as excluding temporary episodes. [from *On Education*]

In 1940 adultery was a criminal offence in New York, and the judge therefore took these quotations to show that 'The philosophy of Mr Russell and his conduct in the past is in direct conflict and in violation of the Penal Law of the State of New York.' To appoint Russell, he claimed, would be to offer as a role-model to the students of New York a man who openly encouraged illegal acts. To preserve the virtue of New York's students and to prevent them from breaking the law, it was thus necessary to overturn the board's decision to hire him to teach philosophy.

Having been prevented from appearing in court to defend himself, Russell remained in Los Angeles throughout the hearing. A sympathetic profile in *Life* magazine, written while the case was going on and headed 'Bertrand Russell rides out the collegiate cyclone', was illustrated with photographs showing him lecturing to capacity audiences and relaxing with his family at home. 'With his youthful, red-haired wife, their child and the son and daughter of his second marriage,' the article stated, 'he has settled down to a cheerful and model domestic existence. In the year-long summertime of Southern California, he hopes finally to make his home.' Kate remembers: 'We sat in our house in Los Angeles reading reports in the papers, hearing the news on the radio, receiving letters from New York three and four days after the event.'

When the verdict was announced, Russell was besieged by reporters asking for his reaction. To one he described McGeehan as 'a very ignorant fellow' and suggested that 'As an Irish Catholic, his views were perhaps prejudiced.' To others, he insisted that he disapproved of adultery and that, in any case, sexual morality was *not* his chief interest: 'I am not as interested in sex as is Bishop Manning, who is greatly concerned with it.' Likening himself to Socrates, against whom, he claimed 'precisely the same accusations were brought – atheism and corrupting the young', Russell emphasised the wider issues of academic freedom and civil liberties raised by the judgment: 'All this fuss frightens me. It makes me fear that within a few years, all the intellect of America will be in concentration camps.'

The American Civil Liberties Union took a similar view and tried, by all means at its disposal, to appeal against McGeehan's verdict. It quickly became clear, however, that the City of New York had no intention of allowing the verdict to be challenged. When Osmond K. Fraenkel, the lawyer hired by the Civil Liberties Union to represent Russell, applied for permission to file an answer to the charges made against Russell's character, the application was turned down, first by Justice McGeehan, then by the Appellate Division of the Supreme Court and finally by the Court of Appeals. Meanwhile, lawyers acting for the City of New York informed the Board of Higher Education that they would not be appealing against the verdict, a decision publicly supported by Mayor LaGuardia. When the board tried to hire private lawyers to take up the case, they were told that they could not do so. The city authorities, indeed, showed an indecent haste to close the subject. On 4 April, just a few days after McGeehan had announced his verdict, Mayor LaGuardia published his executive budget in which – so sharp-eyed newspaper reporters noticed (for LaGuardia did nothing to draw attention to the fact) – the funds allocated for the post Russell was to have filled were withdrawn. When the Mayor was asked about this, he replied blandly that this action was 'in keeping with the policy to eliminate vacant positions'. At the next meeting of the City's Board of Estimate, a resolution was passed that stated: 'No funds herein appropriated shall be used for the employment of Bertrand Russell.' Within two months of its announcement, therefore, Russell's appointment had been revoked by law, appeal – either by Russell or by CCNY – had effectively been made impossible, the post itself had been abolished and it had been ensured that no public funds could possibly be used to hire Russell. Though it had become a *cause célèbre*, Russell's appointment at CCNY was now as lost as a cause can be.

The most immediate consequence for Russell of McGeehan's verdict was, of course, that it threatened his livelihood. In his *Autobiography*, Russell claims: 'No newspaper or magazine would publish anything I wrote, and I was suddenly deprived of all means of earning a living.' This is an overstatement. In the six months immediately after the court case, Russell published three journalistic articles, gave nine public lectures and had ten statements, letters and interviews published in the newspapers. But opportunities for making money from journalism and public speaking were scarce compared to what they had been. A proposed lecture tour for the summer of 1940 had to be cancelled because of the nervousness of lecture-hall owners about hiring their premises to a man who could arouse such ferocious controversy.

Even worse was the fact that Russell's academic career seemed to be over. When Russell told *Life* magazine that he hoped to make his home in Southern California, he was no doubt hoping to stay on at UCLA for the remainder of his three-year contract. President Sproul, however, had other ideas. Though he had written in support of Russell during the New York furore, Sproul had no intention of keeping Russell on at UCLA. When Russell tried to withdraw his resignation, Sproul refused. On 30 April, legal proceedings were instituted in Los Angeles to try to ensure Russell's immediate dismissal from UCLA. The case was thrown out of court, but President Sproul's office took the opportunity of making it clear that Russell would not be staying on at UCLA after the summer of 1940.

At the same time, moves were made to get Harvard to withdraw its invitation to Russell to give the William James Lectures. A legislative agent for the City of Boston called Thomas Dorgan wrote to Harvard's President, James B. Conant, telling him of his intention to institute legal proceedings if Harvard stood by its appointment of Russell as William James Lecturer. 'To hire this man', Dorgan wrote, 'is an insult to every American citizen in Massachusetts.' On 14 April, Russell wrote to William E. Hocking, Professor of Philosophy at Harvard, asking him how the matter stood and received in reply a somewhat ambivalent letter. Enclosing a clipping from the *Boston Herald* that reported a statement from Harvard's governing body that it would stand by its appointment of Russell, Hocking nevertheless succeeded in giving Russell the impression that some of the Faculty might prefer it if he withdrew. 'It would be foolish for me to pretend that the university is not disturbed by the situation,' Hocking told Russell. 'The suit promised by Thomas Dorgan ... has some footing in the law of the Commonwealth, though the University is prepared to meet it. But beyond that, there are possibilities of further legislation which might be serious for an institution already an object of dislike on the part of certain elements of the public.' Harvard, Hocking wrote, would fight the threatened suit, not on the grounds of freedom of speech ('for this would make the university appear as protagonist of a claim of right on your part to teach your views on sex-morals at Harvard, a claim certainly uncontemplated in our arrangements and probably untenable in law'), but simply on the grounds that, as an independent university, it had the right to make its own appointments without interference from the law.

Hocking's letter, Russell wrote in reply, 'makes me wish I could honourably resign the appointment to the William James lectures, but I do not see how I can do so without laying myself open to the charge of cowardice and of letting down the interests of the whole body of teachers'. In the face of the impending legal threat, Russell told Hocking, he almost wished that Harvard had backed down, since 'it would be better to be dismissed now, with financial compensation, than to be robbed both of the appointment and of compensation after long anxiety and distress'. In any case, he urged Hocking to let him know of any further legal developments and to urge Harvard to allow him to be made party of any case brought against his appointment: 'I cannot endure a second time being slandered and condemned in a court of law without any opportunity of rebutting false accusations against which no one else can adequately defend me, for lack of knowledge.'

As it turned out, Dorgan's threat to sue Harvard came to nothing and Russell was spared the ordeal of a second court case. Nevertheless, as the end of the summer term of 1940 approached, he did not know where, or even if, he would be employed after he had given his Harvard lectures in the autumn. His correspondence of the time, however, dwells less on his personal anxieties than on the war. When Kingsley Martin, the editor of the *New Statesman*, published a short and sympathetic piece on the furore over Russell's appointment at CCNY, Russell wrote to thank him and took the opportunity to make a public retraction at last of his pacifist stance. 'Ever since the war started', he told Martin, 'I have felt that I could not go on being a pacifist; but I have hesitated to say so, because of the responsibility involved. If I were young enough to fight myself, I should do so, but it is more difficult to urge others. Now, however, I feel that I ought to announce that I have changed my mind, and I would be glad if you could find an opportunity to mention in the *New Statesman* that you have heard from me to this effect.'

It was an opportune moment to make public his support for the war. On 10 May, Winston Churchill had taken over from Neville Chamberlain as

Prime Minister, and three days later, on the very day that Russell wrote to Martin, Churchill made his famous speech to Parliament in which he declared he had 'nothing to offer but blood, toil, tears and sweat'. The speech caught the mood of the British public perfectly. Whatever public support there had been for pacifism and the policy of appeasement before the war was now swept aside in favour of a fervent desire for victory. Up until then, however, the only active fighting seen by British troops had been in the ill-fated campaign to save Norway from Nazi invasion. In May, the German army began its march through Belgium, Luxemburg, Holland and France, and the news that Russell heard on the radio would have been an unbearably depressing series of reports of one Nazi victory after another, and of the British retreat to Dunkirk. On 19 May, as the British Expeditionary Force was being pushed back to the French coast, Russell wrote to his old friend, Robert Trevelyan:

At this moment it is difficult to think of anything but the war. By the time you get this, presumably the outcome of the present battle will have been decided. I keep remembering how I stayed at Shiffolds during the crisis of the battle of the Marne, and made you walk two miles to get a Sunday paper. Perhaps it would have been better if the Kaiser had won, seeing Hitler is so much worse. I find that this time I am not a pacifist, and consider the future of civilisation bound up with our victory. I don't think anything so important has happened since the fifth century, the previous occasion on which the Germans reduced the world to barbarism.

Russell's abandonment of pacifism was published in the *New Statesman* on 8 June, but in the meantime Russell had to defend himself in the American Press against reports that he had given in his lectures a rather pessimistic view of the Allied war effort. On 23 May, the Santa Monica *Evening Outlook* reported Russell as telling his students that the Allied cause was lost. 'It would be better for them to win,' he is alleged to have said in a lecture, 'but not much better.' Russell promptly denied the report, telling the Press (inaccurately, if Fenwick Holmes's memories are correct) that he 'never has predicted a German victory' and emphasising his belief that 'a German victory would be a calamity greater than any in history'. On 11 June Russell issued a fuller statement of his views, which was carried in both Californian and New York newspapers. 'In recent years I was against the war,' he wrote, 'believing that its evils were greater than any Hitler was likely to inflict upon the world':

I have now come to realise that I, in common with almost everybody else, underestimated his power. I did not really believe he could invade England, and the suggestion that he could attack the United States would have seemed to me utterly fantastic. He has now shown that he will go on in his attempt to dominate the world until he is stopped by overwhelmingly superior force.

Terrible as is the cost of war, whoever wins, I think this is one of those rare cases in which the cost of passivity is even greater.

If I were of military age I should now be fighting. If there were any other way in which I could take part in the war I should be only too glad, but I have been told that so far there is nothing for me to do. The Allies do not need men, still less old men – they need machines.

The impression that he had not really considered the possibility of a Nazi invasion of England is, of course, false. In 1936, Russell had not only considered it, but argued that it was a lesser evil than a mechanised, 'scientific' war. Nor was the thought new to him that Hitler would go on expanding his Reich until stopped by superior force – he had said just that in *Which Way to Peace?* and had maintained in the face of it the view that the best option for Britain was a policy of non-resistance. The truth seems to be that, though in 1936 he had been able to face the *thought* of Britain's invasion by the Nazis, when this looked like becoming a reality in 1940, he found that his deep-rooted love of England could not bear it.

When the summer term ended, Russell, together with Peter, Conrad, John and Kate, rented a log cabin on the shore of Fallen Leaf Lake, near Lake Tahoe, high up on the Sierras – 'one of the loveliest places', Russell later said, 'that it has ever been my good fortune to know'. Though he could never quite get out of his mind what was happening in Europe ('The summer of 1940 offered for me an extraordinary contrast between public horror and private delight,' he says in his *Autobiography*), at least he could put behind him the bitterness of the New York controversy. Throughout his life, Russell sought and found solace in nature when he despaired of mankind, and in the Sierras he found a place where, as he put it in a letter to a friend, 'the works of God still hold their own against those of man'. 'We are 6,000 feet up,' he told her, 'with steep mountains all round – giant pines on the lower slopes, bare rock & snow higher up. The scenery is like the Tyrol; upland meadows with wild flowers kept luxuriant by the moisture of the melting snow, endless lakes tucked away in the folds of the mountains, streams and waterfalls & an endless variety of walks.'

The cabin was too small to sleep the entire family, so, while Conrad and his nursery governess slept indoors, the others slept on porches outside. Russell did, however, have a tiny study, where he worked – often sitting stark naked at his desk because of the heat – on the lectures he was to give at Harvard in the autumn. When these were published later in the year as *An Inquiry into Meaning and Truth*, Russell persuaded his British publisher, Allen & Unwin (his American publisher would have none of it) to add to the title page a long list of his academic honours and distinctions, ending with the words: 'Judicially pronounced unworthy to be Professor of Philosophy at the College of the City of New York'.

The title under which the lectures were published is in some ways misleading. They are not principally concerned with the theory of meaning, but rather with the theory of knowledge. As the first sentence of the Introduction announces: 'The present work is intended as an investigation of certain problems concerning empirical knowledge.' Admittedly, it goes on: 'As opposed to traditional theory of knowledge, the method adopted differs chiefly in the importance attached to linguistic considerations', but in the Preface, Russell, thanking his seminar audiences at Oxford and Chicago, writes: 'The discussions at the two seminars did much . . . to diminish the emphasis which I originally placed on the linguistic aspects of the subject.'

In essence, what this amounts to is that Russell's concern throughout the book is with the traditional epistemological question 'is all our knowledge derived from experience?', but he recasts this question into the form 'what is meant by "empirical evidence for the truth of a proposition?"' In keeping with the spirit of the papers he had written in the 1930s, though refining somewhat his views on the relation between logic and psychology, Russell now understands epistemology – the theory of knowledge – to concern itself with an ordering of propositions that is distinguishable both from their logical and their psychological orders. If we were to arrange propositions in their logical order, we would begin with those from which the others could be logically derived. If we arrange propositions in their psychological order, we would begin with those that we believed first. But if we arrange propositions in their *epistemological* order, we would begin with those that provide the foundations of our knowledge – that is, with what Russell calls 'basic propositions'. At the centre of *An Inquiry into Meaning and Truth* is Russell's investigation into 'the relation of basic propositions to experiences, i.e., of the propositions that come first in the epistemological order to the occurrences which, in *some* sense, are our grounds for accepting these propositions'.

Russell's theory is that basic propositions, the grounds for all our knowledge, are all first-hand reports of perceptual experiences and are *caused* by those experiences. For example, if you feel hot, then 'I am hot' will be, for you, a basic proposition. It follows, 'since no one else can have my percepts', that all basic propositions are personal. In a move that would dog Russell's debates with philosophers for the rest of his life, he drew the further inference that all our knowledge is, strictly speaking, not about the world but about our percepts, which, he would insist to his dying day, are, quite literally, in our heads. Exasperated by having repeatedly to defend this view, Russell resorted to ever more polemical and implausible restatements of it, culminating in 1959 in this spectacularly unconvincing argument in *My Philosophical Development*:

. . . I maintain an opinion which all other philosophers find shocking: namely, that people's thoughts are in their heads. The light from a star travels over intervening space and causes a disturbance in the optic nerve ending in an occurrence in the brain. What I maintain is that the occurrence in the brain *is* a visual sensation. I maintain, in fact, that the brain consists of thoughts – using 'thought' in its widest sense, as it is used by Descartes. To this people will reply 'Nonsense! I can see a brain through a microscope, and I can see that it does not consist of thoughts but of matter just as tables and chairs do.' This is a sheer mistake. What you see when you look at a brain through a microscope is part of your private world. It is the effect in you of a long causal process starting from the brain that you say you are looking at. The brain that you say you are looking at is, no doubt, part of the physical world; but this is not the brain which is a datum in your experience. *That* brain is a remote effect of the physical brain. And, if the location of events in physical space-time is to be effected, as I maintain, by causal relations, then your percept, which comes after events in the eye and optic nerve leading into the brain, must be located in your brain. I may illustrate how I differ from most philosophers by quoting the title of an article by Mr H. Hudson in *Mind* of April *1956*. His article is entitled, 'Why we cannot witness or observe what goes on "in our heads" '. What I maintain is that we *can* witness or observe what goes on in our heads, and that we cannot witness or observe anything else at all.

This strange form of epistemological solipsism, according to which everything we see, everything we say and everything we know is confined to the inside of our heads, permitted one great exception: the *structure* of the world. Reverting to the view he had held in *The Analysis of Matter*, which had been criticised so devastatingly by Max Newman, Russell insists that all physics can tell us about the physical world is structural, not substantial. We can know that the events in the world have a similar structure to our percepts, but everything else we infer about the world on the basis of our experience of it is not *knowledge* but guesswork, the inferences in question being not the secure, certain, demonstrable inferences of pure logic, but the uncertain, 'non-demonstrative' inferences that make up both common sense and the bulk of natural science.

When it was reviewed in academic journals by professional philosophers, *An Inquiry into Meaning and Truth* was treated respectfully but without much enthusiasm or agreement.[13] Most philosophers regarded, and still regard, Russell's view that what we *see* is an event in our heads as bizarre, an unfortunate legacy from the British empiricism of the eighteenth century; and many, like Braithwaite had been in 1938, were unpersuaded by Russell's causal theory of meaning. Though Russell took care to engage with the work of contemporary philosophers, such as Carnap, Neurath, Tarski and Wittgenstein, the book did little to improve his reputation among the leading philosophers of the 1940s, which would remain forever rooted in the work he had written before and during the First World War.

Russell had left Los Angeles for the Sierra mountains in the summer of 1940 still unsure what, if anything, he would be doing for a living after his Harvard lectures in the autumn. It seemed unlikely that any university would offer him a position after the New York débâcle, and opportunities for earning money from journalism and lecturing were also sparse. Financial

---

[13] James Conant, however, has told me that Willard Quine once remarked to him that he considered *An Inquiry into Meaning and Truth* to be Russell's most important book. I find this an extraordinary, and barely explicable, judgment.

rescue, however, came from a most unlikely source. Dr Albert C. Barnes, a self-made millionaire and art collector with a taste for offending conventional opinion, had established at Philadelphia a private educational establishment called the Barnes Foundation, which he now invited Russell to join as a philosophy lecturer. Students enrolled at the foundation principally to be given the opportunity to study the extraordinary collection of paintings that Barnes had acquired, which included, among much else, major works by Renoir, Cézanne and van Gogh, as well as a specially commissioned mural by Matisse. The courses taught at the foundation were based on Barnes's own theories of aesthetics as expounded in his book, *The Art in Painting*, which, borrowing from the work of Clive Bell and Roger Fry, emphasised the importance of aesthetic form over historical scholarship. Teaching art students philosophy was hardly the kind of job that Russell had left England to pursue, but in his present situation he could not afford to be particular and he welcomed Barnes's proposal with open arms, inviting him to California to discuss the matter.

As Russell was warned by friends, Barnes was a difficult and pugnacious man, though he was not quite the uneducated oaf that Russell later caricatured him as being (Russell was particularly fond of ridiculing Barnes's mispronunciations of the names of pre-Socratic philosophers). Born in 1872, the same year as Russell, Barnes was brought up in a working-class family, and studied medicine and chemistry before setting up in business as a pharmaceutical manufacturer. Together with his partner, Herman Hille, Barnes developed a new antiseptic medicine, to which he gave the name Argyrol, which proved effective in the prevention of blindness in babies. The product was an immediate and long-lasting success, and, after he bought Hille out of the business in 1907, Barnes became an immensely wealthy man. In 1910 he bought some land in Merion, an up-market suburb of Philadelphia, upon which he built an enormous mansion for himself and his wife. After that, his time was taken up less and less with the running of the A. C. Barnes Company (which could more or less take care of itself) and more and more with indulging his two great passions: social reform and art.

Barnes's social, cultural and political views were idiosyncratic but deeply held. He was fiercely contemptuous of established authority in all its forms and, though proud of the social status his wealth afforded him and hardly a Socialist, saw himself as a champion of the underprivileged, the working class and the black community. Because of these attitudes, he was an unusually enlightened employer, recruiting the few workers that his pharmaceutical factory needed from the poorest sections of Philadelphia society, paying them well and rewarding their loyalty with generous pensions. After he had begun to acquire fine paintings, Barnes even undertook to educate his employees, hanging his paintings in the factory and organising classes for his staff in psychology and aesthetics. Though Barnes's later claim to have organised his business 'on a cooperative basis' is scarcely convincing – he shared neither the decision-making nor the profits – his paternalistic concern for the well-being of his employees was real enough. In return, he commanded the grateful and undying loyalty of many of his staff, at least two of whom, Nelle and Mary Mullen, remained with him from the early days of his partnership with Hille until his death in 1951, maintaining throughout their lives an unswerving devotion to him.

Barnes's passion for art had been aroused at an early age, but, during his years studying medicine and chemistry and then running his business, it had lain dormant. After his move to Merion, however, he decided to use his fortune to acquire great paintings, and in 1912 he went on a buying trip to Paris, where he was introduced to Gertrude Stein and her brother Leo, both of whom had extensive knowledge of the French art world. With Leo Stein as his guide, Barnes began to acquire the Renoirs, Cézannes and Matisses for which his collection became famous, and, within a few years of voracious buying, he had one of the most notable collections of modern paintings in the world.

After he had filled his factory and his home with great paintings, Barnes began to see himself less as an industrialist and more as an educator. Two hours of each working day were set aside for the education of his employees in psychology and aesthetics. Barnes's great intellectual hero was William James, and in seminars and reading groups he took his staff through James's books, *The Principles of Psychology*, *Pragmatism* and *The Varieties of Religious Experience*. They also read the works of John Dewey, George Santayana and Bertrand Russell. In 1917, excited by Dewey's *Democracy and Education* published the previous year, Barnes enrolled in Dewey's seminar class at Columbia University. As a result, Barnes and Dewey became close friends, and Dewey became a regular visitor to Merion.

When the Barnes Foundation was established in 1925, Dewey agreed to be its Director of Education. Housed in a splendid, specially commissioned limestone art gallery in the French Renaissance style, which Barnes had built next to his home in Merion, the foundation was conceived by Barnes to be an institution with a mission to use his art collection for the purpose of teaching art and aesthetics to those sections of society normally excluded from higher education. 'It will be incumbent upon the Board of Trustees', the foundation's by-laws stated, 'to make such regulations as will ensure that it is the plain people, that is, men and women who gain their livelihood by daily toil in shops, factories, schools, stores and similar places, who shall have access to the art gallery.'

What this meant in practice was that if your application to view the paintings was written on headed stationery, or was addressed from one of the better US universities, or if anything about your name, address or style of writing implied membership of a privileged and wealthy élite, you stood almost no chance of having your request granted and a good chance of its being rejected with bizarre rudeness. When the millionaire and art collector, Walter P. Chrysler, applied, for example, he received a reply from 'Peter Kelly' (Barnes), which told him that, though it was apparent from his letter that 'you are very important', it had nevertheless been impossible to show his letter to Barnes 'because he gave strict orders that he is not to be disturbed during his present efforts to break the world's record for goldfish swallowing'. If, on the other hand, your application was hand-written and you were unemployed, underprivileged, a struggling artist or a manual worker, you were very likely to be granted permission to view the paintings and quite likely to be invited to join the foundation's classes.

By the time Russell was invited to join it, the foundation had gained a reputation as an eccentric and isolated institution. In its earliest days, it had among its teaching staff a number of distinguished academics, but they left within a few years, leaving the teaching in the hands of Barnes himself and some of his loyal employees from the Argyrol factory (which was sold in 1929), most notably the Mullen sisters. Barnes made strenuous efforts to forge formal links with the University of Pennsylvania and the Philadelphia Museum of Art, but was rebuffed, leaving him with a more pronounced dislike than ever of the Establishment.

The furore over Russell's appointment in New York in 1940 seems to have convinced Barnes that he and Russell had much in common. Having made an initial approach through Dewey in May, Barnes wrote several letters to Russell in June, providing him with details of the foundation and of the kind of teaching he hoped Russell would offer. After reading his work, from 'The Free Man's Worship' to *Marriage and Morals*, Barnes told Russell, he gathered that his central message was that 'the hope for a better social order lies in the development of intelligence as a guide to living'. 'That general idea', he added, 'is the main root of our enterprise even though we happen to use the material of art to put it over.' In pursuing this aim, Barnes told Russell, 'I've had many doses of the same bitter medicine that you've been forced to swallow recently; for example, in 1923 the principal Philadelphia newspaper printed an editorial denouncing me as a "perverter of public morals" because I exhibited, wrote and talked about such painters as Cézanne and Renoir.'

'I think you'll see in this incident an illustration of how you could function here,' Barnes went on:

> ... granting that life has many phases not many of which have been frankly, honestly and fully presented to people because institutionalised ignorance and prejudice have ganged up on them – as you know, to your sorrow. In short, if you want to say what you damn please, even to giving your adversaries a dose of their own medicine, we'll back you up. We can do it because we are on a par with universities as a chartered institution and we ask no financial support from the politically controlled public treasury.

Though heartened by this friendly and forthright tone, Russell was clearly slightly alarmed by the implication in this letter that Barnes, like the New York City Council, considered *Marriage and Morals* to be representative of his philosophy, rather than of his popular journalism. In his reply, he therefore insisted firmly: 'I should be very reluctant to lecture on sexual ethics, which have quite wrongly been supposed to be my special field. Actually the subject interests me much less than many others and I should be sorry to be diverted from philosophy and history to sociology.' What he suggested to Barnes was that he might lecture on 'different philosophies of the past, and their influence on culture and social questions: for example, Platonism and its influence, or the Romantic movement of the nineteenth century'.

To discuss the matter further, Russell invited Barnes to Lake Tahoe, though he added: 'I am afraid we could not offer you hospitality, as we are living in a tiny log cabin.' At the beginning of August, Barnes flew out to California, arriving at Lake Tahoe in a hired car, accompanied only by a small mongrel dog called Fidèle-de-Port-Manech, which, Barnes claimed, could understand only French. 'We understood in a moment', Kate remembers, 'that he was a man who lived by the adage "Love me, love my dog".' The Russell family had been primed on how important the visit was and how easily offended Barnes was, and, though they found the dog less than lovable, Kate says, 'we survived without catastrophe'.

Sensing, perhaps, how much it meant to Barnes to obtain his services, Russell, despite his vulnerable financial position, was able to drive an impressively hard bargain. After spending a few days with Russell, Barnes agreed to offer him a five-year contract on a salary of $6,000, in return for which Russell would give just one lecture a week on the history of philosophy, beginning with the pre-Socratics and working up, over five years, to the twentieth century (these lectures later became the basis for Russell's best-selling book, *History of Western Philosophy*). When Russell mentioned to Barnes that he would need more money and would therefore have to give outside public lectures to supplement his income from the foundation, Barnes immediately raised his salary to $8,000, which was the figure written into the contract that the two signed on 16 August 1940. 'My personal problems have been solved by a rich patron (in the eighteenth century style) who has given me a teaching post with little work and sufficient salary' was how Russell summed up the deal in a letter to Gilbert Murray of 6 September.

Barnes returned to Philadelphia in triumph and in October announced his appointment of Russell to the local Press, emphasising that, unlike the 'bigoted authoritarians' in New York, he 'wouldn't think of telling any of our staff what they should and should not say'. He also helped to arrange – by providing $2,000 towards the costs – the publication of *The Bertrand Russell Case*, a collection of articles on the CCNY affair edited by John Dewey and Horace M. Kallen, to which Barnes himself contributed a Foreword. Barnes evidently considered that he had secured Russell, not only as a lecturer, but also, like Dewey, as a personal friend and comrade-in-arms. He and Russell, Barnes considered, were fighting the same battles in a common cause: to challenge conventional morality and established privilege in the name of culture, reason, education and egalitarianism.

That this was not how Russell saw it might have become apparent to Barnes in the exchange of letters the two men conducted during the late summer in connection with the problem of finding the Russells somewhere to live. Barnes evidently wanted to be as closely involved in the Russells' choice of home as possible and devoted considerable energy to finding them a suitably grand place in the countryside around Philadelphia, even offering to put $35,000 of his own money towards such a place. All this, however, was gently but firmly rejected by the Russells, and especially by Peter, who insisted on travelling to Pennsylvania herself – refusing Barnes's offer of hospitality in favour of staying with Russell's old friend, Lucy Donnelly – to look for a suitable home. The place she settled on was a 200-year-old farmhouse called 'Little Datchet Farm' some thirty miles from Philadelphia. It was important, Russell explained to Barnes, that he and Peter should have a place where they could work in peace: 'You have given to both my wife and me the opportunity for the sort of life we want, in which, without undue financial worry, we can devote ourselves to serious work, and to writing long-contemplated books. But in order to achieve this we must organise our living on such a scale that I shall not have to do a lot of hack-work to avoid debt.'

The last thing Russell wanted was a repetition of the problems he had experienced at Telegraph House of living in expensive grandeur. But what is also evident in his letters is that he and Peter wanted as little as possible to do with Barnes and the foundation. As far as Russell was concerned, he was being offered by Barnes an opportunity to realise the ambition he had nurtured since his divorce from Dora of leading the kind of quiet, financially secure, contemplative life that was required in order to pursue 'serious work'. He did not want to fight Barnes's battles, nor did he want Barnes to fight his; he wanted only to work in peace in the countryside, undisturbed by the demands of writing journalism or engaging in polemics. His weekly trip into Philadelphia to deliver a lecture on the history of philosophy was regarded by him as a price worth paying in order to realise this ambition, not as a sign of his commitment to Barnes's educational and social aims. After Peter's visit to Philadelphia, Barnes wrote to Russell telling him that he had had to fight with Peter over the house. 'Kiss her for me,' he wrote, 'and tell her I hope to make amends for all the crimes I've committed.' This tone of jocular intimacy was never reciprocated by either Peter or Russell, and by the time Russell began lecturing at the foundation in January 1941, Barnes probably realised that, though he had secured a distinguished lecturer, he had not succeeded in gaining the friendship or support that he was looking for.

At the end of the summer, Russell, Peter and Conrad left California for Harvard, where they lived for the last three months of 1940 while Russell gave his William James Lectures. John and Kate (now eighteen and sixteen respectively) remained in Los Angeles, and it was to be nearly a year before they saw Russell again. In the meantime they both attended UCLA, Kate living in a sorority house and John in what Kate describes as 'a shabby, co-operative house for men, a place for students who could not live at home and could not afford or did not like fraternity life'. There, according to Kate, he made 'some strange but comfortable friends'. Soon after he moved in John wrote to Russell, describing his lodgings as 'undoubtedly tough' and saying that he missed 'the cultured gentleness of the family'. 'Yesterday afternoon', John wrote, 'the Los Angeles afternoon depressed me, and I was sick (not literally) with apprehension and sadness, and generally gloomy.'

Soon afterwards John and Kate received a letter from Dora that could only have added to John's gloom. Since the war began, Dora's situation had become progressively worse. Her school had lost many of its pupils and was losing money at a greater rate than ever before. Its premises, Kingwell Hall, had been requisitioned by the British army, and Dora was in danger too of losing Carn Voel, her beloved Cornish house, upon which a requisition order had also been served. She managed to hold on to Carn Voel by occupying it, moving there in the summer of 1940 with Pat Grace, her two children by Griffin Barry, Harriet and Roddy, and the ten or so pupils that remained of Beacon Hill School. Her financial position was so bad, however, that she was forced to declare bankruptcy. When Pat was called up into the army, she married him, reasoning that she would then at least be entitled to an army pension, should anything happen to him. Meanwhile, the war was brought uncomfortably close to home. While the Battle of Britain was going on in the skies above the English Channel, the prospect of a German invasion was all too real and Porthcurno beach, the scene of many happy Russell family memories, became a mass of barbed-wire entanglements.

Under these circumstances, Dora began to think that her life, too, might be better in the United States than in Britain, and she conceived the idea of asking Russell to provide the US authorities with the necessary guarantees to allow her to enter the country with Harriet and Roddy. Feeling unable to ask him directly, however, she wrote to John and Kate asking them to intervene on her behalf. 'If Daddy is able to pay my money now in dollars over in the USA that should be enough of a guarantee,' she told them, adding that it was useless to expect any help from Griffin Barry: 'he keeps on writing to say he hopes that we will come, but he has no money and he makes no plans'. And, if they would not do it out of loyalty to her, she suggested, perhaps they would do it for Harriet: 'If Harriet were there and you here she would never rest until she got you out. She adores you both and her loyalty never falters.'

John's and Kate's responses inevitably reflected the divided loyalties they had felt ever since the divorce. 'I am just miserably torn in two,' Kate wrote to her father, 'because I can't bear to ask you to do it and I hate to do nothing.' John tried a little bit harder. 'She [Dora] thinks she would be able to get a job here,' he wrote to Russell. 'It is very difficult. She would probably be a nuisance if she got here, but I wish they could come, provided they did not interfere. At any rate the air raids seem to have been wearing if not v. damaging, and not good for the children, so one wishes they were out of England . . . I can send you her letter if you like.'

Russell, predictably, would have none of it. 'I am sorry your mother is worrying you,' he wrote to Kate. 'I have written to John to say why I can't do what she wants. In fact, it would be much more dangerous to cross the Atlantic than to stay at Carn Voel.' Dora, then, was stuck in England, about which Kate's chief regret seemed to be the effect it would have on her half-sister. 'I wish I could have Harry to bring up,' she wrote to Russell.

'Mummy will spoil her – make her fierce and communist and dirty, and she should be better . . . I feel sure that she isn't right among such fanatics. I'm really getting quite unkind about my dear mother, don't you think?' For a year or two after this, Kate stopped writing to Dora. 'I felt I simply couldn't take any more of the harrowing of the emotions to which she subjected us,' she later explained, 'and so I cut her out of my life as far as possible.' John, meanwhile, fell back on the 'strange but comfortable friends' he had made in his scruffy, downtown Los Angeles house.

During the three months they spent in Harvard, Russell, Peter and Conrad lived in an apartment in the Commander Hotel in Cambridge. Concerning Russell's time in Harvard there is a curious and almost complete silence in the documentary record, a silence all the more glaring when one considers how overwhelmingly well-documented the rest of his life is, how prestigious the William James Lectures were, how much these particular lectures mattered to Russell and how much publicity the CCNY affair had attracted just a few months earlier. These lectures represented, after all, the culmination of five years' thinking, writing and lecturing on the problems of meaning and truth. And yet in Russell's *Autobiography* they are allotted just three terse sentences. Nor are there any reminiscences of them by members of Harvard's distinguished philosophy department, nor any reports of them in the local Press. The Harvard *Crimson* ran a brief report on 2 October 1940 concerning Russell's arrival in the city, describing him as: 'Spick and span in gray suit and tie, looking in the best of ruddy British spirits', but of his lectures there is not a word. While he was living in Harvard, newspapers carried reports of other public lectures Russell gave – a talk in Providence on 6 November on the danger of suppressing liberties in wartime, a lecture on 'My Creed' in New York on 18 November, during which he apparently announced a change of heart regarding his views on marriage, another lecture in New York on 30 November, this time on 'Freedom in Time of Stress' – and in various interviews he discussed these social and political themes, but about his William James Lectures on Meaning and Truth, there is nothing. How well attended were these lectures? Did they lead to any interesting or fruitful discussions? Why did Russell himself have so little to say about either them or his time in Harvard? The answers to these questions, perplexingly, seem lost to history.

Towards the end of his oddly unmemorable time in Harvard, Russell contracted bronchitis, which delayed his move to Little Datchet Farm until just after Christmas. John and Kate, meanwhile, spent Christmas in Los Angeles with the philosopher, Hans Reichenbach, who taught John logic and who invited them both to join in his family's celebrations. Evidently missing his children, Russell wrote to Kate on Boxing Day: 'You know, my dear, that though I am dumb and reserved, I love you very much and find your thoughts and moods most interesting.' Both his children wrote him long letters during this period, Kate keeping him informed about her personal life and John sending him pages and pages of confused and rather tedious political analysis. While Kate was flourishing at UCLA, excelling at

her studies and enjoying the freedom of her social life, John was struggling.
Three thousand miles away, Russell did what he could to guide their lives,
recommending that John continue his studies at Harvard the following
autumn and that Kate should apply to nearby Radcliffe. In the event, John
gained a place at Harvard, largely one suspects because of his father, while
Kate gained a prestigious scholarship to attend Radcliffe.

Russell's lectures at the Barnes Foundation began on 2 January 1941.
More than 500 students had asked to attend his course, putting Barnes in
something of a quandary. 'We're swamped with applications from outsi-
ders,' he wrote to Russell in November, 'some of them of the right sort.
What I'd like you to tell me is – how many students do you prefer to have?
We limit our classes to 20, but prefer 15. I'll leave the decision entirely in
your hands.' In the end, sixty-five students were admitted, hand-picked by
Barnes. The only professional philosopher among them was Barrows
Dunham of Temple University, Philadelphia, who recalls that, at Russell's
first lecture:

> Russell talked for about an hour, and then again asked if there were any
> questions or remarks. Silence. He asked again. Again silence. We were all
> in awe of the great man – I perhaps more than any of the others. Nobody
> wanted to risk saying something silly. So then Dr Barnes proclaimed an
> end to the proceedings. Russell was taken into an office to be interviewed
> and photographed by the press. Meanwhile, Dr Barnes came over to me,
> took me by the lapels, hammered on my chest, and said: 'Why didn't you
> fight him?' This was meant as banter in Barnes's heavy style (he was no
> wit). I suppose he could hardly have guessed what a youngish professor
> would do in the presence of fame.

In time, the students became less overawed, and about a year later they
were described in an article on Russell and Barnes by Carl M. McCardle for
the *Saturday Evening Post* as 'besieging' Russell with questions after his
lectures. Russell, McCardle wrote, 'makes his subject understandable and
rather exciting to those even who may never have heard of Pythagoras or
can't tell Aristotle from Plato. He painstakingly writes out difficult names
and subject matter on an old-fashioned blackboard like a rural pedagogue.
Now and then he discusses the sex life of some ancient civilisation with
frankness.' Within a few months, Russell had become immensely popular at
the foundation. On 13 March 1941, Barnes wrote to him in delight and
gratitude:

> One thing I can say in all sincerity is that your lectures are doing more for
> those students than you think or what I thought anybody could do – it's
> no easy job to jump into a group of mixed and very different backgrounds
> and create in all of them a genuine interest that makes them go into the
> subject further on their own in an effort to link up what you give with
> what the other teachers put over in their own classes. Moreover, you've
> endeared yourself to all of them and if I were a Frenchman I'd kiss you

on both cheeks for the benefit you've brought to our efforts to do something worthwhile.

'Don't worry about your work here,' Barnes added, 'take it in your stride of living a peaceful, carefree life, and if I can further that wish in any way, you may count on me to do it.'

Barnes probably did not quite mean what he says here. He was pleased to act as Russell's patron, giving him the means necessary to pursue the quiet, scholarly life he craved, but he seemed also to want from Russell what he had got from Dewey: personal friendship and a heartfelt commitment to the work of the foundation. Russell's failure to give him these things was interpreted by Barnes as a sign of aristocratic aloofness. Russell, Barnes wrote to Dewey, was in theory democratic but at heart he remained an aristocrat.

And it is true that when Russell wrote to his friends in England about his life in Pennsylvania, he expressed little enthusiasm for either Barnes or his foundation, but dwelt instead on the comfortable life that Barnes had enabled him to lead and, in stark and painful contrast, on the grave situation then facing England. 'Life here, with the job I have, would be very pleasant,' he wrote to Gilbert Murray on 18 June 1941, 'if there were no war':

The country is like inland Dorsetshire; our house is 200 years old, built by a Welshman. My work is interesting, and moderate in amount. But it all seems unreal. Fierceness surges round, and everybody seems doomed to grow fierce sooner or later. It is hard to feel that anything is worth while, except actual resistance to Hitler, in which I have no chance to take a part. We have English friends who are going back to England, and we envy them, because they are going to something that feels important. I try to think it is worth while to remain civilised, but it seems rather thin. I admire English resistance with all my soul, but hate not to be part of it.

Characteristically, when faced with a situation hard for him to bear, Russell did his utmost to see the war from an Olympian perspective. In this he was no doubt helped by the nature of his work at the foundation. A lecture course that attempted to cover 2,000 years of philosophy, while setting it in its historical, social and cultural contexts, provided just the right background for taking a broad view of the events unfolding in Europe. A recurring theme in his correspondence at this time was that Europe, in destroying the civilisation it had built up over the centuries, was heading back to the Middle Ages. 'I feel as if we were living in the fifth century,' he told Gilbert Murray. 'Sometimes I think the best thing one can do is to salvage as much as possible of civilisation before the onset of the dark ages.' The Nazi-Soviet pact, he thought, made it clear that the war was one of ideology, a fight between liberalism and the various forms of totalitarianism: 'Last time the alliance with the Czar confused the issue.' When Hitler invaded Russia on 22 June 1941, however, this view of the war was no longer sustainable: for better or worse, the Soviet Union was now Britain's ally. A few months earlier, Russell had foreseen this possibility with grave misgivings. 'Russia, I think, will be the greatest difficulty,' he wrote to Gilbert Murray, 'especially if finally on our side. I have no doubt that the Soviet Government is even worse than Hitler's, and it will be a misfortune if it survives.'

Though he had negotiated from Barnes an extra $2,000 a year to free him from the financial obligation to write journalism, Russell could not resist some of the invitations that came his way to pursue freelance work. As well as giving public lectures on political themes and contributing an article on 'Education in America' to the journal *Common Sense*, Russell also wrote a piece for the *Reader's Digest*, which was published under the title 'A philosophy for you in these times', though Russell's own title, 'On Keeping a Wide Horizon', is more apt. In it, Russell reiterated the view he had expressed repeatedly ever since 'The Free Man's Worship' in 1903 that the best way to deal with despair is to take an impersonal and large view of the world. 'In times such as that in which we are living', he begins, 'it is difficult to avoid becoming discouraged and hopeless. The world is full of things that are almost unbearably painful – wars, persecuted populations, and vast organised cruelties ... Throughout a great part of the earth's surface, humane and rational ways of thinking are being stamped out to serve the purposes of brutal tyrants.' Some people, he goes on, 'are able to avoid despair by living a purely personal life', thinking only of themselves and their children. But this will not do for him, nor, he implies, for any thinking person: 'Sooner or later, the evils without would come crashing in.'

The true answer to despair, Russell insists, is to take a wider view, reminding ourselves of the good things in the world, beginning with the non-human world: 'there are the stars and the sea and the wind in the trees, summer rain and the song of birds in spring':

> It is necessary to remember that the human race, with all its tumults, is only a part, and a small part, of the vast universe. To me it is very consoling to sit and look at a mountain range, which took thousands of ages in the building, and to go home reflecting that it is not after all so bad that the human race has achieved so little in the paltry six thousand years or so of civilisation. We are only at the beginning.

'I cannot tell what methods other people will find most effective for keeping hope alive,' Russell goes on. 'For my part, I find courage in things remote from human passions, such as the waves on a rocky coast, or the silence of mountains; also in those human things that approach them most nearly – the music of Bach and the poetry of Milton, for example. Coming a little nearer to what is difficult to bear in the present, I find assuagement in the contemplation of long periods of history.' There have been, Russell reminded his readers, good periods and bad in history, 'but neither have been lasting. It is our misfortune to live in a bad period, but it will end, and it will end the sooner for keeping hope alive. When the barbarians overran the Roman Empire, the world seemed at least as hopeless, but the dark ages that followed did not last for ever.'

Fearing perhaps that the horizon Russell was recommending was a little *too* wide for their readers, the editors of the *Reader's Digest* cut from the article all these references to geological time and the history of European civilisation – thus depriving the piece of its central theme – and kept only what was most platitudinous, making it appear that Russell's 'philosophy for you in these times' consisted merely of the plea not to give up hope. As it was published, the central message of the article appeared to be summed up thus: 'And so, to the man tempted by despair, I say: Remind yourself that the world is what we make it, and that to the making of it each one of us can contribute something. This thought makes hope possible; and in this hope, though life will still be painful, it will be no longer purposeless.'

The published piece was so radically unRussellian that one reader was moved to write to Russell to complain: 'Was this Russell? The man must have had tongue in cheek. And the piece was so precisely what Reader's Digest would want for its six hundred dollars or so. Good old Pollyannaish admonition!' Springing to her husband's defence, Peter replied to this reader, a Mr Cragg from New York, telling him that the magazine's editors had 'censored out everything that would have identified the article as characteristically Russell'.

On radio, Russell was harder to control, and, in the four broadcasts that he did for the Columbia Broadcasting Company's series 'Invitation to Learning', he made full use of the freedom to be his acerbic self. The series took the form of conversations between Russell and other regulars, including Mark Van Doren, an English professor at Columbia, and Huntington Cairns, a lawyer and critic. Each week, the panel would discuss a particular book, and Russell was invited to join in the discussions of Hegel's *Philosophy of History*, Spinoza's *Ethics*, Descartes's *Discourse on Method* and Lewis Carroll's *Alice in Wonderland*. About *Alice in Wonderland* he was rather lukewarm, while about Descartes he was warmly defensive. Though he dismissed Spinoza's metaphysics ('completely wrong from beginning to end'), he took the opportunity to present and defend to a radio audience his own idiosyncratic version of Spinoza's ethic. While emphasising the importance of what Spinoza calls 'the intellectual love of God', Russell's version rejected Spinoza's God, leaving one with the characteristically Russellian moral injunction to keep a 'wide horizon.'

On Hegel, Russell was outrageously cavalier, offering a taste of the kind of thing he would say about Hegel – and other major philosophers whom he disliked – in his *History of Western Philosophy*. 'I think philosophy has suffered four misfortunes in the world's history,' Russell told his listeners: 'Plato, Aristotle, Kant and Hegel. If they were eliminated, philosophy would have done very well.' Hegel, he claimed, 'always uses words in a Pickwickian sense'. For example: 'Freedom means the right to obey the police, and it means nothing else at all in the works of Hegel'; and the word 'despot' in Hegel means 'an absolute monarch ruling over a country which is not Prussia. That is the definition of a despot.' 'Is that fair?' asked another member of the discussion, a question that would be echoed time and time again by future readers of Russell's *History of Western Philosophy*.

'I just turned on the radio to see if there was any good music on,' wrote Kate from California soon after one of these broadcasts, 'and guess what happened – out came Diddy's[14] voice . . . Diddy, you sound so funny on the radio, so very, very Cambridge.' 'I always forget to say so,' she added as a postscript, 'but I will be overwhelmingly glad to see you again this summer.' Many years later, she admitted that this postscript was 'almost a polite fiction': 'When I was with them [Russell and Peter], I moped and sulked and spoke hardly at all, and they knew nothing of my life, for I so feared their disapproval.'

In fact, the summer of 1941 proved to be something of a watershed in the deterioration of relations between Russell and John and Kate, 'the final completion of the wall', as Kate was later to put it, 'that had been progressively cutting me off from the family'. Left to their own devices in California, nineteen-year-old John and seventeen-year-old Kate had grown independent from Russell, developing – together with the friends John had made at his student lodgings – a way of life that had very little to do with their father. Every afternoon they would take the car that John had been left and drive with friends down to the beach at Santa Monica, where, in Kate's words, they enjoyed 'the ideal lotus-eating California student life'. John's friends, Kate remembers, 'were poor and radical, probably at that time many of them were Communists, bitterly against the capitalist exploitation they saw all around them. The atmosphere must have been much like that of the communes in the sixties, though without drugs or mystical overtones.'

Kate later said that she was happier that summer in Los Angeles than at any other time in her life. Both she and John were extremely reluctant to leave and delayed the long drive east for as long as they could. 'Though I am longing to see you all very much,' she wrote to Russell, apologising for leaving several days later than planned, 'I find myself more and more reluctant to leave here because we are never coming back.' When they finally set off on the ten-day journey, they took with them three of John's friends, who lived in New York. 'After we had seen the Grand Canyon and some of the other colourful sights of the West,' Kate wrote, 'we settled down and drove and drove and drove, through endless hot countryside, with the hot wind blowing in our faces, existing in a torpor from Coke machine to Coke machine.' When they reached Pennsylvania, they sent Russell and Peter a telegram – 'Five of us to arrive small hours' – and on they went, 'swelling with pride', Kate remembers, 'at our own thoughtfulness'.

They finally reached Little Datchet Farm some time between one and two in the morning and went straight to bed. When they awoke, they were greeted with, as Kate put it, 'a good breakfast and a fine scolding':

It appeared that our mature and responsible telegram had not been quite

---

[14] 'Diddy' was the name the whole family came to use to refer to Russell, adopted from Conrad, who, to begin with, had trouble saying the word 'daddy'.

as grown up as we thought. If we had telephoned instead, they would have told us that there was not room for three extra people in the house and that we should stay one more night along the way. We had been thoughtless and inconsiderate and were made to feel duly ashamed of ourselves. John's friends, with whom we had spent a comfortable ten days on the road, now seemed gauche and uncivilised; they felt ill at ease in our home and were glad to be taken to the station, to continue their journey to New York by train.

After their friends had gone, Kate recalls, the 'hot, oppressive Pennsylvania summer became a long ordeal of disappointed expectations and concealed hurt feelings'. As he had done in Oxford three years previously, John withdrew into himself. As Kate never felt any real tie with Conrad (who was then just four years old), and had shut out her father the previous year in Los Angeles ('feeling myself unable any longer to bear the burden of trying to win his approval'), she looked to Peter to be the 'anchor in an unstable world' that she had been 'ever since she came into our lives ten years before'. But Peter 'was adrift herself, confused and depressed by the problems of her personal life and much more in need of help than able to give it'. As Kate looked to Peter for support, so Peter looked to Kate for sympathy, and neither felt able to give the other what she wanted: 'I resentfully withdrew my confidence from her, and each of us was left alone with her unhappiness.'

One of the few moments of light relief from this gloom was provided by an incident, the significance of which seems to have escaped everyone involved. It occurred when the family decided to play a game based on the Ouija-board method of consulting the spirits of the dead, in which the letters of the alphabet are placed in a circle on a table with an upside-down glass in the middle. Each person playing the game places a finger on the glass, which then moves from letter to letter spelling out a message. As Kate later put it: 'If you believe in ghosts, the message is supernatural. If not, it is possibly something one of the participants feels impelled to reveal.' In this case, the message spelt out was: 'John, John it [is] homo', the most natural interpretation of which was that John was (perhaps subconsciously) trying to tell his family about his homosexuality. One can imagine that this would have been an extraordinarily difficult secret for him to reveal, especially as Russell had, in his published works on parenting in the 1920s, gone on record as saying that homosexuality was the consequence of bad parenting, a view also expressed with great vehemence by John's mother, Dora. Ignoring all this, the family laughed heartily at the message. 'We did not realise then that John had tendencies that way,' Kate later said, 'and must have unwillingly driven the glass to expose them. How painfully he must have been embarrassed by our merriment! Our thoughtlessness on that occasion is one of my most distressing memories.'

Remaining steadfastly and wilfully oblivious to the seemingly obvious fact that John had been trying to confess his homosexuality, the family adopted the phrase 'it homo' to describe anyone they thought might be homosexual.

When the dreadful summer came to an end, Kate and John left Philadelphia for Harvard with relief, John to attend Harvard University and Kate to attend Radcliffe. In a letter home to Russell and Peter, Kate described John's roommate, who seemed to her 'very nice'. In fact, she added, 'I am rather annoyed with John for concealing such an amiable roommate from me for so long. But I gather that John has dark suspicions about his being "it homo".' In such ways was the phrase kept alive, no doubt adding to John's embarrassment.

John, as ever, wrote home less frequently than Kate, but the few letters he did send from Harvard reveal a new tone, one of studiedly insouciant disenchantment. On 21 October 1941, he wrote a late reply to a letter from Russell and Peter, explaining that 'one of the reasons I have been so long answering is that I have been engaged in mild dissipation'. 'I have become increasingly convinced', he told them, 'that I would rather become a wastrel & a drunkard, than devote my life to comfortable but stifling living & the writing of cynical & weary books.' A few months later, he wrote: 'Kate has been doing very well, I think; but I am not as interested in studies as I used to be or should be, and it is all very sad.' In another letter, he revealed how he viewed himself in relation to his father by quoting from Erasmus's *In Praise of Folly*:

> For these kind of Men that are so given up to the Study of Wisdom are in general most unfortunate, but chiefly in their children; Nature, it seems, so providently ordering it, lest this Mischief of Wisdom should spread farther among mankind. For which reason 'tis manifest why Cicero's son was so degenerate, and that wise Socrates's children, as one has well observed, were more like their mother than their father, that is to say, fools.

With every letter he seemed – whether consciously or not – to be attacking one fundamental and cherished belief after another of his father's. Discussing the war in October 1941, for example, he expressed dismay that the Allies had done so little to halt Hitler's advances into Russia, adding: 'liberalism in the face of Nazism and Communism goes down very quickly in the struggle for survival'. The following month he wrote that he had attended a church service and had been much impressed: 'I felt that either one ought to be a Catholic, and support a universal Church not degraded or hampered by temporal restriction, or else have a deep personal religion, which would not conflict with the powers that be.' 'People', he added, 'do seem to have a need for religion.'

After the US entry into the war, following the Japanese attack on Pearl Harbor of 7 December 1941, everything changed for John at Harvard. Many of his fellow-students, feeling that they had little chance of avoiding the call-up into the armed forces for three years, decided to 'accelerate' by studying during the vacations in order to finish their BA a year and a half early. John joined them, so that his degree at Harvard was crammed into eighteen months, during which time he rarely came home (one suspects that this, for

him, was one of the attractions of 'accelerating'). He therefore graduated –
with a rather unexceptional, *cum laude* degree – in the New Year of 1943,
after which he went straight back to England to join the Royal Navy.

Kate, meanwhile, was flourishing at Radcliffe, which, she says, she 'loved
from the very first day', and, just as she had at Dartington, dreaded the
vacations when she would have to return to the awful atmosphere at home.
Peter's temper grew so bad during this time that Kate began to look on her
'as a sort of time bomb: one never knew when she would explode'. She was
angry, too, with her father for putting up with Peter's tirades and
unreasonable behaviour. 'It is very difficult', Russell once told her, as if
to explain the situation, 'pretending to an emotion you don't feel all
the time. Even when I am half asleep I have to show affection. I cannot
relax for a moment.' If he thought Kate would sympathise with this, he
was wrong. Instead she was shocked: 'Was this the honesty he had taught
me? Was it kindness? Was it the right treatment for an unhappy,
frustrated wife? Wasn't he only trying to pacify her for the sake of a
quiet life?'

In his 'Private Memoirs', Russell says that Peter's relations with John and
Kate changed greatly over the years. At first she was very nice to them and
they loved her. Then, she took a dislike to John and started to nag at him all
the time, while remaining fond of Kate. Finally, when Kate began to be
interested in young men, Peter turned against her as well.

Kate's recollections, however, are that Russell and Peter were at one on
the subject of her boyfriends. Both of them, she says, 'never liked my boy
friends and they always gave me bad advice'. When, for example, she
wanted to finish a relationship with a particular boy, Russell advised her:

Men (especially American men) are apt to become violent in such
circumstances, and I should most strongly advise you to avoid being alone
with him. If you *must* see him, let it be only when other people are about.
But it would be better not to see him again at all, and put an end to things
by letter . . . You deserve the very best, and I didn't feel as if what he had
to offer was what one would wish.

The disapproval of her boyfriends made Kate's life at home still more
miserable, and, during the summer of 1942, with John away at Harvard
'accelerating', she more or less gave up speaking to Russell and Peter
altogether: 'I simply couldn't talk to them any more about anything . . .
during that summer I was living in sullen isolation, barely speaking to
anyone in the house except about the most routine matters. And since we
were ten miles out of town and gas rationing was in effect, there was not
anyone much else to talk to.'

Kate's explanation of Peter's ferocious temper was that, though flattered
by the attentions of a famous man when she was young (still only thirty-
two), 'she had found marriage to the great man something of a
disappointment. His passion cooled and was replaced by kindly courtesy and

a show of affection thinly unsatisfying to a romantic young woman . . . She was still young and beautiful, and did not relish being put on the shelf as stepmother, mother, housewife, beyond the need for passion.' Kate's explanation of her father's willingness to put up with Peter was that, having seen the damage done to John and herself by divorce, Russell was anxious not to harm Conrad in the same way.

For the third time in his life, Russell found himself living in a hollow shell of a marriage, in which love, passion and affection were replaced by a fragile and brittle courtesy – a courtesy that, in a more subtle form, was every bit as expressive of hurt, anger and disappointment as Peter's histrionic rages. Kate says that Peter exacted from Russell 'the trappings of affection and he paid them to her like a tribute, imagining that she was deceived'; she added: 'I am sure she was not.' Dora had believed Russell's protestations of love and commitment, against all the evidence, right to (and beyond) the end; Peter, clearly did not. When she demanded affection, she received in return a half-hearted pretence of it, and, as her temper grew hotter and hotter, Russell's 'kindly courtesy' grew colder and colder. One night, however, the mask slipped in the most alarming way, when Peter awoke to find Russell attempting to smother her with a pillow. The explanation given, and accepted, was that they had been reading a detective story together that evening and that Russell had been having a dream about committing a murder. The incident, like the phrase 'John it homo', became a family joke; and, as with John's covert confession of homosexuality, the obvious inference that repressed emotions were here finding some sort of release was laughingly avoided.

But whatever Russell felt about Peter in private, in public they presented a united front. During 1942 and 1943 they wrote together several articles and letters to newspapers, concerned with the movement led by Gandhi for Indian independence. The British Government was at this time worried that support for Gandhi's movement in the United States might weaken the strength of the Alliance, and the Russells' intervention took the form of trying to reassure Americans about British policy. As he put it in a letter to Beatrice Webb: 'People here are ignorant about India, but have strong opinions. I have been speaking and writing to try to overcome anti-English feeling as regards India, which in some quarters is very strong.' What this meant in practice was that the Russells spoke in favour of Indian independence – and, in particular, of the offer made by Sir Stafford Cripps in March 1942 of granting India independence after the war (an offer rejected by Gandhi) – while warning of the damaging effects on the war effort of Gandhi's campaigns.

Peter also helped Russell with his lectures, providing, as she had done with *Freedom and Organization*, much of the historical research that he incorporated into his work. Though this help was acknowledged in the Preface to *History of Western Philosophy*, Peter later complained to friends that the extent of her contributions to that book had gone unrecognised. As Leonard Woolf had discovered many years earlier, Peter was extremely prickly about being regarded as a mere appendage to a famous man. She insisted on being treated with due respect. Paradoxically, this often took the form of ostentatiously drawing attention to the aristocratic status she derived from her husband. Phyllis Terry, an old friend of Ted Lloyd's (one of the legally appointed guardians of John and Kate), visited the Russells at Little Datchet Farm and, knowing that Peter's real name was Patricia, asked her how she was to address her: 'She replied that though it was written "Countess" it was pronounced "Lady"!' On another visit, Phyllis took along her small son, whom she introduced to Conrad: 'Peter exclaimed how fascinating it was to see, at such an early age, how different was the child of noble descent from the child of the people!'

It was a form of self-assertion guaranteed to bring out the very worst in Dr Albert C. Barnes, and it was not very long before Peter became an object of ridicule and contempt at the militantly 'democratic' Barnes Foundation. Peter, Barnes was quoted as saying, 'seems to have difficulty in swallowing the impressive title of Lady Russell. It evidently gets stuck just below her larynx, for she regurgitates it automatically.' Peter also aroused the hostility of Barnes's loyal and long-serving assistant, Nelle Mullen. On 31 October 1941, Miss Mullen wrote to Peter, informing her that the foundation's board had received complaints about her behaviour. One of these was that Peter had once burst into the foundation's gallery, interrupting a Press interview with Russell; the other, somewhat ludicrously, was that her practice of knitting during Russell's lectures caused a disturbance. As a result, Peter was told, she was henceforth prohibited from entering the foundation's premises.

The day she received this letter, Peter fired off a characteristically spirited and vitriolic response. Dismissing her altercation with Miss Mullen ('a white-haired lady who approached me, and whose name I did not know') as an insignificant trifle, Peter went on to defend her presence at Russell's lectures on the grounds that 'I have always acted as his assistant in research for and preparation of his lectures [and] when the subject is not one that I have studied, he has wished me to be present, not for my own sake, but for the sake of his lectures, since I cannot assist him adequately with the preparation of any one lecture without a thorough grasp of the whole course.' As for her knitting: 'when I consulted my husband he remarked that I had disturbed no one by knitting at far more difficult and technical lectures at the Universities of Oxford, Chicago, California and Harvard, and that therefore, I might assume that I would be giving no offence.'

It was a letter calculated to further offend the 'democratic' sensibilities of the foundation, and Peter duly received from Nelle Mullen a stinging reply: 'It was sweet of you to tell us how low-class the Foundation is compared to Oxford, Harvard, etc. – in short, that a superior, well-bred, learned, charitable soul should not be informed by barbarians that her presence in their midst is undesirable. How to bear up under the disgrace is our most serious problem at the moment.'

Miss Mullen was, of course, writing with the full support of Dr Barnes, who, when he tried to calm things down in December by writing a mollifying and appreciative letter to Russell, could not resist adding: 'when we engaged you to teach we did not obligate ourselves to endure forever the trouble-making propensities of your wife'. To this Russell gallantly replied: 'I shall continue to do all in my power (including utilisation of my wife's valuable help in research) to make my lectures as good as I am able to make them; but, so far as any personal relationship is concerned, you are mistaken in supposing that there is no quarrel with me, since whoever quarrels with my wife quarrels with me.' Russell, however, had perhaps misjudged the degree of hostility that Peter had aroused. 'I feel you should be informed', Barnes told him, 'that if your wife ever enters the door of our gallery, the "whitehaired lady" whom she tried to bully . . . has been informed officially how to deal with the situation.'

After this, Russell and Barnes entered an uneasy truce that lasted just a year. The tension between the two became public knowledge in the spring of 1942, following the publication in four weekly instalments by the *Saturday Evening Post* of a long article called 'The Terrible-Tempered Dr Barnes', written by Carl McCardle, a journalist hitherto trusted by Barnes. The third instalment of this article was devoted entirely to the relationship between Russell and Barnes and quoted extensively from the acrimonious correspondence between Peter and the foundation (in an uncharacteristic act of openness that he later regretted, Barnes had agreed to give McCardle access to the foundation's files, in return for which the journalist promised to concentrate on the educational work of the foundation). When he was shown the articles immediately before publication, Barnes realised that he had been duped. The article, as perhaps McCardle had intended all along, concentrated on Barnes's personality rather than the foundation's work, and was notably more sympathetic towards Russell than towards Barnes, whom McCardle described as a man who 'has made capital out of rudeness' and 'gets his greatest personal satisfaction out of writing poison pen letters'.

Hurt and outraged, Barnes made an unsuccessful attempt, through his lawyers and through personal contact with the *Post*'s editor, to prevent the article from being published. The *Post*, however, realised it had a story that would gratify the curiosity that Barnes had aroused and not only refused to pull the article, but promoted it with a big publicity campaign. All over town, large posters went up advertising the series on 'Philadelphia's Millionaire Pepperpot'. Barnes went to considerable effort to counteract this publicity by ripping down as many of the posters as he could find and inserting into copies of the magazine a seven-page pamphlet that he had written giving his side of the story. This, of course, merely fuelled the controversy and increased the public's interest, and, in the end, Barnes had to admit defeat and retire from the fray with as much dignity as he could muster. After this public humiliation, Barnes – wounded by the unequal treatment that he and Russell had received – kept an eye out for any excuse he could use to dismiss Russell from the foundation.

His chance came in the autumn of 1942, when Russell agreed to give a series of weekly lectures on political themes at the Rand School of Social Science. The series ran from October to December, and soon after he had given the last one Russell received a letter from the Barnes Foundation informing him that he was being dismissed as from 31 December 1942 for breach of contract. Barnes evidently thought he had a good case. 'The details of the matter', his letter to Russell claimed, 'have been carefully studied in their legal and ethical aspects by properly qualified disinterested persons.' Of course, it was true that he had raised Russell's salary by $2,000 in order to relieve him of the *necessity* of giving public lectures, but, unfortunately for Barnes, it was not written into Russell's contract that he was *not* to do so. Furthermore, when it was reported in the newspapers in November 1942 that Russell's contract did preclude outside lecturing, Barnes (at Russell's request) publicly denied it.

All this Russell made clear in a statement to the Press that he issued soon after receiving his letter of dismissal, announcing that he intended to take legal action against Barnes for not honouring the five-year contract he had signed in 1940. He sued Barnes for $24,000 – the amount of earnings remaining under his contract – and was justly confident of success. However, his case would not be heard until August 1943, and, in the meantime, he, Peter and Conrad had, once more, to face destitution.

To save money, the Russells sublet Little Datchet Farm and moved into a small servants' cottage nearby. Because they themselves could no longer afford to employ servants, Peter now had to do all the housework, cooking and childcare herself, leaving little or no time for the reading upon which Russell had relied for his lectures and which had been for her an important source of self-esteem. As Russell put it in a letter to Gilbert Murray, he and Peter had discovered that the intellectual development of women was a 'perquisite of aristocracy' that, as a result of the 'growing democracy' of modern times, had to be abandoned: 'For us, who imagined ourselves democrats, but were in fact the pampered products of aristocracy, it is unpleasant.'

In the face of the increasing burdens, anxieties and sheer drudgery that her marriage to Russell presented her with, Peter became more and more unstable and repeatedly threatened suicide. On a rare visit home, Kate was shocked to witness the scene of Peter, after taking an overdose of sleeping pills, running around the house clutching telephones in order to prevent Russell from calling a doctor. At last, when Peter fell asleep, Kate asked her father: 'Shouldn't you call a doctor now?' 'I don't think it will be necessary,' Russell replied. 'She has done this before and she never takes enough.'

After graduating from Harvard in the New Year of 1943, John sailed back to England to live with Dora in her new home in London while he waited to join the navy. Some months after he left, Kate wrote to him to tell him how lucky he was to be free from the home life now endured by Russell, Peter and Conrad. 'I don't mean to bother you with all the family unpleasantness now that you are out of it,' she told him, 'but I'm so bothered about it for Diddy's sake. He is very tired and working very hard, and he has a permanently rather hysterical woman to cope with. I know she has plenty of cause and excuse, but I'm still furious on Diddy's account.'

In order to save Russell money on university fees (and also, as she put it, to 'spare myself the misery of another Pennsylvania summer'), Kate decided, like John, to 'accelerate' and stay at Radcliffe for the summer of 1943, so that she could graduate the following year. However, on what she thought would be a brief visit home, Kate fell while climbing a tree and cracked two vertebrae, forcing her to spend much of the summer at Bryn Mawr hospital. A college friend happened to live in Bryn Mawr and her family offered the Russells the use of their house during the summer, while they themselves stayed at their summer house on Nantucket. 'It was a pleasant, well-provided home,' Kate remembers, 'and we filled it with the discord of our lives. I sometimes wondered if the walls did not reflect back our bitterness into the lives of our friends after they returned.'

The move to Bryn Mawr in July 1943 brought with it a change of fortune. In the months immediately prior to the move, Russell and Peter had gone through their leanest period yet. Stripped, for the moment at least, of his income from the Barnes Foundation, Russell – now in his seventies – had to make do on whatever he could earn from freelance writing. Practically every commission that he was offered he accepted, including an invitation from *Glamour* magazine to write an article advising women on what to do if they fell in love with a married man. According to Sidney Hook, Russell confessed to him that this particular piece had actually been written by Peter – Russell had merely signed it. 'Why did you do it?' Hook asked him. 'I did it for $50' came the reply.

Peter, of course, was far more qualified to write on this subject than Russell; falling in love with a married man was, after all, probably the pivotal event in her life. And the advice offered by the article does in places suggest that it was based on Peter's own experience. If you fall in love with a married man, she counsels, then, even if he gets on badly with his wife, 'you must be prepared to be accused of having broken up a perfectly happy home. His wife may even discover belatedly that she loves him very much.' While insisting that sometimes the advantages of such an affair outweigh the disadvantages, in general the article urges caution. If you fall in love with a married man and have no reason to believe either that he is in love with you or that he is unhappy with his wife, it insists, then: 'It is best to avoid suffering for yourself and possibly for others by going away ... What you suffer by going will be nothing to what you would suffer by staying. And the pangs of love are rarely fatal.'

The *Glamour* article was one of the few magazine commissions Russell received during the lean months of early 1943, but the pot was kept boiling, or simmering at least, by the publisher E. Haldemann-Julius, who commissioned from Russell a number of little books (they were scarcely more than pamphlets) for his series *Big Blue Books*. Russell's contributions to this series were: *An Outline of Intellectual Rubbish*, *How to Read and Understand History* and *The Value of Free Thought* (subtitled 'How to Become a Truth-Seeker and Break the Chains of Mental Slavery'), all of which recycled themes that he had published many, many times before and none of which, one suspects, would have taken him more than a day or two to write.

In Bryn Mawr, however, Russell was given the opportunity to devote

himself to more serious writing. His financial position began to improve in
May 1943, shortly before he left Merion, when he was given an advance of
$3,000 – the largest advance he had ever received – by the publishers Simon
& Schuster for *History of Western Philosophy*, the book based on his Barnes
lectures. Accepting this offer meant a break with W. W. Norton, the man
who had been Russell's American publisher up until then and who had
become a personal friend to Russell, John and Kate. Norton had offered
only $500 for the book and, under the circumstances, Russell considered the
loss of Norton's friendship to be a price worth paying in order to accept the
higher offer. In the same month, Russell's case against Barnes reached the
court and Russell was granted, as expected, a summary judgment in his
favour. The only thing left to decide was the amount of damages owed to
him. At a trial in August, this question was settled by awarding Russell
$20,000 – the amount he had sued for minus $4,000, which, the court
decided, was how much Russell could expect to earn from public lectures
during the remaining period of his contract. After an unsuccessful attempt
by Barnes to register an appeal, this amount was duly paid to Russell in
November.

Barnes, naturally, did not take this defeat graciously. The following year,
he published a pamphlet called *The Case of Bertrand Russell vs Democracy
and Education*, in which he accused Russell of having 'no conception of
democracy as a sharing in significant experience'. 'The history of ideas about
which he lectured', Barnes claimed, 'was a history of abstractions torn from
their human context, with not the slightest recognition of the concreteful-
ness of experience throughout all its history':

> In the religious and moral history of the past, Mr. Russell [and how
> much righteous anger one senses behind that 'Mr'] could see mainly an
> occasion for derision and contempt. Above all, he felt so little share in the
> desire of his students to relate the things he was talking about to their
> own experience, that the fear of his ridicule froze on their lips the
> questions that they would have liked to ask. If they learned anything
> whatever of democracy in education from him, it was because he
> presented them with the perfect example of its antithesis.

Russell did not bother to reply to this pamphlet, or even to read it, 'but I
have no doubt it was good reading', he comments laconically in his
Autobiography. By the time the pamphlet was published, Russell could
afford to be utterly indifferent to whatever Barnes thought or said about
him.

With the advance from Simon & Schuster and the legal damages he won
from Barnes, Russell was able to create at Bryn Mawr exactly the conditions
conducive to independent scholarship that he had looked to Barnes to
provide. Moreover, he could surround himself with sympathetic, interested
and informed companions. At the end of the summer, when the Russells
had to give up the home lent to them by the family of Kate's college friend,
they moved into a boarding house near Bryn Mawr College where they

stayed for the rest of the year. Russell's very old friend, Lucy Donnelly, whom he had known since the beginning of the century, lived at Bryn Mawr with her friend, Edith Finch, who taught English at the college. Russell saw much of them both, and, while he renewed his friendship with Lucy, with Edith he struck up a flirtatious relationship that was to prove of great significance in the years to come.

To enable him to pursue his research for *History of Western Philosophy*, Russell was given access to the Bryn Mawr College library, which was, in almost every respect, superior to that at the Barnes Foundation. He also made contact with the philosophers at Bryn Mawr and its neighbouring colleges, Swarthmore and Haverfield. Despite this, the parts of the *History* written at Bryn Mawr are markedly *less* scholarly than those based on the lectures he had given during his two years at the Barnes Foundation.

The aim of the book, announced in its subtitle, of connecting the history of philosophy 'with Political and Social Circumstances from the Earliest Times to the Present Day' is evident in its first two sections, which are devoted to, respectively, ancient Greek and Roman philosophy and the Middle Ages. After that, it is lost sight of, until, by the time the book reaches the nineteenth and twentieth centuries, it seems to be in an almost indecent hurry to draw to a close. Immanuel Kant, thought by many to be the most important philosopher of the modern period, is dealt with in a brief, critical and, by common consent, unsatisfactory chapter; Hegel's vast corpus of work is disposed of in just fifteen pages; and Nietzsche is made the subject of a caricature so broad as to be almost unrecognisable. Moreover, while philosophers of the stature of Kierkegaard, Husserl and Heidegger are not mentioned at all, figures whose influence on the history of philosophy has been comparatively minor, such as Bergson, Dewey and – most bizarrely of all – Lord Byron, are given whole chapters to themselves. The most obvious explanation for this falling off in the quality of the book, for its later lapses into arbitrariness and capriciousness, is that Russell was indeed in a great hurry to finish it. The philosophers dealt with in its later chapters were chosen, one suspects, not on the basis of a careful consideration of their importance in the history of philosophy, but rather because Russell happened to have lying to hand discussions of their work that he had written earlier. Thus, for Bergson he could use his 1912 lecture, for Byron his 1936 article, for Dewey his 1938 article, and so on.

Russell's hurry to finish *History of Western Philosophy* was motivated to a large extent by his desire to deliver it to Simon & Schuster before he returned home to England, which he hoped to do as soon as possible. Writing to Gilbert Murray in April 1943, Russell told him that 'various things I have undertaken to do will keep me here till the end of October; then I shall return to England'. In fact, it was not until May 1944 that Russell was able to sail home. In the meantime he was kept busy, not only with the final parts of his *History*, but with several series of lectures and his own contributions to the volume dedicated to him in Paul Schilpp's *Library of Living Philosophers*.

In the years since their meeting in Chicago in 1938, when Russell and

Schilpp had first discussed the idea of a volume on Russell in this series, Schilpp had been commissioning the essays on various aspects of Russell's work that would constitute the book. By the summer of 1943, he was ready to send most of them to Russell so that Russell could begin writing his replies. The essays came from a wide variety of authors. Some, like Einstein and G. E. Moore, were extremely eminent, while others, such as John Elof Boodin, Justus Buchler and Edgar Sheffield Brightman, were practically unknown. The topics dealt with were equally various. Einstein's contribution was a short and rather bland discussion of *An Inquiry into Meaning and Truth*, while Moore contributed a long, detailed and painstaking criticism of Russell's Theory of Descriptions. Other essays discussed his work on logic, mathematics, language, the mind, science, metaphysics, ethics, religion, social and political philosophy and education. In promising to reply to each of these essays Russell was, in effect, undertaking to defend his life's work.

On the whole, he found it an uncongenial task. 'I am amazed how little other philosophers understand me,' he wrote to his erstwhile lover Colette. Quoting Socrates's remark that in heaven no one could stop him arguing, Russell added: 'I have had enough of arguing – I want people who feel things in the same sort of way as I do.' Indeed, though his 'Reply to Criticisms' is long and – especially considering the circumstances in which it was written – impressively thorough, it shows little relish for detailed argument. The essays that receive the longest and most careful replies are those that are most Russellian in content and style. The ones treated most perfunctorily are those that either contain vehement criticisms of Russell or are devoted to social and political themes. Responding to an essay called 'Russell's Political and Economic Philosophy', he remarked that it dealt 'mainly with matters which I should regard as lying wholly outside philosophy'. He was not, for example, going to be drawn into a philosophical debate about the views he had expressed in *Principles of Social Reconstruction*:

> With regard to *Social Reconstruction*, and to some extent with my other popular books, philosophic readers, knowing that I am classified as a 'philosopher', are apt to be led astray. I did not write *Social Reconstruction* in my capacity as a 'philosopher', I wrote it as a human being who suffered from the state of the world, wished to find some way of improving it, and was anxious to speak in plain terms to others who had similar feelings. If I had never written technical books, this would be obvious to everybody; and if the book is to be understood, my technical activities must be forgotten.

Ironically, the one contribution to the Schilpp volume to which Russell did not reply was the most technical of them all: Kurt Gödel's masterly essay 'Russell's Mathematical Logic', by some margin the most noteworthy essay in the entire collection. As his correspondence with Schilpp reveals, Gödel wrote this essay with great care and attached considerable importance to it. The author of one of the most famous mathematical theorems of all time – the celebrated Incompleteness Theorem of 1931 – Gödel was, by 1943, widely regarded as the greatest living logician. Philosophically, he took the kind of Platonist view of mathematics that had inspired Russell's great work in mathematical logic – the view, that is, that regards mathematics as being a body of truths concerning objective reality, a view that Russell had abandoned under the influence of Wittgenstein. When Gödel was invited by Schilpp to contribute an essay on Russell's mathematical logic, therefore, he regarded this as an opportunity to try to win Russell back to the Platonic fold, and the central theme of his essay was that Russell was wrong to forsake his early belief in the actual existence of mathematical entities such as numbers, classes, and so on. 'It seems to me', Gödel wrote in his essay on Russell, 'that the assumption of such objects is quite as legitimate as the assumption of physical bodies and there is quite as much reason to believe in their existence.'

Partly because of the care with which he approached the writing of this article (and partly because he was just that sort of person), Gödel missed the deadline he had been set by Schilpp, and in July 1943, while Russell was writing his replies to the other essays, Gödel was writing to Schilpp pleading for more time to perfect his article. When, on 14 July, Schilpp wrote to Gödel asking if he could send the typescript *as it was* to Russell, Gödel replied by telegram: No. As a result, Russell informed Schilpp that, owing to pressure of time, he would not be able to reply to Gödel's essay. 'I think I will say nothing about Gödel,' he wrote, 'except a postscript that it came too late. In any case it is not likely to be controversial.'

On 25 August, Schilpp, who had still not received a final version of Gödel's paper, wrote to tell Gödel that it was 'very unfortunate indeed' that the book would not contain Russell's reply and to admonish him for not allowing Russell to see an imperfect draft of the paper. 'But,' he added, 'since you refused to give me your permission to send that draft to Lord Russell and since Lord Russell had obligated himself to finish his History of Philosophy by this fall and also to write a series of lectures in October and since, moreover, on top of all this, he is planning to leave the United States for Great Britain in November, I do not see how I can use any more pressure than I have already done to try to get him to reply to your essay at this late date.' The following month, a clearly exasperated Schilpp wrote again to Gödel: 'not having your essay in our possession is now seriously inconveniencing us and holding up the entire project'.

But Gödel's mind was on higher things. That he was holding back Schilpp's publication schedule was a matter of comparative (one is tempted to say complete) indifference to him. What mattered far more was that he had written an article that presented Russell with the opportunity, perhaps even the obligation, to rethink his 'Wittgensteinian turn'. On 19 September 1943, he wrote to Schilpp: 'I must say that I find it extremely unfair towards Russell to publish an article in which he is pretty severely criticised when he is prevented by other obligations from writing a reply ... I can therefore agree to a publication under these circumstances only if this is Russell's express wish . . . I am personally in favour of not publishing my article at all without reply since I wrote it largely for the purposes of a discussion.'

Schilpp replied suggesting that Gödel wrote directly to Russell, and quoting from Russell's letter to him of August in which he had said that he would not reply to Gödel. This prompted Gödel to write to Russell on 28 September 1943, urging him to change his mind and spelling out why he attached so much importance to his own essay: 'your decision seems to be based on the wrong assumption that my article will not be controversial. This is by no means so. I am advocating in some respects the exact opposite of the development inaugurated by Wittgenstein and therefore suspect that many passages will contradict directly your present opinion. Furthermore I am criticising the vicious circle principle and appendix B of Principia, which I believe contains some formal mistakes that make the proof invalid.' 'I doubt very much', he concluded, 'if my article should be published at all without a reply.'

Russell still did not respond to Gödel. The following month when, at long last, he received his copy of Gödel's paper, he wrote to Schilpp saying that it was not possible to devote to Gödel's piece the time necessary – which Russell estimated to be a month – to reply to it properly, and sending him a short note on Gödel to append to his other replies. The note reads:

> Dr Gödel's most interesting paper on my mathematical logic came into my hands after my replies had been completed, and at a time when I had no leisure to work on it. As it is now about eighteen years since I last worked on mathematical logic, it would have taken me a long time to form a critical estimate of Dr Gödel's opinions. His great ability, as shown in his previous work, makes me think it highly probable that many of his criticisms of me are justified. The writing of *Principia Mathematica* was completed thirty-three years ago, and obviously, in view of subsequent advances in the subject, it needs amending in various ways. If I had the leisure, I should be glad to attempt a revision of its introductory portions, but external circumstances make this impossible. I must therefore ask the reader to give Dr Gödel's work the attention that it deserves, and to form his own critical judgment on it.

'I hope it will satisfy him,' Russell told Schilpp. 'Please let him know, as he wrote to me, and I have no time to write to him, being desperately busy.' Thus ended the opportunity for arguably the two greatest logicians of the twentieth century to debate the nature of mathematical logic.

Apparently (so one gathers from the above note) Russell did not realise that Gödel's essay, far from concerning itself merely with the technical ways in which the logic of *Principia* needed amending in the light of subsequent work in mathematical logic, was essentially a plea for a fundamental change in Russell's philosophical approach to the subject, a reversal of the 'Retreat from Pythagoras' that Russell himself regarded as one of the most important developments in his philosophical thinking.

When Russell met Gödel the following summer in Princeton, he seemed surprised to find that Gödel subscribed to the Platonic view of mathematics. In his *Autobiography*, Russell says that, while living in Princeton, he used to go once a week to Einstein's house 'to discuss with him and Gödel and Pauli'. The discussions, he remarks, were disappointing, 'for, although all three of them were Jews and exiles and, in intention, cosmopolitans, I found that they all had a German bias towards metaphysics'. Gödel, he writes mockingly, 'turned out to be an unadulterated Platonist, and apparently believed that an eternal "not" was laid up in heaven, where virtuous logicians might hope to meet it hereafter'. Soon after Russell's death, this passage was drawn to Gödel's attention by Kenneth Blackwell at the Russell Archives. In his reply (which, characteristically, he never posted), Gödel drew attention to some inaccuracies in Russell's account: first (not that it matters, he stressed), he was not Jewish; second, the impression given by Russell that they had several meetings was false – he could remember only one. Finally, Gödel wrote:

> Concerning my 'unadulterated' Platonism, it is no more 'unadulterated' than Russell's own in 1921 when in the *Introduction to Mathematical Philosophy* he said: 'Logic is concerned with the real world just as truly as zoology, though with its more abstract and general features'. At that time evidently Russell had met the 'not' even in this world, but later on under the influence of Wittgenstein he chose to overlook it.

Russell's unwillingness to take Gödel seriously is revealing of the extent to which, by 1943, mathematical logic had simply ceased to be important to him. Whatever Gödel had to say about *Principia* could not be of any great philosophical significance, he seems to have thought, because logic itself – contrary to what he had earlier believed – was of no great philosophical significance. This attitude is revealed also in the plans that he was formulating towards the end of 1943 for future philosophical work. In a document called 'Project of Future Work', presumably written for his publishers, Russell wrote that what he wanted to do after he had finished his *History* was a book attempting to systematise the kind of reasoning used in science, which, he emphasised, was quite distinct from the kind of reasoning systematised in formal logic. The latter, which Russell called 'demonstrative inference', was, he says, systematised for late antiquity and the Middle Ages by Aristotle and for the modern age by mathematical logic. It 'has its importance in mathematics,' he wrote, 'but outside mathematics demonstrative inference hardly occurs'. In science, the kind of reasoning used and accepted is not that captured in formal systems of logic – whether Aristotle's or *Principia Mathematica*. It is, rather, what Russell calls 'non-demonstrative', 'in the sense that the conclusion *may* be false when the premises are true and the reasoning is correct'. However: 'When the likelihood of such falsehood is very small, it may be ignored in practice.'

Russell's project, then, was to analyse and systematise the kind of 'non-demonstrative inference' upon which science is built. 'It should not be very difficult', he claims, 'to arrive at a few fairly simple principles which would be logically equivalent to the kinds of inference that are accepted in scientific method. Such principles would constitute a canon.' In October 1943 Russell was invited to give a series of five lectures at Bryn Mawr College on this theme. Called 'Postulates of Scientific Method', the lectures were open to the public and were, according to Paul Weiss, then a philosopher at Bryn Mawr, a 'tremendous success':

> Despite torrential rains students, faculty and others came from Swarthmore, Haverford and Philadelphia in considerable and increasing numbers. His ideas and personality, his comments and illustrations have been discussed widely and vehemently in the classes and in the halls.

The synopsis that survives of these lectures shows them to be a development of the ideas outlined in 'Project of Future Work'. In the first lecture Russell emphasised the 'limitations of deductive logic': in the second he outlined the kind of 'probable inference' that is used in practice (including the practice of science); and in the final three lectures he attempted to analyse in detail the presuppositions of natural science, stressing that these were based neither on logic nor on perception, but rather on certain 'metaphysical assumptions as to the nature of the universe'. The truth of these assumptions cannot be demonstrated either by logic or by experience, but nevertheless: 'We all in fact believe in them, whatever, as philosophers, we may pretend.' The task Russell now set himself was to articulate those assumptions and to show how the 'edifice of scientific knowledge' is built upon them.

In the New Year of 1944, Russell received some extraordinarily good news that would allow him to pursue this task in what were for him the most congenial circumstances imaginable: the Council of Trinity College, Cambridge, had unanimously agreed to offer him a five-year Fellowship beginning the following autumn. It is not entirely clear what prompted the college to make this offer, but behind the scenes lobbying to bring Russell back to Trinity had been going on for some years. In 1942, the Trinity mathematician, G. H. Hardy, prompted by misrepresentations in the Press of Russell's turbulent past relations with his old Cambridge college, had published a detailed history of those relations in a book called *Bertrand Russell and Trinity: A college controversy of the last war*. In it, Hardy emphasised that the quarrel between Russell and Trinity over Russell's activities during the First World War had, contrary to what was repeatedly said in the Press, been healed a long time ago, first by the offer (turned down by Russell) of a lectureship in 1920 and secondly by the invitation to give the public Tarner Lectures in 1925. 'All the world of learning knows that there was a quarrel between the College and one of its most famous members,' Hardy's book ends; 'could it not be told in language which leaves no possibility of misunderstanding that the quarrel has since been healed?'

After Russell's dismissal from the Barnes Foundation, Peter wrote to Hardy telling him that it was still being reported in the States that Russell had been 'disowned' by Trinity. Hardy passed her letter on to George

Trevelyan, the Master of the college, who wrote to Peter in the spirit of Hardy's book, telling her that, though 'there was trouble during the last war, . . . that hatchet was buried as long ago as 1920'. 'The last thing that had occurred between Trinity and your husband', Trevelyan continued, 'was that in 1925 the College appointed him to give the triennial Tarner Lectures on the Philosophy of the Sciences . . . Nothing has since occurred to disturb our amicable relations.' Meanwhile, the Trinity philosopher and former student of Russell's, C. D. Broad, was agitating for Russell's return, prompted by reports of his financial problems in the States.

Whether it was Broad, Hardy or Trevelyan that convinced the Council of the college to issue its invitation of 1944 is now impossible to say, but Russell was, in any case, delighted by it and accepted immediately. His old friends Alfred and Evelyn Whitehead certainly knew what it meant to him. 'Our warmest congratulations,' they wrote on 3 January. 'It is exactly what ought to have happened.' Writing to Kate to let her know the good news, Russell told her: 'I am very glad about it – it heals the old wound of 1916. This makes it definite that I must be in England next autumn.'

By this time, relations between Kate and Peter had reached their lowest point, and, for the first time since she had been in America, Kate did not spend Christmas with her father, preferring to stay with college friends than to return to Peter's hysterics. 'I hate not seeing you for Xmas,' Russell wrote to her. 'You and I get on with each other very well provided we do not attempt to include Peter,' he said in another letter. 'Unless you would find seeing me a bore, I will try to arrange some way of meeting.' His chance came in early 1944, when he gave a series of ten weekly lectures on 'Philosophies in Practice' at the Rand School of Social Science in New York. Every Wednesday he stayed overnight at the Hotel Lafayette in New York and, as Kate puts it, 'I wrote to him there as if I were a mistress carrying on a clandestine affair.' Kate had now decided to return to England after graduating in the summer, a decision of which Russell, of course, was informed before Peter. This gave rise to one among many occasions on which Russell urged his daughter to practise petty deception. On 3 February, he wrote to her: 'will you write me a letter *soon* addressed to Peacock Inn, Princeton, saying you have decided to go home, as if you were saying it for the first time, and so written that I can show it to Peter?' 'Was this the man', Kate wondered, 'who had taught us to be honest and fearless at all times?'

Apart from his weekly trips to New York, Russell lived in Princeton for the last months before his return to England. 'The society of Princeton was extremely pleasant,' he wrote in his *Autobiography*, 'pleasanter, on the whole, than any other social group I had come across in America.' In his 'Private Memoirs', Russell recounts with some glee what he describes as Peter's humiliation in Princeton at the hands of a homosexual Spanish mystic with whom she had fallen in love. According to Russell, Peter went to see this man on Good Friday, believing that she and he would make love together, only to be told he preferred to go to Mass. Afterwards, when they left Princeton, Russell says, scarcely concealing his pleasure at the thought, he was told that this man was in the habit of making fun of Peter. Who the man was, he does not say.

Faced with Peter's affairs with other men, Russell now made attempts to stir back into life one of the great love affairs of his past, that with Colette (Constance Malleson). Colette, whom Russell had not seen for more than twenty years, was now living in Norway, where Russell wrote to her, telling her of his imminent return to England. 'Will you come home when it is possible?' he asked her. 'I hope so.' Telling her of the Schilpp volume, he wrote: 'For my part, I have had enough of arguing – I want people who feel things in the same sort of way as I do. They are few – which brings me back to the hope that we shall meet in England.' He ended the letter: 'Goodbye dearest Colette – with very much love'.

In May, after a long wait for the necessary permission to be granted, Russell finally set sail for England, taking with him the bulky manuscript of *History of Western Philosophy*, now finished but not yet published. He had been in America for six years, during which his marriage had fallen apart, his relations with his oldest two children had come under intense strain and he had attracted the most vicious public opprobrium he had ever suffered. But he had, at last, succeeded where he had failed in 1938: to regain the acceptance of the university that, fifty years earlier, he had described as his 'home'.

9
THE BOMB GOES OFF

The England to which Russell, Peter and seven-year-old Conrad returned in the summer of 1944 was in many ways an unfamiliar place to them. Though the prevailing mood in the country was one of optimism, the living conditions after five years of war were – especially by the standards of the United States – almost unbearably grim. The blackout was still in force and almost every basic necessity was in short supply and rationed by the Government. On 6 June, a few days before Russell's ship reached Britain, the D-Day offensive began, and within a week Hitler retaliated by unleashing his 'secret weapon'. Every day, between 100 and 150 V-1 flying bombs ('doodlebugs', as they came to be called) rained down on the South of England, causing a second evacuation of women and children from London and a return to the blitz conditions of 1940. Even though their last years in America had been marked by financial anxieties and stringent economies, it took a long time for Russell and, especially perhaps, Peter to grow accustomed to the austerities and hardships of British wartime life.

Peter and Conrad travelled separately from Russell: they on board the *Queen Mary* and he with a military convoy that proceeded, he said, 'majestically at the speed of a bicycle'. Though he left the States before them, they overtook him and were settled into Peter's mother's house in Sidmouth, Devon, by the time the military convoy carrying him arrived at the Firth of Forth. He immediately took a night train to London and the following day was reunited at last with his family.

Or at any rate, he was reunited with *one* of his families. Much as Peter might at times wish it were otherwise, Conrad was not Russell's only son, and as soon as he was settled Russell lost little time in getting in touch with John, whom he had not seen for more than a year and whom he had reason to fear he might never see again. After joining the Royal Navy the previous year, John had spent most of his time in London learning Japanese, in preparation, so he thought, for being sent as a naval officer to the Far East. In fact, when his course ended in August, he was kept in London until the following March, when he was posted, in strict secrecy, to Washington, where he was set to work translating Japanese documents. In June 1944, however, neither John nor Russell knew what lay in store for him and, as far as Russell knew, he had just two months in which to renew his relationship with his son before he was sent off to fight. As soon as he reached Sidmouth, therefore, Russell wrote to John, telling him his schedule: he would be at Peter's mother's until the end of July and would then spend a weekend with the Currys at Dartington (where Russell and Peter intended to send Conrad) before coming up to Cambridge on 1 August. 'If you happened to be at Dartington when we are there it would be nice,' Russell wrote. 'In any case I hope you will come to Cambridge . . . I can put you up in College.'

In the event, John did not see Russell in Dartington and did not visit him in Cambridge until October. In the meantime, he stayed with Dora in her house in Kilburn, London. Having left the United States in the New Year of 1943, John had been living with Dora for more than a year and sharing with her, Pat, Harriet and Roddy the perils, but also the warm companionship, of surviving in a war-torn city. He was later to look back on this period as a time when he at last established some sort of intimacy with one of his parents; he was developing, too, close and affectionate relationships with his half-brother and half-sister. For the first time since he left England in 1939, and quite possibly for the first time since his very early childhood, John felt part of a close and supportive family – one, he began to feel, that needed him just as much as he needed it.

It bothered John, however, that the two sides of his family were kept separate, and from this time on he began to dream of healing the old wounds and uniting all his parents, step-parents, siblings and half-siblings into one united family. It was, he felt, a task in which only he could succeed. The previous year, he had made a start by interesting himself in Conrad's education. Knowing that Russell wanted Conrad to attend Dartington, John had gone to see Curry, its headmaster, to ask him about it and had reported back to Russell, then still in the States, that Curry advised Russell to find a place near Dartington to live, so that Conrad could attend the school as a day-pupil. Knowing also that Russell and Peter were short of money, John wrote to his father in January 1944:

> As you have not had a chance to give Conrad a Trust, what with the swirling multitudes of the bigoted and stupid, I propose that I should make some arrangement before leaving for the East, where God knows what may happen, whereby the interest of the Trust, over which I have control, should be used for Conrad's education. I have no control over the capital until I am 25, as was arranged, but I could stipulate that if I am alive, even though in the remoter corners of the earth, it could be made over into his name when I reach that age.

'If I do not make an arrangement like this,' John added ominously, 'my ambitions and cravings, and the excessive expenditures in which officers are invariably involved, will run away with it, and it will become dissipated and worthless.'

Without asking him what he meant by this last sentence, Russell accepted with gratitude John's offer to help pay for Conrad's education and in his first letter to his son upon arriving at Sidmouth told him that, before they met in Cambridge, 'I should be very glad if you arrange about the money for Conrad.'

Conrad did not start at Dartington until September 1945. In the meantime, Dora, again with help from John, arranged to send Harriet and Roddy there in the autumn of 1944. In John's mind this was no doubt one step towards the extended family unity that he craved, but, as it turned out, the helpful interest he took in the education and well-being of all three of his half-siblings was to lead, within a year, to the most acrimonious family dispute in which he had yet been involved.

Meanwhile, John was delighted to welcome home his beloved sister Kate, who returned to England in August 1944, after graduating from Radcliffe not only with top honours but with a prize for the best student at either Harvard or Radcliffe. She had, if she had wanted to take it, a glittering career ahead of her in the States, having been offered no fewer than two professorships at American universities, but it had been decided the previous summer that she, along with her brother and her father and stepmother, would return to England. 'We were all', she writes, 'getting restless for home.' And so, despite the attractions of remaining in the States, which by 1944 included a lover who was a member of the US armed forces, she kept to the plan to return to Britain.

It was a decision she came to regret almost as soon as she arrived. With Russell, Peter and Conrad still in Sidmouth, Kate travelled down to Cornwall to spend the summer with Dora, John, Pat, Roddy and Harriet. She went there, she says, 'intending to establish a mature and friendly relationship' with her mother. After all, she was now twenty-one years old and recognised across the Atlantic as what she had always been: a brilliantly intelligent and resourceful person. But before she knew what was happening, she became 'sucked into a new dependency'. At the end of the summer she moved, not to Cambridge to be with Russell, but into the already crowded house at 72 Dartmouth Road, Kilburn. By this time Dora, having given up Beacon Hill School, had been working for about a year for the Reference Division of the Ministry of Information, which was then housed in a London University building just behind the British Museum (that is, practically next door to Duchess House, where John was learning Japanese), and she had little trouble finding a wartime job at the Ministry for the extremely well-qualified Kate. Thus, by the autumn, Dora had Kate and John living with her and working alongside her.

Russell, whose hostility to Dora was relentless, no doubt viewed these developments with alarm and suspicion. As he and Peter did not yet have a home of their own, however, he could do little to prevent John and Kate from, in effect, returning to Dora. In any case, even had they a home of their own, it was not at all clear either whether John and Kate would risk living again with Peter or whether Peter would agree to their doing so.

At the end of the summer, Russell moved up to Cambridge to live in the splendid rooms made available to him at Trinity while he looked for a house to buy. Meanwhile, Peter and Conrad were housed in what Russell describes as 'squalid rooms in a lodging house'. 'There they were underfed and miserable,' he writes in his *Autobiography*, 'while I was living luxuriously in College.' Finally, towards the end of September, with the money he had been awarded in court from Barnes, Russell was able to buy a house in Babraham Road, Cambridge, called Grosvenor Lodge. 'We shall in a very short time be able to put you up . . . if you don't mind some discomfort,' he wrote to Kate. 'Peter means to make nice rooms for you and John when possible, but at first they will be unfinished.' By 14 October, the house was in a fit enough state for Peter to feel able to have Kate for the weekend, but the visit produced another fierce quarrel between the two, after which Kate received an angry letter from Peter and an apologetic one from Russell. 'Whatever happens,' Russell told her, 'I am determined that friction between her and you shall not affect relations between you and me. If she doesn't want you, or you don't want to stay in her house, I can put you up in a hotel and entertain you in college . . . However, it will be *much* better if you can write her a letter that will cause her anger to diminish.'

John stayed away from Grosvenor Lodge until November, when he and Kate were invited for the weekend before his twenty-third birthday. When they arrived, Russell met them at the station and then took them on a tour of Cambridge, showing them with pride the great colleges and his own rooms in Trinity. 'Then,' reports Kate, 'with some apprehension, we took a bus out to the house to face the uncertainty of Peter.' Though John and she were on the alert for emotional booby-traps, Kate records, everything seemed fine at first: 'Then came the explosion.' During the war, it was customary when visiting people to take with you little packets of scarce basic necessities such as butter, sugar, tea, and so on, together with your ration books. If you forgot to do this, it was extremely difficult for your host to provide enough food. John, Kate says, 'was hopelessly vague about that sort of thing' and she had not been back in England long enough to realise the importance of it. Thus they arrived empty-handed and were blasted for their thoughtlessness by Peter. 'We bowed our heads before the storm,' Kate writes, 'apologised for our lack of consideration and departed as soon as possible, promising ourselves not to return.'

When they got back to London, they mentioned the incident to Dora and Pat, who immediately made up a parcel of food and sent it off to Cambridge to compensate for what John and Kate had consumed. This merely provoked Peter to further fury 'and the silly package of rations went back and forth several times'. After this, John and Kate decided it would be wiser to stay away from Grosvenor Lodge, and for the next few years Russell saw very little of his eldest children. 'I don't wonder that you feel you don't want to risk staying again,' Russell wrote to John, '. . . but I hope you & Kate will relent. It is very painful to me that my house should be a place you don't want to come to.'

According to Russell's *Autobiography*, John and Kate were not the only ones who did not want to visit his house. 'I could have been happy in Cambridge,' he writes of this period, 'but the Cambridge ladies did not consider us respectable.' It is a remark that echoes an earlier one about his time in Oxford in 1938, when, describing his house in Kidlington, Russell wrote: '[We] lived there for about a year, but only one Oxford lady called. We were not respectable. We had later a similar experience in Cambridge. In this respect I have found these ancient seats of learning unique.'

More hurtful even than these social snubs was the fact that Russell arrived back in Cambridge to find himself out of fashion among the younger generation of British philosophers, among whom Wittgenstein was now the greatest influence. Wittgenstein had spent most of the war away from academic life, but in the autumn of 1944 he too returned to Cambridge. His friend, Norman Malcolm, recalls that, on the rare occasions when both Wittgenstein and Russell attended the Moral Science Club, 'Wittgenstein was deferential to Russell in the discussion as I never knew him to be with anyone else.' On the whole, however, Wittgenstein – like 'the Cambridge ladies' – kept his distance. Writing to his friend Rush Rhees soon after his return to Cambridge, Wittgenstein said: 'I've seen Russell, who somehow gave me a *bad* impression.'

Though Wittgenstein never lost his admiration for Russell's early work in logic, he vehemently disapproved of Russell's popular writing of the inter-war period. 'Russell's books should be bound in two colours,' he once said, 'those dealing with mathematical logic in red – and all students of philosophy should read them; those dealing with ethics and politics in blue – and no one should be allowed to read them.' The work that Russell had published since his return to serious philosophical study in 1936 had made little impact on British philosophers, and the books that he was about to publish – his *History of Western Philosophy* and *Human Knowledge: Its Scope and Limits* – aroused among them polite interest at best and open scorn at worst. Russell's Fellowship at Trinity did not oblige him to give lectures, but he gave them nevertheless, beginning in October 1944 with a course on 'Non-Demonstrative Inference', which expanded the ideas he had expressed in his lectures at Bryn Mawr and which he was to expound at greater length in *Human Knowledge*. These lectures were well attended and popular among undergraduates, but, unlike Wittgenstein's lectures of the same period, attracted little curiosity among professional philosophers.

The truth was that, by 1944, Russell was far better regarded by the general public than he was by the academic élite. In part this was due to the fickle nature of intellectual fashion, but in part also it was a reaction to the fact that Russell had evolved a style of writing – and even of thinking – that was more suited to popular journalism than to intricate philosophical debate. The problem is well illustrated by two magazine articles that Russell published soon after his return to Cambridge, which were of a kind that few serious academics would have either the opportunity or the desire to write. The first was 'What Makes a Woman a Fascinator?', published in *Vogue* magazine on 1 November 1944, in which Russell declared his belief that among the essential qualities that a woman must possess in order to 'enslave a man for life' are: 1. the sort of beauty 'that comes and goes, like a gleam of sun on a stormy day'; 2. 'a certain fundamental indifference to men, combined with a superficial interest in them'; and 3. 'mysteriousness'. The woman who truly fascinates, according to Russell, is thus the one who is, for one reason or another, out of reach. The fascination of which he speaks is, therefore, bound to lead to tragedy. 'For every day purposes,' he admits, 'a pedestrian love that mellows gradually into a contented marriage is no doubt preferable.' But 'tragedy is a part, and an inevitable part, of what gives life splendour, and to wish that tragedy should wholly disappear is no part of wisdom'.

One might read this article as revealing of why Russell found it impossible to find happiness in love; otherwise, as an analysis of the relations between men and women, it seems frivolous and silly. Almost equally so was an article that he published in the *Leader Magazine* in the same month, called 'The Thinkers Behind Germany's Sins', in which he rehearsed once again his view that the philosophers of whom he disapproved were in some way responsible for Nazism. On this occasion, as on so many others, the culprits are identified as Fichte, Hegel and Nietzsche; Fichte for encouraging German nationalism, Hegel for glorifying the Prussian State (and, of course, for defining freedom as 'the right to obey the police'), and Nietzsche for elaborating an 'aristocratic doctrine in ethics' that valued the 'will to power' above the impulse to sympathy. These doctrines, Russell claims, 'combined and vulgarised, make up most of what is distinctive in Nazi political theory'. It is not difficult to imagine how this article would have struck anyone with a serious interest in Fichte, Hegel or Nietzsche – or, indeed, in Nazism.

Of course, in its treatment of Fichte, Hegel and Nietzsche, this latter article was little more than a condensed version of Russell's discussions of those philosophers in *History of Western Philosophy*, which, when it was finally published (the American edition in October 1945, the British edition a year later), was greeted with almost universal disdain by the academic philosophers who reviewed it. Even C. D. Broad, an ex-pupil and admirer of Russell's who had played a hand in getting him back to Cambridge, could not bring himself to overlook the book's outrageous and cavalier superficialities and simplifications. Nevertheless, despite its many flaws (or perhaps to some extent because of them), the book became a runaway best-seller and placed Russell's finances on a secure footing for the rest of his life.

The growing realisation that he was no longer taken seriously by the majority of professional philosophers in Britain hurt Russell deeply, but for the most part he seemed reconciled to the fact that he was no longer writing for them but for the much wider public he had been addressing since the 1920s. Of the twenty or so articles that he published in 1945, only one had anything to do with philosophy, and that was a popular account of logical positivism written for the magazine *Polemic*. Though he continued to lecture and to work on *Human Knowledge*, his energies were directed towards writing political journalism as much as towards debating philosophical issues.

Soon after his return to Cambridge, Russell's reputation among the general public received a further boost when he was taken up by BBC Radio as a regular broadcaster. Russell attributed this acceptance by the British

Establishment to the fact that his opinions on the Second World War were – unlike his opinions on the First World War – entirely orthodox. There is no doubt some truth in this, but his entrée into the BBC was also possibly smoothed by an article he published in September 1944 called 'I am Thankful for the BBC', in which he argued – 'first as a Socialist, and second, as one who has suffered under commercial radio in America' – against the introduction of commercial radio and in favour of the BBC retaining its monopoly. Within a few months of the appearance of this article, Russell was making regular BBC radio broadcasts on political and social themes, lecturing, for example, on 'Britain's Place in the Post-War World' in January 1945 and debating with J. B. S. Haldane the following May on 'Should Scientists be Public Servants?' The man who had been regarded as dangerously subversive in the United States was rapidly becoming, in Britain, the voice of established orthodoxy.

Russell was both pleased and proud of this official acceptance, which helped to confirm him in his conviction that he loved Britain, not only because he happened to be British, but also because there was something inherently lovable about the place. In an article called 'British and American Nationalism', published in *Horizon* in January 1945, he described British nationalism, particularly his own, as 'quasi-biological'. A hen, he said, when scared by a motor-car, will rush across the road in order to be at home, despite thus risking its life, and 'In like manner, during the Blitz, I longed to be in England.' American patriotism, on the other hand, 'is more analogous to party or sectarian loyalty'. The British regard themselves as a family or even a race, a 'happy *breed* of men'; the Americans regard themselves as 'a sacred Cause'. Thus American nationalism, because 'it is not so deeply based on instinct as that of the British, is more vocal, more shrill, and more blatant'. The article ends with a characteristic Russellian plea for the overcoming of nationalist prejudices of all sorts, but even the most casual reader must have identified its general tone as that of patriotic Briton delighted to be back home and relieved no longer to be living in a country which, despite its shrill confidence in being the greatest nation on earth, was 'not biologically a nation' at all.

On 3 February John wrote to Russell and Peter, telling them that Russell's article 'seems to have been liked by many people, though they hardly consider it conducive to good relations'. The following month, John received his orders to go with the Royal Navy to Washington to work with US Intelligence translating Japanese documents. During the previous six months, John had seen Russell and Peter only once or twice. There was mutual avoidance: Peter finding a reason not to accept John's invitation to spend some time over the Christmas period with him, and John writing to Russell, stalling on proposed visits to Cambridge. When the time came to leave, he was prevented for military reasons from telling anybody where he was going, and most of his family still imagined him to be on his way to the Far East. By this time, his family very firmly included Pat, Harriet and Roddy, as well as Kate, Russell, Peter and Conrad. 'It'll seem terribly funny without you at 72 [Dartmouth Road]', fourteen-year-old Harriet wrote to him from Dartington, 'we haven't lived there when you haven't been there yet . . . I'm awfully sorry not to see you again, but the sooner you go the sooner you'll be back. Hope you have a lovely time – am sure you will as long as there's enough whiskey about . . .'

On 6 April 1945, John wrote to Russell to say that the address 'The Burlington Hotel, Washington' would find him, and that 'My first impressions of the town are favourable.' After that, for the rest of the war, his address was always given as 'HMS *Saker*' at the British Fleet Mail Office in New York, though in fact he was living throughout this period in Washington. Within a few days of being in Washington, John had a chance meeting that seems, given his preoccupation at this time with his extended family, to have been almost determined by fate: while walking around town he happened to come across none other than Griffin Barry, whom he had not seen for more than ten years. At first, John did not recognise him. Griffin struck him, so he told Harriet in a letter written some time later, to be 'an ill, tired dyspeptic, irritable and sunken old man, who thought he was very charming [and] seemed to have no real interest in anything'. By this time Griffin was embittered and unemployed, though still chasing dreams of being a famous writer. He had been living in Washington since the 1930s, when he went there to work on a publicly funded 'New Deal' post.

As John was looking for a place to live and Griffin for a tenant, John moved into Griffin's flat and remained his flatmate for the rest of his time in Washington. The two of them quickly became very close and were soon exchanging confidences. As John had just spent the last year and a half living with Dora, Harriet and Roddy, his arrival presented Griffin with the perfect opportunity to express his grievances about how Dora had treated him since their break in 1932, and his frustrated longing to re-establish contact with his two children, whom he had not seen for more than ten years. John listened sympathetically as Griffin told him how much it hurt him to be separated from Harriet and Roddy and how upset he was that Dora insisted on their retaining the surname 'Russell'. In return, John found someone with whom he could at last openly discuss his deepest secret, hints of which he had been dropping to his friends and family for the last few years.

In his letters to Russell, John spoke repeatedly of his 'cravings' and of 'pursuing vice' while on leave from the navy, but, as Russell never asked, John never spelt out what he meant. Once he phoned Russell in Cambridge from London in a troubled state, but was not able to tell Russell what the matter was. 'You sounded as if you had been having a bad experience you couldn't talk about,' Russell wrote to him the following day, urging him to come to Cambridge and stay in college: 'I don't like to think of you in London just now. Come if you possibly can.' But John did not come, and the secret remained buried. Similarly, in letters to his old Dartington friend, Jackie Gordon (whom both Dora and Russell regarded as John's girlfriend and even as his fiancée), John wrote of 'dark secrets' that he never revealed. It was only after living with Griffin, who was himself bisexual, that John felt able to come clean, confessing to Kate and others that, during the time he was living in London with Dora, he used to go out into the blackout in the hope of a casual homosexual encounter and that, in Washington, he would pay for sailors to sleep with him. 'Did you know that John has been a homosexual for years?' Kate wrote to her mother, telling her that this secret 'has been eating into him hidden away behind his sweet kind face'.

In Griffin, John found someone who was almost a family member and yet who would not be shocked by revelations of homosexual encounters. Among John's papers after he died was a report of a dream he had had while living with Griffin, which seems to express his feelings about the secret he had kept for many years and also, perhaps, provides some insight into the kind of life John shared with Griffin in Washington. In the dream, Griffin takes John to see a naval captain about his homosexuality, who in turn refers him to a psychiatrist. The psychiatrist tests John by showing him pictures of men and women, asking him which he likes best. The answer is the men, though the psychiatrist tells John there is some hope for him, after John says that he likes the poses of the women better than those of the men. The psychiatrist then warns John against going to a club that he and Griffin have been to for homosexual encounters, as it is crooked and full of thieves:

Griffin tried to explain to me which place, but I could not get it clear, so he took me, and wandered in daftly against my advice as I knew he could not take care of himself. Still he insisted daftly and we went in. It was a mixture of a cave and a barn, with many recesses and layers & hidden rooms & complex stairs, dark, but lighted with torches, and built of soft rock light, so that parts of it were hollowed out into recesses under overhanging cliffs. There were prostitutes (female) in a state of decay reclining in tattered clothes & looking drugged. There were drug addicts and spitting old men with broken physiques and hopeless looks in their eyes, and bent gaits. There were young kids looking gay but hopeless. Several people m & f from the office, or rather their faces, were there; but no one important to me. We met someone, who suggested we should go somewhere in a corner; and I was suspicious, knowing it was dangerous, as G did but would not admit it; but a fight began, in wh. both of us fought off sailors (of a hideous & mean-minded sort) and old men drooling who attacked. Some underworld King or other connected with politics & the city grafts gave the signal for this to start, & controlled the whole place, which was thoroughly crooked & petty. Finally Griffin was overpowered & carried off, and I fought them off successfully and got out and then realised Griffin was not there & that he could not be left inside. I went in again. The faces seemed to have changed, & it looked better, but the same evil current ran through underneath. Everyone was very polite to me, and I was deceived in one part of my nature, though not at bottom; and I went on in a sort of wary trust. I heard G's voice muffled in the distance, saying 'help, 6th floor first door, do you know where it is?' I shouted into the dark upper layers of the place, 'Yes, be along in a minute.' Then silence as if suddenly muffled from Griffin. I wandered upstairs with frantic anxiety to find G, through galleries [of] imploring voices of men, & clawing hands of women on the galleries of the higher floors, wh. I fought off with crusading zeal. Then I met a man in air raid warden's clothes who offered to take me to G, whom he had seen somewhere. I trusted him as he was polite & looked competent, though doubts & fears & anxiety for G assailed me. I went with ARW through a door, just had time to see G gagged & suspended by thumbs on a rack, and was almost dead, then looked at ARW and saw he had changed into one of the horrible old men I had seen earlier, saw that I was trapped, and was smothered (either by him alone or with assistance from the many other people in this room at the top of the dive none of whom offered to help me, & all wrecked) with a sweet-smelling substance, which made me unconscious except of being thrown into a sawdust corner (dark and small) to rot. No further memory existed.

I woke up trembling with fear, found I had slept on my belly with face in pillow, and that it was only 12 p.m. Slight indigestion; a cigarette; and resolved to write this out at once, the most vivid and terrifying dream, with fear running through from the beginning, that I have had for years.

While in Washington John was dreaming about psychiatric treatment, in London Kate was actually receiving it. She had been depressed ever since she returned to England. Her relations with Dora, Pat, Russell and Peter were strained, and, unlike John, she was unable to feel any sense of comradeship among the dismal war conditions in London. She had arrived, she later said, 'in time to spend a few anxious nights on a metal bunk in a subway station, but not in time to feel myself a part of the heroic resistance to Hitler':

All I felt was shame at having escaped so much, along with even greater shame at my inability to take in stride the discomforts the others had already endured for so long.

'I shrank into a solitary cell of depression,' she writes, 'which was sufficiently obvious to worry my father when I reluctantly visited him again in Cambridge.' Russell, who had years ago convinced himself that Kate was potentially mad, convinced her to see a psychiatrist at Guy's Hospital. The psychiatrist in question, Dr Gillespie, was, according to Kate's recollection, 'tall and cold, with pale hair and pale blue eyes behind glasses, a very unforthcoming person':

I was quite sure I didn't want to tell him *anything* about my secret, shameful self. I went to see him several times, making the long trip to the hospital, but I never trusted him enough to tell him what I really felt about anything . . . In the end, he discontinued the visits, and I sank back into my lonely apathy. It was a depressing experience.

Dr Gillespie suggested to Kate that the source of her problems might lie in the complex of her feelings about John: her devotion to him, her sense of being rejected and unwanted by her parents in comparison with him and her guilt at feeling jealous of him. All this Kate rejected, though Russell was inclined to take it more seriously. 'I shouldn't wonder if there were more than you think in his suggestions *re* John,' he wrote to her, 'you know what tricks the unconscious mind can play.'

Kate knew, however, that the real cause of her depression was the melancholy position she found herself in with regard to the conflict between her parents, stranded as she was in a no-man's-land between them. Having sided with her father against her mother, she found herself excluded from her father's side because of Peter and strenuously resisted being thrown on to the other side. 'I had begun to feel', she later wrote, 'that I could not make a life for myself in England and that I must at any cost get far away from all the family except John, who was already gone.' When her job at the Ministry of Information came to an end, she applied for a postgraduate scholarship at Radcliffe, was enthusiastically accepted and so, 'a little over a year after I had come home, I was off again across the Atlantic'.

Though Kate's wartime job ended with the defeat of Germany in May 1945, John's war did not finish until Japan surrendered in August. Almost as soon as it did so, John unleashed a kind of war of his own, a war against his family. At least, that is how most members of the family saw it. John saw it differently. As far as he was concerned, what he was trying to do was bring an end to years of war between his mother and his father and lay the foundations for a lasting peace. In his mind, there was some sort of connection between the end of the Second World War and what he hoped would be the end of the rift between the various members of his family. If the great nations of the world could stop fighting each other, he seems to have reasoned, why could the Russells not do so? It was a forlorn hope, but, for a few months, the energy he put into the attempt was extraordinary. That it came to nothing and resulted only in yet more acrimony seems to have broken his spirit irreparably. After 1945, John would never do anything again with the boldness, outspokenness and determination with which, between August and November of that year, he tried to patch up the cracks in his family. It is doubtful that Russell ever realised how much it cost his son to make the attempt, or how much he suffered from its failure.

The issue that started it was the conflict that had been developing throughout the previous year between Peter and Dora over sending their respective children to Dartington School. Harriet and Roddy had been at Dartington since September 1944 and Conrad was due to start there in September 1945. Peter, however, was very anxious that no connection should be made, either by the staff and students at the school or by Conrad himself, between Dora's children and her son. She therefore asked Dora to change her children's surname from Russell to either Barry or Pat's surname, Grace (both Russell and Peter rather pointedly insisted on referring to Dora as 'Mrs Grace' after her marriage to Pat, despite the fact that she continued to call herself Dora Russell). Neither Harriet nor Roddy cared one way or the other, but Dora vehemently refused, partly out of a principled objection to doing *anything* that Peter asked her to do and partly because it meant a great deal to her that she and *all* her children – John, Kate, Harriet and Roddy – were a single family. Thus, she insisted, if John and Kate were Russells, then so were Harriet and Roddy.

Meanwhile, for months John had been hearing Griffin Barry's side of the story and his own wish that Harriet and Roddy could bear his name. The issue might seem fairly trivial, but to everybody involved it had great symbolic importance. To John, it was a symbol of the ways in which the older members of the family dug their heels in over silly questions, while the children they were fighting over suffered. Having got to know and like Harriet and Roddy, he was determined that they should not have to endure the kind of divisive bitterness that had scarred his and Kate's childhoods. He therefore took it upon himself to settle the issue by trying to knock some sense into Dora and Peter. On 16 August, just two days after the Japanese surrender, he wrote Peter a very long and strongly worded letter, urging her to adopt a more conciliatory and 'civilised' manner towards Dora and her children. To her, and to Dora (to whom he wrote an equally long letter two days later), he expressed, in a way in which he had never felt able to before, the pain he himself had suffered in the past as a result of familial disputes. 'I have always been too mild with my family,' he told Peter, 'and have never adequately let them know my opinion of them, and of their actions. It is time this ceased, for it is the result of a hang-over from the earlier times when any tactless or unpremeditated remark might have been used by one parent against the others, either legally or psychologically.'

His letter, he said, was 'addressed to the whole family: you, Diddy, Dora, Griffin and Pat; and to their actions over the past 12 years or so'. He was the only person in the family who could speak frankly about its problems, he claimed, 'since for Kate the only solution is to break with it completely, and all the others are either committed to a certain position, or are in the power of those who are'. The truth that it fell to him to point out, John wrote, was that all the older members of the family 'have constantly failed to behave in a civilised manner . . . They have failed as the nations have failed; they have been unable to dispense with war as an instrument of policy.' His hope in writing like this, he told Peter, was that the children of the family, 'whose happiness still to a great extent depends on the civilisation of their parents and the opposing parts of the family', might avoid the kind of bitterness that had had such a devastating effect on him and Kate: 'I have no hope of seeing the elders escape their fate, but I do hope to see the children quit of it as far as possible, and free of the follies of their elders.' What he wanted for himself, he said, was to retain the affection he had for Russell, Peter, Dora, Pat and Griffin and 'the opportunity to esteem them'. Going over the old ground of Russell's divorce from Dora, he insisted that, if anyone had considered Harriet's and Roddy's interests, then Russell would have divorced Dora, rather than the other way round, leaving Dora free to live with Griffin and the children bearing Griffin's name. Harriet and Roddy, he reminded Peter, were entitled to as much consideration as Conrad: 'I feel you must realise this.' Apologising for speaking so bluntly, John ended by saying: 'it would have been weak not to do so, and it has been weighing on me. I hope that the whole family will have the strength in future to behave in a civilised way, and to say things in direct communication, straight out, without intrigue, suspicion and suppression, and the darkness which goes with them.'

His letter to Dora of 18 August was no less blunt. Urging her to accede to the demands of both Peter and Griffin to change her children's name to Barry, John told her: 'their being called Russell, although it may suit with the ideals and spirit in which they were conceived and born, is plainly a legal and moral lie . . . in any case, those ideals and that spirit have not worked, and it is time the members of the family faced the fact'. About Griffin, John spelt out another unpleasant truth: 'I do not think you realise how much effect your break with him and your affection for Paul [Gillard] had on him, or seems to have had on me.' John left his strongest words, however, for Dora's incessant quarrelling with Peter: 'I am sick and tired of trying to gather up the shattered fragments of people and emotions left strewn about in bleeding squalor after your respective tantrums and follies.' A few days later, John followed this letter up with a somewhat shorter one to Pat, urging him, for Harriet's and Roddy's sakes, not to stand in the way of an 'arrangement' between Griffin and Dora, should Griffin come to England. 'I have never been able to say things against my parents in relation to Kate and myself,' John told Pat, 'and this is an opportunity to say what I have felt, on behalf of Harry and Rod, for whom I have a very, very great liking . . . I shall never forgive either you or Dora or Griffin if you do not work a great deal harder for the happiness of Harry and Rod than my father and stepmother and Dora worked for Kate's and mine.' If they did not succeed, John wrote, then Harriet and Roddy would – like John and Kate before them – have 'to deny their own interests and suppress their own feelings in the interest of sparing their parents, what in fact means that they will have to be parents to their parents'.

John had never spoken or written like this before and nobody knew quite how to deal with it. In her reply of 25 August, Dora sounded more hurt than angry. His letter, she told John, 'jolted me as no financial worry, no human or animal querulousness could ever have done. For if you and I are not to understand each other after the time we have spent together here then indeed I can have little further faith in human understanding and must only hope that the age of hurling atom bombs about wholesale will come soon.'

Peter, it seems, did not reply at all. Instead, Russell replied on her behalf with, one gathers, two rather fierce letters, accusing John of ignorance, misunderstanding, pomposity and self-righteousness. The letters have not survived (John, presumably, destroyed them), but John's angry response to them gives some idea of both their tone and their content. In his letters to Dora and Peter, John had to a large extent excused his father from responsibility for the family troubles 'since he more than anyone had something to do for the world which was far more important than any family squabbling'. But now John pulled no punches. 'When I first read your letter,' he told Russell, 'I was very angry indeed. But my feeling soon changed to one of uncontrollable laughter and deep amusement. The thought of you in the role of the stern Victorian father somehow strikes me as quite incredibly ludicrous.' But, he went on, 'that you should have said those things fills me with a deep ease and peace of mind, for they show an attitude of such deep-seated triviality and arrogance that I do not feel that I have in any degree to be concerned with you any more ... You have evidently missed the whole point of my letter, and in fact the whole point of my view of things.'

Russell must have said something in his letters to John about what it meant to be a Russell, to which John retorted:

It is not only the tone of your letter which strikes me as arrogant and trivial, and which makes me see with amusement that you really think it more important to be the descendant of your ancestors than to be a person on your own; it is also that in neither of your letters is there the least consideration or even mention of Harry and Rod or their happiness, which anyone with any kindness at all, whatever their feelings to those children's mother, could not ignore as irrelevant, and which is what this row is really about. Nor are your remarks about Dora, which have a very different tone from hers about you, any less trivial and arrogant. She at least has done me and herself the honour to reply on more or less equal terms.

'I am surprised', John told Russell, 'that after giving me all the education & care that you have, for which I shall always be grateful, you should seriously believe that you can get away with writing a letter on stilts.' He was also surprised 'that you should take an attitude towards this quarrel which strikes me as so small and petty'. His letter to Peter, he insisted, had not been intended (as it had evidently been interpreted by Russell and Peter) as a series of insults, but rather 'as an effort to introduce a new spiritual climate into the family, which it very badly needs'.

Russell, evidently, had seen in John's letter little more than a series of criticisms of the way he and Peter had handled family matters since Russell's divorce from Dora, and he seems to have devoted most of his letters to John to a defence of his actions during those years and a reminder to John of how much he had done for him. To John, this seemed an almost wilful missing of the point, and it was this that made him so angry and led him to accuse Russell of superficiality, triviality and arrogance. Russell, in turn, interpreted John's angry reply as a breaking-off of relations and did not respond to it. It was left to Kate to write to John on Russell's behalf, telling John how hurt his father had been by his last letter and explaining to him that Russell did not see John as trying to heal the family wounds, so much as launching an unprovoked and unjustified attack on him personally. In a letter to Russell of 15 October, therefore, John tried once again to explain that his criticisms of Russell and Peter, like those of Dora and Griffin, were motivated not by hatred and a desire to break off relations, but by precisely the opposite. 'I feel that among people who are at all robust', he told Russell, 'it ought to be, and usually is, possible to have a slanging match without serious injury to the other side':

> I have felt, in relation to you and Peter, that if I expressed my sense of the failure of the family caused by the quarrels between you and Dora (whether these were primarily caused by Dora or not) there would be scenes and explosions. As there have been so many scenes and explosions in the family, and as I do not like to hurt people's feelings, which is no doubt a weakness, I have never expressed the feelings, and have therefore felt cowed and stifled and enervated when in the house at Cambridge or in Pennsylvania. Now, through having berated Griffin Barry for not doing more about his children (for I have a great affection for them, and they deserve a lot) I am at last able to berate everybody; and if it is painful to you, I am sorry, but I assure you it is necessary to me, if I am ever to be able to quarrel with people and remain friendly with them.

But quarrelling with people and remaining friendly with them was just what Russell had never been able to do. John, of course, realised this and saw it as one of the greatest threats to the kind of family warmth he craved. 'What I meant by civilised behaviour in my first letter', he explained to Russell, 'was being able to quarrel . . . but still with some sense of warmth and contact with the object of vituperation. The basic sense of failure I have had in regard to this family is that you and Dora were not able to quarrel in this way, or to retain the warmth which must have existed between you before the great break up.' If John did not force himself to quarrel with those he loved, he told his father, he felt he would 'never be able to have differences with people without being coldly cruel to them'. Acknowledging that he had perhaps been unjust to Russell on several points and that there were many things in the past that he did not understand, John tried to get his father to see that 'at least my motives are comprehensible'. They were, he spelt out: 'the welfare & happiness of the family as a whole, and my own survival and emergence from the morbidity which has oppressed me for some years, and from which I have not had the strength even to attempt to escape until now'.

'Perhaps I *am* mad,' John wrote, 'perhaps some demon did take hold of me to make me write to you as I did, but on careful scrutiny I honestly don't think so.' Airing his grievances – even if they were not justified – was not a sign of madness, but a necessary step towards the retention of sanity. 'I wish I could get across to you the essential fact that one cannot survive with such tenderness as has existed in the family, and with such terrible fear of hurting feelings or being hurt':

> I was grieved to hear from Kate that you had taken my first letter to Nubbles [Peter] as an attack on you for having stood up to Dora. This seems to me a stupid interpretation of it; and you cannot seriously suppose that I was not grateful for being able to stay at Dartington and come to the USA . . . I think it would do the whole family good to come

together, all ten of them: you & Peter, & Conrad, Kate, myself, Harry and Rod, Dora, Griffin and Pat, and then let each one spout his little piece about the injuries the others had done him or her . . . For my part, I do not see how you can continue to exist without making some effort . . . to tell yourself and to tell Dora to stop being so melodramatic and establish some sort of friendliness between you, because you are both great people and it is foolish to behave like squabbling brats.

Russell did not respond to this letter either, and a week later John fired off another long letter, this time to Peter, trying once again to explain that his purpose in raising old quarrels was to get closer to his father, not to break away from him. 'I have, perhaps foolishly, hoped', he told Peter, 'that by cauterising the various wounds it might be possible to heal them.' Hoping to give Peter some insight into his own wounds, John traced the history of his withdrawal from his parents:

> I have been trying to think when it was that my sense of strain began. I had a sense of intimacy with you and with my father until after the time at Hendaye. I think the strain began when I was at Beacon Hill during the last year I was there . . . Kate and I complained of being unhappy at Beacon Hill, and, as I remember, though vaguely, we told you both about it, and both of us wrote letters to Dora about it . . . This was, I believe, a necessary step in our being able to go to Dartington, and as such it had to be done; but I remember feeling deeply uncomfortable about it at the time.

From that point on, he wrote, things got worse, 'and intimacy with my father, and therefore with you, and intimacy with my mother, began to be lost increasingly'. Intimacy with his father was never restored, but 'I recovered it with my mother in London through joint struggles against bombs, flying bombs, rockets and so on.' His first letter to Peter, he told her, 'was a stumbling and incompetent effort to restore intimacy with my father through you . . . I hoped my father would see what the effort was that I was making . . . and it was his failure to see it which provoked my ferocious letter in reply . . . I expected in answer to that letter an equally ferocious but animally warm one from Diddy, or at least a trace of understanding of what it was all about . . . I did not expect silence from him.' He could stop saying things that hurt people in the family, John conceded: 'But I am not willing to be satisfied with a half-relation, in which we could still go on in the old way, and which would in many ways be the easiest and most effortless way out; but which would leave one with the desire to scream.'

One is reminded by John's letters of the letters Dora wrote to Russell at the time of their divorce. One hears the same anguished demand for some kind of emotional response, the same frustration at not being able to break down the barriers Russell erected whenever he felt hurt or in danger of being hurt. During the months that he was writing these agonised cries for understanding and sympathy from Russell and Peter, trying desperately to explain to them his emotional state and its history, John was writing equally long and impassioned letters to his mother. In their criticisms of the way he had been treated in the past, these were equally severe, if not more so. He was especially critical, for example, of Dora's attempt during the divorce to gain sole custody of John and Kate and of her resistance to their going to Dartington. But from Dora he got what he was looking for: a human response. On the immediate question of Harry's and Roddy's surname, Dora backed down, agreeing to call them Barry and also allowing Griffin to pay their school fees, thus providing him with a means of re-entry back into their lives. But, more than this, Dora was prepared to see in John's letters an attempt to break his long silence and to explain how he had felt over the years about being the child of fiercely divided parents. Moreover, she was prepared to admit that there was some point in going over this old ground, some point in John's frenzied attempts to understand himself and to make others understand him too. 'I wish very much that you had told me what was on your mind before you went,' she wrote to him on 9 October, 'for talk elucidates things so much more easily than long disputations across the Atlantic.' She also tried to explain to him the fruitlessness of any attempt to reconcile her with Russell: 'Your father is irreconcilable as far as I am concerned, and I must confess that although against everything I have cherished a certain pride in him all these years, that has now grown dim. Lord Russell is not the Bertie I knew.' Besides, she tried to convince John, his lack of a united family was not a handicap but a liberation: 'What has been the good of trying to set you free of family ties, if you do not accept that freedom?' To this, John responded: 'this is like saying, what is the use of freeing people from hunger if they still want to eat?' 'If we had been brought up in an orphanage,' he added, 'we might be free of family ties.'

Just before she set sail for the States at the end of October, Kate wrote to Russell telling him that she wished to stay out of the quarrel with John, saying that she was far too fond of them both to take sides, 'although I think John has behaved very badly'. Like Russell, and perhaps influenced by him, Kate was inclined to think of John's colossal effort to achieve reconciliation within the family as an expression of youthful rebellion and an assertion of independence: 'If it is honestly and genuinely necessary for John to break away so thoroughly in order to grow up, then I'm afraid I can't really blame him for it.' When she was back at Radcliffe, Russell wrote to her: 'I miss you very much – I should in any case, but the loss of John makes me feel your absence even more than I otherwise would.' 'I have implored John to stop writing about the family tangle,' Russell went on, 'but he goes on and on. I hope he will give it up some day. The root of the matter is that he likes his mother better than me.'

Poor John felt misunderstood by everybody concerned. Having tried to overcome the conflicts within the family, he was universally regarded as having taken one side or the other; Dora accused him of siding with Griffin, Russell of siding with Dora, and Griffin of siding with the Russells against the Barrys. Meanwhile Kate understood him to be, like her, trying to break free from family entanglements altogether. By November, John was forced to admit defeat. 'I guarantee to write no more about family matters after this letter,' he wrote to Russell:

. . . it only remains for me to say that I am sorry to have hurt you to no purpose; I hoped the purpose might be achieved; but it has not been. I have merely been needlessly cruel, and it would have been better to let all the sleeping dogs lie, since this is the outcome. But it is easy to be wise after the event; and I still think it was worth the gamble from my point of view to begin with. I did desire, quite seriously, to restore a contact with you (as I have desired this with my mother) which has been lost earlier. My method has been faulty, and has met with failure. I am only grieved to have spent so much effort and caused so much pain towards an object which, it now appears, was completely unattainable. There is nothing you can do about it, or I; so that's an end of that.

Russell's last word on the subject was given in a letter to Kate: 'I want to be on good terms with John again, but this requires no discussion of the past. I have got over being angry with him, though I cannot be as fond of him as I was.'

John's last word was a document called 'General Statement', in which he summed up the quarrel, taking responsibility upon himself for the failure of his strenuous attempts to heal the family wounds. 'The row is now ended,' the document begins, 'and I want to make certain general aims I had in it clear':

I hoped for great things from it, not only for myself but for everyone. I hoped it might be possible to melt the deep bitterness which there has been in the family; I hoped that out of the cruelty of everyone to everyone, myself included, after last summer, it might be possible to draw forth something warm and human . . .

In particular, I hoped for happiness for myself, for freer relations between all of us, for harmony between Griffin and Dora so that Harry and Rod could have a background more emotionally secure than we did, for freer relations between Diddy and Peter and me, and ultimately for better relations between Diddy and Dora, and between Peter and Dora . . .

It was, I suppose, an arrogant, foolish, ignorant, inconsiderate ideal, and the effort to attain it was bound to be costly and to cause pain . . . It was also, I suppose, a semi-religious aim: I hoped that in spite of all the hurts there might still be enough love in all of us to enable everyone to love everyone else, or at least to be able to bear themselves humanely and humanly and without fear towards each other. I wanted this partly as a cry from my own unhappiness, partly because I felt it to be a good thing in itself, which would, if attained, make all of us happier. And I wanted it partly because I felt that, while we all make pretensions towards reforming the world, we are not really justified either in desiring or in expecting it to be a better place until we have attained sufficient goodness in ourselves to be worthy of it if it were better, and to assist it in becoming so.

. . . there was a terrible arrogance in my taking it upon me, as if I knew, to tell everyone what to do, and in my effort to bend everyone to my view, as if their own were not entitled to respect . . . above all [it has failed] because there are things which people can do to each other which are so injurious as to prevent any future revival of human feeling between them.

'But', John concluded, 'I still think the ideal I was fighting for was a good one.'

It was shortly after this that John wrote the short story mentioned earlier, 'Mr von Sohn's Reputation', in which a diplomat makes peace between two warring countries by taking upon himself the sins of both.

In real life, of course, the two sides remained unreconciled, although for a while an uneasy peace was restored. Conrad went to Dartington in September 1945, where he sometimes chanced upon Harriet and Roderick Barry without suspecting that there was any familial connection between them. On one occasion, Harriet was waiting to see the school nurse when she saw Conrad sitting outside the nurse's room reading a letter from Kate. Harriet had also that day received a letter from Kate. When the two fell into polite conversation, Conrad told her that the letter he was reading had come from his half-sister in the United States. 'That's a coincidence,' remarked Harriet, 'I too have a half-sister in America and I too received a letter from her today.'

Upon Russell and Peter the effect of John's outburst was to place a strain upon their fragile marriage that it could not withstand. In the immediate aftermath of John's attempt to lacerate the family wounds, Peter made a suicide attempt that, for once, Russell took seriously. In his 'Private Memoirs', he says that, though Peter often professed to be attempting suicide, only one such attempt was genuine. This was in Cambridge at the beginning of 1946, when Peter found a bottle of sleeping pills that Russell had neglected to hide and, in front of him, swallowed the entire contents, laughing bitterly and derisively. She then sank into a coma, but the doctor succeeded in saving her life by means of a stomach pump.

To outsiders this was represented as an 'accident' or an 'illness' from which Peter needed to recover. With help from his old friends, Clough and Amabel Williams-Ellis, together with their friend, Rupert Crawshay-Williams, Russell began looking for a house in North Wales to which Peter could retire, while he stayed in Cambridge. Crawshay-Williams found a suitable house in the pretty village of Ffestiniog, not far from Portmeirion, and by March 1946 Peter was able to move in. 'Peter is gone to live in N. Wales,' Russell wrote to Kate on 10 March, 'and we shall only be together during Conrad's holidays.' He added forlornly: 'As the family disintegrates, your affection is an increasing comfort to me.'

With Peter gone, Russell sought comfort elsewhere, flirting with Irina Wragge-Morley, the wife of a Cambridge academic, trying to stir some life back into the flirtation with Gamel Brenan that he had started before the war (she, however, was having none of it) and taking steps to revive his ancient love affair with Colette, who had returned to England from Scandinavia at the end of the war. As soon as Peter was out of the way, Russell wrote to Colette, telling her that he would henceforth be living on his own in Cambridge during term time. Colette took the hint, invited him to London and within a few weeks she believed – and had reason to believe – that their affair would, after a break of nearly thirty years, be resumed. 'Every moment of my visit to you was a joy,' Russell wrote to her on 21 March 1946. 'I wonder how soon, if ever, we shall meet again.' A week later, he told her: 'I am very very happy that things are as they are between us.'

But, with Peter's psychological state more precarious than ever and Russell committed to being with her and Conrad during their son's school holidays, it was difficult for Russell and Colette to see each other as often as they would have liked. Russell's letters to Colette during the summer and the autumn contain repeated apologies for being unable to meet. 'My affairs have been very complicated for some time,' Russell wrote to her in October, '& there are dangerous possibilities that I have to avoid.' Presumably he meant that he would have to be careful not to antagonise Peter, lest he should lose Conrad. 'When we met,' Russell said in the same letter, 'I expected things to turn out differently. I am very very sorry.'

Soon afterwards Colette returned to Sweden. She and Russell continued to exchange affectionate letters and they both conspired with publishers, governments and universities to secure Russell an invitation to Scandinavia so that they could meet again, but Colette's hopes that Russell would leave Peter and return to her were groundless, and not just because he was worried about losing Conrad. In an unpublished statement about the deterioration of his marriage to Peter, probably written in 1949, Russell says that her jealousy of Colette was misplaced, and, as if to prove it, points out, rather bluntly and ungallantly, that Colette was by this time middle-aged, very fat, nearly stone deaf and without any traces of her former beauty. This, it seems, was why things between Russell and Colette turned out differently from what he had expected when he arranged to meet her in the spring of 1946. To Colette herself, however, Russell gave a very different impression. 'I long with all my heart to see you again,' he told her in a letter of 8 December 1946, and for the next three years that sentiment was echoed again and again in his letters to her. 'My dearest Colette,' he wrote to her on 26 April 1947, 'I hate to have the time go by without any opportunity to carry on the re-birth of our mutual affection which began last year in London. I do hope you will come back to England some time'; and a year later, he told her that he was 'very very glad . . . that what has been between us is still so very much alive'. Small wonder, then, that Colette took three years to realise that Russell did not, after all, want a romantic and sexual relationship with her.

Another reason why Russell withdrew from resuming his affair with Colette was that, after Peter had been in North Wales for a few months, some sort of reconciliation, albeit temporary, between her and Russell was effected. She still refused to spend any time in Cambridge, however, so Russell acquired for her a small flat in London, where, during term time, he spent one or two days a week. By 26 April 1947, he was writing to Colette that things were looking up for him on all fronts:

> A year ago I was poor, it seemed that my marriage was coming to grief, John was quarrelling violently with me & I was constantly ill so that I got no work done. Now all these troubles have cleared up. And my work goes well.

His philosophical work at this time centred on the completion of *Human Knowledge: Its Scope and Limits*, which, in July 1947, he reported to be 'nearly finished'. By this time, *History of Western Philosophy* had already gone through several reprints, both in England and the United States, and Russell seems to have entertained hopes that *Human Knowledge*, too, would find a wide readership. In its Preface, Russell declared that it was addressed 'not only or primarily to professional philosophers, but to that much larger public which is interested in philosophical questions without being willing or able to devote more than a limited amount of time to considering them'. Indeed, he went further:

> I think it is unfortunate that during the last hundred and sixty years or so philosophy has come to be regarded almost as technical as mathematics. Logic, it must be admitted, is technical in the same way as mathematics is, but logic, I maintain, is not part of philosophy. Philosophy proper deals with matters of interest to the general educated public, and loses much of its value if only a few professionals can understand what is said.

Coming from the joint author of *Principia Mathematica*, one of the most technical and inaccessible contributions to philosophy ever written, these are remarkable sentiments. Remarkable, too, that the man who in 1914 had claimed that philosophy was 'indistinguishable from logic' should now be insisting that logic was not even a part of philosophy. If Russell really believed what he said in this Preface – and there is no reason to think that he did not – then it would seem to follow that he had come to regard his earlier work, not just as mistaken, but as not belonging to 'philosophy proper' at all. In the Preface to *Human Knowledge*, he writes: 'The Prophet announced that if two texts of the Koran appeared inconsistent, the later text was to be taken as authoritative, and I should wish the reader to apply a similar principle in interpreting what is said in this book.' He meant that what was said in the later parts of the book should take authority over the earlier parts, but he must surely have wished a similar principle to be extended to his lifetime's corpus of work.

If so, he was to be bitterly disappointed. He was particularly hurt by a review of *Human Knowledge* by Norman Malcolm, Wittgenstein's friend and disciple, which ended by saying:

> Anyone who feels grateful to Russell, as I do, for the splendid work he did in philosophy and logic during the first twenty years of this century, is likely to regard the present book with considerable regret.

Malcolm accused Russell of slipshod language and careless thought, and of not even *trying* to think through philosophical questions seriously: 'The style is jaunty and bouncy and reminds me of the patter of a conjurer who wishes to entertain, dazzle and bewilder the customers. I have the impression that the author, after writing philosophy for so many years, is not tired, but callous.'

Malcolm's review was especially harsh, but the view that *Human Knowledge* was inferior to Russell's earlier work was, and still is, almost unanimously held by professional philosophers. It is not just that in trying to reach an audience outside academia Russell had expressed himself in the 'jaunty' style of which Malcolm complains; it is also that both the questions raised in *Human Knowledge* and the solutions to them offered by Russell seemed, in the late 1940s, to be hopelessly out of date. The central problem discussed by the book is how to avoid scepticism about the external world, when, as David Hume had pointed out in the eighteenth century, all our knowledge of it comes from experience and no valid, demonstrative chain of reasoning can be found that establishes the *truth* of our sense impressions – that is, that links how things *appear* with how they *are*. Russell's proposed answer to this problem is to suggest that to logic (demonstrative inference) and our sense impressions there must be added certain principles of 'non-demonstrative inference', which he calls 'postulates of scientific method' or 'premises of science', which, as it were, fill in the gaps between appearance and reality. Russell then lists five such 'postulates', including, for example, 'the postulate of spatio-temporal continuity', which 'allows us to believe that physical objects exist when unperceived'.

There are two basic problems with this approach, pointed out trenchantly by Norman Malcolm and more gently by many others. The first is that, as Russell concedes, scepticism cannot be *refuted* by means of his postulates, because it is always open to the sceptic to demand to know *why* these postulates are to be accepted. And to this Russell has no answer other than to insist that no one, in fact, sincerely doubts them. No one, that is, sincerely doubts the existence of the world. This is no doubt true, but it makes Russell's postulates rather redundant. As Malcolm puts it: 'They [Russell's postulates] are supposed to justify the belief in a world of common objects lying "beyond our percepts"; but what they do is nothing more than to *assert*, in obscure language, this belief.'

The second problem is that Russell, influenced by Hume, begins with the assumption that, if scepticism is to be avoided, the existence of the external world has, somehow, to be inferred from the existence of private mental events, for, as Hume famously put it, 'the only existences, of which we are certain, are perceptions'. In the face of Wittgenstein's famous assault on this assumption in his influential 'Private Language Argument', it was generally dropped by late twentieth-century philosophers and, with it, the 'problem of knowledge' as this was formulated by Hume and, after him, Russell. In other words, the very question to which *Human Knowledge* is addressed is one that most philosophers had, by the middle decades of the twentieth century, come to think misconceived. Small wonder, then, that Russell's answer to it has attracted very little interest.

Russell was hurt, disappointed and bewildered by the cool reception his work received from philosophers in the period after the Second World War. He kept a copy of Malcolm's review of *Human Knowledge*, which he annotated, and a copy of an even more scathing review, this time of *History of Western Philosophy*, written by another of Wittgenstein's friends and disciples, Yorick Smythies. *History of Western Philosophy*, Smythies wrote, 'embodies what seem to me the worst features of Lord Russell's previous more journalistic works, but it is of poorer quality than any of these'. Severely criticising both the style and content of the book, Smythies concluded: 'I fear that Lord Russell's book will teach successfully a popular substitute for thinking and for knowledge, and that it will both appeal to and stimulate slipshod thinking.'

Rupert Crawshay-Williams, the man who helped Russell find a house for Peter in North Wales, reports that when he first got to know Russell he was surprised at his need for reassurance about his philosophical work. Rupert and his wife, Elizabeth, 'simply could not believe that anyone so guaranteedly worthy of his eminence could possibly entertain any self-doubts'. However: 'We soon came to realise how much, at that moment, Bertie needed encouragement. Even so, we were astonished at the sheer extent of his demand.' When Russell discovered that Crawshay-Williams and, to a lesser extent, his wife, had an amateur interest in philosophy, he would bring draft chapters of *Human Knowledge* along with him for discussion whenever he visited the Crawshay-Williams' house. It soon became apparent that Russell was looking for encouragement as much as criticism. 'It was very important', Crawshay-Williams recalls, 'that I should find an opportunity at least two or three times in a session of saying how impressed I was not merely by the conclusion of some argument but in particular by the cogency with which it was presented.' As Crawshay-Williams shared Russell's view that the book provided the definitive solution to an important traditional problem of philosophy, he was well placed to give Russell the reassurances he craved. However, when the book was published and reviews by philosophers began to appear, Crawshay-Williams could see that Russell's anxieties about not being appreciated by the academic community were not morbid fantasies, but well-grounded fears: 'The book was indeed valued at a much lower level than he had hoped.' Like Russell, Crawshay-Williams was inclined to attribute this entirely to vagaries of intellectual fashion, and tried to convince Russell that he ought not to have minded its lukewarm reception as much as he did. After all, 'it *was* a definitive work', and, though 'Russell very naturally found it galling that no one should notice this', Crawshay-Williams felt that he should have taken comfort from the fact that 'it was not thought to be wrong or beneath notice; it was simply out of fashion'. Nevertheless, as Crawshay-Williams concludes: 'The fact remains that Russell had produced a large and comprehensive work on the subject which was nearest to his intellectual heart, and that it produced little response from the philosophers to whom it was addressed.'

Of course, if one takes its Preface seriously, then the book was not primarily addressed to philosophers, but 'to that much larger public which is interested in philosophical questions without being willing or able to devote more than a limited amount of time to considering them'. Here too, however, Russell was to be disappointed by the response. The book was felt by general reviewers to be too difficult for a non-academic public, and it did not, like *History of Western Philosophy*, enjoy a particularly large sale. Russell was irritated by this almost as much as he was by its disregard by professional philosophers, and when he next published a collection of essays he called it *Unpopular Essays*, explaining in a rather peevish Preface:

> A word as to the title. In the Preface to my *Human Knowledge* I said that I was writing not only for professional philosophers, and that 'philosophy proper deals with matters of interest to the general educated public'. Reviewers took me to task, saying they found parts of the book difficult, and implying that my words were such as to mislead purchasers. I do not wish to expose myself again to this charge; I will therefore confess that there are several sentences in the present volume which some unusually stupid children of ten might find a little puzzling. On this ground I do not claim that the essays are popular; and if not popular, then 'unpopular'.

While Russell's philosophical work was falling rather flat, disdained by academics and ignored by the general public, his public statements on politics were attracting a great deal of attention. Russell's long-held view that effective international government was the only means of avoiding wars between advanced nations, and thus of preserving civilisation, seemed to acquire a new urgency and relevance in the post-war period. The growing tension between the Soviet Union and her wartime allies seemed all too likely to lead to another war, and the dropping of two atom bombs on Japan in August 1945 showed the unprecedented horror to which another war might lead; showed, in fact, that one could without hyperbole speak of the possible self-destruction of all mankind. The apocalyptic vision of civilisation destroying itself through the power of its science and technology, which

Russell had expressed in countless articles and books since the 1920s, now looked prophetic. Indeed, it was now shared by anyone who cared to contemplate the probable outcome of a Third World War.

For decades Russell had been arguing that the only realistic way of establishing an international government that would be both effective in preventing war and committed to democracy would be for the United States to use its military power to dominate the rest of the world. Now, when America had sole possession of the most devastating weapon mankind had ever known, the time seemed ripe to press this case more insistently. In a series of speeches and journalistic articles, beginning in September 1945, Russell argued passionately that, in order to preserve peace, America had to act firmly and immediately to impose its will on the rest of the world and, in particular, on the Soviet Union. From the very beginning these articles had a bellicosity that contrasted markedly with the pacifist views he had expressed in the 1930s. In an article called 'What Should Be British Policy Towards Russia?' in September 1945, for example, Russell argued that, since 'before long Russia, no doubt, will have as good (or bad) a bomb as that of the Americans', it was of fundamental importance that Soviet power be contained quickly and asserted that this could not be achieved by a 'policy of appeasement such as we pursued towards Germany until after Munich'. A month later he published an article called 'What America Could Do with the Atom Bomb', in which he made clear how he imagined Soviet power to be contained:

> Whatever measures are to be taken to prevent another world war must be taken during the brief period of American supremacy, and must be enforced by a vigorous use of that supremacy.

'The immense power for good or ill conferred by the atomic bomb', Russell argued, should be used by the Americans 'wisely, and with no undue shrinking from the responsibilities which this power confers'.

In private correspondence, Russell was more blunt about what he had in mind and what he feared. To Gamel Brenan on 1 September, for example, he wrote:

> I think Stalin has inherited Hitler's ambition for world dictatorship. One must expect a war between USA and USSR which will begin with the total destruction of London. I think the war will last 30 years, and leave a world without civilised people, from which everything will have to built afresh – a process taking (say) 500 years.

'There is one thing and one thing only', he added, 'which could save the world, and that is a thing which I should not dream of advocating. It is, that America should make war on Russia during the next two years, and establish a world empire by means of the atomic bomb.'

In a speech to the House of Lords in November, Russell gave a more measured assessment, arguing that the best hope was to get the Russian

Government 'to see that the utilisation of this means of warfare would mean destruction to themselves as well as to everybody else ... I cannot really doubt that if that were put to them in a convincing manner they would see it. It is not a very difficult thing to see.'

Behind Russell's comments on the international situation of this time lay not only a concern to prevent the suicide of humanity, but also a fierce detestation of Stalin's regime. In 'What America Could Do with the Atom Bomb' he even went so far as to say that he preferred 'all the chaos and destruction of a war conducted by means of the atomic bomb to the universal domination of a government having the evil characteristics of the Nazis'. In the same article he proposed an international confederation, led by the United States, which would enforce a monopoly on nuclear weapons. Russia should be invited to join this confederation, and if it refused, then 'the conditions for a justifiable war ... would all be fulfilled. A *casus belli* would not be difficult to find.'

In warning of the danger of Soviet expansionism and in urging the Western Allies to take a firm stance in the face of it, Russell, for almost the first time in his life, found himself at one on matters of international politics with the British Government. Though the Labour regime elected in the summer of 1945 was in many ways the most Socialist government Britain had ever had, it was, as Russell was delighted to discover, 'at least as anti-Russian as Churchill'. In his speech to the Lords in November, therefore, he went out of his way to praise the stance taken against Russia by the Prime Minister, Clement Attlee, and his Foreign Secretary, Ernest Bevin.

Russell's attitude to the Soviet Union was, during the early phases of the Cold War at least, even closer to Winston Churchill's than it was to the Labour Government's. Indeed, after June 1946, when the Soviets rejected the American proposal to establish an international authority to control atomic weapons (the so-called 'Baruch Proposal'), Russell's articles and lectures on the subject made Churchill's famous 'Iron Curtain' speech of 5 March 1946 look mild in comparison. As Russell put it to Gamel Brenan: 'I hate the Soviet Government too much for sanity.' The policy he had earlier stated he would 'never dream of advocating', that of using the atom bomb to establish American hegemony, he now began to advocate openly and insistently. As he put it in a lecture to the Royal Empire Society in 1947:

I think you could get so powerful an alliance that you could turn to Russia and say, 'it is open to you to join this alliance if you will agree to the terms: if you will not join us we shall go to war with you'. I am inclined to think that Russia would acquiesce; if not, provided this is done soon, the world might survive the resulting war and emerge with a single government such as the world needs.

In a private letter to an American academic called Walter Marseille a few months later, Russell said that he did not, after all, think the Russians would acquiesce. On the contrary: 'I do not think the Russians will yield without war.' And in this war, he thought, 'the Russians, even without atomic bombs, will be able to destroy all big towns in England'. Nevertheless, 'Even at such a price, I think war would be worth while', for 'I have no doubt that America would win in the end' and 'Communism must be wiped out and world government must be established.'

Russell's advocacy of a firm, even bellicose, line with Russia was motivated not only by his fear of the Russians acquiring atomic bombs and thus precipitating a calamitous atomic world war, but also by his horror of the thought of Russian domination of Western Europe. 'If Russia overruns Western Europe,' Russell said in his letter to Marseille, 'the destruction will be such as no subsequent re-conquest can undo. Practically the whole educated population will be sent to Labour camps in N.E. Siberia or on the shores of the White Sea, where most will die of hardships and the survivors will be turned into animals (Cf. what happened to Polish intellectuals).' A war fought against Russia, even before she acquired atomic bombs, would, he acknowledged, lead to the loss of millions of lives and the destruction of many great European cities, but this he preferred to being governed by the Soviets. It was, as he himself emphasised, the exact reversal of his view in the 1930s about how Britain should respond to the Nazi threat. As he put it in a letter to Albert Einstein: 'I favoured appeasement before 1939, wrongly, as I now think; I do not want to repeat the same mistake.' At this time many books appeared describing the horrific conditions inside Soviet Russia, and Russell publicly applauded as many of them as he could, writing, for example, a Foreword to Frieda Utley's moving memoir, *Lost Illusions*, and an enthusiastic review of Arthur Koestler's anti-Soviet collection of essays, *The Yogi and the Commissar*. Ever since his visit to Russia in 1920, Russell had had a clear-eyed view of the faults of the Soviet system that was rare among British left-wingers and he was perfectly prepared to believe – as many Western Socialists were not – the eye-witness accounts of Stalin's murderousness that were beginning to appear in the 1940s. As we now know, these accounts, far from being exaggerated, fell a long way short of presenting the true horror of Stalin's regime.

Russell's dread of Stalin's Russia, then, has been shown to be amply justified. Where he was mistaken, it seems now, was in thinking that the Soviet Union had the means and the desire to occupy the whole of Western Europe. Not that his fears on this subject were entirely groundless. With the seemingly inexorable spread of the Soviet sphere of influence that took place in the mid-to-late 1940s – Bulgaria and Albania in 1946, Poland in 1947, Czechoslovakia and Romania in 1948, and Hungary and East Germany in 1949 – Russell was not alone in fearing that Soviet expansionism would eventually spread to Western Europe. But the Second World War had devastated the Soviet Union more than any other country; taking civilian and military figures into account, nearly twenty million Russians died in the war, and many of its cities and towns were utterly destroyed. With its economy and its infrastructure in desperate need of rebuilding, the Soviet Union was in no position to embark on an invasion of Western Europe. Russell was also mistaken, it seems, about the strength of America's atomic arsenal. In 1945, when Russell first began to talk of the USA coercing Russia into an international agreement through the threat of atomic warfare, the USA did not, in fact, have the capability to do any such thing. It had at that time only a tiny handful of atomic bombs, and no aircraft capable of delivering even that handful to Russian cities. And, by the time America had everything in place to carry out the threat urged by Russell – mass production of atomic weapons, long-range, intercontinental bombers (such as the B-36 and B-52) and airforce bases in Britain from which attacks on Russia could be launched – the Soviet Union had its own bomb.

Thus, as Russell himself came to realise, the USA, even if it was prepared to threaten the Soviet Union with an atomic attack, could not do so at the time that he was advising them to. In his letter to Marseille, in fact, Russell mentions that 'conversations with professional strategists' had convinced him that the USA needed two more years to make such a threat credible and that, therefore, 'the most dangerous period for us is the next two years'. This turned out to be prescient, for it was during those two years that Russia developed its own bomb.

It was not the impracticality of Russell's advice for which he was criticised, however, but its belligerence. The editor of the *New Statesman*, Kingsley Martin, for example, wrote indignantly in an editorial in 1950 that, after the war, Russell 'decided that it would be both good morals and good politics to start dropping bombs on Moscow'. Russell reacted to this with equal indignation and insisted that Martin publish a long letter of refutation, in which Russell admitted urging the Americans to *threaten* the Soviet Union with atomic bombs in order to secure their allegiance to the Baruch Proposal, but denied urging them to start bombing Russia. Two years later he wrote a similar letter to *The Nation* insisting: 'The story that I supported a preventative atom war against Russia is a Communist invention', but again admitting that he did urge the threat of such a war. In the same vein, when criticised by the Cambridge University Labour Club in 1950 for his views on Russia, he replied: 'I have never advocated preventative war, as your members would know if they took any trouble to ascertain facts.' If one disregards the letter to Marseille, these denials can be interpreted as being accurate, in the sense that in all his public utterances Russell insisted that Russia would probably capitulate to the threat of atomic bombing and that, therefore, to advise the USA to issue the threat was not the same thing as advising it to go to war. In the letter to Marseille, however, Russell was unequivocally advocating a preventative war.

Embarrassingly for Russell, that letter was published in 1954, soon after his blanket denials of ever having supported a preventative war. Five years later, in a BBC television interview with John Freeman, Russell was asked: 'Is it true or untrue that in recent years you advocated that a preventative war might be made against Communism, against Soviet Russia?' Russell replied: 'It's entirely true, and I don't repent it.' He went on to defend his earlier advocacy of such a war on the grounds that, at a time when only America had the bomb, the threat of war against the Soviet Union, and even, if necessary, the carrying out of that threat would have been justified by preventing 'the existence of two equal powers with these means of destruction, which is what is causing the terrible risk now'.

What this omits is that in the period 1945-8, when Russell publicly advocated a policy of threatening the Soviet Union with atomic weapons on no fewer than twelve occasions, his hatred and fear of Soviet Communism were such that he defended such a policy, not only on the grounds that it would prevent the possibility of an armed conflict involving *two* atomic powers, but also on the grounds that it would prevent Soviet conquest of Western Europe. And he had said this publicly as well as in private correspondence. In a lecture he delivered at Westminster School in November 1948 (subsequently published in *Nineteenth Century and After* in January 1949), for example, Russell declared: 'Either we must have a war against Russia before she has the atom bomb, or we will have to lie down and let them govern us.' In the discussion that followed the lecture he made clear, as he had done in his letter to Walter Marseille, that he considered government by the Soviet Union to be so awful that war would be preferable. Indeed, at Westminster he went further, saying, in reply to a questioner, that if the aggressive Russian policy were persisted with, there were three alternatives: 1. war with Russia before she has atomic bombs, 'ending fairly swiftly and inevitably in a Western victory'; 2. war with Russia after she has the bomb, 'ending again in Western victory, but after frightful carnage, destruction and suffering'; and 3. submission. Of these he considered the third alternative to be the worst, 'so utterly unthinkable that it could be dismissed'. This is not exactly *inconsistent* with the argument he gave in his defence to Freeman (for, after all, he could claim that, even if Russia had acquired the atom bomb before the US declared war on her, they might still not be 'equal powers'), but it is nevertheless significantly different in emphasis.

In a letter to *The Listener* following the broadcast of his interview with Freeman, Russell, referring to his earlier denial that he had ever advocated preventative war, made the extraordinary claim that when he wrote that denial (his letter to *The Nation* in 1953) he had 'completely forgotten that I had ever thought a policy of threat involving possible war desirable' – a claim that he repeated in his *Autobiography*, where he writes:

> The arms race became inevitable unless drastic measures were taken to avoid it. That is why, in late 1948, I suggested that the remedy might be the threat of immediate war by the United States on Russia for the purpose of forcing nuclear disarmament upon her . . . My chief defence of the view I held in 1948 was that I thought Russia very likely to yield to the demands of the West.
>
> . . . at the time I gave this advice, I gave it so casually without any real hope that it would be followed that I soon forgot I had given it. I had mentioned it in a private letter and again in a speech that I did not know was to be the subject of dissection by the press. When, later, the recipient of the letter [Walter Marseille] asked me for permission to publish it, I said, as I usually do, without consideration of the contents, that if he

wished he might publish it. He did so. And to my surprise I learned of
my earlier suggestion. I had, also, entirely forgotten that it occurred in
the above-mentioned speech.

This explanation of his denials is a good deal *less* plausible than the
denials themselves. Indeed, it is demonstrably false at almost every turn.
The view that the Soviet Union should be coerced into acceptance of
international control of atomic weapons by the threat of war was not one
that he expressed only on two occasions 'in late 1948'; it was one he
expressed over and over again for the three years following the Second
World War. And it is not possible to believe that he had forgotten having
held this view in the denials he issued in 1950–3, because in those very
denials he admitted having urged the *threat* of war (what he was denying
was that this amounted to urging a preventative war). Finally, in the letter to
Marseille of which he speaks, his 'chief defence' of his view is certainly not
that Russia was likely to yield to the threat; on the contrary, on that
occasion, he explicitly expressed the view that Russia was *unlikely* to yield.
His chief defence of a belligerent attitude towards Russia, in that letter and
on many other occasions, was that a war with Russia was justified if it was
necessary to prevent the spread of Stalinist rule to Western Europe.

Clearly, after 1948, Russell became extremely embarrassed by his war-like
pronouncements of the previous three years. He continued until Stalin's
death in 1953 to make bellicose remarks about the Soviet Union, insisting,
for example, that war with the Soviet Union – even nuclear war – would be
preferable to coming under Soviet rule, but he abandoned his advice that
diplomatic negotiations with the Soviet Union over the issue of arms control
should include the threat of atomic bombardment and now sought to
distance himself, in one way or another, from that advice. Why? The
answer, I think, lies in the Press reaction to his Westminster speech of
November 1948, which threatened to make him a political embarrassment to
the Labour Government, which, up until then, had used him as a kind of
more or less official spokesman. Although this speech was of a piece with
things that he had said many times before, it was much more widely
reported than the others and provoked a good deal of hostile criticism. The
day after the speech, the *Reynolds News* carried an editorial accusing Russell
of peddling a 'message of death and destruction' and of asking his audience
to resign themselves to 'an endless orgy of killing, to the destruction of
cities, to the poisoning of the fruitful earth by atomic radiation'. Lord
Russell, the editorial went on, 'advances the oldest and most blood-drenched
fallacy in History: "the war to end wars"'.

In fact, this last accusation was perfectly true, though less of Russell's
Westminster speech than of an earlier one, a talk he had given to the New
Commonwealth Society in 1947, in which he had said: 'If there is war, the
main issue should be the creation of an international government; and if this
is its outcome, the next great war may be the last.' Nevertheless, after other
newspapers had picked up on his Westminster speech and simplified its
message under the slogan 'attack Russia', Russell felt compelled to act.

Significantly, the first thing he did was to apologise to the Prime Minister, Clement Attlee, for any embarrassment these Press reports had caused him. Then he wrote to the newspapers denying that he had urged war on Russia, but admitting to having urged 'that the democracies should be *prepared* to use force if necessary, and that their readiness to do so should be made perfectly clear to Russia'. After that, Russell dropped the idea that the threat of war was a sensible means of pursuing arms-control negotiations with the Soviet Union and confined himself to a resolute insistence that any sign of Soviet military aggression should be met with armed force, a line more in keeping with British foreign policy.

The furore over Russell's Westminster speech came at the height of his respectability among the British Establishment. In the previous month he had travelled to both Norway and Berlin to act as an unofficial spokesman for the British Government and in the month afterwards he was due to give the first in the prestigious series of Reith Lectures sponsored by the BBC, an honour of which he was deeply conscious and very proud. The climax of this period of respectability came the following year when he was awarded the Order of Merit, the highest honour that the British Government can bestow upon an individual. Despite later making light of them, it is clear that these official honours meant a great deal to Russell; clear too that the last thing he would have wanted in 1948 is to lose the esteem in which he was held by the Labour Government.

In his *Autobiography*, Russell slightly overplays the extent to which, on his visits to Norway and Berlin, he was acting as a representative of the British Government. He says, for example: 'the Government sent me to Norway in the hope of inducing Norwegians to join an alliance against Russia', making it sound almost as though he were there on official Foreign Office business, as part of the negotiations that led up to the creation of NATO. In fact, his visit was sponsored by the British Council and its purpose was to influence public opinion in Norway, rather than to take part directly in political negotiations. His invitation came from the British Ambassador to Norway, Sir Laurence Collier, who happened to be an uncle of Rupert Crawshay-Williams. What Collier hoped for from Russell, as he explained to Crawshay-Williams, was a series of public lectures that would allow Norwegians to see and hear for themselves 'a vigorous and intelligent exponent of Western European ideals who was determinedly opposed to Communism and, indeed, to any form of totalitarianism for reasons transcending either Conservative or Socialist politics'. In the event, Russell gave three lectures that were, Collier reported, 'very much on the lines which I had been hoping for'.

Russell's first lecture was to have been at Trondheim on 2 October 1948, but this had to be cancelled owing to a much-publicised accident. The sea-plane carrying Russell from Oslo to Trondheim blew over in a stormy gale just as it touched the water on arrival and sank, killing all nineteen passengers in the non-smoking compartment. Russell, together with the other passengers in the smoking compartment, was able to swim to the safety of a rescue boat and was then rowed to the shore some miles from

Trondheim. When he arrived at his hotel, Russell found himself besieged by reporters, one of whom asked him what he was thinking of when he was in the water. 'I thought the water was cold,' replied Russell, resisting the invitation to claim that his thoughts had been on the nature of mysticism and logic. 'I was glad you were impressed by the profundity of my reflections while in the water,' he wrote to Crawshay-Williams. 'My time in Norway was very agreeable; I loved both the people and the country. Now I am off to Berlin, which will be less agreeable but more interesting.'

Russell's visit to Berlin, which, remarkably, he undertook just a few weeks after he had nearly lost his life off the coast of Norway, *was* sponsored by the Foreign Office. Berlin had by that time been under blockade by the Soviet Union for five months, during which the Allies had kept supply lines to the city open through the use of military aircraft. Russell's task during the airlift was to give morale-boosting lectures to the troops carrying it out and to the people of Berlin, helping to persuade them, as he put it in his *Autobiography*, 'that it was worth while to resist Russian attempts to get the Allies out of Berlin'. Specially for the occasion he was made a member of the armed forces and issued with a military passport, 'the first and only time', he wrote, 'that I have been able to parade as a military man'.

Russell's visits to Norway and Berlin were widely reported in the newspapers, establishing Russell in the public eye as a leading supporter of, and to some extent a spokesman for, British foreign policy during the Cold War. To Russell, this publicity was entirely welcome. Crawshay-Williams tells a revealing story about a time when he organised a dinner party in order to introduce Russell to Patrick Blackett, the Nobel Prize-winning physicist:

> Bertie arrived a little before the others; and we took the opportunity of showing him a long article about him in some American paper . . . 'What a *lot* about me!' said Bertie, licking his lips. And he settled himself down to read. About five minutes later the Blacketts and the Huntingdons arrived simultaneously. They took off their coats and then we led them through into the kitchen. As we all stood in the kitchen doorway, with me prepared to do the introductions, Bertie rather reluctantly paused in the middle of his reading – but without lifting his eyes from the paper – and said: 'I'm very sorry; I cannot pay attention to anybody. I am *reading about myself.*'

In this context, it must have been alarming to Russell to wake up on 21 November 1948, the day after his Westminster speech and a month after his visit to Berlin, to find his speech reported under headlines such as 'Russell Urges West to Fight Russia Now', 'Earl Russell Calls for Atom War', and so on.

Perhaps this partly accounts for the studied moderation, even blandness, of Russell's BBC Reith Lectures on 'Authority and the Individual', the first of which, 'Social Cohesion and Human Nature', was broadcast on 26 December 1948. The theme of these lectures was essentially the same as *Principles of Social Reconstruction* and *Freedom and Organization*, though expressed with a good deal less passion and fewer provocative asides: society, if it is to survive, must tame the aggressive instincts that lead to war, but it must not, in doing so, repress those bold and adventurous individuals whose creativity is the origin of all original thinking and so of all progress. One might have expected Russell at this time to illustrate this well-worn theme with some inflamed rhetoric about the tyranny of the Soviet Union, but on this occasion he erred on the side of caution, with the result that the essential banality of his central thesis was laid uncomfortably bare. Many readers of *Authority and the Individual* have found themselves agreeing with everything Russell says, without feeling that they have learnt anything from it at all. As Alan Ryan has put it in *Bertrand Russell: A Political Life*: 'Anyone who failed to feel after the Second World War that individual initiative had to be satisfied in a peaceful fashion and social order preserved in a non-tyrannical fashion would have been very eccentric indeed.'

After the Reith Lectures were finished (the last one was broadcast on 30 January 1949), Russell hoped to take a break from both philosophy and politics. His plan was to retire to North Wales for two months in order to finish his autobiography, and then to travel to the Continent at the end of March, where he had engagements in Marseilles and Rome, before taking up an invitation from a friend he had met in America called Daphne Phelps to spend a holiday at her home in Taormina on the island of Sicily. As it turned out, however, the complications in his personal life prevented him from getting on with his autobiography, and the discord that had been building up in his marriage to Peter for nearly ten years finally erupted in a dramatic showdown in Sicily that brought about the end of the marriage and a permanent (and permanently acrimonious) separation.

In his 'Private Memoirs', Russell says that his separation from Peter was brought about partly by a dispute about money and partly by her mistakenly believing that he intended to resume relations with Colette. The dispute about money, he says, arose when, following the success of *History of Western Philosophy*, he told Peter that he proposed to make a new will leaving part of his money to John and Kate, having previously written a will leaving everything to Peter. At this, he claims, Peter burst out crying, saying that he obviously no longer loved her. In another statement, written nearer to the events, he expands upon this, saying that the trouble started when he suggested that the royalties on *Authority and the Individual* should go to John, to which Peter replied that she had done half the work on the book and that she was not willing to see John receive the money, forcing upon Russell the alternative proposal to change his will in John's favour, a proposal Peter met with floods of tears. After this, Russell says, came the more serious matter of his relationship with Colette.

Peter's suspicions regarding Colette are all too understandable. In May 1948, Russell had, at last, secured an invitation to Sweden that would allow him to see Colette again after her departure from England two years previously. The invitation came from the publishers of the Swedish edition of *History of Western Philosophy* and involved giving four public lectures, two in Stockholm and two in Uppsala, after which he was free to spend a few days with Colette in Mariefred, thirty miles west of Stockholm. Russell may, as he said later, have thought that Colette was by this time too old, too fat and too unattractive to consider as a lover, but he certainly gave her the impression that he wanted to resume their affair. He suggested to Colette that she return to Britain and, in a letter written on 29 June 1948, told her that Peter had expressed the hope that Colette would settle in North Wales, rather than (as Colette had originally intended) Scotland.

When Colette arrived in Ffestiniog the following September, Peter was in London, so, when Conrad went to spend a night away with a friend, Colette and Russell were left alone. 'It was utter perfection,' Colette wrote to her friend, Phyllis Urch. 'As we walked up the hill in darkness . . . he said, very emphatically, "We should never have parted." '

A few months later, however, when Russell returned to Wales to work on his autobiography after finishing the Reith Lectures, Colette discovered that things were a good deal more complicated than she had thought. Russell confessed to her that he had begun an affair with a woman called Ragnhild ('Nalle') Kielland, the wife, so Colette learnt, of a somewhat 'strict' husband. Nalle Kielland was a Norwegian woman, whom Russell had known since the 1930s when she had sent her children to Beacon Hill School. During his visit to Norway in October 1948 he had met her again and began an affair with her that seems to have weakened his interest in Colette.

In a long letter to Phyllis Urch written on 17 March 1949, Colette tried to summarise the increasingly tangled situation, as it had been explained to her by Russell. Peter was at this time again in London and Russell was about to set off for the Continent with Conrad. When Colette remarked that Peter must be disappointed not to be going with them, Russell replied: 'Not at all. She'll get far more pleasure from acting the sick, martyred wife, than from seeing France and Rome and Taormina.' Colette had hoped to provide Russell with a 'peaceful, working holiday' during their time together in Ffestiniog, but she told Urch: 'It has been nothing but discussions of painful matters.' Peter, having found out about Russell's affair with Nalle Kielland, had written him a six-page letter 'with everything she has against him; and saying, in very crude language indeed, how *noble* she'd been to marry him!' According to Colette, Peter phoned Russell three times a day, and so did Nalle, leaving Russell and Colette little time to do anything but discuss the wretched state of Russell's marriage: 'he tells me that he does everything he can to prevent her from knowing how bored he is with the shreds his marriage is reduced to'. Two things especially worried Russell: the first was that Peter might sell or let the cottage in Ffestiniog, which, for tax reasons, had been made over to her; the second was that she might leave Russell, taking Conrad with her. 'You may wonder where I come into all this,' Colette wrote. 'Well, I don't intend any plans dependent on Peter.' She had given up the idea of buying a place close to Russell in North Wales and now intended to return to Sweden: 'an unsatisfactory end to a curious episode'.

After what had obviously been a difficult few days, Colette drove Russell 'through bleak rain-sodden country wrapped in mist and fog' to the railway station at Bala, where he boarded the train for London. Meanwhile, she returned to the Ffestiniog cottage. 'I will creep into your big bed tonight,' she wrote to Russell, 'to have the ghost of that kind of closeness, as well as the "coldness of interstellar spaces".' Before he left for Marseilles, Russell spent a few nights in London, which gave Colette just enough time to forward to him a letter that arrived at Ffestiniog from Nalle. The following day, a parcel – also bearing Nalle's name and address as sender – arrived. Immediately, Colette telegraphed Russell asking him what to do with it. With just a few hours to go before his flight left for France, Russell telegraphed back that she was to open the parcel (which contained the typescript of his autobiography), put the typescript in his desk and destroy anything else the parcel might contain.

Russell's confidence that Peter would prefer to stay in London than be with him and Conrad in Sicily turned out to be misplaced. After he had been in Taormina just a few days, Peter arrived unexpectedly and was handed a letter addressed to Russell. The letter was from Colette and, from it, Peter learnt that she had been mistaken to believe that Russell's relationship with Colette was one of friendship only, for Colette still wrote to Russell as a lover. The response was as predictable as it was violent. 'There has been an immense upheaval,' Russell wrote to Colette on 2 April 1949, 'involving at best an amicable separation . . . I am afraid Peter has written you disagreeable letters. It is all disagreeable & I feel I have been incompetent. Please forgive me.' Two weeks later, he wrote again, saying that Peter 'suddenly left this place & went home, saying she couldn't stand me another minute, & intended never to see me again. I *think* this will be permanent.'

The event that triggered Peter's final storming off seems rather harmless and trivial, though one has to bear in mind the months – even years – of deceit, rancour and discord that had preceded it. Russell's hostess, Daphne Phelps, had invited him to accompany her and a few friends, including Julian Trevelyan and Mary Fedden, on a moonlight picnic and fishing expedition led by a Sicilian friend of hers called Rocco. Conrad ('an insistent child of 11 who could be tiresome,' Phelps later remembered) was not invited and Peter said she felt too ill to go. Rocco, knowing that they would catch nothing, brought along a large fish that he grilled on a wood fire and plenty of local wine. Under a beautiful full moon they ate and drank happily until midnight, by which time everybody (with the exception of Mary Fedden, who had to drive back along perilous mountain roads) felt pleasantly inebriated. 'This is most disgraceful,' Russell, clearly enjoying himself, was heard to remark. 'I'm as drunk as a lord. But it doesn't matter because I *am* a lord!' When they arrived back at Phelps's home, Russell needed some help up the garden terraces and the plan was to escort him safely to his room, where he could sleep it off without Peter being any the wiser. Unfortunately, however, Peter was still up. As Phelps remembers it:

The door was flung open and there was Peter furiously pale in a scarlet dressing gown which, I had time to notice, clashed with her hair. As Bertie and I stood there blinking in the sudden light, she screamed hysterically, 'Daphne, how dare you go out without Conrad, you know how he adores fishing (I didn't). Daphne, you ought to be ashamed of yourself.' Bertie lit his pipe in silence, escaped to the lavatory and locked himself in.

Yelling at Julian Trevelyan that it was 'a man's job to put my senile, drunken husband to bed', Peter rushed upstairs and slammed the door. The next morning she ordered a taxi to take her to the airport, where she took the next flight back home.

Conrad took his mother's side, and for the remaining few days of their holiday, while Russell told his hosts how nice it was to be among people who 'are not nasty to me all the time', Conrad told them repeatedly what 'disgusting wine-bibbers' they all were. When they arrived back in England, Conrad rejoined Peter, who was adamant in her determination never to see Russell again and told him that she would never speak to him again unless Russell promised never again to see Colette.

The situation was now a dreadful mess. When Peter arrived back from Sicily, Colette was still in the cottage at Ffestiniog, so she went to the flat in London, where she opened yet another letter to Russell from Colette, containing yet more unflattering references to herself and confirming her in her conviction that Colette and Russell had been conspiring for months to live together. 'I have been such a fool,' Peter wrote to Elizabeth Crawshay-Williams. 'It was my idea that she should settle near us. She was looking for a place in Scotland, but I thought it would be nice for him to have her near; as he gets old he has so few old friends left. And it was my idea that she should stay in our cottage while she got her own ready.' She had no idea, she went on, that Russell and Colette were still lovers until she saw Colette's letter to him in Sicily, for 'Bertie has told me all along that he loved me and me only . . . he said he was not too keen on having her so near, as he found her rather silly and boring and gushing and her deafness was very tiring.'

However, Russell, far from conspiring to live with Colette, was actually trying to get rid of her. When he wrote to her from Sicily telling her about the 'upheaval' caused by Peter's discovery of her letter, he told her that 'for the present it would be unwise for me to see you' and asked her to leave the cottage at the beginning of May; and when he returned from Sicily, he moved temporarily into a cottage on the Portmeirion estate until Colette was safely out of the Ffestiniog cottage and back in Sweden. In the early months of the summer, Colette wrote affectionate letters to Russell, but was then told that she must not write any more in case Conrad discovered them. By the autumn, Colette's friend, Phyllis Urch, considered her close to a nervous breakdown. Russell hardly ever wrote to her and in October even forgot her birthday. During a visit to London at the end of October, Colette wrote to Russell suggesting a meeting and describing herself as being on the point of collapse. The reply was hardly comforting: Russell wrote saying that he thought they had better not meet for a while, but that he would be in London at the beginning of December and thought they could meet then. This meeting however, he ended curtly, must not cause scandal. On 3 January 1950, Colette wrote Russell a long letter intended as a final farewell. 'It would not be a great exaggeration', she told him, 'to say that the best of my life has gone into caring for you and has twice brought me to the verge of a breakdown: after China and now':

> The price you have paid in order to comply with your needs has been heavy. I expect you would still say that if hell is the price of heaven, it is worth paying the price. I would say the same. It is our misfortune that your heavens have been my hells, and – in the long run – your own.

'A world in which the word like has replaced the word love does not seem to me a world worth having,' Colette wrote. 'In the distant past I was able to disperse your spectres because I loved you, passionately and tenderly, even when involved elsewhere. You cannot now disperse my spectres because your love is entirely absent.'

When Russell returned from Sicily to find Peter firm in her resolve to leave him, he wrote to Colette that he felt 'happy like a man let out of prison'. But he was not about to step into a different kind of prison. The unflattering things he had said to Peter about Colette were true: he found her cloying and her deafness, particularly, got on his nerves, a fact he made little effort to disguise, even from Colette. ('Only you, of all the people I know, make me feel my deafness,' Colette wrote in her farewell letter. 'If others did, I should know you had good reason to make much of it. But they never do. Nor did it worry us at all – in Sweden. But the molehill grew to be a mountain – at Ffestiniog.') For the moment, his affair with Nalle Kielland provided Russell with ample compensation for the loss of Colette, while the loss of Peter needed no compensation. What hurt him much more than either of these was the loss of Conrad, who, after the summer of 1949, lived solely with his mother and did not see Russell again for nearly twenty years.

After Colette had vacated the Ffestiniog cottage in May, Peter collected her belongings and moved – with Conrad – to Morwenstow in north Cornwall. Conrad had been unhappy at Dartington, where he had been bullied, and, since the autumn of 1947, had been educated at home. At the time of Russell's separation from Peter, a decision had been reached to send Conrad to Eton, where, it was felt (primarily, one gathers, by Peter), that the intellectually precocious son of Earl and Countess Russell would feel more at home. (Russell's acquiescence to this plan is no doubt a sign both of his acceptance by and of the British Establishment and of his disenchantment with the radical views on education he had held in the 1920s.) Conrad could not start at Eton until the autumn of 1950, so in the meantime lived with his mother in Cornwall. Initially the plan had been for him to spend his holidays – Easter, summer and Christmas – with Russell in Ffestiniog, but this was abandoned after Conrad insisted that he wanted nothing more to do with his father.

Russell could, of course, have gone to the courts to enforce his legal right to see his son, but, after what had happened to his other two children, he refused to do so. As he put it in a letter to Kate: 'I remember how bad divided loyalty was for you & John. So for the moment I do nothing.' It was an act of genuine self-denial and one that cost Russell dearly. As Conrad grew up to become a successful and confident scholar, both at school and at university, and then established himself as one of the foremost British historians of his generation, Russell was forced to watch his achievements from a distance, hearing everything at second hand. Meanwhile, Peter's hatred for Russell remained unabated. So much so that she told Conrad that if he ever had anything to do with his father, she would never speak to him again. True to her word, when, in 1968 (at a time when Conrad was in his thirties and Russell well into his nineties), Conrad did eventually reunite with Russell, Peter broke off contact with her son and has never seen him or spoken to him since.

For nearly a year after the separation Russell lived alone at Ffestiniog, in need not so much of a lover as of a family. 'I grow morbid,' he wrote to Kate, '& reflect what a failure I have made of my life, as a husband & as a father. I have tried to think the fault was other people's but the repetition seems to show that it can't be.' Kate had by this time established a life for herself in America independent from her parents, her step-parents and, to a large extent, her past. After a few years at Radcliffe, she had decided that what she really wanted to be was not a successful academic, or a career woman of any sort, but a wife and mother in a stable, conventional marriage. Seeking 'diligently for a man who would help me realise my vision', she found Charles Tait, a graduate student in languages at Harvard with the personality and the ability to be the reliable husband, father and family provider she was looking for. After consulting her father and getting the response she was seeking ('My advice is: *Marry at once*'), Kate married Charles in the spring of 1948 and brought him to England the following summer to receive the approval – duly given – of Russell, Peter and Dora. By the time Russell and Peter separated, Kate and Charles were back in Cambridge, Massachusetts, planning their family and their future together.

John's life was, as ever, more unsettled. Like Kate, he had tried to establish an independent life for himself in America, but by 1949 he was back in England, his affairs spinning dangerously out of control. This gave Russell the opportunity to re-enter his son's life, in order to give John the support he evidently needed and himself the chance both to undo some of the damage that had been done to his relationship with John after the quarrel of 1945 and, to some extent, to compensate for the loss of Conrad by reacquiring some kind of family.

Since the quarrel in 1945, much had happened to John – too much for him to cope with. Towards the end of that year, he had gone to Cambridge, Massachusetts, to attend a party given by Kate (then newly arrived at Radcliffe) and some of her friends. There he had met an old friend of his from Harvard called Maurice Friedman, who before the war had been a radical Socialist, but was now deep into mysticism and psychoanalysis.

Friedman had for some months been a member of a therapeutic commune of the type that would become popular in the 1960s. Based in Chapel Hill, North Carolina, it was called the 'Creative House' and its members practised what they called 'psychodrama', a kind of therapy that aimed to release and overcome suppressed emotions through the dramatic enactment of symbolic suicides and murders (the murder of one's parents, for example). By November 1945, the time of the party in Cambridge, Friedman had fallen in love with another member of the group, a nineteen-year-old girl called Susan Lindsay, the daughter of the American poet, Vachel Lindsay. Two months earlier, Susan had given birth to a baby daughter, Anne, the father of whom was an estranged previous boyfriend. Entranced by both Friedman and Susan, and convinced that 'psychodrama' might be the answer to his own problems, John became a member of the Chapel Hill group. Friedman and Susan were married in December 1945, but, within a very short while, Susan and John fell in love with each other and, after only two months of marriage, Susan left Friedman for John. By March 1946, John was announcing that he planned to marry Susan as soon as she could be divorced from Friedman.

Leaving aside John's homosexuality (which he evidently believed he could overcome if only he could find the right woman), a further complication to this already bizarre situation was that back in England he was considered to be more or less engaged to Jackie Gordon, his old friend from Dartington. In November 1945, around the time of the party at Radcliffe, John had written to Dora saying that he hoped to arrange for Jackie to come over to America so that they could get married. Then, on 10 March 1946, an understandably confused Dora wrote to John:

> Jackie rang me up two days ago and said that she had had a letter from you. She came to see me about this and I understand from her that you want to marry a girl called Sue who is the wife of a friend of yours, and although quite young, has a baby. Jackie also said that you 'believed in God'.
> ... John, what's the matter with thee, lad? And why don't you write home about it?

The one thing Dora found to applaud in John's otherwise perplexing behaviour was his apparent determination to embrace heterosexuality. 'For a very long time', she wrote in a later letter, 'I had feared you might have this phase of trouble over homosexuality ... You have seen, very rightly, that this can become a horrible prison if one cannot get through the phase.'

So concerned was she about John's headlong rush into an unsuitable marriage that Dora phoned Russell to discuss it with him. This was the first that Russell had heard of it, and he immediately wrote to Kate asking for any information she might have. This prompted Kate to reveal to Russell, as she also revealed to Dora, the story of John's homosexual adventures during the war. 'Your account of John's imbroglio is a masterpiece of clarity,' Russell replied. 'I am not at all surprised about the homosexuality; I refused to submit his letters to the censor for fear they should reveal something of the sort (when we were returning from America).' Kate's view of Susan was that she was 'poised on a knife edge and might become either a saint or a lunatic with a little nudge in one direction or another'. Of the proposed marriage, she told Dora: 'It may go terribly wrong & be a dreadful thing, or it may be the making of both John & Susan. Nobody can tell yet. But let me assure you that, whatever comes of it, it is much better than what was going on before. John was on the edge of utter decay & this has pulled him out if it.' As for John's believing in God, Kate told Dora:

I don't see [why] he shouldn't. I don't myself, nor am I likely to, but many people do & it doesn't make them less good. John had far more strength in him than I knew, but not quite enough for the monstrous load he had to carry. If he can find the extra in belief in God, well so he may. Try to see him as a suffering individual rather than a thinking spirit. Ideas are in the end a small part of most lives, though John has pretended to have them all of his. There was little among the store of ideals to help him in this battle – they have been mostly impersonal & rather negative & not at all competent to deal with emotional chaos.

For his part, Russell felt somewhat reassured about John's forthcoming marriage (if not about his religious leanings) by Kate's level-headed assessment of the situation. 'I agree with you that it *may* do him a lot of good,' he wrote to Kate, 'but the dangers are very great. I have written him a letter of general sympathy and goodwill. I certainly will not join with Dora in any attempt at interference.' Russell's letter – the first after their quarrel of the previous year – came as a great relief to John, who replied with details of his plans: he intended to marry Susan in the summer, when he hoped to be released from the navy, then travel to England in the autumn before settling down in America. In a subsequent letter, Russell recommended to John the advice he had given in *The Conquest of Happiness* (presumably one of the store of ideals that Kate later dismissed as being 'mostly impersonal & rather negative & not at all competent to deal with emotional chaos') that personal happiness should be achieved, not through dwelling on one's own feelings, but through the adoption of a 'wide horizon'. Could John not stop thinking about himself and his family and start thinking instead about the atom-bomb and the Soviet threat? To this John replied:

I wish it were possible to do this, I am constantly trying to do it, and am increasingly able to do it as the eruption and ferment subside. In time, I may even be less cock-a-hoop about getting over my difficulties, and less pleased with all the rabbits which have been pulled out of the hat, less proud of my past ailments. But I do not think this is in any sense separate from the Russian danger or from the atom-bomb. In fact, for most of the people involved, the ferment and confusion started on a more hectic course about the time the atom-bomb went off. I know it was about then I wrote the first disturbing letter; as if the atom-bomb had made us all less sure of our foundations and forced further enquiry. I know the others had their progress much intensified about that time. And both the Russian danger and the atom-bomb are not primarily technical political or institutional problems, but human problems.

On the subject of his homosexuality, John told Russell what he wanted to hear: that it was Dora's fault:

> If I could have told you about homosexuality, it probably would have stopped. There was nothing you could have done but what you did: be friendly and kind in spite of it all. I hope I have not hurt your feelings again, though you are probably quite used to it by now. A good deal of my trouble with homosexuality was due, I think, to Dora's dominance and overpoweringness, and the kind of vortex there is round her. But I must write to her about that.

One thing John and Susan had in common was a history of family trauma. Susan's father, Vachel Lindsay, had achieved considerable fame in the 1920s through his lecture tours and theatrical public recitals of his poetry. Particularly popular at the time was 'The Congo', a long, strongly rhythmic evocation of primitive magic and ritual, which Susan knew by heart and would often recite in the dramatic and slightly deranged manner of her father. In December 1931, when Susan was just five years old, Vachel, who had suffered for years from severe mental illness, committed suicide by drinking Lysol. It was Susan who discovered the body. Like John, Susan had lived all her life under the shadow of her father's fame and remained emotionally crippled by her family history; just as John never quite recovered from the rancorous divorce of his parents, so Susan remained forever haunted by her father's madness and suicide. For these reasons, the bond between them was deep but precarious. In a letter to Dora of 1 April 1946, John did his best to explain:

> Susan is a very remarkable person indeed. She has had to struggle against a kind of schizophrenia in herself, and has successfully come out of the struggle ... Like me, she has had to go through a long series of promiscuous and unreal sexual relationships in order to reach emotional stability and happiness, which each of us has found in the other.

'There is, of course,' he added, 'no guarantee that she will not leave me at the end of 6 months, as she has sometimes done with other men she has lived with at times – But there is equally no guarantee that I won't suddenly leave her for a sailor.'

John's plan of returning to England with Susan in the autumn of 1946 turned out to be unduly optimistic. Susan's marriage to Friedman was dissolved in July, leaving her free to marry John the following month, but then John decided that he wanted to formally adopt Susan's baby girl, Anne, and they had to wait until November for the paperwork to go through. By this time Susan was seven months pregnant, and John had left the navy and got a job working for the United Nations Food and Agricultural Organisation, based in Washington. On 16 January 1947, Susan gave birth to another baby girl, whom she and John named Sarah (because, John explained to Russell, 'her sister is called Anne and Queen Anne was such friends with Sarah, Duchess of Marlborough'), and the following summer John was eventually able to return to England, accompanied now by a twenty-one-year-old wife and two baby daughters.

On 5 August 1947, Russell wrote to Kate to tell her that 'John & his family arrived safely & I have seen a great deal of him & Susan, all the more owing to Peter & Conrad being in Wales.' His first impressions were favourable: 'I find, rather to my surprise, that I like her very much . . . John seems happier & saner than at any time since he was 10.' He would be sorry, he told Kate, if John could not find a job in England and had to return to the United States, 'as all their friends there seem to be lunatics'. After this, however, 'because of the virtual hatred between John & Peter', as Russell put it in a later letter to Kate, he saw little of John for the next two years: 'I have had no difficulty in forgiving John for his outbursts during his brainstorm, but Peter is implacable.' For the first two years of their married life in England, therefore, it fell to Dora to provide John and Susan with the practical support they so clearly needed ('Susan doesn't think as ill of Dora as I hoped,' Russell remarked ruefully to Kate).

From the start it was clear to everyone who met them that John and Susan could hardly look after themselves, let alone care for two small children. To begin with, they stayed with Dora at her home in Kilburn, but they left after a month, because Susan could not get on with Dora and told her that she and John needed to live in a place of their own 'out of family rows'. By this time, Griffin Barry had returned to England, and, for a while, to Dora's great exasperation, he, John, Susan and the little girls shared a large and expensive house in St John's Wood, North London. John, Dora wrote to Kate in September 1947, 'seems like one sleep walking all the time':

> It is the part that G[riffin] B[arry] plays in the affair that makes it most worrying to me . . . I fear now that GB has attached himself to both of them in a way that will be very bad for them and for everybody concerned. Susan believes GB to be a brilliant writer who has never really got a chance, instead of an idle Irishman who had thrown away more chances than most of us get in two lifetimes, and poor John with a brilliant father and those two boosting him up naturally wants to achieve beyond his powers. And what powers he had are being dissipated by the perpetual confusion in which they all three live.

'I wish to goodness I could talk to your father about John,' Dora told Kate. 'But any move there would only be misunderstood.' Like Dora, Kate was alarmed at the situation. 'John is an ass,' she wrote to her mother. 'Griffin is his real evil genius & could easily ruin him, I think. I wish the man could be kept away.'

Encouraged by Griffin and Susan, John started to entertain dreams of earning his living as a writer and devoted much of his time to writing short stories, though to please his mother and to enable him and Susan to stay on at the luxurious house they had chosen to live in, he applied for several temporary Civil Service jobs and eventually obtained a position at the Treasury. Even so, he had to recognise that the house in St John's Wood was beyond his means, and in 1948 he and his family moved into a more affordable small flat in Cambrian Road, Richmond. In July 1948, Susan gave birth to yet another daughter, whom she and John named Lucy, after Russell's lifelong friend Lucy Donnelly, who died that summer.

At Cambrian Road, things started to fall apart badly. John and Susan were simply not able to deal with the strains and responsibilities of bringing up three small children in a tiny London flat. They employed a very competent nanny called Miss Griffiths to take care of the children during the day, but when she was not on hand to deal with them, the children were neglected. Neighbours complained – in person, by letter and through solicitors – about the distressing screaming of children that could be heard coming from 19 Cambrian Road every night. As one neighbour, quoted in a solicitor's letter, put it: 'It sounds as though a child has been shut up somewhere and keeps calling to be let out.' Basic house care was neglected and additional complaints were received about blocked drains, old beds and furniture blocking up the passage and rubbish strewn all over the garden. The complaints fell on deaf ears. John, when he returned home from his Civil Service job, would sit alone in a room, either writing or playing his accordion very loudly and very badly (the cause, inevitably, of yet more complaints from the neighbours), while Susan resumed the 'long series of promiscuous and unreal sexual relationships' that John had hoped she would give up after marriage.

A few years earlier, at the age of twenty-five, John had come into possession of about £4,000, the capital of the Trust Fund that Russell had set up for him and a sum which, had it been used wisely, was large enough to have provided John and Susan with a secure financial foundation. The money, however, was quickly being squandered, first on the house in St John's Wood and then on very expensive psychoanalysis for both John and Susan. John justified this expense to Dora on the grounds that he was 'investing in himself', but, to family members, it seemed that the only effect of the psychoanalysis was to encourage John and Susan to become increasingly preoccupied with themselves at the expense of those around them. Kate was probably echoing the views of the whole family when she wrote to Dora: 'What is the *matter* with John & Susie? . . . They seem to want some kind of perfect harmony of souls & before they get it they will have destroyed their children's chances of ever being reasonably happy.'

By the time of Russell's separation from Peter in the spring of 1949, John had given up his job at the Treasury in order to concentrate on his writing and it was clear that, unless someone stepped in to help them soon, John and Susan, having used up his capital on psychoanalysis, would find themselves destitute. In the summer of that year John, Susan and the children visited

Russell in Ffestiniog and a plan was hatched that seemed to be to everybody's mutual advantage, one that would solve the problems both of Russell's loneliness and of John and Susan's financial incompetence. Russell would buy a large, four-storey house in Richmond and, while he occupied the two top storeys, John and Susan would occupy, rent-free, the ground floor and the basement. They would have the benefit of Russell's servants and their children would be provided for by Russell's more than adequate income, thus relieving John and Susan of the obligation to earn money and providing them with the opportunity to concentrate on their writing, John on his short stories and Susan on her poetry. For his part, Russell would once more have a family around him, one that supported him emotionally, while he supported it financially.

A suitable house in which to execute this plan, 41 Queen's Road, was quickly found, but it took months for the necessary repairs and conversion work to be completed. Meanwhile, Russell waited impatiently in Ffestiniog, while John and Susan supervised arrangements in Richmond. At the beginning of January 1950, Russell, having spent a rather forlorn Christmas alone in Wales, was writing to Kate telling her how much he was looking forward to moving to Richmond in a week's time. Two months later he wrote again: 'Some optimists maintain that the Richmond house will be habitable before I die.' It was not until May that he was able to relinquish the Ffestiniog cottage and move into the house at Richmond. Meanwhile, the letters he received from John and Susan were as concerned to report on the progress of their psychoanalysis as on the progress of the building work. On 11 March, John wrote to say that he and Susan would be able to move into the upper part of the house in two weeks' time, while they supervised the building work still to be done to the lower part and that, since his capital was almost used up and 'the day of our bankruptcy is marching upon us', they would soon no longer be able to afford analysis. When that happened, he claimed, he would get a job and Susan would devote herself to looking after the house and children. The analysis had, in any case, John believed, accomplished its task; it 'has already brought us a long way nearer the point where suicide, insanity or divorce are unlikely, so the future does not feel as melancholy as, on financial grounds, it may look'.

In fact, the future was a good deal worse than anyone could have predicted. John never did succeed in earning a living, Susan resolutely refused to devote herself to her house and her children, and all three of the evils that John had sought to avoid through analysis – suicide, insanity and divorce – were, eventually, inflicted upon the unfortunate occupants of 41 Queen's Road, Richmond. Of the six members of the Russell family who moved into the house in 1950 – John, Susan, Anne, Sarah, Lucy and Russell himself – only Russell emerged to pursue a tolerably happy life.

10

41 QUEEN'S ROAD

Number 41 Queen's Road, Richmond was, and is, a large, but otherwise fairly unremarkable suburban house. However, moving there in the spring of 1950 was for Russell an act charged with emotional significance. Queen's Road adjoins Richmond Park and is but a short walk away from Pembroke Lodge, the house in the park in which Russell was brought up by his grandmother, Countess Russell, after the death of his father in 1876. Russell's association with Pembroke Lodge ended with his marriage to Alys in 1894 and he rarely, if ever, returned to it after that. However, as the first few chapters of his *Autobiography* show, the house, and especially its garden, left a deep and lasting impression upon him. Pembroke Lodge had never actually belonged to the Russell family; it belonged, rather, to the Crown. Queen Victoria had given it to Russell's grandfather, Lord John Russell, when he was Prime Minister in the 1840s, originally for his lifetime, and then, after his death, for that of his widow. After Countess Russell died in 1898, Russell's Aunt Agatha continued to live there by royal favour for a few years until she moved, in 1902, to live with her brother in Sussex. After that, the house reverted to the Crown. In 1950 it was used, as it still is today, by the Royal Parks Commission; half of it as flats for park-keepers and the other half as a tea shop.

On 12 May 1950, almost immediately after moving into Queen's Road, Russell took a walk through the park to revisit his childhood home and was shocked and depressed by what he saw. Returning there, he wrote that evening, 'produced a mood of almost unbearable melancholy'. What had happened to the house was bad enough, but still more distressing was to see what had been done to his beloved garden, his place of refuge as a child and the scene of almost all his happy childhood memories:

> Half the garden is lovely: a mass of azaleas and bluebells and narcissus and blossoming may trees. This half they have carefully fenced in with barbed wire (I crawled through it), for fear the public should enjoy it. It was incredibly like Blake's Garden of Love, except that the 'priests' were bureaucrats.

In his *Autobiography*, he bitterly accused the Government of ordering the ruin of the house and of deliberately destroying its historic interest as a result of discovering 'what they did not know until they were told, that it had been the home of famous people'.

Seeing his past desecrated and destroyed by people who were indifferent to him and his family revived in Russell that feeling to which he was often prone when he became depressed, the feeling that he was a spectre that did not quite belong in the corporeal world. Returning to Richmond, he later said, 'produced a slightly ghostly feeling, and I sometimes found it difficult to believe that I still existed in the flesh'. Over fifty years earlier, after being given the devastating news that there was inherited madness in his family, Russell had written of the 'perpetual gloom which hangs like a fate over P[embroke] L[odge]' and had described the house as 'like a family vault haunted by the ghosts of maniacs'. 'I am haunted by the fear of the family ghost,' he had written then, 'which seems to seize on me with clammy hands to avenge my desertion of its tradition of gloom'. Now, with all traces of his famous and illustrious family removed from Pembroke Lodge, he began to feel more than ever a part of that tradition; not outside the vault looking in, but inside the vault looking out on to a world in which he and his family appeared as no more than spectral remnants of a past so distant that no one could recall it.

Russell's sense of isolation and alienation from the modern world was probably heightened, rather than alleviated, by the fact that, shortly before he returned to Richmond, he renewed contact with an almost forgotten figure from his distant past, one of the few people left alive who could still remember the Pembroke Lodge of his grandmother's day. His first wife, Alys, with whom he had fallen in love at first sight back in 1889, when she had seemed to him the embodiment of beauty and freedom of spirit, was now a frail and rather lonely woman of eighty-two. Since her separation from Russell in 1911, her life had been devoted to looking after her brother, Logan Pearsall Smith, a talented writer but, especially as he got older, a querulous and difficult man. When Logan died in 1946, Alys left the house they had shared in St Leonard's Terrace, Chelsea, and moved just round the corner to Wellington Square, to live with her great-niece, Julia Strachey, to whom she was known as 'Aunty Loo'. With Logan out of the way, Alys blossomed somewhat and became more assertive and self-possessed, even to the extent of giving BBC radio talks on her early life.

It was a sign of Alys's growing confidence in old age that it was she who initiated the renewed contact with Russell. She had never stopped loving Russell and, throughout the previous three decades, had kept a close eye on the Press for reports of his activities. Among her effects when she died was a large collection of newspaper clippings that she had built up over the years recording the major events, scandals and achievements of his life: reports, for example, of his marriage to Dora, his decision not to use his title (upon which Alys had scrawled: 'except Bertie will bother when he is in the House of Lords'), his divorce from Dora, his marriage to Peter, the furore over his New York appointment, and his award in 1949 of the Order of Merit. This last was, as Alys well realised, an honour of which Russell was extremely proud, and on 9 June 1949, soon after the award was announced, Alys, knowing that Peter had just left him, felt emboldened to write Russell a letter of congratulations. 'Dearest Bertie,' she wrote, 'I feel I must break the silence of all these years by sending thee a line of congratulation on thy OM. No one can rejoice in it more heartily than I do, just as no one was more sorry for the prison sentence and thy difficulties in America. Now I hope thee will have a peaceful old age, just as I am doing at 81, after a stormy time with Logan.'

To Alys's unfettered and excited delight, Russell responded warmly to this letter, suggesting that they should meet 'at least once before we die'. Three months later, Alys wrote again. She was, she told Russell, in the process of writing her memoirs and had written a brief paragraph about their marriage, a copy of which she enclosed, promising to change it if he did not like what she had written. The paragraph read:

> Bertie was an ideal companion & he taught me more than I can ever repay. But I was never clever enough for him, & perhaps he was too sophisticated for me. I was ideally happy for several years, almost deliriously happy, until a change of feeling made our mutual life very difficult. A final separation led to a divorce, when he married again. But that was accomplished without bitterness, or quarrels, or recriminations, & later with great rejoicing on my part when he was awarded the OM. But my life was completely changed, & I was never able to meet him again for fear of the renewal of my awful misery, & heartsick longing for the past. I only caught glimpses of him at lectures or concerts occasionally, & thro' the uncurtained windows of his Chelsea house, where I used to watch him sometimes reading to his children. Unfortunately, I was neither wise enough nor courageous enough to prevent this one disaster from shattering my capacity for happiness & my zest for life.

Alys sent this in September 1949 to Russell's address in Ffestiniog, but for some reason it never reached him and another three months went by before it was returned to her marked 'not known'. In January 1950, Alys tried again, and this time received another warm reply from Russell saying: 'What thee says about our marriage is very generous and fills me with shame.' Again he suggested meeting, and so, on 6 February 1950, Russell finally came to Wellington Square for lunch. 'Meeting again after 39 years was an extraordinary experience,' Alys wrote in her diary. She and Russell had talked about 'everything except his wives & our feelings':

> I was awfully excited & quite ill for a week afterwards, but am now settled down & very happy in the memory of his presence, & in the hope of seeing him again, when he has settled at Richmond. For the first time since June 1902 I want to live & am really tho' not completely happy.

Above this last remark, Alys added: 'until I know what he feels about the past!'

After receiving from Russell a thank-you letter for this lunch, confirming that he intended to see her again when he moved to Richmond, Alys wrote in her diary that she was 'so happy that I am crying with joy. I feel I shall burst with happiness & can hardly bear it'. A few days later, she described feeling 'depressed & weepy' but cheered up by the suggestion of a friend that 'Bertie shd. divorce Peter & make "an honest Countess of me"'.

Whether Russell realised what hopes he was arousing in Alys is difficult to say, but in any case, a week or so after he moved into Queen's Road, he agreed to fall in with Alys's plan to celebrate his seventy-eighth birthday at Wellington Square, together with John and Susan and six of Alys's nieces and nephews. Alys was unimpressed with Susan ('not attractive') and disappointed that John bore so little resemblance to Russell, but she pronounced John nevertheless 'a charming and simple young man'. A few weeks later, Alys's diary gushes: 'O joy, O joy, Bertie has just told me that he would like to dine here tomorrow night. How can I wait till then?' When the day came, she prepared for it with uncharacteristic attention to her appearance, wearing a pink ribbon in her hair. That evening at dinner Russell talked about his separation from Peter and his heartbreak at losing Conrad, and generally struck Alys as 'more like his old self, less formal & polished & more jolly & sympathetic'. Russell evidently stayed the night and Alys described the following morning as 'the happiest . . . of my life for 50 years'.

Her health now declining sharply, Alys had just seven months left to live, a great part of which, her diary reveals, was spent dreaming that Russell would return to her. For most of this time, Russell was out of the country, first in Australia and then in the United States, and, while he was away, Alys counted the days until his return and waited anxiously for letters from him:

Bertie has been gone one day & will not be back for another 69.
(19 June 1950)

Only 63 days now till Bertie's return.
(25 June 1950)

4 weeks gone, only 42 days more . . . I long to know how he is & what he is doing & feeling; my darling Bertie, I love thee so.
(16 July 1950)

5 weeks gone & only 35 days to wait . . . alas! no letter from Bertie, a real disappointment.
(23 July 1950)

When a letter from Russell finally arrived, Alys read it and reread it 100 times, 'tho' I know it by heart of course'. She evidently hoped that Russell would come to see her immediately after his arrival back from Australia, but in this she was disappointed. A few days after he got back he phoned her to say that he could not see her for a few weeks because of his backlog of correspondence; then, when he finally came, he struck her as 'sad & dispirited & remote'. 'How I wish I cld bring a little happiness into his life!' Alys wrote in her diary that night. 'But my love can be sad with his, & I can suffer with him tho' he will not accept my comfort, or perhaps cannot.'

When Russell failed to answer her next letter, Alys – breaking a rule she had made to herself – phoned him, but was told that he was preparing his lectures for America and would not have time to see her before he left. Another two months of anguished separation followed, broken only by a single letter from Russell in November. 'It makes me ecstatically happy to hear from him,' Alys wrote. 'I am a silly old fool.' By this time she was seriously ill with bronchitis, coughing blood and often too tired to do anything but lie in bed thinking of Russell:

> I so often feel too poorly nowadays to read or write that I am thankful to find so much occupation & happiness in just thinking about Bertie – his great usefulness & successes & good health, & also about seeing him again & of the many questions I want to ask him, & things I want to say to him. I can remember happily our engagement & the 8 years of our happy married life ... I am a lucky woman, & if I have suffered it has been worth it.
> (3 December 1950)

The following day, Alys saw Russell for the last time before she died, when he came to tea and, she reported, 'took a little more interest in me & my doings, & asked what was the matter with my health for the first time'. For the next few weeks, Russell found one excuse after another for not coming again and, when Alys broke her rule for a second time and phoned him, he told her in a 'dry & distant' voice that he was desperately busy, but that he would come to tea the following week. The last two entries in Alys's diary record her disappointment that this promise was broken and show her desperate determination to find some sign, however small, that she still meant something to him:

> Still Bertie doesn't telephone nor come, & I feel dreadfully sad. From 3 to 4 every day after my nap I have a fit of the blues, & cry & long so much to see him that I can hardly bear it.
> (1 January 1951)

> Sent B a comic picture of reminder of our honeymoon, & rec'd a note of acknowledgement with apologies (of overwork) for not coming & ending up 'Much love, Thine own B'. It is the first sign of affection he has shown me, & it makes me perfectly happy. It looks as if he really cares for me a little.
> (12 January 1951)

Nine days later she died. As she lay dying, the phone rang and she tried valiantly to answer it herself. 'After all,' she was reported as saying, 'it might be Bertie.'

In their different ways, Pembroke Lodge and Alys were, for Russell, reminders of a bygone age, an age in which everything had seemed more hopeful, more stable, happier. The contrast between the world in which he had grown up and that in which his grandchildren were now growing up was made sharper and more painful by sharing a house with John and Susan, whose confusions, anxieties and inadequacies seemed to Russell somehow characteristic of their generation. On the same day that he revisited Pembroke Lodge and returned to Queen's Road in a 'mood of almost unbearable melancholy', Russell wrote the following reflections on the effect upon him of living with his son and his daughter-in-law:

> I suffer also from entering into the lives of John and Susan. They were born after 1914, and are therefore incapable of happiness. Their three children are lovely: I love them and they like me. But the parents live their separate lives, in separate prisons of nightmare and despair. Not on the surface; on the surface they are happy. But beneath the surface John lives in suspicious solitude, unable to believe that any one can be trusted, and Susan is driven beyond endurance by sharp stabs of sudden agony from contemplation of this dreadful world. She finds relief in poetry, but he has no relief. I see that their marriage will break up, and that neither will ever find happiness or peace. At moments I can shut out this terrifying intuitive knowledge, but I love them both too much to keep on thinking about them on a level of mundane common sense. If I had not the horrible Cassandra gift of foreseeing tragedy, I could be happy here, on a surface level. But as it is, I suffer. And what is wrong with them is wrong with all the young throughout the world. My heart aches with compassion for the lost generation – lost by the folly and greed of the generation to which I belong. It is a heavy burden, but one must rise above it. Perhaps, by suffering to the limit, some word of comfort may be revealed.

Far from exhibiting the 'terrifying intuitive knowledge', and 'Cassandra gift of foreseeing tragedy' of which Russell here boasts, his comments on John and Susan seem for the most part to be curiously banal and distant statements of the obvious. By 1950, it took no great powers of perception to see that John and Susan were deeply troubled individuals, especially if – like Russell – you had for years been receiving anguished accounts from John of his miseries and torments and had been given detailed descriptions by both John and Susan of their psychoanalysis and the problems it was designed to solve. Nor did it take very much forsight to see that their marriage was unlikely to last; it was readily apparent to everybody who met them. What is not immediately obvious is why Russell attributes their problems to the fact that John and Susan were born after 1914. After all that John had written to him in 1945, could he really not see more direct and personal causes of his son's suffering?

One supposes that he could, and that, though the ostensible subjects of these reflections are John and Susan, their real subjects are Russell himself, the hopes he had entertained for his own generation before the First World War and his disappointment at seeing those hopes crushed by everything that had happened since. Russell had hoped that his generation could spread civilisation to all corners of the globe; instead it had visited death and destruction upon the world on a previously unimagined scale. And, of course, Russell's hopes for John's generation had been even more ambitious; John, he had hoped, would be a model of nothing less than a new, better kind of person, a person free from fear, inhibition and irrationality. Living with John and seeing the 'suspicious solitude' into which he had withdrawn could not but have been a daily reminder of how utterly and cruelly those hopes and ambitions had been thwarted. Perhaps there was even some comfort to be derived from the thought that what was wrong with John was wrong with 'all the young throughout the world'.

Seeing at close quarters the 'separate prisons of nightmare and despair' in which John and Susan lived, and viewing them as typical of their generation, no doubt helped to inspire Russell to devote his next book, and some of the lectures he prepared for his visit to Australia, to the theme of hope; the hopes, rather than fears, that the modern world presented to the young generation. As he puts it in his *Autobiography*:

I suspected that I had too much emphasised, hitherto, the darker possibilities threatening mankind and that it was time to write a book in which the happier issues of current disputes were brought into relief. I called this book *New Hopes for a Changing World* and deliberately, wherever there were two possibilities, I emphasised that it *might* be the happier one which would be realised.

He then goes on to reproduce the final paragraph of the book, a paragraph in which he urges mankind to dispense with the 'old myths that allow us to go on living with fear and hate – above all, hate of ourselves, miserable sinners'. Man, he claims, 'needs for his salvation only one thing: to open his heart to joy, and leave fear to gibber through the glimmering darkness of a forgotten past':

He must lift up his eyes and say: 'No, I am not a miserable sinner; I am a being who, by a long and arduous road, has discovered how to make intelligence master natural obstacles, how to live in freedom and joy, at peace with myself and therefore with all mankind.' This will happen if men choose joy rather than sorrow. If not, eternal death will bury man in deserved oblivion.

By implication, the cause of John's suffering, of the 'suspicious solitude' in which he lived and of the 'nightmare and despair' that he shared with

Susan, was held to be, not the 'new morality' of Russell and Dora, but precisely the opposite: the sense of sin engendered by the old religious morality against which Russell and Dora had campaigned. In other words, the problem with John was not that he was modern, but that he was not modern enough; not, after all, that he was born after 1914, but that he had not fully embraced the opportunities to shake off the old morality that had been made available to his generation. In the following passage from *New Hopes for a Changing World*, echoing as it does Russell's description of what he saw in John and Susan 'beneath the surface', it is hard to resist the thought that he has John explicitly in mind:

There are many men and women who imagine themselves emancipated from the shackles of ancient codes but who, in fact, are emancipated only in the upper layers of their minds. Below these layers lies the sense of guilt crouching like a wild beast waiting for moments of weakness or inattention, and growing venomous angers which rise to the surface in strange distorted forms. Such people have the worst of both worlds. The feeling of guilt makes real happiness impossible for them, but the conscious rejection of old codes of behaviour makes them act perpetually in ways that feed the maw of the ancient beast beneath.

And how does one slay the beast beneath? 'It is only necessary to open the doors of our hearts and minds to let the imprisoned demons escape and the beauty of the world take possession.' In place of the old, destructive morality, Russell says, he would put 'encouragement and opportunity for all the impulses that are creative and expansive'. The 'new hopes' he had to offer in 1950 were, then, substantially the same as the old hopes he had offered in 1915 in *Principles of Social Reconstruction* and in countless works since.

Shortly before he moved into Queen's Road, Russell wrote to Kate:

I find John's company very agreeable in spite of the fact that I don't respect his character. He would be utterly sunk if I did not help him financially. I have arranged that what he gets now shall be deducted from his share when I die. There is one respect in which I think both he & Susan are justified to a certain degree: they both have very considerable literary talent & I don't like to see talent wasted.

A few days after settling in, he wrote again telling Kate: 'It is very nice to be living here – we have a lot of good talk & I love the children.'

Though Russell was during this period relatively wealthy (thanks mainly to the sales of *History of Western Philosophy*), the costs of keeping John, Susan and their children in the style to which Russell himself had become accustomed were considerable. As well as living in the house rent-free, John and Susan had the advantage of Russell's housekeeper to keep their part of the house in reasonable order and a nanny – paid for by Russell – to look after their children, who when they reached school age were sent, at

Russell's expense, to a private boarding school in Sussex. (The school, Kingsmuir, was run by a protégée of A. S. Neill called Lucy Francis and was modelled on Neill's own school, Summerhill.) In return for providing all these benefits, Russell received only 'good talk' and the promise of enabling John and Susan to fulfil their literary ambitions.

In a legal document prepared a few years later, Russell complained: 'Throughout this period John made little or no effort to earn a living':

> I however did not feel able to be too severe with John as when I went to a psychoanalyst whom he was consulting I was told that if he were compelled to work he would probably commit suicide.

Russell nevertheless made some efforts to find John a job. On 21 May 1950, he wrote to his publisher Unwin to ask whether there was any chance of John 'being able to get any sort of job in some publishing house'. John, Russell wrote, 'has charm & manners & produces a good impression at interviews or business conversations'. Unwin's reply, however, was not encouraging: 'Openings do occasionally arise in the University Presses for someone with your son's qualifications, but not often.' In any case, Unwin told Russell, jobs in publishing were badly paid and the work was boring and routine. Altogether, he advised, John would be better off working in a bank.

On 18 June, just a month after moving into Queen's Road, Russell set off for a lecture tour of Australia, organised by the Australian Institute of International Affairs (AIIA). He took with him the talks that he subsequently developed into *New Hopes for a Changing World*: a set of three on 'Obstacles to World Government' and a set of two on 'Living in the Atomic Age'. In various forms, these supplied the material for public lectures in Sydney, Melbourne, Brisbane, Canberra, Adelaide and Perth. In most of these cities Russell also gave private addresses to branches of the AIIA, though, for the most part, the same material was used for these as for his public lectures. He also gave a large number of interviews to the Australian Press and recorded a few radio broadcasts for the Australian Broadcasting Corporation, including one the day after he arrived in Australia on 'The Asian Threat', in which he gave advice on how to keep Australia a white man's country.

Though there was some concern among members of the AIIA about the repetitions in Russell's talks, they were generally a huge success, all of them well attended and most of them enthusiastically received by Press and public alike. The biggest problem facing the organisers was that of protecting Russell from the scores of people who wanted to meet him and the dozens of invitations he received to attend dinners, address meetings, give interviews and write articles. A personal assistant called R. P. Greenish was given the task of acting as a buffer between Russell and the Australian public, and he saw to it that Russell was given at least two hours a day of solitude and also arranged various sightseeing trips for Russell, including excursions to Alice

Springs, the Barrier Reef, the countryside of southern Queensland and the Western Australian outback.

Less successful than his public lectures were the university seminars that Russell gave at Melbourne and Sydney. Though he insisted on speaking on the social impact of science, the philosophers in the audience insisted on asking him about his earlier philosophical views, irritating him by neglecting his later philosophical work, by asking him to defend philosophical views he no longer held and by implicitly refusing to accept that he had interesting things to say on social and political subjects. There was frustration on both sides and Russell was no doubt pleased to leave university audiences behind in favour of the less critical audiences attracted to his public performances. On 21 August 1950 he flew back to London. In a talk recorded for the ABC, he left Australians with the remark: 'I leave your shores with more hope for mankind than I had before I came among you.'

In fact, despite the calculated optimism of his public talks, Russell returned to England with a good deal *less* hope for mankind than he had felt before he left for Australia, though this was not because of anything he saw or heard in Australia but because, while he was there, the Korean War broke out, bringing with it, so Russell believed, the immediate prospect of global nuclear war. Though it is rarely mentioned in the secondary literature, the Korean War marked a crucial turning point in Russell's political thinking, the point around which he swung from the extreme and belligerent anti-Sovietism of the late 1940s to the equally extreme and belligerent anti-Americanism of the 1960s.

What changed Russell's thinking was the event that he had predicted, but which came sooner than he, or most Western observers, could have guessed: the development by the Soviet Union of its own atomic weapons. The Soviet Union exploded its first atomic bomb on 29 August 1949, thus changing the entire nature of the Cold War. As Russell was quick to announce, the arguments he had advanced in the immediate post-war period for American world hegemony no longer carried any weight, dependent as they had been upon an American monopoly over atomic weapons. Now that the Soviet Union had its own atomic force, Russell believed, it could not be bullied into accepting international government and any attempt to coerce it would greatly increase the risk of unleashing world atomic war upon the European nations. He therefore looked on in alarm as the USA reacted to the Soviet bomb by massively escalating its atomic capability and by pressing ahead as quickly as possible with the development of the hydrogen bomb. Adding to his anxieties was the anti-Communist hysteria that was gripping the United States in the wake of Mao Tse-tung's proclamation in October 1949 of China as a Communist republic. In February 1950, 'McCarthyism' was born when the Republican senator, Joseph McCarthy, announced that he had the names of fifty-seven 'card-carrying communists' in the US State Department. A 'creed war' of the kind that Russell had been prophesying since the 1920s seemed to be building up, only this time carrying with it the very real danger of the cataclysm that haunted Russell's political thinking: the total destruction of civilisation.

It was in this context that Russell reacted with horror to the news on 25 June 1950, just a few days after his arrival in Australia, that the Soviet-backed Communist republic in North Korea had launched a surprise attack on South Korea, in an effort to overthrow its US-backed right-wing nationalist regime. Within days, the South Korean capital, Seoul, had fallen and the United Nations Security Council (in the absence of the Soviet Union, which was at that time boycotting the UN) authorised troops under the unified command of the US general, Douglas MacArthur, to repel the North Koreans. With North Korea's neighbour, China, almost certain to come to its aid, and the USA seemingly bent on a mission to protect the world by force from the Communist threat, it did not take much imagination to foresee how the Korean conflict could become the catalyst for the global creed war that had long been the stuff of Russell's worst nightmares.

Russell's first thought was to return home to England to see to the safety of John, Susan and the children. He thought that, if a world war were to come, they had better get away from London. 'He is not sleeping well,' George Caiger, the General Secretary of the AIIA, reported to another member of the committee on 30 June. 'The international situation is worrying him.' Though, somewhat against his impulse, he stayed in Australia, Russell did everything he could to see to his family's safety from the other side of the world. On 2 July, he wrote to Crawshay-Williams asking him to look out for a suitable house in North Wales in which to house John's family. 'I fear I am asking a lot of you,' he said, 'but as soon as my work is over & I get to bed, I am haunted by nightmares of atomic death, & here, where I know no-one, they drive me nearly mad.'

On 7 July, John, responding to Russell's anxieties, wrote to him advising him not to cut his Australian visit short because of the danger of war. 'The risk of general war is certainly greater than at any time since the Berlin blockade,' John conceded. 'But everyone here is taking it calmly.' John's analysis of the situation was, in some ways, more balanced and better judged than Russell's own. 'So far', he wrote, '[global] war does not look imminent':

I think it is only a matter of days before the Americans are driven out of Korea.[15] Of course it will not stop there: the US will want to recover S. Korea even if driven out . . .

There are, I think, certain hopes in the situation . . . it will enable the US to perceive the consequences of Republican policy, and to learn that Communism in the East is a force far more powerful than they dream . . . Given time there will be a revulsion of feeling against bolstering up the rotten S. Korean government even in the US, for Truman's acts have not been legal, and the absence of China and Russia from the security council makes a mockery of the moral case for this war . . . If the US goes on

---

[15] The American army was at this time suffering heavy losses and, by the end of August, the North Koreans had captured the whole of South Korea, except the area around the port of Pusan. It was only after the US counter-offensive, begun on 15 September, that the tide turned.

trying to impose free enterprise Americanism in far eastern countries where in practice it means opium-peddling, black-market, corruption, stinking administration and peasant starvation because there is no land reform, the west will lose the battle all through the Far East because we shall have no friends but quislings and no way to win but with our own lives and money and material, and nothing good to offer the countries if we do win, e.g., in Indo-China & Malaya as well as Korea.

For himself, John did not particularly dread the threat of war. It might, he told Russell, 'suit me personally very well: I should probably be called up and sent, with Peter Swann, whom I like, to Tokyo, which I should enjoy.' With regard to the safety of his family, John was altogether less urgent than Russell had been, possibly because he was writing at a time when his family looked in danger of disintegrating. Susan and he had separated, he told Russell. Susan had gone off to Harlech, presumably to be with her latest lover, while John was staying at a friend's house in North London. Meanwhile, the children were at Queen's Road, being cared for by their nanny. In response to Russell's concerns, John had written to Susan, suggesting that she look for a furnished cottage in Wales to rent for the summer, but 'I have yet to hear whether she can, or whether she will be able to do it so quickly.' In the meantime, he and Susan would remain separated until they succeeded in patching up their differences. On the outbreak of the Korean War, John wrote: 'My first feelings were to rally round and forget friction, but I think this is wrong. Just because Stalin and Truman have gone a little further down the road to crazy violence is no reason why we should any of us give up our right to private spite. Our differences remain until they are cleared up, if they can be':

I am having a rest from everything – no Susan, no children, no job: I don't even think if I can avoid it: nothing but analysis . . . I am lonely, but I feel curiously tranquil. Perhaps this is deceptive: there is nearly always more turmoil below. But at least at the moment it is curiously delightful: I am not at the beck and call of nagging passions and inconvenient hungers, and my analysis is making progress . . . I am hoping, of course, that Susan and my differences will have gone before you come back; but I think this is optimistic. I shall see her again in early August, when my analysis stops for six weeks.

On the whole, it could not have been a very comforting letter to receive. Russell was no more convinced by John's arguments than he was by those put to him by the Australian Foreign Secretary, the Australian Governor-General and the British High Commissioner, all of whom tried to convince him that it was unlikely that the Korean War would escalate into a world war. A deep gloom had descended upon Russell, quite at odds with the optimism that, in public, he claimed to be bringing to and taking from Australia. 'Even if the present war does not spread,' he wrote to Crawshay-Williams on 26 July, 'Korea has made a world war soon much more likely':

The only hope I see is that Americans may be frightened of their failure. But I don't expect that. So I strongly favour getting a house in Wales, & it should be got *now* before people are alarmed in England.

'Even if there is no war now,' he wrote a week later to Crawshay-Williams's wife, Elizabeth, 'there will be one soon':

I am very gloomy about the world. It seems Korea will not lead to a world war, but there remain Formosa, Indo-China, Hongkong, Persia, Turkey, & Finland, not to mention Tito. I don't see how, with America in its present mood, we are to get through the next two years without a clash.

This mood persisted in the weeks following his return to England at the end of August, which no doubt partially accounts for the impression he gave Alys of being 'sad & dispirited & remote' when he came to see her on 12 September.

Within two months of arriving back from Australia, Russell had to leave for the United States to fulfil an obligation he had made to give a two-week course in philosophy at Mount Holyoke College for Women in New England. Before he did so, he published in the *New York Times Magazine* an article called 'If we are to survive this dark time . . .' in which he revealed the state of mind with which he viewed the world war that was, he had now persuaded himself, both imminent and inevitable. As always, he reminds himself and his readers of the wisdom of taking a 'wide horizon' when considering the appalling suffering that mankind is about to inflict upon itself. He also, perhaps somewhat surprisingly, insists that: 'In spite of some alarmists, it is hardly likely that our species will completely exterminate itself.'

But what is interesting about the article is that, despite the alarm with which Russell had watched the recent hardening of American attitudes towards Communism, he does not utter one word of criticism against the United States and goes out of his way to show that his own anti-Sovietism is as strident as ever. The view expressed in the article is that the impending war against the Soviets is, though certain to be almost unimaginably dreadful, both inescapable and worth fighting. Indeed, the article reads almost like the speech of a general to his troops before a great battle, reminding them what they are fighting for and instilling in them a conviction as to the justice of their cause. 'Courage, hope and unshakeable conviction will be necessary,' Russell writes, 'if we are to emerge from the dark time spiritually undamaged. It is worth while, before the actual danger is upon us, to collect our thoughts, to marshal our hopes, and to plant in our hearts a firm belief in our ideals.' What we are fighting for, he insists, is a conception of human life that values, not the State, but individuals – individuals 'who, as far as is humanly possible, are happy, free and creative'. We in the West 'believe that each individual should have his proper pride . . . We attach importance to the diminution of suffering and poverty, to the increase of knowledge, and the production of beauty and art.'

'The Russian Government', Russell goes on, 'has a different conception of the ends of life', one that regards the State as divine and the individual as of no great importance: 'In the Soviet world human dignity counts for nothing':

It is thought right and proper that men should be grovelling slaves, bowing down before the semi-divine beings who embody the greatness of the State. When a man betrays his dearest friend and causes him, as penalty for a moment's peevish indiscretion, to vanish into the mysterious horror of a Siberian labour camp; when a schoolchild, as the result of indoctrination by his teacher, causes his parents to be condemned to death; when a man of exceptional courage, after struggling against evils, is tried, convicted, and abjectly confesses that he has sinned in opposing the Moloch power of the authorities, neither the betrayal nor the confession brings any sense of shame to the perpetrator, for has he not been engaged in the service of his divinity?

'It is this conviction that we have to fight,' Russell declares, 'a conception which, to my mind and to that of most men who appreciate what the Western world stands for, would, if it prevailed, take everything out of life that gives it value, leaving nothing but a regimented collection of grovelling animals. I cannot imagine a greater or more profound cause for which to fight.'

In the many newspaper interviews that Russell gave during his visit to the States in the autumn of 1950, he struck a similar note: urging Americans to support a rapid rearmament against the Soviet threat and arguing that the use of the atomic bomb against the Soviet Union, though dreadful, would be justified if it curtailed Stalin's expansionist ambitions. Russell's deep love for China, however, seems to have prevented him from extending to Mao's regime the implacable loathing he felt for Stalin's – in any case, the threat of Chinese expansion in the Far East worried him far less than the threat of Soviet expansion in Europe – and he was therefore unable to sympathise with the particular form of violent anti-Communism that the Korean War had aroused in the United States. Throughout October, as MacArthur's forces moved victoriously through Korea towards the Chinese border and MacArthur began to make public his wish to press on *into* China, Russell became increasingly horrified. Though he was able to contemplate the atomic bombing of Moscow with relative equanimity, the atomic bombing of Peking was a prospect he found unendurable. His view was summed up in the headline under which his Press conference of 15 November was reported in the *Manchester Guardian*: 'Fists for Russia and a Smile for Peking'.

By the time of this Press conference, the newspapers were more than usually interested in Russell because, on 10 November 1950, it was announced that he was to receive the Nobel Prize for Literature. Russell was in Princeton when the news reached him. His course at Mount Holyoke had finished a day or two previously, but, while there, he had accepted an invitation to deliver a series of public lectures called the Matchette

Foundation Lectures at Columbia University in New York, starting on 14 November. To fill the days in between the two engagements he had gone to Princeton to give a talk on 'Mind and Matter' and to renew contact with Einstein and others whom he had got to know during his time in Princeton in 1944. So it was that, while having dinner with the Princeton physicist, Robert Oppenheimer, Russell received a phone call telling him that he had won the Nobel Prize.

His reaction was one of mystified delight. If there had been a Nobel Prize for philosophy, or even for mathematics, it would not have been so surprising to hear that he had won it, but for *literature*? Susan Russell, in a memoir of her father-in-law, has written: 'He was very funny about the Nobel Prize; quite as taken with – and suspicious of – the gold trumpet grandeur as a kid who had accidentally won a prize and secretly rather liked it – but wasn't quite sure he wasn't being mocked.' In his *Autobiography*, Russell rather adds to the mystery by saying that the prize was given to him 'somewhat to my surprise' in recognition of the literary merits of *Marriage and Morals*. In fact, the citation does not mention any specific work, but says that the award was made 'in recognition for his varied and significant writings in which he champions humanitarian ideals and freedom of thought'. In presenting the prize, Anders Österling, the Secretary of the Swedish Academy, mentioned *History of Western Philosophy*, *Human Knowledge*, *Sceptical Essays* and the essay 'My Mental Development' (in Schilpp's volume devoted to Russell), and remarked:

> It is not his achievements in special science that the Nobel Prize is primarily meant to recognise. What is important from our point of view is that Russell has so extensively addressed his books to a public of laymen and, in doing so, has been so eminently successful in keeping alive the interest in general philosophy.

In other words, it was specifically *not* for his incontestably great contributions to philosophy – *The Principles of Mathematics*, 'On Denoting' and *Principia Mathematica* – that he was being honoured, but for the later work that his fellow philosophers were unanimous in regarding as inferior. Russell's ambivalence about this can only have been heightened by the knowledge that, before him, the only philosopher to have been awarded the Nobel Prize for Literature was the one against whose influence he had campaigned tirelessly and vehemently for forty years: Henri Bergson. One thing that Russell was *not* ambivalent about, however, was the £11,000 that came with the prize. 'The money, as you say, is nice,' he wrote to Rupert Crawshay-Williams. 'I try to think I like the honour equally, but I don't.'

When Russell arrived in New York on 14 November to give the Columbia lectures, he was greeted by the largest crowds he had ever drawn. 'Good Lord, Lord Russell,' a newspaper reporter was heard to say to him, 'anybody would think it was *Jane* Russell they were here to see instead of just a philosopher.' Julie Medlock, a New York literary agent who had been employed by Columbia University to look after Russell, wrote: 'People were lined up 3 and 4 deep all the way around two blocks in the hope of getting in by some miracle, or at least hearing the piped voice, or catching a glimpse of Lord Russell in person. The crowd roundly cheered as we drove up.' The hall hired for the occasion, the McMillan theatre at Columbia University, was obviously insufficient to hold everybody and two additional halls were wired up so that the overflow could at least hear the lectures, even if they could not actually see Russell.

What these huge crowds heard was a set of three lectures on 'The Impact of Science on Society'. These had been given, together with three others, earlier in the year at Oxford, and Russell had no doubt used some of the material from them in the seminars he gave on the same theme at the Australian universities he visited in the summer. Despite the fact that this time the lectures were treated as newsworthy events (the *New York Times* carried daily summaries of them), for anyone who had read any of Russell's popular writing over the previous three decades they would have contained little that was new. In the first, 'Science and Tradition', he rehearsed his familiar argument that, since the eighteenth century, the 'scientific outlook' has been steadily and continuously eroding religious traditions. In the second, 'General Effects of Scientific Technique', he argued that, though scientific methods of agriculture and medicine had been to the advantage of advanced civilisations, scientific warfare threatened to end civilisation itself. In the third, 'Science and Values', he ran through, yet again, his old arguments against the pragmatist theory of truth (quoting at length from his 1907 paper on the subject) and, having insisted that truth and power are not the same thing, urged his listeners to value science because it offered the former, not because it offered the latter.

In arguing for the value of rationality over sentimentality, Russell used an example that would have struck anyone who could remember his political writings of the 1930s as a piece of extraordinary barefaced cheek. In the face of the suffering of others, he remarked, you could take a variety of attitudes: if you were a sadist, you could enjoy it; if you were completely detached, you could ignore it; if you were a sentimentalist, you could persuade yourself that it was not so bad as it appeared; 'but if you feel genuine compassion you will try to apprehend the evil truly in order to be able to cure it'. A sentimentalist, he went on, will accuse you of being 'coldly intellectual' if you adopt this last attitude, and 'will claim to have a tenderer heart than yours, and will show it by letting the suffering continue rather than suffer himself'. For example, he added, 'the men who made the Munich surrender would pretend, (a) that the Nazis didn't go in for pogroms, (b) that Jews enjoy being massacred . . . Such men are not "coldly intellectual".' Presumably, he was hoping that no one in New York that night could remember that at the time of the Munich agreement he had publicly congratulated Neville Chamberlain for saving Europe from war.

After the lectures were finished, Russell travelled to Washington to see Kate. By this time, her husband, Charles, had abandoned his postgraduate studies at Harvard for a job at the US State Department and Kate had, in turn, abandoned hers in order, as she put it, 'to start my real life's work, the raising of a family'. At the time of Russell's visit, they were living in a tiny Washington flat and Kate was six months pregnant with her first baby. To her lasting dismay, when she opened the door to greet her father, he did not recognise her. 'I did not think', she wrote later, 'I had changed beyond recognition in two years.'

Back in New York, Russell had a less awkward and more satisfying reunion with Edith Finch, whom he had last seen in 1944, when she was living with Lucy Donnelly in Bryn Mawr. After Lucy's death in 1948, Edith had moved into an apartment in Manhattan's Upper East Side. By the time Russell left for London, he and Edith had sown the seeds of what would turn out to be the most durable love of his life. He also left for England with a promise from Julie Medlock to arrange another, far more lucrative, lecture tour of the States the following year.

Overshadowing Russell's personal triumphs and pleasures during this visit to the States, however, was the worsening political climate. On 27 November, China carried out its threat to intervene in the Korean War, reversing the gains made by MacArthur by sending into North Korea a huge army of some 200,000 men, which quickly drove back the UN forces under MacArthur's command. The fear that this would be the trigger to unleash atomic retaliation by the USA was so strong that the British Prime Minister, Clement Attlee, made a special trip to Washington to secure an assurance from President Truman that he had no intention of using the bomb in the Korean conflict. Attlee also tried, unsuccessfully, to persuade Truman to agree to recognise Mao's regime as the legitimate government of China and to admit Communist China into the United Nations. In an article called 'Why America is Losing her Allies', published soon after arriving back in England, Russell committed himself wholeheartedly to Attlee's policies, writing:

> . . . those who dislike communism – and I yield to none in my horror of the Communist regime – if they are not blinded by hysteria, consider that the policy recommended by the British government in favour of negotiation with China, is to be preferred to the American policy of outright condemnation of China, not only on grounds of expediency, but also on moral grounds.

Still more repugnant to Russell than American policy over China and Korea, however, were the witch-hunts begun by Senator McCarthy, which threatened to undermine completely Russell's image of America as the defender of democratic liberties. Summing up his reactions in a letter to Crawshay-Williams of 3 December 1950, a few days after his return to Richmond, Russell wrote: 'America was beastly – The Republicans are as wicked as they are stupid, which is saying a great deal. I told everybody I was finding it interesting to study the atmosphere of a police state, which didn't make me popular except with the young.'

A week later he was in Sweden to receive the Nobel Prize, an occasion he describes in his *Autobiography* as enjoyable and pleasant, 'though very grand'. Unlike other prize-winners, he was not a bit daunted by having to dine and make conversation with diplomats and royalty and he clearly enjoyed every minute of it. As he put it to Crawshay-Williams: 'It is nice being treated like a Christmas tree!' His acceptance speech, 'Politically Important Desires', further added to his celebrity when it was made into a gramophone record. Its message was that 'If politics is to become scientific . . . it is imperative that our political thinking should penetrate more deeply into the springs of human action.' In particular, politicians should develop and master the science of mass psychology, for 'Politics is concerned with herds rather than with individuals, and the passions which are important in politics are, therefore, those in which the various members of a given herd can feel alike.' The politically important desires, then, are those that compel us to co-operate with other members of our own herd and to fear and hate other herds. With regard to the former, Russell advises toleration with those who do *not* co-operate with the herd, for, while some will be idiots and criminals, others will be prophets and discoverers. And with regard to the fear and hatred of other herds, Russell advises a spirit of enlightened self-interest, which will see that it is in the interests of the herd, not to fight other herds, but to live in peace with them. 'I would say, in conclusion,' he ended, 'that if what I have said is right, the main thing needed to make the world happy is intelligence. And this, after all, is an optimistic conclusion, because intelligence is a thing that can be fostered by known methods of education.'

The general message, then, does not differ from (literally) thousands of others that Russell delivered in his lifetime. In the detail, however, one can discern a significant shift in his political allegiances. Whereas, only three months previously, he had written that he could not imagine 'a greater or more profound cause for which to fight' than the defence of the Western conception of human life against the threat posed to it by Soviet Communism, in this speech he sounds as though he considers the ideological differences between the Western democracies and the Soviet Union to be but a cloak for herd hostilities, a correct psychology of which he claims to be a necessary prerequisite for sound political thinking:

The atom bomb and the bacterial bomb, wielded by the wicked communist or the wicked capitalist as the case may be, makes Washington and the Kremlin tremble, and drives men further and further along the road towards the abyss. If matters are to improve, the first and essential step is to find a way of diminishing fear. The world at present is obsessed by the conflict of rival ideologies, and one of the apparent causes of conflict is the desire for the victory of our own ideology and the defeat of the other. I do not think that the fundamental motive here has much to do with ideologies. I think the ideologies are merely a way of grouping people, and that the passions involved are merely those which always arise between rival groups.

Upon his return from Sweden, Russell resolved to live a less hectic life, the lecture tours of the previous year having left him feeling exhausted. 'I have had my fill of lecturing recently', he wrote to Unwin, 'and one of the advantages of the Prize is that it will enable me to do less of it.'

For most of the following year, Russell stayed at home in Richmond, concentrating on writing and becoming more involved in the lives of John, Susan and the girls. The memoir of Russell by Susan mentioned earlier suggests that, for a time at least, the two of them developed an intense, perhaps even a romantic, relationship. Susan later told a number of people that she and Russell even had sexual relations, though it is unclear how much credence should be given to this. In her memoir, she speaks of Russell having 'a sensual wisdom in the back of his eyes, of a man who knows how to handle women, like an Arab who knows horses', and remarks: 'I was taken with him at first; then, after a while, I began to love him in the slightly timorous manner in which one would love a natural phenomenon, like the thunder and lightning, or Niagara falls.' She also claims: 'Diddy loved me; I think, first, because I liked him, and then because, in some sort of way, I managed to understand him.'

In Russell's correspondence of the time, and in his surviving papers, there is nothing to suggest that he loved Susan, or even that he liked her very much. In his letters to Edith (which grew increasingly affectionate during the year of 1951), Russell often mentioned Susan, but almost invariably with disapproval, particularly of her reckless and indiscriminate sexual promiscuity. In May, for example, in the course of describing to Edith the peculiar kind of marriage enjoyed by Elizabeth and Rupert Crawshay-Williams ('She is strictly monogamous, he very much the reverse, & yet they are perfectly happy, which is odd'), he told her that, during a visit to Queen's Road, Rupert had spent the night with Susan, but then, as soon as he had gone, Susan took up with another visitor, the philosopher Hans Reichenbach, after a few days with whom she disappeared suddenly to France, presumably with another lover:

Now she writes happily from Paris showing no signs of returning; we don't know who she is with. John & Hans sit about comparing notes on her character & behaviour & I contribute an occasional side-light. It is very like Dostoevsky. She is a mermaid or a witch or an odalisque – she says 'I love you true', but the sedge is withered – I am upset by it because of John, who struggles to hate her but can't. She has sucked the life out of him for years.

In an earlier letter Russell had written that Susan 'is very unkind to John & I try to get him to feel indifferent towards her, but in vain'.

It was at this time that Russell was completing the task of turning his Australian lectures first into a series of BBC broadcasts and then into a book, *New Hopes for a Changing World*. When the book was finished, he wrote to Rupert and Elizabeth Crawshay-Williams that in it he had 'told America what I think of MacArthur, & the Evening Standard what I think of sex in America, & John what I think of sex in 41 Queen's Road'. It is not difficult to find in the book forthright condemnations of MacArthur (who is described as believing that 'After we have killed a sufficient number of millions of Chinese, the survivors among them will perceive our moral superiority and hail MacArthur as a saviour'), but identifying the passages in which he tells John what he thinks of sex in 41 Queen's Road requires a little guesswork. My own guess is that he had in mind the parts of Chapter 1, 'Current Perplexities', in which he describes the fear and uncertainty produced by the threat of atomic war as balking 'the impulse to every irksome effort' and generating 'a tone of frivolous misery mistakenly thought to be pleasure', together with the passage quoted earlier in which he analyses the plight of those who *imagine* themselves free from 'the shackles of ancient codes' but who, in fact, underneath the surface, are still captives of the guilt engendered by the old morality. Those who believe that he slept with Susan, however, might also see some faint allusion to 41 Queen's Road in the following:

> I think that sexual morality owes its origin to the fear of jealousy. Probably the oldest part of sexual morality is the incest tabu, which is obviously necessary if family life is not to be disrupted by jealousy.

Why does he link the taboo against incest with jealousy here? Would it not have been more natural for him to attribute it to the genetic dangers of inbreeding? Was he perhaps thinking of the disruption to family life at 41 Queen's Road caused by jealousy?

One does not have to believe that Russell and Susan actually slept together in order to imagine John feeling intensely jealous of the affection and admiration that Susan felt for his father, which are abundantly evident in her memoir. Susan's memoir shows too some insight into the sides of Russell's character that he normally reserved for lovers and very close friends. 'Diddy was prickly and irritable,' she writes, 'and so damned hypersensitively sensitive that it was agony to be in his presence; and when I began to realise the amount of suffering he had simply lived with, in utter silence, I was breathtaken and nearly overwhelmed.' Evidently, the two of them had discussed literature at some length, and she comments perceptively on his love of the great English poets ('He was as full of Shelley and Milton as the English countryside is'), and on his psychological understanding: 'He had a queer faculty on occasion of being able to enter, directly, in the sense of utterly primary experience into one's feelings, moods, conscious and half-conscious thoughts, and could, on occasion, anticipate or state them.' She also comments knowingly on his vulnerability, his constant need for flattery and reassurance, and the effects these had on his relations with others:

> . . . he often used to think he had done nothing at all, and feel despairing. Quite really; and one had to cheer him up . . .
> People were very cruel to him when he was little; and he has had an awful time all his life trying to do the right thing by them: and not having

it come right. This worried him a lot; and he used to try to figure it out. He often felt miserable, because he felt he'd never got it quite right. I think this was because he left out the kind of effect somebody like him was going to have on people. His personality was such that, even though he was very good with children, and very sensitive and considerate with people, he was the sort of person who was just likely to send people rocketing off into explosions.

Only a very well-armoured person would have been immune to the sheer incredible dynamic power of that presence; strong people would be hurled off at a tangent by it, and sensitive people would be likely to be disintegrated nervous wrecks after a while. Diddy desperately needed warm and sensitive human contact all his life; so much of him was impersonal. He valued it (as a human being) above all else; and it was, for these reasons, the most difficult thing in the world for him to have.

Reading the memoir, one has the unshakeable impression of its having been written by someone who knew and understood Russell well, someone who had spent many hours discussing with him those things that meant most to him. One feels, too, a deep sense of gratitude to Russell for encouraging her in her literary ambitions. She evidently felt that, in this respect, she was following in the footsteps of T. S. Eliot (whose name and whose poem about Russell, 'Mr Apollinax', recur frequently throughout the memoir). As Susan saw it, just as Russell had recognised Eliot's talent in 1915 and encouraged him to devote himself to poetry, so he now felt moved to do the same for her. And one further feels that this was primarily why Susan wrote the memoir (which survives among Russell's papers): to let Russell know how flattered and grateful she was of being considered worthy to be Eliot's successor:

> . . . he has had this way of finding people at intervals whom he thought ought to be encouraged. I appear to be one of them. I must say he is a wonderful encourager; and I *am* much encouraged. Whether or not I turn out to have been worth it is, of course, quite another thing.

In this respect, at least, Susan was not fantasising. It was part of Russell's purpose in shouldering the financial burdens of John's family to encourage both John and Susan in their literary ambitions. After his failed attempt to secure John a publishing job, he tried to interest Stanley Unwin in publishing John's short stories. Shortly before he left for America in the autumn of 1950, Russell invited Unwin to Queen's Road in order to introduce him to John and Susan, and then wrote to him saying: 'I shall be curious to hear your verdict on my son's satirical story.' This, too, came to nothing, but Russell persevered, trying, whenever the opportunity presented itself, to find a publisher for John's work. With regard to Susan, Russell told Edith and others that he thought she had considerable ability as a poet and among his papers is a file containing a number of her poems typed on Russell's own typewriter. A poem of hers that he thought

particularly highly of was 'Whisky City', an allegorical description of two
lovers, who, by diving together into the sea to their deaths, preserve their
love for ever:

> Sing a song for the swimmers,
> who died and died well;
> who died and died truly
> in death, as in life
> finding life's loving truly
> in the cold and broken death
> of life's last entry
> of the last recall
> the womb of death most surely
> the sweetest womb of all.

The poem ends: 'For in all life's laughing loving, death, in death's green
womb, is here'. Its central idea – akin to the themes Russell discerned in the
work of his favourite novelist, Joseph Conrad – seems to be that, if we are
not to live on life's surface, we need to shake off fear and dive to the perilous
depths below, thus risking our own destruction. Or to put it another way:
self-preservation requires superficiality.

But if Russell encouraged Susan, she also encouraged him. The thing she
seems most keen to emphasise in her memoir is how enormously *impressed*
she was by him and the huge scale of his achievements. 'When he went out
of the house, it felt as though ten people had suddenly left':

He is a combination of a genius, a saint, a hero, and an honest human
being; any one of which would be enough to make people wish to
minimise him. If he had failed, of course, everybody would have a
glorious time sympathising. But he has not failed; and it is hard for
people either to comprehend or to accept – because this is such an usual
phenomenon – the magnitude, the incredible magnitude, of his success.

'He never ceased to be a marvel,' she wrote, 'or to astonish one with what
he was or he did next.'

In fact, after finishing *New Hopes for a Changing World*, what Russell did
next *was* fairly astonishing, and one imagines that he was inspired to do it by
living with John and Susan and by winning the Nobel Prize for Literature.
In the late summer of 1950 he decided to turn his attention to the writing of
short stories. His only previous foray into this form of writing had not been
encouraging. Nearly forty years earlier, he had written an autobiographical
story called *The Perplexities of John Forstice*, which he had abandoned after
no less an authority than Joseph Conrad had advised him against devoting to
it the considerable time and effort that would have been required to turn it
into a decent work of literature.

Now that he was a Nobel Laureate, however, and living with a woman
who considered him to be a literary genius of almost immeasurable

magnitude, his confidence returned. Was there also an element of competition in his decision to try his hand at the very form of writing to which John had devoted himself for years? Certainly John's daughter, Sarah, thinks so. In her memory, the harmony of her childhood home at 41 Queen's Road was first destroyed by the rivalry between her father and her grandfather over the writing of short stories. Russell, she thinks, was trying to show his son that, even on John's own ground, he could beat him. An echo of this view is contained in Susan's memoir when she writes: 'one had to leap about like hell to keep up with him on one's own familiar ground, if he decided he wanted to explore it'.

For whatever reason, Russell was determined to have another attempt at proving himself as a short-story writer and devised an elaborate method for receiving, this time, opinions on his efforts that would be unaffected (for better or for worse) by the knowledge of their author. Perhaps he felt that Conrad had been unduly influenced by the preconception that, as a logician and mathematician, Russell could not be any good at writing fiction. In any case, when he submitted his first short story, 'The Corsican Ordeal of Miss X', to the magazine *Go* (a 'travel and leisure' magazine published in association with *The Sunday Times* in London), Russell asked that it be published anonymously and that readers be invited to submit comments on the story and to guess its author. Accordingly, when the story appeared in the December 1951 issue of the magazine, readers were informed only that it 'was written by a very famous English author' and were asked to: 'Name him if you can and give, in not more than 500 words, any reflection, appreciation or criticism which suggests itself. If you cannot name him, never mind, send in your comment alone.' A prize of £25 was announced for the best entry.

The results were no more encouraging than Conrad's earlier judgment had been. 'The plot was feeble . . . There is nothing to hold the attention,' wrote one reader. Another pronounced the story 'pompous and over-written', while yet another commented that 'improbability dominates the whole and extinguishes every spark of *normal* human emotion in his characters'. As to the author, most readers guessed either Somerset Maugham or Osbert Sitwell. The prize went to a Miss Munro, who was astute enough to rule out Somerset Maugham on the ground that he 'is a professional story-teller which lets him out'. 'The effect of this lamentable extravaganza', she wrote, 'is to suggest that the author has (1) no sense of humour, (2) a very high opinion of himself.' Her guess was that this 'tosh' was written by Charles Morgan.

To the almost unanimous view that this was a very poor short story indeed, there were only two exceptions: Sarah Gibbs, who thought 'Evelyn Waugh might have written this absolutely delightful story', and Lola Greer, who wrote: 'In this intriguing and witty story I see the fine Italian hand of that famous English writer (and artist) The Honourable Winston Churchill . . . Whoever the author, congratulations to him.' Both women gave as their address 333 East 43rd Street, New York (where Edith used to live), and both asked that, if they won the competition, the £25 should go to their friend: Miss Edith Finch. Clearly Susan was not the only one determined to encourage Russell in his fledgling career as a short-story writer.

By this time, in fact, Edith had become the most important person in Russell's life. After their meeting in New York during Russell's visit to the United States in the autumn of 1950, they began writing to each other as lovers, and, in the spring of 1951, Edith moved to London, primarily, one assumes, to spend more time with Russell. When she returned to New York for a brief visit to stay with friends in May 1951, Russell wrote to her almost every day to tell her how much he loved and missed her. By the end of the year it was probably understood by both of them that, as soon as Peter legally divorced herself from Russell, Edith would become his fourth wife.

Though Russell's marriage to Edith was, without doubt, the happiest of his life, Edith remains a somewhat elusive character, refusing somehow to come out of the shadows in any of the surviving descriptions of her. Born in 1901, she was brought up in New York, studied English Literature at Bryn Mawr and at St Hilda's, Oxford, and settled in Bryn Mawr in a house she shared with Lucy Donnelly for over twenty years. Though she occasionally taught at Bryn Mawr, she was never a career academic. She was, however, the author of two biographies, one of Dr Carey Thomas, the President of Bryn Mawr, and the other of the poet Wilfred Scawen Blunt. She is remembered by Russell's grandchildren as a rather remote and frosty figure: neat, precise, impeccably dressed and dauntingly well-mannered. 'She was the sort of person one would never dream of putting one's arm around', as one friend of the family put it to me.

The dominant impression one has of Edith is of someone who decided, at the age of fifty, to devote herself utterly to Russell, her admiration of whom seems to have been entirely without reservation or criticism. When Russell left for New York in October 1951, on what was to be his final lecture tour of the United States, Edith wrote to him from London:

Welcome to New York, my darling Bertie, to my fantastic home town! . . . Perhaps ordinarily I have as you say, no great wish for power, I don't know; yet at the moment I long for one overwhelming power. But you will think it is a mean desire since I long for it only to one end, not to help all mankind directly as you would do but to protect you from the visitations & fatigues & possible discouragements of life amongst my compatriots . . . I long simply to protect you, wherever, whenever, against whatever, & to make you happy & at peace.

Though this final lecture tour was to prove to be the most lucrative of all (Russell returned from it in November $10,000 richer), in many ways he rather regretted having agreed to do it. The itinerary was more packed and exhausting than ever, the agent who arranged it, Julie Medlock, got on his nerves and he hated being away from Edith just when their relationship was blossoming. Moreover, the aspects of the American political climate that had so alarmed and depressed him the previous year – particularly the tendency to divide people into just two camps: zealous American patriots and evil

Communists – had, if anything, grown worse. On his arrival in New York on 20 October, Russell was asked by reporters why he had been delayed for so long going through immigration. 'I had to satisfy your authorities', he replied, 'that I was not suffering from smallpox or communism.'

For the most part, Russell's public lectures centred on the fairly bland and inoffensive themes of *New Hopes for a Changing World*, but this did not prevent him from being denounced in the American Press as a 'learned fool' who preached 'unconventional and Marxist opinions'. Russell courted especial controversy in Indiana, where he had been engaged to speak at Purdue University on 1 November. As it happened, an article that he had written for the *Manchester Guardian* fiercely attacking the Indiana educational system had been published the previous day. The occasion for Russell's attack was a statement by the Indiana State Superintendent of schools to the effect that young American people should be taught that their government was the best in the world and to 'discredit definitions and descriptions used by foreign governments of such words as Social Revolution, Communism, Fascism, Totalitarianism, Police State, Dictatorship, Welfare State, Bureaucracy, Conservatives, Liberals, Capitalism, Socialism, Communal Enterprise and Propaganda'.

Russell's reaction to this egregious and exuberant example of McCarthyite zeal was to meet it with a characteristic mixture of satirical overstatement and heavy-handed irony:

> Every honest man (honest men are only found in America) knows that Mr Acheson is a Communist, that Mr Attlee is a Communist, and that Communism is so catching that anybody whose second cousin once met a Communist at a party is likely to be infected . . .
>
> In Germany under Hitler and in Russia under Stalin nobody ventured upon a political remark without first looking behind the door to make sure that no one was listening. When I last visited America I found the same state of things there. As we all know, America is not a 'police state'. It is true that Senator McCarthy's emissaries and his allies in the FBI are perpetually snooping and that if by some misfortune you were to quote with approval some remark by Jefferson you would probably lose your job and perhaps find yourself behind bars. But this, of course, is done in the defence of liberty.
>
> We all know that England is a 'welfare state' and that this proves that England is only half-heartedly opposed to Moscow . . .
>
> The education authorities of the state in question will, I am sure, agree that the indoctrination which they advocate is not 'propaganda'. It is not 'propaganda' because it is teaching doctrines with which they agree.

Implying that America was a repressive 'police state', comparable to Nazi Germany and Stalinist Russia, struck many of Russell's erstwhile supporters – including, most notably, Sidney Hook – as outrageous, and involved Russell in acrimonious controversies in the letters pages of the *Manchester Guardian* and elsewhere, which would rumble on for months. In Indiana, though, there was neither time nor opportunity to debate the issue. The topic of his talk at Purdue – 'The Physical Conditions of Thinking' – gave little scope for discussing his views on McCarthy and the FBI, and as soon as it had been delivered Russell left town, staying in Indiana, he wrote to one correspondent, 'just long enough to avoid getting lynched'. From there Russell went to Ohio, and then to West Virginia and North Carolina, all in the space of four days. After his last engagement, he wrote to Edith: '*Nothing* will induce me to come again. Absolutely nothing either pleasant or interesting has happened to me, except Kate & David.' This last was a reference to a brief interlude in Washington, where he was able to spend a few hours with Kate and to see his first grandson, David. 'Kate is completely transformed by having a child,' he told Edith, 'it is lovely to see, & makes me happy about her. You can't say I am wrong to think so much about making money – I don't think they would have ventured on a child if I hadn't been able to help.'

Edith, meanwhile, had been seeing rather more of John and Susan than she really wanted. In a letter written a few days after Russell's departure for America, she told him about her encounter with them the previous day. Having arranged to meet them for lunch at a Chelsea restaurant at 1.30, she felt obliged three hours later ('even the waiters had left sometime before we tottered forth into Sloane Square') to invite them back to her house, where John, who had brought along 'a whole briefcaseful', spent hours reading his own writings into Edith's tape recorder. Not to be outdone, Susan (who 'hadn't brought any of her mss.') took down from the shelves the *Oxford Book of Poetry* and read into the machine a number of Russell's favourite poems. As they were enjoying themselves so much, they phoned to cancel a previous dinner engagement and carried on recording throughout the evening. At ten o'clock, they all 'dined on tinned mushroom soup, tinned hash, tinned peas, cheese, coffee & hock'. Finally, at midnight, 'a little foggily & groggily', John and Susan called a cab and returned to Richmond, 'promising to return next week . . . with more mss. to record'. 'How right you were when you said authors delighted in reading their own works,' Edith told Russell, adding, somewhat unconvincingly, 'O well, it will be fun to see them anyway.'

True to his word, after Russell returned from the United States at the end of 1951 he never went back. With the fortune he had earnt from that lecture tour, and with a devoted and protective lover at home, he had little need or urge to travel, and he spent the following two years at Richmond, living quietly and concentrating on his writing. During the first half of 1952 the focus of his work was the completion of his *Autobiography*, which, in an act of symbolism reminiscent of his completion of *The Principles of Mathematics* on the last day of the nineteenth century, he finished on 18 May 1952, the date of his eightieth birthday. In contrast to the 1931 draft, the book now finished on a note of contentment. Living in Richmond with John, Susan and their three children he described as 'a pleasant experience, giving the pleasures of family life without its responsibilities', but the chief source of his happiness – 'a very profound happiness, such as I had not expected to know during my remaining years' – he emphasised was his relationship with Edith. 'At the moment of my eightieth birthday', he wrote, 'I am aware of a greater contentment and sense of peace than at any previous period of my life.'

In 1931, Russell had appended to his *Autobiography* an 'Epilogue' that gave a relentlessly gloomy summation of his life, both public and private, up to that point. In politics, he wrote then, the 'downfall of England' depressed him by abolishing the tradition into which he had been born and thus preventing him from handing over the spirit of that tradition to his son: 'The feeling of impending doom gives a kind of futility to all activities whose field is England.' In philosophy, he found himself, under the influence of modern physics, relapsing into a metaphysical Idealism 'not unlike Berkeley, without his God and his Anglican complacency'. And, overall: 'When I survey my life, it seems to me to be a useless one, devoted to impossible ideals ... when I am alone and idle, I cannot conceal for myself that my life had no purpose and that I know of no purpose to which to devote my remaining years. I find myself involved in a vast mist of solitude both emotional and metaphysical, from which I can find no issue.'

Now, twenty years later, he took stock again and drew up a rather different balance sheet: 'My work is near its end, and the time has come when I can survey it as a whole. How far have I succeeded, and how far have I failed?' Among the failures, rather curiously (as if it were, somehow, his own fault), he listed the lamentable state of the world: 'Communists, fascists and Nazis have successively challenged all that I thought good, and in defeating them much of what their opponents have sought to preserve is being lost.' Philosophically, his failure is now described not as a relapse into metaphysical Idealism, but as the abandonment of his earlier belief in a Platonic eternal world of unassailable mathematical truth. Another 'inner failure' he mentions is that he 'set out with a belief that love, free and courageous, could conquer the world without fighting', but 'ended by supporting a bitter and terrible war'.

'But', he writes this time, 'beneath all this load of failure I am still conscious of something that I feel to be victory.' This victory, it turns out, consists in maintaining, despite everything, an allegiance to the truth, a belief in the possibility of 'a world of free and happy human beings', and a commitment to a personal and social vision that imagines a society 'where individuals grow freely, and where hate and greed and envy die because there is nothing to nourish them'. In these respects, 'the world, for all its horrors, has left me unshaken'.

Russell's eightieth birthday became the occasion for a media celebration of his life and achievements, which showed just how far his public reputation had changed in the twelve years since his vilification in New York in 1940. In the UK and the USA, there was a stream of newspaper articles and radio and television broadcasts paying tribute to him. Though Russell affected to find this all rather wearisome ('I am utterly sick of being 80!' he remarked to Julie Medlock), he contributed to it in no small measure, publishing in the *New York Times* an article called 'Advice to those who want to attain 80'; writing two separate articles called 'The Next Eighty Years' (one for the *Observer*, the other for the *Saturday Review of Literature*); making a broadcast for BBC Radio entitled 'Reflections on my Eightieth Birthday'; and taking part in an NBC-TV broadcast, the transcript of which was later published as 'My First 80 Years'.

Though for the time being at least he regarded his *Autobiography* as a finished work, he did not wish to see it published until after his death ('and', he wrote to Stanley Unwin, 'there are a few other people as old as me, or older, who had better be dead before it is published'). The importance he attached to it, however, can be seen in the enquiries he made to Unwin about how best to protect the manuscript in the event of nuclear war. 'I do not think it would be safe anywhere in London, or New York, or Washington,' he told Unwin, 'as all these cities are likely to be radio-actively disintegrated before long.' Did Unwin, he asked, have 'a safe receptacle in the country for MS'? Alternatively, would Unwin like to have several proofs printed now, 'so that there might be copies in several places'? In the end, Unwin agreed to deposit the manuscript in a safe in his office, and there it remained for the next ten years.

Despite his unwillingness to see the book published during his lifetime, Russell made extensive use of it in a series of four radio broadcasts that he gave for the BBC in the summer of 1952 under the generic title 'Portraits from Memory'. The portraits in question were of some of his old friends: Alfred North Whitehead, John Maynard Keynes, Lytton Strachey (the last two together in one broadcast), D. H. Lawrence, and Sidney and Beatrice Webb. Though none of them was without the occasional barbed remark, the portrait of Lawrence was especially acidic. Lawrence, Russell alleged, 'had such a hatred of mankind that he tended to think both sides [in the First World War] must be right in so far as they hated each other'. He also accused Lawrence of developing 'the whole philosophy of Fascism before the politicians had thought of it'. Lawrence had been dead for twenty years when this broadcast was made, but his wife, Frieda, was still alive and well and living in New Mexico. When the transcript of the talk was published in *Harper's*, Frieda responded with a surprisingly mild letter to the magazine. Calling Lawrence an exponent of Nazism, she wrote, is 'pure nonsense. You might as well call St Augustine a Nazi.' Her letter ended: 'I am convinced that, in some secret corner of himself, Russell has another image of a young Lawrence who was his friend and not the fantastic monster he makes him out to be.'

Frieda died in 1956, and therefore would not have seen the version of Russell's portrait of Lawrence that finally appeared in his *Autobiography*, which differs from the BBC talk by including a paragraph on Frieda herself, revising his earlier statement about Lawrence's Nazism only to the extent of attributing it to Frieda's influence:

Lawrence, though most people did not realise it, was his wife's mouthpiece. He had the eloquence, but she had the ideas. She used to spend part of every summer in a colony of Austrian Freudians at a time when psycho-analysis was little known in England. Somehow, she imbibed prematurely the ideas afterwards developed by Mussolini and Hitler, and these ideas she transmitted to Lawrence, shall we say, by blood-consciousness.

With his *Autobiography* out of the way, Russell turned next to writing more short stories, undeterred by the inauspicious reception given to 'The Corsican Ordeal of Miss X' by the readers of *Go*. On 23 May 1952, he wrote to Unwin: 'You may have noticed that I have broken out in a new place and taken to writing fantastic stories. I doubt if they are the sort of thing that you like publishing, but that remains to be seen. I have always remained grateful to you for publishing my *Social Reconstruction* at a moment when I was at the nadir of unpopularity.' The following day he wrote again, telling Unwin that he had now written three such stories, which, he insisted, were 'not intended to be serious or to have any sort of moral, but merely to amuse'. Unwin, naturally, replied that he would be 'delighted' to see the stories, but, when they arrived, he fell silent on the subject too long for Russell's comfort. On 27 June, Russell wrote again:

> With regard to my short stories, it was my intention to write more of them so as to make an adequate volume if, in the judgment of people whom I could respect, they were worth publishing. I do not gather from you whether or not you consider them completely worthless. The Corsican story was published completely anonymously in one issue of 'Go'. The others have not been published at all. I have some others in my head and if it seems worth while I can probably get them written sometime before the end of September, but it is not the sort of writing that I am used to and I cannot form any critical judgment myself. I shall be grateful for some help from you.

Faced with what must surely be the weakest attempts at fiction ever written by a Nobel Prize-winner for Literature, Unwin evidently did not quite know what to do. Finally, on 3 July, he wrote to Russell:

> I should like to talk to you some time about your short stories, which have now been studied by no fewer than five readers. I should say that on balance the verdict of four is unfavourable and one favourable, though all are agreed that anything under your name would sell. The ideas behind the stories are all excellent and entertaining, but they are developed much more slowly than is the fashion with short stories today. We are, of course, ready and willing to publish anything of yours and are quite sure we should make a success of it, but definitely to encourage you to devote energy to writing of this kind, unless you find it diverting to do so, is rather a responsibility.

The reader who was favourable turned out to be one of the directors of the Bodley Head, a publishing firm associated with Unwin, so a solution to

Unwin's dilemma was reached whereby Russell was offered a contract for the stories, provided they could be published by the Bodley Head, rather than under the Unwin imprint.

This was all the encouragement Russell needed, and, within a month, he had finished the other two stories required for the collection, which was duly released to a bemused public the following year under the title, *Satan in the Suburbs and Other Stories*. Before publication, Russell sent a copy of the title story to a writer and publisher whom he had got to know called Stefan Themerson, and received in reply the most gratifyingly extravagant praise. 'I don't know much about how *Candide* was written', Themerson wrote to Russell (in a letter that he immediately forwarded to Unwin), 'or about the people who first had the chance of reading it, but – turning one after the other the pages of your typescript . . . I felt like one of those 18th century readers, I felt an immense affinity with them, and felt your presence as they must have felt Voltaire's . . . You are concerned with sorrows, not with tears; with joys, not with laughter; you squeeze out all the artifice of trying to be naturalistic.' Russell received similar encouragement from Edith, who wrote to Unwin that Russell's short stories seemed to her, 'both in matter and form', to place Russell 'amongst the great masters of the art'.

Critics and the book-reading public begged to differ and the stories collected in *Satan in the Suburbs* quickly sank into obscurity. There are signs, however, that Russell attached a great deal of importance to his short stories and that he was both disappointed and surprised by the unenthusiastic reception they received. In the Preface that he wrote to *Satan in the Suburbs*, he emphasised, as he had done in his letter to Unwin, that they were not written for any serious purpose, but were simply intended to be interesting or amusing. This led many readers to suppose that they were meant to be funny, and they were therefore read – if at all – as failed attempts at humour from a philosopher, who, having reached the age of eighty, wanted to write merely to enjoy himself. Disappointed with this reaction, Russell insisted later that these stories did, after all, serve a very serious purpose. The writing of them, he claimed, 'was a great release of my hitherto unexpressed feelings and of thoughts which could not be stated without mention of fears that had no rational basis'.

That emotional repression is a central theme in Russell's fiction is evident to anyone who has ever read his short stories carefully (that is to say, to very few people), but that these stories provide a release of Russell's *own* repressed feelings is much less obvious. Once this is understood, however, the importance that he attached to them becomes easier to grasp, and the stories themselves, particularly the title story, take on a much richer, and rather dark, significance. It is no coincidence that the stories were written at a time when Russell was completing his *Autobiography*. 'Satan in the Suburbs', especially, is a piece of disguised autobiographical revelation, and to understand just *what* it reveals, it has to be read alongside Russell's *Autobiography*, especially his account of his early life and his portrait of D. H. Lawrence.

Russell's brief friendship with Lawrence in 1915 ended with each accusing the other of hating the whole of mankind. In a brutal letter that brought Russell to the edge of suicide, Lawrence told him:

> You are simply *full* of repressed desires, which have become savage and anti-social. And they come out in this sheep's clothing of peace propaganda . . . You are too full of devilish repressions to be anything but lustful and cruel . . . The enemy of all mankind, you are, full of the lust of enmity. It is *not* the hatred of falsity which inspires you. It is the hatred of people, of flesh and blood. It is a perverted mental blood-lust. Why don't you own it.

In his portrait of Lawrence, Russell hit back with a very similar denunciation, describing Lawrence as 'a sensitive would-be despot who got angry with the world because it would not instantly obey':

> When he realised that other people existed, he hated them. But most of the time he lived in a solitary world of his own imaginings, peopled by phantoms as fierce as he wished them to be. His excessive emphasis on sex was due to the fact that in sex alone he was compelled to admit that he was not the only human being in the universe. But it was because this admission was so painful that he conceived of sex relations as a perpetual fight in which each is attempting to destroy the other.

However, Russell admits, his first reaction to Lawrence's fierce letter was one of despair: 'I was inclined to believe that he had some insight denied to me, and when he said that my pacifism was rooted in blood-lust I supposed he must be right. For twenty-four hours I thought that I was not fit to live and contemplated committing suicide. But at the end of that time, a healthier reaction set in, and I decided to have done with such morbidness.'

'Satan in the Suburbs', however, shows that Russell was not *quite* done with such morbidness, for among the 'fears that had no rational basis' that are expressed by the title story is the fear that Lawrence was right: that Russell really *was* 'the enemy of all mankind'. The central character of the story, the demonic Dr Mallako, might be regarded as a literal personification of Lawrence's phrase 'devilish repressions' and, as such, a self-portrait of Russell himself, as seen through Lawrence's attack on him and his own fears that Lawrence had some deep insight into his character. In his *Autobiography*, Russell says that the story was in part suggested to him by a stranger he met in Mortlake (a suburb of London not far from Richmond), who, when he saw Russell, crossed the road and made the sign of the Cross. This clearly caused Russell to think: what if he *were* the devil? What if the emotional repressions he had just finished chronicling in his *Autobiography* *had* created in him the all-consuming hatred of which Lawrence had accused him?

In the story, Dr Mallako, from his respectable home in Mortlake, wreaks havoc on the lives of his neighbours by encouraging them, first to reveal, and then to act upon the less respectable sides of their natures: the destructive jealousies, hatreds and ambitions that previously they had kept hidden and unexpressed. The nameless narrator of the story is a scientist who watches in dismay as his neighbours, one by one, fall under Mallako's influence. The doctor's power, the scientist realises, comes from his ability to read secret thoughts and bring them out into the open, 'like monsters of the deep emerging from their dark caves to bring horror to the crews of whalers'. This realisation is a challenge to the scientist's hitherto optimistic view of human nature, and he begins to despair at the thought that *all* people, even the most conventional and respectable, have a dark side; that each and every one of them has some nasty secret about themselves that they keep hidden. Reflecting on this, the scientist becomes 'increasingly filled with a general detestation of mankind'. Possessed with the desire to punish the sinful – that is, the entire human race (indeed, *all* living things) – he builds a device designed to boil all the water on earth, contemplating with satisfaction as he does so the vision of the planet getting hotter and drier until it is no longer able to support life. After which, he reasons, 'there will be no more Sin' and the earth will be as beautiful and as innocent – because as bereft of life – as the moon.

When the machine is built, the scientist goes to see Dr Mallako in order to gloat at his triumph over the sin that Mallako represents. The doctor, however, spots a flaw in the machine's design and informs the scientist that it will not work. But, Mallako suggests, why do the two of them not co-operate on a machine that *will* work, for, as he explains, he too loathes mankind, not self-righteously, but in a spirit of revenge. 'You imagine in your miserable way that you hate mankind,' Mallako tells the narrator. 'But there is a thousand times more hate in my little finger than in your whole body. The flame of hate that burns within me would shrivel you to ashes in a moment.'

When Mallako explains why he is possessed by such all-consuming hatred, he describes an emotionally deprived and repressed childhood strikingly similar to the one described in Russell's *Autobiography*. At the age of six, he says, he lost both his parents, after which he was put in the care of a religious and philanthropic old lady, towards whom he bore deep feelings of resentment and contempt, which, however, he repressed in order to win her approval and so continue to receive her kindness. What follows is one of the most impassioned pieces of writing in Russell's entire oeuvre, one in which it requires little imagination to see expressed the feelings he had buried for years about his grandmother:

She was persuaded that I was a good little boy. She adopted me, and educated me. For the sake of these benefits, I put up with the almost intolerable boredom that she inflicted upon me in the shape of prayers and church-goings and moral sentiments, and a twittering sentimental softness to which I longed to retort with something biting and bitter, with which to wither her foolish optimism. All these impulses I restrained. To please her I would go on my knees and flatter my Maker, though I was at a loss to see what He had to be proud of in making me. To please her I would express a gratitude I did not feel. To please her I would seem always what she considered 'good'.

'Since her death my material circumstances have been easy,' Mallako goes on, 'but never for one moment have I been able to forget those early years . . . the friendlessness, the dark despair, the complete absence of hope – all these things, in spite of subsequent good fortune, have remained the very texture of my life.' In consequence, 'There is no human being, no, not one, whom I do not hate. There is no being, no, not one, whom I do not wish to see suffering the absolute extremity of torment.'

The narrator, appalled by such depths of hatred, shoots Mallako and disguises the death as suicide. Later, he marries and tries to forget the entire episode, but in his nightmares he is haunted by the ghost of Mallako, who taunts him: 'You think I'm defeated, do you? . . . You think you have recovered your sanity, do you? . . . Do you not know that my power is spiritual and rests unshakeably upon the weakness in yourself? If you were half the man that you pretended to be . . . you would confess what you have done . . . Confess? Nay, boast.' Eventually, the scientist can take it no more and shouts to the world that he has killed Mallako and is proud of it, whereupon his wife, who has been worried about his mental state for some time, becomes alarmed and summons the authorities to have him committed to a lunatic asylum. The story ends with the scientist reflecting on the irony that, at the moment he recovered his sanity by confessing his deeds (thus ending years of 'devilish repressions'), he was declared insane. As he waits to be taken off to the asylum, he remarks: 'Nothing stretches before me but long dreary years of solitude and misunderstanding.'

If Mallako represents Russell as seen by Lawrence, and the scientist represents Russell as seen by himself, then the story can be read as Russell's attempt to lay the ghost of self-doubt that Lawrence's attack had induced. However, the triumph is, to say the least, an ambivalent one. After all, the scientist *does* want to – indeed, *intends* to – kill the entire human race. To be sure, he does so out of moral indignation at the wickedness of mankind rather than out of vengeful spite – as Russell puts it, his murderous designs are 'redeemed by the purity of a noble passion' – but is the difference so great? Russell wrestles with this question several times throughout the story, but his attempts to make clear the moral gulf that exists between Mallako and the scientist are strikingly unconvincing. If anything, he makes Mallako's hatred of mankind *more* intelligible and sympathetic than the scientist's own misanthropy, which appears, despite Russell's efforts to the contrary, weird and chilling. With Mallako, the situation is relatively straightforward: he hates people because he has suffered deeply at their hands. The scientist, on the other hand, one feels, is fooling himself, both when he justifies his decision to kill all life on earth by appealing to a higher morality and – at the moment he decides to kill Mallako – when he convinces himself that his hatred of humanity was, after all, 'only a passing madness'. As the scientist listens to Mallako's account of his early suffering and his consequent hatred of mankind, he reflects:

> That he [Mallako] was wicked was my most profound belief. If he wished
> to destroy the world, then it must be wicked to destroy the world. When
> I had thought that I would destroy it, I had enjoyed the vision of
> cleansing power. When I thought that he would destroy it, I had only a
> vision of diabolic hate. I could not permit his triumph.

Though it was surely not Russell's intention, these reflections illustrate
rather than refute Lawrence's central point. In his ferocious diatribe against
Russell, Lawrence had insisted that behind Russell's apparently pacific
condemnation of the war lay hidden a fierce and aggressive misanthropy, a
desire to 'jab and strike'. What Lawrence despised was the attempt to dress
this hatred up as a reasoned moral stance. A similar criticism might be
levelled at the self-deluded scientist in 'Satan in the Suburbs' who imagines
that there is something 'noble' in his desire (nay, decision) to wipe out all
life on earth. If one finds troubling the scientist's claim to have 'enjoyed a
vision of cleansing power' while contemplating universal death, and if one is
unpersuaded that *his* desire to kill all of mankind is somehow morally
superior to Mallako's, then one might say to him, paraphrasing Lawrence:
'It is *not* the hatred of wickedness which inspires you. It is the hatred of
people, of flesh and blood. Why don't you own it?'

'Satan in the Suburbs' may, then, be the most deeply revealing piece of
autobiographical writing that Russell ever produced. However, its old-
fashioned, formal and rather arch style prevented readers from seeing this
and the number of people inclined to take Russell's short stories seriously
remained very small. Frustrated by this, Russell told Unwin that for his
second collection of stories he would 'add a preface telling the reader when
he may laugh and when he should weep. Otherwise people will think that all
the stories are meant to be funny.' It is a remark that echoes the words of
Joseph Conrad in his book *A Personal Record*: 'There can be nothing more
humiliating than to see the shaft of one's emotion miss the mark of either
laughter or tears. Nothing more humiliating!' Russell had intended to *move*
his readers and, humiliatingly, had missed the mark. In the Preface to the
second collection, *Nightmares of Eminent Persons and other stories*, he
therefore fulfilled his promise to Unwin and announced: 'It is only fair to
warn the reader that not all the stories in this volume are intended to cause
amusement. Of the *Nightmares*, some are purely fantastic, while others
represent possible, though not probable, horrors. *Zahatopolk* is designed to
be completely serious.' In a separate Introduction to the ten 'Nightmares' he
further emphasised the point by insisting that his themes were the deeply
serious ones of madness, sanity, fear and unconscious terror:

> The following nightmares might be called 'Signposts to Sanity'. Every
> isolated passion is, in isolation, insane; sanity may be defined as a

synthesis of insanities. Every dominant passion generates a dcminant fear, the fear of its non-fulfilment. Every dominant fear generates a nightmare, sometimes in the form of an explicit and conscious fanaticism, sometimes in a paralysing timidity, sometimes in an unconscious or subconscious terror which finds expression only in dreams.

Despite these very direct pleas to be taken seriously, *Nightmares of Eminent Persons*, like *Satan in the Suburbs* before it, was dismissed as embarrassingly inept whimsy. Each nightmare, one reviewer wrote, was nothing more than a 'cute little fantasy, as impish as it is artless'. 'When logicians with a sense of humour start toying with story telling,' the same reviewer wrote, 'their mighty brains behave like elephants playing dancing mice.'

Nightmares of Eminent Persons was to be Russell's last foray into fiction writing. After it was finished, he turned his attention to moral philosophy. As he had admitted in his 'Reply to Criticisms' in the Schilpp volume, Russell was dissatisfied with what he had written in the past on questions of ethics. In particular, he was dissatisfied with the view he had long held, and expressed in a multitude of places, that moral judgments were merely subjective expressions of emotional preferences. According to this view, there is no *truth* in ethics, only a series of – sometimes conflicting – emotional reactions. Thus, while one can object, say, to murder, cruelty and racial discrimination, one cannot say that one is *right* to object to these things. For someone who was both a fervent moralist and a logician, this was clearly an uncomfortable view to hold, and Russell devoutly hoped to find some more objective basis for the moral positions he held with such vigour and passion.

At the time of writing *Human Knowledge*, Russell had written nine chapters on ethics for possible inclusion in the book, in which he outlined a view that was at least a partial retraction of his earlier subjectivism. Admitting that he found it 'intolerable to suppose that when I say "cruelty is bad" I am merely saying "I dislike cruelty" or something equally subjective', he rather tentatively put forward a theory according to which ethical statements *were* objectively true or false; however, what they were true or false *about* were human emotions, particularly 'the emotion of approval and the feeling of enjoyment or satisfaction'. Russell's idea was that acts that lead to approval could be (objectively) defined as 'good', while those leading to disapproval were 'bad'. The problem with this, of course, is that, as Russell himself had emphasised on many occasions, it not infrequently happened that whole communities agreed in their approval of things he thought wicked (war, the subjugation of women, the persecution of Jews, etc.), while strongly disapproving of things that he himself thought morally unobjectionable (adultery, homosexuality, atheism, etc.). Was Russell prepared to embrace a view of 'ethical knowledge' according to which his own vehemently held moral opinions were in danger of being included among those known to be objectively false?

For whatever reason, Russell was evidently as dissatisfied with these nine chapters as with everything else he had written on the subject and he left them out of *Human Knowledge*, perhaps unpersuaded by his own argument that ethics was, after all, a branch of knowledge. In October 1953, however, a few months after finishing *Nightmares of Eminent Persons*, Russell wrote to Unwin suggesting a 'compendium, with some additions, of my more important books on political theory', the first part of which would be his discarded chapters on ethics from *Human Knowledge* and the other parts made up of selections from his journalism, his public lectures and his books on politics (*Power*, *Authority and the Individual*, *New Hopes for a Changing World*, etc.). The title he suggested was *Human Society: Diagnosis and Prognosis*. A few weeks later, he wrote again to say that he had abandoned the idea of a compendium in favour of 'a new book with the same title'.

The result, delivered to Unwin in December 1953, was *Human Society in Ethics and Politics*, an uneasy and not altogether successful attempt to create a wide-ranging survey of moral and political issues, which passed from the nine chapters on theoretical ethics previously written to a discussion of the questions dominating international politics in the mid-1950s. As always when Russell wrote on politics, theoretical rigour soon gives way to sermonising, and the book ends with a plea to human beings to 'develop their godlike potentialities to the utmost' – that is, to use their knowledge of science, not to kill each other, but to create a society 'more infused with imagination and knowledge and sympathy than anything that is possible to those condemned to live in our present gloomy epoch'. Sounding uncomfortably like the scientist in 'Satan in the Suburbs', Russell writes:

> Sometimes, in moments of horror, I have been tempted to doubt whether there is any reason to wish that such a creature as man should continue to exist. It is easy to see man as dark and cruel, as an embodiment of diabolic power, and as a blot upon the fair face of the universe.

Within a few pages, however, Russell's attitude to mankind – again like that of his fictional counterpart – switches from hatred to love, from despair to hope, and he concludes by announcing that he is 'unconquerably persuaded' that men of 'courage, hope and love' will triumph over 'Malenkov and his opposite number as they prepare the extermination of mankind'.

From a theoretical point of view, the book is unsatisfying. This is not only because no use whatever is made in the second half of the ethical theory developed in its first half (indeed, it is scarcely mentioned), but also because there is a very clear tension between the moral feelings Russell expresses and the theory that he claims to believe. For example, the feeling he expresses above, that mankind is a 'blot upon the fair face of the universe', is on his own theory of ethics unintelligible. According to his theory, the *only* things to which moral values are applicable are human emotions and human actions in relation to human emotions and desires. A desire can be judged wicked (for example, the desire to cause suffering to others) and an action can be condemned as morally bad if it leads to the suffering of others, but the idea of judging the whole of mankind as wicked makes no sense at all on this theory. In an addition to his *Autobiography* written in the 1960s, Russell says that what he considered most important about *Human Society* was 'the impossibility of reconciling ethical feelings with ethical doctrines'. In fact, the book does not discuss this impossibility; indeed, it explicitly denies that such a reconciliation is impossible. What it reveals, however, is that Russell himself found it impossible to reconcile his ethical feelings with his ethical doctrines.

One of the few gestures Russell makes in the book towards bringing together his ethical theory with his substantive moral judgments is in the Preface, where he says that the point of including the theoretical sections is to answer his critics who say that he has no right to make moral judgments on political questions, since he does not believe in the objectivity of moral judgments. 'I do not think this criticism is valid,' Russell writes, 'but to show that it is not valid requires certain developments which cannot be altogether brief'. Hence his nine chapters leading up to the conclusion that ethical judgments can, after all, be factual statements of objective truth, rather than merely subjective expressions of emotional preferences. Within a month of publishing *Human Society*, however, Russell, in a review of A. J. Ayer's *Philosophical Essays*, appeared to show that he had already abandoned the theoretical justification he had offered for regarding moral judgments as objective statements. Singling out for especial praise Ayer's essay 'The Analysis of Moral Judgments', Russell declared himself 'in pretty complete agreement' with it. According to Ayer, though, as Russell himself emphasises, moral judgments are not objective statements of fact but, indeed, subjective expressions of emotion. When, in 1960, the philosopher D. H. Monro published a critical essay on 'Russell's Moral Theories', Russell replied:

I am not, myself, satisfied with what I have read or said on the philosophical basis of ethics. I cannot see how to refute the arguments for the subjectivity of ethical values, but I find myself incapable of believing that all that is wrong with wanton cruelty is that I don't like it. I have no difficulty in practical moral judgments, which I find that I make on a roughly hedonistic basis, but, when it comes to the philosophy of moral judgments, I am impelled in two opposite directions and remain perplexed. I have already expressed this perplexity in print, and I should deeply rejoice, if I could find or be shown a way to resolve it, but as yet I remain dissatisfied.

And this, more or less, remained his last word on the subject, thus committing him, as he was painfully aware, to two directly incompatible beliefs: 1. that his moral judgments about political questions were *right*; 2. that the words 'right' and 'wrong' were not applicable to moral judgments.

Throughout 1952 and 1953, Russell's life at Richmond had been quiet, orderly and almost serene. However, on Christmas Day 1953, less then two weeks after he had delivered *Human Society* to Unwin, the household at 41

Queen's Road suffered a dramatic upheaval from which it never recovered. What exactly happened is to some extent shrouded in mystery. Russell's story is that, after Christmas dinner, John and Susan suddenly announced that they were 'tired of children' and left the house never to return, 'taking the remainder of the food, but leaving the children'. No explanation by John or Susan of their apparently bizarre behaviour on this fateful Christmas Day survives, but, in various legal documents, Dora has insisted that Susan left because she could no longer stand living with Edith, and John followed because he could not bear to lose Susan. Neither, according to Dora, intended to leave their children permanently in the care of Russell and Edith.

Edith moved into Queen's Road after she and Russell married on 15 December 1952, and immediately began to impose more order on the domestic arrangements than had previously prevailed. She objected to the irregular mealtimes and late nights that John and Susan had become used to and let it be known that she disapproved of their feckless lifestyle and their apparently irresponsible attitude towards their children. The closeness that Susan had enjoyed with Russell before Edith's arrival came abruptly to an end, and she and John began to spend more and more time with their friends in London, in particular with Griffin Barry, who at this time was living in a flat in Mecklenburgh Square, Bloomsbury. When John and Susan walked out of Queen's Road, they went immediately to Griffin's flat, where they lived for the next four months.

It seems unlikely that John and Susan intended to leave their children in the care of Russell and Edith, for it was obvious that the couple were not, at that time, in a position to take on such a responsibility. Both Russell and Edith were ill with flu that Christmas, and Russell was due to go into hospital soon afterwards for a prostate operation. It seems more likely that John and Susan, as they had so often in the past, assumed that the children – who would return to their boarding school in January – would be looked after for the remainder of the Christmas vacation by their nanny, Miss Griffiths. In the New Year of 1954, John and Susan bought a cottage in North Devon, which, though small, they evidently intended to be a family home for themselves and their children.

Meanwhile, with Russell in hospital, Edith took charge of the situation. On 2 February, she wrote to Kate that the children were 'safe & happy at school' and that 'as soon as Bertie is stronger we can make plans':

> I feel sure that *something* can be worked out so that they will not be hurt. You may be assured that they will be as well cared for and cherished as is possible because Bertie cares more to have them given a good and happy start than almost anything else in the world. So don't worry about them.

When Russell came out of hospital, he himself wrote to Kate, telling her that, though John and Susan no longer lived at Queen's Road, their children might spend their Easter holidays there. John, Russell wrote, 'is a wastrel who would let his children go to the workhouse rather than do a little honest work, so I have to support them'.

In fact, in his own haphazard and inadequate way, John *was* making plans to support his family. Not only did he acquire the cottage in Devon, but he also took active steps to make a career for himself as a writer, securing from Russell's friend, Stefan Themerson, a contract to publish a novel called *Abandon Spa Hot Springs* in a series of books published by Themerson's company, Gaberbocchus Press. Like many writers, John seems to have had an exaggerated notion of how much he might expect to earn from a first novel, and Russell and Edith were probably right not to take his plans entirely seriously. Nevertheless, John was trying to keep his family together, and in this struggle he had to contend not only with his own lack of experience and worldly knowhow, but with his wife's capriciousness. In the spring of 1954, Susan, apparently indifferent to the plans that she and John were ostensibly making to settle their family in Devon, moved to North Wales to take up an invitation from Susan and Euan Cooper-Willis to live and work on the Portmeirion Estate.

In May, John decided to follow Susan and set off on his bicycle to North Wales. Travelling at the rate of fifty to sixty miles a day, he reached Portmeirion four days later. As soon as he arrived, on 19 May, he wrote a series of letters – to Griffin Barry and other friends in London, to his half-brother Roddy and to his father's solicitor, C. B. Drover at Coward, Chance & Co. – telling them that he and Susan had found a cottage large enough to house them, their children and Miss Griffiths, and that they had both been offered summer jobs at the Portmeirion Hotel. All in all, he sounded confident that he, Susan and their children could make a fresh start for themselves in North Wales.

In the meantime, however, Russell and Edith had been taking steps to have the children taken out of John's and Susan's hands. Just before he set off for Wales, John was advised in person by Russell's solicitors that his father intended to make the children wards of court. John 'said at once that he was quite opposed to such a proceeding', Drover wrote to Russell, 'since he himself had been a ward of court and he knew the difficulties and inconveniences that this entailed. He then went on to say that it was his intention to take full responsibility for the children.' In the light of this, Russell was advised that he would not succeed in making the children wards of court unless he was able to produce 'very strong evidence of neglect'. In an effort to compile such evidence, Russell instructed Drover to obtain as many statements as he could bearing witness to the fact that John and Susan were unfit to look after their children. Russell and Edith themselves provided such statements, and, as soon as John left for Wales, Dora received a letter from Drover asking her to call and see him at his office. When she arrived, she was asked to sign an affidavit to the effect that, to her knowledge, the children were being neglected by their parents. She refused to do so. In a subsequent letter to Drover dated 20 May (the day after John arrived in Portmeirion), Dora wrote:

As I said at the interview, I do feel very strongly that we should be able to arrange matters as a family, without recourse to the Court. That is a decisive step, and it may well be that John would be thoroughly able to look after the children in every way before long. I cannot stress too strongly that I feel John to be the one in need of encouragement and sensible psychological help at present, if he is not to go to pieces entirely – the children at present are in much better shape than he is.

She was more right than she could have known. In Wales, things went from bad to worse for John and, within a few months, he did indeed 'go to pieces entirely'. To begin with, his suggestion that the children should come to stay with him and Susan in North Wales during their holidays was rejected by Russell and Edith, who insisted instead that the children should spend the first half of their summer holiday in Richmond and the second half in Cornwall with Dora. They had, of course, no legal right to insist upon this, but, as Edith pointed out in a letter to Louis Tyler (another solicitor at Coward, Chance & Co.), since 'John and Susan had abandoned the children', Miss Griffiths' wages and the bills for the children's travel, food and clothing had been paid by Russell. As John and Susan by this time had no money, except what they earnt from their summer job at Portmeirion and the small allowance that Russell paid John, the children and their nanny would be able to come to North Wales only if Russell paid for them to do so. As he refused to do this, John and Susan had no choice but to submit to Russell's wish that the children stay in Richmond. Though clearly unhappy with this, John and Susan tried to work around it, and Susan travelled to Richmond to see her children and to help Miss Griffiths look after them. Perhaps inevitably, however, she quarrelled with Russell and Edith and soon returned to Wales. In a decision he later had cause to regret, John took Susan's side in the quarrel and, in July, was summoned to Richmond by Russell to be told that, if he had no intention of returning to Queen's Road, then he had to remove his belongings immediately. To anything he did not remove, he was told, he would lose any claim of ownership.

Having been separated from his children, estranged from his father and cut off from the house that had been his family home for three years, John then lost Susan. When, after his uncomfortable visit to Richmond to collect his belongings, he returned to Portmeirion, he was told by Susan that she had fallen in love with another man. This was Christopher Wordsworth, a talented and bohemian writer, whom Susan had met at a party given by the Cooper-Willises. Upon meeting Wordsworth, Susan took a fancy to him straight away. Her first words to him were, 'I am a poet's daughter, you have a poet's name – save me from these effete aristocrats.' As Susan and Wordsworth were now living together, John had to find somewhere else to live. After staying for a while with Susan and Euan Cooper-Willis, he decided that the only thing open for him to do was to begin divorce proceedings against Susan and to leave Portmeirion. But where was he to go? As he needed looking after and was no longer welcome at Richmond, he turned to his mother, who was spending the summer at Carn Voel, and set off on the long bicycle ride down to Cornwall. When he arrived there, Dora later wrote, she found him 'hard and embittered, though to some degree relieved from the worry and responsibility of his wife'.

In the late summer and autumn of 1954, while John lived with Dora, first in Cornwall and then in London, his mental state deteriorated sharply. Worried about his children, and distraught at losing his wife, he also because increasingly anxious about money. *Abandon Spa Hot Springs* was published in September and received a couple of favourable reviews, but it did very little to improve his financial situation, which took a turn for the worse when he received an income-tax demand for £1,500, a sum that neither he nor Dora could possibly afford to pay. After a plan to publish a book on the history of the Russell family came to nothing (Longman's, the prospective publishers, offered him only a very small advance), John applied without success for a number of routine clerical jobs. In his petition for divorce from Susan, he asked for custody of the children and seemed determined, somehow, to provide for them. Susan was entirely happy with this plan, and she and Wordsworth co-operated fully with John's solicitors in order that the divorce could go through the courts as quickly as possible, even providing, for example, a written confession of their adultery.

On 10 October, when John's solicitors had finished drawing up the divorce petition and were ready to serve it on Susan, Dora – in an effort to wrest control of the children away from Russell – wrote to Russell's solicitor, Tyler, telling him that 'John has been discussing with me the question of the children's Christmas holidays':

I am quite prepared to arrange to have them here or in Cornwall, or, indeed, to take over with John the responsibility for arranging their holiday plans in general, so that there need be no further anxiety on this score.

In reply (as ever when dealing with Dora, through his solicitor) Russell wrote that, though he was 'not particularly anxious to have the children for Christmas day', he would like to have them for the last week of their Christmas holidays; in any case, he thought it 'a little premature to make arrangements for future holidays until John's plans are more settled'.

Clearly John was not going to have full care and control of his children until: (a) the divorce was complete and he had legal custody of them; (b) he was able to provide financially for himself and his family. On both counts, he grew increasingly nervous, writing anxious letters to his solicitors asking them how much longer it would be before his divorce was heard and applying for any job he thought himself even remotely qualified to take. By November, Dora was extremely worried. 'I have John on my hands,' she wrote to Kate at the beginning of the month, 'terribly damaged psychologi-cally by the last seven years . . . he's as near a complete breakdown as ever I've seen – I believe he could even have gone crazy – but don't say anything of that, in case it gets round to him.' By the end of the month, John, according to Dora, 'began to show signs of persecution complex, said he would be arrested if he went out and might be hanged'. She thought of consulting a psychiatrist and phoned Russell in order to discuss the matter, but Russell was steadfast in his unwillingness to deal with her except via lawyers.

On 1 December, John wrote again to William George & Co., the solicitors dealing with his divorce, begging them to tell him when it might be finalised. 'Please let me know if any action on my part is required at all,' he pleaded. 'I shall be much relieved when the matter is completed.' On 16 December, he received the bad news that there was 'considerable congestion' in the divorce courts, and 'we are unable to obtain any precise information as to when your case will be heard, but it is expected that it will be early in the New Year'. Two days later, John set out from Dora's flat in Hampstead to visit his daughters at Queen's Road. While he was there, Russell, alarmed at his mental state, arranged for his own doctor, Dr Boyd, and a psychiatrist called Desmond O'Neill to come and remove John to the psychiatric ward at Guy's Hospital, where he was diagnosed as suffering from 'a serious delusional state of insanity' and given insulin to induce him into a coma. The doctor dealing with him at Guy's, T. A. Munro, subsequently wrote informing Russell and his solicitors that John 'may remain seriously mentally ill for at least six months to a year if not longer'.

To have his son go insane was the realisation of Russell's very deepest fears. Sixty years earlier, his grandmother had attempted to dissuade him from marrying Alys by revealing to him the extent of inherited madness in the Russell family. Though unsuccessful in their stated aim, Lady Russell's revelations had a profound effect on Russell. The fears generated by his grandmother, Russell wrote in his *Autobiography*, 'have never ceased to trouble me sub-consciously. Ever since, but not before, I have been subject to violent nightmares in which I dream that I am being murdered, usually by a lunatic.' The same kind of fear, he writes, 'caused me, for many years, to avoid all deep emotion and live, as nearly as I could, a life of intellect tempered by flippancy'. Reflecting on 'the tragedies, hopeless and unallevi-ated, which have made up the lives of most of my family', Pembroke Lodge came to seem to him 'like a family vault haunted by the ghosts of maniacs' and he came to feel 'as though a doom lay on the whole of my family and I were vainly battling against it, to escape into the freedom which seems the natural birthright of others . . . I am haunted by the fear of the family ghost, which seems to seize on me with clammy hands to avenge my desertion of its tradition of gloom.'

For a while, he had tried to convince himself that, by applying 'scientific psychology' to the upbringing of his children, he would triumph over these fears and produce a son who was not only sane, but a model of psychological well-being. Now, despite the confidence he had expressed in *On Education* and in innumerable articles about the effects of the proper methods of parenting, he was faced with the hardest fact he would ever have to bear: in the opinion of those trained in the 'science of psychology', upon which he had built such hopes for himself and society, his son was insane.

Quite *how* hard it was for him to bear this fact can be seen in his attempts to avoid facing it. In the final parts of his *Autobiography*, though he refers once or twice to his son's 'illness', he never mentions the nature of that illness, still less the emotional effect it had on himself. And when John was admitted to Guy's Hospital, Russell made no attempt to see him, preferring to discuss his medical condition with doctors and his legal and financial problems with lawyers. Talking to John himself, Russell seemed to assume – whether about John's psychological problems, the custody of his children, the divorce from his wife or anything else – was a waste of time. John was mad, irrational, and there was simply no point in consulting him about anything.

Dora's attitude could not have been more different. As soon as she learnt that John had been taken into hospital, she rushed there to see him. For the first two weeks that John was in Guy's, he spent most of his time in deep comas induced by insulin. Nevertheless, Dora went to see him every day. By the end of December, he was able to talk and even write letters. As one might expect, his conversation and his correspondence were those of a confused mind. For example, he became obsessed with a young girl called Daphne, whom he had met on a visit to his daughters' school shortly before his breakdown and whom he imagined was being hidden from him. If he could only find Daphne, he seemed to think, everything would be all right. Writing to Kate on 31 December 1954, John told her that his problem was not that he was insane, but that he did not have the 'guts' to find Daphne. 'Do write to me again,' he urged Kate, 'it is a great comfort to me to hear from you, as you are one of the few people who can understand the particular way in which I muck things up. No one else seems to.'

A week later, John wrote again to Kate, this time with a much more sane, and indeed perceptive, analysis of his difficulties. Apart from 'elements of incipient psychosis', he told her, his problem was that he was 'more generally – as a character, a person, a personality – more or less continuously in a world called Hell'. This Hell was a divided world in which he was called upon to take sides; the world, in other words, created by the divorce of his parents. The reason he was 'aged approx. 14 at 33', he wrote is that 'at 14 I *would* be 33'. Having spent his life trying to avoid taking sides, he now found himself unable to negotiate his way through the world's divisions:

> I *must* now think for myself and take *my* line. Then *they*, whoever they are, will not be able to drag me hither and thither. But this, which it is essential that I should do, is impossible because when I wish to, behold I am a jelly-fish.

Kate and Dora had the patience and sympathy to look for the gems of insight and good sense buried among John's confused ramblings. Not so Russell, who, from the moment John was diagnosed as insane, simply wanted him certified and out of the way, so that his affairs could be dealt with by those more competent to handle them. Russell seemed to attach particular importance and urgency to the task of steering John's divorce from Susan through the courts as quickly as possible. While John was still in Guy's Hospital, Russell instructed his own solicitor, Tyler, to take over the handling of the divorce case, which he did with exemplary speed and efficiency. First he persuaded the divorce court to accept a written affidavit from John in place of a personal appearance, then he wrote the affidavit and went to Guy's Hospital to get John to sign it, and finally he produced a statement from Dr Munro to the effect that, though John was too ill to attend the proceedings, he was not too ill to understand the matters in question and his written evidence could therefore be accepted by the court. The hearing took place on 9 February 1955. John's case – or, more specifically, the case presented on his behalf – was accepted, and on 16 April the divorce became absolute. Much to Russell's relief, Susan was no longer Viscountess Amberley.

Nor, after the divorce hearing, did she have any legal rights with regard to the care and control of her children. Remarkably, though Russell's solicitors submitted to the divorce court Dr Munro's statement that John was 'seriously mentally ill' and would remain so for up to a year, they were nevertheless successful in persuading the court to grant custody of the children to him. Presumably this was on the understanding of the court that, for at least the following year, the children would be in the care of Russell and Edith. Certainly, this was how Russell and Edith understood it. As far as they were concerned, the children were now their responsibility, and they were concerned to protect them, not only from John's fate, but also from John himself.

On 21 January, John was told that he was to be transferred from Guy's to the Holloway Sanatorium in Virginia Water, Surrey. Finding some pretext to phone Dora, he asked her to come at once and, when she arrived, announced that he would *not* go away to the country but would, instead, be returning home with her. Dora agreed to look after him and phoned Russell to tell him what had happened and to ask him to meet her to discuss John's situation. To this, according to Dora's account, Russell 'replied that he [John] must be put into a home and if I did not agree there was nothing to discuss'.

Russell believed that Dora had actively dissuaded John from going to the Holloway Sanatorium and he was furious with her for interfering. 'I have just heard from my father that you were responsible for getting John out of the clinic,' Kate wrote to her, 'if so, I think you made a big mistake':

> It is quite untrue that all John needs is a good woman's love & a stable life . . . He needs expert help for a long time & protection from all the family pressures (including you, painful as this may be) which have contributed to his collapse . . . For God's sake, Mummy, think of *John*, his own self & happiness & best interests.

When Dora replied telling Kate that it was at John's insistence that he had come to live with her – and, indeed, that she had tried to persuade him to remain in hospital – Kate immediately relented: 'I might have known my father would not have it exactly straight.'

While Russell was determined to leave the care of John in the hands of the medical authorities and have as little to do with him as possible, Dora was equally determined that John should be treated as a person and not just as a legal and medical problem. As ever, therefore, they pulled their son in opposite directions, Russell constantly on the lookout for signs that John was certifiable, and Dora on the lookout for signs of improvement in his mental state. At the beginning of March, Dora managed to secure John a job as a telegraphist, but on his first day of work he became confused and had to return home. Remembering that before Christmas he had been more stable in Cornwall than in London, Dora then took him to Carn Voel for a month. She asked Russell to allow John's children to spend part of their Easter holidays in Cornwall, but he refused.

When Dora and John returned to London after Easter, they became involved in a dreadful two-month-long battle with Russell over the question of whether or not John should be placed permanently, against his will, in psychiatric care. During this time John was incarcerated in no fewer than three different psychiatric institutions. What prompted the battle was Russell's fright at seeing John peering in through the windows of 41 Queen's Road. While living with Dora in Hampstead, John would often go wandering about London on his own, sometimes to keep imaginary appointments for job interviews, sometimes to find Susan, but most often to look for 'Daphne'. On several such occasions he ended up at Queen's Road, and, though he was not allowed in, he would prowl around outside, going from room to room, looking in through the windows, apparently convinced that Daphne was hidden somewhere inside the house. Deeply shaken by this, Russell wrote to Tyler on 11 May 1955, telling him: 'John's visits here are very frightening. Not only Griff and Dinah [the housekeeper], but also my wife and I, feel uncertain from moment to moment as to what he will do.' Russell and Edith were about to go away to North Wales for four weeks and, Russell told Tyler:

> I should wish, if it were in any way possible, to make sure that he [John] will not come here either alone or with his mother while my wife and I are away. As his mother insists upon having the care of him it is up to her to do what she can about this. Could you write to her explaining the situation here and the desirability of keeping John away while we are absent? My relations with her are not such that I can do this myself.

Tyler, it seems, felt unable to write to Dora the kind of letter Russell suggested, but, while Russell and Edith were in Wales, steps were taken to get John out of the way. On 15 May, Dr O'Neill wrote to Dora advising her that John should be admitted to St Andrew's Hospital, Northampton. Dora persuaded John to go there as a voluntary patient, but after one night he wrote to her saying that he missed being at home and he signed himself out. A few days later, Dr Boyd arrived at Dora's flat with an Emergency Order, signed by Dr O'Neill, committing John for seven days to the Priory Mental Hospital at Roehampton. Before he would agree to go, John – now worried about and suspicious of his father's attitude to him – typed and signed a short note that he hoped would, to some extent at least, protect him from Russell and from the lawyers and doctors he employed:

To all whom it may concern.

During my illness I wish my mother Mrs Dora Winifred Grace of the above address to be consulted and to have authority to deal with my affairs and matters relating to me and my children.
John Russell

Dora accompanied John to the Priory and persuaded him to enter it without too much fuss. When, some days later, he escaped, Dora came and persuaded him to go back. She then left for Cornwall for a week's holiday, after extracting from the doctors at the Priory an assurance that no action would be taken to disturb John until her return. However, the Priory was an extremely expensive private institution, and when Russell objected to the costs, Dr O'Neill arranged, with Russell's consent (though without consulting Dora, who was still in Cornwall), for John to be transferred under sedation to the Holloway Sanatorium in Surrey, the very institution to which he had a few months earlier refused to be transferred. When John woke up to find himself at Holloway, he became terrified and screamed and banged on the door to be let out, whereupon he was put into a padded room and prescribed further insulin treatment. When Dora phoned the Priory from Cornwall and learnt what had happened, she rushed to the Holloway Sanatorium to see John and then wrote a long letter to Tyler objecting to the way in which her son had been treated. Solitary confinement in an institution, Dora wrote, 'is extremely bad for him, since he depends very much to keep in touch with reality, on some talk and companionship with people he knows and who appreciate him'. Again, she urged Tyler to persuade Russell to meet her to discuss John's problems. There was, she insisted, 'a very great deal to discuss':

We cannot get John well or help him when he begins to be fit for life again, until we tackle the causes of the breakdown; which are crystal clear to me, and which require the utmost co-operation between the household at Richmond and myself . . . Is it not possible for his father to come back before the course of insulin is undertaken, supposing that it is decided on? We could then have the fullest consultation both lay and medical and John would be able to know that all those who care for him have reached some sort of unity through their affection for him.

'And please', Dora ended, 'do not take this matter lightly, but try to get hold of his father at the earliest possible moment. In such a case as John's, when he feels that he has lost everything, that he is unwanted and uncared for, the cure does not lie solely with chemistry or even with psychiatry.'

Tyler sent Dora's letter on to Russell in Wales, urging him to 'go and see the people at Virginia Water' as soon as he returned, but rather discouraging him from having anything to do with Dora, since 'I am dubious about her attitude generally'. In this respect, Tyler was preaching to the converted, and Dora's pleas to meet Russell, repeated in several subsequent letters to Tyler, remained unheeded.

The problem facing Russell and his doctors was that the seven-day order committing John to psychiatric care expired a few days after he arrived at Virginia Water. After that, he was (officially at any rate) a voluntary patient. Nevertheless, when he tried to escape by climbing over a wall, he was picked up – still wearing his dressing gown – and returned to the sanatorium. 'Naturally, he does not like to be shut up,' Dr O'Neill wrote to Russell, 'but I fear this is really necessary at the present time, as if he had any freedom at all he would run away.' However, at Virginia Water, neither Dr O'Neill nor Dr Boyd had any control over John's treatment, which was now in the hands of the Medical Superintendent at Holloway Sanatorium, Dr McDonald. On 14 June, McDonald wrote to O'Neill saying that in his opinion John was suffering from schizophrenia and should be given further insulin therapy ('in view of the fact that previous ECT made no lasting impression on the illness'). But, added McDonald: 'I am afraid his treatment as a voluntary patient is going to be rather a sticky problem . . . I very much doubt that he will accept a full course of treatment voluntarily.' The 'full course' involved a further three months at Holloway, and John showed every indication of signing himself out before that could be completed. According to McDonald, what John most wanted was to go to Richmond and reconcile himself with Russell: 'he himself thinks that if he were able to spend a couple of weeks with his father he would become perfectly all right'.

Passing this letter on to Russell, O'Neill commented: 'I take it . . . that if John is to remain and undertake the full course of insulin treatment he will need to be certified.' In the meantime, Russell, having returned from Wales, had been to Holloway himself to see John and to discuss his condition with Dr McDonald. John, Russell told O'Neill, 'expressed a very intense wish to get away from the Sanatorium', but Russell himself seemed determined to avoid that at any cost and sounded impatient for John's permanent certification: 'I do not quite understand the reason for not certifying him now as it seems to be quite clear that he is certifiable.'

The permanent certification of someone, however, is not something to be undertaken lightly, carrying with it, as it does, the loss of quite fundamental legal rights (had John been certified, he would have lost, among other things, the right to vote as well as the right to succeed his father as Earl Russell and take up his place in the House of Lords), and the authorities at Holloway were understandably reluctant to take this step. For the time being, in any case, it was unnecessary, since John was persuaded to stay at Holloway as a voluntary patient and to submit himself to further insulin treatment. In the meantime, while Dora visited John at least twice a week,

Russell stayed away. Dora, however, would not let the matter drop and persisted in phoning and writing to Tyler, begging him to persuade Russell to meet her to discuss John's future. John, she insisted, needed to re-establish his familial relationships with his father and his children, and she and Russell needed to meet face to face to discuss how best this could be achieved. 'His refusal now and before has upset me terribly,' she wrote in one of many such letters. 'Surely, after two new marriages and more than 20 years, it should be possible for John's father and mother to meet to try and help him as regards himself and his children? There are things about John's feelings proper only to be discussed between his parents, who could really help and which should not be the subject of the exchange of legal letters.'

When these pleas fell once more on deaf ears, Dr O'Neill, rather surprisingly (since his fees were still being paid by Russell), took up Dora's case. On 28 June, he wrote to Tyler informing him that John had agreed to stay at Holloway to complete his course of treatment, adding: 'It seems to me now that the real, and major problem is the question of John's future':

> I should like to suggest, therefore, that a Conference be held at my rooms at Harley Street with Lord Russell, Mrs Grace, yourself, a doctor from the Holloway Sanatorium, and myself, in order to discuss what is to become of John. I realise, of course, that there are difficulties in such a meeting, the chief problem being possible disagreement between the parents, but I feel nevertheless that it is important to hold such a Conference.

Seeing in this letter nothing more than a trick of Dora's, Russell refused O'Neill's invitation.

A few days later, when Dora visited John at Holloway, he complained bitterly that Russell had been to see him just once and vehemently insisted that he needed to talk to his father. The following day, Dora phoned Tyler, saying that Russell must visit John more often, since their son was becoming very restless. About an hour later, John walked into her flat, having escaped from Holloway and hitch-hiked back to London. His intention in escaping, he told her, was to see his father. When Dora received a phone call from Holloway, she told them where John was and promised to return him after she had taken him to Richmond. John, however, announced that he was not going back to the sanatorium. What he really wanted to do, he said, was to move back into Queen's Road, where, he was convinced, he could return to a normal life.

The next morning, 1 July 1955, Dora therefore phoned Russell, who agreed to meet John, so long as he came on his own. Feeling apprehensive about this, Dora followed John to Richmond, and, as she was coming out of the train station, met him coming back. His meeting with his father had lasted about ten minutes, just long enough for Russell to tell John that he could not, after all, move back into his old home. Outraged, Dora took John back to Queen's Road. At first, Russell seemed inclined to shut the door in their faces, but then he said he would talk to Dora so long as John stayed outside. According to Dora, Russell looked frightened when he saw John and said, 'He can't come in here.' 'I can't see why not,' Dora replied. 'I want to talk to you and he can sit in another room and wait.' At this Russell relented, and he and Dora had the discussion about John that Dora had been asking to have for months. In a letter to a friend the following day, Dora said that the conversation was quite amicable:

> I told his father many things about John's feelings and attitudes which were quite news to him ... he did not appear to know that John loved every corner of the house [41 Queen's Road], felt it to be his home and longed to be there again with his children ... He still said he thought John was not really well and I said I supposed anyway he would not be fully well even when discharged from hospital but would still have to do the final stages of his cure himself and he would need care and I felt he would have to be at Richmond either now or later or we should not get him well at all.

While Dora and Russell were talking, Edith came into the room to tell Russell that there was a phone call for him. He left the room, and when he came back told a surprised Dora that John could stay for lunch, since Russell did, after all, want to speak to him. Taking it as natural that she was not included in this invitation, Dora left, telling John that he should phone her when he was ready to leave and she would come and collect him. Later that afternoon, Dora received a phone call from John, telling her that doctors had arrived at Richmond to serve a committal order on him and that he therefore had no choice but to return to Holloway Sanatorium.

This new Emergency Order gave Russell another seven days in which to get John certified, and he did not waste any time. His petition for John's certification was heard before a magistrate at a rapidly convened Board of Control meeting at Holloway Sanatorium on 7 July, the day before John's order expired. The law that governed this procedure, the Lunacy Act of 1890, gave a person appointed by John the right to be present at the hearing; unfortunately, it did not oblige the petitioner or anyone else to give notice to that person that the hearing was taking place. Thus Dora knew nothing about it until the afternoon of 7 July, when she phoned the sanatorium and was told that the question of John's certification was about to be decided. She at once took a taxi to Virginia Water, but arrived too late to attend the meeting and was shown into the waiting room to await the verdict. Presently the magistrate, two members of the Board and a doctor came into the waiting room to tell Dora that the petition had been unsuccessful. The decision reached was that, though John's condition was serious, he was not certifiable. As the sanatorium was unwilling to take the risk of continuing insulin treatment with a voluntary patient who was also an escapee, John was to be discharged the following morning. The expectation of the Board was clearly that John would move back into Queen's Road to live with his father and his children, but when the Board's decision was communicated by phone to Russell, he flatly refused to have John back and it therefore fell, once again, to Dora to take him home and look after him.

Now that John was not, in the eyes of the law at least, considered insane, Dora hoped that Russell's fear of him, and his evident determination to protect John's own children from him, could be overcome. In this, however, she was to be disappointed. When the girls came home from school, Russell and Edith immediately took them to North Wales to spend the summer at Plas Penrhyn, a house on the Portmeirion peninsula that had recently come on to the market and which Russell was thinking of buying. This Dora learnt from Russell's solicitors, when she contacted them to ask if arrangements could be made for John to see his daughters. The solicitors, she discovered, had not been told that Russell's attempt to certify John had failed and were under the impression that John was still in hospital. In petitioning for his certification, it seems, Russell had acted alone, without consulting his solicitors either about the conduct of the case or its outcome.

The failure of the petition had not changed Russell's attitude at all, except possibly by hardening it against John and, especially, Dora. Meanwhile, though John had legal custody of his children, he had practically no access to them; and though legally considered sane, he clearly needed looking after and remained unfit for work. Upon Dora, therefore, fell the twin tasks of caring for John and of trying to effect some kind of reconciliation between him and his father in order to re-establish his relationship with his daughters. In this she was indefatigable, but to no avail. Her letters to Russell's solicitors requesting meetings remained unanswered, and when she invited the girls to spend two weeks of their summer holidays in Cornwall with her and John, she also received no reply. In an effort to enforce his legal guardianship of the children, John wrote to their nanny, Miss Griffiths, demanding to know when he could see them, but received in reply a letter from Russell giving him two dates at the end of the summer when he could visit the girls in Richmond. Russell, however, insisted that if John came to Queen's Road, he was to come without Dora. This John was unwilling to do, because after his last visit to Richmond, he was terrified that his father might attempt yet again to have him committed to an asylum and certified. He therefore wrote to Russell declining the invitation to Richmond and telling him that he would, instead, see his children at school when they returned there in the autumn.

Towards the end of the summer, Dora wrote to Tyler, asking for an urgent meeting to discuss John's affairs and pleading with him to urge upon Russell a more sympathetic attitude to both her and John. Her own finances, she told him, were in a desperate state and were made much worse by the burden of looking after John, who simply refused to go into hospital and yet needed more or less constant attention. Having access to his children, she argued, would do a great deal to improve John's psychological well-being, as would being invited back to his own flat at Queen's Road – or indeed any sign that his father had some feelings for him other than bitterness, anger and rejection. The letter ended: 'You cannot go on acting as if John did not exist.'

Forwarding this letter to Russell, Tyler remarked: 'I suppose that I ought to see Dora when she comes back from holiday but I shall be glad to have your comments before replying.' Russell's comments came by return of post and were predictably harsh. John could come back to Richmond when he was better, Russell told Tyler, but not while he was still 'terrifying to everybody'. In any case, 'It is not his own flat. It is a part of my house in which I allowed him to live rent free.' As for the problems that Dora had in caring for John, they were, as Russell saw it, entirely of her own making: 'if, as Mrs Grace admits, John needs a degree of care which normal adults do not require he must get this care in an institution. So long as his mother will not face this, the resultant trouble and expense must fall upon her.'

When this (like all Russell's comments to her) was communicated to Dora via his lawyers, she gave up the attempt to get Russell to discuss John's affairs face to face and hired a lawyer of her own, an able and wily Scotsman called Lewis Taylor. For the rest of Russell's life, his ongoing struggle with Dora was conducted as a battle of wits between Tyler and Taylor, a war of attrition in which Taylor was able to score some surprising victories. Within a few months, for example, he was able to reverse Russell's attitude towards the expenses incurred by Dora in looking after John. On 14 November, after a great deal of persistence, Taylor set up a meeting between Tyler, himself and Dora, in which Tyler (on Russell's behalf) promised to pay Dora a quarterly allowance of £50 for looking after John. Though not exactly generous (it was a good deal less than Russell would have had to pay a sanatorium), it represented, at least, some recognition on Russell's part that, in looking after John, Dora was doing something that needed to be done and that Russell himself had no intention of doing. It carried with it, however, what was, from Russell's point of view, an important condition. As Taylor's notes from the meeting put it:

> The stipulation was that Lord Russell should not be bothered . . . as he felt that John was something which he could not cope with and whilst he did not agree with Mrs Grace on a great many things which she was doing he was content to let her carry on.

These notes reveal that, earlier in the negotiations, Russell had made his offer of financial support conditional on Dora and John leaving London and moving to Cornwall, 'but Mr Tyler said that this was not now being insisted on'. With the Christmas holiday approaching, the question arose as to when and how John should see his children. Russell and Edith were planning to take them to Wales for the whole of the Christmas vacation, and, although John was invited to join them, this invitation was issued only after Tyler had been told that John was hardly likely to make the trip alone to Portmeirion, especially as Plas Penrhyn was so close to the cottage in which Susan was living with Wordsworth. Dora's suggestion that she should have the children at her house during the holidays was rejected by Tyler, who felt sure that Russell would not consent to it. In the end, it was agreed that, though 'it should not be a definite term of the arrangement', John should meet his children for tea once or twice during the Christmas period. However, it was stressed, in order to arrange this, that 'there should be no direct bothering of Lord Russell'. Tea with the girls, like everything else, should be arranged through Tyler's office. As Russell saw it, the deal amounted to this: in exchange for £200 a year, he was to be relieved of the responsibility of taking care of John and, perhaps most importantly, was to have no further contact with Dora.

An indication of Russell's resolve in this respect was given at the beginning of December, when John expressed a wish to see his father to try, once more, to overcome the mutual fear and suspicion that had, for years now, characterised their relationship. He phoned the Richmond house and received no answer, so Dora phoned later and left a message with the housekeeper that John would like to come to tea and that she would see that he got there safely and would bring him home. To Russell, this sounded uncomfortably as if Dora herself was coming to tea, and the next day she received the following letter:

Dear Dora,
    I understand that you are proposing to bring John tomorrow when he comes to tea. I hope you will not do this. If I am to see him, I wish to see him tête-à-tête. If he does not wish to see me sufficiently to come unescorted, I would rather put off a meeting until he feels differently. If he is not fit to come by himself, he cannot be as much restored as you have been contending.
    Yours,
    Russell

And so John, 'looking very smart and tidy' (as Dora was keen to emphasise in a letter to her solicitor), went on his own to tea at Richmond and, inevitably, it was a melancholy and disappointing occasion. Russell, John told his mother, looked tired, and John felt sad because 'the whole place there is so different now'. It made him think of Susan and his children, and of how badly things had turned out, and he returned home to his mother chastened and in no great hurry to repeat the experience.

At the start of the children's Christmas holiday, before they were taken off to Wales, they came to Dora's flat for tea. 'They were in fine spirits,' Dora wrote the next day, 'and happy to see their Daddy', though John became obsessed with the idea that Susan should have been there too. So Dora wrote to Susan, telling her what had happened to John since their divorce and asking her if she would be prepared to meet him, since 'it would do him good if he could see you and talk with you'.

Dora's request evidently presented Susan with a dilemma that she did not know quite how to resolve, and it was not until after Christmas that Dora received a reply from Christopher Wordsworth, saying that Susan had not been well herself for the past month and that she had written a letter to Dora but, characteristically, had not posted it. 'There is pain for everyone everywhere all the time in all this,' Wordsworth wrote. 'I am not sanguine that it can yet be alleviated.' This was followed by a note from Susan herself, telling Dora that she did not feel strong enough to see John and enclosing her original reply to Dora's letter, in which she wrote:

> I do not see the children now. I expect this is just as well; there are too many stray persons in their lives; & no way for me to help; and I am sure I shall not be welcome . . . I do not suppose I shall ever see any of you again – that is, it seems unlikely. I would like to send my love to Roddy, if that is possible. I suppose those three poor children will grow up in a sort of (modified!) Pembroke Lodge atmosphere, but I suppose there are worse things.

Though there was little here to bring much comfort to either John or Dora, Susan had put her finger on a very striking and ominous aspect of the whole business. The situation of the little girls at 41 Queen's Road – Anne, ten; Sarah, eight; and Lucy, seven – carried very strong echoes of the situation that Russell and his brother Frank had faced when, at the ages of three and ten respectively, they were put into the care of their grandparents. The chief difference, of course, was that the girls' parents were still alive. In that respect, their situation was even closer to the nightmare Russell had had at the age of twenty-one, when he dreamt that his grandparents had deceived him, that his mother was not dead, but mad and hidden away in an asylum. What gave rise to this dream was Russell's feeling that there must be some horrible secret about his parents, since his grandparents spoke so rarely of them. And, when they did mention them, it was in tones of hushed disapproval that gave the strong impression that they had been very wicked and that Bertie and Frank were better off without them. At 41 Queen's Road, therefore, Russell did not just write his *Autobiography*; he re-created it.

The thought that John regarded 41 Queen's Road as his natural home alarmed Russell so much that when he returned from Wales in the New Year of 1956, he put the house up for sale and made plans to make at Plas Penrhyn a permanent home for himself, Edith and the girls. Of course, he said nothing about this to either Dora or John. Nor did he tell them that he intended taking the girls out of Kingsmuir School and sending them to Moreton Hall, a conventional private school for girls in Shropshire. It fell to Louis Tyler, who had been appointed by Russell as a Trustee of a fund he had set up for the girls, to point out to Russell that 'it would be unwise merely to notify John that you intend to move the children to the proposed school, without giving John any opportunity of comment'. After all, John was – thanks largely to Russell and Tyler themselves – the children's legal guardian. 'I do not mean by this that you should allow yourself to be unduly held up,' Tyler wrote to Russell, but certain legal formalities had to be observed. Accordingly he had written to John, enclosing a copy of the school brochure, and had also spoken to Dora on the phone: 'What she told me was helpful from the angle that it would be difficult for her or John to interfere.

She said John was still unable to make decisions. I asked that John should ring me Tuesday morning latest.'

Of course John did not ring Tyler, and the plan to move the children to Moreton Hall went ahead. At the beginning of July, Dora learnt from the newspapers that Russell was leaving Richmond and moving to Wales. She immediately phoned Queen's Road and complained to Miss Griffiths that John should have been consulted about this, since he looked upon the Richmond house as his home. In any case, he still had belongings such as furniture there, which Russell had no right to sell or move without John's consent. In response, Russell wrote to Tyler, explaining that he had, two years previously, asked John to remove anything from the house that he considered his and to give up any claim to anything he left. He therefore instructed Tyler to write to Dora 'and explain to her that I neither possess nor have disposed of anything belonging to John'. 'I think', he added, 'you had better withhold the next £50 quarterly payment to her until we see what her reaction to the above letter is.'

A few days later, Dora was hit by another family tragedy. On 9 July 1956, her son, Roddy, at the age of twenty-four, was the victim of a terrible mining accident that injured his spine and condemned him to a wheelchair for the rest of his life. The accident happened at a Yorkshire coal-mine where Roddy had gone to work in exchange for being exempted from military service as a conscientious objector. Now Dora had both her sons to look after.[16] On 20 July, she called an urgent meeting between herself, Taylor and Tyler, to discuss her now desperate situation and to ask whether, now that Russell was moving to Wales, there was any chance of her, John and Roddy renting 41 Queen's Road. It was then that she was told that the house had already been sold.

In her despair, Dora wrote a long letter to Russell, telling him about Roddy and giving, yet again, a history of John's life and struggles, and pleading with him to take a more sympathetic attitude. 'After things were settled up last November', Dora wrote, 'I hoped that we might get some co-operation, that you would all ring him up now and then, write to him about the children, take pains to arrange for him to see them.' When she told John that she would have to find a place with a ground floor and a garden for Roddy, she wrote to Russell, John said that the Richmond house would be just the thing: 'To him it was the home he had left for his children with the furniture and all, so that they should not be deprived. To learn that it is all broken up without a word to him or to me is a dreadful shock to us both.' In his (much shorter) reply, Russell expressed surprise that John should feel that way about the house. After all, when he and Susan left Queen's Road, 'I asked John point-blank if he thought of coming back and he said that he did not . . . Their departure was a blow to all I had hoped from the house, a

---

[16] Or so she thought at this time; in fact, as it turned out, Roddy went to live with his sister, Harriet, in a flat in Broadhurst Gardens, Hampstead, where he was well-looked after and lived a surprisingly full and independent life.

bitter wound to my affection for John, and the source of a great deal of unexpected expense.'

Without realising how much she was testing Russell's patience, Dora replied to this letter directly to him, rather than – as the financial settlement agreed in November 1955 demanded – through his solicitor. After describing further the situation regarding Roddy, she wrote, apropos of John seeing his children during the summer: 'In September, perhaps I might bring him down to the neighbourhood [of Portmeirion] for a short time, if he will come.' Upon reading this letter, Russell immediately forwarded it to his solicitor, together with the following note:

Dear Tyler,

I enclose a letter from Dora for you to keep. You will observe that she suggests coming to our neighbourhood with John sometime. I should be grateful if you will let her know that, while we are at all times willing to see John, I am not willing to see Dora except for business purposes in the presence of my lawyer and I do not wish her to come to this house, even in my absence, except in similar circumstances.

The claim that Russell was 'at all times willing to see John' should not be taken at face value. The steps that he took in the summer of 1956 would, as Russell well knew, make it extremely difficult for John to see either his children or his father. In moving himself, Edith and John's children to Plas Penrhyn, and in transferring the girls to a school in Shropshire, Russell was quite consciously making a clean break, quite deliberately making both himself and the children inaccessible to John. After moving to Wales, Russell did not see his son again for the rest of his life, except for one brief meeting in 1960. He continued to deal with Dora through their respective lawyers, and, whenever she proved troublesome (which was often), he threatened to withhold her £50 quarterly allowance. Under no circumstances would he be persuaded to meet her face to face. Meanwhile, Dora struggled to cope with John, who was never again able to work or look after himself, and Russell got on with the task of saving humanity.

11

'REMEMBER YOUR HUMANITY
AND FORGET THE REST'

On 23 December 1954, as John lay in an insulin-induced coma in Guy's
Hospital, Russell made the most dramatic and widely celebrated radio
broadcast of his life: 'Man's Peril'. Designed as a 'solemn appeal to mankind
to turn back from universal suicide', the broadcast achieved its impact by
spelling out, in the starkest possible terms, the fact that, with the advent of
the hydrogen bomb, mankind now had the power to wipe out all life on
earth. Quoting a succession of military experts to the effect that a world war
would now threaten total destruction, Russell put the following 'dreadful
and inescapable' question to his listeners: 'Shall we put an end to the human
race: or shall mankind renounce war?' The broadcast ended with words that
would, over the ensuing years, be quoted over and over again:

> There lies before us, if we choose, continual progress in happiness,
> knowledge, and wisdom. Shall we, instead, choose death, because we
> cannot forget our quarrels? I appeal, as a human being to human beings:
> remember your humanity, and forget the rest. If you can do so, the way
> lies open to a new Paradise; if you cannot, nothing lies before you, but
> universal death.

These sonorous phrases marked Russell's return to public life, after the
years of relative political inactivity that had followed his 1951 lecture tour of
the USA. During those years, the world had changed a great deal. In the
UK, Attlee's Labour Government had been replaced by a Conservative
Ministry, headed by the rapidly ageing Winston Churchill; in the USA, the
Democratic President Truman had been replaced by the Republican
Eisenhower; and in the USSR, the death of Stalin in March 1953 had made
possible the creation, under Nikita Khrushchev, of a far less repressive
regime. The net effect of these changes of government on Russell was to
weaken still further his previously passionate commitment to the Western
side in the Cold War, and to accelerate his progress towards a neutral stance,
which saw the threat facing mankind as neither Communism nor capitalism
but the conflict between the two. The Korean War, which in 1950 Russell
had been certain would lead to global nuclear conflict, ended in stalemate in
July 1953, with an armistice agreement that maintained the division between

North and South. However, new areas of potential conflict were emerging all the time, and meanwhile the consequences of global war escalated exponentially.

On 1 March 1954, at Bikini Atoll in the South Pacific, the USA successfully tested a usable H-bomb for the first time, and, though it was to be twenty months before the Soviet Union tested an H-bomb of its own, no informed observer in 1954 doubted that the Soviet Union would, sooner or later, have its own arsenal of thermonuclear weapons. The danger of even testing these weapons was revealed to the world a few weeks after the Bikini test, when it was discovered that the crew of a Japanese fishing boat (ironically called the *Lucky Dragon*) had returned to port suffering from radiation sickness caused by the fallout from the H-bomb, despite fishing some seventy miles away from the test site – that is, well outside the official 'danger zone'. Evidently, the danger from the fallout was much greater than had previously been estimated. When one considers that the official estimate was that the bomb tested at Bikini was 600 times more powerful than the atom bomb that destroyed Hiroshima, one begins to see why, at the end of 1954, the world was ready to listen to Russell's plea to do *something* to avert the peril that now faced the whole of mankind.

But what *could* be done? The hope that the use of hydrogen bombs might be prohibited, Russell told his listeners, was illusory, since whatever agreements were reached in times of peace would no longer be considered binding as soon as war broke out. War itself must be abolished. But how? Neither side in the Cold War could declare itself unwilling to go to war without putting itself at the mercy of the other side, so the only hope, Russell suggested, lay with the neutral countries, which somehow must convince the participants in the Cold War that the issues that separated them must not be decided by war. On the subject of how this was to be achieved, 'Man's Peril' contained a surprisingly specific proposal:

> I should like to see one or more neutral powers appoint a commission of experts, who should all be neutrals, to draw up a report on the destructive effects to be expected in a war with hydrogen bombs, not only among the belligerents but also among neutrals. I should wish this report presented to the governments of all the Great Powers with an invitation to express their agreement or disagreement with its findings. I think it possible that in this way all the Great Powers could be led to agree that a world war can no longer serve the purposes of any of them, since it is likely to exterminate friend and foe equally and neutrals likewise.

Among the huge correspondence that Russell received in response to 'Man's Peril' was a letter from the French physicist, Frédéric Joliot-Curie, dated 31 January 1955, in which he urged Russell to support the idea, already put forward by the World Federation of Scientific Workers (of which Joliot-Curie was President), of an international conference of eminent scientists. They would collectively produce an 'objective statement' on the threat of nuclear weapons and also on 'the potential benefits of scientific discovery'. In some ways, of course, this idea bore obvious similarities to Russell's proposal in 'Man's Peril' for a 'commission of experts'. However, it was an essential part of Russell's plan that the commission should be appointed by, and composed of, *neutrals*, and as Joliot-Curie was a member of the Communist Party and the World Federation of Scientific Workers was widely regarded as a Communist front organisation, a conference arranged under their auspices would hardly fit the bill. In his letter to Russell, Joliot-Curie admitted that 'lingering reservations and suspicions' had hindered the response to his proposed conference, but, he went on, 'Such doubts would vanish if some great, universally respected figures, such as yourself, gave the support of their great authority to the idea.'

As Russell well realised, there was a danger here that he was being flattered into lending his name to, and thereby conferring respectability upon, what was essentially a Communist Party initiative. Though Joliot-Curie was a Nobel Prize-winner and the most eminent nuclear physicist in France, he was an extremely controversial figure. In the 1930s he had been one of the pioneers in the discovery of nuclear fission, and one of the first to recognise its potential military importance. A lifelong Socialist, he had fought with the French Resistance during the war, and joined the Communist Party in 1942. After the war, he was appointed by President de Gaulle as the first High Commissioner of the French Atomic Energy Commission, but in 1950 he was removed from this post because of his Communist Party loyalties. During the Korean War he had been at the centre of a fierce controversy because of his widely disputed claim to have investigated and confirmed the Communist accusations that the United States was using germ warfare in Korea. Sidney Hook, an erstwhile friend and collaborator of Russell's, had been particularly incensed by what he saw as this misuse by Joliot-Curie of his scientific prestige and had asked all American Nobel Prize-winners to sign a letter to Joliot-Curie, asking him to join them in an objective scientific investigation of the charge or to withdraw his allegation. The only person to refuse to sign Hook's letter was Albert Einstein, who told Hook that, though he was disappointed by Joliot-Curie's insincerity, he did not want to put his name to something that would serve only to fan the flames of ideological conflict.

After weighing up the pros and cons of being publicly associated with such a figure, Russell replied to Joliot-Curie on 4 February, rejecting his idea of a conference, but keeping alive the possibility that the two might collaborate somehow in warning governments and the general public about the dangers of nuclear weapons. With regard to the obvious difficulty that Joliot-Curie was a partisan rather than a neutral in the Cold War, Russell sought refuge in his long-standing and deep-seated view that science *itself* was neutral, whatever the ideological commitments of individual scientists. As he put it to Joliot-Curie: 'We all have our prejudices in favour of one side or the other, but in view of the common peril it seems to me that men capable of scientific detachment ought to be able to achieve an intellectual neutrality, however little they may be neutral emotionally.'

On 11 February, Russell wrote to Einstein himself, urging him to support the idea of getting 'six men of the very highest scientific repute, headed by yourself, to make a very solemn statement about the imperative necessity of avoiding war'. This statement, apart from making a 'clear and dramatic impression upon the public', would, Russell proposed, be used to further the idea he had put forward in 'Man's Peril' of appealing to neutral states to appoint a commission of neutral scientists to draw up a report on the probable effects of nuclear war, which would then be published and presented to the governments of the Great Powers. 'Neutral nations', Russell argued in his letter to Einstein, 'are more likely to consider such a scheme favourably if they know that there is important support for it in countries which are not neutral.' In this respect, the fact that Joliot-Curie was well known to be a Communist made him an ideal candidate to be one of the six eminent signatories to the statement that Russell had in mind, so long as his presence was counterbalanced by American atomic scientists, who, though 'anxious to find some way of preventing atomic disaster', could not be accused of Communism. Could Einstein help in securing the collaboration of any such people?

As to what such a statement would contain, Russell provided Einstein with a list of five points which, taken together, amount more or less to 'Man's Peril'. Among the points he emphasised were that 'it would be wholly futile to get an agreement prohibiting the H-bomb' and that 'in any attempt to avoid atomic war the strictest neutrality is to be observed'. For this reason, Russell insisted, 'if eminent scientists can be induced to make a pronouncement, it would be a good thing if some were known Communists and others known anti-Communists'.

Einstein responded favourably to Russell's letter and, by April, Russell had a draft of the statement to send to Einstein and the other invited signatories. This draft was essentially a shortened version of 'Man's Peril', written after consultation with the Cambridge physicist, Eric Burhop, a Communist and leading member of the World Federation of Scientific Workers, who had been urged to see Russell by Joliot-Curie. The result of Burhop's intervention was what Russell described in a letter to Joliot-Curie as 'important changes with a view to conciliating Communist opinion'. The best guess as to what those changes amounted to is the inclusion of the following paragraph, which is, indeed, the only place in which the statement departs substantially from the text of 'Man's Peril':

Although an agreement to renounce nuclear weapons as part of a general reduction of armaments would not afford an ultimate solution, it would serve certain important purposes. First, any agreement between East and West is to the good in so far as it tends to diminish tension. Second, the abolition of thermo-nuclear weapons, if each side believed the other had carried it out sincerely, would lessen the fear of a sudden attack in the style of Pearl Harbor, which at present keeps both sides in a state of nervous apprehension. We should, therefore, welcome such an agreement though only as a first step.

This is startlingly different from the view Russell had expressed to Einstein that an agreement to prohibit nuclear weapons would be 'wholly futile', and one cannot help feeling that Russell had here given way, not only to Communist opinion, but also to Communist interests. For the abolition of thermonuclear weapons in April 1955 would obviously have been more in the interests of the Soviet Union (which did not at that time actually have any) than in those of the United States (which did). When he was asked about this passage, Russell made clear that, for him, the emphasis lay not on the abolition of thermonuclear weapons, but on the phrase 'as part of a general reduction in armaments'. Asked, in particular, whether he favoured the renunciation of nuclear weapons by the West on moral grounds, he replied:

No, most emphatically not. I do not think that is the right way to go about it ... If you can induce the Communist world to reduce its armaments to a degree that is as important for us as would be that renunciation of thermo-nuclear weapons, then you have got a real step forward. But I do not want to see thermo-nuclear weapons abolished if you are not going to get from the other side a *quid pro quo* which is really of equal military importance.

For his part, Eric Burhop clearly felt that the statement represented a compromise on both sides. 'Of course he [Russell] remains a convinced advocate of World Government,' Burhop wrote to his colleague Pierre Biquard on 8 April. 'But he has carefully refrained from referring to that in the document. On our part we believe that peace can only be secure when capitalism and imperialism have been eliminated. But we also do not insist on saying this in the document. That is as it should be.'

Russell, indeed, considered World Government to be the only means of abolishing war, and in the middle of April he travelled to Rome and Paris to address meetings of the Parliamentary World Government Association. On 18 April, on his way from Rome to Paris, he heard the shocking news that Einstein had died. 'I felt shattered,' he later wrote, 'not only for the obvious reasons, but because I saw my plan falling through without his support.' When, however, he arrived at his Paris hotel, he found waiting for him a letter from Einstein agreeing to sign the statement.

While in Paris, Russell had a long discussion with Joliot-Curie, in which they went through the statement sentence by sentence. However, any hopes that Joliot-Curie might have had of making further substantial changes to the document had been scotched by Einstein's death, since Russell was determined above all to keep Einstein's signature, and, therefore, the document as signed by him. After trying unsuccessfully several times to change the statement, Joliot-Curie hesitated to sign it himself until the very last moment, when he finally agreed on condition that one or two qualifications were added as footnotes. The most telling of these was after the question: 'Shall we put an end to the human race; or shall mankind renounce war?', to which Joliot-Curie wanted to add: 'as a means of settling

differences between States', presumably because he did not want to
renounce war, or, anyway, violent revolution, as a means of settling
differences *within* states.

The taint of Communism put off some of the big names that Russell
hoped would sign the statement, including, most notably, Otto Hahn and
Niels Bohr, but, by the end of June, he had succeeded in obtaining the
signatures of nine of the most eminent scientists in the world, eight of whom
were Nobel Prize-winners. As well as Einstein, Joliot-Curie and Russell
himself, the signatories were: Max Born, Percy Bridgman, Leopold Infield,
Hermann Müller, Linus Pauling, Cecil Powell and Hideki Yukawa. Few of
these names would have meant very much to the general public, but, from
the point of view of gaining publicity for the statement, this mattered little,
since not only had Einstein signed, but his signature could fairly be
represented as the last public act of his life, thus guaranteeing maximum
media and popular interest.

Capitalising on this rather grim piece of good fortune, Russell, together
with the *Observer* newspaper, organised a press conference at Caxton Hall in
London, at which the 'Russell-Einstein Manifesto' (as it came to be called)
would be launched. Needing someone to chair the press conference, who
would be able to field any technical questions that might be asked, Russell,
after receiving several rejections, turned to Joseph Rotblat, a Professor of
Physics at St Bartholomew's Hospital Medical College in London, who had
worked in Los Alamos and whom Russell had got to know a year earlier
when they appeared together on a BBC television programme discussing the
consequences of the Bikini test. Rotblat (whose signature was added to the
document) turned out to be the ideal choice; and he has subsequently
devoted his life to the ideals expressed in the document, a devotion for
which he was rewarded with the Nobel Peace Prize in 1995.

The date fixed for the Caxton Hall meeting was 9 July 1955. Immediately
beforehand Russell had what he describes (twice) in his *Autobiography* as a
'dreadful week'. The invitations to the meeting sent out to journalists and
broadcasters said only that 'something important of world-wide interest' was
about to be published, without saying what it was. Thus, as the date of the
meeting approached, Russell was besieged with enquiries from journalists
wanting to know what this important piece of news might be. 'All day long',
Russell remembered, 'the telephone rang and the door-bell pealed.' This
happened to be the week that Russell's petition to certify John came before a
magistrate, and so 'when the telephone was not ringing about that subject
[the Caxton Hall meeting], it was ringing to give me most distressing news
about my elder son's illness'.

Not surprisingly, given the strain he was under, at the meeting to launch
the statement Russell made a couple of slips that showed, perhaps, that his
mind was not fully on the job. First, he described Rotblat as 'Director of
Research in Nuclear Physics in Liverpool', a mistake that Rotblat graciously
affected not to notice, but the shame of which, Russell later recalled,
'swelled to immense proportions in my mind. The disgrace of it prevented
me from even speaking of it.' Then, much more seriously and more

embarrassingly, Russell not only left Max Born's name off the list of signatories, but even said that Born had refused to sign. 'This was a serious blunder on my part,' he later said, 'and one that I have never stopped regretting.'

Despite these slips, the meeting went extremely well. The hall was packed, and the following day newspapers around the world gave front-page coverage to 'Einstein's Last Warning'. After the meeting was over, Russell left for Wales for a holiday with Edith and John's daughters, and when he returned to Richmond at the end of the summer, his time was taken up with World Government conferences, first in Paris and then in London. It was therefore not until 1956 that he could give his full attention to the problem of how best to implement the manifesto's call for a conference of scientists to 'appraise the perils that have arisen as a result of the development of weapons of mass destruction, and to discuss a resolution in the spirit of the appended draft'.

In this, he enlisted the help of Joseph Rotblat, Cecil Powell and Eric Burhop (Joliot-Curie being by this time too ill to take an active part), who became in effect the organising committee. The arranging of an international conference is almost invariably a time-consuming and difficult task, but in this case it was especially long-winded, because it was felt necessary that the invitations to attend the conference should be sent out under the names of all the signatories to the Russell-Einstein Manifesto. Thus, before they could begin to invite people, they had to send out to all the signatories a draft of the letter of invitation to the conference, together with a list of proposed participants. This preliminary process itself took several weeks, and, in the event, two signatories to the manifesto, Percy Bridgman and Hermann Müller, refused to put their names to the letter of invitation. It was not until the end of August that invitations could finally be sent out to an agreed list of thirty-five scientists from around the world, and by the time their responses began to come back (of those, twenty-three agreed to take part), the political events of the autumn of 1956, particularly the Suez and Hungary crises, had made it look doubtful that the conference could take place at all.

In pursuit of his original intention that the conference should take place under the auspices of a neutral state, Russell had hoped that it could be held in India. In the New Year of 1955, immediately after making the 'Man's Peril' broadcast, but before the Russell-Einstein Manifesto had been drawn up, Russell had taken the opportunity of meeting Nehru during his visit to London, and had received from him a warm response to the idea that India might play host to the neutral 'commission of experts' envisaged in Russell's broadcast. This was followed up in February 1956 by Cecil Powell, who secured from Nehru a promise that the conference proposed by the Russell-Einstein Manifesto could be held in New Delhi, shortly before the Indian Science Conference, due to take place there in January 1957. The Anglo-French invasion of Suez in October, and the subsequent closure of the Suez Canal in November, made this plan impractical, and, on 22 November 1956, letters were sent out to all the participants telling them that the conference had been cancelled.

The idea, however, was not yet completely dead. Earlier in the year, immediately after the publication of the Russell-Einstein Manifesto, Russell had received a letter from Cyrus Eaton, a wealthy Canadian industrialist, offering to host the proposed conference at his home in Pugwash, Nova Scotia. Russell now wrote to Eaton and received in reply confirmation that the offer still stood. So it was that what became known as the 'Pugwash Movement' was inaugurated in July 1957, when twenty-one scientists from both sides of the Iron Curtain (including seven from the USA and three from the USSR) met at Pugwash to discuss the dangers of nuclear weapons and to pass resolutions urging their governments to renounce war. They did so under three headings: 1. The hazards of atomic energy; 2. The control of nuclear weapons; 3. The social responsibilities of scientists. Russell himself was unable to attend because of illness, but he was kept in close touch with the proceedings by letter and phone.

At this first conference, a 'Continuing Committee' was established to organise further conferences. Russell, naturally, was elected Chairman of the committee and was subsequently made President of the Pugwash Movement, but really, from this point on, his role in the movement was that of a founder and inspirational figurehead, rather than that of an active participant. At the third Pugwash Conference in Austria in 1958 he gave a presidential address, and at its conference in London in 1962 he gave a speech on the founding of the movement, but, by and large, he left the tasks of organising, and even attending, the conferences to others. Though in its early years the Pugwash Movement attracted the attention of the US Security Forces, who suspected it of being a Communist front organisation, in time the obvious sincerity of the scientists taking part in its meetings (of which, to date, there have been about 250) established for it an impeccable reputation as a sober and respectable body that governments could trust, listen to and learn from, and it is widely credited with having been responsible for the partial Test-Ban Treaty of 1964. It still exists today, its reputation enhanced by the 1995 Nobel Peace Prize, which was awarded, in equal parts, to Joseph Rotblat, now President of Pugwash, and the Pugwash Conferences on Science and World Affairs.

As the Pugwash Movement became respectable, Russell's interest in it declined. Though he was happy to lend it moral support, it was not, in truth, his kind of political movement. Low-profile annual conferences of scientists giving long, intricate papers on detailed questions of technology, or even of social and political policy, were not for him (at one of the few conferences he attended, he was heard to remark, as a scientist exceeded his allotted time with a particularly long address: 'now is the time to drop the bomb'). He longed for something more direct, more dramatic, something that would, like 'Man's Peril' and the Russell-Einstein Manifesto, hit the headlines. Moreover, he wanted the general public, and the leaders of the world, to listen, not only to good sense and reason, but to *him*, Bertrand Russell. It was telling, in this respect, that in his presidential address at the

1958 Pugwash Conference in Austria, Russell invoked the name and memory of his grandfather, Lord John Russell, recalling how Lord John had attended a diplomatic conference in Vienna 103 years previously and had pressed for peace with Russia. 'I, alas, cannot speak for the British Government,' Russell told his audience on that occasion, 'but I equally stand for peace.' The comparison with his grandfather is revealing. Russell wanted to be treated, like Lord John had been, as an equal by the leading statesmen of his day. And he wanted to be seen by the general public as a person with something important to say about world affairs and the plight of mankind, something to which the political leaders of the day *ought* to listen.

In November 1957, these desires found their purest expression in an open letter to President Eisenhower and Premier Khrushchev that Russell published in the *New Statesman*. Beginning 'Most Potent Sirs', the letter sought to convince the respective heads of the two most powerful countries in the world that, on the most important questions, their interests did not diverge, but rather coincided. In particular, Russell argued, they had a joint interest in: 1. The continued existence of the human race; 2. The international control of nuclear weapons (that is, in preventing the ownership of such weapons from spreading to more and more countries); 3. The reduction of military expenditure; 4. The dispersal of 'the pall of fear which at present dims the hopes of mankind'.

What Russell suggested was that Eisenhower and Khrushchev should meet 'in a frank discussion of the conditions of co-existence', seeking 'such agreements and such adjustments in the world as will diminish future occasions of strife'. In a typical piece of Russellian utopian rhetoric, the letter ended: 'I believe that if you were to do this, the world would acclaim your action, and the forces of sanity, released from their long bondage, would ensure for the years to come a life of vigour and achievement and joy surpassing anything known in even the happiest eras of the past.'

This open letter is most naturally read as a piece of journalism, but in his *Autobiography* Russell reveals that, in his mind, it was a serious attempt to influence policy. Explaining his reasons for writing the letter, he writes: 'I felt that I must again do something to urge at least a modicum of common sense to break into the policies of the two Great Powers, Russia and America.' He was encouraged in this exaggerated notion of his place in world politics when, to the amazement of everyone concerned, Khrushchev actually replied, though of course the reply was sent not to Russell personally, but to the *New Statesman*. Sensing an opportunity to make effective propaganda, Khrushchev conceded Russell's argument that peaceful co-existence between the USSR and the USA was in everybody's interests and claimed that the Soviet Union, despite the USA's belligerent attitude, had tried – and would continue to try – to pursue peace. Khrushchev laid particular emphasis on the importance of abolishing nuclear weapons. 'The Soviet Union', he wrote, 'considers that the danger of atomic war will only be removed finally and completely when the manufacture and use of atomic and hydrogen weapons will have been completely prohibited and the stockpiles destroyed.'

The letter demanded some kind of response from the United States, and two months later the Secretary of State, John Foster Dulles, replied on Eisenhower's behalf. Instead of emphasising, as Khrushchev had done, his agreement with Russell's points, Dulles chose to argue that certain aspects of Communism (for instance, its commitment to class warfare and revolution) were *inherently* violent, while the 'creed of the United States is based on the moral law'. Therefore, he argued, 'it is necessary that at least that part of the Soviet Communist creed should be abandoned in order to achieve the peaceful result which is sought by Lord Russell and all other peace-loving people'. This provoked a further long letter from Khrushchev, in which he defended Communism at great length, but, with a nod towards Russell's original letter, ended by insisting that 'there is no need for either the Soviet Union or the United States of America to renounce its own ideology'.

The correspondence was rounded off on 5 April 1958 with a final word from Russell, who described Khrushchev and Dulles as 'rival fanatics, each blinded to obvious facts by mental blinkers'. The particular obvious fact he had in mind was that: 'If we grant for the moment the hypothesis of each, that the victory of his system would be a boon to the human race, it still does not follow that either side should favour a war in which both sides, as well as non-participants, will be exterminated.' Actually, neither Khrushchev nor Dulles said or implied that it *did* follow, nor did either of them speak in favour of war in any context. Nevertheless, Russell went on: 'This is so simple and so obvious that one cannot but be amazed at the incapacity of intelligent men to grasp its consequences.' What he had in mind, presumably, was that *if* they could see the consequences of this 'obvious fact', then both Dulles and Khrushchev would appreciate the need for peaceful co-existence. However, this too missed the mark. For neither Khrushchev nor Dulles had argued *against* peaceful co-existence; Khrushchev had argued warmly in favour of it, and Dulles had argued, not that it was undesirable, but that, given the nature of Communism, it was impossible – an argument that echoes some of Russell's own earlier pronouncements.

Despite heaping scorn on both sides, Russell was clearly more impressed (or perhaps 'flattered' is the word) by Khrushchev's long letters than by Dulles's rather terse rejoinder. 'I think', he wrote in his summing up, 'that Mr Khrushchev comes nearer than Mr Dulles to advocating the sort of policy which is called for.' He then rather curiously singled out as 'the most hopeful passage I can find in his letter' Khrushchev's suggestion that 'a strict prohibition on atomic and hydrogen weapons' should be imposed immediately – a suggestion Russell had repeatedly dismissed as 'futile'. Indeed, just a few months before his letter to Eisenhower and Khrushchev, Russell had argued that the abolition of the hydrogen bomb was not only not possible, but undesirable. 'I'm not in favour of its abolition', he had said in an interview in May 1957. 'Fear is a great and effective force in human nature. The H-bomb is a real deterrent.' In a private letter to Lord Simon in October 1958, he appealed to the same kind of argument, when, in expounding the view that the USA's nuclear force provided an effective defence of Western democracies, he wrote: 'Consider the question: Why does Russia not occupy Western Berlin? I see no answer except fear of America.'

Summing up his reactions to the correspondence in his autobiography, Russell wrote: 'The righteously adamantine surface of Mr Dulles's mind as shown in his letter filled me with greater foreboding than did the fulminations and, sometimes, contradictions of Mr Khrushchev. The latter seemed to me to show some underlying understanding of alternatives and realities; the former, none.'

As Russell got older, he increasingly took personally every dissent from his views, rendering him incapable of distinguishing between criticism of his opinions and attacks on *him*. This tendency had always been apparent in his political writing, where he often seemed unable or unwilling to admit that honest disagreement with him was possible, but in the 1950s this attitude began to spread to his philosophical writings as well, which often struck a note of wounded pride and personal pique. After his return to Cambridge in 1944, Russell had been dismayed to discover that Moore and Wittgenstein were held in greater regard by the younger generation of philosophers than himself. Now, in the 1950s, he discovered that even Frege, whose work had been neglected until Russell drew attention to it, was admired more than he was, especially at Oxford, which had by this time taken over from Cambridge as the leading centre of British philosophy.

Between 1954 and 1959, Russell published a series of articles attacking Oxford philosophy, which served to alienate him still further from the leading philosophers of the day. Two of those philosophers, Gilbert Ryle and Peter Strawson – both singled out for particularly venomous attacks by Russell – were puzzled by the tone of his polemics against them, since they both had a profound admiration for Russell, which they expressed publicly on a number of occasions. Their admiration, however, did not take the form of accepting without question everything that he said. As Strawson once put it, when asked about Russell: 'Of course he is vastly superior, intellectually, to anyone here. But I wish he wouldn't think that we ought all therefore to agree with him!'

In 1950, Strawson published an article in *Mind* called 'On Referring', which contained what many people at the time took to be devastating criticisms of Russell's celebrated Theory of Descriptions. Russell did not know of the existence of this article until 1956, when Rupert Crawshay-Williams drew it to his attention, whereupon Russell wrote a rejoinder called 'Mr Strawson on Referring', which was published in *Mind* in July 1957. At the root of the difference between Russell and Strawson was that, whereas Russell's interest in descriptive phrases was technical and motivated by his concern to develop a formal theory of logic that was free from contradiction and adequate for his purposes in *Principia Mathematica*, Strawson's interest was in analysing how descriptive phrases are actually used in ordinary language, and his central point was that, from this point of view, Russell's theory was inadequate. Though, in his reply to Strawson, Russell made one or two telling points in defence of his original theory and its technical motivation, the effectiveness of his argument was weakened by its over-polemical tone and by his determination to represent Strawson's interest in the pragmatics of ordinary language as marking him out as a member of the 'Cult of "Common Usage"', upon which Russell had, in a radio talk broadcast a few years earlier, heaped abuse as a philosophical movement that was insincere, trivial and ignorant.

Strawson was slightly embarrassed by Russell's article, which he considered unworthy of the great philosopher that Russell had once been, and he did not deign to reply to it, thus incensing Russell, who, ever afterwards, referred to Strawson – only half-jokingly – as 'the enemy'. Relations between the two did not improve until 1962, when, at A. J. Ayer's prompting, Strawson managed to temper Russell's ire with a tactful and mollifying letter.

Russell's other chief 'enemy' was Gilbert Ryle, who, as Waynflete Professor of Metaphysics at Oxford and editor of *Mind*, was at that time, and for many years to come, the most influential figure in British philosophy. In 1957, Ryle had irritated Russell by accepting a rather second-rate article for *Mind* called 'Infinity', by E. R. Emmett, which consisted entirely of an attack on Russell's early views on mathematics, and particularly his view, derived from Georg Cantor, that there exist infinite numbers. What, understandably, exasperated Russell about this article was its apparent ignorance of the body of work on mathematical logic to which Russell's own discussions on the notion of infinity had been a contribution. In a terse and scathing reply to Emmett, which Russell sent to Ryle for inclusion in *Mind*, he drew attention to this ignorance and the errors to which it led. 'The subject of infinite numbers', Russell sniffed, 'is a technical and not very easy branch of mathematics, and those who have not studied it cannot hope to say anything sensible about it.' Though he eventually agreed to publish Russell's reply, Ryle initially tried to talk him out of it, appealing to him to withdraw it for his own sake, an appeal that angered Russell and struck him as 'sheer hypocrisy'.

Like a boxer coming out of retirement to have one last attempt at regaining his title, Russell was determined to have a public spat with Ryle, and in 1958 he published a review of Ryle's most celebrated book, *The Concept of Mind*, despite the fact that it had, by then, been in print for nearly ten years. The point on which Russell was especially concerned to do battle was Ryle's insistence that mental events – thoughts, beliefs, and so on – are not *essentially* private, upon which, Russell alleged, Ryle was 'astonishingly slap-dash and content to let dogmatic assertion take the place of refutation of adverse theories'. To Russell, it seemed obvious that, for example, dreams, pains and thoughts are private events, which can, if we wish them to, *remain* private and inaccessible to others. Ryle had maintained that mental events invariably have external manifestations; pains, for example, are made known to others by groans and other expressions of suffering. 'Evidently', Russell wittily remarked, 'none of his friends are Stoics.'

Russell's greatest scorn, however, was reserved for Ryle's neglect and apparent ignorance of science: 'He seems to believe that the philosopher need not know anything scientific beyond what was known in the time of our ancestors when they dyed themselves with woad.' Like Strawson, Ryle angered Russell by not replying to what had obviously been intended as an opening shot in a public confrontation.

Soon after writing his review of Ryle, Russell fulfilled a long-standing promise to Stanley Unwin to produce a purely intellectual autobiography. The result, *My Philosophical Development*, takes the reader through the various stages of his thought in an engagingly lucid and stimulating way and is essential reading for anyone interested in the development, not only of Russell's work, but also of twentieth-century English-speaking philosophy in general. The climax of the book is its penultimate chapter, 'The Retreat from Pythagoras', in which Russell summarises his intellectual journey as a gradual and sometimes agonistic abandonment of the Pythagorean vision that had motivated his early work on mathematics. In the final chapter, 'Some Replies to Criticism', Russell could not resist collecting together his polemical writing about Oxford philosophy, which, he alleges, concerns itself 'not with the world and our relation to it, but only with the different ways in which silly people can say silly things'. In including his articles on Ryle and Strawson in this chapter, Russell clearly meant to represent them as the leading figures in this 'silly' movement. The chapter begins with some prefatory remarks in which Russell comes close to confessing the personal pique that motivated his attacks:

> It is not an altogether pleasant experience to find oneself regarded as antiquated after having been, for a time, in the fashion. It is difficult to accept this experience gracefully.

Despite the inclusion of these articles in *My Philosophical Development*, however, the Oxford philosophers still refused to rise to Russell's bait, and the public controversy that he wished to have with them remained a one-sided outbreak of hostilities.

In 1959, Russell was offered another chance to bait Ryle, which he seized upon eagerly and this time provoked at least some response. The occasion was the publication of *Words and Things*, a polemical attack on Oxford philosophy by the sociologist Ernest Gellner. Like Russell, Gellner regarded the philosophers at Oxford as constituting a single 'School of Ordinary Language Philosophy', which trivialised the subject by reducing it to linguistic analysis. This ignored the differences between the philosophers at Oxford and led Gellner, as it had previously led Russell, to conflate Ryle's philosophy of mind and Strawson's metaphysics with the work of *real* linguistic philosophers like J. L. Austin. Russell, of course, was delighted by Gellner's attack on his 'enemies' and offered to contribute a Preface to *Words and Things*, endorsing Gellner's views. In the Preface, Russell wrote that Gellner's book 'deserves the gratitude of all who cannot accept the linguistic philosophy now in vogue at Oxford'. He also took the opportunity to add some fresh abuse of his own, pillorying Oxford philosophers as genteel classics scholars who had taken refuge in the trivialities of linguistic philosophy as a means of protecting themselves from the fact that, in a world that had been transformed by science and democracy, they were ossified relics of a bygone era. The philosophers at Oxford, Russell sniped, 'do not reject *all* learning, but only such as is not required for a First in Greats – i.e., such as has been discovered since the time of Erasmus'.

When the book was published, a review copy was sent to *Mind*, but Ryle returned it to the publisher with a note explaining that he would not commission a review, since: 'Abusiveness may make a book saleable, but it disqualifies it from being treated as contribution to an academic subject.' Upon learning of this, Russell immediately wrote a letter to *The Times*, saying that he found Ryle's attitude 'deeply shocking', since it suggested that 'all books that do not endorse Professor Ryle's opinions' were to be 'boycotted in the pages of *Mind*' – in which case, Russell wrote, 'that hitherto-respected periodical will sink to the level of a mutual-admiration organ of a coterie'. This prompted a flurry of further correspondence on the subject, including a defence by Ryle of his editorial decision not to review the book and another letter from Russell, arguing that, even if Gellner's book *had* been abusive, this was no reason not to review it. The dispute attracted the attention of other newspapers and magazines, and inspired the writer Ved Mehta to produce an extended discussion of the controversy in his delightfully written book, *Fly and the Fly Bottle*. Starting off with a view sympathetic to Russell and Gellner, Mehta went to Oxford himself to meet some of the despised 'ordinary language philosophers' and discovered that, contrary to the attacks made upon them, they were indeed a very diverse group. As part of his research for the book, Mehta went to meet Russell and found him slightly unwilling to discuss anything so unimportant when the future of humanity lay in the balance:

> When we were comfortably settled with our tea, he began interviewing me. Why was I concerned with philosophy when my life was in peril? I should jolly well be doing something about the atomic bomb, to keep the Russians and Americans from sending us all up in flames. Anyone might personally prefer death to slavery, but only a lunatic would think of making that choice for humanity.

Russell had indeed decided to 'forget the rest', and his controversy with Ryle over Gellner's book was to be his last contribution to philosophical debate. His only other piece of writing after this that was even ostensibly on philosophy was an article entitled 'The Duty of a Philosopher in This Age', written in 1964, which he contributed to a collection of essays in honour of Paul Schilpp, called *The Abdication of Philosophy*. However, this was not really on philosophy at all, but rather on the threat of nuclear weapons, and might indeed be regarded as an elaboration of his remarks to Ved Mehta. For the duty of a philosopher in this age, Russell argued in this piece, was to forget philosophy and to study 'the probable effects of a nuclear war':

> He must, then, devote himself, by whatever means are open to him, to persuading other people to agree with him as to these effects and to joining him in whatever protest shows the most chance of success.

'If they do not fulfil this duty', Russell insisted, 'they are accomplices in mass murder.' Looked at like this, in the last ten years of his life, though Russell wrote no more on philosophy – indeed, precisely in not writing any more on philosophy – he was perfectly fulfilling the duties of a philosopher.

The popular image of Russell as a campaigner against nuclear weapons is so deeply ingrained that it is not often realised how odd it was, on the face of it, that, when the Campaign for Nuclear Disarmament was launched in February 1958, Russell should be elected its President. After all, in the years immediately prior to this, he had argued repeatedly and consistently that the abolition of nuclear weapons would be futile. Why, then, was he prepared to spearhead a movement whose popular slogan was 'Ban the Bomb'? The answer lies in Russell's conviction that, though little would be gained by the renunciation of nuclear weapons by the Great Powers, the USA and USSR, something at least would be gained by *Britain*'s renunciation of nuclear weapons. As he had said in his letter to Eisenhower and Khrushchev, Russell regarded the potential proliferation of nuclear-armed countries as one of the most urgent dangers facing mankind. Nothing could be done to prevent the USA and USSR from manufacturing nuclear weapons, but, he thought, something could be done – and *must* be done – to prevent other countries from joining the 'nuclear club'. Britain could play a leading role in this, he believed, by unilaterally abandoning its own nuclear programme. As he put it in a letter to *The Times* on 18 March 1958: 'British renunciation of the bomb would make it more possible for America and Russia to agree, as they easily could, that no other Power should possess the bomb.'

Having formulated this view, Russell characteristically came to regard it as the only view consistent with common sense, and became inclined to think that anyone who rejected it must either lack intelligence or positively want to see the spread of nuclear weapons to all the nations of the world and (therefore) the total destruction of human life. Among those who rejected it were the leaders of the Labour Party, who, at the party's annual conference in 1957, had succeeded in gaining support for the view that Britain needed its own nuclear weapons in order to avoid going 'naked in the international conference chamber'. In Russell's eyes, not only was this view mistaken, but the people who urged it were 'murderers'. When Rupert Crawshay-Williams tried to explain how it was possible for his friend, John Strachey (then a Labour Party spokesman on defence), to come honestly to a different conclusion and to support his party's line, Russell became angrily indignant. 'You and John Strachey,' he thundered at Crawshay-Williams, 'you belong to the murderers' club.' A few weeks later, during another discussion on the subject of nuclear weapons, Russell suddenly, 'in a voice of fury', said to

Crawshay-Williams: 'The next time you see your friend John Strachey, tell him I cannot understand why he wants Nasser to have the H-bomb.'

Thus it was that Russell backed the Campaign for Nuclear Disarmament with all the moral fervour with which he had, more than forty years earlier, supported the No-Conscription Fellowship. He took no part in CND's widely publicised Aldermaston marches, but in public talks, journalistic articles and letters to the Press, Russell lent CND his support by putting the unilateralist case as forcefully and as often as he could. On 11 February 1959, Russell, together with Lord Simon, succeeded in tabling a debate on Britain's nuclear deterrent in the House of Lords, but their motion for unilateralism gained little support and had to be withdrawn. At about the same time, his book *Common Sense and Nuclear Warfare* was published and came to be regarded by CND supporters as providing them with a rigorously argued defence of their slogans.

In fact, it is possible to discern in the book a certain distance from the rhetoric of CND that brings to mind the uneasy alliances Russell had made in the past with political movements inspired by religious or moral absolutism – his collaborations, for example, with Quakers in the No-Conscription Fellowship, and with Anglican priests in the Peace Pledge Union. The Chairman of CND, Canon Collins, was, like the Reverend Dick Sheppard of the Peace Pledge Union, a man whose involvement in political activism was ultimately founded on his Christian convictions. For him, it was simply *wrong* for Britain to own weapons of mass destruction, whatever the political realities might be and whatever interests might be served by such ownership. That Russell so often found himself allied to religiously inspired political movements is, of course, no coincidence, given the element of moral absolutism that invariably accompanied his own political convictions. However, in keeping with his moral philosophy, though Russell was content to have absolutist moral *feelings*, he was not content to base his arguments upon them.

Thus *Common Sense and Nuclear Warfare* is relatively free from the moral arguments about the inherent wickedness of nuclear weapons with which CND came to be associated. Nor does Russell make the question of nuclear *disarmament* the central issue. Indeed, in Chapter VI, 'Disarmament', he explicitly rejects this view, arguing that even multilateral disarmament should be seen as 'a palliative rather than a solution'. The question of Britain's unilateral disarmament, the central focus of the entire CND movement, is relegated to an appendix, and, though Russell endorses the policy, it is clear that he thinks the fundamentally important questions lie elsewhere. Of far more urgency to Russell was the abolition of nuclear tests, which, he says, 'is within the sphere of immediate practical politics'. A general agreement to suspend nuclear tests would, Russell insists, 'prevent the spread of nuclear weapons to Powers which at present do not possess them'.

After that, Russell's policy prescriptions for saving the human race become rather vaguer, and, as he admits, somewhat utopian. 'I think the next step', he writes, 'should be a solemn joint declaration by the United

States and the USSR to the effect that they will seek to settle their differences otherwise than by war or the threat of war.' The book then becomes bogged down in a confused discussion of strategic, military and territorial questions, the moral of which seems to be that, if goodwill could prevail, then *some* solutions to these complex problems could be found that did not involve the threat of global war. Russell ends with a familiar plea to mankind to overcome its tendency to fanaticism and nationalism, and to reform its education so as to make such goodwill possible.

With regard to policy prescriptions, one of the few things that is clear from the book is that, though Russell fervently believed that Britain should give up its nuclear weapons, he did not think that this, by itself, would do much to avert the danger facing humanity. As for the removal of American nuclear forces from Britain and the rest of Europe, which was another important element of CND's campaign, Russell remarks that he did not think this would be practical, 'except as a sequel to an enforceable agreement for the abolition of nuclear weapons'. And, as he had earlier doubted that such an agreement could be concluded 'until there is a genuine readiness on both sides to renounce war as an instrument of policy', this threw him back to the position of 'Man's Peril' that the really important thing was to abolish, not weapons, but war itself. 'We must find a way of avoiding all wars,' he says. And his solution to that problem was, as always, World Government, or, as he puts it in *Common Sense and Nuclear Warfare*, an 'International Authority'. He recognises, however, that the establishment of such an authority is unlikely, since: 'while the East–West tension retains anything like its present acuteness, neither side would submit to any International Authority unless it could dominate it'.

The perspective offered in *Common Sense and Nuclear Warfare* is resolutely global, concerned not with the choices facing Britain, but with the choices facing mankind as a whole. Indeed, at times the perspective is even wider than that. In the opening chapter he discusses, with visceral recoil, the suggestion made by the US Air Force to use the moon as a 'retaliation base' from which to launch counter-attacks against the Soviet Union. Recalling the scientist in 'Satan in the Suburbs', who had argued that the moon was beautiful and innocent *because* it was lifeless, Russell writes: 'when I read of plans to defile the heavens by the petty squabbles of the animated lumps that disgrace a certain planet, I cannot but feel that the men who make these plans are guilty of a kind of impiety'.

From this global, or even astronomical, perspective, CND's concerns looked rather local. Still more so was the preoccupation of CND with changing the policy of the British Labour Party, a matter that, as Russell reveals in his *Autobiography*, he approached from such a lofty height that his attitude to it bordered on disdain:

As most of its [CND's] upholders were drawn from the Labour Party, it went to work upon the Parliamentary Labour Party. My own view was that the matter was one that transcends Party politics and even national boundaries. As this reasonable view, as it seemed to me, failed to grip the public imagination, I was willing to uphold the Campaign in its efforts. The means towards the end that we both desired mattered less than its achievement. Perhaps, I thought, if the Labour Party *could* be persuaded to support the Campaign, we might be a short step towards the goal.

Openly disdainful was his attitude towards the Aldermaston marches, which he described as a 'yearly picnic', a 'subject of boredom or distress or hilarity', which 'converted very few of those hitherto unconverted'. What he wanted was a platform from which to address the world at large – not just Britain, not the British Labour Party and certainly not the few thousand supporters of CND, already converted to the cause, who made the annual trek from Aldermaston to London, accompanied by skiffle bands, jugglers and clowns. Within a few years of launching CND, Russell was offered such a platform, or at least the appearance of it, by the young American radical, Ralph Schoenman. His gratitude for this was so great that he adopted Schoenman as the son and political heir he had once hoped John would be, and allowed Schoenman to lead him on the strangest political journey of his life, a journey that was to culminate in the bizarre spectacle of Russell, in the name of peace, issuing calls for global guerrilla warfare.

In the meantime, John remained part of the 'rest' that Russell hoped to forget when he remembered his humanity. After his move to Wales in the summer of 1956, Russell did not see John for four years; nor did he write to him or even send him birthday greetings. In September 1956, when Lucy, John's youngest daughter, asked Russell when she could see her father, she was told that John was welcome at Plas Penrhyn at anytime, but, as Dora pointed out in a letter to her solicitor: 'A general invitation of this kind is obviously absurd, since John would never travel there himself, and my offer to accompany him down was rewarded with an insult.' John would not see Russell without Dora, and Russell would not contemplate being in the same room as her, or even in the same house, so father and son remained estranged.

At Plas Penrhyn, Russell and Edith made a comfortable home for the children, to which all three became deeply attached. Russell and Edith were, it is true, rather old to be looking after young children, but their neighbours, the Cooper-Willises, had daughters of roughly the same age, so the girls were not quite as isolated at Plas Penryhn as Russell had been as a young boy at Pembroke Lodge. And, though their relations with Edith recalled Russell's own relations with his grandmother (they found her intimidatingly cold and correct), the girls – Lucy and Sarah particularly – became genuinely and warmly fond of their grandfather. Anne, constantly reminded that she was not really a Russell, felt rather differently. At Moreton Hall School, the girls, especially Lucy, did exceptionally well in their studies, and all in all they seem to have been happy and settled in the new life that Russell and Edith had created for them.

One cloud on the horizon was the close proximity of Susan, who, when Russell moved into Plas Penrhyn, was still living a short walk away in the cottage she shared with Christopher Wordsworth. Susan's attitude to her children, and to the rather bizarre situation in which she now found herself, appears in her surviving letters to be rather mixed and contradictory. At Christmas 1955, she sent presents to the girls via Edith, accompanied by a note chastising Edith for not letting her know that the children had been in North Wales the previous summer and saying how sorry she was to have been 'ostracised'. Then, a week or so later, she wrote to Dora, apparently willing to accept the fact that she never saw her children and more or less content to surrender them to the 'Pembroke Lodge atmosphere' which she supposed them to be suffering with Russell and Edith. After Russell, Edith and the children moved permanently to Plas Penrhyn, Susan wrote occasional letters, begging Russell to lend her money, but showed no interest in either seeing or hearing about her children, and when Anne came to visit her during the Christmas holidays of 1956, Susan refused to have anything to do with her.

During this period, Susan and Wordsworth were desperately short of money, and Susan's mental state was deteriorating in a way that paralleled John's breakdown of 1954, except that, where John became paralysed with confusion and indecision, Susan became angry, violent and unpredictable. Sometimes she would wander off into the Welsh hills and not return home for days; on other occasions she would physically attack her lover with bottles, wine glasses or whatever else she could find. At the end of 1958, what was then known as the 'Duly Appointed Officer' appeared at the cottage with an Emergency Order committing Susan to psychiatric care, and she was taken away to a hospital in the nearby village of Llanrwst, where she was diagnosed as suffering from 'sub-acute paranoia'. Wordsworth never saw her again, and Susan, like John, never really recovered her mind. In a long, undated letter to her brother, Nick, shortly after she received her diagnosis, she wrote:

> The Russell lot have behaved abominably about me, or towards me. I hate the misery they caused me. Not a crust of bread, or a word of thanks for keeping their unspeakable son out of the British Press, & the Lord Russell's reputation – now that he is dignified – unblemished.

Susan spent the rest of her life in North Wales, sometimes in psychiatric hospitals and sometimes in tiny houses that she shared with lovers, but always in poverty and never quite sane. As she got older, she grew increasingly alarming: thin, grey-haired, wild-eyed and unkempt. From time to time in the 1970s her daughters would succeed in tracking her down, and invariably found her appearance disturbing and her conversation unintelligible. When she died, in 1990, the local authorities had great trouble in finding anybody to inform of her death. They eventually traced Kate, who was then living in Cornwall and who, though she had not seen Susan for about forty years, was deemed to be her closest living relative. Kate was then able to put the authorities in touch with Susan's brother, Nicholas, who immediately flew to Wales and was, among Susan's relatives, the only mourner at her funeral.

In 1958, John emerged from his years of torpor sufficiently to buy himself a typewriter and to dedicate himself to what he called his 'magnum opus'. He also took to writing long, hand-written letters to his friends and relations, including his father and his daughters. Initially Dora took this as an optimistic sign that he was recovering, but when she looked at some of the things he was writing, she was dismayed to discover that they consisted mostly of incoherent rants, sometimes autobiographical, sometimes quasi-religious and, occasionally, obscene. The letters he wrote to his children at school were intercepted by the headmistress, who considered them unsuitable for young girls, while those he sent to Russell were forwarded to Russell's solicitor as proof that John was certifiable.

'John and Susan both get continually further from sanity,' Russell wrote to Kate on 11 March 1959. 'I don't know how long they can be kept out of institutions.' Two months later, he told her plaintively: 'John is become quite insane & Conrad won't speak to me – It is a pity you are so far away.' By this time, it was three and a half years since he had seen John, and ten since he had seen Conrad, who was now in his early twenties and, having gained a first-class degree from Oxford, was embarking upon what was to become a very distinguished career as a professional historian. All this Russell had to hear indirectly, since Conrad, at his mother's insistence, would have nothing to do with him.

Kate's separation from him was, on the face of it, less final and insurmountable. What kept them apart was merely the Atlantic Ocean, a barrier far easier to overcome than the gulf that now separated him from both his sons. Even so, Russell had not seen her since his last visit to America in 1951, and was therefore delighted when he learnt that she and her family would be coming to England in the summer of 1960.

Kate was now in her late thirties and the mother of three – David, aged nine; Anne, aged seven; and Jonathan, aged five – and much had happened to her since Russell last saw her. After the birth of her second child in 1953, Kate had become depressed. Looking for a solution to her unhappiness in her father's *Conquest of Happiness*, she had failed to find it. Its message that puritan morality was the cause of unhappiness offered her little. Indeed, it served only to increase her sense of failure by implying that, since she had been brought up free from puritanism, she *ought not* be unhappy: 'Either that or my father was mistaken'. She decided that he was mistaken and sought help instead from a psychiatrist, from whom, she wrote, 'I began to see that it was possible to feel anger and fear and even envy without being contemptible; it was conceivable that people might like me even if I stopped trying to be a model of all the virtues.'

Her liberation from her upbringing was completed shortly later when she became converted to Christianity. Psychiatry had helped her to accept her own imperfections, but she still craved an answer to the question: what is the purpose of living? Again she looked to her father's books for an answer. She read *Sceptical Essays*, *Unpopular Essays*, *In Praise of Idleness* and *Marriage and Morals*, 'but they all offered the same solutions: reason, progress, unselfishness, a wide historical perspective, expansiveness, generosity, enlightened self-interest. I had heard it all my life, and it filled me with despair.' She found her answer in Christianity, and, ironically, in the very doctrine of original sin that had been such a burden to her father. The utopian hopes of her parents had left her with a sense of inadequacy for failing to live up to their fantastic aspirations – an inadequacy that was compounded by the feeling that, on her parents' terms, the sense of guilt she felt was entirely inexplicable: 'The doctrine of original sin gave to me, when I came to understand it, the same sense of intoxicating liberation my father had received from sexual emancipation. It was *normal* for me to be bad, and I need not feel ashamed.' What was more, God could be relied upon to *forgive* her her sins and to love her unconditionally, whereas: 'My earthly father loved me only when I was good (or so I believed).' Now, with a husband, three small children and a faith in herself and in God that owed nothing to her father, she felt ready to see Russell once more, hoping to convince him that, in Christianity, she had found, not only the answer to her problems, but also the certainty and purpose for which he himself had been looking all his life.

Kate also wanted to see Dora, whom she had not seen since her mother's visit to New York in 1954. The arrangements as to when and for how long she should visit each parent in turn were protracted and involved, and brought back to Kate the horrors of her divided childhood loyalties. 'In all these years', she wrote to Dora, 'I have lost the art of the diplomatic go-between. No wonder poor Ja [John] went bats with it! I hope I shall manage not to offend either of you, because I love you both.'

In the end, she went to Plas Penrhyn first, where she found the memories evoked were mostly pleasant ones. Russell, she wrote:

> sat in his armchair by the fire, with his feet on the same old lovely rug, surrounded by his ivories and his Chinese paintings, his books and all the remembered friends of my childhood, just as he had always done. The whole room, even the whole house, seemed an extension of my father's character. Small and old, a bit deaf and a trifle frail, he sat there in his slippers, pouring tea by the fire, like any old man. But out from him radiated his spirit: his wit, his learning, his love of beauty and passion for truth, reflected on the walls around him and spreading out from the house all over the country and the world. I felt his greatness more then, as we sat quietly over tea in Plas Penrhyn, than at any other time.

He was, Kate recalls, 'a perfect grandfather', telling her children the same stories he had told her as a child, and giving them 'wonderful presents and grandfatherly bits of money'. Kate and her family stayed – at Russell's expense – at Portmeirion Hotel, and were provided with a rented car in which to explore the beautiful Welsh countryside. Every day they had a tea party with Russell and Edith. 'It was so overwhelmingly luxurious', she writes, 'that I was almost embarrassed.'

And yet, even at the height of her admiration of and gratitude towards her father, Kate felt dissatisfied at the lack of real communication that existed between the two of them. She had wanted to 'tell him about God', to share the joy of her Christian faith with him and to justify herself to him: 'I did not want him to think I had swallowed a lot of nonsense and prejudice for the sake of a specious peace of mind.' But she did not get the chance. As the four of them – Russell, Edith, Charlie and Kate – sat around the fire, the talk was of politics, and, says Kate, 'I could never break through to real talk.' In the end, as she hugged him goodbye, she resigned herself to the fact that it was 'too late for storms of emotion, too late to stand up and justify myself against him, defending my values by attacking his'. And so: 'There seemed no solution but to look at each other with love as we drifted apart on our separate rafts of belief.'

From Wales, Kate and her family went to Cornwall to stay with Dora. From opulent serenity, she now entered chaos: Dora had staying with her not only John and his three girls, but also Roddy and Harriet, together with her husband, Chris Unwin. Kate and her family went off to the nearby beaches every day, and she remembers everything in Cornwall as being perfect, 'except for the people, with whom I experienced my usual difficulties'. At Cornwall, as at Wales, Kate was subjected to incessant tirades on the subject of John's children. Who should look after them? Who should have legal custody of them? Should they divide their time equally during their holidays between their grandfather and their grandmother? Should John be allowed to see them? To Kate, the arguments and the way they were presented ('my mother's righteous indignation and my father's cold correctness') sounded horribly familiar: 'I felt the old panic of my childhood returning as I listened, the old impulse to leap up and run away, run for hours along the cliffs and never come back.' When the time came to return to the States, Kate felt 'the usual mixture of sorrow at leaving the country and relief at escaping from the family'.

After Kate's departure, the quarrel between Russell and Dora over the future of John's daughters developed, as she had feared, into something horribly reminiscent of the battle that had been fought years earlier over her and John. The issue was not where the girls should live and who should look after them – everyone was agreed that Russell and Edith were best equipped to take on that responsibility – rather, it concerned the legal question of who should have custody of the girls.

By 1960, Russell felt that, though the arrangements he and Edith had made for the girls since 1954 had worked quite well, they needed to be placed on a legal footing. He was nearing ninety, the girls were entering their teenage years (Anne was by now fifteen, Sarah thirteen and Lucy twelve) and something needed to be done, Russell felt, to ensure the continuity of their lives after his death. As things stood, they would, in all likelihood, be sent to live with John and Dora after Russell's death, and this he was determined to avoid. He therefore took steps to gain legal custody of the girls for himself and Edith, in order to ensure that after his death Edith could continue to look after them without fear of interference from Dora and John.

As soon as she heard of this, Dora prepared to fight the case with all the means at her disposal, enraged at the thought that Edith should be looked upon as the girls' 'real' grandmother, while she and John continued to be excluded from their lives. Her motive in this was to defend the interests of John, whom, she felt, had ceased to be regarded by Russell as a human being as soon as he had suffered a nervous breakdown. The consequent isolation of the girls from their father was, Dora felt, bad for them, but also, more especially, bad for John, undermining his confidence and compounding his sense of rejection by Russell.

In her campaign against Russell's order for custody, Dora had the staunch support of her solicitor, Lewis Taylor, who had, by this time, formed a protective affection for both Dora and John and a sense of outrage at the way Russell had treated his son. Russell, Dora wrote to Taylor in connection with the custody battle, had 'no right to extend his power and cruelty beyond the grave'. Dora also tried to enlist Susan's support, but received in reply only a note saying that she was glad that 'Lord and Lady Russell' were proposing to take custody of her children and that she was sure Edith was very fond of them. For Russell's part, the very worst outcome would be joint custody with Dora, and again and again he instructed his solicitor that 'if the court were to decide in favour of such joint custody, I should withdraw'.

And so began a long and destructive battle between Russell and Dora, not only on the legal question, but also for the hearts of the children. Dora insisted that the girls spend some time with her and John during their holidays, and, while they were there, she would attempt to persuade them of the harm Russell had done to John and to convince anyone who would listen that John's mental health was improving and would improve still further, if only he could see more of his children. Her greatest success was with Lucy, the youngest and cleverest of the children, who began increasingly to take John's side against her grandfather.

In the face of Dora's implacable opposition, Russell withdrew his claim for custody and settled instead for claiming 'care and control' of the girls for himself and Edith. This case came before the judge on 25 July 1960, during Kate's visit to North Wales. The judge, in the words of Russell's solicitor, Tyler, 'remarked that he was concerned that the children should be allowed in the company of an obvious schizophrenic at any time', and insisted that the question of custody be reopened. Before making a decision on that, however, the judge wanted to see a Welfare Officer's report.

This move made Dora understandably nervous, knowing how the shambolic and impoverished conditions of the London flat she shared with John would compare in the eyes of authority with the calm, well-maintained home in the Welsh countryside that Russell and Edith could offer the girls. Her only weapon was the loyalty of the girls themselves, whom she hoped would tell the Welfare Officer how much they loved their father. The diary of Lucy, then eleven, tells something of Dora's attempts to win them over. During the Easter vacation of 1960, Lucy records that Dora told them that John and Susan's divorce was Edith's fault and that Russell had taken the girls in 'to try & make it up to him [John]'. She also writes: 'Daddy's miles better, he crochets, makes stamps, goes out, and is even trying to give up smoking!' At the end of her stay with Dora and John, Lucy wrote that she was sorry to leave their London flat – 'It's really home' – and about her father she wrote: 'He's so – well, kind? nice? lovely?'

But Lucy's sympathy for John was overridden by the desire of all three girls to stay with Russell and Edith. Their unanimity on this question was urged by the eldest, Anne, and seconded by the headmistress of Moreton Hall, Bronwen Lloyd-Williams, a long-standing admirer of Russell's, who wrote to Russell's solicitor, Tyler, to say that she was perfectly prepared to sign an affidavit to the effect that it was in the interests of the children to stay with Russell and Edith: 'All the children are proud of and fond of Lord and Lady Russell, who constitute their real background as well as supplying their basic material and other needs.'

The Welfare Officer's report, produced in the autumn of 1960 by a Miss R. N. Nowell, amply bore out Dora's fears. Miss Nowell's sympathies clearly lay with Russell and Edith. Russell, she reports, was 'apprehensive at the thought of the children remaining in the custody of his son' and felt it would be preferable, in the event of his death, for the children to make their home with Edith rather than Dora. He had not prevented the children from staying in London with their father, but this was because he 'has always been assured that their grandmother would see that they would not be left in the entire care of their father'. The implication that something dreadful would otherwise happen to the children was strenuously resisted by Dora, during her own interview with Miss Nowell. John, Dora stressed, posed no threat to the girls: 'Mrs Grace does not in any way feel that harm could come to the children as a result of contact with their father and in fact considers that it is in her son's interest and vitally important from the point of view of his recovery to feel that the children still have affection for him and spend time with him.' After meeting John for herself, Miss Nowell declared him 'not fit, or I think able, to assume any great degree of responsibility'.

Miss Nowell's interviews with the children confirmed that they would rather stay with Russell and Edith. Anne, she reported, found her visits to London depressing, because they made her think of the sad situation of her parents and because she had to listen to Dora's criticisms of Russell. All the girls, however, emphasised that they did not feel apprehensive about being with their father because of his state of mind, and indeed were at pains to tell Miss Nowell of their great affection for him.

Dora received the report on 4 November. 'John has read [it],' she wrote to Taylor, and 'he is adamant about custody. For the first time I saw him really angry and showing fight on this issue.' On the morning before she read the report, Dora wrote to Taylor with a proposal designed to bring John closer, not only to his daughters, but also to his father. She and John, she explained, would be in London rather than Cornwall for the Christmas holiday, and would be joined for Christmas Day itself by Harriet, Chris and Roddy:

So there is to be a family Christmas in Roddy's flat. We should like to have the girls too, and also have pleasure in inviting Lord Russell and his wife to come and take Christmas dinner with us all.

This may surprise you: you would have been still more surprised if you could have seen the pleasure with which John greeted the suggestion. So much so that I decided to write to you at once, in order that you can approach Tyler, or, if you think better, I will write direct to Lord Russell.

John has been making increasing progress, he welcomes people now, especially relatives . . . if Lord Russell will agree, it might mean much happiness for them both.

From Taylor, this invitation went to Tyler, and from him to Russell, who replied on 12 November:

Dear Tyler,

In reply to the letter from Dora of which you enclose a copy: neither we nor John's and Susan's daughters can accept her kind invitation, as we already have invited guests for Christmas dinner. I should be obliged if you would communicate this to Mr Taylor.

We wish the children to spend the whole of the Christmas holidays with us, especially as they have asked to do so and as they spent a large part of their summer holidays with their grandmother.

Yours sincerely,
Russell

In such a manner was Russell family life conducted.

John reacted to this rebuff with hurt and anger ('those who invoke the law do away with the ordinary courtesies of life,' he told Dora), but Dora would not give up. On 18 November, she wrote again to her solicitor, urging the importance of getting John and Russell to see each other. The psychiatrist, Dr Morgan, she wrote, had been to see John and 'agrees with me that it is important to try and bring about a meeting between John and his father'. Russell's cold rejection of her plan to bring them together for Christmas had been all the more hurtful because she had received it on 16 November, John's birthday, reminding her that 'John's father never writes to him either for birthday or Christmas'. The children usually did so, she added, but 'This birthday . . . only Lucy of the three girls wrote to John.' 'I do think', she added, 'that Tyler should know of the set-back to harmony in the entire family relationships that has resulted from these unwise proceedings, undoing much that Dr Morgan and I have worked for for over five years.'

Taylor duly passed on Dora's remarks to Tyler, who passed them on to Russell, who replied (via Tyler) that he would be happy to see John, 'if he were to write to me and express a wish to see me. So far, he has not done this. I cannot accept his mother's assurance that he wishes to see me without some confirmation from him.' Understandably, Dora was suspicious of this response. With the court case for custody coming up, she told Taylor: 'We cannot risk him [John] writing one his odd epistles and having it produced to us in Court thereafter, which BR is quite capable of doing.' As Russell had in fact filed John's earlier letters to him as evidence that his son was dangerously insane, and as he would some years later produce more letters to show that John was unfit even to see his daughters, this fear of Dora's was entirely justified.

Somehow, the deadlock was broken and Russell did, finally, agree to meet John at Roddy's flat after Christmas, without the girls being present, and on the express condition that Dora, too, would not be there. On hearing the news, Dora said, John's face lit up. The meeting, however, which did not take place until March 1961, was not what either Dora or John might have hoped. According to Dora, it was 'formal on both sides', though 'John behaved with great normality, looked very nice, etc.':

Roddy says that Lord R looked at John in a kind of hopeless way, as if he would like to get near to him but did not know how. Of course, one must recognise his great age, all that can be hoped for is that he realises that John exists as a person, and is not out of his mind.

Russell's account was rather different:

I met John in the street while I was looking for Roddy's house. We shook hands, but he remained completely expressionless, showing not a flicker of interest in our meeting. Throughout the subsequent tea-party he remained silent and apparently totally indifferent to the conversation, his eyes throughout quite blank. He ate largely, but otherwise appeared unaware of his surroundings. His clothes were untidy and bizarre, and he did not look clean. I got not the faintest clue to what he might be thinking or feeling and he gave me no indication as to whether he wished or did not wish for further meetings. As far as I could guess, he did not care either way.

This was to be the last meeting that Russell ever had with his previously much-beloved son.

For both sides of this dreadful gulf, the Christmas period of 1960 was dominated by preparations for the custody case – the date for which had been set as 25 January 1961 – with Dora and Russell going over yet again their conflicting accounts of what had happened between them and between John, Susan and Russell. On behalf of Dora, Taylor looked through the legal papers of John's divorce, commenting: 'From the contemporary correspondence one would think that it was Lord Russell who was in a hurry to divorce Susan!' Affidavits were drawn up and scrutinised, and predictably attitudes hardened. In response to reading Dora's affidavit, Edith wrote that nothing would induce her to have anything to do with her. Challenging Dora's account of Russell's break with John, she wrote: 'The estrangement between John and his father is on John's side alone. He has given no evidence whatever to his father of wishing to see him ... The estrangement with John ... arose from the fact that he, with his mother's backing, refused shock treatment which the doctors thought might cure him, which Lord Russell, therefore, advised.' In their instructions to their solicitors, both Russell and Edith gave great weight to reports they had received from Kate of her time in Cornwall with John:

> John's behaviour may seem 'perfectly rational' to Mrs Grace, but, according to his sister and her husband, John was, last August and September, hearing 'voices' and would suddenly burst into laughter because of something they said to him. The children – both his own and his sister's – accepted his 'hearing voices' as a fact like another.

Russell, for his part, told his solicitor both what he would like to do and what he proposed to do:

> What I should like to do:
> say – 'very well. I will not demand custody of the children, nor will my wife. You – Dora – may have, with John, full custody of the children. We will pack the children's belongings & send them to you, and from now on, you may have full care of the children. We shall take no more responsibility for them, and interfere no further' . . . We shall miss seeing the children and having responsibility for them, since we are very fond of them, but we have neither the time nor the energy to devote to the very involved and unpleasant relations with Mrs Grace that any association with the children now entails . . .
> What I propose should be done:
> The proceedings should go through as scheduled on 25 January.

He had, in addition, one crucial question: 'Supposing the Judge gives custody to John (Mrs Grace being his next friend) & me, must I then accept it?' For Russell, it was absolutely paramount that, whatever happened, he should have as little to do with Dora as possible.

Russell's fears were allayed: the judge gave custody to him and Edith, though he insisted that John be given 'free access' to the girls. This provoked new fears. What does 'free access' mean, Russell asked Tyler?:

> You will remember that Miss Lloyd Williams was very anxious that neither Mrs Grace nor John in his present state should visit the school . . . and you will doubtless also remember that we do not wish Mrs Grace or, in his present state (and in this connection the fact, not mentioned by Mrs Grace or his doctor but told to us by Kate and her husband, that John is still so deranged mentally as to hear voices), John to come here. Will it be possible to prevent these happenings under the ruling 'free access'?

If John and Dora were to see the girls, they would have to do so in the privacy of their own home: they could not embarrass the girls at school and they were certainly not welcome at Plas Penrhyn.

In fact, to get Russell to honour the judge's decision to grant John access to the girls, Dora had to fight every inch of the way. So frustrated was Russell that he could not shake Dora off and had to deal with her, whether he liked it or not, that he refused to pay Dora her maintenance. 'In view of the time, energy, etc., that Dora has caused me to expend needlessly in the last months,' he told Tyler, 'I do not feel inclined to pay the March voluntary payment. A condition of these payments, if you remember, was that Dora would leave off badgering me. She has not done so.'

In fact, as time went on, it suited Russell to have the girls spend their holidays with Dora and John, causing Dora to remark to Taylor that Lord and Lady Russell now seemed too busy to bother about the girls. 'I am not in the least surprised', Taylor replied, 'that Lord Russell, having got his Order for Custody, cannot be bothered with them.' The reason for Russell's indifference was not only that he had become very busy, but also that, at the very time of his 'victory' over Dora for custody of the girls, he had found a son and heir who would be an even better substitute than they were for the loss of John and Conrad.

12

RUSSELL'S VIPER

Russell's acrimonious dispute with Dora over the custody of Anne, Sarah and Lucy in 1960 coincided with the entry into his life of the man who would dominate his next six years, and who gradually became, in the absence of John and Conrad, his ersatz son and heir. To the girls, however, and to many of Russell's friends and neighbours, he was known as 'Russell's viper'. His name was Ralph Schoenman, an intense and energetic young American (twenty-four years old when he first met Russell), with bright, staring eyes and a carefully trimmed beard that, with no accompanying moustache, looked like a helmet-strap.

Schoenman had studied philosophy at Princeton and came to London to enroll as a postgraduate student of politics at the London School of Economics. His tutor was Ralph Miliband, one of the founding members of the then burgeoning British New Left movement – a movement that, through Schoenman, was to have a decisive influence on Russell's political thinking and practice throughout the 1960s. The year 1960 was a formative one for the New Left, the year in which its journal, the *New Left Review*, was founded and in which its hopes of real political influence, through the Peace Movement and the Labour Party, were at their height. The Marxism espoused by the New Left was one fiercely independent of the Communist Party. Its leading thinkers, who, at the time, apart from Miliband, included the historian E. P. Thompson and the cultural critic, Stuart Hall, had become disillusioned with the Communist Party since the Soviet invasion of Hungary in 1956 and now advocated a radical Socialism that was neutral with regard to the Cold War.

Intellectually, the fundamental aim of the New Left was to articulate a new kind of Marxist theory, one that freed it from the straitjacket of the Communist Party and that could form the intellectual foundation for a genuinely Socialist Labour Party. Of the Labour Party as it stood, they were deeply suspicious (Miliband's contribution to the very first issue of *New Left Review* was entitled 'The Sickness of Labourism'); they disliked the 'block-vote' of the trade unions and were dismissive of the non-theoretical approach to Socialism that had characterised the party throughout its existence. They were also firmly opposed to the position on defence adopted by Labour's leader, Hugh Gaitskell, seeing in it nothing more than subservience to the United States. On the questions of Britain's possession of nuclear weapons and its membership of NATO, they supported CND, but tended to be condescending about the dependence of CND upon *moral* arguments. The New Left saw themselves as equipping the Peace Movement with a *theory*, an intellectual foundation for its moral indignation, though in time they had to admit that most of the marchers to Aldermaston had little interest in debating such things as historical materialism and the labour theory of value. Socially and culturally, however, the New Left and the Peace Movement overlapped to a considerable extent, each drawing its supporters from the same group of people and meeting at the same coffee-bars and clubs.

In the uneasy alliance between the intellectualism of the New Left and the fervent moralism of CND, Ralph Schoenman had a foot in both camps. As a theoretician, he was never quite taken seriously by the New Left – for instance, he was never published in *New Left Review* – but as a peace activist he was already, before he met Russell, beginning to make waves. In the spring of 1960, at a coffee-house run by the New Left called the Partisan, Schoenman began meeting a group that included Stuart Hall and Ralph Miliband from *New Left Review*, Hugh Brock and April Carter from the Direct Action Committee, and a painter called Gustav Metzger. With them, he conceived an ambitious plan to channel the massive support that CND had attracted into a mass movement of civil disobedience. He had been a member of CND since 1958, but by 1960 had become dissatisfied with the disparity between the seriousness of the issues involved and the apparent frivolity of the methods employed. To be marching from Aldermaston to London, singing songs, while the whole of mankind was in danger of annihilation seemed to him absurd. He was sympathetic to the raids on air-force bases undertaken by the Direct Action Committee, but what he craved was direct action of a more radical kind, involving nothing less than mass resistance to the British Government. In this, he was influenced by quite general political aims, not specifically tied to the issue of nuclear disarmament.

At this time, despite his contacts with Hall and Miliband, Schoenman's general political outlook differed sharply from the Marxist theorising of the New Left. A few years later, partly under the influence of the next generation of New Left intellectuals (Perry Anderson, Robin Blackburn, and so on), he was to embrace the kind of hybrid revolutionary Marxism – part-Maoist, part-Trotskyist – that was characteristic of 1960s' radicals, but in 1960 his politics were still more anarchist than Marxist. He wanted to stir up rebellion, not against this or that particular authority, but against authority itself. The theoretical underpinnings of this attitude, such as they were, were outlined by him in an article that he published in *Peace News* in 1961 called 'Mass Resistance in Mass Society'. Here, his chief intellectual debt seems to have been to the American sociologist, H. H. Wilson, who, in an essay published in 1954 entitled 'The Dilemma of the Obsolete Man', argued, in Schoenman's words, that: 'the values derived from liberal, democratic and socialist traditions were no longer operative and that those who laid claim to them were obsolete men'.

These liberal, democratic and Socialist ideals have been rendered obsolete, Schoenman argued, by the vast power of private companies, such as American oil corporations, 'whose control over planetary resources is maintained at the expense of the agony and starvation of its population in large'. In the face of this awesome power, 'democratic institutions have been emptied of content' and 'the mass society is now a totalitarian society'. This has nothing to do with political ideology, but is due rather to 'vast industrial technology' and is therefore 'as true of Britain as it is of the United States or the Soviet Union'. Thus:

> It should be patently clear that the nature of the conflict with the Soviet Union has nothing to do with an ideological preference for liberal values or civil liberties. The United States is as monolithic and autocratic a society as is likely to be produced . . . Overt coercion . . . is now built into American institutional life and it ramifies throughout the society. It affects work, travel, study and creative activity. It conditions a fear of ideas, and an intolerance that has eliminated serious communication . . . We have created a concentration camp for the mind.
>
> I believe that we must come to understand how ruthless a society the United States has become, and, in particular, the manner in which the controllers require the military crisis they perpetuate in order to retain their hold.

In the interests of industry, then, according to Schoenman, we are compelled to live in a regimented, dehumanised world that strips people of their individual autonomy and reduces them to the level of obedient children. What does all this have to do with nuclear weapons? Well, explains Schoenman: 'I should have thought it quite impossible to challenge the super-state, the organised society and its inhumanity, had that inhumanity not exposed itself in so stark a manner as to threaten an imminent and total annihilation.' So the advent of nuclear weapons is important in revealing to the mass of people the true nature of their 'controllers' to such an extent that they *have* to resist authority in order to survive. In like manner, Schoenman goes on to claim, mass resistance to nuclear weapons would reveal the 'naked violence' of industrialised society: 'We will be exposing it when we show that authority must set up vast camps to cope with our number because we address ourselves to the unlimited horror of our equivalents of Buchenwald and Auschwitz: Aldermaston, Polaris, NATO.' On Schoenman's analysis, therefore, civil disobedience is not a means to an end, but a good thing in itself: 'In mass society human beings are chained by institutions . . . civil disobedience must return to individuals the prospect of a vital participation in the public world.' There is no point in theorising about political ideology; the point is rather to oppose authority so as to reassert the right to resist our mechanised society: 'Our political theorists are strutting in vain over cadavers for our political institutions are empty. The model of our objective should be the General Strike.'

The article is revealing of what may have attracted Russell to Schoenman, for its strengths and weaknesses strongly recall those of D. H. Lawrence's political writing. Like Lawrence, Schoenman is almost embarrassingly unsophisticated about the actual processes of political decision-making, impatient with nuances and prepared to entertain utterly fantastic visions of people being roused to revolutionary activities for purposes that are only very sketchily spelt out. Like Lawrence, too, Schoenman was less interested in detailed questions of political policy and tactics than in very broad questions of, so to speak, the soul of man in industrialised society. Also like Lawrence, he was attracted to iconoclasm for its own sake, Lawrence's call to 'break the shell' of the State finding its analogue in Schoenman's rhetoric about resistance to our 'controllers'. And, as in 1915, so in 1960 Russell may have been attracted to this iconoclasm without quite understanding – or, at least, without taking seriously – the harebrained politics that underlay it. And so, once again, Russell, for most of his life the great apostle of scepticism, was prepared to put aside his own scepticism for the sake of encouraging the passion and energy that he felt were needed to meet the demands of crisis.

When Schoenman wrote to Russell in July 1960 with his proposal to start a campaign of mass civil disobedience, Russell responded encouragingly. After receiving Russell's reply, Schoenman presented himself at Plas Penrhyn and was given a warm reception, as Russell listened patiently to his fantasies of making the Government change its policies on nuclear weapons by forcing them to imprison vast numbers of protesters, some of them eminent and well-known writers, artists, playwrights, and so on. Schoenman's idea, it turned out, was to form a committee of 100 prominent people, all of whom were prepared to go to prison for an illegal protest, much as the suffragettes before the First World War had openly courted the possibility of prosecution. As the members of the Committee were imprisoned, they would be replaced by members of a 'reserve' list, and so, after a while, the Government would be faced with wave after wave of protesters, all willing to break the law and go to prison in order to show up the brutality of a regime that was prepared to risk the destruction of the entire human race in order to promote the interests of mechanised industry. Eventually, Schoenman believed, the Government would have to admit defeat. As he put it in his *Peace News* article: 'If ten thousand have to be carried into court where they refuse to say a mumbling word; if ten thousand have to be jailed – then we shall realise the meaning of civil disobedience and I dare say so will the makers of bombs.'

There is no reason to think that Russell took these fantasies any more seriously than he had taken Lawrence's dreams of 'Rananim' in 1915. It was no part of his purpose to incite a general insurrection against the State; nor did he believe that they would find 10,000 people prepared to go to jail. What he saw in Schoenman's far-fetched proposal, rather, was a method of propaganda that would, he believed, be more effective than the legitimate protests of CND in bringing attention to the danger of nuclear warfare. The Aldermaston marches were, he felt, becoming something of a picnic, unworthy of the attention of newspapers. As he later put it:

> ... so long as only constitutional methods were employed, it was very difficult – and often impossible – to cause the most important facts to be known. All the great newspapers are against us. Television and radio gave us only grudging and brief opportunities for stating our case ... It was very largely the difficulty of making our case known that drove some of us to the adoption of illegal methods. Our illegal actions, because they had sensational news value, were reported, and here and there, a newspaper would allow us to say why we did what we did.

As a reason for going along with Schoenman's plans for mass civil disobedience in the summer of 1960, this sounds perfectly reasonable. But, in many ways, it flies in the face of the facts. There was actually *more* reason to think that the constitutional methods of CND were working in 1960 than at any previous time. The Aldermaston march of that year had been the biggest yet, ending with over 60,000 people in Trafalgar Square, representing all shades of political opinion and a wide range of organisations, including many of the most powerful trade unions in the country. Moreover, the Press coverage had *not* been 'grudging and brief', but widespread, fulsome and largely sympathetic, with favourable reports of the marchers' objectives appearing not only in left-wing papers, such as the *Daily Herald* and the *Daily Worker*, but also in mainstream newspapers such as *The Times*, the *Observer* and the *Daily Mirror*. And, most importantly, there *were* signs that this extensive coverage was having an effect on policy-makers. Many of the large trade unions had adopted the CND policy of unilateral nuclear disarmament and were pressing the Labour Party to do the same. The adoption of extra-parliamentary methods, then, was certainly not forced upon Russell by circumstances; on the contrary, Russell appeared to lose faith in parliamentary methods at precisely the moment they seemed most likely to succeed.

Besides, doing or saying things because of their 'sensational news value' was, as Russell well understood, fraught with danger. For the distinction between what he did to gain attention for his message and the content of that message itself could easily become blurred. How, for example, could he make it clear that he subscribed to Schoenman's methods while distancing himself from Schoenman's aims? How was the public to know that he did *not* support Schoenman's quasi-revolutionary aspirations? And, in lending his name and prestige to a body of ideas to which he did not actually subscribe, was there not a risk of losing his reputation as a man dedicated to the truth?

As the 1960s wore on, these questions became ever more pertinent, but, at the time of Russell's discussions with Schoenman in the summer of 1960, it was quite clear where Russell really stood on the question of the aims of the anti-nuclear movement, for he continued to publish a stream of articles explaining a position that, while changing, was still undeniably his and not Schoenman's. The greatest change in his position during this time was in his attitude towards the United States and its relations with the countries of Western Europe.

A turning point in this development was his call in the summer of 1960 for Britain to withdraw from NATO and declare itself neutral with respect to the two superpowers. This was an issue much in the air during that summer, as opponents of unilateralism within the Labour Party pressed home the claim that giving up nuclear weapons would mean giving up Britain's alliance with the United States and its protection by NATO. Supporters of CND were divided on this issue, with some arguing that neutrality was in itself a good thing for Britain, and others that Britain could unilaterally give up its nuclear weapons while remaining a member of NATO.

Previously, Russell had held this latter position, arguing that Britain should give up only its *independent* nuclear deterrent, and not its alliance with the United States. In the summer of 1960, however, he published in the *New York Times Magazine* an article outlining 'The Case for British Neutralism'. Russell's argument rested primarily on the evidence of American military policy that he had gathered from an article by Herman Kahn, recently published in the journal *Survival*. There, Kahn quoted the American Secretary of State, Christian Herter, as saying: 'I cannot conceive of any President involving us in an all-out nuclear war unless the facts showed clearly we are in danger of all-out devastation ourselves, or that actual moves have been made towards devastating ourselves.' The devastation of Europe, the implication was, would not be enough to force America to retaliate against the Soviet Union with nuclear weapons.

This being so, Russell argued, Britain stood to gain nothing by allying itself to the NATO policy of 'deterrence', since what was being deterred by such a policy was not an attack on Britain but only an attack on the United States. On the contrary, Britain stood to lose much by membership of NATO, since 'Russia has threatened that, in certain circumstances, satellites of the United States will be obliterated if they grant certain favours to the United States . . . if Britain were neutral, Russia would have no motive for attacking it; but, while Britain is useful to the United States, Russia has such a motive.' In this argument, Russell claimed, he spoke both as a patriotic Briton and as a 'friend of humanity'. For, 'every sane man, whether in the East or in the West, must hope that a policy of peaceful co-existence will prevail on both sides', and that neutral nations would be able to mediate between the two blocs so as to make such peaceful co-existence possible. In this way, the neutral nations 'can, not improbably, be the decisive force turning men aside from collective suicide'.

Though Russell spoke here as an individual, the policy that he recommended was being urged upon the Labour Party by a powerful combination of trade union leaders, left-wing Labour MPs, the intellectuals of the New Left and CND itself. Hopes were high that both unilateral nuclear disarmament and withdrawal from NATO would be adopted at the party conference in Scarborough in October 1960. The main barrier to the adoption of such a policy was the Labour leader, Hugh Gaitskell, who was convinced that Britain's membership of NATO was necessary, not only for the protection of Britain, but also for the maintenance of the balance of power between the Western and Eastern blocs that alone could prevent Soviet expansion and nuclear war between the superpowers. Gaitskell made these points in a reply to Russell's article that was published in the same issue of the *New York Times Magazine*, prompting Russell to respond with a letter to the paper that was published on 14 August 1960 and which contained his fiercest piece of anti-American rhetoric so far. 'We were impressed by the seriousness of Hitler's threat to Britain in 1940,' he wrote, 'but it was not nearly as serious as the US threat to Britain at this present moment.'

Despite this exchange with Gaitskell, Russell, for reasons that are left obscure in his many accounts of this period, took comparatively little interest in the manoeuvres – mainly within the trade union movement – that were being conducted to ensure the success of the CND campaign to 'win Labour over'. Schoenman's lack of interest in Labour Party machinations is entirely explicable by his general disdain for parliamentary democracy. As he spelt out in his *Peace News* article, one consequence of his conviction that 'the values derived from liberal, democratic and socialist traditions [are] no longer operative' is that: 'If we hand over our consciences to any political party we will be betrayed.' The policy of the Labour Party was of no concern to Schoenman. But what of Russell? Why was he so apparently uninterested in the fact that a party with every hope of forming the next British Government seemed about to adopt the very policy he had been urging for many years? Did he feel certain that the Labour Party would *not* adopt such a policy? Or that, once adopted, it would soon be revoked? Or was he sceptical that a future Labour Government would implement it, even if it remained party policy while Labour were in opposition? Or could he possibly have believed what he appeared to believe, namely that his aim of changing the Government's policy on nuclear weapons would more likely be achieved by Schoenman's plans of civil disobedience than by a change in the policy of the Labour Party?

Another explanation suggests itself that sees the solution, not in Russell's convictions about political strategy, but in his vanity. Russell himself wrote of Schoenman's 'fulsome flatteries' of him, adding: 'I am by no means immune to flattery. It is so rare as to be sweet to my ears.' On this occasion, Schoenman's flattery took the form of making Russell the centre of the movement he was planning, encouraging him to believe that the best chance he himself had of making a difference to the anti-nuclear cause was through Schoenman's proposal. Russell's desire during this period to be acknowledged as an important figure in world events was as strong as (some would say stronger than) his desire to change Government policy on nuclear weapons. Rupert Crawshay-Williams records that, after his televised debate with Edward Teller in the spring of 1960, Russell delightedly informed him that Teller seemed nervous and afraid. 'If the man who makes the H-bomb is frightened of me,' Russell remarked, 'well, I feel I really must be *somebody*!'

Russell's disenchantment with the constitutional methods of CND may, one suspects, be linked to the fact that, by 1960, he himself was not a pivotal figure in those methods. The resolution to commit the Labour Party to unilateral nuclear disarmament was not to be presented by Russell, but by Frank Cousins, leader of the Transport and General Workers' Union, and its success did not in any way depend upon what Russell thought or said, but on the ability of Labour Party activists to marshal the support of the enormous block-votes of the unions. Russell tellingly recounts that, when he wrote to Cousins to ask his advice on making public the plans he and Schoenman were making, 'Cousins replied to my letter briefly, saying that it did not matter one way or another what I did or said.' Schoenman's success in ingratiating himself with Russell may have rested primarily upon reassuring Russell that it *did* matter what he did and said.

For whatever reason, Russell stayed aloof from the excitement that gripped the Peace Movement in the weeks leading up to the Scarborough conference. While the rest of CND, sensing themselves to be on the brink of their greatest triumph, canvassed opinion within the Labour Party and assessed their chances of gathering enough support to pass the resolution that would be put to the conference by Cousins on 5 October, Russell threw in his lot with the anarchist wing of the movement, meeting Schoenman to iron out the details of the proposed 'Committee of 100'. For the most part, these discussions were kept secret from the executive of CND, and especially from its Chairman, Canon Collins, for whom Schoenman had a great contempt, shared to some extent by Russell. On 3 September, Russell wrote to Collins to tell him that, at the forthcoming CND meeting at Trafalgar Square on 24 September, 'I plan to say something in support of those who practise direct action'. Collins replied that, with the crucial Labour Party conference coming up, he did not think this would be a good idea. Russell then invited Collins to meet him in London on 16 September to discuss Russell's advocacy of civil disobedience, though even then, according to Collins, Russell did not mention the plans he had formed with Schoenman for a mass movement. After consultation with Frank Cousins, Russell reiterated his promise not to rock the boat until after the Labour Party conference.

Meanwhile, he and Schoenman continued to plot their campaign of insurrection (on Schoenman's understanding) or dramatic propaganda (on Russell's), drawing up lists of potential members of the proposed 'committee' and exchanging ideas as to what their first mass act of civil disobedience should be. At an early stage they were joined by the Rev. Michael Scott, a veteran of the Direct Action Committee, and by 11 September the three of them had drafted letters to the potential 100 members of their new movement. Schoenman's name was absent from these letters, which went out signed only by Russell and Scott. The final list of members of the Committee of 100 was impressive, including the film director Lindsay Anderson, the playwrights Robert Bolt, Arnold Wesker and John Osborne, the painter Augustus John and a host of other celebrities, including Sir Herbert Read and George Melly. If the British Government could be forced to imprison such distinguished company, it would undoubtedly have an impact, whether or not it led to the fulfilment of Schoenman's dreams of vast concentration camps bulging with anti-war protesters.

As promised, Russell kept off the subject of direct action in his speech to the Trafalgar Square meeting of 24 September, but, having sent out letters of invitation to the proposed 100 members of the new committee and having canvassed many more potential sympathisers, it was unrealistic to expect the lid to be kept on his and Schoenman's plans until after the Labour Party conference. News was bound to leak, and it did. Canon Collins first heard of Russell's plans of mass civil disobedience from the publisher Victor Gollancz, one of the recipients of an invitation letter. Collins phoned Russell in alarm and was again reassured that nothing would be made public until after the Scarborough conference.

A week before the conference, however, Russell's plans were made public in dramatic fashion. One of the letters, intended for John Connell, the President of the Noise Abatement Society, was sent instead to John Connell, the military historian, a man of devoutly conservative political opinions, who was understandably surprised to find himself being asked to support a campaign of illegal protests. Connell forwarded his letter to George Hutchinson of the London *Evening Standard*, who published the story on 28 September. Other newspapers picked up the story, and in the following days condemnation of Russell's 'conspiracy' was widespread among editorial-writers and columnists. The timing of this publicity for the Committee of 100 could not have been more embarrassing for the executive of CND, fuelling speculation that Schoenman was, in fact, an *agent provocateur*, whose real purpose was to undermine the anti-nuclear movement. Canon Collins hurriedly released a Press statement reiterating the policy of CND of using 'legal and democratic methods of argument, persuasion and demonstration to achieve its aims', and the following day an emergency meeting of the CND executive was held (attended, however, by only four of its twenty-seven members) at which it was reaffirmed that 'Individuals who advocate methods of civil disobedience, whatever their standing, do so without having consulted either the Executive Committee or the rank and file of the campaign.'

Russell and Scott reacted angrily to this affront (as they saw it), and the following week, while the attention of the Press and the Peace Movement should have been concentrated on the momentous vote at the Labour Party conference, it was directed instead towards a fierce internecine squabble between the two elderly leaders of CND. During the week of the conference (beginning 3 October 1960), Collins and Russell met every day at Russell's London house in Hasker Street to discuss what threatened to develop into a damaging split in the CND movement. Both men were furious with each other. Collins was enraged at the disastrous timing of Russell's support for Schoenman's plans, which he believed inflicted lasting damage on the campaign at the peak of its success. 'Just when CND seemed to be flourishing like a green bay tree,' he later wrote, 'the winds of dissent blew into a gale, and the storm broke':

> With the advent of the Committee of 100 came bickerings, misunderstandings, irreconcilable attitudes and strained loyalties which inevitably reduced the effectiveness of the Campaign . . . in my view, particularly coming at the time it did, the launching of the Committee of 100 was a serious blow to the Campaign, and one from which it never fully recovered.

Russell's grievances were more personal. Immediately after the *Evening Standard*'s story on the Committee of 100, he had offered to resign as President of CND, 'should the Executive pass a resolution to that effect'. No such resolution was passed, but the *Daily Mail* of 30 September mistakenly reported that, at its meeting of 29 September, the executive *had* asked for Russell's resignation, if he refused to be bound by the decision of CND's annual conference to use only legal and democratic methods of persuasion. Russell was incensed by this report, for which he irrationally blamed Collins, whom he now considered to be taking upon himself undemocratic powers, dictating to CND members what they should and should not do to promote the cause. As he later put it: 'The chairman of CND made statements to his friends and to the Executive Committee and to the press which, in effect, charged me with starting a new movement behind his back and one not permissible within the rulings of CND.' He and Scott quickly issued a statement to the Press, affirming the right of individual members of CND to follow their conscience with regard to civil disobedience.

Russell and Collins, then, embarked on their series of meetings at Hasker Street in an atmosphere of great mutual suspicion and acrimony. On Russell's insistence, witnesses were present, and a tape-recording was made of the discussions, in case disputes arose later about what had been said. Russell and Collins even managed to quarrel about who should act as witnesses, with Collins refusing to have Scott as Russell's witness and Russell in turn rejecting Collins's suggestion of having Peggy Duff and Kingsley Martin present. In the end, Arthur Goss came as Russell's 'second', and Michael Howard as Collins's. Pettiness was replaced by farce when it became apparent to Collins that Scott and Schoenman *were* present in the house, only secreted in a room upstairs:

> During the discussions Russell would go upstairs, and it was quite obvious that Schoenman and Michael Scott were there to advise him – he would come down and go back on what we had agreed – again, obviously at their instigation. So we went on and on and on.

The central point at issue was that of finding a formula that would allow Russell to remain President of CND without committing either Collins himself or CND as a movement to an acceptance of Schoenman's plans for mass civil disobedience. On Wednesday 5 October, they broke off discussion to hear the news on the radio that Frank Cousins had won his vote: the Labour Party was now committed to a policy of unilateral nuclear disarmament. Pausing only momentarily to absorb this momentous news, the two old peace campaigners resumed their hostilities, and it was not until the following evening that a 'statement of Amity' was agreed upon. This read in full:

The President and Chairman of the Campaign for Nuclear Disarmament wish to make it clear that they will continue to work together in amity for nuclear disarmament, and they hope that in due course a joint statement will be issued by them concerning the subject of the recent press controversy.

They hope that all members of the Campaign for Nuclear Disarmament, those who support civil disobedience and those who do not, will continue as during the last three years to work for the common end.

Signed: Russell (President)
L. John Collins (Chairman)

As the outcome of four days of protracted debate, it was not a very impressive document; as a statement of amicability, it was entirely unconvincing.

After releasing this statement to the Press, Collins went on holiday. By the time he returned a fortnight later, he found that the decision he and Russell had announced of continuing to work together in amity had been unilaterally overturned by Russell. Facing Collins on his return was a letter from Russell addressed to all members of the CND executive tendering his resignation as President, explaining:

My reason for doing so is that I find it impossible to work with the present National Chairman of the Campaign . . . I cannot countenance the chairman of an organisation of which I am president permitting the policy of that organisation to be misstated in public statements which are said to come from him and have not been publicly repudiated by him.

This seems to hark back to the misreporting of Collins's statements about Russell during the last week of September, which, despite the extended discussions during the first week of October and the joint statement of amity, still rankled with Russell. Russell seemed determined to pursue the matter, even after the publication in the *Daily Mail* on 27 October of a letter from Collins in which he directly repudiated the mistaken report. Still not pacified, Russell prepared an article for the *Observer*, giving his version of the controversy. In the opinion of Peggy Duff, an executive member of CND, this article was 'certainly contentious and possibly libellous' and would have damaged the campaign considerably. In a last attempt to smooth Russell's feathers, the CND executive met on 5 November and agreed a resolution regretting 'that false statements, purporting to come from the Chairman, about CND policy and concerning the President's actions, have been made in the Press'. At last mollified, Russell withdrew his *Observer* article.

Regarding Russell's behaviour during these weeks, it is hard to resist the conclusion that he was quite determined to resign as President of CND, whatever Canon Collins did. Peggy Duff has said that, in her opinion, Russell 'probably expected and hoped that the Executive would repudiate the chairman and beg the president to come back', but the evidence suggests that Russell was no longer very interested in what the CND executive did or said, so long as they put on record their repudiation of the Press reports accusing him of bad faith. Russell had fallen out with CND as finally and irrevocably as he had fallen out with his past ideas, his past wives and lovers and his first son. Once he resigned, there was no going back. What is striking about the whole affair is his blindness to the political consequences of his feud with Collins. It never seemed to occur to him that Collins had a point about the timing of Russell's support for Schoenman, or that it was damaging to the whole movement to pursue in print his feud with Collins at precisely the moment when the Press ought to have been concerned instead with CND's victory at the Labour Party conference. The whole basis of Russell's complaint against Collins was that the Chairman was reported to have said something damaging to his, Russell's reputation. But was that, after all, so *very* important? Was it worth splitting the CND movement over?

Another way of looking at it is that the crucial issue was not Russell's reputation, but the right of anti-nuclear protesters to pursue illegal methods of persuasion in pursuit of their aims. There was a strong body of opinion within CND sympathetic to the methods of the Direct Action Committee and likely to be won over to Schoenman's plans of mass civil disobedience. The fact that it was in the interests of 'winning Labour over' to keep this body of opinion quiet during the Labour Party conference may not have seemed as important to Russell as the principle involved. But this interpretation of Russell's actions does not quite fit. After all, Collins conceded at an early stage that individuals who broke the law out of concern to save humanity had his sympathy, if not his support. And the Press reports that implied a more authoritarian attitude towards law-breakers were publicly denied by Collins. Moreover, he had gone out of his way to reach some kind of compromise with Russell in order to prevent Russell from resigning. After issuing his joint statement, after writing to the *Daily Mail* denying their damaging allegations and after joining with other executive members of CND to denounce the lies told in the Press, what more could Collins possibly have done to placate Russell? One is driven to the conclusion that there is *nothing* he could have done. Russell's mind was made up to resign as President of CND and throw his support instead behind the Committee of 100 – convinced in all probability by his conversations with Schoenman in the summer and by the influence upon him of Schoenman's flatteries. As Collins later said: 'Russell was a very vain old man, a great man, a very great man, but a very, *very* vain man.'

The day after he resigned as President of CND, Russell was elected President of the Committee of 100 at their inaugural meeting of 22 October 1960 at the Friends' Meeting House in Euston Road, London. Scott was elected Chairman and Michael Randle, another veteran of the Direct Action Committee, Secretary. Schoenman had no official post, though it was no secret that the new movement was his inspiration. Many of the 'big names' confirmed as members of the original 100 were present at this first meeting, including Lindsay Anderson, John Osborne and Arnold Wesker, ensuring wide coverage in the newspapers, which now, however, began to adopt a tone of amusement rather than hostility at this supposedly subversive conspiracy. The *Guardian* reported some of the proposals put forward concerning what their first action should be: disrupting official functions, such as the State Opening of Parliament or the Trooping of the Colour, jamming the BBC, and kidnapping the Chancellor of the Exchequer on Budget Day were all mentioned as possibilities, suggesting that the movement would be inspired, not by the quasi-revolutionary hopes of anarchists, but by the fertile imaginations of dramatists and film directors.

A movement led by a committee of 100 people was clearly going to have problems reaching decisions, and inevitably no conclusion was reached at this first meeting about what activities the movement would sponsor. Instead, the Committee elected a 'working group' of thirteen of its members, who would make decisions on its behalf. Thereafter, the fiction that there really *was* a 'Committee of 100' was dropped, and the big names became largely irrelevant, deployed only to convince possible recruits that, if they went to prison for supporting the Committee's actions, they would be in good company. Agreement was, however, reached on the general aims of the new movement, which were those articulated in the 'manifesto' drawn up by Russell and Scott published a few days after the meeting as the pamphlet *Act or Perish: A call to non-violent action.* This spoke of the 'vast scheme of mass murder which is being hatched – nominally for our protection, but in fact for universal extermination' by the governments of East and West, and of the need to show 'steadfastness and willingness to suffer hardship and thereby to persuade the world that our cause is worthy of such devotion'. The nearest it came to spelling out the point of the new movement was in its statement that: 'Our immediate purpose, in so far as it is political, is only to persuade Britain to abandon reliance upon the illusory protection of nuclear weapons.' If that could be achieved, the pamphlet claimed, 'a wider horizon will open before our eyes. We shall become aware of the immense possibilities of nature when harnessed by the creative intelligence of man to the purposes and arts of peace.' It ended with what had already became one of Russell's most oft-quoted declarations:

Remember your humanity, and forget the rest. If you can do so, the way lies open to a new Paradise; if you cannot, nothing lies before you but universal death.

Six weeks later, the working group had come up with a solid proposal, and, at a Press conference on 14 December, Russell announced what the first demonstration of the Committee of 100 would be: a four-hour sit-down outside the Ministry of Defence in Whitehall on 18 February 1961, to coincide with the arrival in Holy Loch, at the mouth of the River Clyde, of the submarine tender, the US *Proteus*, which was to serve the US Polaris submarine fleet. To an audience of sceptical journalists, Russell promised that the demonstration would not go ahead unless they received at least 2,000 pledges to take part. The scepticism was not confined to outsiders. 'We'd never had a DAC [Direct Action Committee] demonstration with more than one hundred people!' Michael Randle said later. 'I was very sceptical as to whether we'd get over two thousand.'

Over the next month, thousands of leaflets were distributed, and the Committee waited anxiously for the pledges to come in. In the meantime, Russell returned to Wales to spend Christmas with his granddaughters, having brusquely turned down Dora's request for a family Christmas in London, with John, Russell and the girls getting together for the first time since 1955. The girls were grateful to Russell for getting them out of having to spend Christmas with Dora, and Lucy's diary shows herself delighted with the result: 'We woke up at 5.45 & opened our stockings & everything was wonderful . . . We had some wonderful presents . . . I haven't got over it yet.' Ralph Schoenman was, by now, such a regular visitor to Plas Penryhn that he had almost become part of the family, and on 28 December Lucy records: 'In the morning Ralph came & we went in & talked to him. He gave us each something from India . . . Ralph's quite fun actually.'

Two days later 'Ralph went', and on 3 January 1961: 'Talked with Gpa & Gma from 9.15–10.30 about nuclear stuff. Very depressing. Going to write to Ralph, I think.' Two weeks later, Lucy mentions that she 'spent the afternoon talking to Ralph'. She and her sisters returned to Moreton Hall with handfuls of leaflets and Lucy promised to 'ask people in our form to send them to their parents!' While she was away, her room was used to put Ralph up, and she wrote hoping 'my room wasn't in too awful a state to sleep in'.

While Lucy was learning to accept Schoenman as part of the household, her own future was being decided in court. But, as Russell's long battle to gain custody of her and her sisters was reaching its conclusion, it was becoming clear that the political adventure he had embarked upon with Schoenman would leave him little time to devote to his grandchildren. In the week that the decision was made to grant Russell custody, he was in London to attend an anxious meeting of the members of the Committee of 100 at Kingsway Hall. There it was reported that, although 34,000 leaflets had been sent out, only 500 pledges had been received. With only a few weeks to go, the question was raised: should the demonstration go ahead? The general feeling was that it should, but only if at least 1,200 pledges came in. By 11 February, just seven days before the event, the 2,000 pledges they needed had been received.

On 18 February, then, 'the quietist, most orderly, most impressive

demonstration senior police officers could recall' took place. It began with a
march from Marble Arch to Trafalgar Square, and then, after speeches in
the square, a crowd of several thousand people marched silently down
Whitehall and sat for two and a half hours outside the Ministry of Defence.
Russell, Edith, Schoenman and Scott sat at the front of the adoring crowd,
and, before they left, Russell and Scott taped a message to the door of the
Ministry calling for unilateral disarmament and for 'people everywhere to
rise up against the monstrous tyranny . . . of the nuclear tyrants of East and
West'. Russell was then taken by Schoenman and Scott on a walk around
the crowd, who all cheered wildly.

As a media spectacle, it was irresistible. Television pictures showed a
white-haired prophet sitting with a resolute expression on his face among a
vast throng of young, idealistic followers. 'Why are you doing this?' he was
asked by a reporter. 'Because, if the present policies of the Western
governments are continued,' came the answer, 'the entire human race will be
exterminated, and some of us think that might be rather a pity.' The
impression was successfully conveyed that only those who wish for mass
annihilation could possibly disagree with what Russell was doing. Among
the many people who fell under his spell that day was the poet James
Kirkup, who shared the platform with Russell at Trafalgar Square and
recalls Russell's kindness in helping to calm his nerves about speaking
before such a vast audience. Russell shook Kirkup's hand, 'and I remember
how dry, small, thin and brittle his hand felt in mine: it was like a withered
bird's claw'. When, in February 1970, Kirkup heard of Russell's death, he
remembered his meeting in a poem that captures well the impression that
Russell made on many that day.

In Memoriam: Bertrand Russell

In another February, on a Sunday afternoon nine years ago
I wept for you, and for a world that could reject your voice.

You were so frail, so ancient: yet stronger than us all.
You stood beside me on a platform in Trafalgar Square
among the toothless lions of a tyrannous imperial pride,
under the shadow of Nelson strutting in the falling snow.

Your head was bare, and your wild white hair
blazed like your mind in the wind of whirling flakes.
Your face, the mask of a tragic hawk,
was sad and bitter as you cried your warnings and defiance
at the armed forces of error, the police of Britain,
the criminal politicians, the priests of power, the insane
manufacturers of arms and poison gas and atom bombs,
inhuman profiteers all, sucking the blood of human misery.

You stood alone, before the gathered heads of microphones,
tilted intelligently, raised like vipers, cobras about to strike.
– But, like a saint, or like Apollo, god of poetry and music,
you charmed them into peace. You won their love with love,
with the fearless beauty of your mind, your noble voice.

Whether the event did anything to change public opinion of nuclear
weapons or not, it certainly did much to bolster Russell's reputation among
young people, for whom he was now a saintly personification of reasonable
protest and justifiable rebellion.

By the media and by well-wishers, the event was judged a great success.
What Russell had said was so unobjectionably reasonable (after all, who
would deny that it would be 'a pity' to destroy the entire human race?), and
the crowd so well-behaved, that the Press, the police and everybody else
looked upon the proceedings with sympathetic tolerance. From Schoenman's
point of view, however – and, to a lesser extent, from Russell's – this very
tolerance was a problem. Schoenman had expected to embarrass the
Government into imprisoning vast numbers of eminent people, and yet not a
single person had even been arrested. 'We do not want forever to be tolerated
by the police,' Russell announced at a Press conference on 19 February. 'Our
movement depends for its success on an immense public opinion and we
cannot create that unless we rouse the authorities to more action than they
took yesterday.' 'We want', added Schoenman, 'to put the Government in the
position of either jailing thousands of people or abdicating.'

The sit-down outside the Ministry of Defence, massively and sympathetically reported as it was, forced the Committee to face again the question of
what the point of their call for civil disobedience was. If the purpose was
publicity, as Russell repeatedly said, then they had surely been successful.
But, if the realisation of Schoenman's vision of 'mass resistance to mass
society' was the objective, then they needed to be more provocative.
Throughout February and March, the leaders of the Committee debated
this question in print. In an article called 'Civil Disobedience to Halt
Polaris', published in Peace News on the eve of the Whitehall demonstration,
Schoenman emphasised his rejection of all political parties and ideologies
and insisted that the purpose of illegal protests against nuclear weapons was
to reaffirm the right of individuals to resist the technological society that
alienated them. Allied to Schoenman's argument was that of Michael
Randle, who, in a Peace News article of 10 March, asked: 'Is it Revolution
We're After?' His answer was 'yes': 'Mass civil disobedience means
revolution'. Unilateral nuclear disarmament, he claimed, implied revolution,
'or at least it implies a profound political and social upheaval that will not be
achieved within the framework of existing parties or existing politics'. The
unilateralists within the Labour Party would not stick to their guns, Randle
argued, because the demand for unilateralism was too revolutionary to be
granted without a fundamental change in the 'military and political tradition
of the country, including, alas, the tradition built up in the Labour Party
over the last fifty years'.

In their talk of revolutionising society, Randle and Schoenman spoke for a significant proportion of the activists within the Committee, which became the natural home for the more radical, more anarchist members of CND. But to satisfy the aims of this group, the Committee had to do something that would offend the authorities more than they had managed to do on 18 February. At the end of that year's Aldermaston march at the beginning of April, Schoenman took matters into his own hands by leading a group of about 500 protesters from Trafalgar Square to the US Embassy in Grosvenor Square. This action was unsanctioned by the working group of the Committee and was conducted with far less decorum than the Ministry of Defence protest in February. Six people were arrested and an atmosphere of hostility and violence created when the demonstrators followed the police vans back to the station. There, a pitched battle between police and protesters developed, leading to twenty-five more arrests, mostly for assault. Despite the fact that Schoenman's action involved only a tiny proportion of the people who had joined in the march, it commanded all the newspaper headlines, and a furious Canon Collins felt compelled to issue a statement condemning the protest and dissociating CND from it.

A fortnight later, Russell matched Schoenman's inflammatory actions with inflammatory words when he addressed the first annual conference of the Midlands Region Youth Campaign for Nuclear Disarmament in Birmingham on the subject of 'Civil Disobedience'. Most of Russell's speech consisted of what were by now familiar themes in his public utterances – the folly of nuclear weapons, the advantages to Britain of neutrality, the danger of accidental nuclear war, the impotence of constitutional methods of persuasion, and so on – but what guaranteed newspaper coverage of his speech was his final paragraph. 'We used to think that Hitler was wicked when he wanted to kill all the Jews,' he said:

> but Kennedy and Macmillan and others both in the East and in the West pursue policies which will probably lead to killing not only all the Jews but all the rest of us too. They are much more wicked than Hitler and this idea of weapons of mass extermination is utterly and absolutely horrible and it is a thing which no man with one spark of humanity can tolerate and I will not pretend to obey a government which is organising the massacre of the whole of mankind. I will do anything I can to oppose such governments in any non-violent way that seems likely to be fruitful, and I exhort all of you to feel the same way. We cannot obey these murderers. They are wicked and abominable. They are the wickedest people that ever lived in the history of man and it is our duty to do what we can.

Such words were calculated to destroy the atmosphere of tolerance that had prevailed on 18 February. If Russell really believed that the British Government was composed of 'the wickedest people that ever lived in the history of man' and that Macmillan was worse than Hitler, then, the authorities may have reasoned, he was a dangerous man. And if what he sought was not only to remind people that the extermination of the human race would be 'a pity', but also to convince them that it was their duty to resist the 'murderers' who governed them in any way they could, then the movement that Russell led could no longer be treated as a harmless group of eccentrics, but had to be regarded as a serious insurrectionary force.

The combination of Schoenman's maverick actions and Russell's intemperate rhetoric succeeded in their stated aim of making the Committee intolerable to the authorities, and before their next demonstration – a sit-down in Parliament Square on 29 April – the police gave notice that they intended this time to enforce the law. Russell was too ill to take part (he suffered a bad attack of shingles soon after his speech in Birmingham), but 2,000 people turned up to be faced by 3,000 police, who succeeded in making 826 arrests. It was beginning to look as though Schoenman's dreams of crowding the prisons might materialise, though most of those arrested chose to pay their one-pound fine rather than face imprisonment, which suggested that, even among committee supporters, there was little faith in Schoenman's plans to force the Government's hand. Still, at least this time some celebrities were arrested, including Vanessa Redgrave and John Neville, both of whom, however, accepted bail in order to appear on stage the following night.

Russell spent most of the summer of 1961 at home in Plas Penrhyn, recovering from shingles. In his convalescence he saw through the publication of *Fact and Fiction*, a collection of his radio talks, speeches and articles, which ranged from the series of BBC talks on 'Books that Influenced Me in Youth' that he had given in 1957 to his more recent articles on disarmament and neutrality. Russell also included two new 'Nightmares', and, most oddly, a collection of five dreams that he was at pains to insist were 'exactly as I dreamt them'. This had to be pointed out, Edith wrote to Unwin on her husband's behalf, because 'If the readers do not grasp that fact firmly, the point of the dreams is very considerably blunted.' Quite what the point of the dreams was, however, remains obscure.

Of the five dreams, the first has the famous nineteenth-century Master of Balliol, Benjamin Jowett, remonstrating with the adolescent Bertie about the folly of longing for death; the second has Russell asking God for Noah's Ark in order that he can put it 'somewhere in the suburbs and charge sixpence admission' (only to be told by God that he has already given it to an American); the third has Henry the Navigator taking Russell to a diplomatic congress at which the Chairman remarks that, though royalty has no price, it has 'inestimable value'; the fourth has Russell in Africa, attending an impromptu meeting of the House of Commons, at which the intentions of Prince Napoleon Louis, the son of Napoleon III, are discussed; and the fifth has Russell in an hotel, witnessing the lynching of 'John Elmwood, Communist and Atheist'. The same uncertainty of tone that afflicts Russell's fiction is evident in these dream reports. Are we supposed merely to find them amusing, or to see in them revelations of Russell's character? Just as critics and readers neither laughed nor cried at Russell's fiction, so a discreet silence was maintained in the face of this peculiarly half-hearted invitation to analyse the contents of his subconscious.

Russell also wrote during the summer of 1961 a 'Penguin Special' called *Has Man a Future?*, which added little to his earlier book, *Common Sense and Nuclear Warfare*, except his now familiar argument for British neutrality and a discussion of the problem that was on everybody's mind that summer: the Berlin crisis. In July, the Soviet Union agreed a treaty with the Communist Government of East Germany, which it regarded as superseding the post-war agreements reached at Yalta and Potsdam. This sent a wave of anxiety through the population of West Berlin, who saw in the announcement an imminent threat to their independence from Soviet control. As West Berlin was entirely surrounded by Soviet-controlled territory, the only effective protection that the West could offer it was a threat of nuclear retaliation against any Soviet advance, and, as Russell put it: 'If the threat is thought to be only bluff, it affords no protection. If it is thought to be bluff, but is not, the human race perishes.' The world was, as many statesmen later admitted, on the brink of nuclear war. In the event, the East German Government drew back from a Soviet-backed invasion of West Berlin and, faced with a mass exodus from East to West Berlin, contented themselves instead with the building of the Berlin Wall.

With regard to the question of nuclear weapons, the crisis served to harden attitudes on both sides. On the one hand, it confirmed the view of those who considered the threat of nuclear attack to be the *only* effective means to control Soviet expansion; on the other, it gave credence to the urgent warnings of the Committee of 100 that nuclear warfare and the consequent possibility of human extinction were real and imminent dangers. The Labour Party was swinging to the first of these positions. After his defeat at Scarborough, Gaitskell had successfully mobilised opinion within the party opposed to unilateralism, and, through his 'Campaign for Democratic Socialism', was working hard to overturn the unilateralist policies of the big trade unions. By the summer of 1961 nobody had any doubt that Gaitskell was winning this battle and that the Labour Party conference of that year would reverse its decision to support unilateralism. The scepticism expressed by Michael Randle and Ralph Schoenman about working within the Labour Party would seem to have been vindicated, though many, including Canon Collins, regarded it as a self-fulfilling prophecy. The antics of the Committee of 100 undoubtedly made it easier for Gaitskell to identify unilateralism with the extreme left, and served to alienate moderate opinion from the CND view.

In turn, the Labour Party swing against unilateralism served to undermine the faith of CND members in constitutional methods, and by the summer of 1961 the Committee of 100 had replaced CND in its leadership of the anti-nuclear movement. Thus, while CND began its long, slow decline into political irrelevance, the Committee, for a few months at least, succeeded in its aim to become a genuinely mass movement and a perceived threat to the British Government.

Further evidence of the authorities' changed attitude towards the

Committee was provided on 6 August 1961, the anniversary of the dropping of the atom bomb on Hiroshima. In the morning, the Committee organised a vigil at the Cenotaph, at which Russell and Edith placed a wreath in honour of the Japanese victims. This was attended by about 2,000 people and was, on the whole, quite peaceful, despite being seen as a provocative act by those who preferred to regard the Cenotaph as a memorial to those who had died fighting the Japanese. Things turned ugly in the afternoon at a rally in Hyde Park, attended by a much larger crowd. The use of microphones was banned in Hyde Park, but Russell and the other leaders of the Committee decided deliberately to flout this law ('We were, after all,' Russell later said, 'an organisation devoted to civil disobedience'). This resulted in the spectacle – caught on television cameras – of Russell's speech being interrupted by a policeman snatching the microphone from the outstretched hand of Schoenman, who stood at Russell's side. While the crowd shouted 'Shame' and 'Leave him alone', Russell looked disconcerted, and a faint, satisfied smile momentarily appeared on Schoenman's face.

For their flouting of the law on this occasion, Russell, Schoenman and Randle were summonsed to Marlborough Street Court on 13 September and fined. They were, however, by this time already in prison on a more serious charge: inciting a breach of the peace. The Government had finally decided to treat the Committee as the subversive organisation that Schoenman had always proclaimed it to be, and issued summonses to thirty-seven of its members, including Russell, Edith, Schoenman, Randle and Scott, to be charged under the Justices of the Peace Act of 1361 at Bow Street Court on 12 September. Five of those summonsed agreed to be bound over to keep the peace, but the rest were sentenced to jail for periods of one or two months. The trial, of course, was a major propaganda coup for the Committee – exactly the kind of thing they had been hoping for – and Russell, as he had in 1916, exploited it to the full. To a court crowded with committee sympathisers, he delivered a dignified but rousing defence of civil disobedience, which ended on a crowd-pleasing note of defiance:

> We who are here accused are prepared to suffer imprisonment because we believe that this is the most effective way of working for the salvation of our country and the world. If you condemn us you will be helping our cause, and therefore humanity.
> While life remains to us we will not cease to do what lies in our power to avert the greatest calamity that has ever threatened mankind.

When Russell's sentence of two months was announced, there were cries of 'fascists' and 'poor old man', and medical evidence was produced on his behalf, which had the effect of reducing his and Edith's sentences to seven days. Schoenman was given two months. After the trial, Russell and Edith were taken to Brixton Prison in a Black Maria upon which someone had scrawled 'Ban the Bomb'.

In the short term, the imprisoning of Russell was a triumph for the Committee. It caused a worldwide storm of protest, made the British

Government look absurd and accelerated Russell's elevation to secular
sainthood in the eyes of the rebellious young. In the long term, however, the
furore surrounding Russell's week in Brixton served to disguise the
underlying fact that, in its battle with the Committee of 100, the
Government was winning.

The Committee's next demonstration – a mass sit-down in Trafalgar
Square on 17 September – had to go ahead in the absence of its leaders,
all of whom were now in prison. Responsibility for the action was thus
assumed by Pat Pottle, a twenty-three-year-old anarchist printer, who, in
the absence of Schoenman, Randle and Russell, was elected Secretary. Pottle
faced a situation very different from that which had faced the organisers of
the Committee's first demonstration in February. Tensions were now
running higher on all sides. The Committee had become more militant, the
Government more hostile, the Labour Party completely unsympathetic and
the international situation more grave. Adding to the last of these was the
fact that, following the breakdown of the Geneva disarmament talks on 30
August, both the Americans and the Soviets had resumed nuclear tests.

A few days before the demonstration, the Home Secretary, R. A. Butler,
escalated tension still further by declaring a ban on processions in the
Trafalgar Square area under the Public Order Act. Anyone who turned up
to the sit-down – whether or not they actually sat down – was liable to be
arrested. The atmosphere created by this order, coming on top of the
fervour aroused by the trial, was much to Schoenman's liking, and from
Eccleshall Prison he wrote delightedly to the Russells at Brixton that it was
just like war-time.

In the event, the demonstration was the best-attended yet, with 12,000
people cramming into the square. Clearly, they could not all be arrested, but
the police, acting at times violently and indiscriminately, arrested as many as
they could. Those arrested included an indignant Canon Collins, who was
led away protesting that he was not a demonstrator, but simply an observer.
A similar fate befell the Labour MP, Fenner Brockway, who protested in
vain to the police that he was there with the Home Secretary's permission.
Other prominent people arrested included John Osborne, George Melly and
Vanessa Redgrave. After midnight, according to one observer, the police-
men, 'surly and foul-tempered at the long hours of struggling and at having
weekend leaves cancelled, launched a deliberate and vicious attack against
the scattered remnants of the crowd':

Cameramen were told abruptly that if they filmed another foot they
would be arrested. Demonstrators, onlookers, passers-by – it made no
difference – were punched, knocked down, kicked. Squads of constables
threw struggling civilians into the icy water of the fountain basins.
Middle-aged women were slammed down and dragged by one leg
through puddles, face down against the concrete pavement. Several
people, alarmed by the thug-like brutality erupting in the Square, tried to
flee. They were hauled down from behind and kicked and beaten where
they lay.

Russell, it seems, had been granted his wish that the Committee should not be forever tolerated by the police. In all, 1,314 arrests were made. Russell's own message to the demonstration (given, of course, *in absentia*) was hardly calculated to calm tempers. Its rhetoric was that of the imprisoned revolutionary leader he had perhaps almost convinced himself he was. 'Friends,' it began. 'Along with valued colleagues I am to be silenced for a time – perhaps for ever, for who can tell how soon the great massacre will take place?':

> . . . Kennedy and Khrushchev, Adenauer and de Gaulle, Macmillan and Gaitskell, are pursuing a common aim: the ending of human life.
>
> You, your families, your friends, and your countries are to be exterminated by the common decision of a few brutal and powerful men. To please these men, all the private affections, all the public hopes, all that has been achieved in art, and knowledge and thought and all that might be achieved hereafter is to be wiped out forever.
>
> Our ruined lifeless planet will continue for countless ages to circle aimlessly round the sun unredeemed by the joys and loves, the occasional wisdom and the power to create beauty which have given value to human life.
>
> It is for seeking to prevent this that we are in prison.

The demonstration marked the high point of the Committee's activities, and, for a while afterwards, its leaders were jubilant, thinking that at last they had succeeded in their aim of inspiring mass resistance to the Government. But despite the impressive number of demonstrators, and the almost equally impressive number of arrests, the demonstration had not been an unqualified success, on either Russell's or Schoenman's understanding of what the point of the Committee was. With regard to Russell's stated aim of attracting publicity, this had certainly been achieved. But publicity for what? Most of the coverage in the newspapers concentrated, not on the aims of the protesters, but on their methods, and especially on their battles with the police. There was no sign that this coverage – unlike the sympathetic coverage of the CND marches of previous years – was increasing public sympathy for the unilateralist argument. On the contrary, unilateralism was now perceived to be a vote-loser, which is one reason why Gaitskell had little trouble in persuading the Labour Party to reject it. As for Schoenman's vision of 'filling the jails', most of those arrested again chose to pay their fines rather than go to prison.

Nevertheless, when Russell addressed the next Committee rally in Trafalgar Square on 29 October, he struck a triumphalist note. Since the demonstration of 17 September, he announced, Committees of 100 had been set up in other countries. 'All these people throughout the world must be encouraged,' he implored. 'We must build up – and we must do it quickly – a great world-wide mass movement of people demanding the abandonment of nuclear weapons, the abandonment of war as a means of settling disputes':

Although the time may be short, our movement is gaining strength day by day. I repeat, and shall go on repeating:

We *can* win, and we *must*.

However, as the Committee grew more confident and ambitious, the Government stepped up its pressure. Its next move was to try and get Schoenman deported. His visa had run out in June and had been extended to November, but as he was by then in prison, the Home Secretary announced that it would not be further extended, since 'aliens who helped to organise breaches of the law could not be allowed to stay in Britain'. Through his solicitor, Russell argued that Schoenman's services as a secretary were indispensable to him, and appeals were made on Schoenman's behalf by Fenner Brockway and Michael Foot. Finally, the Home Office relented, on condition that Schoenman gave an undertaking not to be involved in any further law-breaking. This Schoenman was happy to do, and consequently announced that he had resigned from the Committee. Privately, he had no intention of honouring this agreement, but it did at least make it awkward for him to take, publicly at least, a prominent role in the Committee's activities.

Having thus dealt with Schoenman, the Government moved in for the kill. On 6 December, the Committee's offices at 13 Goodwin Street were raided by Special Branch officers with search warrants issued under the Official Secrets Act. Raids were also made on the homes of six leading members of the Committee: Ian Dixon, Terry Chandler, Trevor Hatton, Michael Randle, Pat Pottle and Helen Allegranza. Two days later, the six were arrested on the serious charge of conspiracy under the Official Secrets Act and remanded on bail. The justification for these actions was that the Committee had announced audacious plans for immobilising seven US and nuclear air-force bases on 9 December: at Wethersfield, Ruislip, Brize Norton, York, Bristol, Cardiff and Manchester. The plan was to bus sufficient numbers of Committee members to each of these bases to bring them to a standstill. In reality, the Committee did not have the resources or the organisational ability to carry out this plan, but the Government was sufficiently alarmed to take strong measures. At Wethersfield, in Essex, a twelve-foot wire fence was erected around the perimeter, all leave for local police was cancelled and boards were put up reading: 'Official Secrets Act. Prohibited Entry. Penalty of two years imprisonment'.

The coaches hired to take the protesters to these bases were cancelled at the last minute, and, though the protests went ahead, they were relatively poorly attended and conspicuously failed to achieve their objective. Pat Pottle went into hiding, the other five awaited trial and the possibility of two years in prison, while the rest of the Committee licked its wounds. Within two months the euphoria of 17 September had vanished, and the Committee of 100 had become, in the words of one of its supporters, 'a public spectacle, a group isolated from the general body of public opinion and feeling, a rowdy show to be televised and reported in the press for the interest and amusement of a majority who are not with us'.

By the end of 1961, Russell's enthusiasm for the Committee of 100 was on the wane. Though it was to be another year before he formally resigned his presidency, and many years before the Committee called an end to its activities, it was already clear that its heyday was over. It was also clear that its greatest asset during its heyday had been Russell himself. The sight of the eighty-eight-year-old philosopher sitting defiantly outside the Ministry of Defence had been an inspiration to thousands, and his imprisonment for a week in September had aroused worldwide sympathy, but the fate of the six Committee members who now faced a possible two years in prison attracted, by comparison, very little sympathy or even attention.

Russell did what he could to stir up interest in the six, issuing Press statements condemning the police for their successful clampdown on the air-force demonstrations, and expressing his support for Pat Pottle's decision to evade arrest. But the public, by and large, remained either indifferent or hostile, and the newspapers refused to print the denunciation of the British Government as 'an evil and criminal conspiracy' that Pottle sent them from his hiding place. Even Russell's statements were beginning to lose their news value. According to Christopher Driver, the author of *The Disarmers: A Study in Protest*, 'News editors had begun to wince' when Schoenman 'telephoned from London or Penrhyndeudraeth to transmit yet another "statement from Lord Russell"'.

At a Press conference on 9 February 1962, Pottle eventually gave himself up to the police, and the trial of the six – Pottle, Randle, Hatton, Dixon, Chandler and Allegranza – began at the Old Bailey three days later. The charge was that of conspiring 'to incite divers persons to commit a breach of Section I of the Official Secrets Act 1911, namely for a purpose prejudicial to the safety or interests of the State to enter a Royal Air Force station belonging to Her Majesty at Wethersfield'. Russell and Edith tried in vain to surrender themselves to the police, insisting that they, too, had been guilty of this charge, but the authorities were hardly likely to fall into that trap again. As expected, all six were found guilty, and the judge, ignoring a plea of leniency from the jury, sentenced the five men to eighteen months in prison and Helen Allegranza to one year. The verdicts were another nail in the coffin of the movement, and, after its next big sit-down on 24 March 1962 at Parliament Square, *Peace News* itself was forced to comment that: 'there was something missing in the atmosphere ... a certain coldness, a lack of creative feeling'. Suddenly, it all seemed rather pointless.

By this time, Russell took little active interest in the affairs of the Committee. He stayed away from their meetings in London, presenting his views either through Schoenman or by letter. The arrangement that had been forced on Russell and Schoenman by the British Home Office the previous autumn – in which Schoenman was to work, not for the Committee of 100, but as Russell's personal secretary – came to suit them both rather well. They were, it seems, more devoted to each other than to the committee. Russell had come to rely on Schoenman, not only as a colleague, but also as a friend and even as a family member. For his part, Schoenman was quick to realise that the most potent weapon that he and the

Committee had was the name 'Bertrand Russell', and he began to concentrate his energies on using that weapon, not in the service of a purportedly mass movement, but in direct personal interventions with heads of state and the Press. He was thus content to spend more and more time at Plas Penrhyn, 'drafting' Russell's statements, and leaving the Committee of 100 (now effectively leaderless) to sink into anarchic confusion and obscurity.

At Plas Penrhyn, Anne, Sarah and even Lucy began increasingly to resent Schoenman's intrusion into their family and their grandfather's corresponding lack of interest in them. The process was gradual, and was mixed with a good deal of pride on the girls' part in their grandfather's heroic status among the rebellious young. At school they followed with delight the reports on the radio, the television and in the newspapers of the Committee's demonstrations, and sympathised with Schoenman and the others when they went to prison. But when they returned to Plas Penrhyn during the school holidays they were less delighted to find their grandfather too busy giving interviews and meeting Schoenman, Scott and the other leaders of the Commitee to have time for them. They were also concerned that Russell seemed to be losing touch with their friends and neighbours in Wales. 'Have you seen much of the Cooper-Willises, Crawshays, Amabel & people,' wrote Lucy on 28 October 1961, 'or have you been too entangled in speeches, photographers, reporters, & things? Don't let them crowd the house out, apart from wearing you out!'

When they were in Wales, the girls spent more and more time with the Cooper-Willis family. Anne, the eldest, had always been made aware that she was not – like her sisters – a 'real' Russell, and she looked to Susan Cooper-Willis to provide the parenting that she lacked, either from her real parents or from Russell and Edith. In 1961, she left Moreton Hall and went to live in Stoke, where Susan Cooper-Willis had a factory that produced the Portmeirion pottery. There, Anne received a training in pottery and design prior to going to the Art School at Dartington. Lucy and Sarah also spent much time with the Cooper-Willis family and became close friends with Susan's daughters, Sian and Anwyl, who were both attending Dartington School. Sarah, like Anne, felt somewhat distant from Russell and Edith, especially after Schoenman's intrusion into the family, but Lucy's relations with her grandfather were more intense and complicated. She had formed a deep attachment to Russell and a fascination for his work with the Committee of 100. She, more than her sisters, was excelling at school, and wanted to follow in her grandfather's footsteps to study mathematics at Cambridge. When she was at home, she would cherish her time with Russell, listening avidly to his stories of Trinity and the famous people he had known. She felt immensely proud of him and wanted to form a bigger part of his life. In October 1961, she recorded in her diary that she had 'Dreamt of how I loved Granpa'.

But the love and attention she craved from Russell she received only in insufficient quantities, and, like her sisters, she began to look to other members of her family to fill the void. Anne had made contact with the

Lindsay side of the family in America – their mother's brother, Nick, and his daughters – and the girls discovered that their other grandfather, Vachel Lindsay, had also been famous. In Lucy's mind, this set up a conflict. Who was she more like: Vachel Lindsay or Bertrand Russell? As she pictured herself being more like Vachel Lindsay, her aspiration to be a mathematician (like Russell) gave way to that of being a poet. Russell seems to have responded to this rivalry, and, when Lucy asked for Vachel Lindsay's poetry as a birthday present, he sent her instead his *Nightmares of Eminent Persons*. Lucy wrote back to say that she loved Russell's stories – 'Most of all Zahatapolk. I wish you'd write some more, Granpa' – but the next Christmas she asked again for Vachel Lindsay.

Russell also kept up his rivalry with Dora and John for the girls' affection, and during the summer of 1961, despite being frantically busy with the affairs of the Committee, he found time to engage in lengthy and petty disputes with Dora about how much of the summer the girls would spend with Dora and John, and who would pay their fares to Cornwall and back. His feuds with Dora on these points became so protracted that even his own solicitor grew impatient with them. 'His conduct has been a great deal worse than discourteous,' wrote Taylor to Dora on 19 July 1961, 'and I think his Solicitors realise perfectly well that he has put himself in danger of losing his reputation as a man of principle.'

Russell's relations with John were hardly improved when, during his prison sentence in September 1961, two stories about John were published in the *Daily Express* and the *Sunday Express*. The former was accompanied by a picture of John at Dora's Hampstead flat standing proudly in front of a pair of trousers that were hanging on the wall. 'I crocheted these out of string,' he was reported as saying. 'It took me a long while because I didn't have a pattern. I had to keep trying them on.' The *Sunday Express* piece was headlined 'Lord Russell's son lives as a recluse' and purported to be an interview with Dora, who was quoted as saying of Russell: 'I have a great admiration for him – but like so many great men some of his personal facets are not so admirable.' The motivation behind both stories was clearly to embarrass Russell at a critical moment, and both sent a message to Russell that, even if he chose to ignore his son, the world might not.

At the end of 1961, Dora and Russell again argued about where the girls should spend Christmas, though this time Russell eventually consented to their spending it with Dora and John. Dora, of course, used the opportunity to impress upon the girls her version of what had happened to their father, and on Christmas Eve Lucy wrote in her diary: 'Began to think Gpa's really cruel & agree entirely with Dora. Awful thought.' When, however, she went to Wales the following week, she wrote of how she wished she could spend more time with Russell and Edith: 'I do love them both'. As if they had learnt nothing from their experience with John and Kate, Russell and Dora seemed intent on using the girls to strike blows at each other.

As Susan had pointed out, the upbringing Russell and Edith were providing for the girls was strikingly similar to the upbringing *he* had been given by his grandparents. Like him, the girls grew up with the sense that

there was some dark secret about their parents, something horrible hidden
from them. On 17 February 1962, Lucy recorded a dream giving expression
to this feeling that strongly recalls Russell's own powerful dream, at the age
of twenty-one, about the secret of his mother:

Last night had terrible dream. Walking with Katy, her father & Sheila
[Katy and Sheila being school friends of Lucy's] through the snow down
a brambly hill & up another, came to an Elizabethan house with one solid
slab of ceiling & grass floor, one end open like a garage. At other end
window in middle, & in one corner porter or door-keeper's hole . . . Went
over & looked in – v. dark, & suddenly terrified of something in there.
Tried to shout at top of my voice, but only feeble words came out. Sheila
& co. other side in corner didn't notice or come. Very frightened, felt
something gripping my heart & keeping it there so I couldn't run. Stood
still, more & more & more terror-struck – terror mounting fast & filling
me. Something was going to come out from underneath the half-wall,
which was a counter. A sleeve, or something – someone had been
murdered there & wouldn't let me go. Just as something was coming, I
woke up terrified.

The dream makes one's hair stand on end. What Russell had sensed was a
guilty secret of madness in the family; what Lucy had sensed was a hidden
murder – a murder that would come to haunt her, that would hold her and
not let her go. After Lucy's conversations with Dora, might this not be a
metaphor for the feeling that her beloved grandfather had himself a dreadful
secret, namely that he had destroyed the life of his son?

In an effort to get closer to her grandfather, Lucy, now thirteen years old,
began reading his books. They had a great influence on her. After *Why I Am
Not a Christian* had threatened the conventional Christianity that was an
ingrained part of life at Moreton Hall, she wrote that she no longer knew
whether she was a Christian or not: 'I don't even know if I believe in God.'
Later, she discovered that she had acquired a reputation among her fellow-
pupils as an outspoken atheist. 'Felt miserable,' she wrote. 'It seems
rumours are going round the form – wished we cld. go home.' She then read
Portraits from Memory and 'wished for someone my own age who wld think
of things as I do & like me'. Seeing Schoenman made her feel '*very*
rebellious . . . All convention makes me rebel, rebel, REBEL.' Naturally, she
began to feel that she did not belong at Moreton Hall, and, despite the fact
that she was doing exceptionally well at school and was looked on by its
principal, Miss Lloyd-Williams, as one of its brightest pupils, she thought
of leaving and going to Dartington. She wanted, she told her diary, to: 'Get
out, get away, enjoy life – live it up with (love) (sex) a gang of happy-go-
lucky people . . . Meet boys you can love'. For Christmas, Schoenman had
given her Laurens van der Post's book about the bushmen of the Kalahari,
The Heart of the Hunter, after reading which, she wrote: 'I'd love so to run
naked among African hills under the sun & live on what food I could find.
Like a Bushman.'

It was a critical time for Lucy, and she wrote long letters to Russell, explaining the dilemma she felt in wanting to leave Moreton Hall. What would Miss Lloyd-Williams think? After all, 'I *do* owe her a lot – an awful lot, I suppose.' Her sister, Anne, had advised her to stay at Moreton Hall, both because she owed it to Miss Lloyd-Williams and because her education would suffer if she left. Russell and Edith replied comfortingly, telling Lucy that they were 'surprised and shocked by Anne's attitude', which 'seems to us indistinguishable from that of Victorian parents – an attitude which has for a great many years been derided, and, we think, rightly so'. They supported Lucy's desire to leave for Dartington and had written to the headmaster there, Child, asking if there was a spare place. 'We think', they wrote to Lucy, 'that you ought to go to his place if his reply is favourable.'

The crisis served to bring Lucy closer to her grandfather, upon whom she now depended for advice and guidance, especially after she had tried and failed to establish contact with her mother. On 22 February 1962, she wrote:

I so want to be with G & G more at Hasker Street particularly, to be in on their plans & things – well, no, not that – but to be with them more & meet more people, but they have their own lives to live & I don't know how much of us they like, & at what point, growing nearer to their privacy they get sick of us. I mean, whether they object to us wanting to know & meddle in their plans, see their visitors, etc. I love them very much, but I wonder how far they tolerate our interference & whether they object without saying so. I hope not!

A few days later, she began reading *Has Man a Future?* It prompted lofty thoughts:

Now, while I'm young, I have my nose to the ground, and my eyes. I think only of my life & the lives of those around me. One day the two walls will break off sharply & jagged, & I will embrace the whole world & think & learn to know & understand it. Granpa is very busy, & often deep in his work, but I think he still takes an interest & loves us very much.

When she finished the book, she wrote in unrestrainedly admiring terms:

Enlightening, inspiring, aspiring – a great, great man who will be remembered always & always, if man survives. 'I am writing at a dark moment, & it seems doubtful (or something) that what I write will ever be published, or that, if published, it will be read. Humanity may not survive enough . . .' (July 1961). But the end – a truly wonderful, happy world, aspiring, creative, with love in all men's hearts – the vision of an almost perfect world, with poverty, hunger & disease rare misfortunes – my heart flared up, soaring by inches & for once I thought less of petty human trifles. Thought then that if I could always keep this vision before me, & try to make it materialise (though goodness knows how), – But my visions are always vague & seem impossible, while Granpa's are realistic

& reachable. And I never get my facts straight, only a vague, hazy idea about e.g., for CND arguments. Rested after lunch, read parts of *Fact & Fiction* and *Portraits from Memory*. Gpa felt deep emotions in adolescence. One passage really showed me he will understand & sympathise with everything. Wished much that I could grow up now, quickly, to understand his books & opinions, & talk about them with him, & about my opinions & ideas & aspirations, & loves & hates & desires & deepest feelings of adolescence. But I'm still a child, a wee small thing, & have little to say. I must, tho', because he'll die one day & the world will lose him – he's one man who should live for ever, & ever, & ever . . . I *do* want to be at home. At home! Living & feeling deeply with G & G . . . How I long to! How I hope they do, too.

When she next went home, however, for the Easter vacation of 1962, her hopes were disappointed. The house was dominated by secretaries; not just Schoenman, but also a young man called Jon Tinker, who, like Schoenman, combined the roles of Committee of 100 activist and Russell's personal secretary. One day, Lucy went into the kitchen after Tinker and Schoenman had been arguing: 'Ralph said "O clear out Jon" fiercely, saw it was me & apologised.' At mealtimes, Tinker and Schoenman ate with Russell and Edith, while the girls ate separately. Lucy felt excluded: 'they care more for their visitors than for us! We see less of them, & never eat with them. Tried to eavesdrop – shouldn't – & wish I was included & cld talk with them & take part.' She began to feel that she and her sisters 'don't count':

G & G have one face, one mood, one expression & certain topics of conversation when with us. We aren't in on anything, such as visitors, plans, discussions, & I *do* want to be. If only I was 3 yrs older! . . . We know G & G far less well than their 'permanent visitors' do – & they're no longer visitors – they even asked Jon's advice on a stair carpet! . . . I like him tho', I wldn't mind him around if only, if ONLY we cld all sit around the fire in the evenings after supper & have good talks.

The part of the Easter holiday that she spent in Cornwall was in complete contrast. There, Dora did everything she could to involve Lucy and her sisters in all that was going on, and to make them feel part of the family. Lucy became especially close to Roddy and began to wish that he was her father. When the time came to leave Cornwall, she wrote: 'Didn't want to leave family life'. Dora, naturally, was quick to seize upon and encourage the girls' doubts about Schoenman, telling them that, in her opinion, Schoenman's aim was to make himself Russell's heir and get himself written into Russell's will at John's expense. Anne had her own theory: that Schoenman might actually be Edith's son, so interested in him did she seem.

What is undeniably true is that by now Schoenman, with Edith's approval, had placed himself at the very centre of Russell's life. From March 1962 onwards, Schoenman was busy arranging a grand and elaborate celebration of Russell's ninetieth birthday in May. What he conceived was less a birthday party than flattery on a grand scale. A special concert was to be given at the Royal Festival Hall by the London Symphony Orchestra under Colin Davis; a painting of Russell was commissioned from Hans Erni; Flora Russell was to present him with a bust of Socrates; a commemorative silver plaque was to be made, featuring Russell sitting among his young admirers in Trafalgar Square; and an anthology of tributes was to be printed. For this last – which was also to serve as the programme of the concert – Schoenman collected contributions from a long and impressive list, including A. J. Ayer, David Ben-Gurion, Leonard Bernstein, Niels Bohr, Max Born, Martin Buber, Isaac Deutscher, Kenneth Kaunda, Martin Luther King, Jawaharlal Nehru, Kwame Nkrumah, Joseph Rotblatt, Albert Schweitzer, U Thant and Leonard Woolf. Speeches were also to be given on the night by, among others, Vanessa Redgrave and the Duke of Bedford.

Dora, of course, was not invited to this celebration, and neither were John, Peter or Conrad. Kate was at this time living in England – she and her family having, in the summer of 1961, moved to Plymouth, where her husband spent a year training as an Anglican clergyman, prior to going to Uganda as a missionary priest – but she saw little of her father during that year and did not attend his grand birthday celebration. Lucy and Sarah *were* invited, but only at the last minute and after some urgent importuning from Lucy. On 11 May, a week before Russell's birthday, they heard that they were welcome to attend the special concert on the nineteenth and to join Russell and Edith for a birthday tea at Hasker Street on the eighteenth, the actual day of the birthday. They were, however, to be put up at the Cadogan Hotel in Sloane Square, rather than at Hasker Street. 'Obviously', wrote Lucy, they 'don't want us around more than necessary'.

The birthday tea turned out to be a small, intimate affair. Apart from Lucy, Sarah, Russell and Edith, the only guests were Russell's London housekeeper, Jean Redmond, and of course Ralph Schoenman. According to Lucy, Russell was 'very gay & full of beans'. The birthday cake had nine small candles, one for each decade, and a tall white candle called 'the torch of knowledge'. After tea, Russell and Edith were taken by Schoenman to the Café Royal, where a large dinner party had been arranged by Rupert Crawshay-Williams and A. J. Ayer. About seventy people were there, including E. M. Forster, Julian Huxley and Russell's cousin, the Duke of Bedford, whom Russell now met for the first time. Ayer, Huxley, Bedford and Forster gave speeches, and Russell was able to meet again friends from the distant past, such as Miles Malleson and Arthur Waley.

Ayer and Crawshay-Williams had intended to invite most of the leading British philosophers of the day, but Gilbert Ryle, the most influential of them all, had to be omitted, Edith having furiously insisted to Crawshay-Williams that Russell would not sit down in the same room as him. The reason she gave was that Ryle was, according to Russell, ensuring that British philosophy was dominated by a small clique, which saw to it that no one got a job in philosophy without first being approved by Ryle himself. Crawshay-Williams, however, dismissed this and thought that Russell was still annoyed with Ryle about the row over Ernest Gellner's book, *Words and*

Things. A similar difficulty arose over P. F. Strawson, but, in the end, Crawshay-Williams wrote, 'Strawson did come, and we had to hope that Bertie would not notice'. At the end of the evening, the lights were lowered and an enormous cake with ninety candles was brought out.

The following afternoon, the efforts of Ayer and Crawshay-Williams were outdone by the lavish celebration organised by Schoenman at the Festival Hall. Acting as Master of Ceremonies, Schoenman presided over a programme that included not only the music of the London Symphony Orchestra, but also a long series of presentation-speeches and an even longer series of tributes from around the world. The most extravagantly phrased tribute, naturally, came from Schoenman himself. 'It is difficult for people', Schoenman said, 'to understand imaginatively the meaning of Bertrand Russell's achievement. I try to remind myself of the full meaning of living and working with him, his warmth surrounding word and gesture, the small acts – the minutiae of life':

> Russell. All the excitement remains with him, the energy and the élan . . . It is his sensibility, his passion for language, his hatred for humbug and pedantry, the great sense of irony and paradox which excites every moment in his presence. Wales. He knows every plant by name and the trained eye drinks the sun and the fields . . . This is the Bertrand Russell I cherish and who I want to celebrate. It is the poetry of man, the generosity of which he isn't aware. I want to celebrate the beauty of Bertie, for nothing touches this, not the meanness or the smallness or the hostility of pathetic men, ridden with envy and the poison of their inadequacy. He needs no metaphor.

Russell later claimed that Schoenman's flattery 'was too often so obvious as to make me feel a fool', but on this occasion he soaked it up. 'I was so deeply moved', he wrote of the concert, 'that I felt I could not utter a word.' He did, however, make a short speech, thanking Schoenman and everyone else who had taken part and declaring 'I have a very simple creed: that life and joy and beauty are better than dusty death' and announcing that, having 'embarked upon a course which invites a greater or less degree of persecution and obloquy and abuse', he felt humbled to find himself 'welcomed as I have been today':

> I feel I must try to live up to the feelings that have produced this occasion. I hope I shall; and I thank you from the bottom of my heart.

The celebration made a great impact on Lucy, who the following day wrote: 'I read the programme, & began to be very moved & much affected by all the tributes, & to realise, as Ralph put it, "the beauty of Bertie".' Schoenman had, however, troubled Lucy by forecasting that Russell would be dead by 1 June that year:

> How I hope it's not true! . . . I was beginning to be aware of the beauty,

greatness, love & truth, depth & sincerity of Bertie, & to desire to be like him, & feel I must. I feel for him a great deep love, which embraces everything under his influence & the more I come in contact with him the more it will grow & flourish. I long & long for the summer holidays, & I hope so much, so very very much that he'll live till then, so we may love & revere him for six weeks. Lately I have wished I'd been a generation earlier, or at least a few years so that I cld be one of the crowd of Comm. of 100, but now I wish it so I cld have had longer with him & learned his ideas from him. Here is a great & fine & lovely being, a very very rare one, & Ralph is so lucky. Now, in bed, I feel I've seen him for the last time, & I prayed so hard that it isn't true, fr we, the family, not only lose a grandfather full of love & gentleness & consideration, combined with wit & an inexhaustible mine of knowledge of so many subjects, & a lively, interesting talker, but all his friends, past & present, lose one of the sincerest & most generous men ever to live on earth, & the world loses a great, great man, the purest & sanest & deepest saint ever to live in it.

She had, she wrote, thought all day 'of when Ralph said "I want to celebrate the beauty of Bertie". I want to celebrate the beauty of Bertie. How can you phrase it better? O lovely, lovely Bertie . . . Because of him, I want to love everyone & be true & pure through & through. Under his influence everything is suddenly clear & I begin to see wisdom. His wisdom.' For the next few days, back at school, she thought constantly of her grandfather:

Granpa's influence is so good & brings you out of yourself & draws out the best in you. I'd derive so much from letters if only he wld write. (21 May)

Wish Gpa had more time for us & wrote to us. (28 May)

Want to ask Gpa to teach me history & geometry, & talk for hours & tell us stories. He knows so much, & is so interesting & lively. (29 May)

She thought of how 'lovely' it would be if John could come and stay with them at Plas Penrhyn, and she wrote long, adoring letters to her grandfather, pleading with him to write back. On 31 May, however, she received what she described as a 'short, cold, formal letter from Gpa . . . smelling strongly of secretary'. She decided it was probably written by Jon Tinker:

Made me rage & boil & seethe; Jon writing 'Dearest Sarah & Lucy, we are so looking forward to your return'. I'm surprised tho': it's such a farce & so insincere for Gpa. Especially when I beg him to write letters, truly expressing my feelings & saying things like 'speeches very moving' & meaning them. It becomes nonsensical, wasted & just rather silly, spending love on a stone wall, & saying 'I want to celebrate the beauty of Bertie' etc. If he writes thro secretaries I'd rather have no letter from him.

She decided that the fault was largely Edith's. 'How much happier had we all lived with Daddy, Dora & Bertie! Edith just doesn't fit in . . . O dear Daddy! I wish he'd recover & come to Wales.' John was, however, at this time at his lowest ebb, and Lucy was condemned either to continue 'spending love on a stone wall' or to look elsewhere for the attention, guidance and love that she so craved.

One of the most striking things about the list of tributes that Schoenman gathered for Russell's ninetieth birthday was its inclusion of many world leaders and heads of state. Kenneth Kaunda, the African leader soon to become the first President of Zambia, had praised Russell for awakening the conscience of ordinary people, and declared: 'The debt of mankind to Bertrand Russell for his courage and for his far-sightedness can not be measured . . . [I] hope that the work of Bertrand Russell will continue for many more years.' Nehru, the Indian Prime Minister, wrote: 'I hope that Bertrand Russell will live many years and will continue to add his powerful voice in favour of good causes and more especially for peace.' Nkrumah, the President of Ghana, called Russell 'an elegant prophet of our times', while U Thant, the Secretary-General of the United Nations, wrote that Russell 'deserves the highest recognition that human society and all organisations can accord'.

The importance of these statements was not just that Kaunda, Nehru, Nkrumah and U Thant were important and powerful people; it was that they were exactly the kind of important and powerful people with whom Schoenman wanted Russell to be associated. After all, he could, no doubt, have found many distinguished statesmen from within the British and American Governments willing to pay tribute to Russell's undeniable stature as a philosopher and writer. He might also have obtained a tribute from Khrushchev. What distinguished the particular statesmen he chose was that they were all *non-aligned*, neutral between the US and the Soviet Union. For those, like the thinkers of the New Left, who looked to the so-called 'third world' to provide a new force in world politics – a force that was hostile to American and European imperialism and yet not in thrall to Soviet Communism, which was basically Socialist but entirely free from the taint of Stalinism – these leaders of the newly independent countries of Africa and Asia were the men to whom they looked for leadership. The fact that these leaders were, in turn, prepared to acknowledge Russell as an inspiration seems to have suggested to Schoenman that Russell might have a role to play in international politics akin to that of a head of state. And if Schoenman could help shape the policies of this 'head of state', then he himself could have an influence on world events greater even than the one he had dreamt of as head of the 'mass movement' that the Committee of 100 had aspired to be.

This image of Russell as a world leader was, of course, just as much a fantasy as Schoenman's earlier visions of forcing the British Government to change its policy on nuclear weapons by crowding its jails with eminent people. Stalin's famous question about the influence of the Vatican – 'How many divisions has the Pope?' – was still more pertinent when asked about a 'nonagenarian intellectual in carpet slippers in his cottage in North Wales'. But it had, at least, *some* basis in reality. After all, heads of state, particularly in the third world, *were*, it seemed, prepared to correspond with Russell and even, as it transpired, to treat as important diplomats people he sent to their countries as his 'representatives'. In his *Autobiography*, Russell adds to his account of his ninetieth birthday celebrations the casual remark that afterwards he retired to Wales, 'returning to London only for a few days in July for the purpose of talking with U Thant about international nuclear and disarmament policies'. He mentions this as if it is only natural that the Secretary-General of the United Nations would make time, while in London, to meet him to discuss these far-reaching issues. Related to these discussions was surely the document that Russell reproduces elsewhere in his *Autobiography* entitled 'Suggestions for U Thant Re: Balancing Committee'. This proposes that U Thant should:

> . . . appoint a small committee consisting entirely of members of uncommitted nations which should be charged with the task of investigating matters in debate between East and West, as they arise, with a view to suggesting compromise solutions which both sides could accept without loss of face.
> . . . This 'Balancing Commitee' should publish the suggestions on whatever problems it investigated and seek to rally to the support of these suggestions first neutral opinion and then, if possible, the opinion of Eastern and Western negotiators. The members of the 'Balancing Committee' should command public respect in their several countries but should not be responsible to the national governments of the states from which they come.
> . . . It may be hoped that in time the suggestions of the 'Balancing Committee' would acquire moral authority and be difficult for either side to resist.

Russell's suggestion was not taken up by the United Nations, but it gives a revealing insight into the role he himself hoped to play in world politics. His hope that Britain would itself become a neutral 'uncommitted' nation was, of course, forlorn, but his paradigm of the kind of person suitable for the peacekeeping task he had in mind – one who commanded public respect but was not responsible to a national government, and who would hope to acquire 'moral authority' among the policy-makers of the world – was surely himself. In any case, this was the role he now sought to carve out for himself.

He was supported in this rather vain and grandiose conception of his place in public life by the flatteries of Schoenman, who now began to formulate ambitious new plans concerning how to use the power of the name 'Bertrand Russell'. In the 'Private Memorandum concerning Ralph

Schoenman' that Russell wrote after his split from him, he emphasises Schoenman's 'inflated ego' and speaks of 'the ascendency of the ego over intelligence' that was characteristic of Schoenman's personality, and even of his 'megalomania'. Schoenman's flattery of him, Russell says, was 'an indirect way of inflating his own ego':

On all occasions he used my reputation and any weight that my name might carry to support his own views. And he had a vastly inflated opinion of my importance.

But it was precisely because Schoenman had a vastly inflated opinion of Russell's importance that he was able for so long to use Russell's reputation for his own aims. Russell asks himself in that document why he did not break with Schoenman earlier, without realising that the most persuasive answer is implicit in his analysis of Schoenman's character. His willingness to succumb to Schoenman's manipulations was itself an example of 'the ascendency of the ego over intelligence'.

And so, under Schoenman's influence, Russell now began to see himself as a world leader in his own right. He no longer spoke as President of the Committee of 100, but as Bertrand Russell, the 'prophet of our times', as Nkrumah had called him. And if it was obvious that not everything that went out under the name of 'Bertrand Russell' was actually written by him, well, as he explained, 'the public utterances of almost all Government officials and important business executives are known to be composed by secretaries or colleagues', so why should his utterances be any different? Thus, the process that had already begun of gathering at Plas Penrhyn an entire 'secretariat' was accelerated, and Russell began to send to congresses, countries and heads of state, not representatives of the Committee, but representatives of himself.

One of the first people to act in this new role of Bertrand Russell's personal emissary was a young man called Christopher Farley. After graduating from the University of London with a degree in Modern History, Farley had devoted himself to the Peace Movement, first as a member of the Direct Action Committee and then with the Committee of 100. He caught the eye of Schoenman and was invited to Plas Penrhyn to join Russell's secretariat. In July 1962, Farley was given the task of travelling to Moscow as Russell's representative at the World Disarmament Congress. In common with Canon Collins, Baroness Wootton and others, Russell had been threatened with expulsion from the Labour Party for his support of this congress, which had been organised by the World Council of Peace, a Communist front body that had long been on the Labour Party's list of proscribed organisations.

CND and the Committee of 100 had, by this time, become an embarrassment to the Labour Party. After his success in reversing Labour policy on nuclear weapons in 1961, Hugh Gaitskell's relations with the Peace Movement had gone from bad to worse, and at a Labour rally in Glasgow on 1 May 1962, Gaitskell had denounced anti-nuclear protesters in the strongest terms. 'When it comes to the ballot and to voting in elections,' he said, 'these people are not worth a tinker's curse. They are peanuts. They don't count. Most of them really ought to go back to school.' People who wanted a Labour Government, Gaitskell insisted, should support its official policy; those who could not were 'wrecking our chances' and 'ought not be in the Labour Party at all'. Russell was clearly identified as one of these 'wreckers', and, after the attempt to expel him for his support for the Moscow congress had failed, the Labour Party tried to insist that he had not paid his subscriptions and announced to the newspapers that he was no longer a party member. This turned out to be a mistake and, for the time being, the party was resigned to having Bertrand Russell among its members.

In the event, the Moscow congress was the occasion for a demonstration of civil disobedience that embarrassed the Soviet authorities as much as the Committee of 100's sit-downs had embarrassed the British the previous year. The delegates from the Committee of 100 took with them to Moscow a leaflet produced by its 'Industrial Sub-Committee', which was dominated by a Trotskyist sub-group called 'Solidarity'. Headed 'Against all Bombs', the leaflet attacked the Soviet regime from a quasi-Trotskyist point of view, denouncing it as a Stalinist state that had betrayed the revolution. 'Our struggle is the struggle for new relationships in production and in society,' the writers declared. In both East and West, they argued, the H-bomb served to defend the interests of 'privileged minorities' at the expense of the lives and well-being of the working class. Appealing to common class interests, the leaflet concluded:

> We must have faith only in ourselves, in our ability to transform society. We extend our hands in solidarity with the working people of Russia, over the heads of our rulers and yours. We have already taken up this struggle: it is yours too. Together we must ACT – OR WE SHALL PERISH TOGETHER.

> *WORKERS OF THE WORLD, UNITE!*

The language of the leaflet was a far cry from Russell's own polished prose, and even Schoenman took exception to its Marxist sloganising, but by distributing it at an illegal demonstration in Red Square, the committee did at least succeed in refuting the pro-Soviet bias of which many accused them. Canon Collins and the rest of the CND delegation issued a statement dissociating themselves from what they regarded as an abuse of Soviet hospitality, but Chris Farley, with Russell's backing, took an enthusiastic part in the action, which was criticised in the Soviet Press as the work of a handful of 'smart alecks' and correspondingly applauded in the Western Press. All in all, as Schoenman remarked to Russell, 'the demonstrations in Moscow have done us a powerful service'.

While Farley was in Moscow, Schoenman was in the United States, visiting his parents in California and using the opportunity of being in

America to make contact with eminent and wealthy people known to be well disposed to the Peace Movement. These included Cyrus Eaton, Linus Pauling, Corliss Lamont and the philosopher Rudolf Carnap, all of whom agreed to meet Schoenman because he presented himself as Russell's representative. From them he sought support and – particularly in Eaton's case – money, but by now it was ambiguous whether he sought these things for the Committee of 100 or for Russell's private secretariat. As he put it in a letter to Russell and Edith: 'The fact is, that volume which is turned out as "private" correspondence for Bertie is virtually a major part of the office work of our movement. Yet it is treated as a personal financial responsibility for you.'

By this time, the Committee of 100 and Russell's personal secretariat were two distinct and rivalrous bodies. In 1962, the committee had restructured itself, creating many regional committees which, in theory, were to be overseen by a National Committee. In practice, however, the chief decisions were taken by the London Committee. Until the summer of 1962, the Secretary of this latter had been Chris Farley, but after he joined Schoenman in Plas Penrhyn, his place was taken by Jon Tinker, who by this time had fallen out with Schoenman and was happy to leave Wales to rejoin his friends and colleagues in London. The reorganisation made it rather difficult to say what Russell's role as President of the Committee of 100 amounted to. What was he now President of? The London Committee had no President. At its first meeting, indeed, items 2 and 3 read as follows:

2. That there shall be no President of the London Committee
3. That Earl Russell be invited to become a member of the London Committee.

Clearly, if they wanted to flatter the notoriously large ego of their greatest asset, they would have to do better than that. Misunderstanding the role played in the successes of 1961 by Russell's personal magnetism, the members of the London Committee conceived themselves to be heading a popular movement of anarchist rebellion. Convinced of the support of the masses, they disdained the 'big names' that had attracted attention to the movement at its birth and concentrated instead on winning over the struggling working classes with whom they had declared their solidarity in their Moscow leaflet.

On this misconception that they were a genuinely mass movement, the London Committee attempted to revive their glory days of the previous year by planning a massive sit-down at the Air Ministry in central London on 9 September 1962, announcing that the demonstration would not go ahead unless the committee received at least 7,000 pledges to take part. This was a tall order, and by the last week of August fewer than half the required pledges had been received. Russell accordingly made a statement to the Press that the sit-down was likely to be abandoned, rousing Tinker to fury. What right did Russell have to make such a statement, when, first, he had no executive position on the London Committee, and, second, no decision had by then been reached? Russell duly apologised, and a meeting of the London Committee was hurriedly convened on 2 September at which he made a rare appearance.

At this meeting, Russell appeared to the London activists to be remote, uncomfortable and dictatorial. Among the young, rebellious anarchists and 'libertarian revolutionaries' who now dominated the London Committee, his attitude seemed alien and unsympathetic, while they in turn had no more respect for his prestige and eminence than they had for the rest of the British Establishment. As if descending from a great height to issue his edicts, Russell gave his view that the demonstration ought to be cancelled, listened to objections without replying and then left, leaving behind him an atmosphere of recrimination and hostility. The meeting reluctantly agreed to call off the sit-down, but, to the executive members of the London Committee, it was now obvious that between them and the Russell secretariat an unbridgeable gulf was developing.

The following month this gulf widened, when the Committee witnessed what many of them regarded as the extraordinary spectacle of Russell and Schoenman publicly *defending* the right of a nation (Cuba) to possess nuclear missiles. On 30 October, in the week after the Cuban missile crisis, the London Committee passed a resolution that Jon Tinker should 'arrange a conference with Lord Russell's secretaries to consider an improvement of our relations with Lord Russell'. By this time, however, it was too late, and two weeks later Russell resigned from the Committee. 'I had', he explained in his *Autobiography*, 'become so tried by the folly of some of the leading members of the Committee of 100 during the events of September and by the growing dissipation of the Committee's policies.' Having failed to understand what Schoenman had grasped from the start – the potency of the name 'Bertrand Russell' – the Committee succeeded in alienating the man who, alone, had given it its main claim to the attention of the public. With Pottle, Randle and the others still in prison, it degenerated within a few months into what one historian has called 'a small, crankish group of young extremists who were hardly taken seriously even by many who were sympathetic to unilateralism'.

Meanwhile, the Cuban missile crisis gave Russell and Schoenman the opportunity to present themselves to the world at large as the *de facto* United Nations 'Balancing Committee' they had long aspired to be. The Cuban revolution in 1958 was a favourite *cause célèbre* of the New Left, inspiring in Perry Anderson and Robin Blackburn – the leading members of the increasingly influential new generation of New Left thinkers – the eulogy: 'Neither pure under-developed nor industrial society, neither simple neutralism nor Communism, neither parliamentarism nor autarky, Cuba seems to emerge beyond these classifications as a fresh invention of man in society.' Fidel Castro was a hero of the New Left because, in the early days of the revolution at least, he seemed to embody the hopes of those who looked to the third world to provide a neutral, Socialist leadership. Anderson and Blackburn quoted with approval Castro's claim to be 'standing between the two political and economic ideologies or positions being debated in the world' and his conception of the Cuban revolution as the representative of a new 'humanism' – so-called, Castro said, 'because its methods are humanistic, because we want to rid man of all fears, directives or dogmatisms'.

In the years following the revolution, Castro's Cuba illustrated the problems confronting any nation that claimed to be 'non-aligned'. Faced with the implacable hostility of the most powerful nation in the world, the United States, how could Cuba defend itself *except* by aligning itself with the second most powerful nation, the Soviet Union? It is a moot point whether Castro's conversion to Marxist-Leninism (announced in 1961) was the cause of America's bellicose attitude towards Cuba, or vice versa. However, after the infamous 'Bay of Pigs' fiasco of April of that year, in which an American-backed force of exiled Cubans tried and failed to overthrow Castro's regime, Castro threw in his lot with the Soviet Union, urging them to defend his revolution with nuclear weapons.

As early as February 1962, Russell (or Schoenman writing as 'Bertrand Russell' – it is already hard to distinguish) announced his support for the Cuban revolution in an article written for the Havana newspaper *Revolución*, headlined 'Atacar a Cuba Llevaria a una Guerra Nuclear' ('Attacking Cuba Will Lead to a Nuclear War'). 'The Cuban revolution', he declared, 'deserves hope and encouragement, not blind hostility':

> Vast corporations such as United Fruit are afraid of losing a profitable empire in Latin America. The military-industrial complex needs continual armament and preparation for war if it is to retain its position and power and profits. These forces in the United States, with their paid liars – be they scientists or industrialists or Congressmen – have created a pathological hatred of the Cuban Revolution which is a grave threat to the independence of Cuba, and a grave threat to the peace of the world.
>
> I appeal to the Government of the United States to allow Cuba to solve her own problems without interference. I appeal to the people of the United States to ignore the hysterical speeches of their leaders. I appeal to the Governments and Peoples of Latin America to uncompromisingly reject any measures against the Cuban revolution. Cuba is a sovereign and independent nation, with the inalienable right to solve her own problems as she pleases.
>
> United States action against Cuba could lead to a nuclear war. Such a war would destroy civilisation, and probably the whole human race. Let us remember our humanity, and forget the rest.

The appropriation of this last phrase seems strikingly incongruous. In the manifesto 'Act or Perish' it had been used to urge upon Britain a policy of withdrawal from NATO and unilateral nuclear disarmament. Here, it was being used to urge upon the United States a policy of allowing Cuba to 'solve her own problems as she pleases'. The incongruity arises from the fact that Castro chose to solve his problems in just the same way that the British Government had chosen to solve its problems; namely, by sheltering under the nuclear umbrella of a superpower. Was this, too, an 'inalienable right'? In which case, why should its adoption on the part of the British Government be seen as the criminal act of a 'gang of murderers'?

Of course, the problems facing Cuba were different and more pressing than those facing Britain. In particular, the fear of American invasion was well justified. Kennedy had made no secret of his desire to see the overthrow of the Castro regime and of his continued willingness to support disaffected Cuban exiles, such as those involved in the Bay of Pigs affair. Many Americans wanted to go further, and there was much talk among right-wing American politicians of using US forces to invade Cuba. Such talk naturally made the Cubans nervous, for there is no doubt that, without outside help, Cuba was in no position to defend itself against an American invasion.

Throughout August and September 1962, the Cubans grew ever more alarmed at the apparent intentions of the US Government to intervene in their country, and signalled their alarm to the Soviet Union, the United Nations and, somewhat oddly, to the Russell secretariat. 'In late August', according to Russell's subsequent account, 'the Cuban Ambassador to the UK privately informed me of his Government's anxiety about impending invasion and global crisis over Cuba. I said I should be willing to do what I could to bring caution to the great powers.' Why he should have been approached by the Cuban Ambassador, he does not say. By this time, the fact that he, as an individual, should have diplomatic links with foreign embassies seems to have been taken by Russell as part of the natural order of things. On 3 September, after a second appeal from the Cuban Embassy, Russell issued a statement to the *Guardian* saying:

> The situation in Cuba involves a serious threat to the peace of the world. The Cubans have every right to the Government they wish and if it is a communist Government it in no way justifies American intervention. If the United States invades Cuba it may provoke dangerous warlike action from the Soviet Union. If Russia supplies arms and troops to Cuba the danger of unwise and warlike action by the Americans will be increased with the imminent risk of world war. The situation demands a definite undertaking by the government of the United States not to invade Cuba and by the Soviet Union not to give armed support to Cuba. Precipitate action by either may provoke world-wide disaster.

Perhaps seeing in this statement nothing more than Cuban propaganda, the *Guardian* refused to print it.

In the light of what followed, Russell's statement seems remarkably prescient and his proposals eminently sensible. However, in one important respect it appears ignorant of the facts. For, by 3 September 1962, the Soviet Union had *already*, at Castro's request, provided armed support to Cuba. At the end of August, fifteen Soviet ships were reported to have arrived in Cuba, bringing troops, arms and military advisers. On 29 August, American spy-planes had photographed eight SAM-2 missile sites in Cuba (SAM-2 being the ground-to-air missile that had brought down an

American U-2 spy plane in the Soviet Union in 1960). On 5 September, President Kennedy announced the presence of these missile sites to the Press, stressing that, as the SAM-2 was essentially a defensive weapon, it presented no threat to the United States. But, he added ominously, if the US discovered any evidence that offensive weapons were being supplied to Cuba, particularly ground-to-ground nuclear missiles, 'the gravest issues would arise'.

On 16 October, Kennedy was provided with just such evidence in the form of aerial photographs showing the preparation of ground-to-ground missile sites. Resisting appeals from some of his advisers to launch immediate air-strikes against Cuba, he instead announced a blockade of the island: all ships approaching Cuba would either be boarded and searched by US inspectors or sunk. Kennedy's speech announcing the blockade was made at midnight (British time) on 22 October. In it, he called upon Khrushchev to remove the missiles from Cuba and declared his intention of regarding 'any nuclear missile launched from Cuba against any nation in the Western Hemisphere as an attack by the Soviet Union on the United States, requiring a full retaliatory response'. The message was clear: the US was willing to escalate this crisis into a nuclear war, if that is what it took to get the Soviets to back down.

Before Kennedy's speech was made, Russell issued a pre-emptive and sensational Press statement. 'It seems likely', it began, 'that within a week you will all be dead to please American madmen.' Urging everyone to listen to Kennedy's speech that night, Russell pleaded:

> Should there be any suggestion of war or of an action calculated to provoke nuclear war, I urge every human being who loves life to come out in the streets of our country and demonstrate our demand to live and let live. There must not be WAR.

The morning after Kennedy's speech, a frightened world perceived itself to be on the brink of nuclear war. Castro did nothing to allay these fears with his bellicose response to Kennedy, boasting that Cuba now had the means to repel an attack by the US 'imperialists', and taunting the Americans by claiming to find consolation in the thought that 'the aggressors will be exterminated'. In declaring themselves to be resolutely determined to remove offensive weapons from Cuba, Castro insisted, the Americans had shown themselves to be 'resolutely determined to commit suicide'. The Soviet response was more measured, insisting on the right of Cuba to defend itself against American aggression, but emphasising – as Castro markedly did not – the importance of avoiding a nuclear confrontation.

Russell and Schoenman, meanwhile, spent the day issuing a veritable blitz of telegrams and statements, all of them sympathetic to the Soviets and Cubans and fiercely hostile towards the Americans. To Kennedy himself, Russell telegraphed:

> Your action desperate. Threat to human survival. No conceivable

justification. Civilised man condemns it. We will not have mass murder. Ultimatums mean war. I do not speak for power but plead for civilised man. End this madness.

His telegram to Khrushchev struck a conciliatory tone: 'I appeal to you not to be provoked by the unjustifiable action of the United States in Cuba. The world will support caution ... Precipitous action could mean annihilation for mankind.' Telegrams were also sent to U Thant, Harold Macmillan and Hugh Gaitskell, urging them to condemn 'American madness'. Russell also issued a statement to the Press (unpublished) urging people to 'demonstrate and to act against death, and on behalf of human survival'.

Because the British Press refused to report his messages, Russell prepared a leaflet the following day, which was printed by the Cuban Embassy. 'YOU ARE TO DIE,' it began, 'not in the course of nature, but within a few weeks':

WHY?

Because rich Americans dislike the Government that Cubans prefer, and have used part of their wealth to spread lies about it.

WHAT CAN YOU DO?

You can go out into the street and into the market place, proclaiming: 'Do not yield to ferocious and insane murderers' . . .

AND REMEMBER:

CONFORMITY MEANS DEATH. ONLY PROTEST GIVES A HOPE OF LIFE.

Unsurprisingly, this leaflet too was ignored by the Press. Its oversimplification of the issues involved would have been startling had they come from a schoolboy; from one of the greatest thinkers of our age, they were truly astonishing. To overcome the indifference of the Press to Russell's urgent, if unsophisticated, pleas, the Cuban Ambassador offered to pay for full-page advertisements in the Press of anything that Russell cared to say about the crisis. The Press, however, were not receptive to the idea. The Ambassador, Russell claims, 'was perfectly aware that he might find my views contrary to his own, but he was firm in his belief that his county had nothing to fear from examination of the facts surrounding the crisis'. The idea that the Ambassador might be using him to disseminate anti-American propaganda seems not to have occurred to him. Nor does Russell ever mention that the most recklessly belligerent response to the crisis came from the Cuban Prime Minister himself, who was, apparently, the only person involved who seemed actually to welcome the prospect of armed conflict between America and Cuba.

On 24 October, the Press suddenly began to take notice of Russell. The reason was that Khrushchev had chosen to deliver a major public statement of his attitude to the crisis in the form of a reply to Russell's telegram. This was addressed to the world, as much as to Russell himself, and indeed was published by the Soviet news agency, Tass, before it reached Plas Penrhyn. The letter showed an encouraging reluctance on Khrushchev's part to escalate the crisis. 'We shall do everything possible to prevent this catastrophe,' he told Russell. 'The question of war and peace is so vital that we should consider a top-level meeting in order to discuss all the problems which have arisen, to do everything to remove the danger of unleashing a thermonuclear war.'

While denouncing the American blockade as a 'piratic action', Khrushchev notably abstained from insisting on the right of Cuba to be defended by nuclear missiles and from any kind of threatening or belligerent rhetoric. It was clear that, unlike Castro, the last thing Khrushchev wanted was war with the United States. It was, Russell said, 'the first indication of sanity on the part of the possible belligerents that we in this country had been given'. The implication that it had been he himself who had been responsible for making Khrushchev take this sane attitude was one that Russell was later to deny,[17] but, to at least one reporter who interviewed him on the day that Khrushchev's letter was received, he seemed happy to take some credit. 'It seems that for many months one has achieved nothing,' he was quoted as saying, 'but all of a sudden everything changes . . . If this attempt comes off it will be the crowning glory of my life.'

Khrushchev's letter made the front page of newspapers all over the world, most of which headlined his offer of a summit meeting and his generally conciliatory attitude. From the memoirs of Kennedy's special assistant, Arthur Schlesinger, it appears that, within the White House, the letter was interpreted as 'the behaviour of a man begging our help to get off the hook'. This interpretation was confirmed the following day, 26 October, when Kennedy received a private letter from Khrushchev containing a striking climb-down: 'This is my proposal: No more weapons to Cuba and those within Cuba withdrawn or destroyed, and you reciprocate by withdrawing your blockade and also agree not to invade Cuba.' The same day, the world breathed a sigh of relief when Soviet ships carrying arms to Cuba were ordered to turn back.

Khrushchev's dramatic letter to Kennedy was not made public until many years after the crisis, so it was in ignorance of the most significant move in the negotiations so far that, on the same day, Russell fired off another series of telegrams. He had, by this time, received a dismissive reply from Kennedy to his initial telegram, which irritated him by its lateness, its brusque rejection of his criticisms of the US blockade and its insistence that the chief issue at stake was the presence of nuclear missiles in Cuba. 'I think', Kennedy told him, 'your attention might well be directed to the burglars rather than to those who have caught the burglars.' Russell replied to Kennedy begging him not to invade Cuba and asking him to give up US bases in Turkey in return for Cuba's acceptance of the inspection of its bases by the United Nations. 'I am appealing to Dr Castro', he wrote, 'to accept

---

[17] 'I don't suppose I have altered the course of events by a fraction of an inch,' Russell remarked a month after the crisis to his friends, Michael Burn and Rupert Crawshay-Williams. Both, however, felt that he half-hoped they would contradict him. They didn't, incurring the displeasure of Edith, who, according to Crawshay-Williams, 'was of course quite convinced that Bertie had done it all himself'.

United Nations inspection in exchange for your solemn pledge that Cuba will not be invaded.'

His cable to Castro making this appeal urged the Cuban leader to accept United Nations protection and argued that: 'To defend Cuba against American invasion can now mean only the annihilation of the whole human race. I ask you humbly to accept the unwarranted American demands regarding supposed missiles. This would remove the pretext for invasion.' To Khrushchev, Russell first sent a brief telegram assuring him that: 'Your continued forbearance is our great hope', and then a much longer letter, congratulating him further on his caution and suggesting that the Soviets ask Kennedy to abandon his bases in Turkey, Iran, West Germany and Great Britain in return for 'the abandonment of the Warsaw Pact'.

The following day, the US Government was surprised and dismayed to receive a letter from Khrushchev that took a much tougher line than the one they had received only twelve hours earlier. Now, Khrushchev was insisting on a *quid pro quo*: 'We will remove our missiles from Cuba, you will remove yours from Turkey ... The Soviet Union will pledge not to invade or interfere with the internal affairs of Turkey; the US to make the same pledge regarding Cuba.' The coincidence that this new letter contained the very 'compromise' suggested by Russell the previous day forces one to wonder whether Russell had, inadvertently, been instrumental in persuading the Soviets to adopt a harder attitude. On the same day, Castro announced his refusal of U Thant's request to suspend work on the ground-to-ground missile sites, construction upon which, aerial observations had shown, was continuing apace. He also rejected the suggestion that the bases be inspected by the United Nations. Cuba had the right to possess all the arms it thought necessary, he insisted, and any combat plane that invaded Cuban air space would be met with 'our defensive fire'. Following this announcement came news that a US U-2 spy plane had been shot down by one of Cuba's new SAM missiles – its pilot, Major Anderson, becoming the first and, as it turned out, the only fatality of the crisis.

In his earlier telegram to Kennedy, Russell had said: 'After shots have been exchanged it will probably be too late.' That this dire warning proved unfounded after the shooting-down of Major Anderson's plane was due to Kennedy's caution, and to the accurate perception by the US Government that the more belligerent attitudes expressed by the statements and actions of 27 October could be ignored. Instead of reacting to this new bellicose mood, Kennedy acted as if Khrushchev's original offer of 26 October – of withdrawing the missiles in return only for a lifting of the blockade and a promise not to invade Cuba – still stood. Towards the end of the day, on 27 October, he wrote to Khrushchev accepting this 'offer'. The following morning, Krushchev agreed to dismantle and withdraw the missiles. The bases in Turkey were forgotten, and Castro had to rely, not on Soviet military power, but on the word of the President of the United States that his country would not be invaded. The crisis was over, and an overwhelming sense of relief was felt throughout the world. This sentiment was not, however, shared by Fidel Castro, who was apoplectic with rage. As the missiles were leaving his island, a biographer reports:

> Castro's tongue exploded with every scatological and cursing word he could grasp for. He railed at Khrushchev to the editors of *Revolución*, screaming, 'Son of a bitch! Bastard! Asshole!' Later he would call Krushchev a '*maricón*' or homosexual. Then as Castro swore still more, he swung around and violently kicked the huge mirror that hung on the wall. A veritable shower of glass rained down on the office.

Russell responded to the ending of the crisis with a Press statement in praise of Khrushchev ('mankind owes him a profound debt for his courage and his determination to prevent war due to American militarism' and a final telegram to the Russian Premier himself, saying: 'I have never known any statesman act with the magnanimity and greatness that you have shown over Cuba and I wish you to be clear that every sincere and honest being pays you homage for your courage.'

Despite his occasional protestations to the contrary, Russell clearly believed that his telegrams and statements had played an important part in averting catastrophe. To one correspondent, he wrote: 'the solution to the crisis made the week one of the most worthwhile of my entire life'. And, in a television interview with Ralph Miliband in 1965, he stated: 'I'm pretty sure we had some voice in preventing war at the time of the Cuba crisis.' In *Unarmed Victory*, the book he wrote about the crisis a few months after its resolution (the very title of which hints at his own triumph – for in what sense were Khrushchev, Kennedy and Castro 'unarmed'?), he reproduces his statements and telegrams as if they were steps in the negotiations that led to a solution. Moreover, he hints at the beginning of the book that the crisis could *only* have been solved by an individual such as himself. It was, he writes, 'so sudden and so swift that the usual forces making for conciliation had no time to act':

> There was no time for the United Nations to suggest conciliation. There was no time for the neutral nations to suggest compromises. There was no time for pacifist organisations to arrange demonstrations . . . In the time available, only individuals could act.

And so, he implies, the task of conciliation fell to him: 'With little hope of success, I decided that I must telegraph to Kennedy and Khrushchev beseeching them to let the human race continue to exist.'

But what role, exactly, did his telegrams play in effecting the conciliation that more traditional methods were prevented from bringing about? Khrushchev, he hinted in another television interview, wanted an excuse to climb down, and 'an approach from a philosopher, a man with no power, no axe to grind' gave him such an excuse.

In truth, even this somewhat modest claim probably overstates Russell's importance in the affair. At the very least, however, one can say that

Russell's telegram gave Khrushchev the opportunity to hint publicly that he was prepared to withdraw from Cuba rather than risk a nuclear confrontation with the United States, though, no doubt, if Russell had not sent his telegram, Khrushchev would have found some other opportunity to make this clear. For the fact is that climbing down was the only sane course of action left open to him – a fact that Khrushchev did not need Russell to spell out. The US navy, Khrushchev knew, had both the means and the intention to carry out Kennedy's threat to sink any ships that broke the blockade, and the US air force was ready to destroy the missile bases in Cuba at a moment's notice. Khrushchev's thinking in establishing the bases in Cuba had been founded – as he himself admitted in his autobiography – on the hope that they would not be discovered until they were ready to strike. Had this come off, Khrushchev wrote, 'the Americans would think twice before trying to liquidate our installations by military means'. Once the bases had been discovered, *before* they were operationally complete, Khrushchev had no choice but to accede to US demands to remove them.

Kennedy, of course, *did* have a choice; he could have chosen to do as Russell urged, and accepted the presence of nuclear weapons in Cuba as part of its defence, just as the nuclear bases in Britain, Germany and Turkey were accepted as the legitimate means of defending those countries. However, whether this would have made the world a safer place – given Castro's apparent relish for nuclear confrontation with the United States – is at least debatable. One of the oddest things about Russell's account of the crisis in *Unarmed Victory* is its complete silence on the alarming bellicosity displayed by Castro. No mention is made of Castro's inflamed rhetoric during the crisis, of his boasts of having the capacity to exterminate 'imperialists', of the shooting-down over Cuba of the U-2 plane at the height of the crisis or of Castro's disappointment at being denied the means of mass thermonuclear destruction. 'To be willing to risk nuclear war is madness,' Russell writes. 'The US was willing to run this risk.' Even more so was Castro, but Russell, apparently, either did not know this or thought it irrelevant.

The Cuban missile crisis marked an important turning point in Russell's political outlook, away from neutrality and towards sympathy with Communist regimes and movements in their struggles against 'US imperialism' (a phrase that figures largely in *Unarmed Victory*). Not that he became a Communist himself, as he himself was at pains to emphasise. His general position remained that of the 'democratic socialist' that he had been since the First World War, and he remained hostile to both Marxism as a political theory and Communism as a political system ('I dislike Communism because it is undemocratic, and Capitalism because it favours exploitation,' as he put it in *Unarmed Victory*). Nevertheless, as friend and foe alike noted at the time, Russell was no longer neutral in the Cold War. In the Cuban missile crisis, he maintained, 'the Communist side has been the less bellicose', a verdict that shows the degree to which he had blinded himself to the attitudes expressed at the time by Castro and his associates

(Che Guevara was, if anything, still more war-like than Castro in his public utterances during the missile crisis).

Schoenman no doubt helped to nudge Russell in this direction. As he himself later wrote about the crisis: 'Step by step the press of events and our continuous dialogue moved Russell beyond neutrality.' Among those who cherished Russell's neutrality and the moral authority it gave him when speaking on nuclear questions, this shift was noted with alarm. Some of the scientists involved in the Pugwash movement expressed their concerns to Russell directly. Joseph Rotblatt told Russell that he was convinced Schoenman was ruining Russell's reputation, while Max Born wrote to Russell spelling out the misgivings over Russell's published statements on the crisis, which he shared with many others sympathetic to Russell's previously neutral stance:

> I admire very much your energy, but again I am not very happy about some of the wording. It seems to me that right from the beginning you have shown an inclination to put the blame upon Kennedy, and I cannot share your admiration of Khrushchev, still less of Castro.

A similar disquiet about Russell's one-sidedness was expressed by Lord Gladwyn, who put the point in stronger terms:

> At the time of the Cuba crisis you circulated a leaflet entitled 'No Nuclear War over Cuba', which started off 'You are to die'. We were to die, it appeared, unless public opinion could under your leadership be mobilised so as to alter *American* policy, thus allowing the Soviet Government to establish hardened nuclear missile bases in Cuba for use against the United States. Happily, no notice was taken of your manifesto: the Russians discontinued their suicidal policy; and President Kennedy by his resolution and farsightedness saved the world.

In his reply Russell insisted: 'Russia and America had policies leading directly to nuclear war. Khrushchev, when he saw the danger, abandoned his policy. Kennedy did not.' He also reiterated his view that: 'It was Khrushchev who allowed the human race to continue, not Kennedy.' He further challenged the fact, as he had all along, that the Soviet Union *was* establishing nuclear bases in Cuba. 'Neither Mr Macmillan nor Lord Home stated that the missiles in Cuba were nuclear,' he told Gladwyn, as if this proved somehow that they were not. This points to another curious and serious blind spot in Russell's accounts of the crisis. In none of his telegrams and statements during the week of the crisis did he ever acknowledge the existence of nuclear missile sites in Cuba. His telegrams to Kennedy and Khrushchev concentrated almost entirely on the recklessness and illegality of the US blockade, while in that to Castro he urged him 'humbly to accept the unwarranted American demands regarding *supposed* missiles'. In *Unarmed Victory*, he expressed scepticism about the famous aerial photographs of the sites, calling them 'unclear and insufficient as evidence' and declaring that they were 'indicative of nothing in themselves'. Elsewhere in the book, he acknowledged the existence in Cuba of some sort of Soviet missiles, but challenged US statements about their range, claiming: 'It is probable that their range was no more than 500 miles.'

Putting these statements together, one arrives at something like the view that Schoenman was to express many years later: 'The missiles were ground-to-air, without nuclear warheads, and amply lied about by Kennedy to include in their supposed range cities from which he required majorities.' Like Russell, Schoenman ignores the fact that, if Kennedy was lying about the range of the missiles and the warheads with which they were to be fitted, then so was Castro in his claims to be able to 'exterminate' Americans. Since the publication of Khrushchev's *Memoirs*, however (if not before), there has been no room for doubt: the Soviets *were* establishing nuclear missile bases on Cuba, and these missiles had a range of 1,000–2,000 miles.

Russell's and Schoenman's concern to deny the fact of Soviet nuclear missile sites in Cuba – which was not denied at the time of the crisis by either the Soviet or Cuban authorities – is somewhat puzzling. After all, it does not affect Russell's main argument against the US blockade, which was that the blockade was a reckless act of war that courted the possibility of nuclear confrontation with Russia. Russell argued that this action was unjustified, *regardless* of whether the Soviets had nuclear missiles in Cuba. By analogy, he argued, Russia would not be justified in imposing a blockade of Turkey or of Britain, even though the US had nuclear bases in those countries. But if the presence of nuclear bases in Cuba was irrelevant to his argument, and if their presence was implicitly acknowledged by both Russia and Cuba, why was he so concerned to deny it?

The answer, I think, is that Russell was anxious to avoid exposing the obvious incongruity between his attitude to the crisis and his vehement campaigning against nuclear weapons. For, if he acknowledged that the Cubans *had* invited Soviet nuclear bases on to their island, then he would have had to explain why his fierce denunciations of the folly of Britain's defence policy did not also apply to Cuba. If Macmillan was to be called a 'murderer' because he chose to defend Britain with nuclear weapons, then why was Castro not to be similarly condemned?

One cannot help feeling that Russell's odd reluctance to accept the fact of nuclear bases on Cuba connects also with his equally odd silence about the belligerent behaviour of Castro during the crisis and with his own willingness to have the publication of his statements paid for by the Cuban Embassy. Conspiracy theorists might see in these connections evidence that Russell was in the pay of the Cuban Government, but a more persuasive explanation is at hand in the familiar form of Russell's susceptibility to flattery. By the Cuban Ambassador and the Russian Premier he was treated as an important and influential spokesman of world opinion; by Kennedy, on the other hand, he was dismissed as an irrelevance; and by Harold Macmillan he was snubbed altogether. Macmillan did not even bother to reply in person to Russell's urgent telegram. Instead, he sent a brief and frosty reply through his secretary that said simply: 'Your views have been noted.' It may or may not have been true that 'the Communist side has been the less bellicose', but it was certainly true that it had been the more receptive to Russell's image of himself as a world statesman.

The importance to Russell of this aspiration was understood clearly by those closest to him. 'I see Lord John emerging in you, Granpa!' wrote Lucy soon after the crisis, knowing, no doubt, that this is just what he wanted to be told. Lucy, like many of those close to him, shared and bolstered Russell's exaggerated sense of the part he had played in the negotiations. On the day that Khrushchev's letter to Russell was published, Lucy noted in her diary: 'Khrushchev's calling a summit because of telegram from Gpa'; and on the day that Khrushchev agreed to remove the bases, she described the decision as 'A noble step in this horrible game. Largely due to Gpa I think . . . He's saved us.' To Russell himself, she wrote: 'Granpa, you did wonders over Cuba – the first time anyone with political power has reacted – & acted – immediately, with some effect.'

Among his friends in North Wales, the situation was a little more complicated. They were all impressed by the extraordinary energy shown in a man of ninety and by Russell's undoubted sincerity in doing everything he could – no matter how small – to avert catastrophe. But some of them, such as Rupert Crawshay-Williams and Michael Burn, were not really convinced that he had played a major role in bringing about conciliation; others, such as Clough Williams-Ellis, positively disapproved of many of the statements Russell had made. Nevertheless, they felt some show of gratitude was called for and fell in with the plans of Tom Kinsey – a neighbour of Russell's, who did believe that Russell's telegrams had been 'a determining factor in stopping World War III' – for a public celebration of Russell's achievement. This took the form of a procession of local people on 10 November from Penrhyndeudraeth to Plas Penrhyn to thank Russell for saving humanity. The procession was led by a little boy holding a banner aloft that proclaimed: 'Thanks to Bert, We're still unhurt'. Speeches were made and a 'tribute fund' was organised to defray the cost to Russell of all the telegrams he had sent and the phone calls he had made.

At least, this is how most of the locals understood the purpose of the fund. Schoenman, however, had other ideas, and the fund became the focus of a feud between him and Russell's neighbours that resulted in a show of loyalty by Russell and Edith to Schoenman, and a partial alienation of their local friends. Schoenman (who had been away when the fund was originally set up) was given the mundane secretarial task of acknowledging the contributions, but managed to orchestrate a petty and protracted squabble by returning the contribution of Rupert Crawshay-Williams, alleging that he had misunderstood 'the purpose, the spirit, and the propriety' of what Schoenman now referred to as the 'Bertrand Russell Peace Fund'. As Crawshay-Williams was one of people who had set the fund up, he was naturally puzzled to be told that he did not understand its purpose. He was also puzzled that a 'tribute fund' had become a 'Peace Fund', the purpose and spirit of which it was Schoenman's place to decide.

What had incurred Schoenman's displeasure was Crawshay-Williams's scepticism about Russell's role in the crisis, and the fact that he had enclosed with his contribution a jokey note to the effect that he could hardly refuse to contribute to the fund, even had he wished to. After receiving Schoenman's unfriendly letter, Crawshay-Williams wrote to Russell complaining of Schoenman's heavy-handed behaviour – as did other signatories to the fund, asking what authority Schoenman had to reject donations and whether they, too, might have misunderstood the purpose of the fund they had set up. Edith then wrote a long, exasperated letter to one of the organisers, Michael Williams, defending Schoenman, criticising Crawshay-Williams and offering to return all contributions that had been sent under the misapprehension that the fund was for Russell's personal expenses, rather than for his 'work for peace'. Clough Williams-Ellis was brought in to mediate and to smooth ruffled feathers and the 'tempest in a teapot' (as Edith called it) blew over.

Petty though it was, the dispute had long-term effects on Russell's relations with Crawshay-Williams and other members of the self-styled 'Welsh Bloomsbury' set. They could not be invited to Plas Penrhyn when Schoenman was there (which was most of the time), and they became confirmed in their view that Schoenman was having a disastrous influence on Russell and that he was supported in everything he did by Edith (who, Crawshay-Williams thought, was 'bemused' by Schoenman). Cut off from his old friends, Crawshay-Williams believed, Russell was deprived of the benefit of conversation with people who could say to him, 'Come off it, Bertie!' when his opinions became too outlandish, and, therefore, became increasingly vulnerable to the flatteries and machinations of Schoenman.

That Christmas, however, Schoenman was away, so the Crawshay-Williamses could safely be invited to lunch at Plas Penrhyn. 'All the children were there,' recalls Crawshay-Williams. 'Edith organised an extraordinarily complete Christmas for them, with every sort of traditional appendage and with masses of beautiful and carefully chosen presents.' Lucy records that 'Gma treated me – & us all – much less like children, offering us drinks, etc., cigarettes.' However, in some respects, she found herself being treated *too much* like an adult. At the end of the day, she writes, 'when Gpa kissed me goodnight he did it like John, though less long & fervent & I didn't like it. It makes me uncomfortable to have fruitful family relationships express themselves in that form – sex & "love" will take a long while to get me.'

Just before Christmas – indeed, as soon as the excitement over his role in the Cuban missile crisis had died down – Russell had been presented with another opportunity to offer himself as an arbitrator between nations when a border dispute between India and China erupted into armed fighting. The second half of *Unarmed Victory* is devoted to his attempts to mediate in this dispute, though this section of the book has aroused very little interest. Russell believed, however, that the Sino-Indian dispute might escalate into world war. The implausible scenario he envisaged went like this:

Fighting will be resumed, and at first the Chinese will have the

advantage. America and Britain will come to the aid of India, but will find
that they cannot defeat China unless they employ nuclear weapons. They
will employ them. China will compose its differences with Russia, and
Russia also will employ nuclear weapons, not only against India, but also
against the West. Within a few days, the whole world will become as
empty and desolate as the Himalayan passes are now.

Thus, on 8 November 1962, he sent telegrams to Prime Ministers Nehru
and Chou En-lai, urging them to begin a ceasefire. In response, he was
visited by officials from both the Indian and Chinese Embassies, who tried
to convince him of the territorial claims of their respective countries. The
issues involved were complicated, and Russell had to admit that 'it was quite
impossible for me to form any judgment in such an obscure and difficult
matter'. But instead of concluding that he had no business trying to mediate
in a dispute he did not understand, Russell persevered, writing again, not
only to Nehru and Chou En-lai, but also to neutrals such as President
Sukarno of Indonesia, President Nkrumah of Ghana and U Thant, asking
them to act as intermediaries. The fact that he received replies from these
heads of state fuelled still further the fantasy cherished by him and
Schoenman that they were at the very centre of world events and, like
Government spokesmen, they released Press statements delivering their
pronouncements on the issue. The attitudes expressed in these statements
swung from sympathy with India for having its territory invaded by China
to extravagant praise of, and gratitude to, China for offering to withdraw its
troops from the disputed territory. For the most part, these statements were
ignored by the Press.

The problem for Russell was that, because, as he conceded to Nehru, 'the
whole legal position as to the frontier is tangled and controversial', the issue
was not one that could be resolved by simple pleas to avoid the madness of
global nuclear war. His impatience with, and ignorance of, the details of the
dispute thus rather vitiated the effectiveness of his recommendations to
Nehru to accept the terms of the ceasefire offered by the Chinese. How was
he to know that these terms were, in fact, reasonable? How could he evaluate
the justice of Nehru's refusal to accept those terms when he had only a
vague understanding of the rival territorial claims? Undaunted by these
problems, Russell had no hesitation in heaping praise upon the Chinese,
while condemning the Indians for their bellicose nationalism. In withdrawing his troops, Chou En-lai had, Russell appeared to believe – like
Khrushchev before him – made a unilateral gesture for peace, after
becoming persuaded by Russell of the importance of avoiding nuclear war.
The fact that India had received military backing from Britain and the US
had, he seemed to think, less influence on the outcome than his telegrams
and Chou En-lai's desire for peace. The Chinese withdrawal from the
disputed territory at the end of November 1962 could therefore be chalked
up as another 'unarmed victory' for the voice of reason and sanity.

In a curious reversal of his stance on Cuba, Russell, in celebrating the
Chinese gesture of peace, strongly criticised the Indians for accepting

Western military aid. India, he lamented, 'has ceased, in fact, though not in form, to be neutral as between East and West, and has, thereby, increased the chance of world war'. The 'worst blow to the peace of the world', he argued, was that India's 'defection from strict non-alignment' weakened the bloc of neutral powers and altered the balance of power in the West's favour. This, of course, was exactly the argument that neutrals and anti-Communists had put forward about Cuba's alignment with Russia – an argument that Russell had appeared to reject.

Russell's aspirations of playing an important part in resolving the Sino-Indian border dispute turned to farce the following summer, when he sent Schoenman and Pottle (who, after his release from prison in January 1963, was recruited by Schoenman into the Russell secretariat) to India and China to try to negotiate a settlement. 'We were on a diplomatic mission,' Pottle later said, 'and the one thing we certainly weren't were diplomats.' What Pottle and Schoenman knew about the dispute, they learnt from reading a caseload of documents on the twelve-hour flight from London to Bombay. 'I have now read all the main evidence of both parties,' Schoenman wrote to Russell, 'and feel quite smitten with the knowledge of so much petty detail of a pathetic squabble. Nevertheless, we shall treat this quarrel over empty and barren land as the historical drama of immense import it, no doubt, is!'

Once they were in New Delhi, Schoenman wrote that he and Pottle had met the Vice-President of India, Zakir Hussain, and that he was 'convinced that crucial work can be done by us on behalf of and in the name of Bertie to save this situation'. The following week, he wrote again, saying that he and Pottle had been frustrated in their attempts to meet Nehru by 'minor officials', who told them that Nehru would be 'occupied' for at least a month. Refusing to take the hint, they pursued Nehru to Kashmir, went directly to his home and succeeded in spending six hours with him over two days. Nehru, Schoenman told Russell, had been hurt by 'our criticism', but was nevertheless prepared to entrust Schoenman and Pottle with an important secret diplomatic mission to China:

> Nehru has agreed to begin direct negotiations on the whole issue if China will agree to no civilian posts in the Ladakh area vacated by Chinese troops. You will recall that China had informed you that she didn't want Indian posts there but would also forgo her own.[18] Nehru explained that his parliament and the press and the industrialists are hostile and he must move carefully. He instructed *us* to tell Chou En-Lai on his behalf that if Chou will agree to no civilian posts there, he will not insist on Indian posts there.
>
> . . . I think that, if we are careful, we can actually break the deadlock about talks. Certainly Nehru has come round.
>
> . . . Nehru has, in fact, allowed us to mediate on his behalf with Chou, and to return to advise him further.

---

[18] After the Chinese withdrew their troops from the disputed border territory, both China and India kept 'civilian posts' in what had now become a 'no man's land'.

. . . Nehru had a map made up for us and also asked us to keep dark
the role we were playing, naturally enough, because of the hostile Indian
press.

Apparently, it did not strike Schoenman and Pottle that this was an odd
way for Nehru to be conducting delicate negotiations. Nor did they ask
themselves why Chou should respect the *bona fides* of two young men, one
American and one British – neither of whom had any diplomatic experience
or credentials – to speak for the Indian Government. Why should Chou
believe promises made to him by Nehru through Schoenman and Pottle?
And how, if the promises were so contrary to prevailing opinion in the
Indian Parliament and the Indian Press that they had to be made in secret,
could Nehru possibly be sure of delivering on them?

When Pottle and Schoenman reached Peking, their diplomatic mission
took a still more bizarre turn. Though he had stressed the importance of
being careful, and though he appeared to believe that he was bringing a
message from Nehru that could 'break the deadlock' and solve the dispute,
Schoenman – according, at least, to Pottle's account – seemed to do
everything he could to alienate the Chinese. In their hotel room, he would
pick up the phone and sing into it: 'Chairman Mao is a sacred cow'. When
they were given the diplomatic honour of being taken on the lake of the
Forbidden City, Schoenman stripped his clothes off and jumped in for a
swim. When they were shown round the bathrooms of a Chinese prison,
Schoenman asked Pottle in a loud whisper: 'Where does the gas come from?'

On the day that they thought they were finally going to meet Chou En-
lai, they were taken instead to a kind of trial, where they were faced with
about twenty Chinese officials, each of whom stood up in turn to accuse
them of various crimes, most of them arising from Schoenman's misdemeanours. It was, recalls Pottle, 'terrifying . . . a horrible experience'. After
their 'trial', they were taken to meet Chou, who told them that they were
'running dog lickspittles of the American Imperialists' and that he did not
believe this verbal message they had brought from Nehru. To prove that it
was a lie, he would make it public. He did, and Nehru of course had to deny
that he had ever sent such a message, whereupon Pottle and Schoenman
were summoned again by Chou, who told them they were 'two little
amateurs pretending to be diplomats'; under normal circumstances he
would have them imprisoned, but, because they were Lord Russell's
secretaries, they would merely be deported.

Russell later referred to this incident as 'Ralph's infamous folly in China',
and wrote that, as a consequence of Schoenman's behaviour, 'I have never
been able to recover the warmth and friendliness formerly accorded me by
the Chinese Government.' Schoenman's extraordinary behaviour in Peking
notwithstanding, the deeper folly behind his and Pottle's adventures in
India and China was one that they shared with Russell: namely, that of
failing to see the difference between taking part in negotiations and taking
part in propaganda.

13

THE GUEVARIST YEARS

It is a privilege to greet you on the historic occasion of the First Tricontinental Conference of the revolutionary peoples of the world. It is very appropriate that this significant Conference has been held in Havana. Throughout the world, people speak in awe of the extraordinary spirit of the Cuban people. The message that Cuba has for the peoples of the world is one of utter determination in struggling against great odds for liberation from brutal foreign domination and rapacious economic exploitation. It is noteworthy that the meeting in Cuba has been one of solidarity, for solidarity is our overriding responsibility to all those struggling for their emancipation. It is an international struggle and, as an international struggle, it must command our clarity, our loyalty and our full solidarity. I look to the people of Cuba and the courageous men and women who have attended this Conference for the creation of an international of resistance to US imperialism, an international which will embrace the people of the United States itself.

Many of those who have come to Cuba have been fighting, only a few weeks ago, in the forests of Angola, Mozambique, Guinea, the Congo, Venezuela, Peru, Guatemala, Vietnam and in the cities and plains of the Dominican Republic . . .

When I greet you today, my thoughts are with the people of Cuba and their heroism, with Fidel Castro and the great international revolutionary figure, Che Guevara. These are men whose example will be followed by struggling people everywhere.

Asked to name the author of this piece of 1960s' revolutionary rhetoric, very few people, one imagines, would immediately think of Bertrand Russell. And yet these passages are taken from Russell's message to the Tricontinental Conference, held in Havana in January 1966 (the conference at which Che Guevara issued his famous call to defeat 'US Imperialism' through the creation of 'two, three . . . many Vietnams'), and are by no means uncharacteristic of the kind of thing that was published under the name 'Bertrand Russell' between 1963 and 1968. Almost all of his public statements during those years are consistent with the strange supposition that Russell had, somehow, become a disciple of Che Guevara.

The idea of Russell as a Guevarist revolutionary is so implausible that many, even now, refuse to believe that Russell could have uttered such stuff. When a revised version of his Tricontinental speech was published as one of the chapters in *War Crimes in Vietnam*, many were sceptical that Russell had even read it, let alone written it. How could a man who, throughout his long life, had opposed Marxism and campaigned for peace now give uncritical and fawning support to a call to armed Marxist revolutionaries to create a series of guerrilla wars?

Of course, as both Russell and Schoenman admitted, many – perhaps most – of the things published under the name 'Bertrand Russell' during this period were in fact written by Schoenman. And he *was* a disciple of Che, as he made no attempt to hide, either during the 1960s or later. In an article published in 1974, Schoenman stated quite clearly that his and Russell's appeals for revolutions throughout the world were motivated by the desire to 'spread thin the power of American imperialism'. He added: 'This was the substance of Che Guevara's call, and we became involved in his strategy and his fate.' In private conversation, he described himself as being 'very close to Che' and claimed that Che's first wife, Hilda Gadea, the woman credited with having 'politicised' Che, was one of his oldest and closest friends.

But the fact that Schoenman wrote the Guevarist rhetoric signed by Russell (and, occasionally, spoken by him into a tape recorder) is not enough to distance Russell from the views Schoenman expressed on his behalf. For there is little evidence to support the idea that Russell did not know what was being published under his name, that he did not understand it, or (most disappointingly of all) that he did not believe it. Indeed, there is plenty of evidence to the contrary. Russell several times insisted that the Press statements, articles and speeches signed by him represented his views, even while admitting that they had been written by others. Nor will it do to say that Russell was too senile to realise what he was saying in his published utterances. The accounts of people close to him during his last years, and the many interviews he gave at the time, show that he remained in possession of his mental faculties until his dying days.

The fact one is left with is that Russell, deliberately and in full awareness of what he was doing, chose to lend his name and reputation to the parroting of Che Guevara's speeches that Schoenman presented for him to sign. Indeed, one can see evidence of this willingness to put himself at the service of the Cuban revolution even before the Cuban crisis. His article of February 1962 for the Havana newspaper *Revolución*, for example, might be seen as a message of support to the Cubans ('The Cuban revolution deserves hope and encouragement') rather than the appeal to the United States that it purported to be. For, if Russell *really* wanted to appeal to the Americans, why do it, in Spanish,[19] in a Cuban newspaper?

---

[19] The typescript of this article is in English. It is not clear who translated it, but Spanish was not one of the languages Russell knew well.

The links that Schoenman forged with the Cubans were evidently encouraged by Russell – even, as we have seen, to the extent of being willing, during the missile crisis, to have his public statements published by the Cuban Embassy. Nor does it require much imagination to regard *Unarmed Victory* as a book written to please the Cuban Government,[20] not only because of its complete avoidance of the question of Cuban culpability for the crisis, and its silence on the war-like pronouncements of Castro and Guevara, but also because of its reflection of the Cuban Government's line on the rivalry between the Chinese and the Soviets.

Because most readers have taken little interest in its second half, the strange symmetry of *Unarmed Victory* has gone largely unnoticed: in its first half, extravagant praise is heaped upon Khrushchev for generously and selflessly allowing the human race to continue, by not responding to the provocation of the United States; in the second half, Chou En-lai is praised in similar terms for not responding to the provocation of the US-backed Indian Government. Thus, *both* Communist leaders are applauded for being, literally, the saviours of mankind. This position mirrors that of the Cuban Government, which, at the time, was anxious to flatter both Communist superpowers in its desire to receive financial and military backing from both. Russell's endorsement of the policy of 'peaceful co-existence' in *Unarmed Victory* also mirrors the views of the Cuban Government, which, despite Castro's annoyance at having been deprived of nuclear missiles, was willing to pay lip-service to the Soviet policy of avoiding conflict with the USA in exchange for Soviet aid. Later, when the Cuban view (and, especially, that of Che Guevara) swung towards the more belligerent policy of the Chinese, Russell's public pronouncements followed suit.

Of course, it is possible that Russell did not know or care that his opinions were those that would please the Cuban Government, but he was doubtless aware that in January 1963 a 'Message to the People of Cuba' was sent in his name, and that in March of the same year he sent a message to the 'Continental Congress of Solidarity with Cuba' (a manuscript of which survives in Edith's hand). No doubt with Schoenman's encouragement and guidance, Russell was, it seems, happy to declare himself firmly in support of the Cuban revolution and to ally himself with Castro and Guevara. There is little sign that either Cuban leader cared one way or the other whether they had Russell's support, but Schoenman evidently considered that he had secured for the Cubans a valuable ally. In order to convince himself of the importance of this, Schoenman had to play up the importance of Russell's influence on world politics, thereby satisfying his own vanity and feeding Russell's.

Describing the events after the Cuban crisis, Schoenman has referred to 'the prominence Russell now assumed in the world movement'. The scale of the 'movement' that Schoenman imagined Russell to be leading grew all the

---

[20] I am not suggesting that this was the chief motive Russell had in writing the book. Its chief purpose, of course, was to emphasise the peacekeeping role of Russell's telegrams to world leaders.

time. Now, it was not just a mass movement of protesters against the British Government, or even an international peace movement; it was a movement of nations, involving Russell in alliances with 'anti-imperialist' heads of state, fighting the Guevarist fight against American imperialism. In Schoenman's increasingly fevered imagination, a vision of Russell's place in world events was forming that saw him as one of the leaders, along with Ho Chi Minh and Fidel Castro, of co-ordinated and armed resistance to the United States. Flattered though Russell no doubt was by this conception of his importance, even Schoenman admits that Russell had his doubts, that he 'sometimes pulled back when unnerved by the direction his involvement was leading him'. These hesitations, Schoenman writes, 'covered such later occurrences as the aid provided to armed revolutionary struggles . . . or the financial and other support received by us from governments and revolutionary movements'. Nevertheless, Schoenman claims, in weighing up these decisions, 'which were so removed from the political choices facing him in tamer times', Russell 'counted upon and trusted my judgment'.

The process that culminated in the late 1960s with Russell and Schoenman receiving money from 'governments and revolutionary movements' (that is, Cuba, North Vietnam and the National Liberation Front) and then providing aid to 'armed revolutionary struggles' (financing Guevarist guerrilla movements) began at the end of 1962 with Schoenman's attempts at international diplomacy. Intoxicated by his and Russell's contacts with powerful heads of state during the Cuban crisis and the Sino-Indian border dispute, Schoenman began to spend more and more time abroad, meeting prime ministers, presidents and foreign ministers. Wherever he went, he took with him the international prestige of Bertrand Russell's reputation as a philosopher and peace campaigner, and brought back with him confirmation to Russell that his political views and activities did indeed count for something on the world stage.

He began in December 1962 with a trip to the Middle East to meet, among others, Abdul Kassem, the Prime Minister of Iraq, and President Nasser of Egypt. The chief purpose of these meetings seems to have been to enlist support for Schoenman's plans for a new organisation, the Bertrand Russell Peace Foundation, the idea of which had been germinating in his mind since before the Cuban missile crisis.

In early October 1962, Russell had sent out letters to prominent people announcing his intention of creating such an organisation, the aim of which, he then said, was to 'attract substantial financial support from all parts of the world' in order to 'undertake the coordination of efforts on behalf of peace internationally'. This it would achieve by setting up an alternative media, including journals, newspapers and films, which would 'educate the public and create the conditions for resistance'. Pat Pottle puts it differently. The idea, he remarked, was 'that if you could attract enough well-known people to sponsor the Bertrand Russell Peace Foundation, it . . . could attract a lot of money and you could use that money for lots of subversive kinds of projects that normally you wouldn't be able to get money for'.

In Iraq and Egypt, Schoenman and Nick Johnson, another member of the

Russell secretariat, were treated courteously, but promised nothing. 'Although we have not got a cheque from any government,' Schoenman wrote to Russell, 'I am convinced of the importance of this trip for our work. We've put the case for the Foundation to people who can make a substantial contribution and we have hopes which are realistic that help will be coming in due course.' In seeking confirmation of Russell's international importance, however, he was apparently more successful. 'We have been asked at the highest level', he claimed, 'for Bertie's mediation over several outstanding Middle Eastern issues.' According to Schoenman's later account, he had gone to the Middle East 'taking proposals which we [he and Russell] had weighed carefully'. What these proposals were, he does not say, beyond revealing that he and Prime Minister Kassem discussed the nationalisation of the Iraqi oil industry and that these discussions were 'followed in ten weeks by his assassination'.

After they returned to England, Johnson left the secretariat, saying that he wanted nothing more to do with Schoenman or the new foundation. Needing new recruits, Schoenman contacted Pat Pottle immediately after his release from prison in January 1963, and invited him to join the incipient foundation. Pottle agreed and accompanied Schoenman to a meeting with someone from the Cuban Embassy, who, according to Pottle's later recollection, turned up carrying a violin-case with a machine gun inside it. Pottle immediately declined Schoenman's offer of visiting Cuba as Russell's representative, and it fell to Alistair Yule to accompany Schoenman to Havana in March, where they presented Russell's 'Message to the Continental Congress of Solidarity with Cuba', the text of which was published in *Pravda* immediately after its delivery.

At about the same time, Russell launched, through articles and letters to newspapers, an attack on the United States that was the literary equivalent of carpet bombing. Many of these statements were written in what by now one recognises as Schoenman's strident tone of voice. For example, in April 1963 Russell published an article called 'The Myth of American Freedom', which resonates clearly with the ideas and even the phrases of Schoenman's *Peace News* article of two years earlier, 'Mass Resistance in Mass Society'. Like Schoenman's earlier article, it argues that the United States and the Soviet Union are alike in suppressing freedom in the interests of technology, industry and bureaucracy, and that, in the dispute between the two: 'Ideology is largely irrelevant'. Like the earlier article, too, it describes American society (in what one quickly comes to realise is one of Schoenman's favourite phrases) as a 'concentration camp of the mind'. However, in its abuse of the United States, the article goes much further than the earlier piece, accusing the US authorities of 'overt and unabashed police-state techniques' and describing its military leaders as 'semiliterate paranoids with their fingers on buttons'.

The same tone and style characterise Russell's contributions to an acrimonious exchange of letters during March 1963 with John Fischer, the editor of *Harper's Magazine*. In the January edition of *Harper's*, Fischer had taken Russell to task for appearing to advocate US 'surrender' to the Soviet Union. In reply, Russell wrote:

The American Government pursues a policy of genocide. This is a plain statement of fact. You, like Eichmann, acquiesce in this policy and you, like he, have the imperative moral responsibility to demand an end to such a policy.

(The invocation of Eichmann's name as a symbol of moral culpability was another conspicuous aspect of Schoenman's rhetoric. His *Peace News* article had ended: 'Short of this [social revolution] Eichmann stands for Everyman.')

Fischer replied to Russell's letter, trying to correct what he took to be its factual mistakes about the nature of the warning systems used by the US forces, upon which Russell's arguments about the likelihood of accidental war were based. This prompted an even more furious response from Russell, quoting experts in support of his views and ending with another intemperate denunciation: 'it is abominable for a man who edits a journal to be so ill-informed and so prepared to write on subjects of which he has no knowledge'. And so it went on, with Fischer writing in a determinedly measured way and Russell stepping up at every turn his attacks on Fischer himself ('I have no compunction in saying to you that you enhance the prospects of annihilation by your journalism'). Eventually, Fischer called an end to the exchange with a plea to Russell to examine these issues 'with the same intellectual vigour that you once applied to the arguments of G. E. Moore and Wittgenstein'. It was, evidently, difficult for him to believe that he was dealing with the author of *The Principles of Mathematics*.

While Fischer and Russell were debating, among other things, the dangers of accidental war and the justice of the phrase 'semiliterate paranoids' to describe US military leaders, the world was learning something of the truth of what was happening in Vietnam. The official story was that the US had sent a team of advisers to the South Vietnamese Government to help it combat a Communist insurgency led by North Vietnam. The truth was that thousands of US troops had been there for two years, taking part in an appalling and bloody civil war.

The regime backed by the US, led by the dictator, Ngo Dinh Diem, had very little support among the Vietnamese population, and was alienating its people still further by its execution of the so-called 'strategic hamlets scheme'. This was an effort to separate the peasants from the guerrillas by forcibly repopulating them into newly built fortified 'hamlets'. Intended to weaken the influence of the Communist-backed Vietnamese National Liberation Front (the NLF, or 'Vietcong'), it succeeded only in strengthening it enormously. As many of the US forces on the ground discovered, the people they had come to 'protect' from Communism were embracing it enthusiastically as their best hope of overthrowing the despised Diem regime. The South Vietnamese Government further alienated its own population by the vicious and indiscriminate way in which it pursued the war against the NLF, attacking peasant villages with napalm and poisoning the countryside with 'Agent Orange'.

The newspaper reporters sent to Vietnam to cover the war were shocked and disillusioned by the disparity between what they saw and what the American people were being told by politicians, and many of them became determined to challenge the official view. In the first three months of 1963, a series of reports from Vietnam were published in mainstream British and American newspapers that left no doubt about the scale of US involvement and the nature of the Diem regime. These reports naturally came to Russell's attention, and on 22 March he fired off his first protest in the form of a letter to the *Washington Post*. 'The United States Government', he began, 'is conducting a war of annihilation in Vietnam':

> The sole purpose of this war is to retain a brutal and feudal regime in the South and to exterminate all those who resist the dictatorship of the South. A further purpose is an invasion of the North, which is in Communist hands.

The 'real concern' of the Americans in Vietnam, Russell went on, 'is the protection of economic interests and the prevention of far-reaching social reforms in that part of the world'.

It is characteristic of Russell's rhetoric at this time that he should begin on a note almost calculated to alienate his readers and encourage them to dismiss him as a dupe of Communist propaganda. The *Washington Post*, predictably, declined to print the letter, but two other journals were only too keen to accept it: the journal of the British-Vietnam Committee, *Vietnam Bulletin*, and the North Vietnamese magazine, *Cuu Quoc Weekly* (its appearance in the latter prompting a grateful letter of thanks from Nguyen-Huu-Tho, the President of the NLF). On 8 April, the *New York Times* published the letter, together with an editorial admitting that Diem's regime had 'insufficient popular backing' and that napalm had been used by the South Vietnamese, but insisting that Russell's claim about the aim of the Americans being to prevent social reform was 'arrant nonsense'. The day before, the *New York Times* had carried an article by Russell called 'Is Communism a Menace?', in which he had argued that, although Communism *had* been a menace during Stalin's reign, it had now 'been replaced by another menace, namely the fear of Communism'. Russell's acceptance of this view, the *New York Times* editorial argued, had produced in him 'an unthinking receptivity to the most transparent Communist propaganda'.

In a series of letters in response to this editorial, Russell adopted the same tone of righteous indignation and fierce denunciation that had characterised his exchange with Fischer, with the foreseeable result that the *New York Times* stopped printing his letters. The impression created by both sets of correspondence is that Russell was now determined to attack the United States in the strongest possible terms at every opportunity – an impression strengthened the following summer when he sent a message to the Civil Rights Freedom March in Washington that read:

The treatment of the American Negro is an atrocity which has a history
of three hundred years in what is now the United States of America. The
number of Negroes who have died through torture, lonely murder and
systematic maltreatment in this period without doubt is in excess of those
killed by the Nazis in the course of their unparalleled barbarism in
Europe.

'Without doubt'? Was Russell *really* sure that more than six million
Negroes had died in the US through 'torture, lonely murder and systematic
maltreatment'? Even when Russell clarified that his estimate 'referred to the
course of the slave trade, the killing and maltreatment over the generations
and effects of extreme terror on any population', the figure still looked like a
wild exaggeration, the purpose of which was to make the familiar 'worse
than Hitler' claim, which was now beginning to lose its impact through
chronic overuse. As the *New York Times* pointed out, the best estimate of
the total number of black slaves brought to the United States was something
under a million.

Having by now publicly accused the Americans of committing Nazi-style
atrocities at home and abroad, while at the same time lavishing praise on
Khrushchev and Chou En-lai as world peacemakers, Russell had conclu-
sively destroyed any hopes he and others might have retained that he could
fulfil the neutral 'balancing committee' role that he had described to U
Thant the previous year. The only governments he could now expect to
exert any influence upon were those hostile to the United States.
Nevertheless, throughout 1963 Schoenman was sent on trip after trip to visit
heads of state, supposedly to promote the cause of peace. In April, he was in
Israel, where he was received by the Prime Minister, David Ben-Gurion.
Russell, it seems, thought that sending Schoenman to meet Ben-Gurion
would do something to lessen Arab-Israeli tensions. Quite why he thought
that remains a mystery, but he was soon disabused of the notion. When
Schoenman returned, he told Russell (according to Russell's later account)
that he had lectured 'the Prime Minister on his and the Israeli government's
shortcomings' – a lecture, Russell adds, 'naturally resented by its recipient'.
For this, he was ticked off by Russell, who nevertheless continued to send
him round the world to act as a diplomat for peace.

In July 1963, immediately after his and Pottle's abortive attempt to
mediate in the Sino-Indian border dispute, Schoenman intended to return
to Iraq, where he had been hospitably treated seven months earlier by Prime
Minister Kassem. Since then, however, Kassem had been assassinated in the
Ba'athist coup of February 1963, and the new regime, led by Colonel Arif,
refused to grant Schoenman a visa. Possibly, as newspaper reports implied
at the time, this was because he was Jewish, though it seems more likely that
it was because he chose as his companion for the trip his close friend Khalid
Zaki, a man well known to the Iraqi authorities as a staunch opponent of the
new regime and regarded by them as a dangerous revolutionary. Later
dubbed the 'Che Guevara of the Middle East', Zaki worked closely with
Schoenman for many years, and was just as committed to the Guevarist

'tricontinental strategy' of a series of co-ordinated guerrilla movements designed to defeat 'US Imperialism'. In 1968, he died attempting to lead just such a movement in southern Iraq. If Russell's intention in sending representatives to Iraq was to receive the goodwill of, and have an influence upon, Colonel Arif's government, then he could hardly have chosen people less suited to the task than Schoenman and Zaki.

When the Bertrand Russell Peace Foundation was formally launched in September 1963, these foreign trips of Schoenman's – variously ill-fated, unsuccessful and abortive though they had been – were represented as evidence that, if only Russell had enough money, he could do wondrous things for world peace. Listing as examples the 'Cuban crisis, the Sino-Indian border conflict, the Arab-Israeli dispute, the problem of Berlin and the future of central Europe', a publicity leaflet appealing for sponsorship claimed that: 'governments in conflict have welcomed or specifically sought Lord Russell's personal mediation because it has brought an impartial and effective voice to the exchange of proposals and counter-proposals'. Russell, the leaflet went on to claim, 'had been instrumental in helping to ease international crises and to create the conditions for their settlement'.

Still more barefaced in this appeal for sponsorship (given that, since the Cuban missile crisis, Russell had pledged his support for Castro, hailed Khrushchev and Chou En-lai as saviours of humanity and poured forth a stream of anti-American invective likening the USA to Hitler's Germany) was the emphasis on the importance of neutrality. Russell, it claimed, was 'in continual correspondence and contact with heads of neutral states all over the world', many of whom had 'accepted his view that neutralism provides one of the most promising means for resolving international tension'.

As for the purpose of the new foundation, the leaflet said that it intended to 'organise on a scale never before attempted the establishment of our own media of mass communication for the furtherance of international work against nuclear war'. Elsewhere, it promised to establish a newspaper, a printing press, a film unit and a radio station, all with a view to making known the work of the Foundation and serving 'as an international voice for nuclear disarmament'.

As most of the claims made in its fund-raising publicity were either misleading or straightforwardly false, the question persists: what *was* the purpose of the Foundation? In the chapter that he devoted to the foundation in his *Autobiography*, Russell is curiously unhelpful on this question. Though emphasising that 'our purposes necessitated vast sums of money', and revealing that 'many thousands of pounds have been contributed to it' from both individuals and governments, Russell is forced to confess that, when the Foundation was asked what it was doing with all this money, 'we had to speak chiefly in vague and general terms, which carried conviction only to the astute and the already converted'.

One thing is sure: the Foundation's purpose was *not* to campaign for nuclear disarmament. For some time before the foundation was launched, Russell's emphasis on the danger of nuclear weapons had been replaced by an even stronger emphasis on the danger represented by the USA. Nor was its purpose to mediate in international disputes, a task for which neither Russell nor Schoenman was very well equipped. The real answer, confirmed at every stage by the documentary record, is given in Schoenman's 1974 article: the purpose of the Foundation was to make use of Russell's reputation as a campaigner for peace in order to raise support and money for the 'struggle against US Imperialism' as this was conceived by Fidel Castro and Che Guevara.

It is often, and understandably, thought that the focus of Russell's political work in the last few years of his life was the campaign to end the Vietnam War, and it is true, of course, that he, Schoenman and the foundation were unstinting in their opposition to American involvement in Vietnam and in their support for the NLF. However, when one reads through the huge amounts of documents produced by the Foundation, what is most striking is the preoccupation they reveal with Latin America in general and, specifically, with Cuba. From the time of his statement in *Revolución* in February 1962 that US action against Cuba could lead to nuclear war, Russell hardly let an opportunity go by to declare his support for the Cuban revolution.

On 10 October 1962, about two weeks before the missile crisis, Russell received an appeal for support from the 'Continental Congress of Solidarity with Cuba', which was to be held in Brazil. Because of the crisis, the congress was postponed to March 1963, when Russell, via Schoenman and Alistair Yule, sent the message of support mentioned earlier. In this message he said that he was glad the congress would be defending the right of Cuba to choose its own government and asserted that 'the attempt to oppress Cuba . . . is rank imperialism and is totally unjustifiable'. He also sent a paper, to be read at the congress on his behalf, in which he alleged that the Soviet Union, China and the United States ('and all of their satellites') 'believe in mass murder, indiscriminate extermination of entire populations whether belligerent or not, and in systematic genocide', and that, therefore, he took heart from the example of Cuba, which showed 'that there is still present a will to resist'.

When, in the immediate aftermath of the missile crisis, Russell received a telegram from the Cuban Ambassador in London expressing 'our deepest gratitude' to him, he replied fulsomely:

If I have been able to help the people of Cuba in any way during the recent crisis, that is my privilege.

I hope you will never hesitate to approach me at any future date if you believe that there might be anything I could do to further the peaceful independence of Cuba.

The 'Message to the People of Cuba' that Russell sent in January 1963 confirmed his willingness to act on Cuba's behalf. 'I join you in spirit as you celebrate the fourth anniversary of the Cuban Revolution,' the message read, assuring the Cuban people 'that those not partisan to the Cold War are appalled by the bellicosity of the Government of the United States'.

The solidarity between the Foundation and Cuba is seen not only in these direct messages of support, but also in the curiously close shadowing of the public pronouncements of Che Guevara and Fidel Castro evident in the statements released under Russell's name. On 15 August 1964, ten days after the USA began bombing North Vietnam, Che made an important speech in Havana, in which he urged Cubans to think of themselves as part of a single international community of revolutionary states. This included China, the Soviet Union and Vietnam, but also those countries in Latin America and Africa in which revolutionary struggles were taking place. Che mentioned Guatemala and Venezuela, but drew particular attention to Africa, and especially to the Congo, where, he assured his audience, the inheritors of Patrice Lumumba's revolutionary example would surely triumph. In the same month, Russell put his name to a piece called 'Africa and the Movement for Peace', in which – echoing Guevara – he argued that: 'The people of Africa and Asia may be militarily weak, but they are many, and together their governments and the peace groups of the West could accomplish the peace we discuss so lengthily in articles, meetings and conferences.'

The Congo featured heavily, too, in a speech that Che gave in Santiago on 30 November 1964, a few days after the Lumumbist revolutionaries had been defeated in Stanleyville by a combined force of Belgian troops and white mercenaries, supported by the USA. The focus of Che's speech was provided by the alleged massacres committed by the whites in Stanleyville, which, Che said, revealed the 'imperialist bestiality' of the 'Hitlerian hordes'. Six days earlier, Russell had issued a Press statement on the same subject, drawing attention to the 'fact' that: 'an army of white mercenaries, recruited from adventurers and sadists, has been murdering women and children indiscriminately and burning whole villages without cause in the course of its progress through the Congo'. 'Unless the open interference of the Western powers stops,' Russell's statement went on, 'the Congo will become another Vietnam, a danger to world peace and a slaughterhouse for innocent people.'

The day after this Press statement was issued, Schoenman sent Russell an article he had written jointly with Khalid Zaki called 'Death and Pillage in the Congo', which called for the withdrawal of British, Belgian and American troops from the region and prophesied the growth and eventual victory of the Congolese rebellion. When this article was expanded into a book, Russell contributed a Preface to it, which began:

The programme of cruelty and exploitation imposed on the peoples of Africa and Asia has nowhere been more terrible than in the Congo. If there were an international tribunal comparable to that which sat at Nuremberg, the planners of policy in the American State Department and the Bureau of Foreign Affairs in Brussels would be arraigned before that tribunal and found guilty of crimes against a whole people.

'It is time', Russell went on to declare, 'for free African and Asian nations to take positive steps to undermine the servants of the colonial Powers ... We must join together to expose neo-colonialism and its works, and it is to this object that the Bertrand Russell Peace Foundation dedicates itself.'

Meanwhile, Che was conducting meetings with members of the Congolese rebellion and sympathetic heads of African states in preparation for his audacious plan, backed by the Cuban Government, to support the rebels directly by travelling to the Congo himself and taking the leadership of their campaign. On 1 April 1965, Che left Cuba for Africa. Travelling as 'Ramon Benitz', he disguised himself by shaving off his beard and wearing glasses, and arrived in the Congo incognito on 24 April. For seven months he stayed in the Congo, leading an increasingly divided and ineffectual army of rebels, until he was forced to withdraw in November. For much of this time, Schoenman, too, was in Africa, visiting the very heads of state with whom Che had discussed his Congolese adventure. First he went to Ghana, where he stayed for about a month as a guest of President Nkrumah, and then he travelled, in quick succession, to Zambia, Kenya and Uganda. Quite what he did in those countries remains a mystery. On 15 March 1965, he wrote Russell a letter from Ghana that was clearly intended to imply that he had a hand in both writing Nkrumah's speeches and formulating Ghana's foreign policy:

I have had the dilemma of having much to tell you which is important with no discreet way of telling it to you. I have had a series of meetings with the President and his cabinet. The talks concern Congo and Vietnam. They have led to concrete results and I am staying this long because of the request of the President.

If you examine the copy of the memorandum to the President on the subject of Congo you will find the proposals which have been under consideration. They have been accepted and this will lead to certain sections which the newspapers will soon make clear.

The best guess as to what Schoenman is alluding to here is his claim, made openly later to colleagues in the foundation, to have written a speech for Nkrumah calling on the Organisation of African States to expel UN forces from the Congo.

The rest of Schoenman's letter of 15 March 1965 is devoted to the allegation that the USA had made detailed plans to bomb China. The only thing that could prevent this, Schoenman declared, was 'a wholesale shift of the non-aligned world into international concourse with China ... Otherwise the US will treat all the militarily weak countries and their views with contempt.' 'Believe me,' the letter ended, 'I'm doing work here I couldn't do in London.'

Whether or not Schoenman was writing the speeches of African leaders, he was certainly writing Russell's, which by 1965 were, like the articles and Press releases issued under his name, following a distinctly Guevarist line. On 15 February 1965, Russell gave a speech at the London School of

Economics attacking the Labour Government's foreign policy for 'supporting Western imperialism' by siding with the Americans over Vietnam and
the Congo, and more generally for attempting, in league with the USA, to
suppress 'the vast movement for independence which is agitating formerly
subject peoples'.

Five months later, on 11 July 1965, at the World Congress for Peace in
Helsinki, a statement by Russell was read out by Schoenman that many
people present simply refused to believe represented Russell's views. Its
theme was that 'the threat to world peace is American imperialism', since
the USA was determined to suppress, not only the Vietnamese people, but
all struggles for political and economic independence 'throughout Latin
America and the greater part of Africa and Asia'. In support of its call to act
against US aggression (which was generally interpreted as a rejection of the
doctrine of peaceful co-existence between the USA and the Communist
countries), the speech repeated and amplified the claims made by
Schoenman in his letter from Ghana that: 'the men who have power in the
Pentagon, in the Central Intelligence Agency are, at this moment, preparing
to destroy by bombing all of the industrial cities of China'. The speech
caused an uproar, and Russell received a telegram two days later, telling him
that it was essential that he dissociate himself from Schoenman and that
such speeches were discrediting the Peace Foundation. In reply, Russell
confirmed that the speech delivered by Schoenman was indeed 'a message
from me'.

Two months before the Helsinki congress, the rejection of peaceful co-
existence had been the theme of Fidel Castro's May Day speech, after
which, and in pursuit of his call to make war on the United States, he began
preparing for the aforementioned Tricontinental Conference to be held in
Havana in January 1966. The purpose of this conference was to gather
delegates from all the revolutionary guerrilla movements throughout Latin
America, Asia and Africa in order to promote solidarity between them and
the Cuban Government. Che was not actually at the conference, since it was
considered that, after his secret departure from Cuba in April 1965, he
should not appear publicly again in Cuba until he could do so as the
victorious leader of a 'national liberation movement'. He therefore went into
hiding, first in Tanzania and then in Prague, while he planned his next
adventure, which turned out to be in Bolivia, where he went, again under
secrecy, in November 1966.

Though he was not present, it is however for Che's message that the
Tricontinental Conference is best remembered. Asserting that there is no
alternative but to do battle against US imperialism, Che argued for 'total
war'. 'We must carry the war into every corner the enemy happens to carry
it,' he declared. 'To die under the flag of Vietnam, of Venezuela, of
Guatemala, of Laos, of Guinea, of Colombia, of Bolivia, of Brazil – to name
only a few scenes of today's armed struggle – would be equally glorious and
desirable for an American, an Asian, an African, even a European.' The
'dispossessed masses' of the third world must take their inspiration from the
'great lesson of the invincibility of the guerrillas', and must develop 'a

relentless hatred of the enemy' so as to prepare themselves for 'a long, cruel war'. If they could do all that:

> How close we could look into a bright future should two, three or many Vietnams flourish throughout the world with their share of deaths and their immense tragedies, their everyday heroism and their repeated blows against imperialism, impelled to disperse its forces under the sudden attack and the increasing hatred of all peoples of the world.

It was not, one would have thought, a message likely to lift the spirits of a peace campaigner, a man who had once declared that his entire doctrine could be summed up by saying that hatred was foolish and love wise. And yet, at this same conference, the message from Bertrand Russell already quoted was read out, echoing the content, tone and even some of the very phrases of Guevara's own message.

Rather curiously, Russell's message to the Tricontinental Conference exists in four, slightly different, versions. The first, dated 27 November 1965, is the longest and contains the most detailed and sustained attack upon the USA, which, it comes close to saying, is responsible for literally *every* evil in the world:

> In every part of the world the source of war and of suffering lies at the door of US imperialism. Wherever there is hunger, wherever there is exploitative tyranny, wherever people are tortured and the masses left to rot under the weight of disease and starvation, the force which holds down the people stems from Washington.

Acknowledging that he had at one time supported peaceful co-existence with this brutal tyranny, Russell now vehemently renounces such a policy and argues that 'a world of peace and of fraternity has to be fought for'. 'The great opportunity before this Tricontinental Conference', he declares, 'is to forge a new international of resistance to oppression.' This version of his message ends with a list of the guerrilla struggles to which Che had drawn attention in his own message – Peru, Guatemala, Venezuela, Columbia, Vietnam, Thailand, the Congo, the Cameroons – and urges all the people of the world, including those of the United States and Britain, to 'demonstrate and struggle and resist . . . Let us join together to resist US Imperialism.' The second, much shorter, version, dated 8 December 1965, was spoken by Russell into a tape machine and contains more fulsome flattery of the Cubans than the first. It ends: 'I send you my warmest greetings in our common struggle.' The third, dated 10 January 1966,[21] is the one quoted at the beginning of this chapter, which is still more effusive in its praise of Cuba and its leaders, and speaks of it becoming 'crystal clear' that 'the struggle for national liberation is the only secure road to world peace'. This is the version most obviously *not* written by Russell, and, one

---

[21] Actually, it says '10 January 1965', but this must be a typing error.

suspects, the one that was actually read out at the conference. The fourth version appears as Chapter 8 of Russell's book, *War Crimes in Vietnam*, where it is entitled 'Peace Through Resistance to US Imperialism'. In this version, dated simply 'January 1966', all references to Cuba, Cuba's leaders and the Cuban people have been removed, though in all other respects it is recognisably a variant of the same text.

In all its versions, the fundamental message remains the same: world peace can only be secured through the defeat of US imperialism, and the way to defeat US imperialism is through support of Guevarist guerrilla movements throughout the world.

With the Peace Foundation committed to a view so closely tied to a particular branch of Marxist revolutionary thought, it could not hope to attract the diversity of support that Russell's previous campaigns had attracted. The liberals who had supported CND, the anarchists who had been drawn to the Committee of 100, even Soviet-style Communists could not identify themselves with a movement allied, as the Foundation now was, to the specifically Guevarist brand of Trotskyism espoused in Russell's public statements. By 1966, most of the people who had been drawn from the Committee of 100 to join Russell's personal secretariat had left the Foundation, to be replaced by a group of young Trotskyists, including Pat Jordan, Robin Blackburn, Quentin Hoare and Ken Coates, all of whom shared Schoenman's admiration for Che Guevara and his 'strategy'. Christopher Farley was one of the very few people still left from the Committee of 100 (and one of the few associated with Russell who was not a Trotskyist), but, from this time on, he worked as Russell's personal secretary in Plas Penrhyn, rather than at the Foundation's tiny offices in Shaver Street, London.

The Shaver Street offices now became the centre of a flurry of activity designed to ensure that the Foundation played its part in responding to Guevara's call to make war on US imperialism on as many fronts as possible. Next door to the Foundation's offices was the office of the 'Iraqi Students' Society', from where Khalid Zaki was planning his own guerrilla campaign, supported by Schoenman and the Foundation. The war in Vietnam, of course, was the natural focus of attention, and, in order to lend support to the NLF, the Foundation set up the Vietnam Solidarity Campaign, led by Tariq Ali, who accompanied Schoenman on trips to Vietnam to pledge loyalty to the guerrillas and gather evidence of American war crimes. On one of these trips, in May 1966, a message from Russell was broadcast on NLF radio addressed to US soldiers, telling them that they had been lied to by their government about the war and urging them to end their participation 'in this barbarous and criminal war of conquest'. The message also revealed Russell's plans to establish, 'along with world famous figures, Nobel prizewinners, novelists, philosophers, mathematicians' a War Crimes Tribunal 'in order to pass judgment, in most solemn terms and with the most respected international figures, upon the crimes being committed by the United States Government against the people of Vietnam'.

On 20 July 1966, the lengths to which Russell was prepared to go in order to support the NLF were revealed when he sent a telegram to the Russian Premier Alexei Kosygin, urgently appealing to him 'to place part of the airforce of the Soviet Union at the disposal of the Vietnamese'. 'World peace can be served,' the telegram stated, 'not by allowing Johnson a free hand but by unstinting help to the Vietnamese in their just cause – a cause which is the same as that of all oppressed and exploited people.' The bizarre spectacle of Russell, the erstwhile 'prophet of peace', actually encouraging the Soviet Union to take a step that would not only put an end to hopes of 'peaceful co-existence' but would almost certainly result in direct military confrontation between the two nuclear superpowers of the world, naturally took both the Soviet Union and the world's Press by surprise. According to David Horowitz, who was then working for the Russell Peace Foundation, the Soviet Consul in London was so alarmed by this telegram that he summoned Schoenman to a meeting at the Soviet Embassy:

> After explaining to him that sending Russian planes would mean war with the United States, the consul warned: 'Mr Schoenman, people who advocate World War III are either crazy or working for the CIA, and they get into trouble.'

In a Press statement released to explain his reasons for urging Soviet military involvement in Vietnam, Russell said: 'Those who think the danger of world war would be, thereby, increased must reflect that, like Hitler, Johnson is emboldened by appeasement and further reflect that the Vietnamese would be doing no more than defending their people over their own territory.' Apparently, Russell now believed that NLF victory was *so* important that it was worth risking global nuclear war in order to achieve it.

A few months later, at a Press conference in London on 16 November 1966, Russell formally announced his intention to hold an International War Crimes Tribunal to investigate the conduct of the USA in Vietnam. Given the extreme bellicosity of his recent statements on the USA, the impartiality of the tribunal was understandably held in doubt, and, in the British and American Press reports of the announcement, Russell was severely ridiculed. Naturally, he was given an easier time by the Cuban Press, his statements to whom made clear that the tribunal was intended as part of the Guevarist strategy for defeating the USA. 'The historical perspective of our Tribunal in relation to the aggression of imperialism', runs one such statement, 'must be to provide a voice for the conscience of humanity capable of bringing to judgment the continuous crimes and aggression of a counter-revolutionary power':

> The power of the United States and its imperialism will inevitably assume the proportions of genocide in three continents. As the full extent of the menace to human wellbeing becomes documented by our Tribunal, the knowledge gained must be used to mobilise co-ordinated action throughout the world.

'The movements of national liberation in Latin America', the statement goes on, 'provide the central point of resistance to US Imperialism . . . The development of the war in Vietnam is inseparably linked to the policy advanced by Cuba':

Che Guevara's last letter to the Tri-Continental Conference is a programme expressing the most urgent necessity for all who oppose US Imperialism. The determination necessary to create two or three new Vietnams is the sole means of defeating the United States itself. All young people should be guided by this memorable declaration. They should find concrete methods of struggle including direct participation and support for the Latin American revolution.

The tribunal, of course, would cost a lot of money, especially if conceived of as part of an attempt to 'mobilise co-ordinated action throughout the world', and donations to the foundation were running dry. From Schoenman's 1974 article, one supposes that it received some help from the Cuban Government and the NLF, but, in an effort to raise more money, Russell's personal wealth began now to be exploited. His previous intention not to publish his *Autobiography* until after his death was scrapped because of the large advance he was offered for it, and it was published in three volumes between 1967 and 1969, the third volume consisting mostly of hurriedly written and vastly inferior material that was added to the 1952 version at the last minute. All income from it went to the Foundation. Russell also arranged for his huge collection of papers to be sold to McMaster University in Canada, the proceeds from which were also donated to the Foundation. Finally, on 18 November 1966, Russell made a new will, which, apart from the money he left to specific individuals (£5,000 to Kate, £3,000 to his granddaughters, £500 to his housekeeper, and so on), bequeathed to the Foundation (via Edith) everything he owned, including the copyright of his books. (In the original draft of this will, John was to be left nothing, but, under pressure from his lawyers, Russell added a codicil, leaving John £300 – that is, slightly less than his housekeeper.) At about the same time, the Foundation was registered as a limited company, its directors drawn from the band of Trotskyists whom Schoenman had attracted to it.

The tribunal was held over two sessions, the first in Stockholm on 2 May 1967 and the second in Denmark six months later. Russell did not attend either, but at the first an opening address was read out on his behalf by Schoenman. In speaking about the 'feverish effort to conceal American crimes', this made clear in advance what verdict the tribunal would deliver. In a further statement, Russell alleged that 'the United States is behaving in Vietnam as Hitler behaved in Eastern Europe' and declared: 'The great meaning of Vietnam is that the world revolution is continuous.' At the sessions, evidence was heard from a succession of North Vietnamese witnesses, who all testified to US brutality, and from a handful of US soldiers, who confessed to having committed war crimes, and on 1

December 1967 the tribunal announced its findings. To no one's surprise, the USA was found guilty on all counts.

By the time it published its verdicts, the tribunal had made itself, to some extent at least, independent of Russell, Schoenman and the Peace Foundation. At the first session, Schoenman had quarrelled violently with two of the tribunal's leading celebrity supporters, Jean-Paul Sartre and Vladimir Dedijer, both of whom had the independence and the strength of personality to resist Schoenman's attempts to bully them. Sartre was Executive President of the tribunal and Dedijer its Chairman (Russell's official status was 'Honorary President'), and they were evidently more willing to exert the power vested in them by these titles than Schoenman had bargained for. In response to their quarrel with Schoenman, they removed the name 'Bertrand Russell' from the tribunal's title and transferred its headquarters from London to Paris.

By this time, in any case, the focus of Schoenman's interests had shifted to Bolivia, where Che Guevara had been leading a guerrilla movement since the previous November. In a message he sent to a memorial meeting for Khalid Zaki in the summer of 1968, Schoenman revealed that his last meeting with Zaki had been in Paris in the summer of 1967:

> He was leaving for Iraq. I was leaving for Bolivia. When we embraced we were in joy for we were going to the battle for which our lives were a preparation – the revolutionary struggle in which our deaths would be a moment in the suffering of millions.

Officially, at any rate, Schoenman was *not* going to Bolivia to take part in its revolutionary struggle, but to observe, on behalf of the Foundation, the trial of Regis Debray, a French academic and disciple of Guevara, who had gone to Bolivia to take part in the guerrilla movement. After enduring a few weeks of the grim reality of guerrilla warfare, Debray told Guevara that he would be more useful 'on the outside'. Guevara agreed and asked Debray to go back to France and organise a 'support network'. The entry in Guevara's *Bolivian Diary* that records this conversation adds: 'I am to write letters to Sartre and B. Russell, asking them to organise an international aid fund for the Bolivian liberation movement.' On 20 April 1967, while trying to return to France, Debray was arrested by the Bolivian authorities and imprisoned. Under torture, he told the Bolivians what they had, up until then, only suspected: Che Guevara was in their country, leading the guerrilla revolt. From this point on, it was only a matter of time before Guevara was hunted down, defeated and killed; in the event, it took just six months.

In the meantime, Debray remained in Bolivian custody to await trial as a guerrilla collaborator and to undergo further interrogations, not only by the Bolivians, but also by the CIA, who were, of course, interested to know Che's exact whereabouts. Understandably, the Cuban Government was anxious to get Debray out of Bolivia as quickly as possible, and to this end they approached Schoenman, hoping, perhaps, that direct intervention from 'Bertrand Russell' would persuade the Bolivians to release Debray without trial. This approach was presumably made in May, when Schoenman was in Cuba to deliver a 'May Day Message to the Cuban People' from Russell, congratulating the Cubans on their inauguration of the 'World Committee for Vietnam' and making the now familiar pledges of 'solidarity' ('Fidel Castro has our warmest support. Che Guevara struggles for every oppressed person . . . May we together struggle for the Vietnamese victory and for the defeat of American aggression wherever it occurs'). On 15 June, the first signs of a response to the Cuban appeal appeared in a letter signed by Russell to the *International Herald Tribune* newspaper, protesting against the 'arbitrary and harsh treatment' that Debray had received from the Bolivians. The following month a document was circulated to the Cuban Press called 'Replies to Questions by Cuban Journalists by Bertrand Russell', in which, to questions about the guerrilla movement in Bolivia and the 'illegal treatment of Regis Debray', Russell replied:

> The guerrilla movement in Bolivia is confirmation that resistance to the United States' control of the resource of the world is spreading throughout Latin America . . .
> The threat presented to the Bolivian oligarchy by Debray is that he may deepen consciousness in wide sections of people . . . We must mobilise a world campaign in defence of the rights of such scholars as Regis Debray.

Asked what response there should be from Europe to the problems of Africa, Asia and Latin America, Russell replied that it was the duty of 'the European socialist movement' to identify itself with the tricontinental revolutionary movement, and that: 'This identification must express itself not in "charitable" acts of aid or assistance, but in actual participation in the process of liberation.'

To encourage such 'identification', the foundation established a journal called the *Bertrand Russell Peace Foundation London Bulletin*, the first issue of which appeared in August 1967. In almost every article in this issue, appeals were made, more often than not under Russell's name, to support and participate in the Guevarist tricontinental struggle. Its opening piece, for example, was Russell's final address to the Stockholm session of the tribunal, in which he urged: 'The International War Crimes Tribunal must do for the peoples of Vietnam, Asia, Africa and Latin America what no tribunal did while Nazi crimes were committed and plotted.' The *Bulletin* also reproduced Russell's message to the OLAS (Organisation for Latin American Solidarity) conference in Havana in July, which had been delivered on his behalf by Ken Coates:

> I am happy to greet the first Conference of Latin American Solidarity which meets appropriately in Havana, the capital of the first revolutionary nation of the continent . . .
> I hope that the movements for liberation will find ways to co-ordinate

their struggle so that an act of resistance, for example, in Bolivia, will serve to advance the liberation of Uruguay . . .

May this conference succeed in creating a continental resistance.

Among the 'foundation literature' advertised in the *Bulletin* was a pamphlet by Che Guevara entitled *A Common Aspiration: The Overthrow of Imperialism unites Cuba with Africa and Asia*, and among its announcements of foundation meetings, past and present, were the following:

The Foundation has already held one meeting in solidarity with the Latin American struggles ('A Salute to Che Guevara'). A capacity crowd of six hundred attended this meeting at Mahatma Gandhi Hall in London, and the enthusiasm of the audience was great. Further meetings are being planned.

Friday, August 25. *Report from the OLAS conference by Ken Coates. Panel discussion to follow. Mahatma Gandhi Hall, Fitzroy Square, London*

The closing article was a piece on 'The background to the trial of Regis Debray', which argued that it was 'grotesque to accuse Regis Debray of bringing violence and revolution to Bolivia'. What the Bolivians were *really* frightened of, the article claimed, was Debray's ideas: 'Despotism will not tolerate the free expression of ideas. Debray's courage is the antithesis of a dictator's cowardice. His example is profoundly important.' It ends: 'His military trial arouses great concern, and support for Regis Debray mounts daily.' If there had hitherto been any doubts about the aims of the Peace Foundation, its *Bulletin* should surely have laid them to rest.

The *Bulletin* served another purpose, too: when Schoenman left for Bolivia in August 1967, taking with him Perry Anderson, Robin Blackburn and Tariq Ali, he gained admittance to the country by showing his credentials as a journalist for the *Bulletin*. Other than Schoenman, the members of the group were clearly nervous about what they might be letting themselves in for. In La Paz, Ali, who was staying at a different hotel from the others, was alarmed to receive a visit from a mysterious stranger, who turned out to be 'one of Schoenman's contacts'. When they arrived in Camiri, the small town in which Debray was held prisoner, they gave the impression to the other journalists there (of whom there were, by now, a great number) of being quite terrified. When Ali started taking photographs of the Bolivian soldiers, he had a gun pressed to his chest and was told that if he took any more unauthorised pictures of military personnel, he would be shot dead. Then he was arrested by soldiers who suspected him of being a member of Guevara's guerrilla army. Though he was eventually released, the incident clearly unnerved both him and Schoenman, and Ali returned to London. Ten days later, Blackburn and Anderson also returned, having been alarmed by Schoenman's suggestion that they locate Che's camp, hire a jeep and take food and medicines to the guerrillas. Schoenman had, it seems, bribed some Bolivian officers to tell him where Guevara was supposed to be hiding. Unwilling to extend their 'identification' with revolutionary guerrillas to the point of risking death, Blackburn and Anderson beat a hasty retreat and got the next plane back to London, leaving Schoenman to continue the Bolivian adventure alone.

The Debray trial kept being delayed, and, as they waited for something to happen, the Western journalists in Camiri got to know each other pretty well. One of them, Richard Gott, wrote to friends on 10 September 1967 that he had met Schoenman and discovered that his intention was 'to intervene during the first day of the Debray trial and to wave a letter from Bertie and say that the whole affair was quite illegal and should be stopped at once'. All the journalists were astonished at how much money Schoenman appeared to carrying around with him, and in his letter Gott recounts:

> Another nice vignette of the trip was Ralph talking with the leader of the quite powerful Trotskyite party: 'We don't have the money to stage the revolution,' says the Bolivian. 'Tell me,' says Ralph, leaning across the table, eyes glinting, 'just how much would it cost?' I gather that the old Peace Foundation is doing quite well as a result of Bertie's autobiography.

In bribing Bolivian officers to tell him where Guevara was, making plans to free Debray, ostentatiously waving money around and openly offering to fund an armed revolution, Schoenman could not help, one supposes, coming to the attention of both the Bolivian authorities and the CIA.

By the time of Gott's letter, Schoenman had returned to London for three weeks in order to prepare what he later described as 'a full legal document which was acceptable in a legal sense to the military tribunal'. This document was later published in the *Bulletin*, and, though it does indeed make a detailed legal case that the treatment of Debray was in violation of the Bolivian constitution, its primary purpose was clearly to make propaganda on behalf of the Guevarist revolutionary movement. It begins: 'I request the liberty to provide this Tribunal with vital evidence and testimony of Bertrand Russell and of members of the Russell Foundation Commission in Defence of Regis Debray.' Then, after making its legal case, it slips into the familiar language of revolutionary exhortation and fervour:

> You, who feed on death and suffering in Bolivia and throughout Latin America are the criminals who fear Regis Debray. You, who murder the people would keep the world from knowledge of your crimes. The writer threatens the tyrant because the people have stirred . . . and if the tyranny points its bloody finger at Cuba, it is because the people look to Cuba with hope and if the criminals who have the death of the people on their conscience accuse Cuba, it is honour to Cuba to have inspired the people to seek liberation in revolutionary emulation.

Surely, Schoenman must have realised that a Bolivian court would find this very persuasive, and one is forced to conclude that it was written not for the court, but for the world's Press who were covering the case.

At the end of October, Schoenman returned to Camiri, armed with his 'full legal document'. By this time, the Guevarist rebellion had been crushed, Guevara himself had been killed and what remained of the guerrilla army was now being held in the prisons of Camiri. Debray's case finally came to court at the beginning of November, and, as planned, Schoenman attempted to interrupt the proceedings by appealing to the court to accept his document as evidence of Debray's innocence. Predictably, he was then arrested and expelled from the court, to be taken to the prisons holding the captured guerrillas. From there he was taken to La Paz, where he was put into what he later described as 'a cage rather than a cell, because its dimensions were about 2.5 by 5 feet'. After trying to escape, he was recaptured and kept in this 'cage' for a further twenty-seven hours before being taken away to be interrogated. During the interrogation, the US Consul to Bolivia arrived and informed Schoenman that his US passport would be confiscated and that he would be returned to the United States, and not, as he hoped, to England. After some show of resistance to this, Schoenman decided that returning to the USA would be better than being taken back to his cage in La Paz, and he was taken under armed guard to the airport and put on a plane to the United States.

In New York, Schoenman gave an interview to a writer from the *Bulletin*, in which he revealed that he was still hoping to attend the second session of the War Crimes Tribunal, due to be held in Denmark on 20 November. After recounting his adventures in Bolivia, Schoenman emphasised that Guevara's death the previous month had not in any way weakened his own, or the Peace Foundation's, commitment to the Guevarist strategy:

Che Guevara was attempting a continental strategy of liberation in the service of that objective. And in support of those objectives, the Russell Foundation was hoping to make clear to people outside Latin America the need to solidarise with the struggle.

His unnamed interviewer remarked: 'Many people think the only thing the Russell Foundation does is to be involved in the War Crimes Tribunal. Very few people are aware that it has activities in other areas.' To which Schoenman replied:

... the Foundation's interest in the Tribunal extends to the point that the Tribunal can service the anti-imperialist struggle ... So we look on the Tribunal as part of a programme of action, and it pertains to Africa, it pertains to Latin America, and it pertains to other parts of Asia. We have been sending people to and travelling to these different parts of the world, and wherever we travel we try to make contact with the revolutionary struggle of the area concerned. We do what we can to engage in it ourselves, to line up to and to struggle with those people. So certainly the Foundation is involved in these things, whether in

Tanzania, the Congo, Bolivia or other places. I hope to be continuing in that.

It is sometimes claimed that Schoenman was alone in this conception of the Foundation as playing an active part in Che Guevara's call for revolutionary movements in three continents, but a glance at the *Bulletin* during 1967 and 1968 shows that this is very far from the case. Its second issue, published in September 1967 and put together while Schoenman was still in Bolivia, is every bit as Guevarist as the first issue had been. It contains an article by Ken Coates called 'Stokely Carmichael at OLAS', which echoes the view that Che Guevara had repeatedly expressed, that the Black Power movement in the USA was, in some sense, engaged in the *same* struggle as the Vietnamese, the Bolivian and all the other guerrilla movements so often invoked in the context of extolling the virtues of guerrilla warfare. Stokely Carmichael, as Coates puts it, 'speaks for all of us'. To confirm this view, the *Bulletin* reprints the text of Carmichael's speech in Havana, in which he was at pains to identify Black Power with the Latin American revolutionary movements.

In addition, there is Coates's own 'Report from OLAS', in which he praises the 'Homeric proportions' of the Cuban revolution and argues that the 'image of the guerrillas fighting in a hostile environment is also an image for rational men fighting in a totally hostile human environment for elementary rights for the people'. The problems caused to the people of Latin America by disease, poor housing and the lack of education, Coates claims, 'will continue inexorably until the Cuban decision has been taken everywhere throughout the continent'. He thus celebrates 'the stated resolutions of the Conference, which stated that the fundamental road forward for the Latin American revolution was the development of armed struggle'.

Elsewhere in the same issue, Robin Blackburn and Perry Anderson, freshly back from Camiri, contribute 'The Debray dossier', which applauds Debray's 'unerring accuracy' in having identified Bolivia in 1965 as a country ripe for successful revolution and tells of the 'devastating series of military defeats' that Guevara's guerrillas inflicted on the Bolivian army and of 'the sudden coalescence of political opposition behind the guerrilla insurrection' that Guevara had inspired. 'Guevara's name', Blackburn and Anderson gush, 'is calculated to strike dread into any Latin American officer.' Within a month of the publication of this article, Guevara's tiny band of guerrillas – who had scored no significant military victories and had aroused fear rather than support among the Bolivian peasants they had attempted to liberate – had been defeated, and Guevara was lying dead.

With Guevara's death died also the hopes that his message to the Tricontinental Conference had inspired, and the Bertrand Russell Peace Movement began to emphasise other aspects of its work, giving the impression in public that its chief purpose was – and always had been – to pursue the release of political prisoners and to campaign, in some usually unspecified way, for 'peace'. That it had actually been vigorously campaigning for war, for armed struggle against the United States, was forgotten – except by Schoenman. After Guevara's death and Schoenman's Bolivian escapade, most of the Trotskyists who had become directors of the Foundation resigned, leaving it in the hands of Farley, Coates and, nominally, Schoenman himself.

Schoenman's problem was that, after his Bolivian adventure, he was considered by the British and American authorities to be a rather dangerous man, and, stripped of his passport, he was frustrated in his attempts to enter Britain, or any other European country, in order to take up once more the leadership of the now demoralised Peace Foundation. In November 1967, a few days after his interview for the *Bulletin*, Schoenman tried to enter Denmark to attend the second session of the tribunal, but was refused permission to leave the airport. He then tried Amsterdam, Helsinki and Stockholm in his search for an immigration office that would let him in without a passport, but was unsuccessful and had to return to the United States. After being refused entry into Britain in March 1968, Schoenman gained a false passport and entered the country illegally, in disguise, the following June. Two weeks later, however, he was arrested and deported back to the United States.

Schoenman was, by this time, a serious embarrassment to both Russell and the Foundation, and Edith was determined to cut him adrift. One of the reasons Schoenman had returned to England in the summer of 1968 was to discuss with Ken Coates and Christopher Farley the manuscript of the third volume of Russell's *Autobiography*, which Edith had had a hand in writing and which Schoenman believed to be a betrayal of the work he had done for Russell and for the Foundation over the previous eight years. When he returned to New York after his illegal visit to Britain in June 1968, Schoenman wrote a long letter to Coates and Farley, expressing his hurt and outrage at the way he was being treated and listing his grievances against Edith, chief among which was the way she had described his relationship with Russell in the *Autobiography*. In the face of Edith's hostility, Schoenman wrote, 'I have decided to fight back with every weapon at my disposal.' One of these weapons was his directorship of the Foundation. As the *Autobiography* was owned by the Foundation, he argued, 'it is for us to decide to publish or not to publish'. He therefore requested, in his role as a director, that the Foundation should make the decision not to publish the *Autobiography* as it stood. Edith, he suggested, should be told by Farley that the remarks she had put into the book about Schoenman were actionable and should therefore be removed.

In case Coates and Farley were not prepared to go along with this plan, Schoenman had another weapon that he was prepared to use: the truth. The ultimatum he issued to his fellow-directors was this: either they agreed with his demands to remove the remarks about him written by Edith into the *Autobiography* or he would 'write and speak out' about who, exactly, had authored the works published under Russell's name during the previous eight years. As he reminded Coates and Farley: 'We are, as you know, quite dependent upon our claim that we act with the approval of Bertie', and 'It

will be fatuous for us to advance work, published or in film, in the name of
the Russell Foundation, if the 3rd volume of his autobiography demeans me
and indicates political disapproval or absence of confidence.' If the truth got
out, he implied, it would be bad for them all:

> It is not difficult to prove that I have written the major works of Russell
> in these last years with his knowledge and approval. I am, therefore,
> asking you both as directors to take note of my determination and to act
> to avoid this undoubted disaster.

In writing this letter, Schoenman had underestimated: 1. how loyal
Coates and, especially, Farley were towards Edith; 2. how little committed
they now were to the work that the foundation had been doing since 1965
and the Guevarist dreams that had inspired it; 3. the lengths to which all
three of them were now prepared to go to separate Russell from both
Schoenman and the discredited revolutionary politics to which he had
committed the Foundation.

After apparently dwelling for over a year on how to respond to
Schoenman's ultimatum, Coates and Farley finally showed the letter to
Edith and Russell towards the end of November 1969, by which time
Russell was ninety-seven years old and in serious decline. A decision was
reached to counter Schoenman's threat with an alternative account of
Russell's relationship with him, which would carry the authority of having
been written by Russell himself. In fact, the 'Private Memorandum
concerning Ralph Schoenman' was written by Edith, but she read it to
Russell and got him to sign every page of it, together with a note confirming
that it was *his* memorandum. The memorandum not only draws attention to
Schoenman's personal failings, but also rather cleverly gives the impression
that the wilder excesses of the work published and the activities pursued
under Russell's name from 1962 to 1968 were the responsibility, not of the
foundation, but of Schoenman alone, acting without Russell's support and,
often, in defiance of his disapproval. It says that Russell felt that 'Ralph
should be dismissed from the Foundation' in 1966 – that is, the year in
which the Foundation committed itself wholeheartedly to the Guevarist
strategy.

Through the third volume of the *Autobiography* and the memorandum,
history was effectively rewritten, and it was as if Russell had never lent his
support to revolutionary politics, thus confirming what many people had felt
must be true all along. It was not Russell, however, but the Peace
Foundation that was most concerned to put the 'Guevarist years' behind it.
It was decided that Russell's name should no longer be used to lend
credibility to the revolutionary movement announced at the Tricontinental
Conference, and, better still, the impression should be given that this had
never happened, still less that it had happened with the approval of both
Russell and the other directors of the Foundation. Thus, at the end of
November 1969, 'Russell' (or, more likely, Edith) wrote to Schoenman

asking him to provide an undertaking never to use Russell's name to support his own work.

The memorandum was not published until after Russell's death. But, before then, Schoenman was outflanked by a series of steps designed to separate him in the public eye from both Russell and the Foundation and to undermine anything he might say in the future about the work that he and others had done in Russell's name. First, on 9 July 1969, Schoenman was removed from Russell's will as one of the executors and trustees. Then, on 6 September, he was stripped of his directorship of the Foundation. Finally, in December 1969, a Press statement announcing this decision was released under Russell's name, which said:

> Mr Schoenman has not been my secretary for some three and a half years. Resolutions were passed with my full knowledge and approval removing him from membership of the company and the board of the Bertrand Russell Peace Foundation Ltd. some three months ago.
>
> For a considerably longer period than this I have had no contact whatsoever with Mr Schoenman and no knowledge of his activities.

Schoenman, the statement implied, had had no authority to speak and write as 'Bertrand Russell' since the summer of 1966.

It was almost as if the events of the 'Guevarist years' had never happened.

14
THE FINAL VISITATION

Of the material that was added to Russell's *Autobiography* after 1952, one of the few passages that one feels certain was written by him and not by Edith is the following paragraph from the book's Preface:

My life in England, as before, was a mixture of public and private events, but the private part became increasingly important. I have found that it is not possible to relate in the same manner private and public events or happenings long since finished and those that are still continuing and in the midst of which I live. Some readers may be surprised by the changes of manner which this entails. I can only hope that the reader will realise the inevitability of diversification and appreciate the unavoidable reticences necessitated by the law of libel.

In this apology for the dullness of the new material (for that is what it amounts to), what seems particularly striking is Russell's insistence that, in the later years of his life, its private part became *increasingly important*. Because the last few chapters of his *Autobiography* are concerned almost entirely with public events, and because his political activities in the last decade of his life received so much attention in the media, it is customary to ignore this private aspect and to write about Russell as if his last few years were spent entirely on political campaigning. This, of course, is not true.

What is true is that the separation between the public and private aspects of Russell's life was never greater than in his last six years. While 'Bertrand Russell' spent his time pouring out, with demonic energy, an endless stream of Press statements, letters to the newspapers, articles and messages to conferences on a bewildering variety of political subjects, Bertrand Russell himself spent his nonagenarian years more quietly at home in North Wales. And while the concerns of 'Bertrand Russell' centred on the struggle against 'US imperialism', those of Bertrand Russell centred on himself and his family.

In considering the relation between Russell and his public pronouncements during the last years of his life, we seem faced with two equally implausible pictures. The first is of a lifelong opponent of Communism and war, who, in his nineties, suddenly becomes fervently committed to the

Guevarist doctrine that the establishment of a stable peace can only be achieved through a series of revolutionary guerrilla wars aimed at defeating the common enemy of mankind: the United States of America. The second is of a helpless old man, who, increasingly out of touch with the outside world, sits at home in North Wales, unaware of what is being said and done in his name.

There is no reason to think that either picture is accurate. In the few glimpses that survive of Russell himself during his last few years – the conversations recorded by his friends, the interviews he gave to the media, and his private correspondence – there is none of the Guevarist rhetoric that one finds in his public statements; equally, there is nothing to challenge Schoenman's claim that everything he did in Russell's name, he did with Russell's blessing.

What one sees, rather, is an extremely old man, whose political vision has become obsessively focused on what he regards as the threat to world peace posed by the aggressive foreign policy of the United States, and who believes that, in opposing that policy, he is doing *something* to make the world a safer place. By lending his name to the activities of Schoenman and the Peace Foundation, Russell evidently believed, he was acting in the interests of humanity. In general terms, then, his position is very clear. On the details, however, he often appears shaky, and on occasions confused and simple-minded. To some extent, this is just as it always had been. Russell had never been an especially sophisticated political thinker. As Beatrice Webb and others had noted long before, he wanted quick answers to political questions and was therefore inclined to oversimplify every issue. It did not help, either, that his political imagination was dominated by the thought that the world was in the hands of irrational murderers – Dr Mallakos – whom it fell to him to oppose with the weapons of reason and kindness. Throughout his life, these tendencies had led him to adopt hasty, ill-considered and intemperate political opinions, but in his extreme old age they forced upon him a view of world affairs that was positively child-like in its refusal to admit nuance and complexity. A phrase that often occurs in the recorded interviews that he made during his last years is: 'It is quite simple'.

For example, in a filmed documentary made in 1965 by Emile de Antonio, Russell, looking tired and not quite comfortable with the situation, is asked by Schoenman why he decided to leave the Labour Party. 'Oh,' he replies, 'because they are a gang of murderers. It is quite simple. I do not approve of murdering ordinary peasants and as long as that is their main activity I do not want to be associated with it.' Asked about Vietnam, he reveals that he thinks American policy is shaped, not by the desire to oppose Communism, but by the imperialistic aim of conquering South Vietnam and its neighbouring countries:

I think America has no shred of right to have any view at all about South Vietnam. I think it is mere imperialism and conquering the country that they think is going to be weak and they can easily conquer. And of course it will be a prelude to conquering a lot of other countries if they do conquer South Vietnam.

American foreign policy in general, he claims, is motivated by 'their desire for world domination. They mean to get the whole world into their financial grip so that nobody anywhere will dare to breathe a word against the American Government.' President Johnson he describes as a 'cheerful murderer', who 'goes in for sending armies to put to death people he does not like'. Asked what, exactly, he thinks is happening in Vietnam, Russell replies: 'It is quite horrible. Quite horrible. They take pregnant women and disembowel them and exhibit their unborn babies. That sort of thing. I shouldn't have known that Americans would act that way.' Later in the film, this allegation is repeated, this time at greater length, when Schoenman shows Russell some photographs of atrocities committed in Vietnam and asks him again what the situation is like for women in the strategic hamlets of that country. In his reply, Russell says that, because the people of Vietnam 'all like the Viet Cong', the men from the villages of the country leave their families to join the guerrillas:

Well, when the men have gone off, the American troops come along, find a lot of women and children, and in one place a number of women were selected by the American authorities and were told that they were to go to the village square where they would be honoured publicly. When they got to the village square they were all pregnant, these women, they were disembowelled, babies taken out and exhibited publicly to the crowd, and the women of course died. And in all the villages they do that sort of thing.

In a filmed interview with Ralph Miliband that Russell made at around the same time, his political emphasis is again on the danger of what he describes as the 'mad' policy of the USA to dominate the world by military force – a policy, he alleges, forced upon the 'ostensible' government led by President Johnson by a 'secret government' consisting of the CIA and the Pentagon. In neither this interview nor the de Antonio film, however, is it clear that Russell supports Che Guevara's 'strategy' for dealing with this threat. In the de Antonio interview he is asked about 'resistance' to US authority, and, though he embraces the notion enthusiastically, he uses the question to look back with nostalgia on the campaigns of resistance in which he had played a part in the past: the movement against conscription during the First World War and the civil disobedience organised by the Committee of 100. The word, evidently, does not call to his mind images of guerrilla fighters in Latin America and Africa. When Schoenman attempts to nudge him more directly into talking about the 'tricontinental strategy', Russell's response shows no real interest in it, nor even any clear recognition of what Schoenman is alluding to, preferring to stick to paranoid fantasies of American intentions:

Schoenman: What do you make of the struggles of different peoples in Africa, Asia, Latin America, to free themselves from economic or military domination, Bertie?

Russell: Well, I entirely support all these efforts but I do not feel at all sure that they will result in peace because the American Government is at present on top of the world and it could, if it liked, exterminate these peoples. I mean take South Vietnam. The Americans can, if they choose, kill all the inhabitants of South Vietnam and put American colonists in their place. That is within their capacity.

In the interview with Miliband, when he is asked what the solution is to the problem posed by American plans for world domination, Russell appeals to the more familiar hope that these plans can be thwarted by the establishment of an effective World Government, which, he says, could be constructed gradually out of a series of federations – a federation of African states, another of Arab states, yet another of Latin American states, and so on. Could this be what Russell thought he was supporting in lending his name to the tricontinental strategy?

Whatever he thought that he, or the foundation set up in his name, was doing to oppose the 'madness' of US foreign policy, of one thing he was quite clear: it was of momentous, global significance. In a letter to the American philosopher, C. W. K. Mundle, written on 19 June 1967, Russell apologised for the lateness of his reply and explained: 'a great deal of work has come upon me, neglect of some of which might jeopardise the continuation of the human race'. This was two weeks after his final address to the Stockholm meeting of the War Crimes Tribunal had been read out by Schoenman, two days before his letter about Regis Debray was published in the *International Herald Tribune*, and about a month before his message to OLAS was delivered in Havana by Ken Coates. Did he *really* think that, if any of these things had not been done, it would have jeopardised the future of the human race?

Well, he thought – and it was important to him to think – that he was doing *something* of global significance, something that would encourage reason and peace to triumph over madness and war. In a manuscript dated simply '1967' (the last piece of his to survive in his handwriting) Russell began: 'The time has come to review my life as a whole, and to ask whether it has served any useful purpose or has been wholly concerned in futility.' Rather oddly, he does not then go on to review his life, but rather the state of the world, urging that: 'The powers must learn that *peace is the paramount interest of everybody*. To cause this to be realised by governments should be their supreme aim.' Asking himself: 'what have I personally contributed?', he answers:

Something perhaps, but sadly little in view of the magnitude of the evil. Some few people in England and USA I have encouraged in the expression of liberal views, or have terrified with knowledge of what modern weapons can do. It is not much, but if everybody did as much this earth would soon be a paradise.

In sending Schoenman to Stockholm to call for the War Crimes Tribunal to 'do for the peoples of Vietnam, Asia, Africa and Latin America what no tribunal did while Nazi crimes were committed', and in sending Coates to Havana to express the wish that OLAS would succeed in finding ways to co-ordinate the revolutionary struggles of armed guerrillas, Russell apparently believed that he was bringing paradise a little bit closer through the dissemination of 'liberal views'.

However, this discrepancy between what was being done by Schoenman and the foundation in Russell's name and Russell's own conception of the 'useful purpose' that he was serving the world points not to the suggestion that Schoenman was acting without Russell's authority, but to the conclusion that Russell was less interested in the *content* of the speeches that were being delivered on his behalf than in the mere fact that they were being delivered. After all, he had explicitly endorsed at least one call for 'peace through resistance to US Imperialism' – the speech Schoenman delivered at Helsinki in 1965 – and it is simply not possible that he was in ignorance of what was being read out under his name at the War Crimes Tribunal. The fact that he chose to lend his name to Schoenman's rhetoric is, then, scarcely in doubt; the question that must be answered is: why? And the answer to that is not that he was attracted to the Guevarist vision of a co-ordinated tricontinental guerrilla movement. The answer is more personal. It is that, through Schoenman, Russell hoped to have his voice heard at an international level – almost, regardless of what it was saying. Through Schoenman, Russell – a deaf old man who could hardly walk to the end of his garden without feeling exhausted – could be quite gloriously active, energetic, controversial and, on an apparently global scale, engaged with political events.

For Russell, the sorry end to his relationship with Ralph Schoenman was, above all, a *personal* disaster. After, as he often put it, he 'lost' John, he looked upon Schoenman as his son. The will he wrote at the end of 1966, leaving everything to the Peace Foundation and making Schoenman his executor and trustee, has an obvious, and great, symbolic significance, which is one reason why the implied claim in his 'Memorandum' that Russell wanted to shake Schoenman off in the summer of 1966 seems so very unconvincing.

Russell often said that one of the joys of being a parent was the feeling that something of one would survive one's death. This is why he attached so much importance to his family tradition and the name 'Russell', why he fought so hard to prevent Dora's children, Harriet and Roddy, from using the name, and why he went to such extreme lengths to erase Harriet's name from *Debrett's* and *Burke's Peerage*. It is also, one suspects, at the root of his desire to have John certified. That the title 'Earl Russell' might one day be inherited by a lunatic filled him with dread. Though he could not confer the earldom upon Schoenman, by making him heir to the Bertrand Russell

Peace Foundation, and by making that Foundation the heir to his property, he could at least do something to ensure that, after his death, his name would live on through the person of Schoenman, and that Schoenman would therefore inherit, as Russell had earlier hoped John would, the political privileges and responsibilities that went with the name 'Russell'. It is no coincidence, one feels, that the will conferring everything upon the foundation failed, in its first draft, to mention John at all.

As well as Schoenman, the other heir of whom Russell entertained great hopes was his granddaughter, Lucy, whose place in the 'increasingly important' private part of his life during his last years was much more significant than is commonly realised. The story of Russell's relations with Lucy is even more tragic than that of his friendship with Schoenman, and, in some ways, reproduces the still deeper tragedy that had been played out for many years between Russell and John.

Though he had fought hard for custody of his granddaughters in 1960, by the time of his death all three – Anne, Sarah and Lucy – had become bitterly estranged from him. Anne had never liked him, and, after leaving Moreton Hall School in 1962, saw little of him. Sarah, the most timid of the girls, never developed a close relationship with him, either. In the incessant war between, on the one side, Russell and Edith, and, on the other, Dora and John, Sarah adopted a neutral line, going to both Plas Penrhyn and Carn Voel whenever the occasion demanded, without committing herself to either side of a divide that she found both alarming and confusing. Her tactic for avoiding discord was, as John's had been, to withdraw into herself.

For Lucy, more intelligent, more intense and apparently more robust than either of her sisters, the situation was very different. She did not just put up with her elderly grandfather for the sake of an easy life; she adored and admired him and looked to him for guidance and support. She was clearly Russell's favourite, and, for a while at least, she was determined to live up to his high expectations of her. When she left Moreton Hall for Dartington in the summer of 1962, she already had nine O-levels. As she was then only fourteen, and British schoolchildren did not normally take O-level examinations until they were sixteen, this was quite an achievement and enough to mark her out as a child of prodigious ability of whom much was hoped.

At Dartington, however, things started to go wrong. In part, this was because she was ill-equipped to cope with the change from a conventional, all-girls school to a progressive mixed school, and consequently neglected her studies and lost her direction. Perhaps more importantly, though, she became increasingly confused and torn by the ongoing battle between her father and her grandfather. Like Russell, Lucy was a determined chronicler of her own life, and, in diaries, memoirs, fictionalised autobiographies and poems, she tried to make sense of the emotional pressures that were, she felt, in danger of sending her insane. Understandably, she was haunted by the fate of her parents. In an unfinished autobiography that she wrote in 1970 she says: 'I was born after madness. I start from there. My life is the going-beyond madness; insanity is axiomatic, and I am the theorem.'

In the same fragment she writes: 'I used to be a cheerful soul with a big grin and a moon face, and anyone with troubles came to me for a warm smile of optimism and a rosy glow.' At Dartington, she says, trying to cope with the conflicting demands of Russell and Edith, Dora and John, her upbringing at Plas Penrhyn and Moreton Hall and the new, relaxed atmosphere in which she now found herself, she was 'beaten into a confused heap of self-conceptions, none of which were acceptable to anyone, not being acceptable to all'.

Her diaries tell the story of this decline from 'cheerful soul' to 'a confused heap of self-conceptions' and reveal how central to that story was the conflict in her mind between her admiration of, and loyalty to, Russell and her love for, and identification with, John. On 9 December 1963, she wrote:

Nobody knows, for example, how John worries me . . . no-one realises the effect he had for a long time on me, seeming to need so much and expect so much . . . My poor Dad, how he longs for attention & love! And this is exactly what I have done. Why? Why did I drive off & attack Bertie & Edith, refuse their love? Well, that is not how it happened, at the time it was only standing up for myself & defying them. They reacted strongly & surprisingly. I was astonished. They didn't love me anymore.

For a while Lucy formed a deep attachment to Dora's son, Roddy, and hoped that Roddy and his wife, Susie, would adopt her. She also looked to Ralph Schoenman for support, but, with the launch of the foundation in 1963, Schoenman spent less and less time at Plas Penrhyn and more and more time abroad. In Cornwall on Christmas Day 1963, in handwriting that suggests that she was either very tired or very drunk, Lucy poured out to her diary her feelings of abandonment and loss:

Nothing's ever the same. I kill everything. Why is nothing the same? Why do I kill everything? . . . Ralph's killed. And I haven't seen him for about 18 months. Roddy's died, I've barely seen him . . . how long is it since I've been home to Wales? *Lost*. Bertie and Edith also quarrelled with and lost. Their love lost, belief in their love lost, belief in them, their ideals, the goodness of their lives lost, all close ties *lost*.

A week later, she was at Plas Penrhyn, reunited with both Russell and Schoenman ('My Ralph, who I always liked from the beginning. Who I got on extremely well with for a while and who was extremely good to me'), but she began to feel that Schoenman was drifting away from her, taking with him the 'Ralph-life – I mean such as he could have introduced me to, had he been my friend'. Then, on 17 January 1964, when she was back at Dartington and reflecting on the diary entries she had written during the Christmas period, it occurred to her that she had written nothing about 'how much I loved Bertie, how much he had my heart, on the day before I left (13th)':

In the morning Edith told me 'your Grandpa would very much like to see you some time before you leave, he hasn't seen anything of you & wondered if you'd be free after tea sometime.' Later, about 4.30pm: 'Your Grandpa is roaring to see you.' Both these went to the quick. We talked, Dartington, my subject – & stick to maths was his advice, with promises to 'talk to you sometime about mathematics', in the summer maybe . . . My sweet, sweet grandadpapa who loves me, I hope, in spite of everything and whom I love best of everything I know . . . I emerge after an hour or ¾ shining throughout, tears in my veins and bright face . . .

Goodbye, he says, goodbye, as if it might be the last time EVER, and it makes me weep.

But while reflecting – or, perhaps, trying to convince herself – that 'Bertie is the search for truth and built of integrity, honesty in all things to the depths of his consciousness', Lucy remembers her father: 'No men are perfect, can I expect him [Russell] also not to humiliate, desert and abandon his unprotected son?'

The diary entry ends with Lucy declaring her loyalty to *both* sides of the dreadful, irreconcilable breach:

God, if I could have one wish and that fulfilled, it would be sanity, fulfillment, reconciliation, happiness in short, for John, and longer still life to Bertie with success & happiness such as he deserves. And the stronger wish, though they do battle equally, is for John, for the weaker, the younger, the one who cannot control or sustain his own life. I will cry like hell when Bertie Granpa dies, I will be sad and weep with all that is in me, but he has had, and from John it has been taken even that which he had.

Later in the same month, she wrote that she was 'grateful kneeling at Bertie's feet, I know he loves me dearly'.

In praying for a long life for Russell and for reconciliation between him and John, Lucy had added a prayer for herself: 'Give me a lover O lord, and be thou blessed! And spare us the pain of parting.' In the Easter term of 1964, this prayer was answered, when Lucy sought and found not one lover but several. As her diary shows, however, this did not ease her problems, but rather added to them by inducing in her deep feelings of revulsion about what she saw as her lack of morality, and anxieties about what Russell and Edith would think if they found out how recklessly promiscuous she had become.

In fact, Russell and Edith were concerned about her moral state at this time, not because of anything they had heard about her sexual behaviour, but because of what they considered to be the potentially dangerous influence upon her of John. In March 1964, towards the end of the Easter term, Russell and Edith approached their lawyers asking them to appeal to the Divorce Court to change the terms of the custody settlement of 1961, which granted John 'reasonable access' to Lucy and her sisters, and to ask the court to impose an order preventing John from seeing his daughters until they were twenty-one.

What prompted this move was Russell's alarm at receiving from John two large packages of his writing, consisting of several 'books', among which were 'Anne's Book', 'Sarah's Book', 'Lucy's Book' and one called 'Review'. All of these books, like the rest of John's writing, were incoherent and manifestly the product of a disordered mind, but what particularly worried Russell and Edith about them was the obscene language in which they were written. This, they thought, indicated that John might pose some kind of sexual threat to his daughters. For example, in 'Anne's Book', John writes:

> 'I did but SEE her passing by
> and yet will I love her till I Die'
> Audience! Do you think that the author of this sentiment was
> SPEAKING the TRUTH
> or do you think he FUCKED her within
> Ye Firste Fyve MINUTES?
> Do you think that if he DIDN'T Fuck her
> Within really the first five minutes
> he was a silly little eunoch-NOBODY?

One of the things that Russell and Edith found especially disturbing about these packages was a bizarre hand-written scrawl on the envelope containing 'Review', which read: 'Do you share my enthusiasm for fashionable necrophily?'

What possibly worried, or anyway angered, Russell still more was the uncharacteristic aggression towards him shown by John in these writings. In 'Sarah's Book' John writes:

> Why, Papa, WHY!
> Art thou such a MISERABLE Bourgeois FOP?
> and such a Cretinous
> Bourgeois IDEALIST?
>
> Why, Pig-Head! Tell Me WHY!!
>
> We need not Now AWAIT Papa's REPLY
> We KNOW he is quite COUTH
> His PROPER Name is RUTH
>
> Poor Papa! OF COURSE you need
> to be BUGGERED!
>
> You are only the MINOTAUR'S Arse!
>
> Goodbye, Heavenly Father!

If you DON'T Like It
why
don't you DO Something?

In the book entitled 'Review' John reproduced a poem by Peter Porter called 'Inspector Christopher Smart Calls', which had been broadcast on the radio and printed in *The Listener* on 27 February 1964, and which John presented as a 'proof' that Russell and Christine Keeler, the prostitute at the heart of the Profumo scandal, were one and the same. The poem contains lines that seem fairly obviously to allude to Russell:

You know that great philosopher on the telly,
The one who still looks randy at eighty-five –
A million selfishnesses have oiled his skin,
A spark of light on his mummied eye
And he'll basilisk your girlfriend
Now, here's the point: get with him, he's history, he's life!

The Profumo scandal had a powerful impact on John's imagination, and afterwards he moved permanently to Cornwall, refusing to live in London, which, he said, was now too corrupt to tolerate. It seems likely, therefore, that the thought he was expressing in 'Review' is that Porter's poem shows the decadence revealed by the scandal to be manifest also in Russell.

Russell found John's writings deeply disturbing, and, in an effort to protect her husband and the girls from any further such disturbances, Edith filed a suit to strip from John his legal right to see his daughters, hoping perhaps that this would stop him writing to his father. On 18 March 1964, Lucy received a phone call from Russell, telling her about John's writings and asking her not to go to Cornwall at Easter, but to spend the entire holiday at Plas Penrhyn. Sensing that it was up to her to act as a peacemaker, she wrote to Russell later that day: 'I was very sorry to hear John has been worrying you, granpa and though I don't know what these letters said it is probably only a temporary setback. We can talk about it when the term ends. Please, whatever he's said, don't be too concerned about it – we can discuss it when I see you both.'

A few days later, Lucy wrote to Dora saying that she was 'very upset that Grandpa has dragged up this old subject again of whether we may visit you and John':

It is all so needless: the whole question was settled years ago and the situation is no different now – except that John is better every time I see him. I can't see any valid reason on earth why Bertie should want to prevent us seeing him.

Echoing many similar sentiments expressed years before by John and Kate, Lucy added:

It is difficult enough to live in two homes which barely communicate and (lately) refuse to meet – there are constantly rival claims on one's loyalties, one senses or imagines that one side would prevent us seeing the other – without these senseless rows which create a division of loyalties in us.

'It is ridiculous', Lucy told Dora, 'to pretend that I don't like being with Daddy or enjoy his company or that it ever does or ever has made me unhappy or worried to be with him . . . If only Granpa knew what he was like to be with!'

In connection with the case, the psychiatrist who had reported on John for previous court hearings, Dr Morgan, was consulted by Dora's lawyer and wrote a letter to be shown to the court, in which he said:

The incoherent writings to which reference has been made represent an attempt on his part to batter his way through the problem in the light of which he became ill. I do not look upon them as a particularly serious manifestation. I have never known him other than extremely gentle. I understand his relationship with his children is excellent . . . I frankly see no reason why he should be deprived of their company, particularly since when the arrangement was made on the previous occasion he has improved greatly.

Edith and Russell had hoped to get the case settled on 25 March, the day on which Lucy's and Sarah's Easter vacation began, in time to prevent them from going to Cornwall for part of the holidays. However, the judge ruled for the case to be adjourned until Dr Morgan had time to examine John again and prepare a more extensive report, giving his professional opinion as to: (a) whether John's mental state had deteriorated, and (b) whether it was dangerous for the girls to be in his company. In the meantime, the terms of the custody order of 1961 remained unchanged, thus obliging Russell and Edith to allow the girls to see their father during the holiday. To prevent this from happening, Tyler advised Russell and Edith to show John's writings to the girls, so that they could see for themselves the potential dangers of being in his company. 'We have discussed the matter with the children,' Edith wrote to Tyler's colleague, Holland, 'and they appear to understand the situation.'

This attempt to make the girls afraid of John incensed both Dora and her solicitor. 'It is not something that anyone in their right mind ought to do to those girls,' Dora wrote. 'I don't mean anything to do with obscenity, but the attempt to undermine their feeling for their father and their confidence in meeting and having family relations with him.' Taylor, sounding even more angry than Dora, agreed that Russell's action was 'wicked', especially as he did not think that Russell and Edith *really* believed that John was a danger to the girls: 'Personally I have little doubt that he instructed Tyler to issue this Summons because he was nettled by some of the personal allusions which were too penetrating to be comfortable, particularly the description of him from the poem in the *Listener* – "A million selfishnesses have oiled his skin".'

As Taylor was quick to point out, Russell and Edith were arguably in contempt of court when they showed John's writings to the girls, and he therefore felt able to take a more aggressive stance in his dealings with Tyler. 'Having failed in their application to the Court to suspend access during the Easter holidays,' he wrote on 13 April, 'your clients have disobeyed the order of the Court and have set out to achieve their own ends by doing themselves the very thing from which they professed to protect the girls.' As this action cast doubt on the *bona fides* of their application, he told Tyler, he would be insisting that both Russell and Edith should attend the adjourned hearing of the summons to face cross-examination on their affidavits.

The prospect of Russell and Edith being cross-examined in court over their attitude to John alarmed them, their solicitors and Schoenman. While Tyler made repeated phone calls to Taylor asking to settle the case out of court, Schoenman persuaded Lucy that – far from being in any danger from her father – she had a duty to spend the last part of her holiday in Cornwall with John, in order to keep Dora happy and the case out of the newspapers. 'From what Ralph said about a public court summons', Lucy wrote in her diary, it seemed that she had to go to Cornwall after all. After spending three weeks at Plas Penrhyn, Lucy's sympathies were now firmly on the side of Russell and Edith:

Dora has no right or reason to make this fuss; what *does* she want, we ask ourselves, to stir up trouble or ah! maybe force B's hand since she believes 'our relation with our father' is being spoilt and adverse influences insinuated against our going there . . . So now off I go to hear long harangues, virulent attacks, sordid in and outs from John's mother, always champion of what J wld. have wanted! . . . It'll be a tough time & I doubt I'll hear anything but this lot for 5 days or so, but for public peace it's worth it. Humour & optimism (& Dad) will see it through.

After a few days in Cornwall, however, Lucy's sympathies swung the other way:

Dora is magnificent – she deserves great fame and (I think) will have it one day . . . Dora gets everything in perspective, I've known her so long . . . I love, fear and admire John. I love & admire Dora warmly.

On 15 May, Dr Morgan submitted his report to the court. John, he wrote, far from getting worse, 'has improved enormously since I first saw him in 1957 and now needs no medication whatsoever'. In his judgment, the writings John had sent to Russell did not provide any evidence either that his mental state had deteriorated or that he posed any threat to his children: 'The obscene passages in his recent writings are no indication of his likely behaviour.' In his report, Dr Morgan also expressed the opinion that John's condition 'is connected with the relationship between him and his father', thus alluding to his earlier remark that John's writings should be interpreted, not as an indication of perverted sexual desires towards his children, but as an attempt to 'batter his way through' the problem of his relationship with Russell.

Clearly, the report offered no support to Edith's petition, but strengthened still further the position of Dora and her lawyer. 'As you advised your clients to show the children the obscene material,' Taylor wrote to Tyler on 8 June, 'have you advised them to show them Dr Morgan's report?' If Russell and Edith had proceeded with the case, they would certainly have lost and, in the process, would have been put through the ordeal of cross-examination. They therefore withdrew.

In the summer of 1964 – sensing, like Dora, Taylor and Dr Morgan, that what had *really* upset Russell about John's writings was the aggression they expressed towards him – Lucy tried to effect some sort of reconciliation. After she returned to Dartington for the summer term, she wrote to Russell, trying to reassure him that 'Daddy has great affection for you'. Any hopes of success were, however, scotched by her sister, Sarah, who on 9 June wrote to Lucy to tell her that: 'G'pa spoke to me at some length abt the question of John coming to Wales, & was remarkably insistent on the impossibility of it. He asked me to make it clear to you that John cldn't come to Wales & imagines you to be very much set on the idea.'

The strain of trying to mediate in an irreconcilable conflict, and of maintaining loyalties that were not only divided but incompatible, imposed an intolerable burden on Lucy, just at a time when she was feeling emotionally adrift and in need of support, and from this time on her life went into a kind of free-fall. In the summer of 1964, she was entered, two years earlier than was usual (she was still only fifteen), for two A-levels – mathematics and English – both of which she failed. This was her first experience of academic failure and its effects were devastating, confirming her in her opinion that she was turning out to be a great disappointment to those who had previously had high hopes of her. The result of her A-level failures, she wrote to a friend, 'is an awful situation between me & my grandparents', made worse by the fact that, spending the summer in Plas Penrhyn without the company of her sisters (both of whom were abroad), she continually managed to upset Edith, who 'you may remember . . . is very much a lady, & easily offended'.

Not only did Lucy feel that she had failed Russell and Edith, but she also felt that they – and all the other adults in her life – had failed *her*. She therefore gave up trying to please them and attempting to live up to their hopes and, deliberately abandoning her reputation as the pleasant and considerate 'cheerful soul with a big grin and a moon face', ceased to care whether she offended them or not. A vignette illustrating her new attitude survives in a description she wrote of the first evening of her Christmas holidays at Plas Penrhyn in 1964: 'Apparently last night I sat up when Gma came in. She said "It's lovely to have you here" & I answered "Nonsense". And went back to sleep.'

The change in Lucy's attitude, and in some respects her whole personality, was noted with dismay by her teachers at Dartington. By March 1965, the headmaster of the school, H. A. T. Child, had become so alarmed that he wrote to Russell, asking whether Russell had noticed the change in Lucy and expressing his concern. Lucy, Child wrote, 'finds co-operation with any adult very difficult' and this was severely affecting her work. Far from looking the safe bet it had seemed a few years earlier, Lucy's chances of gaining a place at Cambridge to study mathematics now looked rather slim. Indeed, 'As things stand at the moment, it would be folly to enter her for Cambridge in the Autumn.' Her teachers were even beginning to wonder whether mathematics was the right subject for her; 'her greatest competence ... has seemed to us to be in languages but she clings obstinately to Mathematics, although often turning up to a class without paper, pen or pencil'.

In Lucy's mind, her own papers reveal, the question as to whether she should study mathematics or a humanities subject was bound up with the question of which of her famous grandfathers – Russell or Vachel Lindsay – she most identified with. Her obstinate clinging to mathematics was, at least partly, the result of her desire to follow the advice and example of Russell. Russell waited to reply to Child's letter until Lucy returned to Plas Penrhyn for the Easter holidays, when, after discussing the situation with her, he wrote Child a brief, curt letter, informing him that Lucy would not be returning to Dartington for the summer term, but would instead be educated privately at home in mathematics and physics. 'As I gather from your letter that you feel that Lucy's withdrawal might be advisable,' Russell's letter ended, 'I take it for granted that you will not object to this late notice of it.' Obviously taken aback by the abruptness of this decision, Child nevertheless responded with a polite and generous letter, telling Russell: 'Until the last term or two we found Lucy a co-operative and easy girl and we are only sorry that we cannot put our finger on what has gone wrong.'

For the spring and summer months of 1965, Lucy lived with Russell and Edith at Plas Penrhyn, travelling to Aberystwyth once a week to receive two hours of private coaching from a mathematician at the University College of Wales called C. F. Gardiner, who admired Russell so much that he named his daughter after him ('Russell Gardiner'). Two hours' tuition a week was obviously not enough to make up the ground that Lucy had lost and living at Plas Penrhyn during the 'Guevarist years' of the foundation was hardly conducive to concentrated study. Besides, she had lost interest in mathematics, as her teachers at Dartington had not failed to notice. In her private musings, she wondered whether mathematics served any useful purpose at all, since it seemed so unrelated to human emotions, and understanding her own emotional life had become her first priority. And so Lucy spent the months before her exams covering innumerable pages with poetry and personal reflections; predictably, she again failed her A-levels.

Among her writings during this period is the following analysis of her relationship with Russell and of her struggle to maintain, in the face of his opposition, things that were 'sacred' to her:

> I am having such a fight here to maintain my identity & morals against my grandfather, the invader ... now, he is making (unconsciously) the force of his ideas & his ingrained *own* morality a person for me to fight. The price or prize of fighting it is my own independence (inward) or his affection & approval, and love (if I lose) ... Unless I can fight my own way, pitting my ideals & ME against him, I shan't ever make anything on my own ... Why is it so dangerous to love your relatives?

'My grandpa despises people who are not well-educated,' she wrote on another occasion, 'especially when they ought to have lived up to his hopes – the worst mistake, to have hopes of your children, etc. What they want to be, and are, is what you have to think important.'

Not far in the background of almost all Lucy's reflections was the troubled history of her family. An image that recurs frequently is that of John trapped in a bubble, which it was somehow Lucy's responsibility to burst, setting John free to reconnect with the rest of the world. She also pictured herself in a bubble, and, in a piece about John, wrote: 'I never understood you till now. Because I am the same.' The inevitable consequence of this identification with her father was the alienation from Russell that is manifestly evident in the following description of her Welsh home:

> Plas Penrhyn
> Inhabited with egg shells & martyrs. Some of them are boilproof. The temperature is variable, regulated by a decrepit relic thermostat from the days when England was generally cooler ... The tireder people among the inmates go to bed early and rise late, thus leaving the more sprightly members of the house free to roam between 10.30p.m. and 11.30a.m., but on no account during other hours ... Reject my warning and you are Doomed; heed it, and safety & Redemption for the Rabid Racking Wrecking Wrangling Rancid Russells may yet be yours.

She also scribbled the following lines about Schoenman:

> Ralph
> Poisoned malicious heart. It desires power raw alone, pure simple power to rule others, despite any little live movements in its heart. I, the Big Man. Why don't you see if you can like yourself before you force others to put up with you?

In July 1965, as soon as her A-level examinations were finished, Lucy took off on a two-month holiday with her sister Anne to France, Spain and Morocco. Anne and Lucy quarrelled violently during this holiday, mostly because of Lucy's wild and self-destructive behaviour. Several times she placed herself deliberately in dangerous situations, with the result that, on at least one occasion, she was raped. Salvation of some kind came in the form of a young Moroccan student called Ahmed, with whom Lucy fell deeply in love. When she returned to Wales in September, her only thought was of being reunited with Ahmed, and she was only dissuaded from returning to Morocco by Russell's promise to invite Ahmed to Plas Penrhyn for Christmas. Russell further undertook to ensure that Ahmed would be allowed into the UK by writing to the Home Office saying that he wished to employ him.

After long discussions with Russell and Edith about her future, Lucy, at their insistence, made yet another attempt to pass A-levels in mathematics and physics, this time by enrolling at the Polytechnic of North West London. She also applied to take the entrance examinations for Oxford and Cambridge. In the meantime, she lived at Russell's Chelsea flat in Hasker Street and waited anxiously for Ahmed to arrive. When he did, Russell took an immediate and deep dislike to him and refused to have him at Plas Penrhyn.

Lucy took her Oxbridge exams in December and, to nobody's surprise, failed them. In March 1966, Russell learnt that Ahmed, who was still waiting for a permit to work in the UK, had been caught stealing books from Foyles Bookshop in London. After writing to the Home Office to say that he did not, after all, wish to employ Ahmed and that he relinquished any responsibility for the Moroccan's maintenance in the UK, Russell then instructed his solicitors to act on Ahmed's behalf in his forthcoming prosecution for theft. While waiting for the case to reach the court, Ahmed was again caught stealing books from Foyles, whereupon Russell wrote to his solicitors asking them *not* to act in Ahmed's defence and expressing a strong desire to see him deported as soon as possible. In order to prevent Lucy from following him back to Morocco, Russell suggested that a court order might be obtained keeping her in the UK.

To Russell's evident irritation, Tyler replied that, even if Russell did not feel able to pay the expenses incurred by Ahmed's defence, he 'could not, for professional reasons, immediately desert Ahmed, since however great a nuisance he is, he is entitled to be defended'. In the event, Ahmed was deported before his case reached the court. On the day that he left, 30 April, Russell wrote a letter to Tyler expressing at length his annoyance with Lucy's irresponsibility: over Ahmed, over money and over her own future. Nevertheless, he emphasised, he and Edith were 'very fond of Lucy' and had made it clear to her that she would be welcome at Plas Penrhyn.

Just a month later, however, on 25 May 1966, Russell wrote to Tyler that he and Edith 'intend to relinquish immediately all legal responsibility and all financial responsibility for Lucy':

We no longer wish to remain her legal guardians and should be grateful if you would pursue your suggestion of arranging for the official solicitor and the court to replace us as guardians and financial providers.

We are ceasing all financial covenants for her support and towards any
fees or other expenses and wish you to arrange this.

Two months before her eighteenth birthday, Lucy – without a home, a
job, a boyfriend or any coherent plans for the future – was on her own.
She was by no means the only person with whom Russell made a break
that summer. A month after he disowned Lucy, Russell wrote to Tyler
suddenly announcing that he no longer wished to retain his lawyer's
services. 'We realise', Russell told him, 'that your main interest must lie in
the large affairs with which you deal and that our business is too small and
too personal to command much of your attention.' He was therefore
transferring his, and the Peace Foundation's, legal affairs to Blanche Lewis
of Theodore Goddard & Co. Clearly shocked by this, Tyler replied that it
was 'with great regret' that he received Russell's letter, adding that, because
he was still worried about Lucy, he thought that he should at least remain
the granddaughters' trustee. When Russell insisted that Tyler and his
colleague, Drover, should step down as trustees in favour of Blanche Lewis
and another member of her firm, Tyler dug in his heels. On 8 July, an
exasperated Russell wrote to Tyler:

Mr Schoenman has told me of his telephone conversation with you this
afternoon and I can scarcely believe it is possible that you would refuse to
conform with my express wishes in so intimate a matter.

But Tyler was not to be bullied, either by Russell or by Schoenman. The
trusteeships, he told Russell, had proved a thankless task, but: 'Be that as it
may, we are of the opinion that we should be failing in our duty to the
beneficiaries if we were to resign':

Mr Schoenman, upon whose advice and views it is clear to us both you
and your wife greatly rely, seems to think that Drover and I are simply
agents to do what we are told. We cannot accept this, and it is our
intention to continue to discharge our duties as trustees in the best
interests of the beneficiaries.
    . . . I do not like to end on a controversial note, but we do ask that Mr
Schoenman should not be the channel of communication between you
and us.

The mention of Schoenman here serves as a reminder that, despite the
impression created by the 'Memorandum Concerning Ralph Schoenman'
that Russell effectively broke with Schoenman in the summer of 1966, it was
precisely during that summer that Schoenman exerted his *most* powerful
influence on Russell's life, both public and private.
    Russell's association with Tyler's firm, Coward, Chance & Co. – a firm
that had represented Russell ever since his divorce from Dora – was not the
only casualty of that influence. On 28 June 1966, just eight days after Russell
had dispensed with Tyler's services, Stanley Unwin was surprised to receive

a letter from Russell, stating that, though hitherto Unwin had acted both as Russell's literary agent and as his publisher, he was henceforth to consider himself Russell's publisher only. He was to be replaced as Russell's literary agent by Deborah Rogers, who would begin by negotiating the foreign rights of Russell's *Autobiography*. A month later, as suddenly as she had been appointed, Deborah Rogers was replaced by Anton Felton of Continuum Ltd. On 3 September 1966, Unwin received from Russell another piece of unwelcome news:

> . . . as I live such a long distance from London and am able to get through less work in a day than I should wish, I might have to do a certain amount of business through my secretary, Mr Schoenman.

Then, on 22 November, Unwin was told that Russell had made a new will, under the terms of which Unwin (who was to have been Russell's literary executor) had been replaced in that role by Edith and Felton. 'This not only removes the burden which I placed on you,' Russell wrote, 'but enables Mr Felton to assist more thoroughly the Foundation which he advises and to which I have recently made various assignments.'

After receiving several insistent demands from Schoenman, demanding to know why so few reviews of *War Crimes in Vietnam* had appeared and why so few foreign rights had been sold, Unwin wrote directly to Russell on 16 January 1967, enclosing copies of his correspondence with Schoenman, together with a plaintive note saying: 'I hope that you will forgive me if my reply to Mr Schoenman shows any sign of exasperation.' This elicited an apology from Russell on Schoenman's behalf, but did not change the nature of the demands made upon Unwin, who throughout 1967 received a series of letters, sometimes signed by Russell, sometimes by Schoenman, all written in the same insistent tone and demanding either urgent payments to the Peace Foundation (on advance of sales of Russell's *Autobiography*) or further steps to promote *War Crimes in Vietnam*.

It is possible that Lucy never knew about Russell's letter to Tyler of 25 May 1966, effectively disowning her. After living in London with Ahmed during the first few months of 1966, she had little to do with her grandfather, and the financial support that she continued to receive from him she received indirectly, through the members of Tyler's firm responsible for administering the trust set up for her and her sisters. In any case, on 14 June, after finishing her exams (which, yet again, she failed), she wrote to Russell as if nothing had happened, asking if she could come to stay at Plas Penrhyn 'for a time'. In reply, she received the following rather cold response from Edith:

> We think . . . that we do not want a visit from anyone whom it is not necessary for us to see on business in the next months. We have devoted the past six months to family affairs and public business has been cut to a minimum. Now its claims must be answered and your grandfather must devote himself to it. As few distractions as possible must be allowed to

interfere with it. It would, in consequence, be most convenient if you do not return to Plas Penrhyn for the holidays but remain where you are.

This was written on the same day, 20 June 1966, as Russell's letter to Tyler ending his association with Coward, Chance & Co. For the following year Lucy lived first at Roddy's house and then at Harriet's. In both places she outstayed her welcome. In an effort to get rid of her, Susie, Roddy's wife, phoned Russell to explain the situation and to urge him to take Lucy off their hands. Like Tyler and Unwin, however, and many other people who tried to make contact with Russell during this period, Susie found herself dealing with Schoenman, from whom some weeks after her call to Wales she received a surprise visit. Schoenman, Susie soon discovered, was far more interested in telling her about the War Crimes Tribunal and its colossal significance than in discussing Russell family problems. After listening to him for what seemed a very long time, Susie remonstrated: 'Yes, but what about Lucy?' 'Ah, yes,' Schoenman replied, 'Lord Russell asked me to tell you that, compared with the Vietnam War, Lucy is a very small problem.'

In 1967, as preparations for the War Crimes Tribunal continued, and the Peace Foundation committed itself with ever greater fervour to Che Guevara's 'strategy', Russell found himself effectively cut off from almost all the personal associations that linked him to his pre-Schoenman past. By the spring, as his ninety-fifth birthday approached, he was feeling deeply his isolation from his family and was beginning to regret the way things had turned out with Lucy and her sisters, which typically he interpreted as *their* rejection of *him*. On 25 April 1967, he wrote to Kate: 'Your branch of the family is the only one that acknowledges me; the rest avoid me & vilify me.' A month later, he wrote to thank her for an especially comforting letter, telling her: 'I have been suffering from a belief that only people who didn't know me well could tolerate me. Dora, Peter, John, Conrad, Sarah, Lucy, seemed to bear this out.' He added: 'If you ever write to Sarah or Lucy, tell them that if they come I will keep Schoenman away while they are here.'

Separated from his family, Russell depended for company at Plas Penrhyn on Edith, Christopher Farley, his friends in the local neighbourhood – particularly Michael Burn and Rupert Crawshay-Williams – and, for a few years at least, the young people who worked for the foundation. David Horowitz remembers being taken to Plas Penrhyn for Russell's ninety-fourth birthday in 1966 (the very month of his apparently final break with Lucy):

When we arrived I was immediately struck by the character of the gathering. There were twenty or so guests, all connected to the Foundation or in some other way to Ralph's activities. All were under 25 years of age. They were Marxist activists, mainly Trotskyists, reflecting Ralph's most recent political enthusiasm . . .

The extraordinary scene in Russell's home reflected the fact that the great man had outlived himself. All his friends were dead, and the world that had been his was gone. Now there were only these children whom Ralph had gathered, who neither were Russell's friends nor had any connection with him, other than the political utility they saw in his name.

It was not quite true, of course, that *all* Russell's friends were dead, but his circle was getting smaller. Crawshay-Williams still saw him regularly and kept notes of his conversations with Russell, from which one can see the way in which he declined in his last few years. He was, of course, remarkably vigorous for a man in his nineties, but his deafness was becoming a serious obstacle to social relations and, because of a mysterious disorder of the throat, he was unable to eat solid foods. He drank whisky heavily, and, though he hardly ever struck people as drunk, his conversation became increasingly formulaic, telling the same stories from his past over and over again. Characteristically of people in their extreme old age, while his long-term memory remained extremely good, his short-term memory became very bad. He was not senile, but, on occasion, especially if he was taking antibiotic drugs, he would seem so. Among the notes Crawshay-Williams took of his meetings with Russell is a description of going to Plas Penrhyn at Christmas 1967 and being astonished to be greeted with the remark: 'Apparently you approve of the Bolsheviks, do you?':

> . . . he [Russell] was completely confused not only as to who we all were but also as to *when* we all were. He seemed to know that I was in some way opposed to him over his current obsession; but he translated this into terms of the 1920s.

A year later Crawshay-Williams records with some relief: 'he was perfectly all here. Of course he was tired and stooped, and very deaf. But he knew exactly what was going on.'

That Christmas, to Russell's very great delight, he was reunited with Conrad, who had by 1968 decided to defy his mother by resuming relations with his father. When, over conversation during drinks, Conrad demonstrated both his memory and his scholarship by producing instantly two quotations, one from Hume and the other from Bentham, Crawshay-Williams writes, 'Bertie looked on with evident fatherly pride.'

To some extent, this reunion with Conrad compensated Russell for the loss of both John and Schoenman. On 5 December 1969, just when the breach with Schoenman became complete and irrevocable, Russell made what might be interpreted as a final small gesture towards renewing contact with John, when he forwarded to him a letter he had received from John's old physics teacher, Dr Holter. 'I thought you might like to see what he says,' Russell wrote, significantly signing off with the word 'love'.

To John, however, the bitterness of the previous fifteen years had cut too deep, and he saw in the short note only the cold reserve he expected to find in a communication from his father. He wrote back:

LETTER TO BERTRAND RUSSELL: or BERTIE,
LORD Now Bertrand Risseole
DIDDY
DADDY
PAPPA; OR PAPA
Or;
The Earl Russell, OM

Darling is how yr letter SHOULD Begin . . .
You Didn't Need To Be So Grudging In The FIRST Place
You Didn't Need
To Hit Out And Be A War-monger:
Thus; Dr Holter, the Professor who taught me physics, enquiring into
the whereabouts of this son,
Thanking Professor Norman J.Holter for his kind words, your humble
servant goes on to remind the reader that THE EMPEROR TAISHO is at
present studying Norman castles.

This was to be the last exchange between the two.

In the New Year of 1970, Russell was suffering from acute bronchitis and
was very weak. By the end of January, he was mostly confined to bed. On 2
February, he was having difficulty breathing and Edith called the doctor,
but by the early evening Russell was dead. It was, in some ways, a lonely
death. Edith was there, of course, but none of the rest of Russell's family
was present.

In his will of November 1966, Russell had given instruction that there
was to be no funeral service, and he made it clear to those close to him that
the place of his cremation should not be made open to the public. He
further stipulated that there was to be no music. Within these rather austere
restrictions, the task of organising Russell's cremation fell to Ken Coates,
who, together with Edith, Farley, Conrad and his wife, was one of the very
few mourners in attendance when, four days after Russell's death, his coffin
was carried off to the furnace. Afterwards, his ashes were scattered over the
Welsh hills. Some time after his death, Lucy wrote to Dora: 'If there are
ghosts to lay, let them be laid, along with our childhoods, among the
magnificent mountains.'

But the ghosts were by no means laid. At his death Russell left two
embittered ex-wives, an estranged schizophrenic son and three granddaughters who felt themselves haunted by the 'ghosts of maniacs', as Russell
himself had described his family back in 1893. John succeeded his father as
Earl Russell and became a regular attender of – and occasional participant in
– the debates in the House of Lords, but he never fully regained his sanity.
He died in 1987. His daughter Sarah was diagnosed as schizophrenic shortly
before Russell's death and has spent much of her time since in psychiatric
care. In an effort to put her past behind her, Anne moved in 1975 to New
Mexico, where she has lived ever since.

Especially haunted was Lucy, who by the time of Russell's death was a
confused and disturbed twenty-one-year-old, without any settled direction
in life. In the summer of 1970, she finally managed to pass some A-levels

and was accepted on a course in anthropology and politics at the University of Kent. At this time, she described her outlook on life to her father, John, as 'a mixture of mythology, metaphysics, religion, science & psychology, with a dash of R. D. Laing and a flavour of LSD culture'.

Continuing to identify herself with John, Lucy shared his distress when, in 1972, a centenary celebration of Russell's life and work was planned at Woburn Abbey, the ancestral home of the Dukes of Bedford (the 'senior' branch of the Russell family). Encouraging John to turn up to the celebration in order to destroy it, Lucy wrote to him:

> For God's sake let's let ourselves out and the Side Down for once in a public nuisance of ourselves. That Mesmeric Family, its name and its nature, pow and power . . . No, I agree with my conscience that in the cause of liberty, looked at one way, I cannot countenance Invitation to Woburn . . . no bowing down before bread or idols or Russell worshippers or *with* them . . . I don't want to say you're anyone's relative, if *I* don't want me to. Time to publish 'The Death of Papa' perhaps. On the other hand, if people hold summit conferences to establish Churches in people's names, which are the names I bear, should I go to the Cross for them without uttering a word on the subject of their ordination? I would like to correct some impressions; I'm not desperate to and will be guided by you if you so wish . . . Anyway, John, I know how you feel.

After the first two years of her course at Kent, Lucy abandoned it and went to Kathmandu, searching for enlightenment. Soon after her return to England she was hospitalised and diagnosed as schizophrenic. Upon leaving hospital, she resumed her itinerant life, moving from place to place, sometimes imposing on friends and family members and sometimes living in squats. By the spring of 1975, it was clear to her that she was not entirely welcome *anywhere*. As a last resort she went to Carn Voel to stay with Dora and John, but, on this occasion, she was unwelcome even there and Dora asked her to leave. In the early morning of 11 April 1975, Lucy caught the bus from Porthcurno to Penzance and got off at the village of St Buryan, where she walked into the churchyard, climbed on top of one of the graveyard monuments, poured paraffin over herself and set herself alight. She was perhaps intending, in imitation of the Buddhist monks and nuns in Vietnam, to sit with her hands clasped in prayer while she burnt to death, but in fact she ran blazing and screaming from the churchyard towards the village blacksmith's shop. There, in the blacksmith's yard, she presented the most awful sight that the blacksmith and his son had ever seen: a human torch in flames, standing with her hand held out as if imploring somebody to help her. They could not tell, so badly was she burnt and so low her screams, whether they were looking at a man or a woman. Shouting for somebody to phone the police and the ambulance, they set about throwing blankets, sacks and carpet on to her to smother the flames. Eventually they managed to put the fire out, but not before she had stopped screaming and, apparently, lost consciousness. The ambulance came and took her to the

West Cornwall Hospital at Penzance, where she died almost on arrival. She was twenty-six years old.

After Lucy's death, Dora enraged Lucy's friends by insisting on regarding her suicide as a protest against the American bombing of Cambodia. They knew that it was no such thing, that her death was not a political statement, but a personal tragedy. Moreover, they felt that to misrepresent Lucy's suffering in this way was to turn a wilfully blind eye to the nature of the tragedy. In November 1967, Lucy had written to Russell from Paris, where, she told him, 'all French youth seems to be pretty active politically'. In what was surely intended as a rejection of Russell's own creed, Lucy added: 'I . . . believe, that in the last analysis human nature and human relationships have a far greater bearing on anyone's life than politics ever could.'

Lucy's life and death might be regarded as the final link in a chain of human relationships that had its beginnings in Russell's upbringing by his grandmother in Pembroke Lodge. It is in this sense that her suicide strikes one as the final visitation of the ghosts that haunted Russell throughout his life.

NOTES AND REFERENCES

Details of the published sources cited below are given in the Bibliography. For unpublished sources I am indebted to a number of individuals and institutions, chief among which is the Russell Archive at McMaster University, Hamilton, Ontario, where I consulted, among other things, Russell's correspondence with his wives, Dora and Edith, his son, John, his granddaughter, Lucy, his daughter-in-law, Susan, his publisher, Stanley Unwin, and his lovers, Ottoline Morrell and Constance Malleson. I also consulted there the large files containing Russell's legal correspondence with Coward, Chance & Co., and Dora's correspondence with her solicitor, Lewis Taylor. At the Russell Archive, too, I was able to consult the unpublished typescripts relating to the Bertrand Russell Peace Foundation that are used in Chapter 13. The copy of Russell's 'Private Memoirs' used for this book was *not* consulted at the Russell Archives, but was given to me by its owner.

Much additional unpublished material, including the typescript of Paul Gillard's novel, *One May Smile*, and the family correspondence between John, Kate, Dora and Lucy, was provided by the large private family archive, now in the possession of Katharine Tait, who very generously allowed me full access to it. Kate also gave me access to the long document she prepared for McMaster (referred to below as *Annotated Letters*) in which she provides a detailed commentary on her correspondence with her father. The letters between Dora and Griffin Barry were consulted by kind permission of their owner, Harriet Ward. The correspondence between Paul Gillard and Dora Russell and the papers relating to Gillard's mysterious death are now in the possession of the International Institute for Social History, Amsterdam. The diaries and correspondence of Alys Russell are owned by Camellia Investments, who allowed me access to them at their London offices. Copies of Susan Russell's letters to her brother, Nicholas, were provided by their recipient. The private papers of Lucy Russell used in the final chapters were given to me by the Cooper-Willis family and are, temporarily, in my possession. Unpublished documents relating to the Committee of 100 were shown to me by the late Nicholas Walter, who had built up a large and impressive personal archive of such documents. The correspondence between Russell, Gödel and Schilpp quoted in Chapter 8 was consulted at the Gödel Archives at Princeton University.

In the citations that follow, Russell is abbreviated as 'BR' and his co-correspondents as follows:

AB	Albert Barnes
GB	Griffin Barry
ECW/RCW	Elizabeth/Rupert Crawshay-Williams
TSE	T.S. Eliot
PG	Paul Gillard
KG	Kurt Gödel
DHL	D.H. Lawrence
CLD	Crompton Llewellyn Davies
CM	Constance Malleson ('Colette')
OM	Ottoline Morrell
GM	Gilbert Murray
AR	Alys Russell
DR	Dora Russell
ER	Edith Russell
JR	John Russell
KR	Katharine Russell
LR	Lucy Russell
PR	Patricia (Peter) Russell
SR	Susan Russell
PS	Paul Schilpp
RS	Ralph Schoenman
LT	Louis Tyler
SU	Stanley Unwin
LW	Ludwig Wittgenstein

1. Fallen Angel: Russell at Forty-Nine

p. 3 'My brain': see *The Diary of Virginia Woolf Volume 2 1920–24*, p. 147

p. 3 'cynical and witty': *The Diary of Beatrice Webb Volume Three 1905–1924*, p. 396

p. 4 'changed everything': *The Autobiography of Bertrand Russell Volume II*, p. 38

p. 4 'I became convinced': ibid., p. 39

p. 5 'achieved that obscure but illustrious fame': quoted by S.P. Rosebaum in 'Gilbert Cannan and Bertrand Russell: an addition to the logic of a literary symbol', *Russell*, 21–2, 1976, p. 16

p. 5 'You are the same Melian': quoted ibid., p. 24

p. 5 'He may be a genius': quoted by A.L. Rowse in *Glimpses of the Great*, p. 1

p. 6 'came in two waves': *My Philosophical Development*, p. 112

p. 7 'different ways': see *The Collected Papers of Bertrand Russell 9*, p. 405

p. 7 'the greatest social philosopher': *Autobiography II*, p. 136

2. Moral Training in the Waste Land

p. 8 'a new emotional centre': *Autobiography II*, p. 150

p. 8 'the boy': Webb, op. cit.

p. 8 'spiritual ancestors': see *The Tamarisk Tree Volume 1*, p. 150

p. 9 'Bloomsbury dinners': ibid., p. 154

p. 9 'I am amazed': BR to OM, 31.1.22

p. 9 'all the characteristics': BR to OM, 31.1.22

p. 9 'that there is no way': *On Education*, p. 203

p. 9 'freed from fear': ibid., p. 205

p. 9 'A generation': ibid.

p. 9 'train the instincts': ibid., p. 203

p. 10 'can be done': ibid., p. 204

p. 10 'Studies in Infant Psychology': see *Scientific Monthly*, Dec. 1921, pp. 493–515

p. 10 'Mothers and nurses': *On Education*, p. 58

p. 10 'in a considerable measure': see *The Collected Papers of Bertrand Russell 10*, p. 165. Russell's review was first published in *The Sun*, New York, 12 May 1928, p. 6

p. 10 footnote: 'Mothers are not to kiss': ibid., p. 164

p. 11 'To the devoted parent': *On Education*, p. 61

p. 11 'The right moment to begin': ibid., p. 60

p. 11 'Take such a matter': ibid., p. 31

p. 12 'if it cries': ibid., p. 60

p. 12 'It is easy': ibid., p. 63

p. 12 'do not minister': ibid., p. 66

p. 12 'Some of these precepts': ibid., p. 63

p. 12 'Whose experience?': *My Father Bertrand Russell*, p. 60

p. 12 'unduly optimistic': *Autobiography II*, p. 151

p. 12 'I think now': ibid.

p. 12 'John had not been doing too well': *The Tamarisk Tree Volume 1*, p. 157

p. 12 'simple domestic bliss': ibid., p. 158

p. 12 'a funny house': ibid.

p. 12 'It is lovely here': BR to OM, 11.5.22

p. 13 'The house is hideous': BR to OM, 19.5.22

p. 13 'In my memory': *Autobiography II*, p. 151

p. 13 'I want him': BR to OM, 17.7.22

p. 13 'infatuated': *The Tamarisk Tree Volume 1*, p. 159

p. 13 'robust again': ibid.

p. 13 'We all tramped the streets': ibid., p. 160

p. 14 'at the height': *Autobiography II*, p. 101

p. 14 'Well, I suppose': quoted in Michael Nedo and Michele Ranchetti (eds), *Wittgenstein: Sein Leben in Bildern und Texten*

p. 14 'to come as the angel of peace': DHL to BR, 14.9.15

p. 14 'a man of a certain imaginative genius': *Autobiography II*, p. 20

p. 14 'perhaps the most perfect example': ibid., p. 98

p. 14 'an essentially timid man': ibid., p. 23

p. 14 'It is a long time since I have heard from you': LW to BR, undated

p. 15 'The Chinese are gentle': *The Problem of China*, p. 166

p. 15 'Can Chinese virtues': ibid., p. 10

p. 16 'The . . . danger': ibid., p. 13

p. 16 'showed that something is wrong': ibid.

p. 16 'The Chinese have discovered': ibid., p. 17

p. 16 'demand Western science': ibid., p. 251

p. 16 'if, when they have become safe': ibid.

p. 16 'Obstacles to Free Thought': The Moncure Conway Memorial Lecture, London, 24 March 1922, published in *The Freeman*, 24 and 31 May 1922 and reprinted as 'Free Thought and Official Propaganda' in *Sceptical Essays*, pp. 112–28

p. 16 'My plea throughout this essay': *Sceptical Essays*, p. 128

p. 17 'Hopes and Fears as Regards America': *New Republic*, 15 and 22 March

1922, reprinted in *Bertrand Russell's America Volume One 1896–1945*, pp. 220–7

p. 17 'Apart from the Russian Revolution': *Bertrand Russell's America Volume One*, p. 220

p. 17 'by its very nature': ibid., p. 227

p. 17 'Practically all advanced opinion': ibid.

p. 17 'American radicals': ibid., p. 224

p. 17 'it is impossible': *The Problem of China*, p. 179

p. 17 'Socialism in Undeveloped Countries': *The Atlantic Monthly*, May 1922, pp. 664–71, reprinted as Chapter VI of *The Prospects of Industrial Civilization*

p. 17 'Socialism in Advanced Countries': *The Kaizo*, July 1922, pp. 104–14, reprinted as Chapter VII of *The Prospects of Industrial Civilization*

p. 17 'The ultimate victory': *The Prospects of Industrial Civilization*, p. 103

p. 17 'relapse': ibid.

p. 17 'We cannot': ibid., p. 107

p. 17 'The future of mankind': ibid., p. 109

p. 17 'upon the path': ibid.

p. 18 'so long and destructive': ibid.

p. 18 'After reverting': ibid.

p. 18 'a belief in socialism': ibid., p. 117

p. 18 'capable of increasing': ibid., p. 120

p. 18 'abandon the class outlook': ibid.

p. 18 'breeds strife': ibid.

p. 18 'a gain to the community': ibid.

p. 18 'It is in this way': ibid.

p. 18 'All land and capital': ibid., p. 89

p. 19 'Bertrand Russell is a gentleman': Webb, op. cit., p. 402

p. 19 electoral address: see *Autobiography II*, pp. 163–4

p. 19 'As I watched': *The Tamarisk Tree Volume 1*, p. 166

p. 19 'I am delighted': BR to OM, 17.11.22

p. 19 'Writing and speaking': 'To Members of the National Committee', 18.5.17

p. 20 'the whole romantic movement': see 'Dr Schiller's Analysis of *The Analysis of Mind*', *The Journal of Philosophy*, 19, Nov. 1922, pp. 645–51, reprinted in *The Collected Papers of Bertrand Russell 9*, pp. 39–44

p. 20 'I dislike the heart': *Collected Papers 9*, p. 39

p. 20 'precarious and deceptive': ibid.

p. 20 'What little': ibid.

p. 20 'as one may call': ibid., p. 41

p. 20 'the more abstract': ibid., p. 40

p. 20 'Vagueness': *The Australasian Journal of Psychology and Philosophy*, 1, June 1923, pp. 84–92, reprinted in *Collected Papers 9*, pp. 147–54

p. 20 'Physics': *Collected Papers 9*, p. 154

p. 21 'almost all thinking': ibid., p. 147

p. 21 'By studying the principles of symbolism': ibid.

p. 21 'All language is vague': ibid.

p. 21 'Science is perpetually trying': ibid., p. 153

p. 21 'almost wholly unintelligible': quoted ibid., p. 145

p. 21 'When I pointed out': ibid., p. 146

p. 23 'It is probable': *The ABC of Atoms*, p. 11

p. 23 'The outcome': ibid., p. 15

p. 23 'Is the world "rational"': ibid., p. 170

p. 24 '... although this statement': ibid., p. 149

p. 24 'Our imagination': ibid., p. 153

p. 24 'I am prepared': BR to SU, 22.2.24, quoted in *Collected Papers* 9, p. 234

p. 25 'When he got here': BR to DR, 23.3.23

p. 25 'I work all morning': BR to OM, 12.5.23

p. 25 'bored and depressed': Miranda Seymour, *Ottoline Morrell: Life on the Grand Scale*, p. 333

p. 25 'sitting among heaps of nappies': ibid.

p. 26 'I have seen several people': OM to BR, 9.12.23, quoted ibid.

p. 26 'involves reading': BR to Cambridge University Press, 21.10.23

p. 26 'Leisure and Mechanism': *The Dial*, 75, Aug. 1923, reprinted as Chapter IX of *The Prospects of Industrial Civilization*

p. 26 'I have hopes': *The Prospects of Industrial Civilization*, p. 155

p. 26 'If excellence is to survive': ibid., p. 160

p. 26 'Somehow': *The Tamarisk Tree Volume 1, p. 167*

p. 26 'the intoxication': ibid., p. *166*

p. 26 'Farewell to the theatre': DR to C.K. Ogden, quoted ibid. p. *167*

p. 26 'I knew': ibid.

p. 27 'breathing space': BR to OM, *30.9.23*

p. 27 'delightful': BR to OM, *14.10.23*

p. 27 'It gives me very great pleasure': TSE to BR, 15.10.25, see *Autobiography II*, p. 173

p. 28 'After seeing': *Autobiography II*, p. 18

p. 28 'that part of the present': T.S. Eliot, 'The Idea of a Literary Review', quoted in Gladys Garner Leithauser and Nadine Cowan Dyer, 'Bertrand Russell and T.S. Eliot: their dialogue', *Russell*, 2(1), summer 1982, pp. 7–28; quotation p. 20

p. 28 a letter to the *Daily Mail*: see Peter Ackroyd, *T.S. Eliot*, p. 143

p. 28 'pure Toryism': ibid.

p. 28 'Science and Civilization': *Daily Herald*, 16, 19, 20 and 21 Nov. 1923

p. 28 'The conclusions': see *Daily Herald*, 16 Nov. 1923, p. 4

p. 29 'dangers inherent': *Icarus*, p. 6

p. 29 'This power': ibid., p. 49

p. 29 'the possibility': ibid., p. 53

p. 29 'Science enables': ibid., p. 57

p. 29 'Science is no substitute': ibid., p. 58

p. 29 'it is of the greatest importance': ibid., p. 61

p. 29 'even if we knew': ibid., p. 62

p. 29 'Men's collective passions': ibid., p. 63

p. 29 'leading to the gradual formation': ibid.

p. 30 'Can Men Be Rational?': *The Rationalist Annual*, Oct. 1923, pp. 23–8, reprinted in *Sceptical Essays*, pp. 36–42

p. 30 'all solid progress': *Sceptical Essays*, p. 41

p. 30 'To preach': ibid., pp. 41–2

p. 30 'That's the worst of Bertie': *The Diary of Beatrice Webb Volume Four 1924–1943*, p. 71

p. 31 'felt it would be faint-hearted': *The Tamarisk Tree Volume 1*, p. 168

p. 31 'Their whole campaign': BR to OM, 9.12.23

p. 32 'The child is fat and large': BR to OM, 31.12.23

p. 32 'A Motley Pantheon': *The Dial*, 76, March 1924, pp. 243–5

p. 32 'One is immediately struck': T.S. Eliot, 'A Commentary', *The Criterion*, 11(7), April 1924, p. 233

p. 33 'One does not like him': Woolf, op. cit., p. 295

p. 34 'I can never think': *The Tamarisk Tree Volume 1*, p. 168

3. How to be Free and Happy

p. 35 'On arrival': BR to OM, 2.6.24

p. 35 'I am really': BR to DR, 18.4.24

p. 35 'The people I meet': BR to DR, 14.4.24

p. 35 'there is something about Americans': BR to DR, 13.5.24

p. 35 'are *quite* dreadful': BR to DR, 18.4.24

p. 35 'I don't feel': BR to DR, 23.4.24

p. 35 'the money growing more': BR to DR, 14.4.24

p. 35 'I have no difficulty': BR to DR, 3.4.24

p. 36 'a nice host': BR to DR, 9.5.24

p. 36 'a Jew': BR to OM, 2.6.24

p. 36 'a pathetic lonely soul': BR to DR, 23.4.24

p. 36 'To my great relief': BR to DR, 18.4.24

p. 36 'I see': BR to DR, 9.5.24

p. 36 'the lack of sincerity': BR to DR, 1.5.24

p. 36 'I was away from home': BR to DR, 23.3.24

p. 36 'I dream about you': BR to DR, 28.3.24

p. 36 'smiling deliciously': BR to DR, 9.5.24

p. 36 'I long to see': ibid.

p. 36 'Little Kate': DR to BR, 19.5.24

p. 37 'I like': BR to DR, 1.5.24

p. 37 'in the presence': *New York Times*, 4 April 1924, quoted in *Bertrand Russell's America 1*, p. 9

p. 38 'Mr Scogan: see Aldous Huxley, *Crome Yellow*, Chapter XXVII

p. 38 'I foresee': see *Bertrand Russell's America 1*, p. 95

p. 38 'When an institution': ibid., p. 96

p. 38 'The Harvard Union': ibid., p. 97

p. 38 'If we had socialism': ibid., p. 92

p. 39 'he says "yes"': BR to DR, 4.5.24

p. 39 'I got the best of it': BR to DR, 7.5.24

p. 39 'I will have my fling': BR to DR, 30.4.24

p. 39 'I did not say': BR to SU, 8.12.24

p. 39 'In America': *Bertrand Russell's America 1*, p. 98

p. 39 'My time': BR to OM, 2.6.24

p. 39 an odd piece: see *Autobiography II*, pp. 172–3

p. 40 'Americans have': BR to OM, 25.6.24

p. 40 'It is *so* delicious': ibid.

p. 40 'Anyone who takes these debates': Max Eastman, *Great Companions*, p. 139, quoted by Ronald W. Clark in *The Life of Bertrand Russell*, p. 535

p. 40 'I should like to chuck politics': BR to DR, 18.4.24

p. 40 'I dread getting nominated': BR to DR, 4.5.24

p. 40 'to retire from the world': BR to Kallen, 29.9.24

p. 41 'was delicious': BR to OM, 25.6.24

p. 41 'who was generally timid': *On Education*, p. 69

p. 41 'I cured him': ibid., p. 71

p. 41 'very carefully': ibid., p. 75

p. 41 'If we had been more indulgent': ibid.

p. 41 'I think an irrational fear': ibid., p. 71

p. 41 'I am fairly certain': ibid., p. 73

p. 41 'When he showed cowardice': ibid.

p. 42 'Impressions of America': *The New Leader*, 22 Aug. 1924, reprinted in *Bertrand Russell's America 1*, pp. 228–31

p. 41 'The American Intelligentsia': *The Nation and the Athenaeum*, 11 Oct. 1924, reprinted in *Bertrand Russell's America 1*, pp. 232–5

p. 42 'there is reason for fear': *Bertrand Russell's America 1*, p. 231

p. 42 'I know so little of America': BR to Kallen, 29.9.24

p. 42 'purposes mutually beneficial': see J. Ramsay MacDonald to BR, 31.5.24, *Autobiography II*, p. 147

p. 42 'Memorandum': see *Autobiography II*, p. 148

p. 42 'a highly immoral character': see minutes of a meeting between Sir Eyre Crowe and Lord Phillimore, 3 June 1924, quoted in Clark, op. cit., p. 509

p. 44 Whitehead wrote to *Mind*: Whitehead to the editor of *Mind*, 5.11.25

p. 45 not 'quite right': Whitehead to BR, 24.5.23, see Victor Lowe, *Alfred North Whitehead: The Man and His Work Volume II*, p. 275

p. 45 letter to his mother: see Wittgenstein, *Letters to C.K. Ogden*, pp. 77–9

p. 45 'Ramsey's diary: now in the possession of Ramsey's sister, Margaret Paul

p. 45 'talked about identity': Ramsey's diary, 2.2.24

p. 46 'to lunch with Russell': ibid., 3.2.24

p. 48 'the theory of real numbers': *Principia Mathematica* (second edition), Introduction, p. xiv

p. 48 'had exhausted his interest': Webb, op. cit., p. 71

p. 48 'Philosophy in the Twentieth Century': *The Dial*, 77, Oct. 1924, pp. 271–90, reprinted in *Collected Papers 9*, pp. 451–66

p. 48 'Dr Whitehead's recent books': *Collected Papers 9*, p. 451

p. 48 'are useful': ibid.

p. 48 'Bergson, like the pragmatists': ibid., p. 457

p. 48 'is merely': ibid.

p. 48 'a temperamentally inactive man': ibid., p. 458

p. 49 'all knowledge': ibid., p. 460

p. 49 'great truths': ibid., p. 466

p. 50 'I have been watching': BR to DR, 13.5.24

p. 50 'All through 1924': *The Tamarisk Tree Volume 1*, p. 174

p. 50 'true political education': ibid., p. 175

p. 50 'I don't feel': BR to DR, 9.5.24

p. 51 'fortunately': *The Tamarisk Tree Volume 1*, p. 177

p. 51 'Naturally': ibid., p. 178

p. 52 'I was told': ibid., p. 179

p. 52 'For me personally': ibid.

p. 52 'British Labour's Lesson': *The New Republic*, 41, 31 Dec. 1924, pp. 138–9

p. 52 'Since the General Election': BR to OM, 20.2.25

p. 53 'In London': BR to OM, 2.1.25

p. 53 *What I Believe*: first published as a book by Kegan Paul in March 1925, subsequently reprinted in *Why I am not a Christian*, pp. 43–69, and *The Basic Writings of Bertrand Russell*, pp. 367–90

p. 53 'the earth': *The Basic Writings of Bertrand Russell*, p. 371

p. 53 'The good life': ibid., p. 372

p. 53 'There is probably': ibid., p. 387

p. 53 *Hypatia*: reprinted in *The Dora Russell Reader*, pp. 1–43
p. 54 'it is the progressive working woman': ibid., p. 6
p. 54 'Let us freely admit': ibid., p. 14
p. 54 'We want better reasons': ibid., p. 26
p. 54 'Men and women': ibid., p. 41
p. 54 'The intellectual': ibid., pp. 38–9
p. 55 'Dora was badly beaten': BR to OM, 17.3.25
p. 55 'I am getting back': BR to OM, 20.2.25
p. 55 'The Philosophical Analysis of Matter': published (for the first time) in
        Collected Papers 9, pp. 276–84
p. 55 'The logical problems': ibid., p. 276
p. 55 'what we call': ibid., p. 284
p. 56 'above the heads': BR to DR, 25.1.25
p. 56 'One gets the impression': ibid.
p. 57 'There never seems to be time': BR to OM, 14.10.25
p. 57 'I know a lot': BR to SU, 17.3.25
p. 57 'I have begun to understand': BR to OM, 21.8.25
p. 57 'A thousand ancient fears': *On Education*, p. 149
p. 57 'lack of novelty': BR to Horace Liveright, 31.10.25
p. 57 'If existing knowledge': *On Education*, p. 204
p. 57 'We do not do so': ibid.
p. 58 'I feel so happy': BR to OM, 21.8.25
p. 58 'Last year': ibid.; see also *The Tamarisk Tree Volume 1*, p. 191
p. 58 'Mummy is angry': ibid., p. 181
p. 58 'Day after day': ibid., pp. 180–1
p. 58 'Life is short': BR to DR, 28.3.25
p. 59 'We are both overworked': BR to OM, 14.10.25
p. 59 'John loves his school': BR to OM, 17.10.25
p. 59 'disordered imagination': see *On Education*, p. 83
p. 59 'in spite of the fact': ibid., p. 149
p. 59 the syllabus: see *Collected Papers* 9, p. 485
p. 60 'Psychology and Politics': *The Dial*, 80, March 1926, reprinted in *Sceptical
        Essays*, pp. 153–61, and *Collected Papers* 9, pp. 355–62
p. 60 'In the present age': *Sceptical Essays*, p. 154
p. 60 'political opinions': ibid., p. 153
p. 60 'In such important acts': ibid., p. 158
p. 60 'The essence of education': ibid., p. 156
p. 60 'would be easy': ibid., p. 161
p. 61 'Freedom in Society': *Harper's Magazine*, 152, March 1926, reprinted in
        Sceptical Essays, pp. 129–39
p. 61 'Americans': *Sceptical Essays*, p. 130
p. 61 'The British police': ibid., p. 134
p. 61 'Miss McMillan': ibid., p. 138
p. 61 'The people': ibid., pp. 129–30
p. 62 'a moderately reasonable being': see 'Confessions', *The Little Review*, May
        1929, pp. 72–3
p. 63 review of Trotsky: 'Trotsky on Our Sins', *The New Leader*, 26 Feb. 1926,
        reprinted in *Trotsky's Writing on Britain*, pp. 260–3
p. 63 his reply: 'Once More on Pacifism and Revolution', *Derites Kak Cherti*, May
        1926, reprinted in *Trotsky's Writings on Britain*, pp. 169–82
p. 64 'an aristocratic attitude': *The Tamarisk Tree Volume 1*, p. 198

p. 64 'the class basis of "service"': ibid., p. 151

p. 64 'when the class question': ibid.

p. 65 'pregnant': ibid., p. 183

p. 65 'lived in a flat': ibid., p. 184

p. 65 'For this': ibid.

p. 65 'A general strike': *Daily Mail*, 3 May 1926, quoted in Robert Graves, *The Long Weekend: A Social History of Great Britain 1918–1939*, p. 165

p. 65 'My first impulse': *The Tamarisk Tree Volume 1*, p. 186

p. 66 'Rather nervously': ibid.

p. 66 'Oh, how comely': see ibid., p. 187

p. 66 'She is a born proletarian leader': BR to OM, 15.6.26

p. 66 'heart and soul': BR to OM, 10.5.26

p. 66 'I think the Govt.': BR to OM, 10.5.26

p. 67 'a most lovable man': BR to OM, 15.6.26

p. 67 'To this day': *The Tamarisk Tree Volume 1*, p. 187

p. 67 'the sell-out': ibid.

p. 67 'a sort of Jeanne D'Arc': BR to OM, 15.6.26

p. 67 'half scoundrels': BR to OM, 15.6.26

p. 67 'On the Use of a General Strike': *The New Leader*, 28 May 1926, pp. 3–4

p. 68 'The Danger of Creed Wars': first published in *The Socialist Review*, May 1927, pp. 7–19, reprinted in *Sceptical Essays*, pp. 162–75

p. 68 'I do not think': *Sceptical Essays*, p. 170

p. 69 'I look upon the coming strife': ibid., p. 173

p. 69 'As to the methods': ibid., p. 174

p. 69 'Perhaps in time': ibid.

p. 69 'strangely solitary': *Autobiography II*, p. 38

p. 69 'fundamental delusion': *Sceptical Essays*, p. 173

p. 70 'One feels disaster': BR to OM, 10.5.26

p. 70 'What you say': BR to Dewey, 15.6.26

p. 70 'against national': Dora Russell, *The Right to be Happy*, Preface

p. 70 'People of our time': ibid., p.v

p. 71 'till we no longer believe': ibid., p. 29

p. 71 'Mr Russell's "Causal Theory of Perception"': see *Mind*, April 1928, pp. 137–48

p. 71 'matter is less material': *The Analysis of Matter*, p. 7

p. 71 'the traditional separation': ibid., p. 10

p. 71 'Physics': ibid.

p. 71 'can be included': ibid.

p. 72 'Many thanks': BR to Max Newman, 24.4.28, published in *Autobiography II*, p. 176

p. 72 'important book': A.S. Eddington, review of *The Analysis of Matter* in *Journal of Philosophical Studies*, 1928, pp. 93–5

p. 72 'the physicist': ibid.

p. 72 'By physical inquiry': ibid.

p. 72 'it may be left vague': ibid.

p. 73 'haunting nightmare': *Autobiography II*, p. 158

p. 73 'the cruelty': ibid.

p. 73 quoted Frank Ramsey: see *My Philosophical Development*, p. 130

p. 73 'what I do *not* feel': ibid.

p. 73 'cosmic impiety': see 'Bertrand Russell talks to God (and Ralph Miliband)', *The Spokesman*, March 1970, pp. 18–23

p. 73 'Bertrand Russell's Confession of Faith': *Jewish Daily Forward*, 24 April 1927, pp. 3, 11

p. 74 'metaphysically old-fashioned': see *Collected Papers 9*, p. 315

p. 75 'He is disintegrating prejudice': Webb, op. cit., p. 71

p. 75 'Behaviourism and Values': *The Century Magazine*, 113, Dec. 1926, pp. 148–53, reprinted in *Sceptical Essays*, pp. 69–75

p. 75 'If you want a child': *Sceptical Essays*, p. 72

p. 75 'ever since': ibid., p. 69

p. 75 'feeling and knowing': ibid., p. 70

p. 75 'I cannot cease to admire': ibid., p. 75

p. 76 'Bertie thinks': see *The Tamarisk Tree Volume 1*, p. 189

p. 76 'The surrender': ibid.

p. 76 'The Harm that Good Men Do': *Harper's Magazine*, 153, Oct. 1926, pp. 529–34, reprinted in *Sceptical Essays*, pp. 84–92

p. 76 'does not drink': *Sceptical Essays*, p. 85

p. 76 'is known to smoke': ibid., p. 86

p. 77 'the standards of "goodness"': ibid., p. 90

p. 77 'Official morality': ibid., p. 92

4. The New Morality

p. 78 'Bertie rather feared': *The Tamarisk Tree Volume 2*, p. 7

p. 79 'He thought well of the book': *The Tamarisk Tree Volume 1*, p. 190

p. 79 'We were disappointed': *The Tamarisk Tree Volume 2*, pp. 26–7

p. 79 'chiefly for the Americans': BR to OM, 23.7.27

p. 80 'Things that Have Moulded Me': *The Dial*, 83, Sept. 1927, pp. 181–6, reprinted as the 'Introduction' to *Selected Papers*

p. 80 'do the ninety-nine per cent': *Selected Papers*, p. xvi

p. 80 'A radical reform': ibid., p. xvii

p. 80 'you will take home': Feakins to BR, 20.6.27, quoted in *Bertrand Russell's America 1*, p. 103

p. 80 'The New Philosophy of America': *New York Times*, 22 May 1927, reprinted in *Bertrand Russell's America 1*, pp. 244–8

p. 80 'a philosophy of life': *Bertrand Russell's America 1*, p. 244

p. 80 'best work': ibid., p. 245

p. 81 'is due': ibid., p. 246

p. 81 'so great a boon': ibid., p. 248

p. 82 'The Future': *Jewish Daily Forward*, 26 June, 3, 10 and 17 July 1927, reprinted as 'Some Prospects: Cheerful and Otherwise' in *Sceptical Essays*, pp. 176–89

p. 82 'Biologically': *Sceptical Essays*, p. 185

p. 82 'will decide': ibid., p. 187

p. 82 'central authority': ibid., p. 177

p. 82 'I am an international socialist': ibid., p. 179

p. 82 'If our civilisation continues': ibid.

p. 82 'Why I Am Not a Christian': first published as a booklet by the Rationalist Press in April 1927, reprinted in *Why I am not a Christian and Other Essays* in 1957

p. 83 'primarily': *Why I am not a Christian*, p. 25

p. 83 'whole conception': ibid., p. 26

p. 83 'the Christian religion': ibid., p. 25

p. 83 'the sort of intellectual arguments': ibid., p. 20

p. 83 'We want': ibid.

p. 83 'the recognition': quoted in Ackroyd, op. cit.

p. 83 'humility': ibid.

p. 83 'Mr Russell': T.S. Eliot, *The Dial*, 1927, quoted in Ackroyd, op. cit., p. 163

p. 83 'essentially a low Churchman': T.S. Eliot, review of *Why I am not a Christian*, *Criterion*, Aug. 1927, pp. 177–9

p. 83 'should know': ibid., p. 179

p. 84 'Just as': ibid.

p. 84 'Everything has turned out': see *Autobiography II*, p. 173

p. 84 'is a thousand times worse': ibid., p. 174

p. 84 'What you suggest': ibid.

p. 85 'He was compelled': ibid., p. 153

p. 85 'intolerably cruel': ibid.

p. 86 'Poor Everard': Elizabeth von Arnim, *Vera*, p. 307

p. 86 'a mere maiden lady': ibid., p. 45

p. 86 'always a wife behind': *The Tamarisk Tree Volume 1*, p. 154

p. 86 'Ah, when I look at you': ibid.

p. 86 'very sighful': see *Autobiography II*, p. 174

p. 86 'you owe her everything': Lady Agatha Russell to BR, dated simply 'August 1926'. The 1952 typescript of Russell's autobiography reveals that he had intended to include this long letter immediately after the letters from his brother Frank that appear in *Volume II*, pp. 174–5. What persuaded him to change his mind we do not know, but the letter does not appear in the final version. In the 1952 typescript it occupies pp. 595–600

p. 87 'a malicious old lady': *The Tamarisk Tree Volume 1*, p. 154

p. 87 'acid old spinster': *Autobiography II*, p. 174

p. 87 'Vera had never understood him': *Vera*, p. 29

p. 87 'if one looked': ibid., pp. 29–30

p. 87 'You do not realise': 1952 typescript of Russell's autobiography, p. 597

p. 88 'lost our childhood happiness': *My Father Bertrand Russell*, p. 69

p. 88 'he seems': ibid., p. 16

p. 88 'my father's skill': ibid., p. 18

p. 88 'My father': ibid., p. 31

p. 88 'He stands': ibid., p. 37

p. 88 'Kate is proving amazingly intelligent': BR to OM, 23.7.27

p. 88 'women are': *Marriage and Morals*, p. 71

p. 88 'but I am afraid': BR to OM, 23.7.27

p. 88 'in my memory': *My Father Bertrand Russell*, p. 16

p. 89 'Dora speaks': BR to GB, 16.2.33

p. 89 'profoundly shocked': BR to DR, 26.8.27

p. 89 'To a Hannah': *The Tamarisk Tree Volume 1*, p. 198

p. 89 'For some weeks': Roy Randall to BR, 8.9.27

p. 89 'In my anger': Roy Randall to DR, 21.9.27

p. 90 'I have a silly kind of feeling': DR to BR, 23.2.28

p. 91 'I am afraid': BR to DR, 6.11.27

p. 91 'I have often been hurt': BR to DR, 9.11.27

p. 91 'I feel you despise me': BR to DR, 20.10.27

p. 91 'You do me a wrong': DR to BR, 17.11.27

p. 91 'you want the children': ibid.

p. 91 'It would give you': BR to DR, 6.11.27

p. 91 'is really desperately in love': DR to BR, 24.10.27

p. 91 'There is absolutely no doubt': DR to BR, 4.11.27
p. 91 'It was all a folly': BR to DR, 20.10.27
p. 92 'When she goes away': BR to DR, 21.10.27
p. 92 'I should be infinitely happier': BR to DR, 28.11.27
p. 92 'no hope': BR to DR, 20.10.27
p. 92 'as trivial and superficial': quoted in Clark, *The Life of Bertand Russell*, pp. 535–6
p. 92 'roused by democratic indignation': ibid.
p. 92 'I wanted to enjoy myself': BR to DR, 11.10.27
p. 93 'Is trial-marriage moral or immoral?': first published in the *Jewish Daily Forward*, 25 Dec. 1927, reprinted as Chapter 19 of *Bertrand Russell on Ethics, Sex and Marriage*
p. 93 'I am much disgusted': BR to Lindsey, 14.1.30, quoted in *Bertrand Russell's America 1*, p. 107
p. 93 'The first Christmas': *The Tamarisk Tree Volume 1*, pp. 201–2
p. 94 'sinister': see *Autobiography II*, p. 154
p. 95 'Shall we say': BR to DR, 7.5.27
p. 95 'The parents': *Autobiography II*, p. 154
p. 95 'was to establish': ibid.
p. 95 'was teased': *My Father Bertrand Russell*, p. 76
p. 95 'no topic': ibid., pp. 95, 97
p. 95 'John and I': ibid., p. 97
p. 96 'The complete happiness': *Autobiography II*, p. 155
p. 96 'Those years': *My Father Bertrand Russell*, p. 98
p. 97 'My Own View of Marriage': *The Outlook*, 148, 7 March 1928, reprinted as Chapter 20 of *Bertrand Russell on Ethics, Sex and Marriage*
p. 97 'the whole institution': *The Tamarisk Tree Volume 1*, p. 203
p. 98 'that voice': ibid., p. 205
p. 98 'was to have': ibid.
p. 98 'Both of us': ibid.
p. 98 'I'm afraid': DR to BR, 23.4.28
p. 98 'has got over the shock': DR to BR, 18.8.28
p. 98 'a night': *The Tamarisk Tree Volume 1*, p. 206
p. 98 'looked ghastly': ibid., p. 207
p. 98 'Living as an artist': DR to BR, 3.8.28
p. 98 'I contemplate going away': BR to DR, 12.11.28
p. 99 'bored to extinction': BR to DR, undated, but probably Nov. 1928
p. 99 'My love for Bertie': *The Tamarisk Tree Volume 1*, p. 208
p. 99 'Bertie's severe Victorian upbringing': ibid.
p. 99 'Science and Education': *St Louis Post-Despatch*, 9 Dec. 1928, reprinted in *Basic Writings*, pp. 615–19
p. 99 'has become accustomed': *Basic Writings*, p. 619
p. 99 'As I comforted John': *The Tamarisk Tree Volume 1*, p. 209
p. 100 'Your Child and the Fear of Death': *The Forum*, 81, March 1929, pp. 174–8, reprinted as 'Stoicism and Mental Health' in *In Praise of Idleness*, pp. 159–67
p. 100 'I think that very intense affection': *In Praise of Idleness*, p. 163
p. 100 'Whoever has to deal': ibid., p. 166
p. 101 'passing malady': review of *The Modern Temper* by Joseph Wood Krutch, *The Nation*, 128, 10 April 1929, p. 428
p. 101 'I think Mr Krutch is right': ibid.

p. 101 'enthusiastic persons': ibid.

p. 101 'It seems to me now': GB to DR, 23.5.29

p. 102 'Children are the purpose of marriage': *Marriage and Morals*, p. 151; unless otherwise stated, the citations from *Marriage and Morals* are from the 1985 Unwin Paperbacks edition

p. 102 'felt by the great majority of men': ibid., p. 131

p. 102 'A man who desires a child': ibid.

p. 102 'A child': ibid., p. 129

p. 102 'should not': ibid., p. 148

p. 102 'even after': ibid., p. 152

p. 103 'To this I can testify': ibid.

p. 103 'The obligations of parents': ibid., p. 201

p. 103 'There can be no doubt': ibid.

p. 103 'Where illegitimate children come in': ibid., p. 149

p. 104 'it is in this case': ibid., p. 146

p. 104 'A boy hates his father': ibid., p. 124

p. 104 'considerable experience': ibid., p. 125

p. 104 'centre the heterosexual feelings': ibid.

p. 104 'if a woman is happy': ibid.

p. 104 'It seems on the whole fair': *Marriage and Morals* (first edition), p. 209

p. 104 'women are on the average': *Marriage and Morals* (1985 edition), p. 71

p. 105 'There is no sound reason': ibid., p. 171

p. 105 'The habit': quoted (without reference) in Caroline Moorehead, *Bertrand Russell: A Biography*, p. 382

p. 105 'The sterilisation of the unfit': *Marriage and Morals*, p. 166

p. 105 'be very definitely confined': ibid., p. 167

p. 105 'can be decided': ibid., p. 168

p. 106 'From the standpoint': ibid., p. 173

p. 107 'if law and custom': ibid., p. 131

p. 107 'It would, I believe': ibid., p. 132

p. 107 'On this subject': *The Tamarisk Tree Volume 1*, p. 68

p. 108 'courtly behaviour': ibid., p. 223

p. 108 'Griffin and I': ibid., p. 211

p. 108 'we had': ibid.

p. 108 'hear all you have to say': BR to DR, 12.8.29

p. 108 'put by and invested': *The Tamarisk Tree Volume 1*, p. 217

p. 109 'So long': BR to OM, 21.9.29

p. 109 'Women do not': *New York Times*, 26 Sept. 1929, quoted in *Bertrand Russell's America 1*, p. 111

p. 109 'Well, they're not quite as bad': ibid., p. 114

p. 109 'If the American people': ibid.

p. 110 short piece: 'Socialist Government in England', *Jewish Daily Forward*, 9 June 1929

p. 110 second article: 'MacDonald Government Makes Rapid Strides', *Jewish Daily Forward*, 8 Sept. 1929

p. 110 'Rabbi Louis Newman': see *Bertrand Russell's America 1*, p. 115

p. 110 'has scenery': BR to DR, 3.11.29

p. 110 'full of people': BR to DR, 13.11.29

p. 110 'Homogeneous America': *The Outlook and Independent*, 154, 19 Feb. 1930, pp. 285–7, reprinted in *Bertrand Russell's America 1*, pp. 256–61

p. 110 '"Thou God seest me"': BR to DR, 16.10.29

p. 110 'There is something incredibly wrong': BR to Rachel Brooks, 5.5.30, quoted in *Bertrand Russell's America 1*, pp. 115–16

p. 111 'Shall I just let it be': DR to BR, 1.11.29

p. 111 'against the biological basis': *Marriage and Morals*, p. 149

p. 111 'nervous disorders': ibid., p. 201

p. 111 'ALL RIGHT': BR to DR, 14.11.29

p. 111 'My Darling Love': BR to DR, 14.11.29

p. 111 'I have reason': *The Tamarisk Tree Volume 1*, p. 223

p. 112 'Barry has no legal rights': BR to DR, 24.11.29

p. 112 'I don't believe you': DR to BR, 5.12.29

p. 113 'Is Modern Marriage a Failure?': both sides of this debate were published in *Debate! Is Modern Marriage a Failure?*, New York, 1930, and reprinted as Chapter 22 of *Bertrand Russell on Ethics, Sex and Marriage*

p. 114 'Since it involves arguing': BR to G.E. Moore, 11.3.30

p. 115 'His theories': BR to G.E. Moore, 5.5.30

p. 115 'The book was written': *Autobiography II*, p. 156

p. 115 'Now, on the contrary': *The Conquest of Happiness*, p. 14

p. 115 'If a person tells me': see Maurice Drury, 'Conversations with Wittgenstein, in Rush Rhees (ed.), *Recollections of Wittgenstein*, p. 112

p. 115 'One of Mr Krutch's': *The Conquest of Happiness*, p. 27

p. 115 'I have by no means': ibid., p. 29

p. 116 'in a more courageous': ibid., p. 30

p. 116 'capable of providing': ibid., p. 151

p. 116 'parents feel': ibid., p. 152

p. 116 'the feeling': ibid., p. 154

p. 116 'The parent': ibid., p. 156

p. 116 'There is no heaven–sent instinct': ibid., p. 158

p. 116 'children are as apt': ibid., p. 159

p. 116 'Professional moralists': ibid., p. 189

p. 117 'a man should': ibid., p. 187

p. 118 'I felt sick': *The Tamarisk Tree Volume 1*, p. 226

p. 118 'one of the most beautiful women': *My Father Bertrand Russell*, p. 105

p. 118 'were left': quoted in Clark, op. cit., p. 553

p. 118 'Anyone would think': ibid.

p. 118 'unpublished autobiographical novel': *One May Smile*, the typescript of which is now in the possession of Katharine Tait

p. 119 'popped to and fro': see *The Tamarisk Tree Volume 1*, p. 227

p. 119 'We soon learned': ibid., p. 228

p. 119 'There was every sign': *The Tamarisk Tree Volume 1*, p. 229

p. 120 first draft of his *Autobiography*: now in the Russell Archives

p. 120 'I tried to accept': 1952 typescript of *Autobiography*, p. 567

p. 120 'When you look back': Hayden Church to BR, 27.11.30

p. 120 his reply: published (minus the last sentence) in the *Sunday Express*, 8 March 1931

p. 121 'Looking back now': *The Tamarisk Tree Volume 1*, p. 234

p. 121 'I have no second daughter': see Robert C. Marsh, 'Talking with Russell: 1951–55', *Russell* 15(1), Summer 1995, pp. 21–35, quotation on p. 34

p. 121 'talk over': *The Diary of Beatrice Webb Volume Four*, p. 244

p. 121 'My wife': quoted ibid.

p. 121 'to withdraw': ibid.

p. 121 'What interested me': ibid.

p. 121 'he had become convinced': *The Tamarisk Tree Volume 1*, p. 244

p. 121 'or to give': BR to Lord Marley, 29.3.31

p. 122 'such as divorce': BR to Fenner Brockway, 29.3.31

p. 122 'I like their conduct': BR to Gilbert Murray, 8.3.31

p. 122 'hogwash': quoted in Caroline Moorehead, *Bertrand Russell: A Life*, p. 409

p. 122 'In return': *The Scientific Outlook*, p. 103

p. 122 'stating that recent advances': ibid., p. 105

p. 122 'the general public': ibid.

p. 122 'what they have said': ibid.

p. 123 'The reconciliation': ibid., p. 100

p. 123 'It belongs': ibid., p. 102

p. 123 'the cold breath': ibid., p. 103

p. 123 'That this is a misfortune': ibid., p. 104

p. 124 'Thus it is only': ibid., p. 273

p. 124 'the seeker after power': ibid., p. 275

p. 124 'the lover': ibid.

p. 124 'When I come to die': ibid.

p. 124 'men should not be': ibid., p. 279

p. 125 'Epilogue': dated 11 June 1931, this appears in *Autobiography II*, pp. 159–60

p. 125 'My activities': ibid., p. 160

p. 125 'only thoughts exist': *The Scientific Outlook*, p. 82

p. 125 'And what of philosophy?': *Autobiography II*, p. 160

p. 126 'When I survey my life': ibid.

p. 126 'My personal life': ibid., p. 159

p. 127 'Mankind is divided': see *In Praise of Artificiality', Mortals and Others*, p. 24

p. 127 'Now I am a married man': see 'Marriage', ibid., p. 39

p. 128 'Though unostentatious': ibid., p. 8

p. 128 'On Being Edifying': see ibid., pp. 96–7

p. 128 'On Feeling Ashamed': ibid., pp. 154–5

p. 128 'would like to': see 'Interest in Crime', ibid., p. 146

p. 129 'The foundation': *The Tamarisk Tree Volume 1*, p. 238

p. 129 'any child': ibid., p. 239

p. 130 'In my second marriage': *Autobiography II*, p. 192

p. 130 'I have often thought': *The Tamarisk Tree Volume 1*, p. 240

p. 130 'I had wanted': DR to BR, 18.8.31

p. 131 'Did Peter tell you': BR to DR, late Oct. 1931

p. 131 'I don't mind': BR to DR, 21.11.31

p. 131 'I feel that': BR to DR, 29.11.31

p. 132 'I hate': BR to DR, 21.11.31

p. 132 'Christmas at Sea': *New York American*, 13 Jan. 1932, reprinted in *Autobiography II*, pp. 156–8

p. 133 'resolved to break off': quoted in Clark, op. cit., p. 555

p. 133 'I was still in love': ibid.

p. 133 'I now think': *The Tamarisk Tree Volume 1*, p. 240

p. 133 'I want to spend': BR to DR, 22.1.32

p. 133 'I wish very much': BR to DR, 29.11.32

p. 133 'I know you will hate': BR to DR, 31.1.32

p. 134 'we tried': DR to BR, 4.2.32

p. 134 'a deep & indestructible affection': BR to DR, 9.2.32

p. 134 '& it naturally frightened': DR to BR, 11.2.32

p. 134 'Don't take Peter's mood': BR to DR, 15.2.32

p. 134 'The things': BR to DR, 20.3.32
p. 134 'He is not sure': BR to DR, 7.4.32
p. 135 'entirely out of character': *The Tamarisk Tree Volume 1*, p. 244
p. 135 'must also have been': ibid., p. 246
p. 135 'We were never closer': ibid., p. 249
p. 136 'I am persuaded': BR, legal statement, 4.5.34, p. 6

5. Divorce

p. 137 'The effect': *Autobiography*, 1952 typescript, p. 567
p. 141 'And this is the thing': DR to BR, 9.11.32
p. 141 'she has worked hard': BR to DR, 12.11.32
p. 141 'You seem to forget': ibid.
p. 141 'what I have left': DR to BR, 27.12.32
p. 142 'jokes and folly': *My Father Bertrand Russell*, p. 111
p. 142 'She listened': ibid., p. 109
p. 143 'I suppose': CLD to BR, 23.9.32
p. 143 'to clear out': DR to BR, 9.11.32
p. 143 'drove me crazy': Edmund Wilson, *The Thirties*, p. 401
p. 143 'unctuous': ibid.
p. 143 'Exactly like a woman': ibid., p. 354
p. 143 'when a Jew': ibid.
p. 143 'Griffin and I': Edmund Wilson to John Dos Passos, 11.5.33, see Wilson, *Letters on Literature and Politics 1912–1972*, p. 230
p. 143 'home': ibid.
p. 144 'it may, just possibly': GB to DR, 18.11.32
p. 144 'you never meant': GB to DR, 1.1.33
p. 144 'More than you think': GB to DR, 1.1.33
p. 144 'poor fellow': GB to DR, 5.1.33
p. 144 'a magnificent letter': GB to DR, 14.3.33
p. 144 'for it seems to me': GB to BR, 7.2.33
p. 145 'Dora speaks': BR to GB, 16.2.33
p. 145 'by reason': GB to DR, 14.3.33
p. 146 'I simply cannot': GB to BR, 12.4.33
p. 146 'Bertie was very charming': PG to DR, 23.9.32
p. 147 'Poor old Basil!': *One May Smile*, p. 195
p. 147 'George could divine': ibid., p. 232
p. 147 'To my mind': ibid., p. 234
p. 147 'could not but admire': ibid.
p. 147 'thrown back': ibid., p. 235
p. 148 'has the same kind of claim': ibid., p. 237
p. 148 'something of his relation': *The Tamarisk Tree Volume 1*, p. 283
p. 148 'Basil was a man': *One May Smile*, p. 238
p. 148 'which, in a less exalted mood': ibid.
p. 149 'Quite frankly': PG to DR, 2.3.33
p. 149 'since the Cornish climate': BR to DR, 14.2.33
p. 149 'about Griffin': *The Tamarisk Tree Volume 1*, p. 264
p. 149 'a romantic idea': ibid.
p. 150 'I have been talking': GB to DR, 31.5.33
p. 150 'I told him': GB to DR, 31.5.33
p. 150 'You intimate': GB to DR, 1.11.33
p. 150 'a man in whom': *The Tamarisk Tree Volume 1*, p. 267

p. 150 'and we did the work': ibid.

p. 150 'Darling': GB to DR, 24.5.33

p. 151 'As a free lover': GB to DR, 1.11.33

p. 151 'I thought': see *The Tamarisk Tree Volume 1*, p. 267

p. 151 'I can understand': DR to BR, 25.7.33

p. 152 'fully expected': *The Tamarisk Tree Volume 1*, p. 270

p. 153 'I guessed': ibid., p. 270

p. 153 an odd event: see ibid., p. 268

p. 153 'wondered': ibid., p. 270

p. 153 'As I knew': DR, 'Statement regarding the death of Paul Gillard on October 31 1933', p. 6

p. 154 'led by': PG to DR, 27.7.33

p. 154 'I have fairly definite proof': PG to DR, 22.9.33

p. 154 'one of the chief blokes': ibid.

p. 154 'terrifying journey': *The Tamarisk Tree Volume 1*, p. 269

p. 154 'He was convinced': ibid., p. 270

p. 155 'I could not seem': ibid., p. 271

p. 155 'he did not confide': ibid.

p. 155 Accounts differ: these include witness statements collected for the inquest on 3 November and further statements collected by Dora Russell in January and May 1936. All statements are now in the International Institute for Social History, Amsterdam

p. 156 'Night after night': *The Tamarisk Tree Volume 1*, p. 273

p. 158 'Please keep the original': BR to CLD, 7.11.33

p. 158 'take no notice': CLD to BR, 11.11.33

p. 158 'I think your advice': BR to CLD, 12.11.33

p. 158 'If there is a breakdown': CLD to BR, 14.12.33

p. 159 'In asking Dora': BR to CLD, 20.2.34

p. 160 'I will stick at nothing': BR to CLD, 5.3.34

p. 161 'I took a dislike to Gillard': Mary Bailey, legal statement dated 8.3.34

p. 162 'I should of course': BR to CLD, 11.5.34

p. 162 'The last time': BR, legal statement, 4.5.34

p. 162 'What disturbed me': BR, affidavit, 12.6.34, p. 10

p. 162 'faithful maid Nelly': OM to CLD, 2.5.34

p. 164 'all involved': *My Father Bertrand Russell*, p. 106

6. Forward to the Past

p. 165 'spend more time': BR to DR, 22.1.32

p. 165 'in spite of all the corruption': *The Diary of Beatrice Webb Volume Four*, p. 282

p. 167 'The Modern Midas': *Harper's Magazine*, 166, Feb. 1933, pp. 327–34, reprinted in *In Praise of Idleness*, pp. 49–62

p. 167 'a single world Government': *In Praise of Idleness*, p. 57

p. 168 'the forces of the State': *Education and the Social Order*, p. 153

p. 168 'the powers of education': ibid., p. 31

p. 168 'Negroes': ibid., p. 34

p. 168 'I gave up writing pot-boilers': *Autobiography II*, p. 190

p. 169 'during the next ten years': ibid., p. 150

p. 169 'if I could afford it': BR to SU, 8.3.32

p. 169 'I do not want to write': ibid.

p. 170 'to trace the opposition': *Freedom and Organization 1814–1914*, p. 8

p. 170 'the Tories': ibid., p. 67

p. 170 'a lovable man': ibid., p. 124

p. 170 'The Great War': ibid., p. 7

p. 170 'The same causes': ibid., p. 510

p. 170 'the support of historic continuity': *Autobiography II*, p. 157

p. 171 'The history of society': Lord John Russell, *An Essay on the History of the English Government and Constitution from the Reign of Henry VIII to the Present Time* (second edition), London, 1823, p. vii

p. 171 'exemplified to this day': ibid.

p. 172 'I was quite frightened': KR, *Annotated Letters*, disc 1, p. 11

p. 172 'Peter went to work': *My Father Bertrand Russell*, p. 115

p. 172 'I, however': ibid., p. 123

p. 173 'ashamed of my unfairness': ibid., p. 127

p. 173 'All through the Dartington years': ibid., pp. 126–7

p. 173 'If that happens': DR to GB, 2.2.35

p. 173 'I swear': ibid.

p. 174 'I have much regretted': *The Tamarisk Tree Volume 1*, p. 262

p. 174 'It is terribly shocking': GB to DR, 19.11.33

p. 174 'I did': ibid.

p. 174 'Your rehearsals': GB to DR, 18.12.33

p. 174 'I can love a comrade': DR to GB, 2.2.35

p. 174 'haggard, dishevelled and distraught': *The Tamarisk Tree Volume 2*, p. 4

p. 174 'I took Pat Grace': *The Tamarisk Tree Volume 1*, pp. 286–7

p. 175 'had been living': ibid., p. 287

p. 175 'in some kind of espionage': ibid.

p. 175 'funny and kind': KR, *Annotated Letters*, disc 1, p. 40

p. 175 'vulgar and ugly': ibid.

p. 175 'I enjoy writing history': BR to Norton, 31.3.33

p. 175 'another big book': BR to SU, 16.12.33

p. 175 'spring from the cult': ibid.

p. 176 preliminary notes: held by the Russell Archives

p. 176 'The Revolt against Reason': *The Political Quarterly*, 6 Jan. 1935, pp. 1–19, reprinted as 'The Ancestry of Fascism' in *In Praise of Idleness*, pp. 49–62

p. 176 'induction is a habit': *In Praise of Idleness*, p. 65

p. 176 'among all the successors': ibid.

p. 176 'there is English truth': ibid., p. 81

p. 176 'Between these different "truths"': ibid.

p. 177 'Bertie held': J.M. Keynes, *Essays in Biography*, p. 449

p. 177 'who invented': *In Praise of Idleness*, p. 79

p. 177 'the Hitlerite madness': ibid., p. 75

p. 177 'a Fascist movement': ibid., p. 80

p. 178 'Why I am neither a Communist nor a Fascist': *New Britain*, 2, 31 Jan. 1934, reprinted as 'Scylla and Charybdis, or Communism and Fascism' in *In Praise of Idleness*, pp. 82–90

p. 178 'there is no philosophy of Fascism': ibid., p. 87

p. 178 'an element of free growth': ibid., p. 90

p. 178 'that Communism and Fascism': ibid., p. 82

p. 179 'the decay of formality': see 'Stilted Manners', *New York American*, 23 Nov. 1934, p. 25

p. 179 'good manners': see 'Polite Lies', *New York American*, 14 Dec. 1934, p. 27

p. 179 'peace will come': see *The Sunday Referee*, 30 Dec. 1934, p. 10

p. 180 'The spread of the scientific outlook': *Religion and Science*, p. 244

p. 180 'The threat': ibid., p. 251

p. 180 'the human race will stagnate': ibid., p. 252

p. 181 'State ownership': *In Praise of Idleness*, p. 92

p. 181 'the defeat': ibid., p. 94

p. 181 'strongest argument': ibid., p. 109

p. 181 'The world': ibid., p. 112

p. 181 'the absence': ibid.

p. 181 'nationalisation': ibid.

p. 181 'it may be safely assumed': ibid., p. 114

p. 182 'Suppose England and France': *Which Way to Peace?*, p. 141

p. 182 'Because the Danes': ibid., p. 136

p. 182 'Having no longer': ibid., p. 139

p. 182 'When disarmament': ibid.

p. 183 'if, suddenly': ibid., p. 140

p. 183 'what is harsh and silly': ibid., p. 142

p. 183 'There would be little objection': ibid., p. 143

p. 183 'if we refrained': ibid.

p. 183 'unconsciously insincere': *Autobiography II*, p. 191

p. 184 'to pass out': J. Middleton Murry, *The Pledge of Peace*, p. 9

p. 184 'This movement': ibid.

p. 184 'has meant': ibid., p. 10

p. 184 'if we could educate': *Which Way to Peace?*, p. 145

p. 184 'Admiration of the Germans': ibid., p. 107

p. 185 'In the present temper': ibid., p. 89

p. 185 'it is argued': ibid.

p. 185 'the probability': ibid., p. 90

p. 185 'The Germans': ibid., p. 156

p. 185 'If Russia': ibid., p. 58

p. 185 'humanity': ibid.

p. 185 'after a successful campaign': ibid., p. 156

p. 185 'the United States': ibid.

p. 185 'it would be less disastrous': ibid.

p. 186 'Having remained': BR to GM, 3.3.37, see *Autobiography II*, p. 245

p. 186 'If I were young': BR to Kingsley Martin, 13.5.40, see ibid., p. 233

p. 186 'never seriously envisaged': ibid., p. 191

p. 186 'The hope of preserving peace': *Which Way to Peace?*, p. 109

p. 186 'When the weight of America': ibid., p. 98

p. 186 'if I were an American': ibid., p. 80

p. 186 'The Case for US Neutrality': *Common Sense*, 8 (3), March 1939, pp. 8–9, reprinted in *Bertrand Russell's America 1*, pp. 296–8

p. 187 'inflamed': *Bertrand Russell's America 1*, p. 297

p. 187 'Fear of America': see 'US can avert war, declares English leader', *The Times-Picayune*, 4 April 1939, p. 5

p. 187 'auto-obituary': 'The Last Survivor of a Dead Epoch', *The Listener*, 12 Aug. 1936, reprinted as 'Obituary' in *Unpopular Essays*, pp. 188–90

p. 187 'politically . . . as isolated': *Unpopular Essays*, p. 190

p. 187 'In the Second World War': ibid., pp. 189–90

p. 187 'His life': ibid., p. 190

p. 187 'Aristocratic Rebels': see 'Aristocratic Rebels: Byron and the Modern World', *Saturday Review of Literature*, 12 Feb. 1938, pp. 16, 18. This formed the basis for the chapter on Byron in *A History of Western Philosophy*, pp. 716–21

p. 187 'Did you ever read': BR to GM, 9.4.43, see *Autobiography II*, p. 251

p. 188 'Moving matter about': see *In Praise of Idleness*, p. 21

p. 188 'The Superior Virtue of the Oppressed': *The Nation*, 144, 26 June 1937, pp. 731–2, reprinted in *Unpopular Essays*, pp. 69–75

p. 188 'an ingenuity': *Unpopular Essays*, p. 74

p. 188 'Admiration of the proletariat', ibid., pp. 74–5

p. 189 'On Being Modern-minded': *The Nation*, 144, 9 Jan. 1937, pp. 47–8, reprinted in *Unpopular Essays*, pp. 76–81

p. 189 'suppresses': *Unpopular Essays*, p. 78

p. 189 'money rewards': ibid., pp. 78–9

p. 189 'A certain degree': ibid., p. 81

p. 189 'one of the most fascinating books': Leonard Woolf to Margaret Llewelyn Davies, 30.12.36, see *Letters of Leonard Woolf*, p. 243

p. 190 'she had a Puritan dislike': *The Amberley Papers 1*, p. 144

p. 190 'no longer important': ibid., p. 262

p. 190 'In Amberley': *The Amberley Papers 2*, p. 250

p. 190 'flat and dull': ibid., p. 573

p. 191 'attractive vision': Webb, op. cit., p. 370

p. 191 'It is to be hoped': ibid.

p. 191 'I have largely wasted it': ibid., p. 373

p. 192 'Would you': see *Letters of Leonard Woolf*, p. 333

p. 192 'I really don't think': ibid.

p. 192 'as a result': BR to KR, 30.10.35

p. 193 'I used to enjoy his company': Gerald Brenan to Frances Partridge, 8.2.70, quoted in Jonathan Gathorne-Hardy, *The Interior Castle: a Life of Gerald Brennan*, p. 520

p. 193 'violent vituperation': Gerald Brennan, *Personal Record*, p. 265

p. 193 'I like him': see ibid., p. 262

p. 193 'outside his philosophy': ibid., p. 264

p. 193 'deeply impressed': ibid., p. 269

p. 193 'What he really wanted': ibid.

p. 194 'Outside his philosophical works': ibid., pp. 264, 272

p. 194 'I found them rather dull': ibid., p. 267

p. 194 'I regret': Gerald Brenan to BR, 18.11.36

p. 194 'I am so tired of seeing people': quoted in Kenneth Hopkins, 'Bertrand Russell and Gamel Woolsey', *Russell*, 5 (1), summer 1985, pp. 50–65, quotation on pp. 57–8

p. 194 'From the first': quoted ibid., p. 62

p. 195 'it was very hard': Gamel Brenan to Alyse Gregory, autumn 1945, quoted ibid., p. 63

p. 195 'it leads to such difficulties': Gamel Brenan to Alyse Gregory, probably Dec. 1952, quoted ibid., p. 62

p. 195 'We do not know anyone else': BR to Gerald and Gamel Brenan, 22.6.37, quoted in Gathorne-Hardy, op. cit., pp. 314–15

p. 196 'the rule is': KR, *Annotated Letters*, disc 1, p. 93

p. 196 'What upsets me': ibid., p. 95

p. 196 'When you were here': BR to KR, 7.5.36

p. 196 'I was just beginning': KR, *Annotated Letters*, disc 1, p. 97

p. 196 'Mr von Sohn's Reputation': eventually published in *Five Stories* by John Conrad Russell, pp. 11–18

p. 197 'I dreamed': BR to KR, 24.9.36

p. 197 'What fun': BR to KR, 5.10.36

p. 197 'This seems': KR, *Annotated Letters*, disc 1, p. 109

p. 197 'I had known': ibid., p. 97

7. Back to Philosophy

p. 199 'it is an extraordinary rest': BR to OM, 20.9.17

p. 199 'worked on the problem': *Autobiography II*, p. 191

p. 199 'would never do': ibid.

p. 199 'On Order in Time': *Proceedings of the Cambridge Philosophical Society*, 32, May 1936, pp. 216–28, reprinted in *Collected Papers 10*, pp. 124–37

p. 200 'I think you have done': BR to W. van O. Quine, 6.6.35, see *Collected Papers 10*, pp. 213–14

p. 200 'which may not': ibid., p. 124

p. 200 'The Limits of Empiricism': *Proceedings of the Aristotelian Society*, 36, 1935–6, pp. 131–50

p. 201 'so that they might have': LW to BR, undated, but probably autumn 1935; see Wittgenstein, *Letters to Russell, Keynes and Moore*, p. 102

p. 201 'Broad or no Broad': LW to BR, undated, but probably November 1935; see ibid., p. 103

p. 201 Rush Rhees: in conversation with the author

p. 201 preliminary notes: see *Collected Papers 10*, pp. 652–75

p. 202 'The pain and the cry': ibid., p. 670

p. 202 'knowledge is not derived': ibid., p. 671

p. 202 'These are the things': ibid., p. 674

p. 203 'we can understand': ibid., p. 327

p. 204 'Finitism in Mathematics': *Mind*, 44, 1937, pp. 186–203

p. 204 'The finitist': ibid.

p. 204 'we can understand': *Collected Papers 10*, p. 327

p. 205 'the youngest': 'Philosophy and Grammar', first published in *The London Mercury*, March 1936; this review of Ayer is reprinted in *Collected Papers 10*, pp. 331–3

p. 205 'led to a view': ibid., p. 331

p. 205 'the word "God"': ibid.

p. 205 'Determinism and Physics': *Proceedings of the University of Durham Philosophical Society*, 9, March 1936, pp. 228–45, reprinted in *Collected Papers 10*, pp. 67–80

p. 205 'best working hypothesis': *Collected Papers 10*, p. 80

p. 205 'unavoidable working hypothesis': ibid.

p. 205 'scientific knowledge': ibid.

p. 206 'I gather': BR to Norton, 30.11.36

p. 206 'pulling wires': Norton to BR, 4.1.37

p. 206 'I have become': see *Autobiography II*, p. 214

p. 207 'It is hardly worth': BR to G.E. Moore, 18.2.37; see ibid., p. 215

p. 207 'I should *very much* like': BR to Norton, 18.2.37

p. 207 'physically worn out': Webb, op. cit., p. 386

p. 207 'I look forward': Desmond MacCarthy to BR, 16.3.37; see *Autobiography II*, p. 215

p. 208 'Do you think': BR to OM, 6.7.37

p. 208 'that numbers are needed': *The Principles of Mathematics*, p. xi

p. 208 'The formalists': ibid.

p. 208 'is a more serious matter': ibid.

p. 209 'consequences even more drastic': ibid., p. x

p. 209 'would make a clean sweep': ibid.

p. 209 'I have gone back to philosophy': BR to OM, 25.9.37

p. 209 'only one Oxford lady': *Autobiography II*, p. 194

p. 209 'was certainly not neglected': A.J. Ayer, *Part of My Life*, p. 214

p. 209 'On the Scope of Empirical Knowledge': *Erkenntnis*, pp. 267–74

p. 210 'On Verification': *Proceedings of the Aristotelian Society*, 38, 1937–8, pp. 1–20, reprinted in *Collected Papers 10*, pp. 345–59

p. 210 'The logical tendency': *Collected Papers 10*, p. 353

p. 210 'is emotional': ibid., p. 358

p. 210 'The Relevance of Psychology to Logic': *Aristotelian Society, Supplementary Volume: Action, Perception and Measurement*, 17, 1938, pp. 19–41, reprinted as Appendix VIII in *Collected Papers 10*

p. 211 'Problems of logic': see *Collected Papers 10*, pp. 625–6

p. 211 his reply: see Russell, 'The Relevance of Psychology to Logic', *Aristotelian Society, Supplementary Volume 17*, pp. 43–53, reprinted in *Collected Papers 10*, pp. 362–70

p. 211 'which first led me': *Collected Papers 10*, p. 362

p. 211 'I hold': ibid., p. 369

p. 211 'largely in agreement': *Aristotelian Society, Supplementary Volume*, 17, 1938, p. 54

p. 211 'your time would be your own': Richard P. McKeon to BR, 25.3.38

p. 212 'I have very little hope': BR to OM, 10.4.38

p. 212 'poisoning of the nervous system': see Miranda Seymour, *Ottoline Morrell: Life on the Grand Scale*, pp. 412–13

p. 212 'The news is a terrible blow': BR to Philip Morrell, 22.4.38

p. 212 'I still hold': *Autobiography II*, p. 193

p. 212 'be concerned': *Power*, p. 9

p. 213 'just as we teach children': ibid., p. 207

p. 213 'If human life': ibid., p. 71

p. 214 'was a time': *My Father Bertrand Russell*, p. 128

p. 214 'like an animal at bay': ibid., p. 129

p. 214 'There he stayed': ibid.

p. 214 'his brief': ibid.

p. 214 'I can still remember': KR, *Annotated Letters*, disc 1, p. 180

p. 215 'that this would': ibid.

p. 215 'What your mother stands for': DR to KR, 30.6.38

p. 215 'What really troubled her': KR, *Annotated Letters*, disc 2, p. 9

p. 215 'Peter was not used': ibid., p. 26

p. 215 'We are not really a camping family': ibid.

p. 215 'in despair': BR to Gamel Brenan, 15.9.38

p. 215 'an extreme pacifist': *New York Times*, 26 Sept. 1938, quoted in *Bertrand Russell's America 1*, p. 127

p. 215 'I am afraid': ibid.

8. Russell in America

p. 219 'several hundred townspeople': see Gary Slezak and Donald W. Jackanicz, '"The town is beastly and the weather was vile"', *Russell*, 25–8, 1977, pp. 5–20

p. 220 'occupied': *Autobiography II*, p. 217

p. 220 'The town is beastly': ibid.

p. 220 'During a chilly fall day': Slezak and Jackanicz, op. cit., pp. 13–14

p. 220 'Russell was brilliant': quoted ibid., p. 11

p. 221 'Russell had the felicitous ability': quoted ibid.

p. 221 'We used to have': *Autobiography II*, p. 217

p. 221 'eliminate': quoted in Slezak and Jakanicz, op. cit., p. 12

p. 221 'I remember Russell': ibid.

p. 221 limerick: quoted ibid., p. 11

p. 222 'those clustered': quoted ibid., p. 13

p. 222 'has been delivering': *The Pulse*, Nov. 1938, p. 27, quoted ibid., p. 13

p. 222 'The Role of the Intellectual in the Modern World': published in *The American Journal of Sociology*, Chicago, 44, Jan. 1939, pp. 491–8

p. 222 'I have been speaking': ibid., p. 491

p. 222 'was out of all proportion': quoted in Slezak and Jackanicz, op. cit., p. 16

p. 223 'agreed': ibid., pp. 16–17

p. 223 'It has been done': BR to Schilpp, 13.3.39

p. 223 'a large, slow-moving mind': BR to OM, 22.3.14

p. 223 'unwilling': BR to OM, 21.2.21

p. 223 'Dewey's New *Logic*': *The Philosophy of John Dewey*, pp. 137–56, reprinted in *Collected Papers 10, pp. 145–60*

p. 223 'industrialism': *Collected Papers 10*, p. 145

p. 224 Dewey's rejoinder: *The Philosophy of John Dewey*, pp. 527, 544–9, reprinted as Appendix IX in *Collected Papers 10*

p. 224 'Mr Russell's confirmed habit': *Collected Papers 10*, p. 628

p. 224 report of his visit: see *The Michigan Daily*, 19 Feb. 1939, pp. 1, 2

p. 224 'If America becomes a belligerent': *Bertrand Russell's America 1*, pp. 297–8

p. 225 'A war for democracy': ibid., p. 297

p. 225 'nine people out of ten': BR to Dora Sanger, 5.11.38

p. 225 'Even if': BR to Curry, April–May 1939

p. 226 'If you and John': BR to KR, 15.4.39

p. 226 'About going to America': JR to BR, Easter 1939

p. 226 'It seems': JR to BR, 7.6.39

p. 226 'I am afraid': DR to KR, 30.6.39

p. 226 'When someone comes': ibid.

p. 227 'We had to listen': KR to BR, 20.6.39

p. 227 'It is odd': KR to BR, 7.7.39

p. 227 'As I stood': *My Father Bertrand Russell*, p. 132

p. 227 'how glad': *The Tamarisk Tree Volume 2*, p. 86

p. 227 'Dora was seriously ill': *Annotated Letters*, disc 2, p. 22

p. 228 'One is that': *Autobiography II*, pp. 217–18

p. 228 'I cannot resist': quoted in *Bertrand Russell's America 1*, p. 130

p. 228 'It was very kind of you': ibid.

p. 229 'No wonder': *Annotated Letters*, disc 2, p. 123

p. 229 'Though my father': *My Father Bertrand Russell*, p. 135

p. 229 'inadequate': see *Autobiography II*, p. 218

p. 229 'was done': *My Father Bertrand Russell*, p. 136

p. 229 Fenwick W. Holmes: see 'Bertrand Russell at U.C.L.A.: a Reminiscence', *San Jose Studies*, Fall 1992, pp. 28–43

p. 230 'I try to remain': BR to Robert Trevelyan, 22.12.39, see *Autobiography II*, p. 239

p. 230 'much less agreeable': ibid., p. 218

p. 230 'a satisfactory substitute': BR to Lucy Donnelly, 22.12.39

p. 230 'We were all unhappy': *My Father Bertrand Russell*, pp. 143–4

p. 231 'awkward and overweight': ibid., p. 142

p. 231 'I looked better': ibid., p. 139

p. 231 'was rendered difficult': *Autobiography*, 1952 typescript, p. 629

p. 231 'whose company': ibid., p. 628

p. 231 'feared to say': *My Father Bertrand Russell*, p. 145

p. 231 'It is with a deep sense': Ordway Tead to BR, 29.2.40

p. 232 'a man who': quoted in 'How Bertrand Russell was Prevented from Teaching at City College, New York' by Paul Edwards, which was published as an appendix to *Why I am not a Christian and Other Essays*, pp. 165–99; the quotation appears on p. 166

p. 232 'Can anyone': ibid.

p. 232 'who are so confused': ibid.

p. 232 'professor of paganism': ibid., p. 167

p. 232 'a desiccated': ibid., p. 167

p. 232 'a disgrace': quoted in *Bertrand Russell's America 1*, p. 137

p. 232 'to protect': see Edwards, op. cit., p. 167

p. 233 'unaware': see *Bertrand Russell's America 1*, p. 137

p. 233 'finding one corner': quoted in Edwards, op. cit., p. 168

p. 233 'The hue and cry': quoted in *Bertrand Russell's America 1*, p. 139

p. 234 'In other circumstances': quoted ibid., p. 141

p. 234 'If you can find': Daniel Bronstein to BR, 15.3.40, ibid.

p. 234 'on hearing': ibid., pp. 141–2

p. 234 'the fair name': quoted ibid., p. 146

p. 234 'a dog': see Edwards, op. cit., p. 169

p. 235 'tarred and feathered': ibid.

p. 235 'delighted': BR to *New York Times*, 21.3.40, quoted *Bertrand Russell's America 1*, p. 149

p. 235 'It still seems': quoted ibid., p. 150

p. 235 'The issue': see ibid., p. 149

p. 235 'constitute a danger': ibid., p. 152

p. 236 an affidavit: see ibid., pp. 152–3

p. 236 'was as anxious': *Autobiography II*, p. 219

p. 236 'vicious, nasty lie': quoted in *Bertrand Russell's America 1*, p. 154

p. 236 'Have we got to': ibid.

p. 237 'If I find': ibid., p. 155

p. 237 'Mr Russell': ibid., p. 156

p. 237 long statement: see Edwards, op. cit., pp. 174–90

p. 238 sympathetic profile: *Life*, 8 (14), 1 April 1940, pp. 23–5

p. 238 'We sat in our house': *My Father Bertrand Russell*, pp. 147–8

p. 238 'a very ignorant fellow': see *Bertrand Russell's America 1*, p. 157

p. 238 'I am not as interested': ibid.

p. 238 'precisely the same': ibid.

p. 238 'All this fuss': ibid.

p. 239 'in keeping': quoted ibid., p. 163

p. 239 'No funds': ibid.

p. 239 'No newspaper': *Autobiography II*, p. 219

p. 239 'To hire this man': quoted in *Bertrand Russell's America 1*, p. 169

p. 240 'It would be foolish': William E. Hocking to BR, 30.4.40, see *Autobiography II*, p. 230

p. 240 'makes me wish': BR to Hocking, 6.5.40, ibid., p. 231

p. 240 'Ever since': BR to Kingsley Martin, 13.5.40, *Autobiography II*, p. 233

p. 241 'At this moment': BR to Robert Trevelyan, 10.5.40, ibid., pp. 240–1

p. 241 'It would be better': quoted in *Bertrand Russell's America 1*, p. 176

p. 241 'never has': ibid.

p. 241 'In recent years': ibid., p. 177

p. 242 'one of the loveliest places': *Autobiography II*, p. 220

p. 242 'The summer': ibid.

p. 242 'the works of God': BR to Lucy Silcox, 20.7.40

p. 242 'The present work': *An Inquiry into Meaning and Truth*, p. 11

p. 243 'the relation': ibid., p. 18

p. 243 'since no one else': ibid., p. 139

p. 243 'I maintain': *My Philosophical Development*, pp. 25–6

p. 246 'It will be incumbent': see Howard Greenfeld, *The Devil and Dr Barnes*, p. 75

p. 246 'you are very important': ibid., p. 130

p. 247 'the hope': AB to BR, 24.6.40, quoted ibid., p. 202

p. 247 'I should be very reluctant': BR to AB, 20.7.40, quoted ibid., p. 203

p. 248 'I am afraid': ibid.

p. 248 'We understood': *My Father Bertrand Russell*, p. 149

p. 248 'My personal problems': BR to GM, 6.9.40, see *Autobiography II*, p. 248

p. 248 'bigoted authoritarians': quoted in Greenfeld, op. cit., p. 206

p. 249 'You have given': BR to AB, 24.8.40, ibid., p. 205

p. 249 'Kiss her': AB to BR, 1.11.40, ibid., p. 206

p. 249 'a shabby': *My Father Bertrand Russell*, p. 150

p. 249 'some strange': ibid.

p. 249 'undoubtedly tough': JR to BR, 12.9.40

p. 250 'If Daddy': DR to JR and KR, 23.9.40

p. 250 'I am just': KR to BR, 13.10.40

p. 250 'She thinks': JR to BR, 7.10.40

p. 250 'I am very sorry': BR to KR, 22.10.40

p. 250 'I wish': KR to BR, 25.11.40

p. 251 'I felt': *Annotated Letters*, disc 4, p. 27

p. 251 'Spick and span': quoted in *Bertrand Russell's America 1*, p. 184

p. 251 'You know': BR to KR, 26.12.40

p. 252 'We're swamped': AB to BR, 1.11.40, quoted in Greenfeld, op. cit., p. 206

p. 252 'Russell talked': ibid., p. 207

p. 252 'makes his subject': see *Bertrand Russell's America 1*, p. 190

p. 253 'Life here': *Autobiography II*, p. 250

p. 253 'I feel as if': BR to GM, 6.9.40, ibid., p. 248

p. 254 'Russia, I think': BR to GM, 18.1.41, ibid.

p. 254 'Education in America': *Common Sense*, 10, June 1941, pp. 163–6, reprinted in *Bertrand Russell's America 1*, pp. 308–14

p. 254 'A philosophy for you in these times': *Reader's Digest*, Oct. 1944, pp. 5–7, reprinted in *Collected Papers 10*, pp. 644–5. 'On Keeping a Wide Horizon', the paper as originally written by Russell, can be found in *Collected Papers 10*, pp. 452–7

p. 254 'In times such as that': *Collected Papers 10*, p. 452

p. 254 'are able to avoid': ibid.

p. 254 'there are the stars': ibid., p. 453

p. 254 'I cannot tell': ibid., p. 454

p. 254 'but neither': ibid., pp. 253–4

p. 255 'And so': ibid., p. 644

p. 255 'Was this Russell?': Alliston Cragg to BR, 24.10.41, quoted ibid., pp. 450–1

p. 255 'censored out': PR to Cragg, quoted ibid., p. 451

p. 255 four broadcasts: see ibid., pp. 491–530

p. 255 'completely wrong': ibid., p. 516

p. 255 'I think philosophy': ibid., p. 500

p. 255 'always uses words': ibid., p. 499

p. 255 'Freedom': ibid., p. 496

p. 255 'an absolute monarch': ibid., p. 499

p. 256 'I just turned on the radio': KR to BR, 5.4.41

p. 256 'almost a polite fiction': *Annotated Letters*, disc 4, p. 12

p. 256 'the final completion': ibid.

p. 256 'the ideal': ibid.

p. 256 'were poor and radical': ibid.

p. 256 'Though I am longing': KR to BR, 12.6.41

p. 256 'After we had seen': *My Father Bertrand Russell*, p. 151

p. 256 'Five of us': ibid.

p. 256 'swelling with pride': ibid.

p. 256 'a good breakfast': ibid., p. 152

p. 257 'hot, oppressive Pennsylvania summer': ibid., p. 154

p. 257 'feeling myself': ibid., p. 153

p. 257 'anchor': ibid., p. 154

p. 257 'was adrift': ibid.

p. 257 'I resentfully withdrew': ibid.

p. 257 'If you believe': *Annotated Letters*, disc 5, pp. 8–9

p. 257 'We did not realise': ibid.

p. 258 'very nice': KR to BR and PR, 7.5.42

p. 258 'Kate has been doing very well': JR to BR, 29.1.42

p. 258 another letter: JR to BR, 14.4.42

p. 258 'liberalism': JR to BR, 21.10.41

p. 258 'I felt': JR to BR, 19.11.41

p. 259 'loved': *My Father Bertrand Russell*, p. 154

p. 259 'as a sort of time bomb': *Annotated Letters*, disc 5, p. 88

p. 259 'It is very difficult': *My Father Bertrand Russell*, p. 158

p. 259 'Was this the honesty': ibid., pp. 158–9

p. 259 'never liked': *Annotated Letters*, disc 4, p. 105

p. 259 'Men': BR to KR, 11.1.42

p. 259 'I simply couldn't': *Annotated Letters*, disc 5, p. 47

p. 259 'she had found': *My Father Bertrand Russell*, p. 158

p. 260 'the trappings': ibid.

p. 260 'People here': BR to Beatrice Webb, 31.1.43, see *Bertrand Russell's America 1*, p. 202

p. 261 'She replied': Phyllis Terry to KR, 10.1.77

p. 261 'seems to have difficulty': quoted in Greenfeld, op. cit., p. 209

p. 261 'a white-haired lady': PR to the trustees of the Barnes Foundation, 1.11.41; see ibid., pp. 210–12

p. 261 'It was sweet of you': Nelle Mullen to PR, 5.11.41, ibid., pp. 212–13

p. 262 'when we engaged you': AB to BR, December 1941, quoted ibid., p. 213

p. 262 'I shall continue': ibid., pp. 213–14

p. 262 'I feel you should be informed': ibid., p. 214

p. 262 'has made capital': quoted ibid., p. 219

p. 263 'The details': AB to BR, 28.12.42, ibid., pp. 221–2

p. 263 'perquisite of aristocracy': BR to GM, 9.4.43, see *Autobiography II*, pp. 251–2

p. 263 'Shouldn't you call a doctor': *Annotated Letters*, disc 5, p. 40

p. 263 'I don't mean to bother you': KR to JR, 13.9.43

p. 264 'spare myself': *My Father Bertrand Russell*, p. 160

p. 264 'It was a pleasant, well-provided home': ibid., p. 162

p. 264 an article: 'If you fall in love with a married man', *Glamor*, April 1943, pp. 68, 94, 99–100

p. 264 'According to Sidney Hook: see Hook, 'Bertrand Russell: A Portrait from Memory', *Encounter*, March 1984, pp. 9–20, especially p. 18

p. 264 *Big Blue Books: How to Read and Understand History* (1943) and *The Value of Free Thought* (1944) were subsequently reprinted in *Understanding History and Other Essays*, Philosophical Library, New York, 1957; *An Outline of Intellectual Rubbish* (1943) was reprinted as Chapter 7 of *Unpopular Essays*. Haldemann-Julius had earlier (1942) published Russell's *How to Become a Philosopher*, reprinted in *Collected Papers 10*, pp. 535–81

p. 265 'no conception of democracy': quoted in Greenfeld, op. cit., p. 227

p. 265 'but I have no doubt': *Autobiography II*, p. 222

p. 266 'various things': BR to GM, 9.4.43, ibid., p. 251

p. 267 'I am amazed': BR to CM, 16.8.43

p. 267 'mainly with matters': *The Philosophy of Bertrand Russell*, p. 729

p. 267 'With regard': ibid., p. 730

p. 268 'It seems to me': ibid., p. 137

p. 268 'I think I will say nothing': BR to PS, 8.8.43

p. 268 'very unfortunate': PS to KG, 25.8.43

p. 268 'not having': PS to KG, 16.9.43

p. 269 'Dr Gödel's most interesting paper': *The Philosophy of Bertrand Russell*, p. 741

p. 269 'I hope it will satisfy him': BR to PS, 11.10.43

p. 270 'to discuss': *Autobiography II*, p. 224

p. 270 'Concerning': KG to Kenneth Blackwell, 1971, quoted in John W. Dawson, 'Kurt Gödel in Sharper Focus', in *Gödel's Theorem in Focus*, edited by S.G. Shanker, London, 1988, pp. 1–16, quotation on p. 8

p. 270 'Project of Future Work': see *Collected Papers II*, pp. 117–18

p. 270 'It should not be very difficult': ibid., p. 118

p. 271 'tremendous success': quoted ibid., p. 114

p. 271 synopsis: see ibid., pp. 118–20

p. 271 'We all in fact': ibid., p. 120

p. 271 'All the world of learning': G.H. Hardy, *Bertrand Russell and Trinity*, p. 58

p. 272 'there was trouble': George Trevelyan to PR, 12.3.43

p. 272 'Our warmest congratulations': see *Autobiography II*, p. 257

p. 272 'I am very glad': BR to KR, 6.1.44

p. 272 'I hate not seeing you': BR to KR, 30.12.43

p. 272 'You and I': BR to KR, 16.12.43

p. 272 'I wrote to him': *Annotated Letters*, disc 6, p. 1

p. 272 'Was this the man': ibid., p. 8

p. 272 'The society of Princeton': *Autobiography II*, p. 224

p. 273 'Will you come home': BR to CM, 16.8.43

9. The Bomb Goes Off

p. 274 'majestically': *Autobiography III*, p. 15

p. 275 'If you happened': BR to JR, undated, but surely June 1944

p. 275 'As you have not': JR to BR, 22.1.44

p. 276 'We were all': *My Father Bertrand Russell*, p. 160

p. 276 'intending': ibid., p. 166

p. 276 'sucked': ibid.

p. 277 'squalid rooms': *Autobiography II*, p. 16

p. 277 'We shall': BR to KR, 30.9.44

p. 277 'Whatever happens': BR to KR, 18.10.44

p. 277 'Then': *My Father Bertrand Russell*, p. 167

p. 277 'Then came the explosion': ibid.

p. 277 'was hopelessly vague': *Annotated Letters*, disc 6, p. 32

p. 277 'We bowed our heads': *My Father Bertrand Russell*, p. 168

p. 277 'and the silly package': *Annotated Letters*, disc 6, p. 32

p. 277 'I don't wonder': BR to JR, 22.11.44

p. 277 'I could have been happy': *Autobiography III*, p. 16

p. 278 'lived there': *Autobiography II*, p. 194

p. 278 'Wittgenstein': Norman Malcolm, *Ludwig Wittgenstein: A Memoir*, p. 57

p. 278 'I've seen Russell': LW to Rush Rhees, 17.10.44

p. 278 'Russell's books': *Recollections of Wittgenstein*, p. 112

p. 278 'What Makes a Woman a Fascinator?': *Vogue*, 1 Nov. 1944, pp. 130, 175

p. 279 'The Thinkers Behind Germany's Sins': *Leader Magazine*, 18 Nov. 1944, p. 6, reprinted in *Collected Papers II*, pp. 368–70

p. 279 'combined and vulgarised': *Collected Papers II*, p. 368

p. 279 popular account of logical positivism: see 'Logical Positivism', *Polemic*, 1, Nov. 1945, pp. 6–13, reprinted in *Collected Papers II*, pp. 148–67

p. 280 'I am Thankful for the BBC': *Reynolds News and Sunday Citizen*, 24 Sept. 1944, p. 2, reprinted in *Russell*, 18, summer 1975, pp. 15–17

p. 280 'British and American Nationalism': *Horizon*, 11, Jan. 1945, reprinted in *Bertrand Russell's America 1*, pp. 338–49

p. 280 'quasi-biological': *Bertrand Russell's America 1*, p. 339

p. 280 'In like manner': ibid.

p. 280 'is more analogous': ibid.

p. 280 'not biologically': ibid.

p. 280 'It'll seem terribly funny': Harriet Barry to JR, 5.3.45

p. 281 'an ill, tired, dyspeptic': JR to Harriet Barry, 19.10.45

p. 281 'You sounded': BR to JR, undated

p. 282 'Did you know': KR to DR, 5.4.46

p. 282 report of a dream: found among John's papers at Carn Voel. It is dated 'Sep 5' (presumably 1945)

p. 283 'in time': *My Father Bertrand Russell*, p. 168

p. 283 'tall and cold': ibid.

p. 284 'I shouldn't wonder': BR to KR, 14.5.45

p. 284 'I had begun to feel': *Annotated Letters*, disc 6, p. 57

p. 284 'a little over a year': *My Father Bertrand Russell*, p. 169

p. 286 'I have never been able': JR to Pat Grace, 30.8.45

p. 286 'since he more than anyone': JR to PR, 16.8.45

p. 286 'When I first read your letter': JR to BR, 10.9.45

p. 289 'I have, perhaps foolishly, hoped': JR to PR, 4.11.45

p. 290 'this is like saying': JR to DR, 19.10.45

p. 290 'although I think': KR to BR, 13.10.45

p. 290 'I miss you': BR to KR, 1.12.45

p. 291 'I guarantee': JR to BR, 19.11.45

p. 291 'I want': BR to KR, 11.1.46

p. 291 'General Statement': a copy of this (undated) was found among John's papers

p. 292 'That's a coincidence': told to the author by Harriet Ward

p. 293 'I am very very happy': BR to CM, 27.3.46

p. 293 'My affairs': BR to CM, 13.10.46

p. 294 'nearly finished': BR to CM, 16.7.47

p. 294 'indistinguishable from logic': see 'On Scientific Method in Philosophy' (1914), *Collected Papers 8*, pp. 55–73, especially p. 65

p. 295 'Anyone who feels': Norman Malcolm, 'Russell's *Human Knowledge*', *Philosophical Review*, Jan. 1950, pp. 94–106

p. 295 'The style is jaunty': ibid., p. 106

p. 295 'They are supposed': ibid., p. 105

p. 296 'embodies': Yorick Smythies, review of *History of Western Philosophy*, *The Changing World*, 7 (1), pp. 72–81

p. 296 'I fear': ibid., p. 81

p. 296 'simply could not believe': Rupert Crawshay-Williams, *Russell Remembered*, p. 47

p. 296 'It was very important': ibid., p. 43

p. 297 'The book': ibid., p. 50

p. 297 'it *was*': ibid., p. 100

p. 297 'The fact remains': ibid.

p. 298 'What Should Be British Policy Towards Russia': *Forward*, 39 (38), 22 Sept. 1945, p. 4

p. 298 'What America Could Do with the Atom Bomb': see 'Humanity's Last Chance', *Cavalcade*, 7 (396), 6 Oct. 1945, pp. 8–9, reprinted in *Bertrand Russell's America Volume 2 1945–1970*, pp. 311–14

p. 298 speech to the House of Lords: see *Parliamentary Debates* (Lords), 28 Nov. 1945, reprinted in *Has Man a Future?*, pp. 19–24, and by Dora Russell in *The Tamarisk Tree Volume 3*, pp. 70–5

p. 299 'to see that': *Has Man a Future?*, p. 22

p. 299 'all the chaos': *Bertrand Russell's America 2*, p. 312

p. 299 'the conditions': ibid., p. 314

p. 299 'at least': BR to Gamel Brenan, 20.10.45

p. 299 'I hate the Soviet Government': BR to Gamel Brenan, 15.1.46

p. 299 a lecture to the Royal Empire Society: see 'The International Bearings of Atomic Warfare', *United Empire*, 39, Jan.–Feb. 1948, pp. 18–21

p. 299 'I do not think': BR to Walter Marseille, 5.5.48

p. 300 'I favoured appeasement': BR to Einstein, 24.11.47

p. 301 'decided': Kingsley Martin, *New Statesman*, 18 Nov. 1950

p. 301 'long letter of refutation: see 'Lord Russell and the Atom Bomb', *New Statesman*, 21 April 1951, pp. 448, 450

p. 301 'The story': *The Nation*, 17 Oct. 1953, p. 320

p. 301 'I have never': BR to Harvey Cole, 30.11.50, quoted in Clark, op. cit., p. 657

p. 301 that letter was published: see '1948 Russell vs 1954 Russell', *The Saturday Review*, 37 (42), 16 Oct. 1954, pp. 25–6

p. 301 television interview: 'Face to Face with John Freeman', broadcast by the

BBC on 8 March 1959, published in *The Listener*, 19 March 1959, pp. 503–5

p. 302 a lecture he delivered at Westminster: see 'Atomic Energy and the Problems of Europe', *The Nineteenth Century and After*, 145, Jan. 1949, pp. 39–43

p. 302 'Either we must have': quoted in Moorehead, op. cit., p. 469

p. 302 in reply to a questioner: *The Nineteenth Century and After*, 145, Jan. 1949, p. 43, quoted in Clark, op. cit., p. 655

p. 302 letter to *The Listener*: see *The Listener*, 28 May 1959, p. 937

p. 302 'The arms race': *Autobiography III*, p. 18

p. 303 'message of death': *Reynolds News*, 21 Nov. 1948

p. 303 a talk he had given to the New Commonwealth Society: see 'International Government', *The New Commonwealth*, 9, Jan. 1948, pp. 77–80

p. 304 'that the democracies': see BR's letter to the *Observer*, 28 Nov. 1948, p. 3; the same letter was published in *The Times*, 30 Nov. 1948, p. 5

p. 304 'the Government': *Autobiography III*, p. 21

p. 304 'a vigorous': see *Russell Remembered*, p. 51

p. 304 'very much': ibid., p. 52

p. 305 'I thought': see *Autobiography III*, p. 21

p. 305 'I was glad': see *Russell Remembered*, p. 53

p. 305 'that it was worth': *Autobiography III*, p. 20

p. 305 'Bertie arrived': *Russell Remembered*, p. 57

p. 305 'Russell Urges': *New York Times*, 21 Nov. 1948, p. 4

p. 305 'Earl Russell': *Daily Worker*, 22 Nov. 1948

p. 306 'Anyone who failed to feel': Alan Ryan, *Bertrand Russell: A Political Life*, p. 167

p. 307 'It was utter perfection': CM to Phyllis Urch, 12.9.48

p. 308 'I will creep': CM to BR, 17.3.49

p. 308 'suddenly left': BR to CM, 15.4.49

p. 308 'an insistent child': Daphne Phelps, letter to the author dated 18.6.96, upon which the account that follows is based

p. 309 'I have been such a fool': PR to Elizabeth Crawshay-Williams, dated 'Easter Sunday' [1949]

p. 309 'for the present': BR to CM, 2.4.49

p. 310 'happy like a man': BR to CM, 26.4.49

p. 311 'I remember': BR to KR, 11.4.50

p. 311 'I grow morbid': BR to KR, 7.1.50

p. 311 'diligently': *My Father Bertrand Russell*, p. 170

p. 311 'My advice': BR to KR, 7.2.48

p. 312 'For a very long time': DR to JR, 29.3.46

p. 312 'Your account': BR to KR, 23.5.46

p. 313 'poised on a knife edge': *Annotated Letters*, disc 6, p. 12

p. 313 'It may go terribly wrong': KR to DR, 23.5.46

p. 313 'I don't see': KR to DR, 5.4.46

p. 313 'I agree with you': BR to KR, 23.5.46

p. 313 'mostly impersonal': KR to DR, 5.4.46

p. 313 'I wish it were possible': JR to BR, 15.4.46

p. 315 'her sister is called Anne': JR to BR, 25.4.46

p. 315 'because of the virtual hatred': BR to KR, 12.10.47

p. 315 'I have had no difficulty': BR to KR, 6.11.47

p. 315 'Susan doesn't think': BR to KR, 12.10.47

p. 315 'seems like one': DR to KR, 27.9.47

p. 315 'John is an ass': KR to DR, 16.10.47

p. 316 a solicitor's letter: Abbott, Sturgess & Co. to Coward, Chance & Co., 12.9.49

p. 319 'What is the *matter* with John': KR to DR, 4.2.49

p. 317 'Some optimists': BR to KR, 3.3.50

10.   41 Queen's Road

p. 318 'produced a mood': *Autobiography III*, p. 89

p. 318 'Half the garden': ibid.

p. 319 'what they did not know': ibid., p. 69

p. 319 'produced a slightly ghostly feeling': ibid.

p. 319 'perpetual gloom': see 'A Locked Diary', 20–1 July 1894, *Collected Papers 1*, p. 65

p. 319 'like a family vault': ibid., p. 66

p. 319 'I am haunted': ibid., pp. 65–6

p. 319 a large collection of newspaper clippings: now in the possession of Camellia Investments

p. 320 'at least once': BR to AR, 20.1.50

p. 320 'Bertie was an ideal companion': see *Autobiography III*, p. 47

p. 320 'What thee says': BR to AR, 6.3.50

p. 320 'Meeting again': Diary of Alys Russell, 1.3.50

p. 321 'so happy': ibid., 6.3.50

p. 321 'depressed & weepy': ibid., 21.3.50

p. 321 'not attractive': ibid., 18.5.50

p. 321 'O joy': ibid., 2.6.50

p. 321 'more like his old self': ibid., 5.6.50

p. 321 'the happiest': ibid.

p. 321 'tho' I know it by heart': ibid., 25.7.50

p. 322 'sad & dispirited': ibid., 12.9.50

p. 322 'It makes me': ibid., 16.11.50

p. 322 'took a little more interest': ibid., 4.12.50

p. 322 'dry & distant': ibid., 27.12.50

p. 323 'After all': quoted in Clark, op. cit., p. 637

p. 323 'I suffer also': *Autobiography III*, p. 89

p. 324 'I suspected': ibid., p. 31

p. 324 'old myths': see ibid., p. 32; see also *New Hopes for a Changing World*, p. 217

p. 325 'There are many': *New Hopes for a Changing World*, p. 16

p. 325 'I find John's company': BR to KR, 11.4.50

p. 325 'It is very nice': BR to KR, 21.5.50

p. 326 'Throughout this period': BR, affidavit dated 28.12.59

p. 326 'Openings': SU to BR, 23.5.50

p. 327 a talk recorded for the ABC: 'My Impressions of Australia' – see *Daily Telegraph*, 24 Aug. 1950, p. 8, and *The Australian Outlook*, 4, September 1950

p. 328 'He is not sleeping well': quoted in Nicholas Griffin, 'Russell in Australia', *Russell*, 16, winter 1974–5, pp. 3–12 (quotation on p. 9)

p. 328 'I fear I am asking a lot': see *Russell Remembered*, p. 65

p. 329 'Even if the present war': ibid.

p. 330 'Even if there is no way now': ibid., p. 66

p. 330 'I am very gloomy': ibid., p. 67

p. 330 'If we are to survive this dark time': *New York Times Magazine*, 3 Sept. 1950, pp. 5, 17–18, reprinted in *Basic Writings*, pp. 682–7

p. 330 'In spite of': *Basic Writings*, p. 687

p. 330 'Courage': ibid., p. 682

p. 330 'who, as far as is humanly possible': ibid., p. 683

p. 330 'believe that each individual': ibid.

p. 332 'He was very funny': Susan Russell, 'Lasting Impressions of Bertie Russell', an unpublished typescript found among Russell's papers and now in the possession of the Russell Archives, p. 5

p. 332 'somewhat to my surprise': *Autobiography III*, p. 30

p. 332 'in recognition': quoted by Irving Polonoff in 'Bertrand Russell', *British Winners of the Nobel Literary Prize*, pp. 168–201, quotation on p. 201

p. 332 'It is not his achievements': quoted ibid., p. 198

p. 332 'The money': BR to RCW, 3.12.50, *Russell Remembered*, p. 58

p. 332 'Good Lord': from 'Bertrand Russell so Fondly Remembered', an unpublished memoir by Julie Medlock, quoted in Clark, op. cit., p. 639

p. 332 'People were lined up': ibid.

p. 333 'but if you feel': *The Impact of Science on Society*, p. 103

p. 333 'to start my real life's work': *My Father Bertrand Russell*, p. 175

p. 334 'I did not think': ibid.

p. 334 'Why America is Losing her Allies': *The Wichita Beacon*, 5 Feb. 1951, reprinted in *Bertrand Russell's America 2*, pp. 327–8

p. 334 'those who dislike communism': *Bertrand Russell's America 2*, p. 328

p. 334 'America was beastly': *Russell Remembered*, p. 58

p. 334 'though very grand': *Autobiography III*, p. 31

p. 335 'It is nice': *Russell Remembered*, p. 67

p. 335 'Politically Important Desires': published as Part Two, Chapter II, of *Human Society in Ethics and Politics*, reprinted in *Basic Writings*, pp. 468–78

p. 335 'If politics is to become scientific': *Basic Writings*, p. 468

p. 335 'Politics': ibid., p. 477

p. 335 'I would say': ibid., p. 478

p. 335 'The atom bomb': ibid., p. 476

p. 336 'I have had my fill': BR to SU, 23.11.50

p. 336 'a sensual wisdom': Susan Russell, op. cit., p. 1

p. 336 'I was taken with him': ibid., p. 4

p. 336 'Diddy loved me': ibid., p. 7

p. 336 'She is strictly': BR to ER, 31.5.51

p. 336 'Now she writes happily': BR to ER, 31.5.51

p. 336 'is very unkind': BR to ER, 28.5.51

p. 336 'told America': BR to CW and ECW, 20.5.51; see *Russell Remembered*, p. 69

p. 337 'After we have killed': *New Hopes for a Changing World*, p. 10

p. 337 'the impulse': ibid.

p. 337 'I think that sexual morality': ibid., p. 178

p. 337 'Diddy was prickly': Susan Russell, op. cit., p. 2

p. 337 'He was as full of Shelley': ibid.

p. 337 'he often used to think': ibid., p. 5

p. 338 'he has had this way': ibid., p. 7

p. 338 'I shall be curious': BR to SU, 13.9.50

p. 339 'Whisky City': this was included in a collection of Susan Russell's poems, typescripts of which are preserved among Russell's papers

p. 339 'When he went out of the house': Susan Russell, op. cit., p. 4

p. 339 'He is a combination': ibid., p. 8

p. 340 Sarah thinks so: Sarah's opinion was passed on to me by her sister, Felicity

p. 340 'one had to leap': Susan Russell, op. cit., p. 3

p. 340 'The plot was feeble': this and the other responses to *Go*'s competition that are quoted here survive among Russell's papers

p. 341 'She was the sort of person': Barry Lock in conversation with the author

p. 341 'Welcome to New York': ER to BR, 16.10.51

p. 342 'I had to satisfy': quoted in *Bertrand Russell's America* 2, p. 28

p. 342 'discredit definitions': see ibid., p. 32

p. 342 'Every honest man': 'Democracy and the Teachers', *Manchester Guardian*, 30 Oct. 1951, pp. 6, 8, quoted in *Bertrand Russell's America* 2, pp. 32–3

p. 343 'just long enough': BR to Harold Kastner, 15.11.51, quoted in *Bertrand Russell's America* 2, p. 33

p. 343 '*Nothing* will induce': BR to ER, 5.11.51

p. 343 'Kate is completely transformed': BR to ER, 29.10.51

p. 343 'even the waiters': ER to BR, 22.10.51

p. 343 'a pleasant exprience': *Autobiography*, 1952 typescript, p. 652 (remark cut from the published version)

p. 343 'a very profound happiness': ibid.

p. 344 'At the moment': ibid., p. 654

p. 344 'Epilogue': see *Autobiography II*, pp. 159–60

p. 344 'My work is near its end': *Autobiography III*, pp. 222–3

p. 344 'I am utterly sick': Medlock, op. cit., quoted in *Bertrand Russell's America* 2, p. 49

p. 345 'and there are': BR to SU, 29.3.53

p. 345 'I do not think': BR to SU, 29.3.53

p. 345 the portrait of Lawrence: *The Listener*, 24 July 1952, pp. 135–6, reprinted in *Harper's Magazine*, Feb. 1953, pp. 93–5; see also *Portraits from Memory*, pp. 104–8, and *Autobiography II*, pp. 20–4

p. 345 surprisingly mild letter: *Harper's Magazine*, April 1953, reprinted in Frieda Lawrence, *The Memoirs and Correspondence*, pp. 447–8

p. 345 'Lawrence': *Autobiography II*, p. 23

p. 347 'I don't know much': Stefan Themerson to BR, 4.8.52

p. 347 'both in matter and form': ER to SU, 23.8.56

p. 347 'was a great release': *Autobiography III*, p. 35

p. 348 'You are simply *full*': DHL to BR, 14.9.15

p. 348 'a sensitive would-be despot': *Autobiography II*, p. 23

p. 348 'I was inclined': ibid., p. 22

p. 349 'like monsters': *Satan in the Suburbs*, p. 15

p. 349 'increasingly filled': ibid., p. 55

p. 349 'there will be no more Sin': ibid., p. 57

p. 349 'You imagine': ibid., p. 60

p. 349 'She was persuaded': ibid., p. 61

p. 350 'You think I'm defeated': ibid., p. 64

p. 350 'Nothing stretches': ibid., p. 66

p. 351 'That he was wicked': ibid., p. 62

p. 351 'add a preface': BR to SU, 26.4.53

p. 351 'There can be nothing': Joseph Conrad, *A Personal Record*, p. xvi

p. 352 'cute little fantasy': quoted in Moorehead, op. cit., p. 495

p. 352 'intolerable to suppose': *Human Society in Ethics and Politics*, p. 110

p. 353 'compendium': BR to SU, 1.10.53

p. 353 'a new book': BR to SU, 31.10.53

p. 353 'develop their godlike potentialities': *Human Society*, p. 238

p. 353 'Sometimes': ibid., p. 237

p. 353 'unconquerably persuaded': ibid., p. 239

p. 354 'the impossibility': *Autobiography III*, p. 34

p. 354 'I do not think': *Human Society*, p. 7

p. 354 'in pretty complete agreement': *Collected Papers II*, p. 175

p. 354 'I am not': *Collected Papers II*, p. 310

p. 355 'tired of children': *Autobiography III*, p. 70

p. 355 'is a wastrel': BR to KR, 28.2.54

p. 356 'said at once': C.B. Drover to BR, 7.5.54

p. 357 'John and Susan': ER to LT, 14.7.54

p. 357 'I am a poet's daughter': quoted by Christopher Wordsworth in conversation with the author

p. 358 'hard and embittered': DR, 'Statement for Affidavit', undated, but probably 1960, p. 8

p. 358 'not particularly anxious': BR to LT, 12.10.54

p. 358 'I have John': Dr to KR, 7.11.54

p. 358 'began to show signs': DR, 'Statement for Affidavit', op. cit., p. 8

p. 359 'a serious delusional state': Dr T.A. Munro to LT, 14.1.55

p. 359 'may remain': ibid.

p. 359 'have never ceased': *Autobiography I*, p. 85

p. 359 'the tragedies': *Collected Papers 1*, pp. 65–6

p. 360 'elements of incipient psychosis': JR to KR, 9.1.55

p. 361 'replied that': DR, 'Statement for Affidavit', op. cit., pp. 8–9

p. 361 'I have just heard': KR to DR, 12.3.55

p. 362 'I might have known': KR to DR, 21.3.55

p. 363 'To all whom it may concern': JR, 22.5.55

p. 363 'is very bad for him': DR to LT, 5.6.55

p. 364 'go and see the people': LT to BR, 14.6.55

p. 364 'Naturally': Dr Desmond O'Neill to BR, 6.6.55

p. 364 'I take it': O'Neill to BR, 17.6.55

p. 364 'expressed': BR to O'Neill, 21.6.55

p. 365 'His refusal now': DR to LT, 19.6.55

p. 366 'According to Dora: see *The Tamarisk Tree Volume 3*, p. 209

p. 366 'I told his father': DR to 'Vincent' (surname unknown), 2.7.55; a copy of this letter was in the files of Dora's solicitor

p. 367 'You cannot go on': DR to LT, 6.9.55

p. 368 'I suppose': LT to BR, 10.9.55

p. 368 'terrifying': BR to LT, 12.9.55

p. 368 'The stipulation': Taylor's notes dated 14.11.55

p. 368 'it should not be': ibid.

p. 369 'Dear Dora': BR to DR, 7.12.55

p. 369 'looking very smart': DR to Proud, 9.12.55

p. 369 'They were in fine spirits': DR to SR, 22.12.55

p. 369 'it would do him good': DR to SR, 22.12.55

p. 369 'There is pain': Christopher Wordsworth to DR, 27.12.55

p. 370 'I do not see the children': SR to DR, undated, but presumably December 1955

p. 370 'it would be unwise': LT to BR, 19.5.56

p. 371 'and explain to her': BR to LT, 5.7.56

p. 371 'After things were settled': DR to BR, 21.7.56

p. 371 'I asked John': BR to DR, 23.7.56

p. 372 'In September': DR to BR, 27.7.56

p. 372 'Dear Tyler': BR to LT, 30.7.56

11. 'Remember Your Humanity and Forget the Rest'

p. 373 'Man's Peril': *The Listener*, 30 Dec. 1954, pp. 1,135–6, reprinted in *Portraits from Memory*, pp. 215–20, and *Basic Writings*, pp. 729–32

p. 373 'solemn appeal': BR to Eileen Molony (of the BBC), 24.11.54

p. 373 'dreadful and inescapable': *Portraits from Memory*, p. 217

p. 373 'There lies before us': ibid., p. 220

p. 374 'I should like': ibid., p. 219

p. 376 'important changes': BR to Joliot-Curie, 17.6.55

p. 376 'Although an agreement': see *Has Man a Future?*, pp. 57–8

p. 377 'No, most emphatically not': BR at the Caxton Hall press conference, 9 July 1956, quoted in Clark, op. cit., p. 691

p. 377 'Of course': quoted ibid., p. 673

p. 377 'I felt shattered': *Autobiography III*, p. 74

p. 377 'as a means': see *Has Man a Future?*, p. 57

p. 378 'dreadful week': see *Autobiography III*, pp. 76, 79

p. 378 'All day long': ibid., p. 76

p. 378 'swelled': ibid., p. 78

p. 379 'This was a serious blunder': ibid.

p. 380 'now is the time': see Cyrus Eaton, 'Now is the Time to Drop the Bomb', in J.E. Thomas and Kenneth Blackwell (eds), *Russell in Review*, pp. 3–4

p. 381 'I, alas': BR, address to Vienna Pugwash Conference, 20 Sep. 1958, quoted in Clark, op. cit., p. 683

p. 381 open letter: *New Statesman*, 23 Nov. 1957, p. 638, reprinted in *The Vital Letters of Russell, Khrushchev, Dulles*, London, 1958, and *Basic Writings*, pp. 726–8

p. 381 'in a frank discussion': see *Basic Writings*, p. 728

p. 381 'I believe': ibid.

p. 381 'I felt': *Autobiography III*, p. 102

p. 381 'The Soviet Union': Khrushchev, *New Statesman*, 21 Dec. 1957, pp. 845–6, quoted in *Bertrand Russell's America 2*, p. 104

p. 382 'creed of the United States': Dulles, *New Statesman*, 8 Feb. 1958, pp. 158–9, quoted in *Bertrand Russell's America 2*, p. 106

p. 382 'it is necessary': see *Bertrand Russell's America 2*, p. 107

p. 382 'there is no need': Khrushchev, *New Statesman*, 15 March 1958, pp. 318–22, quoted ibid., p. 108

p. 382 'rival fanatics': Russell, *New Statesman*, 5 April 1958, pp. 426–7, quoted ibid., p. 108

p. 382 'I think': ibid., p. 109

p. 382 'I'm not in favour': see interview with Russell, *Daily Mail*, 15 May 1957, p. 6

p. 383 'Consider the question': BR to Lord Simon, 17.10.58

p. 383 'The righteously adamantine surface': *Autobiography III*, p. 102

p. 383 'Of course': quoted in a letter from Kevin Holland to Professor Jensen, 22.10.58

p. 383 'On Referring': *Mind*, 59, 1950, pp. 320–44

p. 384 'Mr Strawson on Referring': *Mind*, 66, 1957, pp. 385–9, reprinted in *Collected Papers II*, pp. 630–5

p. 384 'Cult of "Common Usage"': broadcast on BBC radio on 23 Oct. 1952, published in the *British Journal for the Philosophy of Science*, Feb. 1953, pp. 303–7, and reprinted in *Collected Papers II*, pp. 610–14

p. 384 'Infinity': *Mind*, 66, 1957, pp. 242–9, reprinted as Appendix V in *Collected Papers II*

p. 384 terse and scathing reply: 'Mathematical Infinity', *Mind*, 67, 1958, p. 385, reprinted in *Collected Papers II*, p. 364

p. 384 'sheer hypocrisy': quoted in Holland to Jensen, op. cit., 22.10.58

p. 384 a review of Ryle's most celebrated book: 'What is Mind?', *Journal of Philosophy*, 55, Jan. 1958, pp. 5–12, reprinted in *Collected Papers II*, pp. 635–42

p. 384 'astonishingly slap-dash': *Collected Papers II*, p. 637

p. 385 'Evidently': ibid.

p. 385 'He seems to believe': ibid., p. 638

p. 385 'not with the world': *My Philosophical Development*, p. 230

p. 385 'It is not': ibid., p. 214

p. 386 the Preface: reprinted in *Collected Papers II*, pp. 642–4

p. 386 'deserves the gratitude': *Collected Papers II*, p. 642

p. 386 'do not reject': ibid., pp. 643–4

p. 386 'Abusiveness': Ryle to (presumably) Victor Gollancz, 29.10.59, quoted in *Collected Papers II*, p. 607

p. 386 'deeply shocking': BR to *The Times*, 3.11.59

p. 386 'When we were comfortably settled:': Ved Mehta, *Fly and the Fly Bottle*, p. 39

p. 387 'The Duty of a Philosopher in This Age': *The Abdication of Philosophy*, pp. 16–22, reprinted in *Collected Papers II*, pp. 457–63

p. 387 'the probable effects': *Collected Papers II*, p. 459

p. 387 'If they do not': ibid., p. 457

p. 388 'You and John Strachey': *Russell Remembered*, p. 106

p. 388 'in a voice of fury': ibid., p. 108

p. 388 'a palliative': *Common Sense and Nuclear Warfare*, p. 47

p. 388 'is within': ibid., p. 37

p. 389 'I think the next step': ibid., p. 38

p. 389 'except as a sequel': ibid., p. 61

p. 389 'until there is': ibid., p. 51

p. 389 'We must find a way': ibid., p. 29

p. 389 'while the East–West tension': ibid., p. 65

p. 389 'when I read': ibid., p. 19

p. 390 'As most': *Autobiography III*, p. 104

p. 390 'yearly picnic': ibid.

p. 390 'A general invitation': DR to Proud, 5.9.56

p. 391 'Pembroke Lodge atmosphere': SR to DR, undated

p. 391 'The Russell lot': SR to Nick Lindsay, undated

p. 392 'John is become quite insane': BR to KR, 21.5.59

p. 392 'Either that': *My Father Bertrand Russell*, p. 181

p. 392 'I began to see': ibid.

p. 393 'but they all offered': ibid., p. 182

p. 393 'The doctrine': ibid., pp. 187–8

p. 393 'My earthly father': ibid., p. 188

p. 393 'In all these years': KR to DR, 5.4.6;

p. 393 'sat in his armchair': *My Father Bertrand Russell*, p. 193

p. 394 'It was so': ibid., p. 195

p. 394 'tell him about God': ibid., p. 196

p. 394 'I did not want': ibid.

p. 394 'I could never break': ibid.

p. 394 'except for the people': ibid., p. 197

p. 394 'my mother's': ibid., pp. 179–80

p. 394 'I felt': ibid., p. 180

p. 394 'the usual mixture': ibid., p. 197

p. 395 'no right': DR to Taylor, 28.1.60

p. 395 'Lord and Lady Russell': SR to DR, 14.2.60

p. 395 'if the court': BR to LT, 14.1.60

p. 395 'remarked': LT to BR, 25.7.60

p. 396 'to try': LR, diary, 6.4.60

p. 396 'Daddy's miles better': ibid.

p. 396 'It's really home': ibid., 31.4.60

p. 396 'All the children': Bronwen Lloyd-Williams to LT, 8.10.59

p. 396 'apprehensive': Miss R.N. Nowell, Welfare Officer's Report, presented in court 25.1.61

p. 396 'John has read': DR to Taylor, 5.11.60

p. 397 'So there is to be': DR to Taylor, 4.11.60

p. 397 'those who invoke the law': quoted in DR to Taylor, 18.11.60

p. 398 'if he were': BR to LT, 23.11.60

p. 398 'We cannot risk': DR to Taylor, 18.12.60

p. 398 'formal on both sides': DR to Taylor, 9.3.61

p. 398 'I met John': BR to LT, 18.3.61

p. 398 'From the contemporary correspondence': Taylor to DR, 29.11.60

p. 399 'The estrangement': ER, 'Comments on affidavit by Mrs Grace on 20 Jan., 1961', 23 Jan. 1961

p. 399 'John's behaviour': instructions to counsel, Jan. 1961

p. 399 'What I should like to do': BR, 'Telephone conversation with Tyler 23 Jan. '61'

p. 399 'Supposing the Judge': ibid.

p. 399 'You will remember': BR to LT, 28.1.61

p. 400 'In view of the time': BR to LT, 29.6.61

p. 400 'I am not': Taylor to DR, 20.9.62

12. Russell's Viper

p. 402 'Mass Resistance in Mass Society': *Peace News*, 25 Aug. 1961, reprinted in David Boulton (ed.), *Voices from the Crowd: Against the H-Bomb*, pp. 106–10

p. 402 'the values': Boulton (ed.), op. cit., p. 106

p. 403 'whose control': ibid.

p. 403 'democratic institutions': ibid., p. 107

p. 403 'It should be patently clear': ibid.

p. 403 'I should have thought': ibid., p. 108

p. 403 'We will be exposing': ibid., p. 109

p. 403 'In mass society': ibid., p. 110

p. 403 'Our political theorists': ibid.

p. 404 'If ten thousand': ibid.

p. 405 'so long as': from a speech called 'Civil Disobedience' that Russell delivered to a Youth CND conference in Birmingham, 15 April 1961; see *Autobiography III*, p. 139

p. 406 'The Case for British Neutralism': *New York Times Magazine*, 24 July 1960, pp. 10, 35–6, reprinted in *Fact and Fiction*, pp. 263–73

p. 406 'I cannot conceive': quoted in *Fact and Fiction*, p. 267

p. 406 'Russia has threatened': ibid., p. 266

p. 406 'every sane man': ibid., p. 265

p. 407 'We were impressed': *New York Times Magazine*, 14 Aug. 1960, pp. 90–1, reprinted in *Bertrand Russell's America 2*, pp. 125–7

p. 407 'if we hand over': Boulton (ed.), op. cit., p. 110

p. 407 'I am by no means': see 'Private Memorandum Concerning Ralph Schoenman', *Black Dwarf*, 14, 5 Sept. 1970, reprinted as an appendix in Clark, op. cit.; for quotation, see Clark, p. 807

p. 407 'If the man': *Russell Remembered*, p. 127

p. 408 'Cousins replied': *Autobiography III*, p. 111

p. 409 'legal and democratic methods': quoted in Christopher Driver, *The Disarmers: A Study in Protest*, p. 113

p. 409 'Individuals': ibid., p. 114

p. 410 'Just when CND': Canon J. Collins, *Faith Under Fire*, p. 318

p. 410 'should the Executive': quoted in Richard Taylor, *Against the Bomb: The British Peace Movement 1958–1965*, p. 65

p. 410 'The chairman of CND': *Autobiography III*, p. 111

p. 410 'During the discussions': Collins in conversation with Richard Taylor, quoted in Taylor, op. cit., p. 75

p. 411 'The President and Chairman': see ibid., p. 66

p. 411 'My reason for doing so': BR to CND Chairman and executive members, 21.10.60

p. 411 'certainly contentious': Peggy Duff, *Left, Left, Left*, p. 174

p. 412 'that false statements': see Taylor, op. cit., p. 67

p. 412 'probably expected': Duff, op. cit.

p. 413 'Russell was a very vain old man': Collins in conversation with Richard Taylor, quoted in Taylor, op. cit., p. 75

p. 413 *Act or Perish*: reprinted in *Autobiography III*, pp. 137–9

p. 414 'We'd never had': Randle in conversation with Richard Taylor, quoted in Taylor, op. cit., p. 198

p. 414 'We woke up': LR, diary, 25.12.60

p. 414 'spent the afternoon': ibid., 15.1.61

p. 414 'the quietest': *Observer*, 19 Feb. 1961, quoted in Taylor, op. cit., p. 199

p. 415 'people everywhere': ibid.

p. 415 'and I remember': James Kirkup, *Me All Over: Memoirs of a Misfit*, p. 90

p. 415 a poem: see Kirkup, ibid., pp. 91–2

p. 416 'We do not want': *Guardian*, 20 Feb. 1961, quoted in Taylor, op. cit., p. 200

p. 416 'We want': quoted in Driver, op. cit., p. 118

p. 416 'Civil Disobedience in Halt Polaris': *Peace News*, 17 Feb. 1961

p. 416 'Is it Revolution We're After?': *Peace News*, 10 March 1961

p. 416 'Mass civil disobedience': ibid., quoted in Taylor, op. cit., p. 217

p. 417 'Schoenman took matters into his own hands: based on Taylor's account (ibid., p. 201); see also Driver, op. cit., p. 120

p. 417 'Civil Disobedience': see *Autobiography III*, pp. 139–45

p. 417 'We used to think': ibid., p. 144

p. 418 'exactly as I dreamt them': *Fact and Fiction*, p. 194

p. 418 'If the readers': ER to SU, 22.3.61

p. 418 five dreams: see *Fact and Fiction*, pp. 194–7

p. 419 'If the threat': *Has Man a Future?*, p. 117

p. 420 'We were, after all': *Autobiography III*, p. 115

p. 420 'We who are here accused': ibid., p. 145

p. 421 'surly and foul-tempered': Herb Greer, *Mud Pie: The CND Story*, p. 59, quoted in Driver, op. cit., pp. 158–9

p. 422 'Friends': see 'A Message from Bertrand Russell', *Autobiography III*, p. 146

p. 422 'All these people': ibid., p. 149

p. 423 'aliens': Driver, op. cit., p. 123

p. 423 'a public spectacle': ibid., p. 125

p. 424 'an evil': ibid., p. 130

p. 424 'News editors': ibid., p. 143

p. 424 'there was something missing': quoted in Taylor, op. cit., p. 240

p. 425 'Dream of how': LR, diary, 25.10.61

p. 426 'Most of all Zahatapolk': LR to BR, 16.6.62

p. 426 'I crocheted': *Daily Express*, 18 Sept. 1961

p. 426 'Lord Russell's son': *Sunday Express*, 17 Sept. 1961

p. 426 'I do love them both': LR, diary, 4.1.62

p. 427 'I don't even know': ibid., 8.5.61

p. 427 'Felt miserable': ibid., 17.10.61

p. 427 'wished for': ibid., 20.1.62

p. 427 '*very* rebellious': ibid., 26.1.62

p. 427 'Get out': ibid., 2.2.62

p. 427 'I'd love': ibid., 5.2.62

p. 428 'I *do* owe her': LR to BR, 18.1.62

p. 428 'surprised': BR and ER to LR, 22.1.62

p. 428 'We think': BR and ER to LR, 22.1.62

p. 428 'Now, while I'm young': LR, diary, 24.2.62

p. 428 'Enlightening': ibid., 4.3.62

p. 429 'Ralph said': ibid., 30.3.62

p. 429 'they care more': ibid., 14.4.62

p. 429 'don't count': ibid., 17.4.62

p. 429 'Didn't want to leave': ibid., 9.4.62

p. 430 'Obviously': ibid., 14.5.62

p. 430 'very gay': ibid., 18.5.62

p. 431 'Strawson did come': RCW, notes in preparation for *Russell Remembered*

p. 431 'It is difficult': this and extracts from the other tributes collected for the occasion were published in a commemorative programme called *Into the 10th Decade: Tribute to Bertrand Russell*

p. 431 'was too often': see 'Private Memorandum Concerning Ralph Schoenman', Clark, op. cit., p. 807

p. 431 'I was so deeply moved': *Autobiography III*, p. 123

p. 431 'I have a very simple creed': ibid., p. 124

p. 431 'I read the programme': LR, diary, 20.5.62

p. 431 'How I hope': ibid.

p. 433 list of tributes: extracts from these can be found in *Into the 10th Decade*

p. 434 'nonagenarian intellectual': see Clark, op. cit., p. 745

p. 434 'returning to London': *Autobiography III*, p. 124

p. 434 'Suggestions for U Thant': see ibid., pp. 149–50

p. 435 'the ascendency': see Clark, op. cit., p. 804

p. 435 'an indirect way': ibid.

p. 435 'the public utterances': *Autobiography III*, p. 164

p. 436 'When it comes': quoted in Driver, op. cit., p. 135

p. 436 a leaflet: a copy of this in the possession of the late Nicholas Walter was consulted by the author

p. 437 'The fact is': RS to BR, 13.7.63

p. 437 '2. That there should be': Minutes of the London Committee of 100, shown to me by Nicholas Walter

p. 438 At this meeting: the account that follows is based on conversations with Nicholas Walter

p. 438 'I had': *Autobiography III*, p. 125

p. 438 'a small crankish group': quoted in Taylor, op. cit., p. 242

p. 438 eulogy: see P. Anderson and R. Blackburn, 'Cuba, Free Territory of America', *New University*, 4, 1960, pp. 17–23; see also R. Blackburn, 'Prologue to the Cuban Revolution', *New Left Review*, 21, 1963, pp. 52–91

p. 439 'The Cuban revolution': original article published in *Revolución*, 15 Feb. 1962, pp. 1, 6; English translation published in *Bertrand Russell's America 2*, pp. 146–7

p. 440 'In late August': *Unarmed Victory*, p. 23

p. 440 'The situation': ibid.

p. 441 'It seems likely': ibid., pp. 29–30

p. 441 'Your action desperate': ibid., p. 31

p. 442 'I appeal to you': ibid., pp. 31–2

p. 442 'YOU ARE TO DIE': ibid., p. 32

p. 442 'was perfectly aware': ibid., p. 33

p. 443 'We shall do everything': ibid., p. 36

p. 443 'the first indication': ibid.

p. 443 'It seems that': BR, interview in the *Caernarvon and Denbigh Herald and North Wales Observer*, 26 Oct. 1962, p. 10

p. 443 'the behaviour of a man': Arthur Schlesinger, *A Thousand Days: John F. Kennedy in the White House*, p. 821, quoted in Al Seckel, 'Russell and the Cuban missile crisis', *Russell* 4 (2) winter 1984–5, pp. 253–61

p. 443 'This is my proposal': see Robert E. Kennedy, *Thirteen Days*, p. 89

p. 443 'I think': see *Unarmed Victory*, p. 45

p. 443 'I am appealing': ibid., p. 46

p. 444 'To defend Cuba': ibid., p. 47

p. 444 'Your continued forbearance': ibid., p. 46

p. 444 'We will remove': see Kennedy, op. cit., p. 94

p. 444 'After shots': see *Unarmed Victory*, p. 38

p. 445 'Castro's tongue': Georgie Anne Geyer, *Guerrilla Prince: The Untold Story of Fidel Castro*, p. 292

p. 445 'mankind owes him': *Unarmed Victory*, p. 51

p. 445 'I have never known': ibid., p. 53

p. 445 'so sudden': *Unarmed Victory*, p. 8

p. 445 'With little hope': ibid.

p. 446 'To be willing': *Unarmed Victory*, p. 60

p. 446 'I dislike Communism': ibid., p. 13

p. 446 'the Communist side': ibid.

p. 447 'Step by step': Schoenman, 'Bertrand Russell and the Peace Movement', in

George Nakhnikian (ed.), *Bertrand Russell's Philosophy*, pp. 227–52, quotation on p. 248

p. 447 'I admire very much': Max Born to BR, 5.12.62

p. 447 'At the time': Lord Gladwyn to BR, 3.11.64, see *Autobiography III*, pp. 192–4

p. 447 'Russia and America': BR to Gladwyn, 14.11.64, ibid., pp. 194–7

p. 447 'humbly to accept': *Unarmed Victory*, p. 47

p. 447 'unclear': ibid., p. 42

p. 448 'The missiles': see Schoenman, op. cit., p. 248

p. 449 'I see Lord John': LR to BR, 10.12.62

p. 449 'Khrushchev's calling a summit': LR, diary, 24.10.62

p. 449 'A noble step': ibid., 28.10.62

p. 449 'Granpa': LR to BR, 14.11.62

p. 450 'tempest in a teapot': ER in her notes on Clark's biography of Russell (now in the possession of the Russell Archives)

p. 450 'All the children': *Russell Remembered*, p. 142

p. 450 'Gma treated me': LR, diary, 25.12.62

p. 450 'when Gpa kissed me': ibid.

p. 450 'Fighting will be resumed': *Unarmed Victory*, p. 108

p. 451 'it was quite impossible': ibid., p. 71

p. 451 'the whole legal position': ibid., p. 99

p. 452 'has ceased': ibid., p. 105

p. 452 'worst blow': ibid., p. 106

p. 452 'We were on a diplomatic mission': Pat Pottle in conversation with the author

p. 452 'I have now read': RS to BR, 16.6.63

p. 452 'convinced that crucial work': RS to BR, 19.6.63

p. 452 'our criticism': RS to BR, 28.6.63

p. 453 Pottle's account: Pat Pottle in conversation with the author

p. 453 'two little amateurs': ibid.

p. 453 'Ralph's infamous folly': Private Memorandum, see Clark, op. cit., p. 806

13. The Guevarist Years

p. 454 'It is a privilege': BR, 'Message to the Tricontinental'. There exist four typescript versions of this message; this one is dated '10 January 1965', though, surely, 10 January 1966 is meant

p. 455 'spread thin': Schoenman, op. cit., p. 250

p. 456 'the prominence': Schoenman, op. cit., p. 248

p. 457 'sometimes pulled back': ibid., p. 242

p. 457 'that if you could attract': Pat Pottle in conversation with the author

p. 458 'Although we have not': RS to BR, 18.12.62

p. 458 'taking proposals': Schoenman, op. cit., p. 248

p. 458 'The Myth of American Freedom': *Frontier*, April 1963, pp. 5–8, reprinted in *Bertrand Russell's America 2*, pp. 356–60

p. 458 'Ideology': *Bertrand Russell's America 2*, p. 359

p. 458 'concentration camp': ibid., p. 357

p. 458 'overt': ibid., p. 356

p. 458 acrimonious exchange: see ibid., pp. 162–75

p. 459 'The American Government': BR to John Fischer, 4.3.63, ibid., p. 163

p. 459 'it is abominable': BR to Fischer, 15.3.63, ibid., p. 167

p. 459 'with the same': Fischer to BR, 4.4.63, ibid., p. 172

p. 460 'The United States Government': BR to the *Washington Post*, 22.3.63, see *Bertrand Russell's America 2*, p. 181; see also *War Crimes in Vietnam*, p. 31

p. 460 'been replaced': 'Is Communism a Menace?', *New York Times Magazine*, 7 April 1963, pp. 35, 168, 170, 173

p. 460 'an unthinking receptivity': see *Bertrand Russell's America 2*, p. 182

p. 461 'The treatment': BR, message to the Civil Rights Freedom March in Washington, 28.8.63, see ibid., p. 219

p. 461 'the Prime Minister': see Clark, op. cit., p. 806

p. 461 publicity leaflet: the copy consulted by the author is now in the possession of Professor Adam Roberts

p. 462 'our purposes': *Autobiography III*, p. 159

p. 462 'we had to speak': ibid., p. 162

p. 463 'the attempt to oppress Cuba': BR, 'Message to the Continental Congress of Solidarity with Cuba', 21.3.63

p. 463 'If I have been able': BR to Dr Frederico de Cordova, Cuban Ambassador in London, 14.11.62

p. 463 'I join you': 'Message to the People of Cuba', Jan. 1963

p. 464 'The people of Africa': 'Africa and the Movement for Peace', typescript dated August 1964, p. 4, published as 'Africa can stop this nuclear madness', *Africa and the World*, Oct. 1964, pp. 8–11

p. 464 'an army': press statement, 24.11.64

p. 466 'supporting Western imperialism': see *Autobiography III*, pp. 205–15, quotation on p. 213

p. 466 a statement by Russell: BR, message to World Congress of Peace, Helsinki, 11.7.65; see 'Bertrand Russell: The Threat to World Peace is American Imperialism', *Peking Review*, 13 July 1965, p. 21

p. 466 'a message from me': see Clark, op. cit., p. 810

p. 466 'We must carry': *Venceremos! The Speeches and Writings of Che Guevara*, edited by John Gerassi, p. 581

p. 467 'How close': ibid., p. 583

p. 467 'How close': ibid., p. 583

p. 467 four slightly different versions: the fourth is published as Chapter 8 of *War Crimes in Vietnam*; the other three survive in typescript in the Russell Archives

p. 468 'in this barbarous': see *War Crimes in Vietnam*, p. 111

p. 469 a telegram: a copy of this survives in the Russell Archives, together with the accompanying press statement

p. 469 'After explaining': David Horowitz, *Radical Son*, p. 141

p. 469 'Those who think': BR, press statement, 20.7.66

p. 469 'The historical perspective': BR, 'Message to Cuba. Answers to Marta Rojas', May 1967

p. 470 'feverish effort': see 'Russell Condemns US "Brutality"', *Daily Telegraph*, 1 May 1967, p. 25. The speech was published in full in *Against the Crime of Silence*, pp. 49–51

p. 470 'the United States': see 'The International War Crimes Tribunal and the Nature of the War in Vietnam', *Bertrand Russell's America 2*, pp. 406–7

p. 471 'He was leaving for Iraq': RS, message to a meeting in London on 17.8.68 to mark the death of Khalid Zaki

p. 471 'I am to write': *The Bolivian Diary of Ernesto Che Guevara*, p. 150

p. 472 'Fidel Castro has our warmest support': BR, 'May Day Message to the Cuban People', 7.4.67

p. 472 'The guerrilla movement': BR, 'Replies to Questions by Cuban Journalists', dated (by hand) 'c. July '66', but this must be wrong, so presumably July 1967 is the correct date

p. 472 'The International War Crimes Tribunal': see 'Towards a new morality', *Bertrand Russell Peace Foundation London Bulletin*, 1 Aug. 1967, p. 2

p. 472 'I am happy': ibid., p. 4

p. 473 'grotesque': 'U.S. counter-insurgency in Latin America. The background to the trial of Regis Debray', ibid., pp. 12–13

p. 473 'one of Schoenman's contacts': Tariq Ali, *Street Fighting Years*, p. 146

p. 474 'to intervene': Richard Gott to 'Nick and Michael', 10.9.67

p. 474 'a full legal document': see *Bertrand Russell Peace Foundation London Bulletin*, 5, summer 1968, p. 7. The document is published in full as 'The suppressed evidence of Ralph Schoenman', ibid., pp. 40–52

p. 474 'I request': ibid., p. 40

p. 475 'a cage': ibid., p. 8

p. 475 'Che Guevara': ibid., p. 12

p. 475 'the Foundation's interest': ibid.

p. 476 'speaks for all of us': *Bertrand Russell Peace Foundation London Bulletin*, 2, Sept. 1967, p. 10

p. 476 'Report from OLAS': see ibid., pp. 12–23

p. 476 'The Debray dossier': ibid., pp. 24–30

p. 477 'I have decided': RS to Coates and Farley, 29.6.68

p. 478 was written by Edith: so, it seems, one must infer from Edith's notes on Clark, op. cit., in which she remarks: 'That B "dictated" the memorandum about RS to me is untrue. Nor does B anywhere, I think, say that he did. It is characteristic of Clark's slovenliness to translate "I told my wife what I wished her to type and she has typed it" into "dictate".'

p. 478 'Ralph should be dismissed': Clark, op. cit., p. 815

14. The Final Visitation

p. 481 filmed documentary: a transcript of this, headed 'Recorded Interview with Bertrand Russell 22 November 1965', was consulted at the Russell Archives

p. 482 filmed interview: a copy of this was obtained by the author from the Russell Archives

p. 483 manuscript dated simply '1967': published as 'The Last Testament of Bertrand Russell', *Independent*, 24 November 1993

p. 485 unfinished autobiography: this and the other papers of Lucy Russell's quoted in this chapter are among the papers that Lucy left with her friends the Cooper-Willises shortly before she died

p. 486 'My Ralph': LR, diary, 6.1.64

p. 487 'grateful kneeling': LR, diary, 27.1.64

p. 488 several 'books': consulted at the Russell Archives

p. 489 'Inspector Christopher Smart Calls': see Peter Porter, *Collected Poems*, Oxford, 1983, pp. 75–6. The lines quoted in the text are given as they were transcribed from the radio by John Russell

p. 489 'very upset': LR to DR, 22.3.64

p. 490 'The incoherent writings': Dr Morgan to Taylor, 22.3.64

p. 490 'We have discussed': ER to Holland, 4.4.64

p. 490 'It is not something': DR to Taylor, 6.4.64

p. 490 'Personally': Taylor to DR, 24.4.64

p. 491 'From what Ralph said': LR, diary, 21.4.64

p. 491 'Dora has no right': ibid.

p. 491 'Dora is magnificent': ibid., 24.4.64

p. 492 'Daddy has' LR to BR, 17.5.64

p. 492 'Apparently': unless stated otherwise, the quotations from Lucy's papers that are given in this chapter come, as this one does, from loose sheets that Lucy preserved but did not arrange in any discernible order

p. 493 'finds co-operation': H.A.T. Child to BR, 3.3.65

p. 493 'As I gather': BR to Child, 27.3.65

p. 493 'Until the last term': Child to BR, 1.4.65

p. 495 'could not': LT to BR, 25.4.66

p. 496 'We realise': BR to LT, 20.6.66

p. 496 'with great regret': LT to BR, 1.7.66

p. 496 'Be that as it may': LT to BR, 1.8.66

p. 498 'Yes, but what about Lucy?': story told to the author by Susie Barry

p. 498 'I have been suffering': BR to KR, 22.5.67

p. 498 'When we arrived': Horowitz, op. cit., p. 149

p. 499 'Apparently': although this episode does not appear in *Russell Remembered*, Crawshay-Williams's account of it survives in the large collection of his notes of conversations with Russell, now in the Russell Archives

p. 500 'if there are ghosts': LR to DR, 20.4.71

p. 501 'a mixture': LR to JR, 19.1.71

p. 50 'For God's sake': LR to JR, undated, but probably April 1972

p. 501 'In the early morning of 11 April: this account of Lucy's death is based on contemporary newspaper reports. See 'Lady Lucy is Killed in Churchyard Blaze Ritual', *News of the World*, 14 April 1975; 'Lady Lucy Russell named as blaze victim', *Western Morning News*, 14 April 1975; and 'Woman in flames was daughter of Earl Russell', *Western Evening Herald*, 14 April 1975

p. 502 'all French youth': LR to BR, 29.11.67

BIBLIOGRAPHY

T he excellent three-volume *Bibliography of Bertrand Russell* by Kenneth Blackwell and Harry Ruja (Routledge, 1994) is an indispensable tool for anyone researching Russell's life and work. Without it, it would have been almost impossible to keep track of the immense output of journalistic articles that Russell sustained throughout the second half of his life. What follows is not an attempt to duplicate the effort involved in the production of that magnificent work, but simply a list of the works that were consulted in the writing of this book.

The amount of secondary literature on Russell's later moral and political writings is very small compared to the vast number of commentaries on his early philosophical work. However, many useful articles can be found in the pages of *Russell: The Journal of the Bertrand Russell Archives*, edited by Kenneth Blackwell and published by the McMaster University Library Press.

Works by Russell

The Collected Papers of Bertrand Russell

Produced by the Bertrand Russell Editorial Project, based at McMaster University, Hamilton, Ontario, and led by the Project Directors, Louis Greenspan and Richard Rempel, this is an ambitious attempt to publish in a uniform edition all of Russell's shorter (i.e., less than book-length) writings, whether previously published or not. After Volume 1, which includes Russell's juvenilia and earliest professional work, the series divides in two: Volumes 2 to 11 containing his philosophical work, and Volumes 12 onwards his personal and political writings. Below are listed the volumes published so far that were used in writing this book. For a list of the volumes used in the writing of my first volume, Russell, *The Spirit of Solitude* see the Bibliography provided there.

Volume 1. Cambridge Essays, 1888–99, edited by Kenneth Blackwell, Andrew Brink, Nicholas Griffin, Richard A. Rempel, and John G. Slater, London, George Allen & Unwin, 1983

Volume 9. Essays on Language, Mind and Matter, 1919–26, edited by John G. Slater with the assistance of Bernd Frohmann, London, Unwin Hyman, 1988

Volume 10. A Fresh Look at Empiricism, 1927–42, edited by John G. Slater with the assistance of Peter Köllner, London, Routledge, 1996

Volume 11. Last Philosophical Testament, 1943–68, edited by John G. Slater with the assistance of Peter Köllner, London, Routledge, 1997

Volume 12. Contemplation and Action, 1902–14, edited by Richard A. Rempel, Andrew Brink and Margaret Moran, London, George Allen & Unwin, 1985

Autobiographical Writings

Russell was a dedicated chronicler of his own life, and kept up a constant stream of memoirs and evaluations of his private and public hopes, disappointments and achievements, from the 'Self-Appreciation' of 1897 to the third volume of his *Autobiography* in the last year of his life. Below are listed, in chronological order, those autobiographical writings not (yet) included in the *Collected Papers*.

1927 'Things That Have Moulded Me', *The Dial*, 83, Sept. 1927, pp. 181–186, reprinted as 'Introduction' to *Selected Papers of Bertrand Russell*, New York, The Modern Library

1930 'How I Was Educated', *John O'London's Weekly*, 23, 19 July 1930, pp. 525–6

1936 '"The Last Survivor of a Dead Epoch"', *The Listener*, 16, 12 Aug. 1936, p. 289, reprinted as 'Obituary (1937)' in *Unpopular Essays*

1938 'My Religious Reminiscences', *The Rationalist Annual*, 1938, pp. 2–8, reprinted in *Basic Writings*

1944 'My Mental Development', *The Philosophy of Bertrand Russell*, edited by Paul Schilpp, pp. 3–20, reprinted in *Basic Writings*

1946 'Eminent Men I Have Known', *Unpopular Essays*, pp. 181–7

1951 'How I Write', *London Calling*, 10 May 1951, reprinted in *Portraits from Memory*

1951 'Memories of My Childhood', *Vogue*, 117, 15 May 1951, pp. 69, 106, 108–10

1952 'Reflections On My Eightieth Birthday', *The Listener*, 47, 22 May 1952, pp. 823–4, reprinted as 'Postscript', in *The Autobiography of Bertrand Russell 1944–1967* (Volume III)

1952 'My First 80 Years', *New York Post*, 25 May 1952, pp. 10–11

1952–3 'Portraits from Memory':

1. 'Alfred North Whitehead', *The Listener*, 48, 10 July 1952, pp. 51–2, reprinted in *Portraits from Memory*
2. 'Maynard Keynes and Lytton Strachey', *The Listener*, 17 July 1952, pp. 97–8, reprinted in *Autobiography*, pp. 70–4
3. 'D.H. Lawrence', *The Listener*, 24 July 1952, pp. 135–6, reprinted in *Portraits from Memory*
4. '"Completely Married: Sidney and Beatrice Webb"', *The Listener*, 31 July 1952, pp. 177–8, reprinted in *Portraits from Memory*
5. 'Cambridge in the Eighteen-Nineties', *The Listener*, 50, 20 Aug. 1953, pp. 307–8, reprinted as 'Some Cambridge Dons of the 'Nineties' in *Portraits from Memory*
6. 'Cambridge Friendships', *The Listener*, 27 Aug. 1953, pp. 337–8, reprinted as 'Some of My Contemporaries at Cambridge' in *Portraits from Memory*
7. 'Bernard Shaw: The Admirable Iconoclast', *The Listener*, 3 Sept. 1953, pp. 380–1, reprinted as 'George Bernard Shaw' in *Portraits from Memory*
8. 'H.G. Wells: Liberator of Thought', *The Listener*, 10 Sept. 1953, pp. 417–18, reprinted as 'H.G. Wells' in *Portraits from Memory*
9. 'Joseph Conrad', *The Listener*, 17 Sept. 1953, pp. 462–3, reprinted in *Portraits from Memory*

10. 'George Santayana', *The Listener*, 24 Sept. 1953, pp. 503, 511, reprinted in *Portraits from Memory*

1953 'Private Memoirs', unpublished typescript, the purpose of which 'is to explain why my relations with women that I have been fond of were until the last unsatisfactory'

1955 'Six Autobiographical Talks':

  1. 'Philosophers and Idiots', *The Listener*, 53, 10 Feb. 1955, pp. 247, 249, reprinted as 'Some Philosophical Contacts' in *Portraits from Memory*

  2. 'Why I Took to Philosophy', *London Calling*, 3 March 1955, p. 9, reprinted in *Portraits from Memory* and *Basic Writings*

  3. 'A Pacifist in Wartime', *London Calling*, 17 March 1955, p. 10, reprinted as 'Experiences of a Pacifist in the First World War' in *Portraits from Memory*

  4. 'War and the Pursuit of Peace', *London Calling*, 24 March 1955, p. 8, reprinted as 'From Logic to Politics' in *Portraits from Memory*

  5. 'A Philosophy of My Own', *London Calling*, 31 March 1955, p. 10, reprinted as 'Beliefs: Discarded and Retained' in *Portraits from Memory*

  6. 'So I Go On Writing Books', *London Calling*, 7 April 1955, p. 10, reprinted as 'Hopes: Realized and Disappointed' in *Portraits from Memory*

1956 'Adaptation: an Autobiographical Epitome', *Portraits from Memory*, pp. 7–17

1957 'Books that Influenced Me in Youth':

  1. 'The Importance of Shelley', *London Calling*, 7 March 1957, p. 4, reprinted in *Fact and Fiction*

  2. 'The Romance of Revolt', *London Calling*, 14 March 1957, p. 10, reprinted in *Fact and Fiction*

  3. 'Revolt in the Abstract', *London Calling*, 21 March 1957, p. 12, reprinted in *Fact and Fiction*

  4. 'Disgust and its Antidote', *London Calling*, 28 March 1957, p. 10, reprinted in *Fact and Fiction*

  5. 'An Education in History', *London Calling*, 4 April 1957, p. 6, reprinted in *Fact and Fiction*

  6. 'The Pursuit of Truth', *London Calling*, 11 April 1957, p. 14, reprinted in *Fact and Fiction*

1959 *My Philosophical Development*, New York, Simon and Schuster, 1959

1967 *The Autobiography of Bertrand Russell 1872–1914*, London, George Allen & Unwin, 1967

1968 *The Autobiography of Bertrand Russell 1914–1944* (Volume II), London, George Allen & Unwin, 1968

1969 *The Autobiography of Bertrand Russell 1944–1967* (Volume III), London, George Allen & Unwin, 1969

Published Correspondence

The Vital Letters of Russell, Khrushchev, Dulles, London, MacGibbon & Kee, 1958

Dear Bertrand Russell: a selection of his correspondence with the general public 1950–1968, edited by Barry Feinberg and Ronald Kasrils, London, George Allen & Unwin, 1969

Dear Russell–Dear Jourdain: A commentary on Russell's logic, based on his correspondence with Philip Jourdain by I. Grattan-Guinness, London, Duckworth, 1977

'Unpublished Correspondence between Russell and Wittgenstein', B.F. McGuinness and G.H. von Wright, *Russell*, 10 (2), winter 1990–1, pp. 101–24

The Selected Letters of Bertrand Russell. Volume 1: The Private Years, 1884–1914, edited by Nicholas Griffin, London, Allen Lane, 1992

Other Writings by Russell

Below are listed, in chronological order, only those works used in the preparation of this volume. The list includes little, therefore, written before 1921. Most of Russell's books have been reprinted many times; after listing the details of the initial publication, I give details of the editions used in writing this book. Most of the newspaper and magazine articles referred to in the text can be found in the books listed below. Where this is not the case, full bibliographic details of the articles cited are given in the Notes and References.

1903 *The Principles of Mathematics*, Cambridge, University Press, 1903; paperback edition, London, Routledge, 1992

1910–13 (with A.N. Whitehead) *Principia Mathematica*, Cambridge, University Press, *Volume I*, 1910, *Volume II*, 1912, *Volume III*, 1913; second (expanded) edition 1925–7; paperback (abridged) edition, Cambridge, University Press, 1962

1916 *Principles of Social Reconstruction*, London, George Allen & Unwin, 1916

1920 *The Practice and Theory of Bolshevism*, London, George Allen & Unwin, 1920; second (revised) edition, 1949

1921 *The Analysis of Mind*, London, George Allen & Unwin, 1921; paperback edition, London, Routledge, 1992

1921 (in collaboration with Dora Russell) *The Prospects of Industrial Civilization*, London, George Allen & Unwin, 1923

1922 *The Problem of China*, London, George Allen & Unwin; 1922; paperback edition, Nottingham, Spokesman Books, 1993

1923 *The ABC of Atoms*, London, Kegan Paul, Trench, Trubner & Co., 1923

1924 *Icarus or the Future of Science*, London, Kegan Paul, Trench, Trubner & Co., 1924

1924 *How to be Free and Happy*, New York, The Rand School of Social Science, 1924; reprinted in *Bertrand Russell on Ethics, Sex and Marriage*

1925 *What I Believe*, London, Kegan Paul, Trench, Trubner & Co., 1925; reprinted in *The Basic Writings of Bertrand Russell*

1925 *The ABC of Relativity*, London, Kegan Paul, Trench, Trubner & Co., 1925

1926 *On Education Especially in Early Childhood*, London, George Allen & Unwin, 1926; paperback edition, London, Unwin Paperbacks, 1985

1927 *Why I am not a Christian*, London, Watts & Co., 1927; reprinted in *Why I am not a Christian and other essays on religion and related subjects*, paperback edition, London, Unwin Paperbacks, 1989

1927 *The Analysis of Matter*, London, Kegan Paul, Trench, Trubner & Co., 1927; paperback edition, London, Routledge, 1992

1927 *Selected Papers of Bertrand Russell*, New York, The Modern Library, 1927

1927 *An Outline of Philosophy*, London, George Allen & Unwin, 1927; paperback edition, London, Unwin Paperbacks, 1989

1928 *Sceptical Essays*, London, George Allen & Unwin, 1928; paperback edition, London, Unwin Paperbacks, 1985

1929 *Marriage and Morals*, London, George Allen & Unwin, 1929; paperback edition, London, Unwin Paperbacks, 1985

1930 *The Conquest of Happiness*, London, George Allen & Unwin, 1930; paperback edition, London, Unwin Paperbacks, 1987

1931 *The Scientific Outlook*, London, George Allen & Unwin, 1931

1931–35 *Mortals and Others: Bertrand Russell's American Essays 1931–35*, edited by Harry Ruja, London, George Allen & Unwin, 1975

1932 *Education and the Social Order*, London, George Allen & Unwin, 1932; paperback edition, London, Unwin Paperbacks, 1984

1934 *Freedom and Organization, 1814–1914*, London, George Allen & Unwin, 1934

1935 *In Praise of Idleness*, London, George Allen & Unwin, 1935; paperback edition, London, Unwin Paperbacks, 1986

1935 *Religion and Science*, London, Thornton Butterworth, 1935; paperback edition, Oxford, University Press, 1967

1936 *Which Way to Peace?*, London, Michael Joseph, 1936

1937 *The Amberley Papers*, Volumes 1 and 2, London, Hogarth Press, 1937

1938 *Power: A New Social Analysis*, London, George Allen & Unwin, 1938; paperback edition, London, Unwin Paperbacks, 1988

1940 *An Inquiry into Meaning and Truth*, New York, Norton, 1940; paperback edition, London, Unwin Paperbacks, 1987

1941 *Let the People Think*, London, Watts & Co., 1941

1942 *How to Become a Philosopher*, Girard, Kansas, Haldeman–Julius Publications, 1942

1943 *How to Read and Understand History*, Girard, Kansas, Haldeman–Julius Publications, 1943

1944 *The Value of Free Thought*, Girard, Kansas, Haldeman–Julius Publications, 1944

1945 *A History of Western Philosophy*, London, George Allen & Unwin, 1946; paperback edition, London, Routledge, 1995

1948 *Human Knowledge: Its Scope and Limits*, London, George Allen & Unwin, 1948; paperback edition, London, Routledge, 1992

1949 *Authority and the Individual*, London, George Allen & Unwin, 1949; paperback edition, London, Unwin Books, 1965

1950 *Unpopular Essays*, London, George Allen & Unwin, 1950; paperback edition, London, Unwin Paperbacks, 1984

1951 *The Impact of Science on Society*, New York, Columbia University Press, 1951; paperback edition, London, Unwin Paperbacks, 1989

1951 *New Hopes for a Changing World*, London, George Allen & Unwin, 1951

1953 *Satan in the Suburbs*, London, The Bodley Head, 1953; paperback edition, Penguin, 1961

1954 *Nightmares of Eminent Persons*, London, The Bodley Head, 1954; paperback edition, Harmondsworth, Penguin, 1962

1954 *Human Society in Ethics and Politics*, London, George Allen & Unwin, 1954

1956 *Portraits from Memory and Other Essays*, London, George Allen & Unwin, 1956

1956 *Logic and Knowledge*, edited by Robert C. Marsh, London, George Allen & Unwin, 1956; paperback edition, London, Routledge, 1992

1957 *Why I am not a Christian and other essays on religion and related subjects*, London, George Allen & Unwin, 1957; paperback edition, London, Unwin Paperbacks, 1989

1959 *Common Sense and Nuclear Warfare*, London, George Allen & Unwin, 1959

1960 *Bertrand Russell Speaks His Mind*, New York, World Publishing Co., 1960

1961 *The Basic Writings of Bertrand Russell*, London, George Allen & Unwin, 1961; paperback edition, London, Routledge, 1992

1961 *Fact and Fiction*, London, George Allen & Unwin, 1961

1961 *Has Man a Future?*, London, George Allen & Unwin, 1961; paperback edition, Harmondsworth, Penguin, 1962

1963 *Unarmed Victory*, London, George Allen & Unwin; paperback edition, Harmondsworth, Penguin, 1963

1964 'The Duty of a Philosopher in This Age', in *The Abdication of Philosophy: Philosophy and the Public Good. Essays in Honor of Paul Arthur Schilpp*, edited by Eugene Freeman, La Salle, Illinois, Open Court, 1976

1967 *War Crimes in Vietnam*, London, George Allen & Unwin, 1967

1969 *Dear Bertrand Russell*, London, George Allen & Unwin, 1969

Posthumously Published Collections of Russell's Writings

The Collected Stories of Bertrand Russell, compiled and edited by Barry Feinberg, London, George Allen & Unwin, 1972

Bertrand Russell's America Volume One 1896–1945, by Barry Feinberg and Ronald Kasrils, London, George Allen & Unwin, 1973

Bertrand Russell's America Volume Two 1945–1970, by Barry Feinberg and Ronald Kasrils, London, George Allen & Unwin, 1973

Essays in Analysis, edited by Douglas Lackey, London, George Allen & Unwin, 1973

Bertrand Russell on God and Religion, edited by Al Seckel, New York, Prometheus Books, 1986

Bertrand Russell on Ethics, Sex, and Marriage, edited by Al Seckel, New York, Prometheus Books, 1987

Works by Others

The works listed below are given in the editions that I happen to have used. In many cases, therefore, the date given will not be the date of first publication.

Ackroyd, Peter, *T.S.Eliot*, London, Abacus, 1985

Ali, Tariq, *Street Fighting Years: An Autobiography of the Sixties*, New York, Citadel Press, 1991

Anderson, C. Anthony, 'Russell on Order in Time', in Savage & Anderson (eds.), *Rereading Russell: Essays in Bertrand Russell's Metaphysics and Epistemology*, Minneapolis, University of Minnesota Press, 1989

Anderson, John Lee, *Che Guevara: A Revolutionary Life*, London, Bantam Press, 1997

Anderson, Perry and Blackburn, Robin, 'Cuba, Free Territory of America', *New University*, 4, 1960, pp. 17–23

Arnim, Elizabeth von, *Vera*, London, Virago, 1988

Ayer, A.J., *Part of My Life*, Oxford University Press, 1977

Bell, Quentin, *Virginia Woolf: A Biography Volume One. Virginia Stephen 1882–1912*, London, Triad/Granada, 1976

—— *Virginia Woolf: A Biography Volume Two. Mrs Woolf 1912–1941*, London, Triad/Granada, 1976

Blackburn, Robin, 'Prologue to the Cuban Revolution', *New Left Review*, 21, 1963, pp. 52–91

Blackwell, Kenneth, *The Spinozistic Ethics of Bertrand Russell*, London, George Allen & Unwin, 1985

Brenan, Gerald, *Personal Record 1920–1972*, New York, Knopf, 1975

Brian, Denis, *Einstein: A Life*, New York, John Wiley & Sons, 1996

Brink, Andrew, *Bertrand Russell: The Psychobiography of a Moralist*, New Jersey, Humanities Press, 1989

Callinicos, Alex, *Trotskyism*, Milton Keynes, Open University Press, 1990

Castaneda, Jorge G., *Companero: The Life and Death of Che Guevara*, New York, Vintage, 1998

Clark, Ronald W., *The Life of Bertrand Russell*, Harmondsworth, Penguin, 1978

—— *Bertrand Russell and His World*, London, Thames and Hudson, 1981

Cocchiarella, Nino B., 'Russell's Theory of Logical Types and the Atomistic Hierarchy of Sentences', in Savage & Anderson (eds), *Rereading Russell: Essays in Bertrand Russell's Metaphysics and Epistemology*, Minneapolis, University of Minnesota Press, 1989

Coffa, J. Alberto, *The Semantic Tradition from Kant to Carnap: To the Vienna Station*, Cambridge, University Press, 1991

Collins, Canon L.J., *Faith Under Fire*, London, 1966

Conrad, Joseph, *The Mirror of the Sea & A Personal Record*, Oxford University Press, 1988

Crawshay–Williams, Rupert, *Russell Remembered*, London, Oxford University Press, 1970

Darroch, Sandra Jobson, *Ottoline: The Life of Lady Ottoline Morrell*, London, Chatto & Windus, 1976

Driver, Christopher, *The Disarmers: A Study in Protest*, London, Hodder & Stoughton, 1964

Duff, Peggy, *Left, Left, Left*, London, 1971

Duffett, John (ed.) *Against the Cime of Silence: Proceedings of the Russell International War Crimes Tribunal*, London, O'Hare Books, 1968

Eliot, T.S., *Prufrock and Other Observations*, London, The Egoist Limited, 1917

—— 'Eeldrop and Appleplex', *The Little Review*, May and Sept. 1917, pp. 7–11 and 16–19, reprinted as *Eeldrop and Appleplex*, Tunbridge Wells, The Foundling Press, 1992

—— 'Style and Thought', review of Russell's *Mysticism and Logic*, *The Nation*, 22, March 1918, pp. 768, 770

—— 'A Commentary', *The Criterion*, April 1924, pp. 231–5

—— Review of *Why I am not a Christian*, *The Criterion*, Aug. 1927, pp. 177–9

—— *The Letters of T.S. Eliot Volume 1 1898–1922*, edited by Valerie Eliot, London, Faber & Faber, 1988

Fried, Richard M., *Nightmare in Red: The McCarthy Era in Perspective*, New York, Oxford University Press, 1999

Gallup, Donald, *T.S. Eliot: A Bibliography*, London, Faber & Faber, 1952

Gathorne-Hardy, Jonathan, *The Interior Castle: a Life of Gerald Brennan*, London, Sinclair-Stevenson, 1992

Geyer, Georgie Anne, *Guerrilla Prince: The Untold Story of Fidel Castro*, Boston, Little, Brown & Co., 1991

Gordon, Lyndall, *Eliot's Early Years*, Oxford, University Press, 1977

—— *Eliot's New Life*, Oxford, University Press, 1988

Gottschalk, Herbert, *Bertrand Russell: A Life*, London, John Barker, 1965

Graves, Robert and Hodge, Alan, *The Long Weekend: A Social History of Great Britain 1918–1939*, London, Cardinal, 1985

Greenfeld, Howard, *The Devil and Dr Barnes: The Life of Albert C. Barnes, the Irascible Art Collector*, New York, Marion Boyars, 1996

Greenspan, Louis, *The Incompatible Prophesies: Bertrand Russell on Science and Liberty in the Political Writings of Bertrand Russell*, Oakville, Ontario, Mosaic Press, 1978

Griffin, Nicholas, 'Russell in Australia', *Russell* 16, winter 1974–5, pp. 9–12

Guevara, Ernesto Che, *Venceremos! The Speeches and Writings of Ernesto Che Guevara*, edited by John Gerassi, London, Panther, 1969

—— *Che Guevara and the Cuban Revolution: Writings and Speeches of Ernesto Che Guevara*, edited by David Deutschmann, Sydney, Pathfinder, 1987

—— *The Bolivian Diary of Ernesto Che Guevara*, New York, Pathfinder, 1994

Hardy, G.H., *Bertrand Russell and Trinity: A College Controversy of the Last War*, Cambridge, University Press, 1942

Harrison, Royden, 'Bertrand Russell and the Webbs', *Russell*, 5 (1), summer 1985, pp. 44–9

—— 'Bertrand Russell: from liberalism to socialism?', *Russell*, 6 (1), summer 1986, pp. 1–38

Hayhurst, Stephen, 'Russell's Anti–Communist Rhetoric before and after Stalin's Death', *Russell*, 11 (1), summer 1991, pp. 67–82

Holmes, Fenwick W., 'Bertrand Russell at U.C.L.A: a Reminiscence', *San Jose Studies*, Fall 1992, pp. 28–43

Hopkins, Kenneth, 'Bertrand Russell and Gamel Woolsey', *Russell*, 5 (1), summer 1985, pp. 50–65

Horowitz, David, *Radical Son: A Generational Odyssey*, New York, The Free Press, 1996

Hughes, Penelope, *Richard Hughes: Author, Father*, Gloucester, Alan Sutton, 1984

Huxley, Aldous, *Crome Yellow*, London, Flamingo, 1994

Ironside, Philip, *The Social and Political Thought of Bertrand Russell: The Development of an Aristocratic Liberalism*, Cambridge, University Press, 1996

Irvine, A.D. and Wedeking, G.A. (eds), *Russell and Analytic Philosophy*, Toronto, University of Toronto Press, 1993

Jager, Ronald, *The Development of Bertrand Russell's Philosophy*, London, George Allen & Unwin, 1972

Jean-Aubry, G., *Joseph Conrad. Life & Letters*, (two volumes), London, Heinemann, 1927

Karl, Frederick R., *Joseph Conrad. The Three Lives: A Biography*, London, Faber & Faber, 1979

Karnow, Stanley, *Vietnam: A History*, London, Century, 1983

Kearns, Marion, 'Alys Russell: a Bibliography', *Russell*, 10, summer 1973, pp. 17–19

Kennedy, Robert E., *Thirteen Days: A Memoir of the Cuban Missile Crisis*, New York, Mentor, 1969

Kennedy, Thomas C., 'The Women's Man from Wimbledon', *Russell*, 14, summer 1974, pp. 19–26

Kenny, Michael, *The First New Left: British Intellectuals After Stalin*, London, Lawrence & Wishart, 1995

Kermode, Frank, *Lawrence*, London, Fontana, 1973

Keynes, John Maynard, *The Collected Writings Volume X. Essays in Biography*, London, Macmillan, 1972

King, James, *Virginia Woolf*, London, Hamish Hamilton, 1994

Kirkup, James, *Me All Over: Memoirs of a Misfit*, London, Peter Owen, 1993

Lackey, Douglas P., 'The Whitehead Correspondence', *Russell*, 5, spring 1972, pp. 14–16

—— 'Russell's Unknown Theory of Classes: The Substitutional System of 1906', *Journal of Philosophy*, 14, 1976, pp. 69–78

—— 'Russell's contribution to the study of nuclear weapons policy', *Russell*, 4 (2), winter 1984–5, pp. 243–252

Lansbury, George, *My England*, London, Selwyn & Blount, 1934

Lawrence, D.H., *D.H. Lawrence's Letters to Bertrand Russell*, edited by Harry T. Moore, New York, Gotham, 1948

—— *The Collected Letters* (two volumes), edited by Harry T. Moore, London, Heinemann, 1962

—— *The Letters of D.H. Lawrence Volume II June 1913–October 1916*, edited by George J. Zytaruk and James T. Boulton, Cambridge, University Press, 1981

Lawrence, Frieda, *The Memoirs and Correspondence*, edited by E.W. Tedlock, Jr, New York, Knopf, 1964

Leithauser, Gladys Garner, 'Spirited Satire: the Fiction of Bertrand Russell', *Russell*, 13 (1), summer 1993, pp. 63–82

—— and Dyer, Nadine Cowan, 'Bertrand Russell and T.S. Eliot: Their Dialogue', *Russell*, 2 (1), summer 1982, pp. 7–28

Lowe, Victor, 'The Development of Whitehead's Philosophy', *The Philosophy of Alfred North Whitehead*, edited by Paul Arthur Schilpp, Northwestern, 1941, pp. 15–124

—— *Alfred North Whitehead. The Man and His Work Volume I: 1861–1910*, Baltimore, Johns Hopkins, 1985

—— *Volume II: 1910–1947*, edited by J.B. Schneewind, Baltimore, Johns Hopkins, 1990

Magee, Bryan, *Confessions of a Philosopher*, London, Weidenfeld & Nicolson, 1997

Malleson, Constance, *After Ten Years*, London, Jonathan Cape, 1931

—— *The Coming Back*, London, Jonathan Cape, 1933

—— *In the North: Autobiographical Fragments in Norway, Sweden, Finland: 1936–1946*, London, Gollancz, 1946

—— 'Fifty Years: 1916–1966', in Ralph Schoenman (ed.), *Bertrand Russell: Philosopher of the Century*, London, George Allen & Unwin, 1967

—— 'The End', *Russell*, 21–2, spring–summer 1976, pp. 25–7

Marsh, Robert C., 'Talking with Russell 1951–55', *Russell*, 15 (1), summer 1995, pp. 11–36

Martin, Kingsley, *Father Figures: A first volume of autobiography 1897–1931*, London, Hutchinson, 1966

Mehta, Ved, *Fly and the Fly Bottle: Encounters with British Intellectuals*, London, Weidenfeld & Nicolson, 1963

Moorehead, Caroline, *Bertrand Russell. A Life*, London, Sinclair–Stevenson, 1992

Moran, Margaret, 'Men of Letters: Bertrand Russell and Joseph Conrad', *Russell*, 2 (1), summer 1982, pp. 29–46

Murry, J. Middleton, *The Pledge of Peace*, London, Herbert Joseph, 1938

Nakhnikian, George (ed.), *Bertrand Russell's Philosophy*, London, Duckworth, 1974

'Other, A.N.' Christopher Wordsworth, 'The Self–Inflicted Wound', *Underdogs: Eighteen Victims of Society*, edited by Philip Toynbee, London, Weidenfeld & Nicolson, 1961

Pais, Abraham, *'Subtle is the Lord ... ': The Science and the Life of Albert Einstein*, Oxford, University Press, 1982

Park, Joe, *Bertrand Russell on Education*, London, George Allen & Unwin, 1964

Partridge, Frances, *Julia: A Portrait by Herself*, London, Gollancz, 1983

Patmore, Brigit, *My Friends When Young. The Memoirs of Brigit Patmore*, edited by Derek Patmore, London, Heinemann, 1968

Perkins, Ray, 'Bertrand Russell and Preventive War', *Russell*, 14 (2), winter 1994–5, pp. 135–54

Quirk, Robert E., *Fidel Castro*, New York, W.W. Norton, 1993

Rhees, Rush, *Recollections of Wittgenstein*, Oxford, University Press, 1984

Roberts, George W. (ed), *Bertrand Russell Memorial Volume*, London, George Allen & Unwin, 1979

Rogers, Ben, *A.J. Ayer: A Life*, London, Chatto & Windus, 1999

Rosenbaum, S.P., 'Gilbert Cannan and Bertrand Russell: an addition to the logic of a literary symbol', *Russell*, 21–2, spring–summer 1976, pp. 16–24

Rowse, A.L., *Glimpses of the Great*, Lanham, Maryland, University Press of America, 1985

Rumble, Greville, *The Politics of Nuclear Defence: A Comprehensive Introduction*, Oxford, Polity Press, 1985

Russell, Dora, *The Tamarisk Tree Volume 1. My Quest for Liberty and Love*, London, Elek Books, 1975; paperback edition, London, Virago, 1978

—— *The Tamarisk Tree Volume 2. My School and the Years of War*, London, Virago, 1981

—— *The Tamarisk Tree Volume 3. Challenge to the Cold War*, London, Virago, 1985

—— *The Dora Russell Reader: 57 years of writing and journalism, 1925–1982*, London, Pandora Press, 1983

—— *The Religion of the Machine Age*, London, Routledge, 1983

Russell, Frank, *My Life and Adventures*, London, Cassell, 1923

Russell, John Conrad, *Abandon Spa Hot Springs*, London, Gaberbocchus Press, 1954

—— *Five Stories*, Penzance, The Triton Press, 1977

Russell, Lord John, *An Essay on the History of the English Government and Constitution, from the reign of Henry VIII to the present time*, London, 1821

Ryan, Alan, *Bertrand Russell: A Political Life*, London, Allen Lane, 1988

Santayana, George, *Persons and Places*, Massachusetts, MIT Press, 1987

Savage, C. Wade and Anderson, C. Anthony (eds.), *Rereading Russell: Essays in Bertrand Russell's Metaphysics and Epistemology*, Minneapolis, University of Minnesota Press, 1989

Scharfstein, Ben–Ami, *The Philosophers: Their Lives and the Nature of Their Thought*, Oxford, Blackwell, 1980

Schilpp, Paul Arthur (ed.), *The Philosophy of Bertrand Russell*, Illinois, Open Court, 1944; revised edition, 1971

Schoenman, Ralph (ed.), 'Mass Resistance in Mass Society', *Voices from the Crowd: Against the H–Bomb*, edited by Daniel Boulton, London, Peter Owen, 1964

—— *Bertrand Russell: Philosopher of the Century*, London, George Allen & Unwin, 1967

—— 'Bertrand Russell and the Peace Movement', *Bertrand Russell's Philosophy*, edited by George Nakhnikian, London, Duckworth, 1974

Seckel, Al, 'Russell and the Cuban Missile Crisis', *Russell*, 4 (2), winter 1984–5, pp. 253–61

Sencourt, Robert, *T.S. Eliot: A Memoir*, London, Garnstone, 1971

Seymour, Miranda, *Ottoline Morrell: Life on the Grand Scale*, London, Hodder & Stoughton, 1992

Sharpe, Tony, *T.S. Eliot: A Literary Life*, London, Macmillan, 1991

Sheehan, Neil, *A Bright Shining Lie: John Paul Vann and America in Vietnam*, London, Picador, 1990

Skidelsky, Robert, *John Maynard Keynes: Hopes Betrayed* 1883–1920, London, Macmillan, 1983

—— *John Maynard Keynes Volume Two: The Economist as Saviour* 1920–1937, London, Macmillan, 1992

Slater, John G., 'Lady Constance Malleson, "Colette O'Niel", *Russell*, 20, winter 1975–6, pp. 4–15

—— *Bertrand Russell*, Bristol, Thoemmes Press, 1994

Slezak, Gary and Jackanicz, Donald W., '"The town is beastly and the weather was vile": Bertrand Russell in Chicago, 1938–1939', *Russell*, 25–8, 1977, pp. 5–20

Stone, I.F., 'Bertrand Russell as Moral Force in World Politics', *Russell*, 1 (1), summer 1982, pp. 7–26

Strachey, Barbara, *Remarkable Relations: The Story of the Pearsall Smith Family*, London, Gollancz, 1980

Tait, Katherine, *My Father Bertrand Russell*, London, Gollancz, 1976

—— *Carn Voel: My Mother's House*, Penzance, The Patten Press, 1998

Taylor, A.J.P., *The Origins of the Second World War*, Harmondsworth, Penguin, 1991

Taylor, Richard, *Against the Bomb: The British Peace Movement* 1958–1965, Oxford, Clarendon, 1988

Thomas, J.E. and Blackwell, Kenneth, *Russell in Review: The Bertrand Russell Centenary Celebrations at McMaster University, October* 12–14, 1972, Toronto, Samuel Stevens, Hakkert & Co., 1976

Trent, Christopher, *The Russells*, London, Frederick Muller, 1966

Trotsky, Leon, *Collected Writings and Speeches on Britain, Volume Two*, edited by R. Chappell and Alan Clinton, London, New Park Publications, 1974

Unwin, Sir Stanley, *The Truth About a Publisher: An Autobiographical Record*, London, George Allen & Unwin, 1960

Utley, Freda, *Lost Illusion*, London, George Allen & Unwin, 1949

Watling, John, *Bertrand Russell*, Edinburgh, Oliver and Boyd, 1970

Webb, Beatrice, *The Diary of Beatrice Webb Volume Two* 1892–1905, edited by Norman and Jeanne MacKenzie, London, Virago, 1983

—— *The Diary of Beatrice Webb Volume Three* 1905–1924, edited by Norman and Jeanne MacKenzie, London, Virago, 1984

—— *The Diary of Beatrice Webb Volume Four* 1924–1943, edited by Norman and Jeanne MacKenzie, London, Virago, 1986

Wilson, Duncan, *Gilbert Murray OM* 1866–1957, Oxford, Clarendon, 1987

Wilson, Edmund, *The Thirties*, London, Macmillan, 1980

—— *Letter on Literature and Politics* 1912–1972, edited by Elena Wilson, New York, Farrar, Straus & Giroux, 1986

Wintle, Justin, *The Viet Nam Wars*, London, Weidenfeld & Nicolson, 1991

Wittgenstein, Ludwig, *Letters to C.K. Ogden*, edited by G.H. von Wright, Oxford, Blackwell, 1973

—— *Letters to Russell, Keynes and Moore*, edited by G.H. von Wright assisted by B.F. McGuinness, Oxford, Blackwell, 1974

Wood, Alan, *Bertrand Russell: The Passionate Sceptic*, London, George Allen & Unwin, 1957

Woolf, Leonard, *An Autobiography* 1: 1880–1911, Oxford, University Press, 1980
—— *An Autobiography* 2: 1911–1969, Oxford, University Press, 1980
—— *Letters of Leonard Woolf*, edited by Frederic Spotts, London, Bloomsbury, 1992
Woolf, Virginia, *The Diary of Virginia Woolf Volume* 2 1920–24, edited by Anne Olivier Bell assisted by Andrew McNeillie, Harmondsworth, Penguin, 1981
Zytaruk, George, 'Lectures on immortality and ethics: the failed D.H. Lawrence Bertrand Russell collaboration', *Russell*, 3 (1), summer 1983

INDEX